Clipper 5.2

A Developer's Guide

DBMS Magazine's Database Foundations Series

Clipper 5.2

A Developer's Guide

Joseph D. Booth, Greg Lief, and Craig Yellick

Foreword by Al Acker, Editor, *Clipper Advisor*

Introduction by David Kalman, Editor-in-Chief, *DBMS Magazine*

M&T Books
A division of MIS:Press
A subsidiary of Henry Holt and Company, Inc.
115 West 18th Street
New York, New York 10011

Printed in the United States of America

Library of Congress Cataloging-in-Publication Data

Booth, Joseph D.
Clipper 5.2: A Developer's Guide / Joseph D. Booth, Greg Lief, Craig Yellick.
p. cm.
ISBN 1-55851-319-1 (book / disk set)
1.Compilers (Computer programs) 2. Clipper (Computer program)
I. Lief, Greg. II. Yellick, Craig. III. Title.
QA76.76.C65B662 1993
005.75'65—dc20

93-13290
CIP

93 4

Cover Design: Lauren Smith Design **Project Editors:** Peggy Watt & Christine de Chutkowski

We dedicate this book to the founding members of the Clipper Widows' Club: our wives! (Sandy Booth, Jennifer Lief, and Heather Yellick.)

Contents

Acknowledgments

The writing of this book is unusual enough to merit explanation. It was accomplished by three authors in three cities. If not for the miracle of modern technology (particularly modems), and the Aquarium shell, writing this book would have been a logistical nightmare.

Joe Booth lives outside Philadelphia, Craig Yellick lives near Minneapolis, and Greg Lief lives in the sleepy state capital of Salem, Oregon. Kathy Uchman, our tireless technical editor, hails from the San Francisco Bay Area. Our faithful proofreaders were similarly far-flung: George Barnabic is from New Jersey, Tod Watts resides in central Illinois, and Matt Amis lives near Puget Sound in the Pacific Northwest.

In addition to the proofreaders listed above, the authors would also like to thank our in-house proofreaders for their tireless assistance: Don Bayne, Ron Bellinger, and Traci Welter. We would also like to say thanks again (and again and again) to Kathy Uchman, without whom this book would not have seen the light of day until sometime in 1992. Thanks also to Ted Means, who wrote the numerous small but vital .ASM routines that make our lives a bit easier.

Finally, the authors would like to thank the editors at M&T Books who helped make this revision of *Clipper 5.2: A Developer's Guide* possible; Brenda Mc Laughlin, Peggy Watt, and Christine de Chutkowski.

The Aquarium Bulletin Board System served as the hub of activity surrounding this book. The Aquarium is a disk-based Clipper technical journal published monthly by Grumpfish, Inc., designed and created by Greg Lief. The Aquarium shell was written entirely in Clipper, and includes an integrated telecommunications link. The Aquarium completely automates the message and file transfer process. Messages can be composed off-line. With the touch of a key, Aquarium dials up the BBS, sends outgoing messages, pulls down incoming messages, and downloads files (if requested). Incoming messages can then be read and responded to off-line.

The authors, technical editor, and proofreaders used the Aquarium to correspond with each other. Rough chapters were posted on the BBS for the proofreaders' review. When finished, the chapters were posted again for the technical editor to download. Whenever anyone had questions, they simply fired off a quick message and got answers virtually immediately. Considering the deadline and vast amount of material to cover, there was no room for wasted effort, and the Aquarium BBS ensured that none was necessary.

An ancient Chinese curse reads "May you live in interesting times". The gifted Clipper 5 architects — Rich McConnell, Basil Hosmer, and Denny Dias — have certainly kept our lives interesting over the past several months. Over the next several years, as you learn more about Clipper 5, you too will live an interesting life full of programming power that is truly limited only by your imagination.

Foreword

Before Computer Associates purchased Nantucket, the fate of Clipper was an unknown. Now, under new leadership, Clipper is sure to continue as the ultimate xBASE application development platform. With its new features, such as replaceable database drivers, Clipper 5.2 adds new power and flexibility to an already formidable array of application development tools.

Clipper 5.01 was light years beyond its original trademark slogan, "The Ultimate dBASE Compiler," and had matured into a powerful and robust programming language. Clipper 5.2 adds to this status and capability, and allows the production of an application with power limited only by the talent and imagination of the programmer.

This book is an excellent reference and tutorial on the visionary world of the new Clipper. Features such as RDD's let you access data formats of several other popular database products. This feature alone makes Clipper 5.2 the single-source answer that makes sense.

For the programmer new to Clipper 5 this book is an excellent reference for learning to use code blocks, multidimensional arrays, and the Clipper objects Get, TBrowse, TBColumn, and Error.You will also find ways to gain the maximum benefit from Clipper's new preprocessor and debugger. Included are program examples that will satisfy the needs of every level of programmer.

Clipper will be supporting the needs of the database programmer well into the 90s. You owe it to yourself to become familiar with all the possibilities Clipper provides. By purchasing this book, you have made an excellent start toward reaping the benefits of programming in the newest Clipper, CA-Clipper 5.2.

—Al Acker, Editor
Clipper Advisor

Introduction

Clipper 5.x's designers had a simple objective: to build a flexible, productive tool to enable the construction of robust, large scale applications. They achieved this goal through inspiration, teamwork, and persistence, yet for all the effort that went into Clipper, it requires you—the programmer—to manually extract its benefits. Clipper is a conceptual framework in which the primary tools are your own thoughts and words expressed programmatically as flow of control, modules, syntax, semantics, events, and messages. More simply, Clipper can only do what you tell it, and that's why this book is so important.

The authors of *Clipper 5.2: A Developer's Guide*—Greg Lief, Joseph D. Booth, and Craig Yellick—are recognized masters of Clipper development. They "speak" the language fluently, and immerse you in techniques, concepts, and code, that will improve your Clipper fluency and make you more productive in solving application problems. To help you master a language, linguists often recommend "total immersion." First you study the formal constructs of a language, then you spend a year in the field. This book melds the formal and informal approaches, using well-structured chapters to convey the benefits of the authors' combined experience in the field. Studying this book provides a "total immersion" program for the developer serious about exploiting the potential of Clipper 5.2.

As a footnote, I attended the Clipper DevCon in Palm Desert, California where the Nantucket folks (Clipper's original developers, who have since sold the technology to Computer Associates) first previewed Clipper 5.0 with its powerful new syntax and new methods. Despite the promised benefits of the new approach, I saw many perplexed faces in the audience when the presentation turned to lexical scoping, code blocks, objects, and modular design. These constructs required new techniques and new ways of thinking about application design and programming. Fortunately, the authors of this book quickly adopted the new techniques and, in turn, taught them to thousands of Clipper developers in magazine articles, newsletters, lectures, and in the earlier edition of this book. With *Clipper 5.2: A Developer's Guide*, the authors once again bring Clipper developers up-to-date on the most productive concepts and techniques for developing serious applications. The immersion continues.

— David Kalman, Editor-in-Chief
DBMS Magazine

Why this Book is for You

Clipper 5.2 represents one of the most advanced applications development systems available today. Whether you have been with Clipper from the beginning, or have just found out about Clipper recently, this book is for you. *Clipper 5.2: A Developer's Guide* is not just a rehash of the reference manual, in it you'll find solid examples and guidelines for developing applications. You will gain an understanding of how Clipper works, and how you can best take advantage of its tremendous power.

This book will be of particular interest to:

- **xBASE programmers who are new to Clipper**. xBASE lets you get away with things that don't belong in a structured computer program. This book will help you unlearn those bad habits and make your code faster, more powerful, and most importantly, much easier to maintain.

In addition, with the release of Clipper 5.2 and its powerful database drivers, you can still use the files and indexes from your favorite xBASE interpreter, and gain the tremendous programming advantages that Clipper has to offer.

- **Clipper Summer '87 programmers who haven't tried Clipper 5**. We too were nervous at first to try all the changes that Clipper 5 introduced. However, we worked through it and saw what Clipper 5 can do. There is no going back to Summer '87. The Summer '87 release of Clipper had its time, but Clipper 5 really shines. After reading this book, you too will feel it is time to put Summer '87 away and bid it a fond adieu.

- **C programmers who are new to Clipper**. While there are many uses for the C language, rapid applications programming is not one of its strong points. Clipper allows you to get a database application up and running much faster than in C. Although you won't need as much grounding in the formalities, this book will get you quickly started into the benefits that Clipper has to offer.

CHAPTER 1

Compiling Your Application

The heart of Clipper 5 is its incredible new compiler. Its many new options make the Summer '87 compiler look anemic by comparison. All these great options will not help you, however, unless you understand what they do, and where and when to use them. This is the main focus of this chapter.

A discussion of the Clipper 5 compiler options would not be complete without also covering the CLIPPERCMD, INCLUDE, and TMP environmental variables. This chapter also touches upon compiler warning and error messages.

Compilers and interpreters

If you had to write all of your programs in machine code, you would probably not be reading this because you would have long since thrown up your hands and sworn off programming. Fortunately, there are numerous high-level programming languages, such as BASIC, FORTRAN, and Pascal. Clipper is in this category as well. All of these languages are easily understood by us humans. A computer, however, does not know what to make of something like:

```
use CUSTOMER new
```

Fortunately, compilers and interpreters bridge this gap. They translate source code (high level) into machine code (low level). The machine or object code can then be grouped with other machine code by a linker to create an executable file. There is still some confusion about the difference between a compiler and an interpreter. A compiler translates source code into machine code, which is then linked (often with other machine code that may be in library files) into an executable file with the COM or EXE extension. Therefore, if you are using a compiled language such as Clipper, there are two steps to creating an executable file: compiling and linking.

An interpreter (such as dBASE or GWBASIC) circumvents the link step by translating your source code to machine code and executing it in one fell swoop. Although this approach may seem desirable, there are two drawbacks to using interpreters. The first drawback is execution speed: When you run a program, each line must be converted to machine code each time it is encountered. Consider the following simple loop:

```
private mtotal
mtotal = 0
use customer new
do while ! eof()
   mtotal = mtotal + customer->balance
   skip
enddo
```

The two statements in the DO WHILE loop must be translated to machine code once for each record in CUSTOMER.DBF. You can imagine what a waste of time this is.

By contrast, a compiler translates each statement to machine code only once, at compile-time. When you subsequently execute the program, the intermediate step of interpreting each line of code is unnecessary, thus netting you a massive gain in execution speed.

The second drawback to using an interpreter is distribution. If you write a dBASE program that must be interpreted, it can be executed only from dBASE. This means that you can distribute your program only to people who own dBASE. By contrast, nearly all compiled languages allow you to create stand-alone executable files, which can then be run without the need for any other supporting programs.

A note about memory: Much has been said about Clipper's well-known love for memory. It is true that a Clipper-compiled executable is not the leanest and meanest program that will ever grace your hard disk. But consider the alternative, an interpreted program. When you run a dBASE program, you must first load dBASE to interpret it. dBASE is quite adept at gobbling up copious amounts of memory. Memory usage is a necessary evil that in light of Clipper 5's Virtual Memory Management system should no longer cause distress to Clipper developers.

Basic syntax

To compile a .PRG file, you must execute the CLIPPER command, followed by the file name and any options you want to use. You do not need to specify the PRG file extension.

The following command compiles MYPROG and, assuming there are no fatal compilation errors, creates the MYPROG.OBJ object file:

```
clipper myprog
```

Instead of specifying a single .PRG file, you may create a .CLP file that contains multiple .PRG file names to be compiled into one .OBJ module. You then use the @ sign directly followed by the name of that file. You do not need to specify the .CLP extension.

The following command compiles the .PRG files listed in TEST.CLP and creates the TEST.OBJ object file:

```
clipper @test
// test.clp
myprog1
myprog2
myprog3
myprog4
```

TEST.OBJ would then contain the compiled contents of MYPROG1.PRG, MYPROG2.PRG, MYPROG3.PRG, and MYPROG4.PRG. Be sure to list each file on a separate line in the .CLP file.

In the Summer '87 version of Clipper, each variable, function, and procedure required an entry in the symbol table. Each variable required 20 bytes of storage space. One of the big advantages to using a .CLP file was to reduce the size of the symbol table.

Suppose that you have the following two .PRG files:

```
// myprog1.prg
private x, y, z
return

// myprog2.prg
private x, y, z
return
```

If these files are compiled into separate .OBJ files (MYPROG1.OBJ and MYPROG2.OBJ) and then linked together to create an .EXE file, the variables **x**, **y**, and **z** would have duplicate symbol table entries, one from each .OBJ file. However, suppose you created a file named TEST.CLP that contained these two lines:

```
myprog1
myprog2
```

If you then compiled TEST.CLP and linked it into an .EXE file, the duplicate symbols would be eliminated. This is because all duplicates are resolved within the same object module.

If you are using the RTLINK linker provided with Clipper, the potential advantage to using .CLP files is nullified because RTLINK automatically removes duplicates from the symbol table. Therefore, it is recommended that you compile your .PRG files separately using the /m compiler option to ignore calls to other .PRG files.

If you are using a third-party linker instead of RTLINK, you might want to consider using .CLP files because not all linkers compact the symbol table. For more information about specific linkers, please refer to Chapter 2, "Linking Your Application."

The Clipper 5 compilation process

If you have worked with any earlier releases of Clipper (particularly Summer '87), you may notice that your Clipper 5 compiles take longer. Do not be alarmed; this delay is because the Clipper 5 compiler is vastly different (and fortunately, a lot smarter) than its predecessors. There are now two stages to the Clipper 5 compile process:

1. A preliminary step has been added to the compilation process: the preprocessor phase. Before your source code is compiled, the Clipper 5 preprocessor scans your .PRG file sequentially for any directives and translates them into source code that can be compiled. These directives can include manifest constants (#define), user-defined commands (#command or #translate), and conditional compilation (#ifdef, #ifndef, #else, and #endif). (For more details on these directives and other mysteries, please refer to Chapter 7, "The Preprocessor.")

2. The preprocessor's output is passed on to the compiler, which steps in and creates the object code (assuming that it does not stumble across any fatal errors in your code). You can redirect this preprocessor output to a file with the /p compiler option to see how the preprocessor translates your source code.

Looking at the preprocessed output is an enlightening experience. During your first several months of experimenting with Clipper 5, you should use the /p option because it provides invaluable insight into both the preprocessor and the internal construction of the language. The better you understand this, the better you will be equipped to write clean, efficient code that takes full advantage of everything Clipper 5 offers.

Compiler options

The Clipper 5 compiler allows a host of command-line options, most of them new. See Table 1.1. (Options that are new to Clipper 5 are identified as such in the discussion of each switch, which follows.) Several of these are crucial during the learning process, and others are necessary throughout the course of Clipper 5 development. Note that all compiler switches are case-insensitive.

Table 1.1 Compiler options

Syntax	*Description*
/a	Automatic memvar declaration
/b	Debug information
/credits	Credits screen
/d<id>[=<val>]	#define <id>
/es	Set exit severity level
/i<path>	#include file search path
/l	Suppress line number information
/m	Compile module only
/n	No implicit starting procedure
/o<path>	Object file drive and/or path
/p	Generate preprocessed output (PPO) file
/q	Quiet
/r[<lib>]	Request linker to search <lib> (or none)
/s	Syntax check only
/t<path>	Drive/path for temporary files
/u[<file>]	Use command definition set in <file> (or none)
/v	Variables are assumed **memvar->**
/w	Enable warnings
/z	Disable logical "shortcutting"

/a

Automatic memory variable declaration

The /a option is reminiscent of the Summer '87 -v option. It instructs the compiler to declare any variable included in a **private**, **public**, or PARAMETERS statement as a **memvar**. You should always use this option because it eliminates ambiguity between memvars and fields. Related to this, you should always refer to fields by preceding them with the corresponding alias:

```
use customer new
mname := customer->lname   // good
mname := lname             // bad
```

Not only does this make clear what is and is not a field, it also saves you valuable time maintaining your programs because you will be able to tell at a glance which work area the field corresponds to. When you have multiple work areas open, this can mean the difference between a quick debug and a gigantic headache.

/b

Debug Information (New)

Clipper 5 includes a source-level debugger that makes debugging a breeze because you can view your source code as your application executes. However, this means you must prepare your application slightly differently if you intend to debug it. In the Summer '87 version of Clipper, you simply compiled your source code without the /l option (thus preserving line number information). You would then link in the DEBUG.OBJ file, and call upon the debugger by pressing Alt-D while running the application.

If you plan to debug a Clipper 5 application, you must include the /b switch, which embeds debugging information in the object file. As with the Summer '87 version, you should also leave the line numbers in the object file. In other words, if you use the /b option, do not use the /l option.

Using the /b option adds approximately 5-7 bytes to your object (OBJ) file per line of source code, which in turn leads to a slightly larger executable file. However, .EXE size is practically a non-issue because the RTLINK linker automatically puts your Clipper code into a dynamic overlay. Therefore, you might want to consider using the /b option on a regular basis. (While you are becoming familiar with Clipper 5, you will probably be doing quite a bit of debugging.)

/credits

Credits Screen (New)

The /credits option displays the name of everyone who was responsible for the development of Clipper 5. This is useful only if you would like to know who to praise or blame.

/d<id>[=<val>]

Define Identifier (New)

The /d option defines an identifier to the preprocessor. <id> is the name of the identifier. You may optionally assign a value, <val>, to the identifier by following <id> with an equal sign and the value. An identifier is a flag that exists solely for the preprocessor. Identifiers are defined in a .PRG file with the #define directive. Through the use of the #ifdef and #ifndef directives, the preprocessor includes or ignores sections of source code based on whether an identifier has been defined.

Identifiers are most commonly used for conditional compilation, which is ideal for debugging or demonstration versions. For example, you might want to have the following debugging code in your .PRG file:

```
// MYPROG.PRG
debug = .t.
*
* elsewhere in the program
if debug
   ? "procname() = ", procname()
   ? "procline() = ", procline()
   ? "readvar() =  ", readvar()
   ? "x = ", x
   ? "y = ", y
   ? "z = ", z
endif
```

Unfortunately, this debugging code will be compiled into your .OBJ file regardless of whether you are using it. Thus, if you ship the production (and presumably fully debugged) version of your program, your .EXE file will be larger than necessary because of the inclusion of the debugging code.

Fortunately, Clipper 5's preprocessor makes it very easy to strip out this debugging code. You should declare an identifier at the top of your program. For example, in the following program, the identifier is named DEBUG:

```
// MYPROG.PRG
#define DEBUG
*
* elsewhere in the program
#ifdef DEBUG
   ? "procname() = ", procname()
  ? "procline()=", procline()
  ? "readvar()= ", readvar()
   ? "x = ", x
   ? "y = ", y
   ? "z = ", z
#endif
```

Because the DEBUG identifier is defined prior to the #ifdef statement, the preprocessor includes the block of code containing procname(), procline(), and readvar() for compilation. Without this, that code would have been omitted from the compiled source code.

Suppose that you want a demonstration version of your program for prospective customers. In previous versions of Clipper, you could structure your code in the following manner to limit the user to 50 records:

```
* MAIN.PRG
demo = .t.
*
* elsewhere in the program
if demo
   if lastrec() > 50
      @ 10, 18 TO 13, 61
      @ 11, 19 say "Limit of 50 records for this demo version!"
      @ 12, 19 say "Call 123-456-7890 now to buy this program!"
      inkey(0)
      quit
   endif
endif
```

You can see that the demo code will be compiled into your .OBJ file regardless of whether you are using the demo limits. However, as with the debugging example, you can get around this easily by declaring an identifier to the preprocessor:

```
* MAIN.PRG
#define DEMO
*
* elsewhere in the program
#ifdef DEMO
   if lastrec() > 50
      @ 10, 18 TO 13, 61
      @ 11, 19 say "Limit of 50 records for this demo version!"
      @ 12, 19 say "Call 123-456-7890 now to buy this program!"
      inkey(0)
      quit
   endif
#endif
```

The /d compiler option makes it much easier to do conditional compiling, because you can #define your identifiers on the command line rather than mucking around with the source code. You can leave the explicit declarations of DEBUG and DEMO out of your source code entirely, and #define them on the command line when you compile:

```
clipper myprog /dDEBUG
clipper myprog /dDEMO
```

You may optionally assign a value to an identifier. For example, assume that the following loop occurs several places in your program, and you want to be able to alter the loop counter by changing only one variable. The easiest way to do this is to define an identifier (or manifest constant) at the top of your program like so:

```
#define LOOP_CNT  500
for x = 1 to LOOP_CNT
   * perform some action
next
```

Further suppose that you want to be able to change this loop counter without changing your source code. With the /d switch, it is easy. Compiling your program with the following command line will result in a loop counter of 1000 iterations instead of 500.

```
clipper myprog /dLOOP_CNT=1000
```

But wait! Did you get a redefinition of #define compile error? That's because you are defining LOOP_CNT twice, once when you fire up the compiler, and again in the source code where you originally #defined it. Fortunately, there is an easy way to solve this problem:

```
#ifndef LOOP_CNT
   #define LOOP_CNT  500
#endif
for x = 1 to LOOP_CNT
   * perform some action
next
```

This directs the preprocessor to define LOOP_CNT only if it has not already been defined.

When you become more accustomed to using preprocessor directives and manifest constants, you will appreciate the utility of the /d option. For more details on the various directives, please refer to Chapter 7, "The Preprocessor."

/ES Exit Severity

Sets the default exit severity level. If warnings are encountered during compilation, the compiler does not set the DOS error level upon exit.

Severity setting	Action
0 [Default]	No action is taken if warnings occur
1	Set DOS error level if warnings occur
2	Set DOS error level AND do not create an OBJ file

/i<path>

Include File Search Path (New)

The /i option appends the specified directory to the front of the path list specified by the INCLUDE environmental variable. You are not required to add a trailing backslash to the path name. The following command line specifies one additional directory, C:\INCLUDE, to be searched for header files:

```
clipper myprog /ic:\include
```

If necessary, you may specify multiple search paths in a semicolon-delimited list. For example, the following command line searches two additional directories, C:\APPS and C:\INCLUDE, for header files:

```
clipper myprog /ic:\apps;c:\include
```

In most instances, though, it will suffice to keep all of your header (CH) files in one directory. The only exception might be certain application-specific header files.

When you compile a program, the Clipper 5 preprocessor looks for header files first in the current directory, then in any directories specified by the /i option, and finally in any directories specified by the INCLUDE environmental variable.

Tip: The preprocessor will search for only the first occurrence of a given header file. Therefore, if you have two versions of the header file, one in the current directory and one in your regular \INCLUDE directory, the former will override the latter.

/l

Suppress Line Numbers

The /l option omits the program's source code line numbers from the object file. This will save three bytes for each line of source code. Therefore, if you compile 1000 lines of source code with the /l option, you will save 3000 bytes in your .EXE file.

As mentioned in the discussion of the /b option, you should avoid using the /l option because size and memory usage is not much of an issue with the RTLINK linker. Also, when (not if) your programs crash, Clipper's error handler will return a line number if you do not use the /l option (rather than a zero if you use the /l option). Your programs will probably crash a great deal as you get accustomed to Clipper 5, so you should prepare to have as much information available as possible for easy debugging.

/m

Compile Module Only

The Clipper 5 watchword is modular. Using the /m option enforces this principle and makes it easier to track compiler errors. As with Clipper Summer '87, this option compiles only the current .PRG file, suppressing the automatic search for any .PRG files referenced in a program file with the DO, SET FORMAT, SET KEY, and SET PROCEDURE commands.

As mentioned during the discussion of .CLP files, the fact that RTLINK automatically removes duplicates from the symbol table makes the /m option more appealing. There is no longer much reason to compile multiple .PRG files into one .OBJ file. The /m option is also particularly useful with MAKE files, which expedite the compile process by recompiling only the source code files that have changed. (See the "MAKE Files" section in Chapter 3 for more details.) By using /m, you can prevent unnecessary recompilation of source code modules that have not been altered, which subsequently streamlines the development process.

/n

Suppress Implicit Starting Procedure (New)

The /n option suppresses the automatic definition of a procedure with the same name as the .PRG file. You should always use this option, and get in the habit of prefacing the first function in your PRG with a FUNCTION declaration.

Why go to this effort? The reason is file-wide (or external) static variables. Suppose that you want the SETTINGS_ array to be visible to every function in SETUP.PRG. You can do this by declaring SETTINGS_ as **static** prior to the first function, as shown in listing 1.1.

Listing 1.1. External STATIC variables

```
// SETUP.PRG
static settings_ := {}    // visible in both MAIN() and MODIFY()

function main
local x
for x = 1 to 5
   aadd(settings_, x)
next
modify()
aeval(settings_, { | a | qout(a) } )
return nil

function modify
local x
for x = 1 to len(settings_)
   settings_[x]++
next
return nil
```

If you omit the /n option, the compiler will create a start-up procedure entitled SETUP. SETUP will then contain only the static declaration prior to MAIN(). At run-time, this will do nothing other than waste your time.

Another desirable side effect of /n is that it conserves memory in your .EXE file. Each procedure and function name must be represented by an entry in the address table as well as an entry in the symbol table. If you compile with /n to remove the unnecessary creation of the startup procedure, you save approximately 125 bytes per object module. This might not sound like a lot but, as all Clipper developers know, when it comes to memory, every little bit helps.

(Note that by declaring procedures or functions as **static**, you can remove them from the address table. For more information on **static** functions and variables, see Chapter 6, "Variable Scoping.")

Remember: If you plan to use file-wide static variables, be sure that you are compiling with the /n switch! Failure to do so will lead to mysterious run-time errors that will drive you crazy. Get in the habit of using the /n switch now, because you will certainly want to use file-wide static variables to take full advantage of Clipper 5.

/o<path>

Object File Drive and/or Path

The /o option defines the name, location, or both of the output object file. The following example compiles MYPROG.PRG to BLAHBLAH.OBJ and places the resultant object file in the C:\OBJ directory:

```
clipper myprog /oc:\obj\blahblah
```

As you may expect, you will get a fatal error if you specify a directory that does not exist. Note: If you want to specify only a path, you must end it with a backslash (\).

/p

Generate Preprocessed Output File (New)

The /p option instructs the compiler to copy the preprocessed output to a .PPO file. This file will have the same name as the .PRG file, and as of this writing there is no way to redirect it to a different file name. Once again, it is highly recommended that you consider use of this option for instructional purposes.

Use the following command to create the file MYPROG.PPO:

```
clipper myprog /p
```

Then examine the .PPO file to see how your code looks to the preprocessor and, thus, the compiler. Do not overlook this simple way to learn about the inner workings of Clipper 5.

/q

Quiet

The /q option suppresses the display of line numbers during compilation, and can save you a few seconds when compiling long .PRG files.

/r[<lib>]

Request Linker to Search <lib> or None (New)

The /r option embeds a library search request into the object file. Libraries are searched to resolve any references that have not been resolved at compile time. For example, if you attempt to compile and link the following program:

```
function main
myfunc()
return nil
```

the linker will be forced to search the Clipper libraries (CLIPPER.LIB, EXTEND.LIB, TERMINAL.LIB, and DBFNTX.LIB) for the missing symbol MYFUNC. The Clipper 5 compiler automatically embeds search requests for CLIPPER.LIB and EXTEND.LIB into your object file. (DBFNTX.LIB and TERMINAL.LIB are usually embedded as well if the compiler deems them necessary.) This means that you do not need to specify the names of these libraries in your link command (assuming that you have specified a LIB environmental variable so that the linker can find them).

Using the /r option will override these defaults, which could in turn cause undesirable side-effects such as dozens of undefined symbols at link time and a premature death at run time. If you use /r without the <lib> parameter, no search requests are embedded. Therefore, you must explicitly name the desired libraries as part of your link command; otherwise, RTLINK will be unable to find them.

You may also specify multiple /r options to embed more than one library search request, as the following command line demonstrates.

```
clipper myprog /rGRUMP /rMYLIB  <-search GRUMP.LIB & MYLIB.LIB
```

/s

Syntax Check

With the /s option, you can check the syntax of the PRG file without generating any object code. The following command will redirect any compiler error or warning messages to the file ERROR.TXT.

```
clipper myprog /s > error.txt
```

/t<path>

Drive/Path for Temporary Files (New)

With the /t option, you can specify a different directory for temporary files generated during compilation. This speeds compilation when you have a RAM disk.

The following example uses RAM disk D to store temporary files:

```
clipper myprog /Td:
```

/u[<file>]

Use Alternate (or No) Command Definitions (New)

The /u option directs the compiler to use an alternate standard header file to preprocess your source code, rather than the defaults found in STD.CH (which are embedded directly into CLIPPER.EXE). The preprocessor searches first in the current directory, then in any directories specified by the INCLUDE environmental variable.

Warning: If you use this option, be prepared to provide redefinitions for all Clipper commands in your alternate standard header file, because the defaults will be completely ignored. If you want to create your own command set, make a copy of the STD.CH file, rename it, and edit the renamed file. You can then specify this new CH file with the /u option.

The following example uses alternate command definitions in the FRENCH.CH header file:

```
clipper myprog /ufrench.ch
```

/v

Variables Are Assumed as M->

The /v option directs the compiler to assume that all references to undeclared or unaliased variable names are either **public** or **private** declarations. This is identical to declaring such variables as **memvar** (or using the **memvar**-> construct).

/w

Enable Warnings (New)

The /w option tells the compiler to generate warning messages for undeclared or unaliased (ambiguous) variable references. This is another option that you are strongly advised to use every time you compile Clipper 5 source code. By doing so, the compiler will warn whenever you forget to declare a variable, which will quickly force you to write cleaner code.

These warnings are annoying at first, especially when they mount into the hundreds (or even thousands). When you begin porting over applications from Summer '87 to Clipper 5, you might want to redirect the warnings to a separate text file — sometimes there are so many warnings that the warning files will be longer than the original source code. Try to suffer through it, because it is the best way to get your variable scoping down pat. When you can compile "quietly" (that is, using the /w option and not getting a single warning), you will know that you are writing true Clipper 5 code.

/z

Disable logical shortcutting

The /z compiler option turns off logical "shortcutting". Shortcutting is a code optimization technique new to Clipper 5. It is employed with statements that utilize boolean operators (.and. and .or.). The default Clipper 5 behavior is to stop evaluating expressions when one tests false (.F.). Take the following code fragment (please):

```
lflag := .t.
*
if lflag .or. myfunc()
   ? "Made it this far"
endif
```

Because LFLAG is true (.T.), Clipper 5 will not bother to evaluate the second clause in the IF statement (namely, MyFunc()). The converse is true when using the .and. clause:

```
lflag := .f.
*
if lflag .and. myfunc()
   ? "Made it this far"
endif
```

Once again, MyFunc() will not be evaluated because LFLAG tests false (.F.). Clipper 5 will therefore realize that the statement must evaluate to false, and thus not bother with the second (or any subsequent) clauses.

However, some programmers relied upon the lack of shortcutting in Summer '87 to perform a chain of events. Under S'87, MyFunc() would have been evaluated in both of the examples shown above. Therefore, if you are planning to compile Summer '87 code that relies upon this behavior under Clipper 5, you should use the /z compiler option.

Please note that any code executed using the macro operator (&) always uses shortcutting. Use of the /z switch will have absolutely no effect in this regard.

Suggested configuration

You should use the following compiler options regularly:

/n	No implicit starting procedure
/w	Generate warnings
/a	Automatic memvar declaration
/p	Generate preprocessed output (PPO) file
/b	Add debugging information to the object (OBJ) file

Save time by using the CLIPPERCMD environmental variable to set these as your default compiler options, rather than having to type them in each time.

The compiler environment

Three environmental variables affect the operation of the Clipper 5 compiler: CLIPPERCMD, INCLUDE, and TMP. Although these settings will be discussed elsewhere, they merit further discussion here.

SET CLIPPERCMD

As mentioned, the CLIPPERCMD environmental variable can save you time by allowing you to establish default Clipper 5 compiler options. Each time that you compile a source code file, anything in CLIPPERCMD is appended to the command. For example, if CLIPPERCMD contained "/N /W", the following compile command:

```
clipper myprog
```

would be treated as though you typed:

```
clipper myprog /n /w
```

The following example sets up the preferred compiler configuration, as mentioned in the preceding section:

```
set clippercmd=/n /w /a /p /b
```

Warning: You must separate these options with a space; otherwise, only the first option is acted upon. (Ignore any examples in the Clipper 5 Norton Guides file that do not include spaces.) For example, the Clipper 5 compiler treats this setting:

```
set clippercmd=/n/w/a
```

as though you had typed:

```
set clippercmd=/n
```

You may continue to specify other command-line options in addition to those listed in CLIPPERCMD. Listing some options in this fashion will lead to side-effects that you should be aware of. The following list covers these side-effects in great detail.

/d (define an identifier for the preprocessor). Even if you have defined one or more identifiers with CLIPPERCMD, you may define more on the command line. However, you cannot redefine an identifier without getting a compiler warning.

/i (#include file search path): You may specify as many additional INCLUDE directories as necessary, in addition to those listed in CLIPPERCMD.

/o (destination OBJ file). If you specify /o on the command line, it overrides any settings in the CLIPPERCMD variable.

/p (generate PPO file). If you have specified /p in CLIPPERCMD, adding it to the command line will toggle the feature off.

/r (library search). You may specify as many additional libraries to search as necessary, in addition to those listed in CLIPPERCMD.

/t (destination for temp files). If you add this to the command line, it will override any /t setting you have in CLIPPERCMD.

/u (standard header file to use). If you specify /u on the command line, it will override the CLIPPERCMD setting (if there is one).

SET INCLUDE

The INCLUDE environmental variable tells the compiler where to search for header (CH) files. The search order is

1. The current directory
2. Any directories specified by the /i compiler option
3. Any directories specified by the INCLUDE environmental variable

The following example instructs the compiler to search the C:\CLIPPER5\INCLUDE directory for header files if they are not located elsewhere:

```
set include=c:\clipper5\include
```

SET TMP

The TMP variable tells the compiler and linker where to create their temporary files. As with the compiler /t option, this is best suited to a RAM disk. The following example directs temporary files to drive D:

```
set tmp=d:\
```

When things go wrong

It should not surprise you to learn that not every Clipper 5 compile will be flawless. There are three categories of compiler error messages: warnings, errors, and fatal errors. The format for all of these types of messages is

```
<filename>(<line>):  Error Cxxxx <message>[: <symbol>]
```

Warnings

Warnings indicate areas where the compiler anticipates problems, such as undeclared variables. Warnings are not fatal to the compilation process, and will not set the DOS return code. Messages in this category always begin with C1. See Table 1.2.

Table 1.2. Compiler warnings

Code	*Explanation*
C1001	Return statement with no value in function
C1002	Procedure returns value
C1003	Ambiguous variable reference
C1004	Ambiguous variable reference, assuming memvar
C1005	Redefinition or duplicate definition of #define
C1007	Function does not end with RETURN

You are going to be seeing a lot of compiler warnings during your Clipper 5 work. The following paragraphs list each warning and its probable cause(s).

C1001: Return statement with no value in function. This is an easy one: You cannot exit a function without returning a value. If you forget to, a default return value of NIL is assumed, which might not be what you intended.

C1002: Procedure returns value. This is the converse of warning C1001. Procedures are not intended to return values. Write functions instead.

C1003 and C1004: Ambiguous variable reference. There are three common reasons for this warning:

1. You forgot to explicitly declare a variable using one of the **static**, **local**, **public**, **private**, **memvar**, or **field** declarations. This means that you may not be taking full advantage of the new **static** and **local** declarations to minimize the EXE size and maximize performance. Do your best to reduce this type of warning, and your applications will benefit greatly.

2. You misspelled the name of a variable. The compiler is quite sensitive to even the smallest typing error.

3. You may have forgotten to #include a header file. If the ambiguous variable is entirely uppercase (for example, K_ESC, K_ENTER, or any of the other inkey() definitions in INKEY.CH), you should check your #include statements first.

C1005: Redefinition or duplicate definition of #define. You may get this warning because you have declared the same identifier both with the /d compiler option and in your PRG file. If you need to declare an identifier in your source code, but also intend to declare it on the command line, bulletproof your source code in the following manner:

```
// the right way
#ifndef LOOP_CNT
   #define LOOP_CNT  500
#endif

// the wrong way
#define LOOP_CNT  500
```

C1007: Function does not end with RETURN. This compiler warning is self-explanatory. Like all compiler warnings*, it will only appear when you compile with the /w option (which you should always use).

Errors

Compiler error messages indicate program errors that may be (and usually are) fatal to the compilation process. After a compilation error, the compiler attempts to recover and continue the compilation process. In most cases, however, it is a lost cause; DOS returns a return code of 1 and the object file is not created. Messages in this category always begin with C2. See Table 1.3.

Table 1.3. Compiler errors

Code	*Explanation*
C2001	Syntax error
C2002	Statement unterminated at end of line
C2003	Syntax error in statement
C2004	Illegal character
C2005	Statement not recognized
C2006	Statement not allowed outside procedure or function
C2007	Unterminated string
C2009	Invalid use of @ (pass by reference) operator
C2010	Incorrect number of arguments
C2011	EXIT statement with no loop in sight
C2012	LOOP statement with no loop in sight
C2013	EXIT statement violates enclosing SEQUENCE
C2014	LOOP statement violates enclosing SEQUENCE
C2015	Illegal initializer
C2016	Name conflicts with previous declaration
C2017	Duplicate variable declaration

* The only exception that we are aware of is warning C1005, which results when you attempt to redefine a previously-established identifier. This warning will appear even if you do not use the /w option.)

C2018 Outer block variable out of reach
C2019 CALL of Clipper procedure or function
C2020 Mistreatment of CALLed symbol
C2021 Redefinition of Clipper procedure or function
C2022 Redefinition of predefined function
C2023 Clipper definition of CALLed symbol
C2024 Unclosed control structures
C2025 ELSE does not match IF
C2026 ELSEIF does not match IF
C2027 ENDIF does not match IF
C2028 ENDDO does not match WHILE
C2029 NEXT does not match FOR
C2030 ENDCASE does not match DO CASE
C2031 CASE or OTHERWISE is not immediately within DO CASE
C2032 TEXT statement error
C2033 Missing ENDTEXT
C2034 Formal parameters already declared
C2035 Invalid declaration
C2036 Mayhem in CASE handler
C2037 Invalid procedure name in DO statement
C2038 Invalid target name in CALL statement
C2039 Invalid selector in send
C2040 Invalid unary inline operator
C2041 Invalid binary operator
C2042 Invalid lvalue
C2043 Invalid alias expression
C2044 Invalid function name
C2045 Target name was used previously in non-CALL context
C2046 SEQUENCE nesting error
C2047 GET contains complex macro
C2048 GET contains both macro and declared symbol
C2049 Code block contains complex macro

C2050 Code block contains both macro and declared symbol

C2051 **local** declaration follows executable statement

C2052 **memvar** declaration follows executable statement

C2053 **field** declaration follows executable statement

C2054 **static** declaration follows executable statement

C2055 Syntax error in #define

C2056 Unexpected end of file in #define

C2057 Label missing in #define

C2058 Comma or right parenthesis missing in #define

C2059 Missing => in #translate/#command

C2060 Unknown result marker in #translate/#command

C2061 Label error in #translate/#command

C2062 Bad match marker in #translate/#command

C2063 Bad result marker #translate/#command

C2064 Bad restricted match marker in #translate/#command

C2065 Empty optional clause in #translate/#command

C2066 Unclosed optional clause in #translate/#command

C2067 Too many nested #ifdefs

C2068 Error in #ifdef

C2069 #endif does not match #ifdef

C2070 #else does not match #ifdef

C2071 Error in #undef

C2072 Ambiguous match pattern in #translate/#command

C2073 Result pattern contains nested clauses in #translate/#command

C2075 Too many locals

C2076 Too many parameters

C2077 Too many parameters

C2078 Circular #define

C2079 Circular #translate/#command

C2086 RETURN violates enclosing SEQUENCE

Common errors. The following are typical Clipper 5 compiler errors that should be easy to cure.

Always be careful to initialize **local** and **static** variables using the in-line assignment operator (:=) rather than the equal sign (=). Forgetting the colon will result in the C2001 syntax error message.

Do not get carried away with the in-line assignment operator. For example, you would not want to use it in the following situation:

```
if inkey(0) := 27  // invalid use of ":="
   return .f.
endif
```

This tells the compiler to assign a value to a function, INKEY(). Naturally, it balks at the thought and displays:

```
C2042 Invalid lvalue error
```

This is what can happen if you do a global search-and-replace to change all equal signs to in-line assignment operators.

local, **static**, **memvar**, and **field** declarations must precede all executable statements in a function or procedure. Failure to do so will result in the C2051, C2052, C2053, and C2054 error messages.

Under Summer '87 and the initial release of Clipper 5, it was possible to RETURN (instead of BREAKing) from inside a SEQUENCE.

```
begin sequence
      *
      return
      *
end sequence
```

CHAPTER 2

Linking Your Application

In Chapter 1, you learned the best ways to compile your Clipper source code. Now it is time to put your compiled code to good use by creating an executable program with it. The next step on the path to execution is linking.

This chapter will discuss the basics of the linking process. We will review the syntax and options for the .RTLINK/5.0 linker. You will learn how to slash your linking time and disk storage requirements with Pre-Linked Libraries, as well as how to manipulate the environment to facilitate and streamline .RTLINK/5.0's operation. We will also touch briefly upon using library managers to examine the contents of library (.LIB) files.

Overview

Although linking is an operation that every Clipper developer undergoes many times during the course of a workday, it remains an arcane subject. Most Clipper developers know very little about the link process. It is obviously difficult to optimize something that you know nothing about, which is why we are going to get to the nitty-gritty of linking right here and now. Wait... don't turn the page! You will be surprised at how simple it is.

As you probably know, the compiler produces code that is readable at the machine level. However, the object (.OBJ) modules it creates do not constitute an executable program by any stretch of the imagination. It is the linker's responsibility to combine these compiled modules into an executable (.EXE) file. (Note that some executable files carry the extension of .COM; however, you will never encounter such a beast when working with Clipper, because .COM files are limited to 64K in size.)

The linker combines objects that have been compiled separately. It must ensure that the compiled modules will be accessible to other code segments. Otherwise, modular programming would be impossible because you would always have to combine all of your procedures and functions into one gigantic .PRG file. Not only is this horrible programming practice, but it would be impossible to implement due to limitations in the number of modules per source code file.

Object modules contain the following three types of symbols:

Public - these symbols are callable from other objects.

Static - these symbols are callable only within the same object (see Chapter 6 for a full discussion of static functions).

External (or **Undefined**) - these symbols are referred to by one object but exist in another object. This is where the linker earns its keep by scanning other objects to resolve external references.

The process of scanning to resolve external symbols occurs in two passes:

Pass 1: the linker first scans the list of public symbols in all of the specified object files. As it finds the symbols, it assigns a segment address to each one. When the linker has finished scanning the object files, if there are still unresolved symbols, it will proceed to search any specified library (.LIB) files.

Pass 2: the linker searches all object and library files again to see if there are any **public** definitions for remaining unresolved symbols. If/when it finds such **public** definitions, it assigns addresses to ensure that the calling symbol will be able to properly locate the called symbol. This procedure is also known as "fixing up". If none of an object's public symbols are referred to by any other objects, the linker will not bother to include it in the executable file.

A Linker's-eye view of symbols

Before we delve into overlays, an example of how the linker deals with symbols would be appropriate. Listing 2.1 presents the DispTime() function, which displays the current time in 12 hour format. This is easily accomplished by passing the system time as a parameter to the Clipper AMPM() function.

Listing 2.1 Display current time in 12-hour format

```
/* DISPTIME.PRG - compile with /N */
function DispTime
? ampm(time())
return nil
```

When you compile DispTime(), the compiler will create the object file DispTime.OBJ. It will put three symbols in the internal symbol table:

1. **DISPTIME** - the name of the primary function, required so that it can be assigned an address.

2. **QOUT** - where did this come from? The "?" output command is translated by the preprocessor into a call to the Clipper QOUT() function. (This will be discussed in much greater detail in Chapter 7.) The QOUT() symbol therefore must be resolved at link-time.

3. **AMPM** - called directly within DispTime(). This must also be resolved at link-time.

At link-time, the linker will attempt to resolve the two external symbols (QOUT and AMPM). Assuming that you do not specify any other .OBJ files, the linker will search libraries as determined by the search requests embedded in the DISPTIME.OBJ file. (As discussed in Chapter 1, the Clipper 5 compiler by default will embed library search requests for CLIPPER.LIB, EXTEND.LIB, DBFNTX.LIB, and TERMINAL.LIB.)

Let's peek at the Clipper libraries to see where QOUT() and AMPM() may be lurking. The best way to do this is through the use of a library manager utility. Microsoft's LIB and Borland's TLIB are popular library managers. They are packaged with each company's respective programming language products. Both of these utilities allow you to generate a list file containing all of the objects and symbols in a .LIB file, along with their sizes and addresses.

The following commands generate the list files CLIPLIST and EXTLIST for CLIPPER.LIB and EXTEND.LIB, respectively.

```
lib clipper,cliplist
lib extend,extlist
```

For more information on using library managers to create your library (.LIB) files, please refer to the sidebar "Creating Your Own Library Files".

If you examine CLIPLIST, you will discover that the QOUT() function is contained in CLIPPER.LIB. In fact, it is part of a larger object module, TERM, which contains various input and output functions. Listing 2.2 shows all of the relevant information of the TERM object module, including its relative offset from the beginning of the library file, code and data size, and all of the public symbols it contains.

Listing 2.2 Snapshot of TERM.OBJ (taken from CLIPPER.LIB)

TERM	*Offset: 0003a260H*	*Code and data size:*	*189aH*
DEVOUT	DISPOUT	LASTKEY	NEXTKEY
QOUT	QQOUT	SETCURSOR	SETKEY
SETPRC	_Now	__ATCLEAR	__BOX
__BOXD	__BOXS	__CLEAR	__COL
__cQOut	__dbgtermx	__DEVPOS	__EJECT
__INKEY0	__INKEY1	__KEYBOARD	__modal_key
__nbuff	__PCOL	__PROW	__ROW
__SETPOS	__SETPOSBS	__termSLR	__XHELP

The linker will spy the public symbol QOUT in the midst of the TERM object, and will therefore link the entire TERM.OBJ into your executable file. This means that all of the other functions will automatically become part of the .EXE. However, this is not necessarily a problem because you will need most of them anyway.

The situation is quite different with AMPM(). If you examine the EXTLIST file you generated a moment ago, you will see that AMPM() is part of the EXAMPLEP object module. Surely enough, AMPM() is one of a series of functions contained in EXAMPLEP.PRG. This file is on the Clipper 5 distribution disks, and contains various and sundry sample functions written in Clipper. Table 2.1 lists these functions along with brief descriptions of each.

Table 2.1 Functions in EXAMPLEP.PRG

Function	*Description*
AMPM( )	Converts a time string to 12-hour format
STRZERO( )	Converts a numeric to a string padded with zeros
DAYS( )	Returns integer number of days from numeric seconds
DBF( )	Returns the alias of the currently selected .DBF
ELAPTIME( )	Returns string showing difference between start and end times
FKLABEL( )	Returns the name of a given function key
FKMAX( )	Returns maximum number of function keys
LENNUM( )	Returns the string length of a numeric expression
MOD( )	Returns remainder of one number divided by another
OS( )	Returns name of current operating system
READKEY( )	Returns number representing the key pressed to exit a READ
SECS( )	Returns numeric seconds as a quantity of the time string
TSTRING( )	Returns 24-hour time string from numeric seconds

When EXTEND library was created at the "factory", the source code in EXAMPLEP.PRG was compiled into one object module (EXAMPLEP.OBJ). This object was added to the EXTEND library (EXTEND.LIB). Listing 2.3 shows all of the relevant information about the EXAMPLEP object in EXTEND.LIB.

Listing 2.3 Snapshot of EXAMPLEP.OBJ (taken from EXTEND.LIB)

EXAMPLEP	*Offset: 00002300H*	*Code and data size:*	*5cfH*
AMPM	DAYS	DBF	ELAPTIME
FKLABEL	FKMAX	LENNUM	MOD
OS	READKEY	SECS	STRZERO
TSTRING			

As you can see, there is a public symbol for each function in the .PRG file. This is not a particularly efficient example of library management, because if you call any of these functions the linker will put all of them in your executable file! To add insult to injury, these functions in turn make calls to other Clipper functions. The linker then must resolve those symbols as well, which further bloats your .EXE file. When the dust clears, you will have over 70K of unnecessary code in your .EXE file.

However, since the source code for EXAMPLEP.PRG is provided with Clipper 5, there is an easy workaround to this inefficiency. Simply pull the AMPM() source code from EXAMPLEP.PRG and put it directly in your program. Listing 2.4 shows a revised version of DISPTIME.PRG that contains both DispTime() and AMPM().

Listing 2.4 Display current time in 12-hour format

```
/* DISPTIME.PRG - compile with /N */
function DispTime
? ampm(time())
return nil

function ampm(cTime)
if val(cTime) < 12
   cTime += " am"
elseif val(cTime) = 12
   cTime += " pm"
else
   cTime := str(val(cTime) - 12, 2) + substr(cTime, 3) + " pm"
endif
return cTime
```

When you compile this, AMPM() will still appear in the symbol table, but it will be resolved at compile-time. Therefore, when it comes time to link the executable file, the linker will not be compelled to pull in the EXAMPLEP object module from EXTEND.LIB.

Creating your own library Files

To save on typing and linking time, it is often expeditious to combine these object (.OBJ) files into one library (.LIB) file. To do this, you will need a library manager utility. Microsoft's LIB.EXE will be used for these examples. The syntax for Microsoft LIB.EXE is:

```
LIB [<Libname>] [<Commands>],[<Listfile>],[<Output>] [;]
```

The <Libname> parameter is the name of the library (the .LIB extension is assumed and therefore not necessary). The <Commands> parameters are of the general format <symbol> <filename>, and must be separated by spaces. The available symbols are shown in Table 2.2.

Table 2.2 Symbols for manipulating object modules

Symbol	*Action*
+	add module name to the library
-	remove module name from the library
*	extract module name without removing
-+	replace module name in library
-*	extract module name and remove

The <Listfile> parameter is the name of the list file to be generated, which lists the module names in the library and the memory required for each module.

The <Output> parameter is the name of the output library file. This is useful if you wish to make a new library that essentially duplicates another with some modifications. If you do not wish to generate a list file or a new output library file, you may follow the <command> parameter with a semi-colon.

Please note that each of these parameters is optional. If you run LIB without one or all of them, you will be prompted for each item.

Examples

Let us suppose that you have three object files that you use in all of your Clipper applications. You wish to combine these into one library file named MYFUNCS.LIB. You do not need a list file, nor do you need a different name for the output library. Here is the command you would use:

```
lib myfuncs +dupes +rec_lock +rec_srch ;
```

This will generate MYFUNCS.LIB, which will contain the four object files. Now, instead of linking in each .OBJ file:

```
rtlink fi mfile, dupes, rec_lock, rec_srch /pll:base50
```

you can merely link in the library like so:

```
rtlink fi mfile li myfuncs /pll:base50
```

Suppose that later you make changes to the source code of REC_LOCK.PRG and recompile it to reflect those changes. You would then update MYFUNCS.LIB with the following command:

```
lib myfuncs -+rec_lock;
```

If you decided later that you did not want REC_LOCK in your library, you could delete it with:

```
lib myfuncs -rec_lock;
```

Armed with this information, you should now be able to put together your own library of Clipper functions.

Overlays

Overlays are a method of permitting large programs to execute in less memory than would ordinarily be necessary. Chunks of code that would usually be relegated to the .EXE file are instead directed to separate sections. These separate sections are not loaded immediately at run-time. Instead, they are pulled into memory only when a procedure or function within them is called by your program. This can significantly reduce your program's required load size. For example, if your load size is 415K and you move 70K of code into an overlay, your load size would be reduced to approximately 345K.

The word "overlay" evokes dismay in any Clipper programmer familiar with PLINK86. Fortunately, the advent of dynamic overlay linkers has made use of overlays completely hassle-free. PLINK86 deals with **static overlays**, whereas .RTLINK/5.0 can use **dynamic overlays**. The words "static" and "dynamic" themselves are polar opposites, as are PLINK86 and .RTLINK/5.0.

Static overlays

Static overlays consist of code stored in sections that occupy the same memory space at run-time. As mentioned above, this was the only method of overlaying available with PLINK86. The biggest disadvantage to static overlays is their unwieldy management. Because the overlays must occupy the same memory space at run-time, you had to be very careful not to call a procedure in an overlay from a procedure in another overlay. The problem is that static overlays are loaded at the object level, rather than the procedure level.

The sample script file in Listing 2.5 illustrates the difficulty in managing static overlays. If for some reason you needed to call a procedure in INVDATA while you were within CUSTDATA, the overlay manager would need to remove the entire CUSTDATA object module from memory in order to load the INVDATA object module. When the program attempted to return to CUSTDATA, it would crash upon not being able to find it. (Always remember that computers are extremely stupid and, despite having a vast supply of memory, quite forgetful.)

Listing 2.5 Sample script file using static overlays

```
BEGINAREA
   SECTION FILE custdata
   SECTION FILE invdata
   SECTION FILE venddata
ENDAREA
```

This marks the beginning of a long series of headaches involving static overlays. Because Summer '87 applications have a voracious demand for memory, Clipper developers have to struggle with PLINK86 to design their overlays so that their programs will not crash. This often necessitates multiple and nested overlays. Spending more time on overlay management than on writing software can be very demoralizing. But with Clipper 5 and .RTLINK/5.0, it is no longer necessary to rely upon static overlays.

Dynamic overlays

Dynamic overlays consist of code that is loaded into a memory pool (or "swap space") at run-time. Dynamic overlays are generally loaded at the procedure level rather than the object level. This effectively eliminates the biggest problem with static overlays, as discussed above. You no longer have to worry about calling a procedure in a different overlay section, because .RTLINK/5.0 can handle it gracefully. Another benefit to dynamic overlays is that you should rarely (if ever) have to concern yourself with nesting overlays or any similar PLINK86 gyrations.

Dynamic overlay linkers generally keep the symbol table in the executable (or "root") area, and put each procedure or function in a separate overlay segment to facilitate loading. However, .RTLINK/5.0 establishes its overlays a bit differently. It divides all of the Clipper-compiled code in your application into fixed-length overlays (which are also referred to as "pages"). These pages may or may not correspond to routines—each page may contain either several small functions, or part of a large one.

As your application runs, .RTLINK/5.0 makes the current page available. As the end of a page is approached, the overlay manager loads other pages into the swap space so that your program will keep running. Because the swap space is of a finite size, as it fills, .RTLINK/5.0 will need to discard pages in order to be able to load new ones. To minimize the need for fetching pages from disk (which would slow performance considerably), .RTLINK/5.0 maintains a profile of which pages are used most often. It can therefore take these pages into account when deciding which pages to discard from the swap space. Clipper 5 automatically determines the size of the swap space for best performance.

There is one limitation to the .RTLINK/5.0 dynamic overlay linker. Only pure Clipper-compiled code can be dynamically overlaid. C and Assembler modules must reside in the root area, along with the .RTLINK/5.0 overlay manager. Regardless of how much Clipper code you have, it will run in a relatively small swap space. This leaves far more memory for your program to work with, which is great news because Clipper applications crave memory.

Table 2.3 illustrates the difference between a Clipper Summer '87 application, with and without overlays, and a Clipper 5 application. Note the drastic increase in free pool memory in the Clipper 5 memory model.

Table 2.3 Memory differences between Summer '87 and Clipper 5

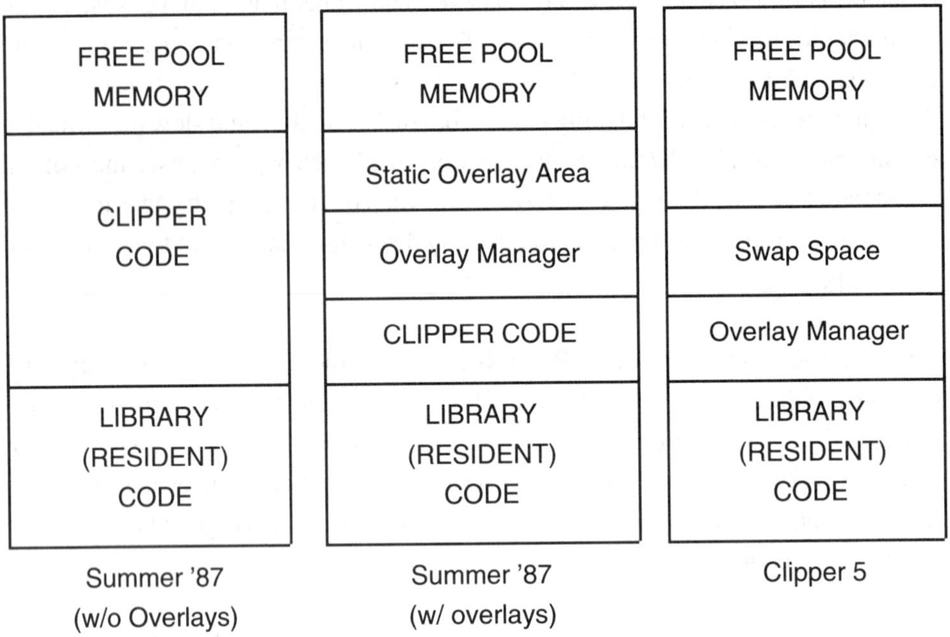

Summer '87 (w/o Overlays)	Summer '87 (w/ overlays)	Clipper 5
FREE POOL MEMORY	FREE POOL MEMORY	FREE POOL MEMORY
CLIPPER CODE	Static Overlay Area	
	Overlay Manager	Swap Space
	CLIPPER CODE	Overlay Manager
LIBRARY (RESIDENT) CODE	LIBRARY (RESIDENT) CODE	LIBRARY (RESIDENT) CODE

Symbol table compression

In earlier versions of Clipper, symbol table bloat was a major source of concern. Each variable name required an entry in the symbol table for the .OBJ file in which it appeared. When the application was linked, PLINK86* did not remove duplicate symbols from the executable file. This resulted in considerable "dead weight" in the .EXE file that accomplished no purpose except to hasten memory problems.

The common practice in Summer '87 was to use .CLP files (also discussed in Chapter 1) to combine multiple .PRG files into one .OBJ file. This forced the compiler to remove the duplicate symbols itself, because duplicates could not be tolerated within the same object module.

* WarpLink, a third-party linker, provides a utility entitled SymPakWL that will compact the symbol table of a Clipper Summer '87 application. Please refer to the brief descriptions near the end of this chapter for more information about WarpLink and other alternative linkers.

However, .RTLINK/5.0 is intelligent enough to automatically remove duplicates from the symbol table in your executable file. This is a major advantage in terms of memory savings, and means that you do not have to bother using .CLP files. You can structure your programs in a more modular fashion, without having to lump all your procedures together into one mammoth file to combat duplicate symbols.

Lazy programmers take heed: This breakthrough does not necessarily mean that you can now resort to sloppy coding! Rather, you should continue to pursue good memory management techniques, such as using arrays instead of memory variables and the reuse of symbol names. For more information on the basic tenets of memory management through symbol reduction (along with many other relevant tips), you have three places to turn:

- Roger Donnay, author of dCLIP, has written several fine articles on the subject of memory conservation for The Aquarium, a disk-based Clipper journal available from Grumpfish, Inc. (Voice: (503) 588-1815, Fax: (503) 588-1980).

- Al Acker has written an excellent "Memory Management in Clipper" tutorial, which is available from Pinnacle Publishing (Voice: (800) 231-1293 or (206) 941-2300).

- Savannah Brentnall and David Morgan wrote an enlightening memory management dissertation in the January/February 1989 issue of Nantucket News, which is available from Computer Associates Corporation (Voice: (213) 390-7923, Fax: (213) 397-5469).

Pre-Linked Libraries

.RTLINK/5.0 allows you to build Pre-Linked Libraries (.PLL) that can radically decrease your development time by speeding the link cycle. A Pre-Linked Library contains code pulled from object and library files that is nearly the same as an executable (.EXE) file. The only difference is that wherever code in the Pre-Linked Library refers to code in the main application, these references must be adjusted (or "fixed up") at run-time.

Each Pre-Linked Library has a corresponding Pre-Linked Transfer (.PLT) file. .RTLINK/5.0 must rely upon the .PLT file at link-time to provide relevant information about the Pre-Linked Library.

Because the code in a Pre-Linked Library is already considered as linked, there is no need for .RTLINK/5.0 to put it in your .EXE file. When you link an executable with a Pre-Linked Library, .RTLINK/5.0 pulls information from the corresponding .PLT file into the (now much smaller) .EXE file.

At run-time, the .RTLINK/5.0 overlay manager will know to look for the .PLL file based on the information embedded in the .EXE file. The PLL and LIB environmental variables (discussed later in this chapter) are used to facilitate this search. At this time, the references in the .PLL file will be "fixed-up" to the code in the main application, the .PLL will be loaded into memory, and your program will begin execution just as if you had created a traditional large .EXE file.

Please note that the entire .PLL file is treated as part of your root (.EXE) area. Memory savings is definitely not one of the advantages of using .PLLs.

Creating BASE52.PLL

If you have not already created the BASE52.PLL file, please take a moment to do so before going any further! First, comb your hard disk for the file BASE52.LNK (see Listing 2.6 in the event that you cannot find it). This is a script file that allows .RTLINK/5.0 to create a Pre-Linked Library containing all the major Clipper 5 subsystems.

Listing 2.6 BASE52.LNK file

```
prelink
output base52

lib clipper, extend, terminal, dbfntx

refer _VOPS, _VMACRO, _VDB, _VDBF, _VDBFNTX
refer _VTERM, _VPICT, _VGETSYS
refer _VDBG

exclude ERRORSYS
```

Make sure that you have a LIB environmental variable that points to the directory containing your Clipper 5 libraries (probably C:\CLIPPER5\LIB). Fire up .RTLINK/ 5.0 with the following command:

```
rtlink @base52
```

This will create two files: BASE52.PLL and BASE52.PLT. Place these in the directory designated for PLL storage (probably C:\CLIPPER5\PLL). Make sure that you have a PLL environmental variable pointing to this directory.

Faster linking

Create a short program that opens a database and issues several @..GET commands. Compile it to an object file. Then link with the following two commands:

```
rtlink fi myprg
rtlink fi myprg /pll:base52
```

You will be stunned by the speed of the second command. For a simple program like the one described above, the link without the .PLL took 27 seconds on a 386/20. With the .PLL, the link time dropped to 7 seconds! That's a time savings of nearly 75%! This should be sufficient to convince you that Pre-Linked Libraries are worth using during your development cycle. When you are ready to ship your application, you can switch back to a full link.

Saving disk space

Although the price of hard disks has plummeted over the past few years, most of us can still use more free hard disk space. .RTLINK's Pre-Linked Libraries give us this freedom by reducing storage requirements for common code.

If you have worked with the Summer '87 version of Clipper, you are probably aware that Summer '87 applications contained a minimum of 150K of overhead. The ubiquitous "hello world" program weighed in at approximately 159K. Granted, Clipper is not the language in which to be writing such a program. Nonetheless, the huge overhead concerned many people who insisted on using this traditional (though inappropriate) benchmark.

Clipper 5 reduces this overhead to about 100K, mainly due to the increased granularity of CLIPPER.LIB. This means that if you do not need certain subsystems, such as the macro compiler or network-related functions, they will not be linked into your executable. (This was not the case in Summer '87, where you got everything whether you needed it or not.) However, 100K is still quite a bit of overhead.

With the use of a Pre-Linked Library, though, you can have .EXE files as small as 4K. As mentioned above, this does *not* mean that you will be able to run a Clipper program in 10K of available RAM! You can confirm this for yourself by linking a one-line program with a Pre-Linked Library. Figure 2.1 shows the output from two link cycles, with and without a .PLL. The program in question contained one statement: "function main".

Figure 2.1 Load size vs. .EXE size

```
253K available
Compiling TEMP.PRG
Code size 32, Symbols 32, Constants 0

D>rtlink fi temp
.RTLink for Clipper Dynamic Overlay Linker/Pre-Linker Version 3.11

(C) Copyright Pocket Soft Inc., 1988-1990. All Rights Reserved.

100K

D>dir temp.exe

 Volume in drive D is MS-RAMDRIVE
 Directory of  D:\

TEMP     EXE    109568 02-27-91  10:36a
               1 File(s)    1580032 bytes free

D>rtlink fi temp /pll:base52
.RTLink for Clipper Dynamic Overlay Linker/Pre-Linker Version 3.11
```

```
(C) Copyright Pocket Soft Inc., 1988-1990. All Rights Reserved.

225K

D>dir temp.exe

 Volume in drive D is MS-RAMDRIVE
 Directory of  D:\

TEMP     EXE      4096 02-27-91  10:36a
        1 File(s)    1684480 bytes free
```

You can see that although the .EXE file created with the .PLL is only 4K, its load size will still be a healthy 225K. In fact, this is more than double the load size of the full-blown .EXE. At run-time the entire .PLL file will be treated as part of the root, which means that its size will be reflected in the load size. Once again, memory savings are not the reason to use Pre-Linked Libraries.

However, the fact that you can produce small .EXEs through the use of Pre-Linked Libraries means that you can save dramatically on storage space. For example, let's suppose that you have ten Clipper applications on your hard disk. At the absolute minimum, those ten .EXE files contain a combined overhead of 1 Megabyte (100K x 10). If you use a Pre-Linked Library to create them, you will remove the overhead from the .EXE files and isolate it entirely to the .PLL file. Assuming that the BASE52.PLL file has a size of approximately 300K, this represents a savings of 700K of storage space.

Remote support

A third advantage to using Pre-Linked Libraries is in the area of remote support. If you do programming work for clients across the state or across the country, you probably spend a considerable amount of time and money transmitting files via modem. The smallest change in your code may mean that you have to send them an entirely new .EXE file. Even with the use of file compression utilities such as PKZIP (TM) or LHARC (TM), you are still facing a long file transfer.

Pre-Linked Libraries will help you reduce your phone bill. Instead of giving your clients a large .EXE file, give them a small .EXE and the corresponding .PLL file. Then when you make modifications (don't call them "bug fixes"), you can send them a small .EXE rather than a gigantic one.

Pre-Linked Library (.PLL) files can be distributed on a royalty-free basis in the same manner as executable (.EXE) files.

.RTLINK/5.0 specifics

Default syntax

The default syntax for .RTLINK/5.0 is "FREEFORMAT". This corresponds exactly to the PLINK86 syntax, as shown in Listing 2.7.

Listing 2.7 .RTLINK/5.0 FREEFORMAT syntax

```
rtlink file <objlist> [lib <liblist>] [<link options>] ;
[output <output file>] | [@<scriptfile>]
```

If you are accustomed to using Microsoft LINK, .RTLINK/5.0 also offers "POSITIONAL" syntax. Listing 2.8 demonstrates POSITIONAL syntax.

Listing 2.8 .RTLINK/5.0 POSITIONAL syntax

```
rtlink <objlist>, [<output>], [<mapfile>], [<liblist>], ;
[<link options>] | [@<scriptfile>]
```

If you prefer always to use POSITIONAL syntax, you can use the RTLINKCMD environmental variable to specify this to .RTLINK/5.0 with the following command:

```
set rtlinkcmd=/positional
```

You may also simply call RTLINK by itself without parameters, in which case you will be prompted for each command. The following FREEFORMAT syntax links the files MAIN, DATA, and REPORTS using the BASE50 Pre-Linked Library and the GRUMP library file. Since no output file is explicitly named, the resulting .EXE will carry the name of the first object file listed (MAIN).

```
rtlink fi main, data, reports lib grump /pll:base50
```

Note that the Clipper libraries (CLIPPER, EXTEND, DBFNTX, and TERMINAL) are not listed. It is not necessary to list them because the compiler will embed library search requests for these libraries in your object modules. If for some reason you do not want these library searches to be performed, you can either use the NODEFAULT link option to suppress the search, or the compiler /R option to cause them not to be embedded. (Please turn back to Chapter 1 if you need more information on /R.)

Script files

You may optionally create an ASCII text file that contains all of the necessary commands to link your executable file. When you are working with extremely involved projects, you will find script files to be much easier to deal with than typing an endless file list each time you link.

If you use the FREEFORMAT syntax, options specified in the script file do not have to be in a specific order. However, if you are using POSITIONAL, the format of the script file must be as follows:

```
<objlist>[<link options>]
[<output>]
[<mapfile>]
[<liblist>]
```

Listing 2.9 shows a FREEFORMAT script file that accomplishes the same purpose as the command line shown above. To link the executable file based upon this script file, you would issue the following command:

```
RTLINK @test
```

Listing 2.9 Sample .RTLINK/5.0 FREEFORMAT script file

```
#test.lnk
file main
file data
file reports
lib grump
pll base50
```

Linker options

.RTLINK/5.0 has numerous options that you can specify either on the command line, in your script file, or as part of the RTLINKCMD environmental variable. If you plan to use certain options on a regular basis, you should definitely make use of RTLINKCMD to save time.

Most of the linker options have different syntax for POSITIONAL and FREEFORMAT mode. If you are using POSITIONAL mode, you must specify options preceded by a forward slash ("/"). FREEFORMAT allows you to omit this slash and the colon (if there is one).

BATCH. The /BATCH option prevents .RTLINK/5.0 from prompting you when it is unable to locate a file. The default setting for this is /NOBATCH.

This option may be used in both FREEFORMAT and POSITIONAL mode. If you are using POSITIONAL, you must use the syntax "/BATCH" (or "/NOBATCH").

BEGINAREA..ENDAREA. These commands designate a static overlay area. All sections specified between these commands (that do not contain Clipper code) become static overlay sections within this static overlay. You may nest these constructs if necessary.

Even if specified within a BEGINAREA..ENDAREA, Clipper-compiled code will still be put in the dynamic overlay. Listing 2.10 creates a static overlay containing REPORT1, REPORT2, REPORT3, and REPORT4.

Listing 2.10 Static overlay construction

```
BEGINAREA
     SECTION FILE report1
     SECTION FILE report2
     SECTION FILE report3
     SECTION FILE report4
ENDAREA
```

However, as previously discussed, in light of the tremendous advantages of dynamic overlays you will probably not be using static overlays much.

DEBUG. This option affects the run-time overlay manager. If used, .RTLINK/5.0 will display a message identifying each overlay as it is loaded into memory at run-time. This option may be used in both FREEFORMAT and POSITIONAL mode. If you are using POSITIONAL, you must use the syntax "/DEBUG".

DEFAULT. By default, .RTLINK/5.0 obeys any library search requests embedded by the compiler. If you wish to override this behavior, you may use the /NODEFAULTLIBRARYSEARCH option (the abbreviated /NODEFAULT will also suffice). This option may be used in both FREEFORMAT and POSITIONAL mode. If you are using POSITIONAL, you must use the syntax "/DEFAULT" (or "/NODEFAULT").

DYNAMIC. This option forces .RTLINK/5.0 to put any subsequent modules containing Clipper code into a dynamic overlay instead of the root (.EXE). This is done by default. If you wish to change this behavior, you can use the RESIDENT option. This option may be used in both FREEFORMAT and POSITIONAL mode. If you are using POSITIONAL, you must use the syntax "/DYNAMIC:<overlayfile>".

EXCLUDE. This option allows you to specify certain symbols that should be excluded from the link. This is useful to avoid duplicate symbols. EXCLUDE may be used in both FREEFORMAT and POSITIONAL mode. If you are using POSITIONAL, you must use the syntax "/EXCLUDE:<symbol>".

Listing 2.11 demonstrates how you could create the BASE50 Pre-Linked Library, excluding the GETSYS symbol.

Listing 2.11 BASE52.LNK file excluding GETSYS

```
prelink
output base52

LIB clipper, extend, terminal, dbfntx

refer _VOPS, _VMACRO, _VDB, _VDBF, _VDBFNTX
refer _VTERM, _VPICT, _VGETSYS
refer _VDBG
exclude getsys
```

EXTDICTIONARY. This option determines whether or not .RTLINK/5.0 is to search the extended dictionary. By default, this search will be performed. If you wish to suppress it, you may use the /NOEXTDICTIONARY option. This option may be used in both FREEFORMAT and POSITIONAL mode. If you are using POSITIONAL, you must use the syntax "/EXT" (or "/NOEXT").

FREEFORMAT. As discussed earlier, this directs the linker to expect FREEFORMAT (PLINK86-style) input syntax. This is the default input mode.

HELP. This displays all linker options on the screen.

IGNORECASE. This option is similar to the Microsoft Link /NOE switch. It determines whether or not case should be significant in symbol and segment names. By default, case will not be significant. If you wish to change this, you should use the /NOIGNORECASE option. This option may be used in both FREEFORMAT and POSITIONAL mode. If you are using POSITIONAL, you must use the syntax "/IGNORE" (or "/NOIGNORE").

INCREMENTAL. This option enables incremental linking of Clipper-compiled modules. Although this option has been ballyhooed, at press time it leaves a lot to be desired. By default, incremental linking is not used, which is probably for the best.

If you are a brave soul and wish to use incremental linking anyway, the syntax is "/INCREMENTAL[:<n>]". <n> is an optional parameter indicating how much buffer space to keep in each Clipper module. Increasing this parameter will have two effects: It will increase the likelihood that an incremental link can be performed (as opposed to a full link); and it will mean a greater amount of wasted space in your executable file.

If you want incremental linking, you should investigate third party linkers such as Blinker and WarpLink.

MAP. This option allows you to generate a map file containing one or more reports about the link session. By default, no map will be created.

There are three available map options:

S - this report shows the name, starting and ending memory addresses, and class and group information for each segment.

N - this report lists each public segment by name. It also shows each segment's memory address in segment:offset format.

A - this report lists each public segment by value. It also shows each segment's memory address in segment:offset format.

This option may be used with both FREEFORMAT and POSITIONAL mode. If you are using POSITIONAL, you must use the syntax "/MAP:<option list>". If you are using FREEFORMAT, you may optionally redirect the map output to a different file with the syntax "MAP=<mapfile>".

MODULE <list>. This option allows you to move segments from specified modules into the current static overlay section.

PLL. As discussed earlier, this option allows you to rely upon a Pre-Linked Library file when creating an executable. This option may be used with both FREEFORMAT and POSITIONAL mode. If you are using POSITIONAL, you must use the syntax "/PLL:<pllfile>".

POSITIONAL. As discussed earlier, this directs the linker to expect POSITIONAL (Microsoft Link-style) input syntax.

PRELINK. This instructs .RTLINK/5.0 to prelink rather than link. When using this option, the .RTLINK output file will be a Pre-Linked Library (.PLL) rather than an executable (.EXE) file. This option may be used with both FREEFORMAT and POSITIONAL mode. If you are using POSITIONAL, you must use the syntax "/PRELINK".

PRELOAD. This option causes the current static overlay section to be loaded into memory before the start of execution. This is contrary to the default behavior of only loading resident (root) sections into memory before execution.

REFER. This command is similar to using an EXTERNAL command in a source code file. It forces the linker to search all libraries in an attempt to resolve the REFERred symbol. It is most commonly used in script files when creating Pre-Linked Libraries. Please refer to Listing 2.6 for an example of its use.

This option may be used with both FREEFORMAT and POSITIONAL mode. If you are using POSITIONAL, you must use the syntax "/REFER:<symbol>", where <symbol> is the symbol to search for.

RESIDENT. This forces any subsequent Clipper-compiled objects to be loaded into the root (.EXE) area. This overrides the default behavior, namely, creating dynamic overlays for all Clipper-compiled code. You may use this option with both FREEFORMAT and POSITIONAL mode. If you are using POSITIONAL, you must use the syntax "/RESIDENT".

SECTION. As discussed earlier, SECTION creates a static overlay section. Segments in any non-Clipper object modules that are specified in subsequent FILE or LIBRARY statements will become part of that section. See the BEGINAREA..ENDAREA discussion for an example of this command.

SILENT. This option merely suppresses any prompts and responses when you are using a script file. You may use this with both FREEFORMAT and POSITIONAL mode. If you are using POSITIONAL, you must use the syntax "/SILENT".

STACK. This option allows you to override the program stack specified in the object module. You may specify a stack size up to 65,535 bytes. The STACK option may be used in both FREEFORMAT and POSITIONAL mode. If you are using POSITIONAL, you must use the syntax "/STACK:<n>", where <n> is the desired stack size.

VERBOSE. This option causes the linker to keep you fully apprised during the link process. You may specify three different levels of information:

0 — nothing. This completely contradicts the point of using VERBOSE. If you should ever find yourself using /VERBOSE:0, you will know that you deserve a vacation.

1 —status messages ("Library Search," "Writing Executable," etc.) and names of all modules as they are linked.

2 —same as 1, but also displays additional status messages (such as "Loading Default Libraries").

This option may be used in both FREEFORMAT and POSITIONAL mode. If you are using POSITIONAL, you must use the syntax "/VERBOSE:<n>", where <n> is the level of verbosity desired.

Linker environment

You learned in Chapter 1 how to manipulate the environment to optimize the Clipper compiler's performance. You can also streamline .RTLINK/5.0's operation by manipulating the following environmental variables.

SET LIB

.RTLINK/5.0 will search directories specified by the LIB variable for any library (.LIB), pre-linked transfer (.PLT), or pre-linked library (.PLL) files that it does not find in the current directory. The .LIB variable will also be used at run-time, if necessary, to ascertain the location of any .PLL files that were used to link the application. (If you link with a .PLL, that information will be embedded in the .EXE file so that .RTLINK/5.0 will know to go hunting for it at run-time.)

The following command placed in your AUTOEXEC.BAT file will direct .RTLINK/5.0 to look for libraries in the C:\CLIPPER5\LIB directory.

```
set lib=c:\clipper5\lib
```

Note that the PLL environmental variable takes precedence over the LIB variable insofar as .PLL and .PLT files are concerned.

SET OBJ

.RTLINK/5.0 will search directories specified by the OBJ variable for any object files not found in the current directory. You may specify multiple paths, separated by semi-colons.

The following command placed in your AUTOEXEC.BAT file will direct .RTLINK/5.0 to search C:\SYSTEM and D:\GRUMP\50 for object modules that it cannot find in the current directory:

```
set obj=c:\system;d:\grump\50
```

If you use the compiler /O option (see Chapter 1) to direct the compiler where to create object files, and use the OBJ environmental setting as described here, you can neatly manage all of your .OBJ files.

SET PLL

The PLL variable is quite similar to the LIB variable, except that it only dictates where to search for pre-linked transfer (.PLT) and pre-linked library (.PLL) files. The following command placed in your AUTOEXEC.BAT file will direct .RTLINK/5.0 to search the directory C:\CLIPPER5\PLL for .PLL and .PLT files.

```
set pll=c:\clipper5\pll
```

As alluded to above, if you do not specify the PLL variable and request .RTLINK/5.0 to use a Pre-Linked Library, the LIB environmental variable will dictate where the linker will search for these files.

SET RTLINKCMD

This variable stores a default set of commands that will be passed to .RTLINK/5.0 whenever you execute it. You may include any or all of the .RTLINK commands discussed above.

The following command placed in your AUTOEXEC.BAT file specifies that FREEFORMAT input mode should be used rather than POSITIONAL. The BATCH option tells the linker not to prompt you when it is unable to locate a file. Finally, it instructs .RTLINK/5.0 to use the BASE52 Pre-Linked Library to build the executable file.

```
set rtlinkcmd=/free /batch /pll:base52
```

SET TMP

Introduced in Chapter 1, the TMP environmental variable instructs both .RTLINK/5.0 and the Clipper 5 compiler where to create their temporary files. As with the compiler /T switch, TMP is best suited for a RAM disk if you have one available. The following command placed in your AUTOEXEC.BAT file will direct the compiler and linker to create their temporary files on drive D.

```
set tmp=d:\
```

Alternative linkers

Although .RTLINK/5.0 is quite adept, our intention is to educate you to all possible alternatives. Therefore, you may wish to investigate the following three dynamic overlay linkers, all of which are worthy of your consideration.

Each linker covers certain aspects that are not included in .RTLINK/5.0. All three linkers will dynamically overlay most C and Assembler objects (along with all Clipper object modules). The following general caveats apply:

- The code must be "well-behaved"—it must use the Clipper Extend System interface for passing parameters, and must not rely on any undocumented Clipper features.

- The code must not handle interrupts.

- The code cannot be self-modifying.

BLINKER

BLINKER is a dynamic overlay linker designed specifically for use with Summer '87 and Clipper 5 applications. It is incredibly fast, and offers blindingly quick incremental linking. Its syntax is entirely compatible with PLINK86 syntax and .RTLINK/5.0 FREEFORMAT syntax.

BLINKER also offers numerous Clipper-specific utility functions, the most important of which is memory packing. This combats memory fragmentation, the bane of Clipper Summer '87 applications. BLINKER also allows you to embed serial numbers and Clipper environmental information directly into your executable file.

BLINKER allows you to create demonstration versions of your programs that limit their execution based on date, length of execution time, or number of calls to the overlay manager. It also includes a wonderful profiling feature that allows you to optimize the logic flow of your program. Blinker version 1.5 includes symbol table compaction.

For more information about BLINKER, contact Assembler Software Manufacturers, Inc. at (804) 353-0137 (fax: (804) 355-1676).

WarpLink

WarpLink is a language-independent linker that is compatible with Summer '87 and Clipper 5. It also links and dynamically overlays C, Assembler, Basic, FORTRAN, and COBOL. As its name implies, it offers breathtaking performance, supplemented by fast incremental linking. It supports .RTLINK/5.0 POSITIONAL syntax; it does not support PLINK86 syntax.

WarpLink includes technology contained in the SMARTMEM (TM) library that allows memory profiling and defragmentation. As mentioned above, it includes a terrific utility, SymPakWL, that compacts the symbol table of your Clipper Summer '87 applications . Also included is a utility allowing you to simulate actual conditions by limiting the amount of memory available for use by your application.

WarpLink can create .COM files directly from object files for small non-Clipper applications. If you work with C or Assembler, this may be an important consideration. Support has just been added for EMS and XMS at both link-time and run-time. Also newly added are a profiler, the ability to split libraries into separate modules for overlaying, and true dynamic link libraries.

For more information about WarpLink, contact Hyperkinetix, Inc. at (714) 573-2260.

.RTLINK/PLUS 4.10

The company that was contracted to produce the Clipper 5 linker has also developed another similar linker. Like WarpLink, .RTLINK/PLUS is language-independent. This linker has caused a lot of confusion in the marketplace because of its similarity to the bundled .RTLINK/5.0 linker. Briefly, major differences between .RTLINK/PLUS and .RTLINK/5.0 are:

- .RTLINK/PLUS virtualizes Clipper code (similar to .RTLINK/5.0's code "paging" but more powerful).
- As mentioned above, .RTLINK/PLUS will allow you to dynamically overlay C and Assembler modules.

Another significant difference is that .RTLINK/PLUS will offer the benefits of .RTLINK/5.0 to your Summer '87 applications. This may be reason enough to consider this linker. .RTLINK/PLUS is also compatible with OS/2 and can interact with CodeView.

For more information about .RTLINK/PLUS, contact Pocket Soft, Inc. at (713) 460-5600 (fax: (713) 460-2651).

Summary

If you did not understand the linking process previously, you should now. You should know the difference between static and dynamic overlays. You have seen how .RTLINK/5.0 will give you more available memory for your applications. You have also seen the many advantages to using Pre-Linked Libraries. Now that you have a thorough grasp on compiling and linking, the next logical step is to discuss how to manage your source code files during the development cycle. Chapter 3 will introduce Clipper's RMAKE utility and give you a solid grounding in the use of MAKE utilities to simplify program management.

CHAPTER 3

Making Your Application

Clipper encourages small, black-box programming modules. By allowing variables and procedures to be visible to only a particular program file, you can ensure that a module cannot interfere with other modules in the program. This tighter program cohesion provides two significant benefits: It improves the capability for writing code that is truly an independent function, and it paves the way for object-oriented program design. By increasing the number of programs in an application, other complexities arise related to the management of the many modules. To assist in this area, Clipper includes a powerful MAKE program.

This chapter describes how MAKE utilities operate, and how the RMAKE utility included with Clipper works. It also includes a brief discussion of other available MAKE utility programs.

Introduction to MAKE

MAKE is a programming utility designed to assist in compiling and linking large applications. The MAKE program reads a text file which contains a list of targets and dependencies. Each target is compared with its list of dependencies. If any of the dependencies have changed, then the target module needs to be rebuilt. The code to rebuild the target is then executed.

Target and dependencies

A target is a file that is created by some sets of operations, most frequently a compilation. Dependencies are the files that are operated upon to create the target. In a MAKE file, the target and dependencies are separated by a colon character ":". This relationship is illustrated below:

```
<target>  :  <dependency(ies)>
operations
```

This relationship can be expressed as:

> You need to create a new target file only if any of the dependent files have been changed. To create the new target file, perform the operations specified.

Date/time stamp

Each file in a DOS directory contains both a date and a time stamp. These dates and times are used for comparison purposes. The target file needs to be recreated if the date and/or time stamp of the dependencies is later than that of the target file. For a simple example, assume the program MENU.OBJ is created by compiling MENU.PRG. The following syntax represents this instruction to a MAKE program:

```
MENU.OBJ  :  MENU.PRG
CLIPPER menu /m
```

This command is interpreted by the MAKE program as follows:

1. Compare the date/time stamp on MENU.PRG and MENU.OBJ.

2. If MENU.OBJ is later than MENU.PRG, do nothing.

3. If MENU.PRG is later than MENU.OBJ, then perform the following line(s) of code:

   ```
   CLIPPER menu /m
   ```

This will create a new MENU.OBJ with a later date/time stamp than MENU.PRG. The next time the application needs to be created, the MAKE utility knows that MENU.OBJ does not need to be recompiled.

While the MAKE utility offers many additional features, the basic concept is to compare files on either side of the colon. The results of this comparison determine whether or not the instructions that follow it are performed.

TOUCH.EXE - A program to alter date/time stamps

There are times when you wish to have the system recompile and relink every program in the application. You could call up each program in an editor, make a minor change, and save the file back to the disk. This action will update the file's date and time stamp. Of course, for systems with more than one or two source files, this hardly seems an efficient method.

Listing 3.1 is a Clipper program that can be used to update the date and time stamp of every file specified.

Listing 3.1 TOUCH.PRG

```
* Program..: TOUCH.PRG
*
parameters file_list
local flist
if file_list <> nil
   flist := directory(file_list)
   aeval(flist, { | afile | Chgtime(afile[1]) })
else
   ? "SYNTAX: touch <file_list>"
endif
return nil

function chgtime(fname)
local fh,one_byte := space(1)
fh       := fopen(fname,2)
if fh > -1
   fread(fh,@one_byte,1) ; fseek(fh,0,0)
   fwrite(fh,one_byte,1) ; fclose(fh)
endif
return nil
```

The program works by loading all matching files into an array. Each element in this array is then evaluated using a code block. The code block calls a UDF which opens the file for read/write access, reads a byte and writes it back to the file. It then closes the file. This action causes the date/time stamp to be updated to the current date and time without changes to the file.

The syntax for TOUCH is:

```
TOUCH <file_list>
```

where <file_list> is any valid wildcard specification, as the examples below illustrate:

```
*.PRG       - All .PRG files.
GL??.PRG    - Only files 2-4 characters long, whose first two
              characters are GL and have an extension of .PRG.
```

Sample MAKE file

Let's look at a complete MAKE file for a realistic application. The environment is as follows:

```
MENU.PRG    - Main system menu
GL.PRG      - General Ledger system
AR.PRG      - Accounts Receivable system
AP.PRG      - Accounts Payable system
```

FUNCS.LIB - Library of windowing functions and printer control functions. The source code for this library is stored in two files:

```
WINDOWS.PRG
PRINTER.PRG
```

The MAKE file for this system is illustrated below:

```
MENU.OBJ     :  MENU.PRG
  clipper menu /m

      GL.OBJ        :  GL.PRG
        clipper GL /m /n

      AR.OBJ        :  AR.PRG
        clipper AR /m /n

      AP.OBJ        :  AP.PRG
        clipper AP /m /n

      FUNCS.LIB    :  WINDOWS.PRG  PRINTER.PRG
        clipper WINDOWS /m /n
        clipper PRINTER /m /n
          lib funcs -+windows
          lib funcs -+printer

    MENU.EXE     : MENU.OBJ GL.OBJ AR.OBJ AP.OBJ FUNCS.LIB
        rtlink    FILE MENU+GL+AR+AP LIBRARY FUNCS
```

Note that the FUNCS.LIB is compared with two files. If either one has been changed, both are recompiled and updated into the library. Several commands may be executed as a result of the comparison. MENU.EXE would be recreated by using RTLINK if any of the object files have been updated or if the library date/time stamp has changed.

RMAKE - Computer Associates' MAKE utility

Included on the distribution disks from Computer Associates is the RMAKE utility program. This program provides complete MAKE capabilities as described above as well as a few additional features. These features include:

- Use of macros to control the MAKE operation.
- Forced creation of target files.
- Display of text to standard output and error devices.

Invoking RMAKE

RMAKE is copied into the \CLIPPER5\BIN directory during the installation process. Your path should include this directory for RMAKE to work.

The general syntax for RMAKE is:

RMAKE <Makefile(s)> <Macros> <Options>

where <Makefile(s)> is one or more MAKE files to process. If no extension is specified, RMK is assumed. Multiple files can be specified and should be separated by a space.

<Macros> are macro definitions in the form of <macro_name>=<value>

Macros defined on the command line take precedence over macros defined in the MAKE file itself or in the environment setting.

<Options> is a list of RMAKE switches. Each switch must be preceded by a slash (/) or a dash (-) character. The valid command line switches are:

B Display debugging information.
D Define a MACRO.
F Force all targets to be created.
I Ignore execution errors.
N Null MAKE, display only.
Q Suppress sign-on message
S Search subdirectories.
U Enable comments.
W Show warnings.
XS Set Symbol table size. The format is /xs<nSymbols>. The default number of symbols is 500.
XW Set internal workspace. The format is /xw<nBytes>. The default size is 2048 (2k) bytes.

The /b option causes messages to be displayed showing the files being compared. If a rule is triggered, a message will be shown indicating why the rule was triggered. These messages are useful when you are debugging your MAKE script.

The /d option provides an alternative syntax to the macro definition parameter. Macros defined with the /d option have the format:

/d<cMacro>:<value> <M>

The /f option forces all targets to be created without comparing them with their dependent files. The effect is the same as running TOUCH.PRG against all dependent files.

The /i option instructs RMAKE to ignore execution errors. Normally, if an operation returns a DOS errorlevel greater than one, RMAKE will stop. This switch allows you to instruct RMAKE to keep processing if a DOS error occurs. Fatal errors from RMAKE, however, will halt the program regardless of this switch setting.

The /n option will display the DOS operations that would be performed without actually executing them. This is referred to as a Null Make.

The /q option disables the display of the Computer Associates logo and copyright notice that RMAKE normally shows when it is first invoked.

The /s option instructs RMAKE to search subdirectories. Normally, RMAKE searches only the current directory for files. By specifying the /s option, RMAKE will search the current directory and all subdirectories as well.

The /u option causes the RMAKE program to treat the # character as a comment. This option will negate all directives in the MAKE file.

The /w option causes RMAKE warning messages to be displayed.

The /xs option increases the default setting of the symbol table size. If you receive one of the following error messages, try increasing the size using the /xs switch:

```
R3006      - Symbol table exhausted
R3008      - String table exhausted
R3009      - File table exhausted
```

The /xw option increases the default setting of the internal workspace. If you receive one of the following error messages, try increasing the size using the /xw switch:

```
R3005      - Internal workspace exhausted
R3020      - Environment exceeds workspace
```

RMAKE environment string

You may specify the default MAKE file name and options in the DOS environment by using the RMAKE environment variable. You cannot, however, use the environment variable for creating default macro assignments. This is due to the fact that DOS does not allow the equal sign to be included in an environment variable. If you wish to assign a macro in the RMAKE environment string, you should use the /d alternative syntax.

The syntax for setting the RMAKE environment string is:

```
set rmake= <filename(s)> <Options>
```

The options would be preceded by the slash or dash character, the same as on the command line. If you receive a DOS error indicating Out of Environment Space, you can increase the environment space by adding the following line to your config.sys file:

```
SHELL=COMMAND.COM /E:1024 /P
```

The increase will not take effect until you reboot the computer.

The options and file names set in the RMAKE variable will be overridden by parameters on the command line if passed when RMAKE is called.

The following example tells RMAKE to search subdirectories and ignore execution errors. The /d option instructs RMAKE to set the value of the macro DEBUG to on.

```
set rmake=/s /i /Ddebug:ON
```

RMAKE return code

RMAKE will return a DOS error code of zero if the MAKE process encounters no errors or an error code of the number one if any errors occurred. This allows the MAKE to be tested within a batch file using DOS errorlevel. For example:

```
rmake acct.rmk
if errorlevel 1 goto problem

echo Make successfully ran...
goto end
:problem

echo A problem occurred during the MAKE program

:end
```

The Clipper compiler also returns a DOS error code of zero if the program compiled successfully or a code of one if an error occurs. Checking the errorlevel is a handy method to redirect the flow in a batch file and perform DOS commands only if the compile or make process was successful.

RMAKE file commands

The make script file should be created with a text editor or a word processor in ASCII mode, i.e. no embedded control codes. This section describes the commands and directives that can be included in an RMAKE file.

Rules. There are two types of rules that can be included in the MAKE file. These rules are:

- Inference rules
- Dependency rules

Inference rules are a set of default actions that should be used for all dependency statements (i.e. target, colon, dependencies set) that are not followed by any operations. If a target file needs to be created and no statements follow the rule, RMAKE will search the inference rules to see how to create the target file. Inference rules allow shortcuts to be created if similar operations require the same actions or rules.

Dependency rules consist of a target file, a colon, and a list of dependent files. The rule is usually followed by a series of DOS commands to be performed to recreate the target file. These rules are basically used to instruct RMAKE how and when to create a new target file.

Creating inference rules. An inference rule has the basic form:

.<dependent extension>.<target extension>

For example, the inference rule:

```
 .PRG.OBJ
Clipper  $** /m
```

establishes that the command Clipper <file name> /m should be executed for any targets that have the extension .OBJ and have dependencies with the extension .PRG. The $** is a macro symbol indicating the dependent file name. Macro symbols are described later in this chapter.

Notice that the target/dependent order is reversed in an inference rule. The dependent extension is listed first and the target extension listed second.

Creating dependency rules. A dependency rule has the basic form:

<target file> : <one or more dependent files>
  [One or more optional DOS commands]

For example, the dependency rule:

```
ACCT.OBJ    :   ACCT.PRG
      Clipper acct /m
```

defines to RMAKE that acct.obj is created by compiling acct.prg with Clipper and the switches /m.

For both inference and dependency rules, the operation to be performed must be indented at least one space from the left margin.

Searching for files. When a file name is specified as a target or dependency, RMAKE assumes the file will be found in the current directory. This search can be expanded by using the /s option as described earlier. In addition, RMAKE supports a MAKEPATH macro that instructs RMAKE where to search for certain types of files. The syntax of the MAKEPATH macro is:

```
makepath[.<extension>]  = <path specification>
```

If MAKEPATH is specified for a particular file extension, only the paths specified will be searched. The current directory will not be searched unless it is included in the path specification. For example,

```
makepath[.PRG]  = "C:\CLIPPER5\SOURCE;C:\ACCT\PROGS"
```

instructs RMAKE to first search the CLIPPER5\SOURCE directory for any program files. If they are not found there, then the ACCT\PROGS directory is searched.

If the file is not found when searching through the MAKEPATH, RMAKE will attach the first path in the macro to the file name. For a target file, this will result in the file being created in the first directory specified. For a dependent file name, this will cause an error to occur since RMAKE cannot find the file.

You can also append to an existing MAKEPATH macro by using the := operator instead of the = operator. For example:

```
makepath[.PRG]  ="C:\CLIPPER5\SOURCE;C:\ACCT\PROGS"
makepath[.PRG]  :=   "C:\LIBRARY\SOURCE"
```

after these two macros are executed, the MAKEPATH value for program files is:

```
C:\CLIPPER5\SOURCE;C:\ACCT\PROGS;C:\LIBRARY\SOURCE
```

If a target or dependent file includes a directory specification as part of the file name, RMAKE will only search that directory, regardless of the MAKEPATH value.

Comments. Comments are notes intended to help clarify the RMAKE files. The RMAKE utility ignores comment lines during its execution. This allows you to include file headers including system name, author, last update time, etc. You may also identify any unusual DOS commands or compilers so that others working on the project will be familiar with the tools needed to recreate the program.

For multi-line comments the syntax is borrowed from the C programming language. The comment delimiters are /* and */. All text between the leading /* and the trailing */ is considered to be a comment and is ignored by RMAKE.

You may also include comments in-line by preceding them with a double slash (//).

The following example shows a commented RMAKE file that illustrates inference rules, dependency rules, and comments.

```
/*  File....: ACCT.RMK
    Author..: Joseph D. Booth
    System .: Accounting Program
    Date ...: January 3, 1993                         */

.PRG.OBJ        // All object files are created with Clipper
Clipper $** /m

.OBJ.LIB        // All library files use Microsoft's LIB
     Lib $* -+$<,,$*
```

```
MENU.OBJ    :  MENU.PRG
GL.OBJ      :  GL.PRG
AR.OBJ      :  AR.PRG
AP.OBJ      :  AP.PRG
WINDOWS.OBJ :  WINDOWS.PRG     // Library windowing functions
PRINTER.OBJ :  PRINTER.PRG     // Library printer functions
FUNCS.LIB   :  WINDOWS.OBJ
FUNCS.LIB   :  PRINTER.OBJ
ACCT.EXE    :  MENU.OBJ GL.OBJ AR.OBJ AP.OBJ FUNCS.LIB
     RTLINK @ACCT
     IF NOT ERRORLEVEL 1 ECHO Success!
```

Line continuation. Long lines in the RMAKE file can be continued by using the backslash character (\) as the last character on the line. For example:

```
library.obj  :  windows.prg  printer.prg  \
               errors.prg
```

If any comments are on the line, they must appear after the line continuation character. For example:

```
rtlink file acct  file ledger   \    // Menu and G/L
       file payroll  lib grump       // Payroll & Grumpfish
```

Since the RMAKE utility ignores comments, the moment it detects the // in-line comment it will stop processing the line. As a result, if the continuation character appears after the comment delimiter, it will be ignored.

Quotation marks. There are times when it is necessary to force the RMAKE program to interpret certain characters literally rather than as commands. For example, DOS uses the backslash as a delimiter between directories and RMAKE uses it as a line continuation character. To tell RMAKE to interpret the symbol as part of the command, include the entire symbol in quotation marks. For example:

```
PROG.EXE  :  PROG.OBJ  d:\library\windows.obj
 RTLINK
```

would be interpreted by RMAKE as

```
PROG.EXE  is dependent upon  PROG.OBJ and D:RTLINK
```

This interpretation would most likely cause a cryptic error message. The proper method for the above example is:

```
PROG.EXE  :  PROG.OBJ  "d:\library\windows.obj"
   RTLINK
```

If you are in doubt as to whether you need quotes or not, use the quotes. Macros will be expanded whether they occur inside or outside of quotation marks.

Directives. Directives are commands to the RMAKE utility program. They allow you to control the processing steps RMAKE performs. All directives are preceded by the # character. If you use the # character for comments (see /u option), you may specify the ! character for a directive instead.

#ifdef. The #ifdef directive allows you to test if a macro has been defined. Its syntax is:

```
#ifdef  <macro_name>
```

If the named macro has been defined either in the RMAKE script or on the command line (using the /d switch), the instructions following the #ifdef directive will be processed by RMAKE. For example, the following instructs RMAKE to compile code with the Clipper debugging information and line numbers if the macro DEBUG has been defined. If the macro has not been defined, the inference rule specifies no line numbers and no debugging information.

```
#ifdef DEBUG
    .PRG.OBJ
           Clipper $** /m /b
#else
    .PRG.OBJ
        Clipper $** /m
#endif
```

All #ifdef directives must be terminated by a corresponding #endif directive.

#ifndef. The #ifndef directive allows you to test if a macro is not defined. It is the opposite of the #ifdef directive. The syntax is:

```
#ifndef  <macro_name>
```

If the named macro has not been defined either in the RMAKE script or on the command line (using the /d switch), the instructions following the #ifndef directive will be processed by RMAKE. The following example sets the MAKEPATH macro for program files if the macro SRCPATH has not been defined.

```
#ifndef SRCPATH
   makepath[.PRG] = "C:\CLIPPER5\SOURCE"
#endif
```

#else. The #else directive allows an alternative set of options to be performed if the comparison fails. It is only valid with a #if directive and its corresponding #endif. The syntax is:

```
#else
```

#endif. The #endif directive is used to terminate the previous #if directive. Its syntax is:

```
#endif
```

#ifeq. The #ifeq directive allows you to test if two strings are the same. One or both strings may be a macro. The macro $* for example, will be replaced with the target file name without an extension. The syntax for #ifeq is:

```
#ifeq <string1> <string2>
```

Since the strings are separated by a space it is necessary to include the strings in quotation marks. The comparison is not case sensitive.

The following example displays a message if the ERRORSYS.OBJ target file needs to be recreated. It compares the string "ERRORSYS" with the macro $*, which will get expanded to the string "ERRORSYS" if the target file needs to be created. See the section on macros for more information about the $* macro.

```
errorsys.obj : errorsys.prg
#ifeq  $* "ERRORSYS"
     echo Errorsys.prg has been modified
#endif
clipper errorsys /m
```

#iffile. The #iffile directive allows you to test if any files are found which match a file specification. Its syntax is:

```
#iffile <file specification>
```

For example, the following directives will cause the macro UPDATE to be defined if the directory C:\APPL contains any files. If the C:\APPL directory is empty, the NEWSYS macro is defined instead.

```
#iffile "C:\APPL\*.*"
   update="TRUE"
#else
   newsys="TRUE"
#endif
```

#include. The #include directive allows you to include a text file of additional commands. Its syntax is:

```
#include "<filename>"
```

The file name may include a path designation and an extension. The #include directive does not use an environment variable or a MAKEPATH macro. It will only search the current directory or the path specifically designated in the file name.

#undef. The #undef directive allows you to remove a user defined macro string. Its syntax is:

```
#undef  <macro_name>
```

#stderr. The #stderr directive allows you to write text to the standard error device. Its syntax is:

```
#stderr  <text>
```

It is useful to have RMAKE display messages for errors it detects. For example the following directive will inform the user that an error has occurred.

```
#stderr  "Problem during LIB update...."
```

#stdout. The #stdout directive allows you to write text to the standard output device. Its syntax is:

```
#stdout  <text>
```

It is useful to have RMAKE display messages for its operations. For example the following directives will inform the user that RTLINK is being performed.

```
#stdout  "RTLINK being performed. Get yourself a"
#stdout  "cup of coffee..."
```

The standard output device and the standard error device are usually the same. You may, however, redirect the standard output into a text file. By providing directives to write to both devices, your script can have the regular RMAKE messages stored in a file and any error messages sent to the screen.

#!. The #! directive allows you to execute any DOS command. Its syntax is:

```
#!  <command>
```

The specified command will be directly executed during the first pass when RMAKE parses the MAKE file script. For example:

```
#! del *.obj
```

Macros. Macros are variables that the RMAKE utility replaces with values when it is executing a line in the script file. These variables may either be predefined, in which case RMAKE knows the values to replace, or user-defined, in which case the script file contains a string of characters which defines the macro.

Predefined. Predefined macros allow you to access the target and dependency information from the last dependency rule encountered. These macro substitutions will be performed during the DOS operations which follow the target dependency pair. These macros will also be expanded if an inference rule is used (i.e. no DOS operations follow the dependency statement.)

Macro	*Meaning*
$*	Target file name without path or extension.
$@	Target file name with both path and extension.
$**	Complete list of dependencies.
$<	File name that triggered the rule.
$?	List of dependencies with a later date/time stamp than the target.

For example, assuming the following files were in the current directory:

```
ACCT.OBJ     01/04/91     11:55am
ACCT.PRG     01/04/91     11:15am
GL.PRG       01/07/91     3:07pm
AR.PRG       01/04/91     9:30am
AP.PRG       01/07/91     2:15pm
```

They are represented with this dependency statement:

```
ACCT.OBJ :ACCT.PRG  GL.PRG  AR.PRG  AP.PRG

$*    would expand to   ACCT
$@    would expand to   ACCT.OBJ
$**   would expand to   ACCT.PRG GL.PRG AR.PRG AP.PRG
$<    would expand to   GL.PRG
$?    would expand to   GL.PRG AP.PRG
```

When using these macros, keep in mind that DOS has a maximum line length of 128 characters. It is possible that a series of file statements being passed to RTLINK could exceed this limit. If possible, redesign the MAKE script to use a link file (see Chapter 2 for more information on link files).

The Clipper compiler accepts only a single file name as a parameter. Be careful when using any macros that can return more than one file name, since the compiler might produce an error. If multiple source files need to be put together, consider creating a CLP file to bind them into a single OBJ file. CLP files are discussed in Chapter 1.

User-defined. In addition to the predefined macros provided by RMAKE, you can define your own macro strings. A macro may be defined on the command line to RMAKE, using the /d option, or in the MAKE script file. The syntax for a macro definition is:

```
<macro>=<value>
```

The value may be any string of characters, including spaces, or it can be a null string. In the MAKE script file, each macro must be defined on a separate line.

A macro value may be surrounded by quotes if need be. The quotes are necessary only if you use a reserved character or trailing spaces. You should not use the following characters in the macro value string:

```
$    -  dollar sign
()   -  parentheses
:    -  colon
.    -  period
%    -  percent sign
```

The libraries might require two steps, a compile and a LIB update operation, to rebuild their target. For example:

```
my_lib.lib    :   windows.prg  printer.prg
clipper windows /n /m
clipper printer /n /m

lib my_lib -+windows
lib my_lib -+printer
```

The finished script file would then appear as follows:

```
acct.obj       :   acct.prg
        clipper acct /m
errorsys.obj   : errorsys.prg
        clipper errorsys /m /n
ledger.obj     :   ledger.prg
       clipper ledger /m /n
sales.obj      :   sales.prg
       clipper sales /m /n
chekbook.obj   : chekbook.prg
       clipper chekbook /m /n
payroll.obj    : payroll.prg
       clipper payroll /m
my_lib.lib     : windows.prg printer.prg
       clipper windows /n /m
       clipper printer /n /m
         lib my_lib -+windows
       lib my_lib -+printer
acct.exe  : acct.obj errorsys.obj ledger.obj sales.obj \
            chekbook.obj payroll.obj my_lib.lib grump.lib \
            acct.lnk
   rtlink @acct.lnk
```

The script file can be enhanced by using inference rules, macros and directives if need be. The RMAKE program provides a high degree of flexibility and capability to the Clipper programmer.

Other MAKE utilities

In addition to RMAKE, several other MAKE utilities are available to the Clipper programmer. These programs are briefly described here, along with information about where you can obtain them. This list is by no means exhaustive. You might already have another MAKE utility on your disk just waiting to be used.

JBMAKE

JBMAKE was written specifically for the Clipper developer. The major benefit of JBMAKE is that it works from your link script file rather than a separate MAKE file. This concept removes the requirement of learning a MAKE file syntax.

JBMAKE is written to work with RTLINK, PLINK86, and BLINKER. It will also support alternate linkers if they work with script file commands similar to RTLINK. The program has several switches to alter its processing. It also displays a summary screen at completion showing status of the compile and link processes. An environmental variable may be defined for default switches.

If you are interested in using a MAKE utility, but do not want to take the time to learn an additional set of commands, JBMAKE offers you the best of both worlds.
To find out more about JBMAKE, contact:

Jeff Bryant
Bryant MicroSystems
3967 North Pacific
Fresno, CA 93705
(209) 226-0306
CompuServe ID: 76416,1462

3PMAKE

3PMAKE is a make utility that is included with the 3PX2 library. It contains a subset of the commands found in Microsoft's Make product. It offers an advantage to other make programs in that dependencies may be listed anywhere in the file. Some make utilities require a particular order for the dependency rules.

3PMAKE supports a DOS variable for setting default switches, inference and dependency rules, and predefined macros. Additionally, user-defined macros are supported.

To find out more information about 3PMAKE, contact:

> 3P Software, Inc
> 1827 Kendrick Street
> Philadelphia, PA 19152-1829
> (215) 725-6068
> CompuServe ID: 73157,2412

Microsoft NMAKE

Microsoft Language products, such as C, Cobol, QuickBasic, etc. include a make utility program called NMAKE. NMAKE supports dependencies and inference rules and has predefined and user- defined macros and directives similar to RMAKE. One syntax difference is that the pound sign (#) is a comment marker in NMAKE, while it is a directive indicator under RMAKE. To use RMAKE with a NMAKE script file, be sure to use the /u option.

Summary

After reading this chapter you should understand what a MAKE utility does and see its benefit on large projects. You should also know how the RMAKE program works and how to create your own MAKE script file.

The tables at the end of this chapter provide summaries of RMAKE options, macros, rules, directives, and error messages.

Reference

Table 3.1 RMAKE options

Switch	*Meaning*
B	Display debugging information.
D	Define a MACRO. Syntax is <macro>:<value>.
F	Force all targets to be created.
I	Ignore execution errors.
N	Null MAKE, display only.
Q	Suppress sign-on information.
S	Search subdirectories.
U	Enable comments.
W	Show warnings.
XS	Set Symbol table size using /xs<nSymbols>.
XW	Set internal workspace using /xw<nBytes>.

Table 3.2 RMAKE macros

Macro	*Meaning*
$*	Target file name without path or extension.
$@	Target file name with both path and extension.
$**	Complete list of dependencies.
$<	File name that triggered the rule.
$?	List of dependencies with a later date/time stamp than the target.
MAKEPATH[.<extension>]	Path for files of a particular file extension.

Table 3.3 RMAKE rules

Inference rules - defaults for dependent rules with no specified actions. The syntax is:

.<dependent extension>.<target extension>
  <ACTIONS>

Dependency rules - Comparison between two file types. The syntax is:

<target file> : <dependent file(s)>
  <ACTIONS>

Table 3.4 RMAKE directives

Directive	*Meaning*
#ifdef	If macro is defined
#ifndef	If macro is not defined
#else	Condition when #if not met
#endif	Termination of #if directive
#ifeq	If strings are equal
#iffile	If file exists
#undef	Undefine a macro
#include	Include the text of a file
#stdout	Write text to standard output
#stderr	Write text to standard error
#!	Execute a DOS command

Table 3.5 RMAKE warnings

Warning	*Meaning*
R1001	Ignoring redefinition of command-line macro
R1002	Target file does not exist: '<filename>'
R1003	Ignoring text

Table 3.6 RMAKE execution/fatal errors

Error	*Meaning*
R2001	Exit n: '<action-line>'
R3001	Too many MAKE files
R3002	Can't open file: '<filename>'
R3003	Invalid option: '<option>'
R3004	Out of memory
R3005	Internal workspace exhausted
R3006	Symbol space exhausted
R3007	String too large
R3008	String table exhausted
R3009	File table exhausted
R3010	Too many actions
R3011	Too many dependencies
R3012	Syntax error: '<token>'
R3013	Unbalanced parenthesis
R3014	#else without #if
R3015	#endif without #if
R3016	Open conditionals
R3017	Unrecognized directive
R3018	Dependency does not exist: '<filename>'
R3019	Circular dependency
R3020	Environment overflows workspace
R3021	Error in redirection
R3022	Cannot execute '<action-line>'

CHAPTER 4

Data Types

A computer system stores information as a string of bits. Through the use of data types, a programmer can impose a logical view on those physical bits. Most programming languages provide several different data types to allow the programmer to work in a higher level mode than the bit level the computer works with.

Clipper supports nine data types. These are listed in table 4.1.

Table 4.1 - Clipper data types

Character
Date
Logical
Memo
Numeric
Array
Code Blocks
NIL
Object

In this chapter we will briefly describe the data types and what they are used for. We will also cover the functions Clipper provides to convert between data types.

Standard data types

The five standard data types are the same five field types allowed in a .DBF file. These five are: Character, Date, Logical, Memo, and Numeric.

Character

The character data type is used to represent strings of individual characters. Examples of character data include:

- Name and address
- Descriptions
- Phone numbers

Character data has the least restrictions imposed on it of any of the data types. A character string may be composed of any number of individual characters. Any character on the ASCII chart (see Appendix A) is valid in a character string. Clipper automatically terminates a character string with a null byte, or CHR(0).

The few restrictions on character data make it a catch-all data type. Phone numbers, for example, are mostly numeric, but contain some punctuation characters. A numeric field will not allow these punctuation characters to be used. Similarly, a zip code, which is a list of numbers, is separated by a dash. Since a dash is only used to denote a negative number, it cannot be used in the middle of a zip code. Character data can be used to represent ten-digit zip codes including the middle dash. A character string is created using the assignment operators.

The data to be assigned to the string is enclosed in a pair of delimiters or it is a value returned from a function. It may also be a combination of the two. For example:

```
<cString> := "Clipper is a powerful language"

<cString> := 'Clipper '+Version()
```

A null character string can be created by using only a pair of delimiters. For example:

```
<cNull_string> := ""
<cNull_string> := []
```

Chapter 21 discusses the character data type in more detail.

Date

The date type is used to represent calendar dates. Clipper stores dates internally in such a way that a variety of operations can be performed on them. You can determine the number of days between two dates by subtracting them, and you can determine a future date by adding an integer value to a date value. The result will be a date value, some number of days in the future.

Clipper supports all dates in the range of January 1, 100AD through December 31, 2999. In addition, an empty date may be created. The syntax for an empty date is:

```
ctod("")
```

Empty dates are always placed first in a sorted list of dates.

A date variable is created by combining digits for the month, day, and year together, along with a separation character. The character to use and the order in which the month, day, and year are combined is determined by the value of the SET DATE command. The default value for SET DATE is AMERICAN. Table 4.2 lists other possible values.

Table 4.2 - SET DATE values

American	mm/dd/yy
Ansi	yy.mm.dd
British	dd/mm/yy
French	dd/mm/yy
German	dd.mm.yy
Italian	dd-mm-yy
Japanese	yy/mm/dd
USA	mm-dd-yy

The syntax for the SET DATE command is:

```
set date <literal value>
```

The literal value must be one of those formats listed in table 4.2. You cannot use a character expression in the SET DATE command although you can macro-expand the value. For example:

```
cDformat := "AMERICAN"
set date cDformat              // Not ok
set date (cDformat)            // Still not ok!
set date &cDformat             // This will work
```

You can also set the date format using the SET DATE FORMAT command. One benefit of the SET DATE FORMAT syntax is that it allows a character string to be used to determine the date format, rather than a literal value. The syntax for SET DATE FORMAT is:

```
 set date format to <cFormat_string>
```

The format string is a combination of the following characters:

```
YYYY  Four digit year
YY    Two digit year
MM    Month number
DD    Day number
```

and a separation character, such as a colon (:), a period (.), etc. The format string must be twelve or fewer characters. Clipper maps the date components onto the appropriate character, i.e. the year is mapped to YYYY, the month to MM, and the day to DD. For example:

```
set date format to "YYYY-MM-DD"
? date()                          // Displays 1991-01-22
mvar := "MM|DD/YY"
set date format to mvar
? date()                          // Displays 01|22/91
```

The SET DATE FORMAT command allows any structure of date to be used as the default date format. You may also store the date format in a memory variable to allow different users to modify their preferred date display.

Dates are discussed in more detail in Chapter 22.

Logical

The logical data type is used to represent a data item which can only have two states, i.e. ON/OFF, YES/NO, etc. Although two possible states can be represented in one bit, Clipper's smallest component is a byte. A logical value in memory and in a disk file occupies one byte of storage.

While logical data has only two states, the character set consists of the characters T, t , Y , y , F , f , N , n. To define a logical value, one of the characters from the character set is delimited by periods. For example:

.T. .t. .Y. .y. - All represent the TRUE state

.F. .f. .N. .n. - All represent the FALSE state

Clipper's preferred syntax is .T. and .F.

Logical values can also be returned from function calls. For example:

```
enough_room := diskspace() > (recsize()*lastrec())
```

In this example the numeric value returned from the Diskspace() function is compared with the result of Recsize() * Lastrec(). If the disk space is larger than the .DBF size, enough_room returns .T.; if not, it returns .F.

In addition, some Clipper functions return logical values. These values can be saved to logical data types as well. For example:

```
Seek "Smith"
was_found := found()
if was_found
   ? "Smith is in the file"
else
   ? "No Smiths in the file, try Jones..."
endif
```

When logical values are sorted, the .F. values always come before the .T. values.

Numeric

Numeric data is made up of the characters zero through nine and a period (.). If the number is negative, a minus sign is used. No other characters may be placed into a numeric field. The enforcement of this restriction allows mathematical operations and calculations to be performed on numeric fields. Examples of numeric fields include:

- Age
- Salary and tax information
- Costs and prices

Numeric data is created by the assignment operator or as the result of an operation. For example:

```
salary := 25000              // Starting salary
bonus  := salary * .10       // Christmas bonus
gross  := salary + bonus
taxes  := gross - 3000
net    := gross - taxes
left   := -500.00
```

In addition, many Clipper functions return numeric values. For example:

```
space  := Diskspace()        // Space available on disk
recs   := Lastrec()          // Number of records in DBF
size   := Recsize()*rec()    // Size of data portion of DBF
```

Memo

The memo data type is essentially a very large character string. The memo field is stored on disk differently than character data is. Character data stored in a .DBF file is a fixed length, while memo data may be variable length.

Once a memo field is in memory Clipper treats it just like character data. All functions and operations which apply to character type data can also be used with memo data.

In addition to the standard string functions, Clipper also provides special functions for handling memos. These are listed in Table 4.3.

Table 4.3 - Memo functions

Hardcr()	Replace chr(141) with chr(13)
Memoedit()	Edit or display a memo's contents
Memoline()	Extract a single line from a memo
Memoread()	Import a text file into a memo variable
Memotran()	Replace carriage returns
Memowrit()	Create a text file from a memo variable
Mlcount()	Count number of lines in a memo
Mlctopos()	Determine byte position for row/column
Mlpos()	Determine offset in memo for a line
Mpostolc()	Determine row/column for a byte position

Memos are covered in detail in Chapter 24.

Additional data types

There are four additional data types available in Clipper. These types cannot be directly represented in a .DBF file. The four are: Array, Code Block, NIL, Objects.

Array

An array is a single memory variable name that can hold more than a single value. The values held are referred to as elements of the array. These are accessed by providing the array name and its element number or index. For example:

```
LOCAL  buf_[3]              // Array called buf_ with three elements
buf_[1]:="Clipper "         // First element is of character type
buf_[2]:=date()             // Second element is system date
buf_[3]:=795.00             // Third element is numeric
```

Element number or index

Array name

The elements in an array can be any valid data type, including another array. Each individual element conforms to the rules of its specific data type. An array allows mixed data types, so element one might be a character string, element two a numeric value, and element three a date.

Arrays are created by a variable declaration statement. Table 4.4 lists declaration statements.

Table 4.4 - Declaration statements

```
DECLARE      array_name [ size ]
LOCAL        array_name [ size ]
PRIVATE      array_name [ size ]
PUBLIC       array_name [ size ]
STATIC       array_name [ size ]
```

The declaration used to declare the array will determine the array's scope. Chapter 6 discusses variable scoping in much more detail.

An array may also be created by enclosing a list of items in curly brackets { }. The items on the list are separated by commas. For example:

```
array := {"Joe","Greg","Craig","Betty"}
```

This statement creates a four element array. Each element contains a character string. The array elements can be mixed data types as well. For example:

```
array := {"CUST_ID","N",8,0}
```

Clipper provides functions which work on the entire arrays, as well as functions which work on array elements. Arrays are discussed in much more detail in Chapter 9.

Code blocks

Code blocks are a new data type that contain compiled Clipper code. They can be compiled either at compile-time with the rest of your Clipper code, or at run-time with the use of the macro operator.

This is a code block in its rawest form:

```
{ | [<argument list>] | <expression list> }
```

Code blocks are delimited by the curly brace characters. (This is the same character used by array declarations.) Code blocks delimit their arguments by the vertical pipe character. If no arguments are present, two pipe characters must be written to distinguish a code block from an array.

A few of the Clipper functions allow a code block to be passed as a parameter. For example, listing 4.1 provides a function which sorts an array by column positions other than the first position. By passing a code block, we can change the method in which ASORT() operates.

Listing 4.1 - ACOLSORT

```
function Acolsort(arr_,col,size)
Asort(arr_,,,;
{|x,y|substr(x,col,size) < substr(y,col,size) })
```

Without the use of code blocks, a column sort could only be done by manipulating the array element to move the sort column to the front of the element. With a code block, ASORT() can handle columnar and descending sorts with miminal effort.

Code blocks are discussed in more detail in Chapter 8.

NIL

NIL is one of the three new datatypes provided with Clipper 5. It is the value that Clipper assigns to declared variables, arrays, and parameters before they are initialized.

Parameter checking/assigning defaults

By far the most significant use of NIL is for parameter checking in your functions. In the past, this was accomplished primarily with the Clipper PCOUNT() and TYPE() functions. Although we learned to live with this arrangement, in retrospect you will see that it was actually quite clumsy.

To illustrate this, let us look at the function ShowMsg() in Listing 4.2. This function accepts three possible parameters: (a) the message to be displayed; (b) the color in which to draw the box; and (c) the color in which to display the message. The latter two parameters are optional. In Summer '87, the general rule for optional parameters was to pass null strings if you wanted to ignore them, so we will construct our function accordingly.

```
ShowMsg("this is a test")
ShowMsg("this is a test", "", "+W/B")
ShowMsg("this is a test", "W/G", "+W/G")
```

Listing 4.2 - ShowMsg

```
* Program...: ShowMsg
*
function ShowMsg
parameter msg, boxcolor, msgcolor
private oldcolor, buffer, leftcol
*** assign box color
if pcount() < 2                    && did not pass second parameter
     boxcolor = 'W/R'
elseif type('boxcolor') != 'C'     && passed a non-character string
```

```
     boxcolor = 'W/R'
elseif empty(boxcolor)          && passed a null string
   boxcolor = 'W/R'
endif
*** assign message color
if pcount() < 3                 && did not pass third parameter
     msgcolor = '+W/R'
elseif type('msgcolor') != 'C'  && passed a non-character string
     msgcolor = '+W/R'
elseif empty(msgcolor)          && passed a null string
   msgcolor = '+W/R'
endif
leftcol = int(76 - len(msg)) / 2
buffer = savescreen(11, leftcol, 13, 80 - leftcol)
oldcolor = setcolor(boxcolor)
@ 11, leftcol, 13, 80 - leftcol BOX " ╔═╗║╝═╚║ "
setcolor(msgcolor)
@ 12, leftcol + 2 say msg
inkey(2)
restscreen(11, leftcol, 13, 80 - leftcol, buffer)
setcolor(oldcolor)
return .t.
```

Look how clunky the test is for the color parameters! First, PCOUNT() is used to determine whether or not the parameters were even passed. Then, we have to verify that the parameters are of character type. Then we have to make one more test to see if the parameter is a null string.

Now let's rewrite this using NIL. Clipper allows you to skip unnecessary parameters simply by placing a comma in the parameter list—you no longer need to use a null string. If a parameter in the formal list has been omitted, it will merely be initialized within the function with the value of NIL. Listing 4.3 contains the NIL version.

Listing 4.3 - ShowMsg - NIL version

```
* Program...: ShowMsg
*
include "BOX.CH"
function ShowMsg(msg, boxcolor, msgcolor)
local buffer, leftcol := int(76 - len(msg)) / 2
// assign box color
if boxcolor = nil.or. valtype("boxcolor") <> "C"
    boxcolor := 'W/R'
endif
// assign message color
if msgcolor = nil.or. valtype("msgcolor") <> "C"
   msgcolor := '+W/R'
endif
buffer := savescreen(11, leftcol, 13, 80 - leftcol)
dispbox(11, leftcol, 13, 80-leftcol, B_DOUBLE + '', boxcolor)
@ 12, leftcol + 2 say msg color msgcolor
inkey(2)
restscreen(11, leftcol, 13, 80 - leftcol, buffer)
return nil
```

This is so much cleaner than earlier releases! Clipper 5.2 includes a DEFAULT TO command that assigns default values if needed. Here it is, live from the Clipper 5.2 header files:

```
#xcommand DEFAULT <v1> TO <x1> [, <vn> TO <xn> ];
          =>
          IF <v1> == NIL ; <v1> := <x1> ; END
          [; IF <vn> == NIL ; <vn> := <xn> ; END ]
```

You can then rewrite these lines:

```
if boxcolor = nil
  boxcolor := 'W/R'
endif
if msgcolor = nil
   msgcolor := '+W/R'
endif
```

as two lines:

```
default boxcolor TO 'w/r'
default msgcolor TO '+w/r'
```

without sacrificing one iota of readability or functionality.

"VOID" functions

Because of the way Clipper is structured, it makes good sense to write functions rather than procedures. However, there will be times when you have a function whose return value is irrelevant. In Summer '87, you might have returned a zero, or a logical, or a null string. In Clipper 5, though, it is neater to return NIL from these types of functions. That way, you will be able to tell at a glance whether a given function's return value has any real significance. This can save you time during the maintenance phase.

Other points

Keep in mind that when you declare static, local, and private variables, they will be initialized to NIL until you explicitly assign them a value:

```
function test
static a
local b
private c
public d
? a      // nil
? b      // nil
? c      // nil
? d      // .f.
return nil
```

Array elements will also be initialized to NIL until you give them a value:

```
function test
local a[4]
? a[1]  // nil
? a[5]  // crash!
return nil
```

Although they are not the flashiest new feature in Clipper 5, NILs will eliminate a lot of messy code. (NIL is definitely a case where you get something for nothing.)

Objects

Objects are a special data type which contains both functions and data. Objects inherit their functionality from a class.

Clipper provides four standard classes; an object is an instance (data and functions) of one of these classes. The four classes are listed in Table 4.5.

Table 4.5 - Standard classes

```
* Error Class
* Get Class
* Tbrowse Class
* Tbcolumn Class
```

With the introduction of objects, Computer Associates has adopted a new approach for solving programming problems: object-oriented programming. Chapters 25 through 27 describe the object classes provided in Clipper.

Determining data type

Clipper provides two functions which can be used to determine the data type of a variable. These functions are TYPE() and VALTYPE(). While the two functions accomplish the same task, VALTYPE() is preferred because it does not perform a macro expansion to determine type. VALTYPE() is therefore faster and can be used on local and static variables. TYPE() cannot be used on local and static variables since they cannot be macro expanded.

TYPE()

The TYPE() function returns a one- or two-character code which represents the data type that the parameter evaluates to. The syntax is:

```
type("<cExp>")
```

where <cExp> is a string containing the expression for which you wish to determine the type. The expression should be enclosed in quotation marks. The expression may be a variable, a function call, or a field name from a database. It may not be a local or static variable declaration (VALTYPE() handles those).

The possible return values are listed in Table 4.6.

Table 4.6 - Type() return values

```
A      Array
B      Code Block
C      Character
D      Date
L      Logical
M      Memo
N      Numeric
O      Object (see Chapters 25 thru 27 for more detail)
U      NIL (returned if LOCAL or STATIC variable passed)
UE     Error in syntax
UI     Type cannot be determined
```

TYPE() and arrays

The TYPE() function will return "A" if its parameter is an array name. If the parameter is an array element, the type of the element will be returned. For example:

```
private emp_list[5]

emp_list[1] := "John"
emp_list[2] := 5500.00
emp_list[3] := .T.
emp_list[4] := date()

? type("emp_list")          // Returns 'A'
? type("emp_list[1]")       // Returns 'C'
? type("emp_list[2]")       // Returns 'N'
? type("emp_list[3]")       // Returns 'L'
? type("emp_list[4]")       // Returns 'D'
? type("emp_list[5]")       // Returns 'U'
```

TYPE() and functions

The parameter passed to the TYPE() function can be a function call. If the function call is a standard Clipper function that is found in CLIPPER.LIB, then the function will be evaluated. The type code returned is based upon the function's normal return value.

If the function being tested is either a user-defined function or a function found outside of CLIPPER.LIB (such as those functions in EXTEND.LIB), then the TYPE() function returns a UI code. This code informs us that the function is linked into the application, but its type cannot be determined. If the function is not linked in TYPE() will return the UE code.

This use of the TYPE() function allows you to design a menu system which only runs programs the client has paid for. For example, the program in Listing 4.4 will check to see if the function being called is linked in. If so, the menu option will be performed. If not, an error message indicating that that option is not available will be displayed.

Listing 4.4 - TYPE() example

```
* Program...: Example of type()
*
local mpick :=1
clear
@ 10,30 to 15,50                        // Draw a box
@ 11,31 prompt "General Ledger      "
@ 12,31 prompt "Accounts Receivable"
@ 13,31 prompt "Accounts Payable    "
@ 14,31 prompt "Payroll             "
menu to mpick
do case
case mpick = 1
    if type("GL()") = "UI"
        Gl()
    else
        ? "General Ledger is not installed...."
    endif
```

```
case mpick = 2
   if type("AR()") = "UI"
       Ar()
   else
       ? "Accounts Receivable is not installed...."
   endif
case mpick = 3
   if type("AP()") = "UI"
       Ap()
   else
       ? "Accounts payable is not installed...."
   endif
case mpick = 4
    type("PR()") = "UI"
       Pr()
   else
       ? "Payroll is not installed...."
   endif
endcase
```

The proper use of TYPE() with functions allows you to create a system in which the menu code does not change if you link in more object files. If your client decides he wants to purchase the payroll module, you merely need to link the PR() object file into his program and send him a new executable. No coding changes are required!

VALTYPE()

The VALTYPE() function returns a one-character code which represents the data type that the parameter evaluates to. The syntax is:

```
valtype(<cExp>)
```

where <cExp> is a variable for which you wish to determine the type. Using VALTYPE(), no quotation marks are needed around the expression. The possible return values are listed in Table 4.7.

Table 4.7 - VALTYPE() return values

```
A    Array
B    Code Block
C    Character
D    Date
L    Logical
M    Memo
N    Numeric
O    Object (see Chapters 25 thru 27 for more detail)
U    NIL
```

The VALTYPE() function evaluates the expression and returns the data type. If the expression is a user-defined function or a function from EXTEND.LIB, VALTYPE() will return the function's return value. (TYPE(), on the other hand, will indicate it can not determine the data type.) VALTYPE() can also process local and static variables. Since these variables have no entry in the symbol table, they cannot be macro-expanded, which prevents the TYPE() function from identifying them.

VALTYPE() is the preferred syntax over TYPE() due to its performance and avoidance of macros.

For example:

```
test _type("THIS IS A TEST OF VALTYPE")

function test_type(id_code)
local arry :={}
? valtype(id_code)                    // returns C
? valtype(arry)                       // returns A
```

Checking parameter types

When parameters are passed to user-defined functions, the parameter scope is defined by how the parameters are coded. For example:

```
function test1(param1)          // param1 is LOCAL

function test2
parameter param2                // param2 is PRIVATE
```

A frequent test of parameters under old releases of Clipper was the following:

```
if type("param2") = "C"
```

Unfortunately, if the TYPE() function was used with param1, it would return a U, since TYPE() cannot handle local variables. It is better to use VALTYPE() or the NIL operator to handle parameter testing.

Type conversions

There are many times when it is necessary to convert data from one type to another. For example: When building an index key which consists of multiple fields, all the components of the key must be of the same data type. Converting the fields to character type data allows you to concatenate the components into a single index key.

When using the ?? or ? for unformatted display purposes, it is useful to create formatted character strings to display data.

Character to numeric

A character field may be converted to a numeric value using one of two Clipper functions. Which function to use and the value returned is determined by the contents of the character field.

ASC(): Character to ASCII equivalent

The ASC() function takes a single character, finds it on the ASCII chart, and returns its rank. Its syntax is:

```
ASC(<character string>)
```

If the character string is longer than one character, the ASC() function only evaluates the leftmost character. The following examples illustrate the ASC() function:

```
? ASC("A")          // Returns 65
? ASC("Clipper")    // Returns 67, upper case C
? ASC("")           // Returns 0, null byte
```

The return value will also be an integer between 0 and 255. The CHR() function is the inverse of the ASC() function. The ASC() can be used to interpret bytes from a file. For example, the function in listing 4.5 reads the first two bytes from an executable file. If the first two bytes are not 77 and 90 respectively, then the file is probably not a valid executable file.

Listing 4.5 - Checkexe

```
* Program...: Checkexe
*
function Checkexe(file_name)
local fh,buf1:=" ",buf2:=" ",retval:=.f.
if (fh := fopen(file_name)) >=0
   fread(fh,@fbuf1,1)
   fread(fh,@fbuf2,1)
   fclose(fh)
   retval := ( asc(fbuf1) = 77 .and. asc(fbuf2)=90 )
endif
return retval
```

This function can be used if your program allows the user to specify a DOS program they wish to run. By checking the first two bytes of the executable file, you can display a less cryptic error message than the DOS error BAD COMMAND OR FILE NAME.

VAL(): Character string to numeric value.

The VAL() function takes a string and attempts to evaluate it as a numeric value. Its syntax is:

```
nValue := val(<character string>)
```

Its inverse function is STR(). VAL() reads the character string and converts it to a numeric value. VAL() will stop reading the character string if it encounters a second period, a non-numeric character, or the end of the string. Any leading spaces are ignored during the conversion. For example:

```
? val("1600 Pennsylvania Avenue")  // displays 1600
? val("     500.712.143")           // displays 500.712
```

Numeric to character

STR(): Numeric to string.

The STR() function takes a numeric variable and returns it as an *unformatted* character string. STR() is the inverse of VAL(). The syntax for STR() is:

```
<cString> := str(<numeric>,<nWide>,<nDec>)
```

The <nWide> and the <nDec> are both optional parameters. If the parameters are not specified, a database field will be returned according to its structure in the database. A memory variable will be returned with at least ten spaces and room for decimal places. The SET DECIMAL command described in Chapter 21 allows you to control the number of decimal places displayed.

If formatting is necessary, refer to the TRANSFORM() function later in this chapter.

CHR().

The CHR() function takes a number between the range of zero and 255 and returns the character at that position on the ASCII chart. Its syntax is:

```
chr(<numeric>)
```

The CHR() function is frequently used to send control codes to a printer. Many printers support an escape sequence which begins with the ESCAPE character. Since the ESCAPE character cannot be entered from the keyboard, CHR(27) could be used instead. Any character which cannot be accessed from the keyboard can be created using the CHR() function.

Table 4.8 lists some commonly used CHR() codes.

Table 4.8 - Common CHR() codes

15 or 27, 15	Condensed print on many printers
171, 172	1/2 and 1/4
218, 196, 191 179 179 192, 196, 217	Single sided box

Date to character

There are several functions for converting date variables into characters. Two of these work with the entire date. These are the DTOC() and the DTOS() functions. The CMONTH() and CDOW() functions work with only part of the date variable.

DTOC(): date to character

The date to character function takes a date variable as a parameter and returns a string representation of the date. The string is created in the format specified by the SET DATE or the SET DATE FORMAT command. If SET DATE has not been specified, the default date format is mm/dd/yy.

The syntax for DTOC() is:

```
<cString> := dtoc(<dVariable>)
```

For example, you could use DTOC() along with PADL() to display a date in the upper right corner of a line of text.

```
? padl( dtoc(date()), 79 )
```

DTOS(): date to string.
The date to string function takes a date variable as a parameter and returns a string in the format:

YYYYMMDD

where	YYYY	represents the four digit year
	MM	represents the numeric month
	DD	represents the day of the month

The return format of the DTOS() function is not affected by the SET DATE setting. It is this string representation of the date that should be used for sorting and indexing dates, since the dates will appear in chronological order. The DTOC() function is more useful for displaying the date in a fashion the end-user is familiar with.

The syntax for DTOS() is:

```
<cString> := dtos(<dVariable>)
```

For example, you could use DTOS() to create an index which will cause the database to appear in chronological date sequence.

```
index on dtos(LOG_DATE) to cust01
```

The DTOS() function can also be used to create concatenated index strings. For example:

```
index on dtos(LOG_DATE)+state  to cust01
```

CDOW(<date>): day of week name, i.e. Monday, Friday.

The CDOW() function takes a date variable and returns the day of the week as a character string. Its syntax is:

```
<cDayname>  := Cdow(<dSomeDate>)
```

For example we can use the CDOW() function to display a date variable in a longer fashion.

```
mdate := Ctod("01/22/89")
? cdow(mdate),mdate      // Displays  Sunday 01/22/89
```

CMONTH(<date>): name of month,i.e. January, December.

The CMONTH() function takes a date variable and returns the month of the year as a character string. Its syntax is:

```
<cMonthname>  := Cmonth(<dSomeDate>)
```

As an example we can use the CMONTH() function to display two dates as a range of months.

```
mdate1 := Ctod("06/05/90")

mdate2 := Ctod("09/15/90")
? left(cmonth(mdate1),3)+"-"+left(cmonth(mdate2),3)
```

This example will display:

```
Jun-Sep
```

Date to numeric

A date's components may also be converted to a numeric form. Clipper provides a function for each part of the date.

YEAR().

This function returns a four digit year from a date variable. The returned value is not affected by the current date format. Its syntax is:

```
<nYear>  := Year(dSome_date)
```

DAY().

This function returns a two digit day of the month from a date variable. Its syntax is:

```
<nDay>  := Day(dSome_date)
```

MONTH().

This function returns a two digit month number from a date variable. Its syntax is:

```
<nMonth>  := Month(dSome_date)
```

It is preferable to use these functions rather than relying upon SUBSTR() to extract date components. Since the date format can be changed, the SUBSTR() function may not always be aware of the positioning of the components. In the AMERICAN date format, the month is the first two positions. In the GERMAN date format, the month is positions four and five.

Character to date

Clipper provides a function to convert a string of characters into a date variable. The characters must form a valid date and will be interpreted according to the current date format.

CTOD().

This function reads a character string and attempts to map it into the current date format. If the string is mapped successfully, a date variable will be returned. Its syntax is:

```
<dVariable> := Ctod(<cFormatted_date_string>)
```

It is important to be aware of the current SET DATE value when using CTOD(). For example:

```
? ctod("01/05/91") // Produces 01/5/91 or January 5, 1991
                   // if SET DATE is AMERICAN and produces
                   // 05.01.91 or May 1,1991 if the SET
                   // DATE format is BRITISH or GERMAN
```

Logical to character/numeric

A logical variable or field may be converted to a character string or a numeric value using the IF() function. The syntax for such a conversion is:

```
<expression> :=if(<logical>,<value if .T.>,<value if .F.>)
```

The IF() function evaluates the logical expression. If TRUE, the second parameter is assigned to the expression. If FALSE, the third parameter is assigned. For example:

```
lVar := .T.
nBinary := if(lVar,1,0)
? nBinary                       // Displays    1
```

For display purposes, we can convert a logical variable to a YES or NO character string. For example:

```
 ? "| CUSTOMER NAME    |  NEW? | BALANCE DUE"
 ? "|_________________ |______|____________"
select customer
while !eof()
  ? " "+customer->cust_name+"  "

  // Convert new_cust (logical) to YES or NO

  ?? IF(customer->new_cust," YES"," NO ")
  ?? " "+str(customer->balance,12,2)
  skip +1
enddo
```

Character/numeric to logical

Any data type can be converted to a logical value by comparing the data type with some value. The general syntax is:

```
<logical>  := (<comparative expression>)
```

The parentheses around the expression are not required, but suggested to make the code easier to read.

Let's look at a couple of examples:

```
is_male := (sex_code = "M")
is_new  := (date()-dAcquired < 365)
enough  := (Diskspace() > (Recsize()*Lastrec()+header())
```

By assigning the results of the comparison to a variable, we can convert data of any type to a logical variable. It is important to note that the comparison operator cannot be colon-equals (:=) if comparing for equality, such as in the sex_code="M" example. As written, *is_male* will have a logical value. If written as (sex_code := "M"), the is_male variable will be assigned the letter "M", which is not what we intended.

Display purposes

It is often desirable to display any data type as a string. This is useful when using the ? or ?? to display data. These commands do not provide any formatting capabilities by themselves. Fortunately Clipper provides a formatting function to allow data to be displayed in a consistent fashion.

TRANSFORM()

Transform takes an expression of any data type and converts it into a formatted character string. Its syntax is:

```
<cString> := Transform <expression>,<cFormat_string> )
```

The <cFormat_string> controls the appearance of the output character string. It consists of a combination of picture templates and function strings. The picture template corresponds to a single character position in the expression. The function string affects the entire expression. Table 4.9 lists the picture templates.

Table 4.9 - Picture templates

```
.     Inserts a period into a numeric expression
,     Inserts a comma into a number expression
*     Displays an asterisk in the place of a leading zero
$     Displays a dollar sign in the place of a leading zero
L     Displays logical values as T or F
Y     Displays logical values as Y or N
!     Convert character to upper case
```

Some template examples are illustrated in listing 4.6.

Listing 4.6 - Transform() template examples

```
* Program....: Template examples
*
? Transform(1500,"  9,999.99")  // produces   1,500.00
? Transform(2500,"***,**9.99")  // produces **2,500.00
```

The function strings available in TRANSFORM() are listed in Table 4.10. These function strings affect the entire variable, not just a character position. A function string must be preceded by the at sign (@) to distinguish it from a character in a template.

Table 4.10 - Function strings

```
@B   Displays numbers left justified
@C   Displays CR after positive numbers
@D   Displays date in the SET DATE format
@E   Displays date in British (dd/mm/yy) format
@R   Non template characters should be inserted in the display
@X   Displays DB after negative numbers
@Z   Displays zeros as blanks
@(   Encloses negative numbers in parentheses
@!   Converts output to upper case
```

If multiple functions are to be used, there should be a single at sign (@) followed by the function letters. For example:

```
x := -1500
? Transform(x,"@Z(")  // produces  (  1500)
```

Combining function strings and picture templates.
Function strings and picture templates can be combined to provide a large range of formatting capabilities. If both are present, the function string must come first and must be followed by a space character. For example:

```
x := 1500
y := -2500

Transform(x,"@Z 999,999.99")    // Produces    1,500.00
Transform(y,"@( ***,***.99")    // Produces (**2,500.00)
```

The TRANSFORM() function is frequently used in printed reports to produce the proper columnar output that is required.

Summary

After reading this chapter you should know what the nine data types in Clipper are, and should know a little about each one. If you want to expand your expertise on various data types, they are covered in more detail in later chapters.

You should also be familiar with the functions used to convert between data types. These functions are particularly handy when you are preparing an index that consists of a mixture of field types.

CHAPTER 5

Operators

Operators are a crucial part of any programming language. They allow us to assign, manipulate, and compare pieces of data. Clipper 5 features a rich set of mathematical, relational, and logical operators. This chapter will discuss all of these operators, and give examples of where and how you can use them.

Given Clipper's many operators, it is quite possible to write extremely complex statements that combine many operations. To avoid confusion, we will also cover precedence rules so that you will have a clear understanding of the order in which operators will be evaluated.

Overview

The Clipper language has always provided us with a good set of operators. However, Clipper 5 goes a step further than prior versions by borrowing some operators from the C programming language, most notably the in-line assignment (":=") operator, increment ("++") and decrement ("--"), and arithmetic (compound) assignment operators. These new operators will allow you to write some incredibly powerful statements. Coupled with the fact that Clipper 5 permits us to put multiple statements on the same line, it will now be very tempting to write code such as the following:

```
y := z := 100; for x := 1 to 100 ; y += x + --z**2 ; next
```

Although this may win you an honorary mention in an obfuscated programming contest, it will make your debugging a real nightmare. Not only is it more difficult to sort through all the statements, but the source-level debugger will not be of much assistance because it only goes line by line (as opposed to statement by statement).

The only good reason to use multi-statement lines is for user-defined commands, where the #xcommand or #xtranslate directive would necessarily force multiple statements to be on the same line.

Clipper 5 operators are divided into five general categories:

- Mathematical
- Relational
- Logical
- Assignment
- Special purpose

Mathematical operators

It is important in any programming language to get a firm grasp on mathematical operators and their precedence. Clipper has eight such operators. Two of them ("+" and "-") can perform more than one operation, and may also be used on date and character expressions.

Table 5.1 shows all of the Clipper 5 mathematical operators.

Table 5.1 Mathematical operators

Operator(s)	*Performs*	*Applicable Data Types*
**, ^	Exponentiation	N
*	Multiplication	N
/	Division	N
%	Modulus (Remainder)	N
+	Add, unary positive	N, D
+	Concatenate	C
-	Subtract, unary negative	N, D
-	Concatenate	C
++	Increment	N, D
--	Decrement	N, D

C = character
D = date
N = numeric

Exponentiation

The exponentiation operator raises one numeric expression to the power of a second. "Raising" a number to a given "power" is generally the same as multiplying it by itself that many times. For example, 3 raised to the power of 3 is 27 (3 * 3 * 3). Any number raised to the power of one is unchanged. Any number raised to the power of zero equals one. When a number is raised to a negative power, it will equal the reciprocal of the positive power. For example, 2 raised to the -2 power would equal .25 (1 / (2 * 2)).

Note that "**" and "^" are functionally equivalent.

Listing 5.1 shows exponentiation examples.

Listing 5.1 Examples of exponentiation

```
? 3  ** 2           // 9
? 10 ** 0           // 1
? 10 ** 2           // 100
? 10 ** -2          // .01
? 10 ** 4           // 10000
? 4  ** 1           // 4
? 16 ** .5          // 4
? 16 ** -.5         // .25
```

Listing 5.2 illustrates bitwise mathematics in Clipper using the exponentation operator. DecToBin() converts a decimal number between 0 and 255 to its binary equivalent. Although Clipper does not support bit fields, there are instances where binary conversion will come in handy, such as translating data from different file formats.

Listing 5.2 DecToBin()

```
/*
   DecToBin(<x>) - converts decimal to binary
   Parameter: <x> = integer between 0 and 255
*/
function DecToBin(x)
local i, buffer := { '0', '0', '0', '0', '0', '0', '0', '0' }

for i := 8 to 1 step -1
   if x >= 2 ^ (i - 1)
       x -= 2 ^ (i - 1)
       buffer[9 - i] := '1'
   endif
next
return (buffer[1] + buffer[2] + buffer[3] + buffer[4] + ;
        buffer[5] + buffer[6] + buffer[7] + buffer[8])
```

Modulus

The modulus operator divides one numeric expression by another and returns the remainder. If you specify a zero divisor, you will get a fatal compiler error.

If you have never used the modulus operator, look for instances in your source code where you perform an operation similar to the following:

```
if x - (y * int( x / y)) = 2
```

This could be replaced by the modulus operator like so:

```
if x % y = 2
```

Listing 5.3 shows examples of the modulus operator in action.

Listing 5.3 Examples of modulus operator

```
? 100 % 10          // 0
? 5 % 6             // 5
? 4 % 3             // 1
? 8 % 3             // 2
? 8 % 0             // compile-time error
```

The MOD() function

dBASE III PLUS' MOD() function is well-known for its quirkiness. The Clipper MOD() function is supplied only for dBASE III PLUS compatibility purposes. It has been entirely superseded by the modulus operator, and its use is not recommended.

Table 5.2 illustrates differences between the dBASE III PLUS MOD() function and the modulus operator:

Table 5.2 MOD() and modulus comparison

		Result of Operation Using		
Dividend	*Divisor*	*Modulus Operator*	*Clipper MOD()*	*dBASE III+ MOD()*
3	0	Compiler Error	Run-Time Error	3
3	-2	1	-1	-1
-3	2	-1	1	1
-3	0	Compiler Error	Run-Time Error	-3
-2	3	-2	1	1

The "+" operator

The "+" operator can take one of three forms:

- Addition — Applicable either to two numeric expressions or a date and a numeric.
- Unary positive — Preceding a numeric by "+" will force this to take a higher level of precedence than other numeric operations (except for unary negative).
- Concatenation — Joins two character expressions (either strings or memos) together.

As you can see, the data types of the operands you specify dictate which operation the "+" operator is expected to perform. Listing 5.4 demonstrates usage of the "+" operator.

Listing 5.4 Examples of + operator

```
/* addition */
? 5 + 100                // 105
? 20 + 103               // 123
? 31 + ctod("12/01/90")  // 01/01/91
? ctod("12/01/90") + 7   // 12/08/90

/* concatenation */
mstring := "Clipper"
? mstring + " 5"        // Clipper 5
? "I love " + mstring  // I love Clipper
```

The "-" Operator

As with "+", the "-" operator can mean one of three things:

- Subtraction — Applies either to two numeric expressions, two dates, or a date and a numeric. The only permutation that is not acceptable here is subtracting a date from a numeric.

- Unary negative — Preceding a numeric by "-" will effectively multiply it by -1. This operation will take precedence over all other numeric operations except unary positive.

- Concatenation — Joins two character expressions (either strings or memos) together. However, unlike the "+" operator, this will remove any trailing spaces from the first expression and tack them onto the end of the returned string.

The "-" operator automatically determines which operation to perform based on the data types of the operands used with it.

Listing 5.5 shows examples of the "-" operator.

Listing 5.5 Examples of - operator

```
/* subtraction */
? 25 - 21                                // 4
? 31 - ctod("12/01/90")                  // run-time error
? ctod("12/08/90") - ctod("12/01/90") // 7
? ctod("01/01/91") - 31                  // 12/01/90

/* unary negative */
mnum = 500
? -mnum                  // -500
? 250 - -mnum            // 750

/* concatenation */
mstring = " Clipper "
? mstring - "5"               // " Clipper5  "
? "I love" - mstring + "5"  // "I love Clipper 5"
? "I love" - mstring - "5"  // "I love Clipper5  "
```

The increment and decrement operators

C programmers have been using these wonderful operators for years. They increase or decrease the value of their operand by one. They can be applied to numeric or date variables or database fields. (Note: If you use these operators in conjunction with a field, you must either preface the field with its alias or declare it with the FIELD statement.)

There are two ways to use the increment and decrement operators. You may use them either before (*prefix*) or after (*postfix*) the operand. If you use the prefix format, the operand will be incremented/decremented before its value is used elsewhere. The postfix format delays the increment/decrement operation until after the rest of the expression has been evaluated.

The increment operator effectively replaces code such as:

```
mvar := mvar + 1
```

with the following:

```
mvar++
```

This representation is far more concise, and will execute a bit faster than the old code. But speed is not the only reason to use them. Convenience plays a far bigger role. The increment and decrement operators are perfect in a wide variety of situations, because you can use them wherever Clipper allows an expression. When you get accustomed to these operators, you will be able to use them to remove many lines of unnecessary source code from your PRG files.

Examples

Suppose that we want to load an array with the first twelve records corresponding to a certain date. Listing 5.6 shows how we would do this with and without the increment operator.

Listing 5.6 With and without increment operator

```
// Without Increment Operator
local finds_[12]
xx := 0
do while customer->date == mdate .and. xx < 12 // limit 12 finds
   finds_[xx + 1] := recno()
   xx    =  xx + 1
   skip
enddo

// With Increment Operator
local finds_[12]
xx := 1
do while customer->date == mdate .and. xx < 12 // limit 12 finds
   finds_[xx++] := recno()
   skip
enddo
```

The first time through the loop, xx will have the value of 1, so the first **recno()** will be assigned to **finds_[1].** After that assignment, **xx** will be incremented by one.

Did you notice that we changed the initial value of **xx** from 0 to 1? This was deliberately leading up to the next example (prefix increment). Now let's see how the prefix increment operator behaves:

```
// With Prefix Increment
local finds_[12]
xx := 0
do while customer->date == mdate .and. xx < 12 // limit 12 finds
   finds_[++xx] := recno()
   skip
enddo
```

The first time through the loop, **xx** will be incremented to 1 before anything else happens. **Recno()** will then be assigned to **finds_[1]**.

Listing 5.7 shows another example of the pre-increment operator in action:

Listing 5.7 Before and after prefix increment operator

```
// Before Prefix Increment Operator
use customer
private names[lastrec()], k
k := 0
do while ! eof()
   k := k + 1
   names[k] := trim(customer->fname) + ' ' +;
               trim(customer->lname)
   skip

enddo

// After Prefix Increment Operator
use customer
private names[lastrec()], k
k := 0
do while ! eof()
   names[++k] := trim(customer->Fname) + ' ' +;
                    trim(customer->Lname)
   skip
enddo
```

As you can see, these are very powerful operators that can greatly change the way that you write Clipper code. However, be sure that you fully understand the difference between *prefix* and *postfix* before you start going crazy with them. Listing 5.8 is another example to further illustrate the difference between the two:

Listing 5.8 Examples of increment and decrement operators

```
yy := 5
zz := --yy          // prefix
? yy                // 4
? zz                // 4
zz := yy++          // postfix
? yy                // 5
? zz                // 4
zz := yy + yy++     // postfix
? yy                // 6
? zz                // 10
zz := --yy + yy     // prefix
? yy                // 5
? zz                // 10
zz := yy + --yy     // prefix
? yy                // 4
? --zz              // 8
? zz                // 8
```

Precedence

The order of precedence for mathematical operators is:

1. Unary positive and negative (+, -)
2. *Prefix* increment and/or decrement (++, --)
3. Exponentiation (**, ^)
4. Multiplication, division, modulus (*, /, %)
5. Addition, subtraction (+, -)
6. *Postfix* increment and/or decrement (++, --)

When you use more than one mathematical operator in an expression, each "sub-expression" is evaluated for each precedence level before subexpressions at the next level are evaluated. All operations are performed in order from left to right.

You can also use parentheses to override this default order. Any subexpressions in parentheses are evaluated first using these precedence rules. If you nest parentheses, the subexpressions will be evaluated beginning with the innermost pair and working outwards.

Example

Let's look at a statement (shown in Listing 5.9) that combines many mathematical operators. We will simplify the expression in each step by applying the operation that takes highest precedence.

Listing 5.9 Precedence evaluation

```
y := 5
x := 24 - --y ^ 5 / 4 ^ 2 % 12 * 6
a.   24 -  4  ^ 5 / 4 ^ 2 % 12 * 6        (prefix decrement)
b.   24 -  1024   / 4 ^ 2 % 12 * 6        (exponentiation)
c.   24 -  1024   /  16   % 12 * 6        (exponentiation)
d.   24 -         64      % 12 * 6        (division)
e.   24 -                 4    * 6        (modulus)
f.   24 -                    24           (multiplication)
g.     0                                  (subtraction)
(x = 0, y = 4)
```

Now let's try that statement again (as shown in Listing 5.10), but add some parentheses to upset the natural order of precedence.

Listing 5.10 Precedence evaluation with parentheses

```
y := 5
x := (24 - --y) ^ (5 / 4 ^ (2 % 12)) * 6
a.    (24 - 4) ^ (5 / 4 ^ (2 % 12))   * 6(prefix decrement)
b.    (24 - 4) ^ (5 / 4 ^    2     )   * 6(innermost parentheses,
                                            modulus)
c.   (24 - 4) ^ (5 /   16          )   * 6(parentheses, exponentia-
                                            tion)
d.   (24 - 4) ^      .31               * 6(division)
e.        20   ^     .31               * 6(parentheses, subtraction)
f.              2.55                   * 6(exponentiation)
g.                                   15.30(multiplication)
```

Relational operators

Just as mathematical operators are vital to a programming language, so then are relational operators. They are used to compare two pieces of data and return a logical True (.T.) or False (.F.) based on the results of that comparison.

Table 5.3 shows the comparisons Clipper 5 allows us to make.

Table 5.3 Relational operators

Operator(s)	*Test*	*Applicable Data Types*
<> != #	Not equal	C, D, L, N, M, NIL
<	Less than	C, D, L, N, M
<=	Less than or equal	C, D, L, N, M
=	Equal	C, D, L, N, M, NIL
==	Exactly equal	C, D, L, N, M, A, O, NIL
>	Greater than	C, D, L, N, M
>=	Greater than or equal	C, D, L, N, M
$	Substring	C, M

```
C = character
D = date
L = logical
N = numeric
M = memo
A = array
O = object
NIL = NIL
```

Equivalence ("=" and "==")

Most of these operators are self-explanatory, but there is still much confusion over the difference between "=" (equal) and "==" (exactly equal). These two operators deviate when it comes to comparing character strings. A test for equality ("=") follows these three rules based on the length of the two strings being compared:

```
? <string1> = <string2>
```

1. If <string2> is a null or empty string (''), the return value is false (.F.).
2. If <string2> is longer than <string1>, the return value is false (.F.).
3. Otherwise, each character of <string2> is compared against its counterpart in <string1>. If all characters in <string2> match <string1>, the return value is true (.T.). Otherwise, the return value would be false (.F.).

By contrast, a test for exact equality ("= =") returns true (.T.) only if the two strings match exactly. Note: if you SET EXACT ON, all equality ("=") tests will be performed in the same fashion as exact equality ("= =") tests. This is very important to remember for those situations where you must test for exact equality. Please refer to Chapter 20, "String Manipulation," for examples of these two types of tests.

Another difference between "=" and "= =" is that you can use the "= =" operator to test two array expressions for equivalence. If both expressions refer to the same array, "= =" will return true (.T.).

Precedence

Unlike mathematical operators, relational operators all take the same level of precedence and are thus evaluated in order from left to right. You can, however, override this order of precedence by using parentheses. In the grander scheme of things, relational operators are evaluated after all mathematical operators.

Listing 5.11 presents more examples of relational operators.

Listing 5.11 Examples of Relational Operators

```
? 5 > 4                    // .T.
? 5 >= 4                   // .T.
? 5 != 4                   // .T.
? 5 != date()              // run-time error—type mismatch
? .T. != .T.               // .F.
? date() < date() + 10     // .T.
? x < NIL                  // run-time error—cannot apply to NIL
? "hi there" = "hi"        // .T.—left string longer than right
? "hi" = "hi there"        // .F.—right string longer than left
? "hi there" == "hi"       // .F.
? "A" < "a"                // .T.
? "the" $ "hi there"       // .T.
? "THE" $ "hi there"       // .F.—search is case-sensitive
```

Logical operators

Logical operators expand upon mathematical and relational operators by allowing you to "join" groups of logical expressions. You can then evaluate these groups of expressions to a single true or false value. They are particularly useful when you need to satisfy several conditions. The logical NOT (.NOT. or !) operator is also perfect for toggling the value of a logical value.

Table 5.4 shows the three Clipper logical operators.

Table 5.4 Logical operators

Operator(s)	*Test*	*Applicable Data Type*
.AND.	Logical AND	Logical
.OR.	Logical OR	Logical
.NOT., !	Logical NOT (negation)	Logical

These operators can be used on logical variables and fields. But you will use them more frequently on expressions that evaluate to a logical value, such as the following:

```
customer->balance <= 250.00
eof()
recno() < 2000
```

Short-circuiting with .AND.

When Clipper 5 evaluates the .AND. operator, if the first operand tests false (.F.), it will immediately return false without bothering to evaluate the second operand. This behavior is different from Summer '87, which would go on to evaluate the second operand even if the first one tested false. This new behavior will allow you to code quite differently. For example, if you wanted to test a variable against a character value in Summer '87, but were unsure whether it had been defined, you would have had to code it in the following manner:

```
if type("mvar") = "C"
   if mvar = "the value"
      * perform action
   endif
endif
```

Clipper 5 lets us combine these two IF tests with the .AND. operator without fear of a run-time error:

```
if type("mvar") = "C" .AND. mvar = "the value"
   * perform action
endif
```

If **mvar** does not exist, the TYPE() function will return "U" (for undefined), and Clipper 5 will not bother evaluating the second operand (**mvar = "the value"**). Summer '87 would evaluate the second operand anyway, causing an undefined identifier error.

By the same token, Clipper 5 will short-circuit an .OR. test if the first clause tests true. Consider the following code fragment:

```
x := 5
y := 10
if y > 8 .or. len(x) > 2
   ? "made it"
endif
```

Under Summer '87 this will meet a bloody end ("Type Mismatch") because of the LEN() test on a numeric. With Clipper 5, though, the first clause **(y > 8)** evaluates to True and the program is smart enough to proceed without bothering to evaluate the second clause. Note that you can still override this behavior via the /Z compiler option (see Chapter 1 for details).

Tip: The preferred method of testing for data type is the new Clipper 5 VALTYPE() function. Major differences between TYPE() and VALTYPE() are that TYPE() relies upon macro substitution, and thus cannot test for local and static variables (discussed in Chapter 6). For more details on VALTYPE(), please refer to Chapter 4, "Data Types".

Precedence

Logical operators are evaluated in the following order:

1. .NOT.
2. .AND.
3. .OR.

When you use more than one logical operator in an expression, each subexpression is evaluated for each precedence level before subexpressions at the next level are evaluated. All operations are performed in order from left to right. You can also use parentheses to override this default order. Any subexpressions in parentheses are evaluated first using these precedence rules. If you nest parentheses, the subexpressions will be evaluated beginning with the innermost pair and working outwards.

In the grander scheme of things, logical operators are evaluated after all mathematical and relational operators.

Examples

Here are two examples of how you could invert a logical variable. One uses the NOT ("!") operator, and one does not. Which do you prefer?

```
monochrome := if(monochrome, .F., .T.)
monochrome := ! monochrome
```

The following statement counts all customers who are in the states of Oregon and California or have a last name of SMITH and deposits the result in the variable **people**:

```
count while customer->state $ "OR.CA" .or. ;
             upper(customer->lname) = "SMITH" to people
```

The following code loops through invoices for a given customer and determines the outstanding balance:

```
mbalance := 0
select invoice
do while  customer->code == invoice->custcode .and. ! EOF()
   mbalance := mbalance + invoice->balance
   skip
enddo
```

Listing 5.12 shows examples of logical operators in action.

Listing 5.12 Examples of logical operators

```
? 5 < 4 .AND. .T.                       // .F. short-circuits
                                        // because 5<4 is false
? 10 = 0 .OR. date() > date() - 10      // .T. (second operand
                                        // is true)
? .NOT. 5 < 4          // .T.  5<4 is false,and .NOT. negates that
? ! 5                   // type mismatch 5 not a logical expression
? ! .T. .AND. ! .F.  // .F.—short-circuits because ! .T. is false
```

Assignment operators

None of the operators we have already discussed would be of much value if you could not assign their results to a variable or database field, now would they? Fortunately, Clipper includes assignment operators for just this purpose. As mentioned previously, Clipper 5 has taken some cues from the C programming language by adding in-line assignment (":=") and compound assignment operators ("<op>=").

Table 5.5 lists the assignment operators at your disposal in Clipper 5.

Table 5.5 Assignment operators

Operator(s)	*Performs*	*Applicable Data Types*
=	Simple assignment	All
:=	In-line assignment	All
<op>=	Compound assignment	C, D, N, M

C = character
D = date
N = numeric
M = memo

In-line assignment

The in-line assignment operator (:=) is used to assign values to variables and fields of any type. The expression to the right of the equals sign is evaluated and then assigned to the variable on the left side of the colon. One of the big advantages of using in-line assignment over the simple assign (=) operator is that you can use the in-line operator anywhere that an expression or constant is allowed, including variable declaration statements.

Examples

When you declare variables, use the in-line assignment operator to initialize them at the same time. Instead of:

```
static counter
local oldrow, oldcol, oldcolor, oldscrn
counter   := 1
oldrow    := row()
oldcol    := col()
oldscrn   := savescreen(0, 0, 24, 79)
oldcolor := setcolor()
```

you can now do this:

```
static counter := 1
local oldrow :=row(), oldcol :=col(), oldcolor :=setcolor(), ;
      oldscrn := savescreen(0, 0, 24, 79)
```

The in-line assignment can (and should) be used to assign multiple variables or fields the same value:

```
customer->fname := mname := "Clipper 5"
```

This is similar to `STORE <exp> TO <var>, <var1>`, with one major difference: You can assign values to fields as well as variables.

LOCAL Caveat: If you want to declare and initialize multiple local variables to the same value, do not use the following syntax:

```
local a := b := c := 1
```

Of these three variables, only the first (**a**) will be treated as LOCAL. The other two (**b** and **c**) will be treated as PRIVATE. This is the way that Clipper 5 was designed to behave, and is *not* a bug. Therefore, you should use the following syntax:

```
local a := 1, b := 1, c := 1
```

Note that the Clipper 5 preprocessor will convert any occurrences of STORE <exp> TO <var> to in-line assignment anyway:

```
// Source Code
STORE 0 TO mrow, mcol, pages

// Preprocessed Output
mrow := mcol := pages := 0
```

You can also use in-line assignment to eliminate redundant code. How often have you needed to assign a value (usually a function call) to a variable and then immediately test that variable?

```
marker1 := AT('{', printline)
if marker1 > 0
   *
endif
```

With the in-line assignment operator, you can remove one of these lines:

```
if (marker1 := at('{', printline)) > 0
   *
endif
```

This statement assigns the value of the AT() call to **marker1**. It then tests if **marker1** is greater than zero. As alluded to earlier in this chapter, the in-line assignment makes it easy for us to write very convoluted code. Resist temptation now, and save yourself a lot of painful debugging later.

Simple vs. in-line assignment

If all you want to do is assign a value to a variable, then the simple and in-line assignment operators are virtually synonymous. However, some programmers (including your humble authors) try to get into the Clipper 5 swing of things by searching for all occurrences of simple assignment ("=") and replace them with in-line assignment (":="). This is a feeble attempt to make their programs look "more like Clipper 5". Not only is this unnecessary, but it will not always work because of the split personality of the "=" operator.

As previously discussed, this operator also serves a relational purpose to test for equality. It therefore returns a logical value: true if the two expressions are equal, or false if they are not. For an illustration of this principle, let's look at this snippet:

```
x = 4
? x = 5            // .F.
? x                // 4
```

When "=" is used as shown in the second statement, instead of assigning a value it will perform an equality test (returning false because **x** is not equal to 5). Consequently, when we test for the value of **x**, it remains unchanged.

In-line assignment is quite different in this regard. If you use it in this type of situation, it will continue to assign the value *and* return that assigned value if asked to do so. With that in mind, let's try that snippet again with in- line assignment.

```
x = 4
? x := 5           // 5
? x                // 5
```

Simply changing each "=" to ":=" will not do, because there will be many instances in your programs where the "=" operator is expected to perform an equality test rather than an assignment. Good examples of this situation are the CASE and IF statements, which must be used with logical values. Changing "=" to ":=" with one of these statements will spell disaster at run-time, as shown in Listing 5.13.

Listing 5.13 In-line assignment caveats

```
#include "inkey.ch"
key := inkey(0)
do case
   case key := K_ENTER     // wrong
      *
   case key := K_ESC    // wrong
      *
   otherwise
      *
endcase
```

```
if mvar := 25      // wrong
   *
endif
```

To reiterate, the equality operator ("=") returns a logical value which suits CASE and IF perfectly. Unfortunately, the in- line assignment operator returns whatever value was assigned. For example, `key := K_ENTER` returns a value of 13 (which, as Spock might say, is definitely not logical). This will result in a run-time error ("argument: conditional").

(K_ENTER is a *manifest constant* in INKEY.CH that represents the INKEY() value of the Enter keypress. For more information about manifest constants, please refer to Chapter 7.)

Compound assignment

These operators perform a mathematical operation and then assign a value to a variable or field. As with in-line assignment, these operators will allow you to make your code more succinct. Additionally, they can be used in expressions and code blocks, whereas their traditional counterparts cannot.

Their format is "<op>=", where <op> is the operation to be performed.

Table 5.6 shows each compound assignment operator.

Table 5.6 Compound assignment operators

Operation	*Equivalent to*	*Operation(s) Performed*
`x += y`	`x := x + y`	concatenation or addition
`x -= y`	`x := x - y`	concatenation or subtraction
`x *= y`	`x := x * y`	multiplication
`x /= y`	`x := x / y`	division
`x %= y`	`x := x % y`	modulus
`x ^= y`	`x := x ^ y`	exponentiation

Listing 5.14 presents examples of compound assignment operators.

Listing 5.14 Examples of compound assignment operators

```
string1 := "Clipper "
? string1 += "5"    // "Clipper 5"
string1 := "Clipper "
? string1 -= "5"    // "Clipper5 "

xx := yy := 10
? xx += yy             // 20
? xx *= yy             // 100
? xx /= yy             // 1
? xx ^= yy             // 10000000000
? xx % 4               // 2

mdate := CTOD("10/01/90")
? mdate += 14          // displays 10/15/90
? mdate += 30          // Halloween!
```

Precedence

Like their relational brethren, assignment operators all take the same level of precedence. However, they differ from all other operators in that they are evaluated *from right to left.*

Compound assignment operators must be viewed a bit differently because they are essentially hybrids between mathematical and assignment operators. Accordingly, the mathematical component of a compound assignment operator will take the same precedence as other mathematical operators. The assignment component will have the same precedence as other assignment operators.

In the grand scheme of things, assignment operators will be evaluated only after all mathematical, relational, and logical operators have been dealt with.

Special purpose operators

Clipper 5 also includes a handful of special purpose operators that are not classifiable in any of the aforementioned categories. These are shown in Table 5.7.

Table 5.7 Special operators

Operator(s)	*Description*
&	Macro operator
->	Alias operator
@	Pass by reference
{ }	Literal array and code block delimiters
[ ]	Array element
( )	Function or grouping

Macro operator

When an ampersand ("&") precedes a character variable or an expression bound in parentheses, this summons the **macro compiler** which compiles expressions at run-time. If the ampersand is used with the name of a variable, the macro compiler will return the value of that variable. This can include any valid Clipper expression, including function calls but not including commands, as shown in Listing 5.15.

Listing 5.15 Examples of macro operator

```
lname := "Jones"
x := "lname"
? &x      // Jones
x := "year(ctod('01/01/91'))"
? &x      // 1991
x := "set decimals to 2"
? &x      // crash!
```

Note: if you plan to embed function calls in a character string in this fashion and then macro compile them at run-time, be sure that you have linked those functions into your application. If they are functions contained in a library (.LIB) file, you may need to declare them EXTERNAL. Otherwise, you may be looking at a "missing external" run-time error when the macro compiler searches in vain for a function that does not exist.

If the ampersand is used with an expression bound in parentheses, the expression will be evaluated first and then the macro compiler will operate on the result. The following example calls the Clipper INDEXKEY() function, which returns the key expression of the specified index. Passing a parameter of zero to INDEXKEY() directs it to look at the controlling index.

```
use customer new
index on lname TO customer
? indexkey(0)       // lname
? &(indexkey(0))   // "Jones"
```

You can substitute text within character strings using the macro operator:

```
fname := “Brutus”
? “Et Tu, &fname”  // Et Tu, Brutus
```

However, this is an exercise in futility. Instead of invoking the macro compiler, we recommend that you concatenate the character strings, which is far more efficient:

```
fname := "Brutus"
? "Et Tu, " + fname
```

Caveat: Static and local variables cannot be macro expanded. Case in point:

```
local lname := "Jones"
x := "lname"
? &x      // run-time error
```

Macros and Memory

The macro is incredibly open-ended but is not without its disadvantages. Macros are slow. In particular, the run-time creation of variables using macros is anathema for the havoc it wreaks upon Clipper's free pool memory. (Free pool memory is the amount of RAM available for your program to use after it has been loaded. For example, if you start with 550K, and the .EXE requires 450K to load, you would have a starting free pool of 100K.)

Each time a variable is created using the macro operator, Clipper takes a chunk out of the free pool memory to store the name of the variable for future reference in a temporary symbol table. The problem is not the memory that these chunks occupy, but rather the memory that they prevent you from using.

The regular symbol table is created at compile-time and has its own space within your program. Unfortunately, the same cannot be said for the temporary run-time symbol table, because Clipper is indiscriminate about where it chooses to create these symbols. As a result, your free pool memory can become badly fragmented, and thus the largest amount of contiguous memory blocks will steadily decrease. This in turn means that if you need to edit a memo of 10K length, although you could have much more than that available, the largest *contiguous* block might be less than that, in which case your program would crash.

This loop creates one thousand variables at run-time:

```
for x := 1 to 1000
   mvar := "test" + ltrim(str(x))
   &mvar := 0
   ? x, memory(0)
next
```

The value of MEMORY(0) will decrease steadily throughout the course of this loop. The worst part is that this memory is lost for the duration of the program, i.e., there is no way to recover it by releasing variables or some such device. Even with Clipper 5's Virtual Memory Management (VMM) system, this type of coding is best left to dBASE. Clipper 5 offers many tools better than macros to solve any programming problem. You should only use macros as a last resort. One such example is the code block, which is often an excellent alternative to a macro. If you feel that you have to use a macro, perhaps you should try using a code block instead. (Please refer to Chapter 8 for more information on code blocks.)

Compiling code blocks at run-time

In Chapter 4 ("Data Types"), we mentioned that the macro operator can also be used to compile code blocks at run-time.

When you compile a code block using the macro operator, you can save the result to a variable. This variable can then be EVALuated later in your program.

```
myblock := &("{ | a | qout(a++) }")
*
*
eval(myblock, 5)    // 6
```

Code blocks can thus be compiled once, and referred to many times throughout the course of your program. By comparison, macros must be recompiled each time they are encountered. The ability to compile code blocks at run-time is crucial to creating a generic database browser with TBrowse. When setting up a TBrowse object, you must specify a code block for each column that dictates what will be displayed in that column. Because the browser must be generic, you cannot hard-code any field names. The following code establishes the columns for a generic TBrowse:

```
local x, browse := TBrowseNew(3, 19, 15, 60), column
use customer new
for x := 1 TO fcount()
   column := TBColumnNew(field(x), &("{ | | " +field(x)+ "}"))
   browse:addcolumn(column)
next
```

The Clipper FIELD() function returns a character string representing the name of the xth field in the database structure. This is then compiled to a code block and used as the basis for the TBrowse column. This would be impossible if code blocks could not be compiled at run-time.

Alias operator

When preceded by a valid alias and followed by an expression, the alias operator ("->") allows you to refer to a field or evaluate an expression in the work area specified by the alias. If the alias points to an unselected work area, the alias operator will automatically SELECT the desired work area, perform the operation, and reselect the previous work area.

This allows you to compact your code by eliminating explicit SELECT statements. For example, if you want to test for EOF() in an unselected work area, there is no need to write:

```
use invoices new
use customer new
set relation to customer->custno into invoices
select invoices
if eof()
   *
endif
select customer
```

when instead you can write:

```
use invoices new
use customer new
set relation to customer->custno into invoices
if invoices->(eof())
   *
endif
```

If you use expressions in this fashion, you must enclose them within parentheses.

```
invoices->(eof())     // proper
invoices->eof()       // will not compile
```

In addition to using Clipper functions with the alias operator, you can refer to your own user-defined functions. For example, suppose you wanted to perform a SEEK in a work area other than the current one. You could write it like this:

```
old_area := select()
select new_area
seek value
select old_area
```

Or you could use the Clipper 5 function dbSeek() as follows:

```
new_area->(dbSeek(value))
```

The reason why you must use a function rather than a command is that the alias operator requries a valid Clipper **expression**. Functions count as expressions—commands do not.

You can easily write your own functions to make full use of the alias operator. To get you started, Listing 5.16 shows a set of small but useful functions that let you do various database-related operations in unselected work areas.
Late note: Clipper 5.01 has added database handling functions similar to these alias functions. The Clipper 5 functions are covered in more detail in Chapter 18.

Listing 5.16 Alias functions

```
/*
   SEEK(<val>) - seek for <val>
   Returns true if found, false if not
*/
function seek(val)
seek val
return found()

/*
   GOTO(<rec>) - jump to Record # <rec>
*/
```

```
function goto(rec)
goto rec
return nil

/*
   TOP() - jump to top of database
*/
function top()
go top
return nil

/*
   BOTTOM() - jump to bottom of database
*/
function bottom()
go bottom
return nil

/*
   DEL(<rec>) - delete current record
   Note: cannot use DELETE(), which is
   a Clipper 5 reserved word
*/
function del()
delete
return nil

/*
   PACK() - pack database
*/
function pack()
pack
return nil

/*
   APPEND() - append blank record
   Returns true if successful, false if not
*/
function append()
append blank
return neterr()
```

```
/*
   ZAP() – zaps database
   Please use judiciously!
*/
function zap()
zap
return nil
```

This code seeks an unselected work area for a record and deletes the record if found, all without a single SELECT statement:

```
test->(top())
if test->(seek(mname))
   test->(del())
endif
```

Chapter 7, "The Preprocessor," shows you how you can add the ALIAS option to many of the database commands.

Pass by reference

When you precede a variable with "@", you are passing it *by reference*. Ordinarily variables are passed to functions *by value*. This means that the function makes a copy of the variable. Any subsequent changes made to the variable in the function affect only the copy. Listing 5.17 demonstrates passing a variable by value.

Listing 5.17 Passing by value

```
mvar := 5
myfunc(mvar)
? mvar          // 5

function myfunc
parameter x
? ++x           // 6
return nil
```

Notice that the value of **mvar** remains unchanged in the higher level function.

When you precede a variable with "@", instead of passing the value of the variable, you are passing the memory address where the variable is stored. Therefore, any changes made to the variable in the lower level function *will change the variable directly*. Listing 5.18 shows how to pass a variable by reference.

Listing 5.18 Passing by reference

```
mvar := 5
myfunc(@mvar)
? mvar          // 6

function myfunc
parameter x
? ++x           // 6
return nil
```

Although the convention is to pass variables by value, there will be some instances where you will want to pass variables by reference so that they can be changed by the function receiving them.

Database fields are always passed by value. This is because they have no memory address per se.

Arrays are handled somewhat differently than variables. Entire arrays are always passed by reference, which means that they can be changed in the lower level function. If you were able to pass an entire array by value, the function would then be forced to make a local copy of every single element in the array! When your arrays are hundreds (or thousands) of elements long, this is simply not practical.

In Listing 5.19 we pass an entire array to MYFUNC(), which changes one of the array's elements.

Listing 5.19 Passing an entire array to a function

```
myarray := { 1, 2, 3, 4 }
myfunc(myarray)
? myarray[3]       // 100
quit

function myfunc(nums)
nums[3] := 100
return nil
```

By contrast, individual array elements are always passed by value. Any attempt to precede them with the "@" operator will result in a compile error, as the following statement demonstrates:

```
myfunc(@a[1])
```

The receiving function therefore makes a copy of the array element and manipulates it, rather than the original. Listing 5.20 demonstrates this concept by passing one element to MyFunc(), which changes it on a local basis only.

Listing 5.20 Passing an array element to a function

```
Myarray := { 1, 2, 3, 4 }
MyFunc(MyArray[3])
? MyArray[3]       // still 3
quit

function MyFunc(num)
? num += 100       // 103
return nil
```

Braces

Curly braces are used to denote the beginning of either a literal array or a code block. Clipper 5 relies upon pipe characters to distinguish between literal arrays and code blocks. Listing 5.21 should help make this distinction clear.

Listing 5.21 Examples of literal arrays and code blocks

```
local array1 := { 0, .T., date(), space(50) }
static array2 := { "Joe", "Greg", "Craig" }
local block1 := { | | myfunc() }
local block2 := { | a, b | qout(a, b) , a += b }
static array3 := { 1, 2, 3, 4, space(10) }     // wrong
```

Note that the declaration of **array3** will not compile. The reason is the call to the Clipper SPACE() function. When you declare static arrays and variables, you can only use constants. Calls to user-defined functions and most Clipper functions are not acceptable, because they are not available at compile-time.

(TIP: The Clipper functions CHR() and ASC() are available at compile-time, so you may use them to initialize static variables.)

Brackets

Left and right brackets ("[" and "]") indicate a reference to an array element. They should be preceded by either a reference to an array, or a literal array. The following examples are both valid and will both display the word "Craig":

```
local a := { "Joe", "Greg", "Craig" }
? a[3]
? { "Joe", "Greg", "Craig" }[3]
```

If you want to refer to an element of a multi-dimensional array, you have two choices in Clipper 5: **[x, y]** or **[x][y]**. For instance, both of these statements will display the number 5, which is the second element of the subarray located at **a[4]**.

```
local a := { 1, 2, 3, { 4, 5, 6} }, x := 4, y := 2
? a[x, y]
? a[x][y]
```

Note that in user-defined commands, brackets have an entirely different meaning. For more information on this, please see Chapter 7, "The Preprocessor".

Parentheses

As we have already discussed, parentheses can be used to override precedence rules when evaluating operators. However, don't forget that parentheses also indicate functions when preceded by a valid function name. Any parameters passed to the function would then be listed between the left and right parentheses.

Summary

Congratulations! You now know everything there is to know about Clipper 5's operators. You understand the fundamental difference between simple and in-line assignment, and know when to use each. You are equipped to make use of increment, decrement, and compound assignment operators to streamline your source code.

Other small but significant things that we discussed include:

- The difference between the modulus operator ("%") and the MOD() function.
- The fact that Clipper 5 will short-circuit the .AND. evaluation if the first expression tests false.
- The difference between passing variables by value and reference.

Finally, you should have no doubts as to the order of precedence for each type of operator. To recap, the overall rule of categorical precedence is as follows:

1. Pre-increment and pre-decrement
2. Mathematical operators
3. Relational operators
4. Logical operators
5. Assignment operators
6. Post-increment and post-decrement

In the coming chapters, we will put all of these operators to work in each and every facet of Clipper 5.

CHAPTER 6

Variable Scoping

Scoping is the study of when and where a given variable is "visible" within your program. It also governs how long the variable retains its value.

This chapter will give you a solid grasp of variable scoping, which you can then use to write more modular programs. In particular, you will be able to take full advantage of the new **local** and **static** declarations to get the maximum power and performance out of Clipper 5.

Overview

In earlier releases, Clipper was positioned primarily as a compiler (and competitor) for dBASE III PLUS. Thus, the Clipper language set has traditionally been patterned after the de facto dBASE standard for compatibility reasons. This direction is good because it swayed legions of dBASE programmers to defect to Clipper, who in turn have kept the language flourishing.

However, dBASE compatibility brings with it several glaring drawbacks, one of which was an utter lack of rigid variable scoping. The only possible variable declarations in the dBASE language are **public** and **private**.

The symbol table

Whenever you refer to these two types of variables, your program must follow a two-step process to derive their values. First, it must look for the name of the variable in a **symbol table**, which is created when you compile your program. The symbol table contains the memory addresses at which the variables' values are stored. Only after your program determines the memory address can it actually determine the variable's value.

Use of the symbol table has two disadvantages:

1. Performance will be more sluggish because each reference to a public or private variable is a two-stage process. Granted, this will probably take no more than a few milliseconds per variable, but as Candice Bergen might put it, "Who would you rather have the time? You or your PC?" If it is easy to reduce execution time, then why not do it?

2. Each public or private variable costs you about 18 bytes in the symbol table. Multiply this by the typical number of variables in one of your applications (hundreds or thousands). If you use 500 variables in an application, that adds up to almost 9K of dead weight in your executable file. Obviously we all want to reduce memory requirements wherever possible, and the symbol table is a good place to start.

   However, we would like to present a word from the devil's advocate:

   > "The implementation of the symbol table is not entirely bad. For example, it allows you to make use of the macro operator to macro substitute variable names at run-time."

For example, consider the following:

```
private mvar, test
mvar := 200
test := "mvar"
? &test          // 200
```

Without an entry in the symbol table, this macro substitution is impossible. However, it is our humble opinion that for the most part, macro substitution is unnecessary and best avoided whenever possible. So many other possible solutions are available in Clipper 5 that macros should be used only as the very last resort.

There are six variable declaration statements in Clipper 5: **private**, **public**, **local**, **static**, **field**, and **memvar**. We will now cover each declaration in great detail, and offer reasons for and against their usage.

Note: the word **function** will be used throughout this chapter to refer to both functions and procedures. However, in Clipper 5 it is preferable to write functions rather than procedures.

Private

Private variables and arrays are visible within the function in which they are declared. They are also visible within any functions called from that function, but not in functions at higher levels.

If you declare a private variable without initializing it, the variable will be assigned the starting value of NIL. If you declare a private array without initializing it, all of its elements will be initialized to NIL.

Besides explicit declaration, private variables are also created when:

- You pass parameters to a function using the **parameters** statement. In the following example, variables **a** and **b** will be treated as private variables.

```
function MyFunc
parameters a, b
```

- You assign a variable without declaring it. In the following example, although only **mvar** is declared as **private**, both it and **mvar2** will be considered as private variables:

```
function Main
private mvar
mvar := "this is private"
mvar2 := "so is this"
```

Scope

Listing 6.1 demonstrates the scope of a private variable.

Listing 6.1 Scope of a private variable

```
// Using Inherited Variables
function Main
MyFunc1()
? mvar     // crash—not visible here
return nil

function MyFunc1
private mvar := 200 // note in-line initialization
MyFunc2()
? mvar     // 416
return nil

function MyFunc2
mvar *= 2
myfunc3()
return nil

function MyFunc3
mvar += 16
return nil
```

Main() calls MyFunc1(), which declares **mvar** as **private**. MyFunc1() then calls MyFunc2(), which in turn calls MyFunc3(). Note that although **mvar** is not explicitly passed as a parameter to either MyFunc2() or MyFunc3(), it is nonetheless visible in both of those lower-level functions, which both change its value.

When control is returned to Main(), **mvar** goes out of scope and is therefore not visible.

Listing 6.2 shows how a **private** variable can be declared in one function but initialized in a lower-level function.

Listing 6.2 Using inherited variables

```
function Main
private mvar
MyFunc()
? mvar    // 300
return nil

function MyFunc
mvar := 300
return .T.
```

When created, private variables "hide" any private and public variables of the same name in higher level procedures. The code shown in Listing 6.3 demonstrates this principle. Note that the values of **mvar** and **whatever** remain unchanged in the higher level function.

Listing 6.3 Visibility of private variables

```
function MyFunc1
public whatever := 2000
private mvar := 20
MyFunc2()
? mvar      // 20
? whatever  // 2000
return nil

function MyFunc2
private mvar := 50, whatever := "testing"
? mvar     // 50
? whatever // testing
return nil
```

Private variables remain in scope until you:

- return from the function in which you declared them to a higher level function
- issue a CLEAR ALL command
- issue a CLEAR MEMORY command
- issue a RELEASE command

"Inherited" variables

The first two examples shown above illustrate a potentially dangerous programming habit: *inherited variables*. This leads to subtle and difficult-to-trace bugs. Imagine that hundreds or thousands of lines of source code separate the functions in these examples. Worse yet, suppose that all of the functions are in different .PRG files! If an inherited variable gets changed by mistake, it may cause incorrect results or a run-time error, which may in turn take hours to track down.

Besides, the use of inherited variables is not at all conducive to modular programming. If you want to write a Clipper 5 function that is truly reusable in every situation, that function should accept only a formal list of parameters. A truly modular function should make no assumptions whatsoever. This includes assuming that undeclared variables will exist when the function is invoked! Therefore, we highly recommend that you begin using the **local** declaration in lieu of **private**.

Notes

- Private variables and arrays may be assigned at the same time that they are declared by using the in-line assignment operator.

- Because **private** statements are considered executable statements, they must follow any **field**, **memvar**, **local**, and **static** statements or else a compiler error will result. The following code snippet demonstrates this.

```
/* bad */
function Main
private mvar
local x

/* good */
function Main
local x
private mvar
return nil
```

- If you redeclare as **public** or **private** an identifier that has already been declared as **field**, **local**, or **static**, in the same source code file, a compiler error will occur.

```
function Main
static x
MyFunc()
return nil

function MyFunc
public x        // whoops!
return nil
```

- Clipper 5 imposes a maximum of 2,048 private and public variables and arrays at any given time during your program.

Public

Public variables are visible to all functions within your application. Once declared, their lifetime is the entire duration of the program unless released.

If you declare a public variable without initializing it, the variable will be assigned the starting value of False (.F.). (This is an exception to the NIL rule—remember it now and save a lot of grief later.) However, if you declare a public array without initializing it, all of its elements will be initialized to NIL, rather than .F.

Scope

The code fragment in Listing 6.4 demonstrates the scope of **publics**.

Listing 6.4 Scope of public variables

```
function Main
MyFunc1()
? mvar          // 416
? marray[1]     // NIL
return nil

function MyFunc1
public mvar := 200
MyFunc2()
? mvar          // 416
? marray[1]     // NIL
return nil

function MyFunc2
mvar *= 2
MyFunc3()
return nil

function MyFunc3
public marray[10]
mvar += 16
return nil
```

Main() calls MyFunc1(), which declares **mvar** as **public**. MyFunc1() calls MyFunc2(), which then calls MyFunc3(). Although **mvar** is not explicitly passed as a parameter to either MyFunc2() or MyFunc3(), it is visible in both of those lower- level functions because it is **public**. In fact, it is also visible in Main() for the same reason.

MyFunc3() declares the array **marray** as **public** but does not initialize it. However, when you declare an array in Clipper 5, its elements are automatically initialized to the value of NIL. When program control returns to MyFunc1() and Main() (which both refer to elements in **marray**), the array is visible because it was declared as **public**.

It is possible to bypass **private** and **public** declarations. For example, if we rewrote MyFunc3() like so:

```
function MyFunc3
if mvar < 100
   public marray[10]
endif
mvar += 16
return nil
```

then **marray** would not be declared because **mvar** is greater than 100 by the time it reaches this function. Our program would subsequently crash when MyFunc1() attempted to refer to **marray[1]**.

Public variables remain in scope until you:

- issue a CLEAR ALL command
- issue a CLEAR MEMORY command
- issue a RELEASE command

Notes

- Public variables may be assigned at the same time they are declared by using the in-line assignment operator.

- As with **private**, **public** statements are considered executable statements and therefore must follow any **field**, **memvar**, **local**, and **static** statements.

- If you redeclare a **field**, **local**, or **static** identifier as **public** within the same source code file, the compiler will get upset and retaliate by refusing to compile your program.

- Clipper 5 imposes a maximum of 2,048 private and public variables and arrays at any given time during your program.

- If you declare a public array by the same name as a previously declared public or private variable, that variable will be destroyed. The following code demonstrates this.

```
function Main
public mvar := 200
MyFunc()
? mvar     // ????
return nil

function MyFunc
public mvar[10]  // goodbye, mvar variable
return nil
```

When you attempt to display **mvar** in Main(), nothing will appear on the screen because it will now be an array rather than a variable.

- For those who actually entertain notions of running your Clipper 5 programs under dBASE III PLUS, the special variable CLIPPER is for you. If you declare the variable CLIPPER as **public**, it will automatically be initialized to true (.T.). The following example assigns the appropriate extension for index files to the variable **ntx_ext**.

```
function Main
public clipper
if clipper
   ntx_ext := "NTX"
else
   ntx_ext := "NDX"
endif
return nil
```

However, the fact that you are reading this book indicates that you want to use Clipper to its fullest extent. To do this, you must abandon the idea of dBASE compatibility, and thus the CLIPPER variable becomes a moot point.

Local

Local variables and arrays are visible only within the function in which they are declared. Though at first glance **local**s and **private**s appear similar, the big difference is that **local**s are not visible to lower level functions.

As with **privates**, if you declare a local variable but do not initialize it, that variable will be assigned the starting value of NIL. Likewise, if you declare a local array without initializing it, all of its elements will be initialized to NIL. Besides explicit declaration, local variables are also created when you pass parameters to a function using list syntax instead of the **parameters** statement. In the following example, variables **a** and **b** will be treated as local variables.

```
function MyFunc(a, b)
```

This syntax, which bears an uncanny resemblance to C, may be somewhat intimidating if you are not accustomed to it. But there are several reasons why you should start using this syntax and abandon the **parameters** statement:

- As already discussed, using **local** instead of **private** means faster execution speed and a smaller .EXE because of the lack of symbols.

- Once you get used to it, you will find the formal declaration syntax to be more instantly readable. You will be able to tell at a glance what parameters your functions are expecting.

Scope

Listing 6.5 demonstrates the scope of local variables.

Listing 6.5 Scope of local variables

```
function MyFunc1
local mvar := 200
MyFunc2()
? mvar              // never gets this far
return nil

function MyFunc2
mvar *= 2           // crash—not visible here
return nil
```

This is a throwback to the inherited variables technique. MyFunc1() declares **mvar** as **local**, then calls MyFunc2(), which attempts to change the value of **mvar**. Because **mvar** is **local** to MyFunc1(), it is not visible in MyFunc2(), and a run-time error quickly ensues. A better way to code this would be to pass a parameter from MyFunc1() to MyFunc2(), as shown in Listing 6.6.

Listing 6.6 Passing a local variable by reference

```
function MyFunc1
local mvar := 200
MyFunc2(@mvar)     // pass by reference
? mvar             // 400
return nil

function MyFunc2(mvar)
mvar *= 2
return nil
```

This time, MyFunc1() passes **mvar** by reference, which means that any changes that MyFunc2() makes will be reflected in the higher level function. (Please refer to the discussion of the "@" operator in Chapter 5 for a thorough comparison of passing by reference and value.)

If you are accustomed to using **privates**, the **local** declaration will require more thought and planning because it completely precludes the possibility of inherited variables. But when you start using **local** instead of **private**, not only will your programs be more efficient and run faster, you will save yourself many hours that you used to waste chasing elusive bugs.

Notes

- Local variables and arrays may be assigned at the same time that they are declared by using the in-line assignment operator.

There are several things to look out for when assigning local variables. First, if you use this syntax to initialize three local variables:

```
local x := y := z := 0
```

only **x** will be **local**. **y** and **z** will be treated as **private**. The proper way to write this is:

```
local x := 0, y := 0, z := 0
```

Another gotcha is that you cannot use a local variable to assign another local variable in the same statement. This code snippet compiles without mishap, but at run-time look out!

```
function password(string)
local x := len(string), midpoint := int((80 - x) / 2)
```

The problem is that the assignment to **midpoint** relies upon the value of **x**. This cannot be done in the statement where **x** is assigned. Therefore, the solution is to break this into two **local** statements:

```
function password(string)
local x := len(string)
local midpoint := int((80 - x) / 2)
```

- When you declare a local variable in a function, that declaration must precede any executable statements (which include **private**, **public**, and even **parameters**). The following example will not compile because the **private** statement precedes the **local**:

```
function MyFunc
private whatever := 100
local mvar := 200
return nil
```

- Local and static variables take precedence over public and private variables, and any database fields of the same name. They do not, however, override variables or fields that have been declared with the **memvar** or **field** declarations.

```
function Main
private mvar := 5
MyFunc()
? mvar      // still 5

function Test
local mvar := 1
? mvar     // 1, not 5
return nil
```

- Macros cannot refer to **local** memvar names because, as mentioned previously, they do not have entries in the symbol table. For situations where you simply *must* continue using macros, you will have to use either **public** or **private** variables.

```
function Main
local mvar := 1
private mvar2 := 5
testing := "MVAR2"   // PRIVATE
? &testing          // 5
testing := "MVAR"    // LOCAL
? &testing          // crash—undefined MVAR
return nil
```

- You must use VALTYPE(), rather than TYPE(), to test the type of a local variable. The TYPE() function relies upon macro substitution to expand its argument (which is why you always have to enclose the parameter within quotes). However, because local variables cannot be macro substituted, TYPE() will be useless upon them.

```
function Main
local mvar := 1
? type('mvar')        // "U" (undefined)
? valtype(mvar)       // "N" (numeric)
return nil
```

- Local variables cannot be saved to or restored from memory (.MEM) files. Be extremely careful of this fact when you attempt to convert all your private variables to **local**. If you must save variables to a .MEM file, you will need to continue using **public** and **private**.

  The following example will create TESTING.MEM, which will contain only the private variables **mvar3** and **mvar4**:

  ```
  local mvar1 := 1, mvar2 := 2
  private mvar3, mvar4
  store "These will be saved" TO mvar3, mvar4
  save all to testing
  ```

- Unlike private and public variables, there is no limitation on the total number of local variables and arrays within your program.

Static

Static variables are similar to **local**s inasmuch as they are only visible within the function where you declare them. However, they vary from **local**s because they retain their value for the duration of your program. This is a difficult concept to grasp, so we will demonstrate it now in Listing 6.7.

Listing 6.7 Static variable retaining value

```
function Main
for x := 1 to 1000
   ? Counter()
next
return nil


function Counter
static y := 1
return y++
```

Each time that we execute the FOR..NEXT loop in Main(), the value returned by Counter() will be incremented. In other words, the first time that we call the Counter() function, the value of **y** will be 1 and Counter() will return 2. The second time that we call Counter(), **y** will retain its previous value of 2, and the function will return 3, and so on.

The reason for this is that when you initialize a static variable, that line of code is handled at compile-time rather than at run-time. This completely flies in the face of **private** and **local** declarations, where the variables must be reinitialized every time you enter the function. Indeed, if we declared **y** as **local** or **private**, then its value would be "reset" to 1 each time we called Counter(), which would always return 2, which is hardly what we intended.

As with local and private variables, if you declare a static variable without initializing it, the variable will be given the value of NIL. In similar fashion, the elements of uninitialized static arrays will automatically be set to NIL.

Scope

Listing 6.8 demonstrates the scope of two static variables.

Listing 6.8 Scope of static variables

```
function Main
static mvar := "testing"
for x := 1 TO 100
   ? MyFunc()
   ? mvar              // "testing"
next
return nil

function MyFunc
static y := 100
return --y
```

Main() declares **mvar** as **static** and executes a FOR..NEXT that invokes MyFunc(). MyFunc() also declares the variable **y** as **static**, and initializes it to 100 at compile-time. Each time MyFunc() is called, it will decrement **y** and return that value. Because **y** is a static variable, it will retain its value for the next time that MyFunc() is called.

mvar will only be visible in Main(), and **y** will only be visible in MyFunc().

Notes

- Static variables and arrays may be assigned at the same time that they are declared by using the in-line assignment operator. However, you may use only simple constants to assign them. Function calls are not acceptable because static variables are initialized prior to run-time. In the following example:

  ```
  static mvar := date()
  ```

  mvar cannot be initialized because the function DATE() cannot be evaluated because you are not yet running the program!

  If you must assign the value of a function to a static variable, be sure to do so at run-time rather than at compile- time:

  ```
  static mvar
  if mvar == nil
     mvar := date()
  endif
  ```

- When you declare a static variable in a function, that declaration must precede any executable statements (which include **private**, **public**, and even **parameters**). The following will not compile because the **public** statement precedes the **static**:

  ```
  function Counter
  public mvar := 'test'
  static mcounter := 0
  return ++mcounter
  ```

You may also declare static variables before the first function or procedure statement in a .PRG file. We will discuss these file-wide statics shortly.

- Static and local variables take precedence over public and private variables, and any database fields of the same name. They do not, however, override variables or fields that have been declared with the **memvar** or **field** declarations. Listing 6.9 demonstrates the precedence of static variables.

Listing 6.9 Precedence of static variables

```
function Main
private mvar := 5
MyFunc()
? mvar      // still 5

function Test
static mvar := 1
? mvar    // 1, not 5
return nil
```

- As with **locals**, macros cannot refer to **static** memvar names because they do not have entries in the symbol table. If you cannot live without macros, you must continue to use either public or private variables.

```
function main
static mvar := "can't find this"
private mvar2 := "no problem"
testing := "MVAR2"  // PRIVATE
? &testing          // "no problem"
testing := "MVAR"   // STATIC
? &testing          // undefined MVAR
return nil
```

- You must use VALTYPE(), rather than TYPE(), to test the type of a static variable. The TYPE() function relies upon macro substitution to expand its argument (which is why you always have to enclose the parameter within quotes). However, because static variables cannot be macro substituted, their TYPE() will always be "U" (undefined).

```
function main
static mvar := 1
? type('mvar')        // "U" (undefined)
? valtype(mvar)       // "N" (numeric)
return nil
```

- Static variables cannot be saved to or restored from memory (.MEM) files. If you must save variables to a .MEM file, you will need to continue using **public** and **private**.
- Unlike private and public variables, there is no limitation on the total number of static variables and arrays within your program.

File-wide static variables

If you declare **static** variables prior to any function or procedure statements, the scope of these variables becomes file-wide and they will be visible in all functions of that .PRG file. You could consider these file-wide **static**s as "limited **public**s"—they are similar to **public**s *but only for that .PRG file.*

Listing 6.10 demonstrates the principle (and power) of file- wide static variables. We have two .PRG files, MAIN.PRG and SCRNSAVE.PRG.

Listing 6.10 Example of file-wide static variables

```
/* MAIN.PRG - compile with /N option */
function Main
@ 0, 0, maxrow(), maxcol() box replicate("*", 9)
Gsavescrn()
inkey(2)
cls
@ 12, 20 say "You are staring at a mostly empty screen"
@ 13, 20 say "Press any key to restore previous screen"
inkey(0)
Grestscrn()
return nil
* EOF main.prg

/*—————————————*/
```

```
/* SCRNSAVE.PRG — compile with /N option */
static buffer

function Gsavescrn(t, l, b, r)
/* establish default window parameters if not passed */
t := if(t = NIL, 0, t)
l := if(l = NIL, 0, l)
b := if(b = NIL, maxrow(), b)
r := if(r = NIL, maxcol(), r)
buffer := { t, l, b, r, savescreen(t, l, b, r) }
return nil

function Grestscrn
restscreen(buffer[1], buffer[2], buffer[3], buffer[4], ;
           buffer[5])
return nil
* eof scrnsave.prg
```

Main() fills the screen with pretty asterisks, and calls Gsavescrn(), a function contained in SCRNSAVE.PRG. Gsavescrn() creates an array of five elements. The first four elements correspond to the top, left, bottom, and right coordinates of the screen buffer to be saved. The fifth and final element contains the actual contents of the screen buffer. This array is saved in the file-wide static variable **buffer**, which is visible only to Gsavescrn() and Grestscrn(). If we attempted to access **buffer** from Main(), our program would crash speedily.

Control returns to Main(), which clears the screen, displays a message and waits for a keypress. Main() then beckons Grestscrn() to restore the previously saved screen. Grestscrn() refers to the **buffer** array, neatly pulling the window coordinates from the first four elements and the screen contents from the fifth.

This is just the beginning of what you can accomplish with the devastating combination of file-wide static variables. In this fashion you can save and restore GETs, SET variables, environmental information, or anything else you can think of. More importantly, you are "encapsulating" the data within the only part of your program that needs to access it.

In Chapter 12 ("Program Design"), we will expand on this concept in two ways:

- File-wide dynamically resizable arrays will make it possible for us to create completely modular "stack-based" functions that will amaze you with their efficiency and brevity.

- File-wide static arrays will allow us to change the way we approach global variables. Switching from **public**s to **static**s will reduce the size of our symbol table (and the .EXE file) and allow our programs to execute more quickly.

There is another very important reason to make the switch. Because public variables are visible throughout the program, they are continually vulnerable to being accidentally changed (or even RELEASEd!). Instead of dragging a set of public variables around for the duration of the program, we will now be able to tuck a set of static variables away in a function where they can rest safely until we need them.

Caveats

If you remember only one thing from this chapter, let this be it: *If you use file-wide static variables, you must compile with the /N option*. We, your humble authors, have made this mistake many times, and cannot overstress the importance of this caveat. (For more information about /N, or any of the many other compiler options, please turn back to Chapter 1.) When you do not use /N, Clipper will create an "implicit starting procedure" for the .PRG file. This starting procedure will render your file-wide static variables completely useless. Consider the code shown in Listing 6.11.

Listing 6.11 Example of file-wide static variables

```
/*  TEST.PRG  */
static marray_ := { 'one', 'two', 'three' }

function Func1(params)
? marray_[1]
return nil
```

```
function Func2(params)
? marray_[2]
return nil

function Func3(params)
? marray_[3]
return nil
```

It works great if you compile with /N, but if you should be unfortunate enough to forget, Clipper 5 will create an implicit starting procedure named TEST. The scope of array **marray_** will now be restricted only to this dummy (in every sense of the word) procedure TEST.

Another situation to watch out for is the duplicate declaration. Suppose that you declare a **local** variable. Later, you decide to make it file-wide **static** because it must be visible in other modules in that .PRG. You declare the variable as static above the top of the first function in the .PRG, and forget to remove the **local** declaration. Gotcha! The **local** declaration will override the **static** and cause you all kinds of grief. Look at the example shown in Listing 6.12.

Listing 6.12 STATIC vs. LOCAL

```
static counter := 0

function Main
local counter := 1  // whoops! forgot to delete this one
? counter           // 1—looking at the LOCAL
MyFunc()
quit

function MyFunc
? counter           // 0—looking at the STATIC
return nil
```

You can see how this would create confusion, so be sure always to delete the **local** declaration immediately.

Static functions

You have already seen that the **static** declaration gives us the power to "hide" data from other functions. You may also use **static** to hide functions from other functions! Declaring a function as **static** restricts its visibility only to other functions within the same .PRG file. This cuts down drastically on function name conflicts.

A prime example of such naming conflicts is the Center() function: Every Clipper programmer has his or her own, and naturally, everyone's syntax is different enough to cause confusion. But now you can hide yours from everyone else's by declaring it as **static**. Consider the example in Listing 6.13, with two separate .PRG files, MAIN.PRG and FUNCS.PRG:

Listing 6.13 Static functions

```
/* MAIN.PRG */
function Main
Whatever()
Center(16, "Ouch!")    // run-time error
return nil

* eof main.prg

/*————————————————*/


/* FUNCS.PRG */
function Whatever
Center(17, "This is a test")
return nil

static function Center(row, msg)
@ row, int((maxcol() + 1 - len(msg)) / 2) say msg
return nil
* eof funcs.prg
```

The Center() function will only be visible to other functions and procedures within FUNCS.PRG. When we call Whatever() from MAIN.PRG, there will be no problem when Whatever() calls Center() because they are both in the same .PRG file. But when we attempt to call Center() directly from MAIN.PRG, the program will crash.

Through the use of static functions, you can thus have numerous functions of the same name throughout your program, as long as they are all contained in separate .PRG files. If you work in a team environment, you will adore static functions not only because they eliminate naming conflicts, but also because they simplify documentation. Suppose that you are working on a module that contains numerous functions:

```
function Entry()
*
return nil

static function Func1()
*
return nil

static function Func2()
*
return nil

et cetera
```

When the time comes for you to distribute your module to the other members of your team, you need only document the parameters required for the Entry() function. They do not need to know about the other static functions, which will only be used within your .PRG file.

Declaring a function as **static** will also reduce the size of your .EXE file by reducing your symbol table. Functions generally require an entry in the symbol table, but the memory addresses of static functions are resolved at compile-time. This can have its downside, as you will discover if you use MEMOEDIT(), ACHOICE(), or DBEDIT() with a user-defined function. Your UDF cannot be declared **static** because those three Clipper functions rely upon macro substitution to access your UDF (which is why you must pass the function name in quotes). Since static functions do not have entries in the symbol table, their names cannot be macro substituted.

By way of demonstration, Listing 6.14 shows a simple user-defined function attached to an ACHOICE(). It processes the **Enter**, **Esc**, and **Spacebar** keypresses.

Listing 6.14 Static functions and ACHOICE()

```
#include "inkey.ch"
function Main
local marray := {'one', 'two', 'three'}, ele
cls
ele := achoice(11, 38, 13, 42, marray, .t., 'MyFunc')
quit

static function MyFunc(status, curr_elem, curr_row)
local key := lastkey()
if key == K_ESC
   return 0
elseif key == K_ENTER
   return 1
elseif key == 32
   @ 20,0 say "You pressed Spacebar! Boy am I smart!"
   inkey(0)
   scroll(20, 0, 20, 36, 0)
endif
return 2
```

Compile and link this, then press the spacebar. Nothing happens! Now remove the word **static** from the MyFunc() declaration. Recompile and link, and try pressing the spacebar again.

Field and memvar

We will discuss these two declarations together because they are somewhat different from the other declarative statements. When you use the **memvar** or **field** statement, you are not "creating" variables as you would with the other declarations. Instead, you are merely telling the compiler that the names you list are to be assumed as either memory variables or fields.

If you have worked with previous versions of Clipper, you are probably painfully aware that fields take precedence over memory variables. For those of you unfamiliar with this phenomenon, assume that the file CUSTOMER.DBF contains a field LNAME:

```
function Main
lname := "Lief"
use customer new
? lname        // ????
```

Rather than displaying "Lief", this function will display whatever is in the field LNAME in the first record of the CUSTOMER database.

When the compiler encounters any names that you have declared as **memvar**, it will automatically precede them with the alias **memvar->**. As you may expect, names declared as **field** will be preceded with the alias **field->**.

Therefore, if you wanted to be certain that LNAME would refer to the variable, you could declare it as **memvar**:

```
function Main
memvar lname
lname = "Lief"
use customer new
? lname        // "Lief"
```

Now all ambiguous (un-aliased) references to LNAME will be assumed to be referring to the variable.

Once again, please remember that declaring something as **memvar** or **field** does not mean that a variable will be created or a database will be opened. These statements neither create nor verify the existence of these identifiers. They are, however, extremely useful in avoiding compiler warnings. For example, if you were coding a report, you might not want to precede each and every field reference with the alias. You could simply declare the fields with **field** as shown in Listing 6.15.

Listing 6.15 Example of FIELD declaration

```
function Rep
local tot := 0
field lname, fname, address, city, state, zip, balance
use customer new
index on lname to temp
set device to print
do while ! eof()
   @ prow() + 1, 1 say trim(fname) + ' ' + trim(lname) + ;
                             if(balance > 0, '*', '')
   @ prow(),    19 say address
   @ prow(),    39 say city
   @ prow(),    61 say state
   @ prow(),    64 say zip
   @ prow(),    73 say balance picture '###.##'
   if prow() > 57
     eject
   endif
   tot += balance
   skip
enddo
@ prow() + 1, 1 SAY 'Total balance outstanding:'
@ prow(), pcol() + 2 SAY tot picture '######.##'
use
set device to screen
ferase('temp.ntx')
return nil
```

If you were to omit the **field** declaration, the compiler would give you a stream of warnings since it would be unable to tell whether you were referring to fields or variables.

Another compiler warning that you may grow tired of is the already infamous GETLIST. GETLIST is a public array that Clipper 5 carries around to ensure compatibility with prior versions of Clipper. If you compile the following code fragment with the /W (warnings) option:

```
function Main
local x := 0, y := 0, z := 0
cls
@ 10, 10 get x
@ 11, 10 get y
@ 12, 10 get z
read
```

you will get several compiler warnings about the variable GETLIST. This is because the preprocessor translates all @..GET and READ commands into function calls that make reference to GETLIST. These warnings are harmless but annoying. To silence the blasted compiler, you need only include this line at the top of your function:

```
memvar getlist
```

As with the **local** and **static** declarations, **memvar** and **field** must precede any executable statements in a function (which include **private**, **public**, and **parameters**).

The scope of **memvar** and **field** declarations is identical to **static**s. If they are declared within a function, their scope is that function only. Like **static**, the **memvar** and **field** declarations may be used before any function or **procedure** statements, in which case their scope will be file-wide. In fact, you may want to consider putting the aforementioned GETLIST squelcher:

```
memvar getlist
```

at the top of your files instead of in each function that refers to GETs. Once again, though, please bear in mind that if you want to use file-wide scope for **memvar** or **field**, you must compile your program with the /N option.

Summary

You now understand the differences among the various declarations. You know that using local variables is infinitely preferable to using privates. You have seen the beginning of what the **static** declaration is going to do for us in Clipper 5. You know how to declare and use static functions and file-wide static variables to reduce naming conflicts and hide data.

Now that you understand scoping (and particularly the concept of file-wide static variables), you will be able to use the modular programming techniques discussed in Chapter 12 to write succinct, powerful, reusable code. These techniques will streamline your development time and help you write more bulletproof programs in less time.

CHAPTER 7

The Preprocessor

When we discussed the Clipper 5 compilation process in Chapter 1, we introduced the preprocessor. If the new compiler is the heart of the Clipper 5 package, then the preprocessor must be the soul. They work hand in hand to make Clipper the completely open-ended language that it has become.

After reading this chapter, you will use the preprocessor to make your programs run faster, be easier to read, and leap tall mainframes at a single bound (if not one, then certainly two). We will demonstrate many ways to use preprocessor directives like manifest constants and user-defined commands to your best advantage.

Overview

C programmers already know the benefits that a preprocessor offers. Now Clipper developers can share in those benefits, because the Clipper 5 release includes its own powerful built-in preprocessor. This feature alone speaks volumes for Computer Associates' conviction in making Clipper 5 a bona fide development language.

A preprocessor looks at your source code and performs certain translations prior to the main compilation step. Based upon its limitless capacity for translation, some Clipper developers have gone so far as to describe the preprocessor as a glorified search-and-replace mechanism. This is in effect like piloting an airplane and never getting it off the tarmac, because the preprocessor does a lot more than search and replace. Its operations include:

- translation (simple and complex)
- inclusion of other files (known in Clipper 5 as "header files" and denoted by the file extension .CH)
- conditional compilation of certain blocks of code (which is great for debugging and/or demonstration versions)

Because the preprocessor is integrated into the Clipper 5 compiler, you are going to be using it whether you know (or like) it or not, so you might as well learn how to make it work to your benefit. In fact, the issue of upward compatibility (making Summer '87 code run under Clipper 5) is neatly addressed by the preprocessor with the STD.CH file. (We will talk more about this file later.)

Manifest constants

Manifest constants are identifiers that the preprocessor acts upon. They have many uses, including improved readability, faster execution speed, and conditional compilation.

Improving readability

With the preprocessor you will now be able to substitute meaningful names instead of cryptic numbers. The **#define** directive allows you to declare **manifest constants**. The syntax for defining a manifest constant is:

```
#define <identifier> [<value>]
```

The preprocessor will sniff out all occurrences of <identifier> in your source code, and replace them with <value> (hence the aforementioned search-and-replace comparison).

Be aware that the preprocessor's substitution for manifest constants is **case-sensitive**. You may wish to avoid problems by adhering to the C naming convention of all uppercase for manifest constants. This is the convention that we will use throughout this book. (Note that you can also define manifest constants without using the <value> parameter. We will discuss this situation in a moment.)

Before we delve into source code examples, be warned that you will see many examples of original source code and preprocessed output with the latter following hot on the heels of the former (and not just in this chapter either). Rest easy — the code that you write is the original source code. The preprocessed output is what it looks like after the preprocessor has finished mangling it. Although you do not have to look at the preprocessed output (let alone do anything with it), we nonetheless recommend that for your first few months with Clipper 5, you make heavy use of the /P compiler option (previously discussed in Chapter 1). This option will create a preprocessed output file, which will have the same filename as your PRG but with the extension PPO. Carefully scrutinize the PPO file to see what the preprocessor is doing to your source code.

Okay, on with the first source code example:

Original source code (.PRG):

```
#define K_DOWN  24
#define K_UP     5
#define K_LEFT  19
#define K_RIGHT  4

if keypress == K_DOWN .or. keypress == K_UP   .or. ;
   keypress == K_LEFT .or. keypress == K_RIGHT
```

Preprocessed output (.PPO):

```
if keypress == 24 .or. keypress == 5 .or. keypress == 19 ;
      .or. keypress == 4
```

(Note that the preprocessor strips out whatever is not translated and leaves blank lines in its wake. There would thus be several blank lines at the top of the PPO file.)

As you can see, it is far more obvious what is happening when you use words rather than numbers. You may have an infinite capacity for memorizing numbers and can recite the entire INKEY() value list in your sleep. But using words in your source code will help the poor soul who will inherit your code next year and be forced to maintain it.

Simply put, we humanoids prefer words and computers prefer numbers, and with the preprocessor there is less need for us to waste time looking up INKEY() values. In fact, Computer Associates provides a header file, INKEY.CH, which contains manifest constants for all of the INKEY() equivalents. Because they use a standard naming convention (K_ENTER, K_TAB, K_CTRL_E, and so on), you will probably never need to look at this file either. Just include it in your programs, and leave the drudgery to the preprocessor.

Another reason to use manifest constants is that the preprocessor will allow you to use as many as 32 characters in a manifest constant as compared to the customary 10 characters in a variable name. You can say a lot more in 32 characters than 10!

Arrays vs. memvars

Although we have not covered arrays yet, you will learn in Chapter 9 how to save memory by using arrays rather than **private** or **public** memory variables to hold field values while editing. This is because you can cut down on the number of symbols in your program, and thus shrink your symbol table (which we discussed at length in Chapter 6, "Variable Scoping").

There is only one drawback to using arrays instead of memory variables — it often leads to unreadable code. But with the preprocessor, we get the best of both worlds: We can use the array but establish manifest constants to give each array element more obvious meaning.

```
local aMemvars[8]

#define MFNAME      aMemvars[1]
#define MLNAME      aMemvars[2]
#define MADDRESS    aMemvars[3]
#define MCITY       aMemvars[4]
#define MSTATE      aMemvars[5]
#define MZIP        aMemvars[6]
#define MFRIEND     aMemvars[7]
#define MBIRTHDATE  aMemvars[8]
```

Then you can write your GETs and actually be able to figure out what is happening:

```
@ 7, 28 get MFNAME
@ 8, 28 get MLNAME
@ 9, 28 get MADDRESS
@ 10, 28 get MCITY
@ 11, 28 get MSTATE
@ 12, 28 get MZIP
@ 13, 28 get MFRIEND picture "Y"
@ 14, 28 get MBIRTHDATE
```

whereas the array equivalent is not going to be a very pretty sight:

```
@ 7, 28 get aMemvars[1]
@ 8, 28 get aMemvars[2]
@ 9, 28 get aMemvars[3]
@ 10, 28 get aMemvars[4]
@ 11, 28 get aMemvars[5]
@ 12, 28 get aMemvars[6]
@ 13, 28 get aMemvars[7] picture "Y"
@ 14, 28 get aMemvars[8]
```

Improving execution speed

Let's review our first example in this chapter, the keypress test. Another way that we could have approached the problem would be to define variables instead of manifest constants:

```
K_DOWN  := 24
K_UP    :=  5
K_LEFT  := 19
K_RIGHT :=  4
```

In prior versions of Clipper, this was the only method available. Many developers used such "pseudo-manifest constants" to improve the readability of their programs. But there are two drawbacks to this method as compared to true preprocessed manifest constants:

- These pseudo-constants are held in the symbol table rather than being resolved at compile-time. This means that whenever they are referred to at run-time, their value must be looked up in the symbol table. Although this does not take a lot of time, it does slow things down by a few clock cycles. Let's do a simple timing test:

```
* using pseudo-constants
TEST := 5
for xx := 1 to 1000
   y := TEST
next

* using manifest constants
#define TEST 5
for xx := 1 to 1000
   y := TEST
next
```

  The second loop runs approximately 10% faster. Another advantage is that the size of your program will be smaller because no symbol table entry is required for the manifest constant (as would be for a traditional memory variable).

- Pseudo-constants are always subject to accidental change during the course of your program. For example, what is to keep you from switching between numeric and character type?

```
* at the top of the program
K_RIGHT := 4

* 3000 lines further down!
K_RIGHT := chr(4)
```

  What would happen the next time your program refers to K_RIGHT? Flip a coin and find out.

You may protest that it is unlikely you would make such a silly mistake. We agree, you are an excellent programmer. However, there is always the possibility that some other programmer will make future modifications to your source code, and they might not be as perfect as you!

While we're on the issue of speed, you can also save time by substituting one-line function calls with preprocessor macros. These are definitely not the same (nor anywhere close) to the traditional dBASE macro (i.e., &something). For the sake of clarity, we will refer to preprocessor macros as **pseudo-functions**. The syntax for defining a pseudo-function is quite similar to that of a manifest constant:

```
#define <function>([<argument list>]) <expression>
```

The preprocessor will track down all occurrences of <function> in your source code, and replace them with <expression>. If you specify an optional <argument list>, those arguments will be substituted into the <expression> based on the names you give them in the <argument list>. For example:

```
#define WHATEVER(exp1, exp2)   exp1 + exp2
x := WHATEVER("ABC", "123")
```

will be preprocessed into:

```
x := “ABC” + “123”
```

Because we specified an argument list (**exp1** and **exp2**), **exp1** assumed the value “ABC”, and **exp2** the value of “123”. The preprocessor was then kind enough to substitute them in the expression **exp1 + exp2**.

If you choose to specify an argument list, you must follow some simple rules:

• No whitespace between the function name and the open parenthesis.

```
#define WHATEVER(exp1, exp2)   exp1 + exp2      // fine
#define WHATEVER (exp1, exp2)   exp1 + exp2     // nope
```

- A closing parenthesis must follow the argument list.

Let's write a pseudo-function Maxx(), which will accept three numeric parameters, and return the maximum of the three. First we will write it as a regular UDF:

```
x1 := 500
x2 := 499
for xx := -1000 to 1000
   yy := Maxx(x1, xx, x2)
next

function Maxx(a, b, c)
return max(if(a > b, a, b), c)
```

Now we will try it again as a pseudo-function:

Original (.PRG):

```
#define MAXY(a, b, c)  max(if(a > b, a, b), c)
x1 := 500
x2 := 499
for xx := -1000 to 1000
   yy := MAXY(x1, xx, x2)  // note uppercase
next
```

Preprocessed output (.PPO):

```
x1 := 500
x2 := 499
for xx := -1000 to 1000
   yy := max(if(x1 > xx, x1, xx), x2)
next
```

The pseudo-function runs 25% faster than the function call (and that is even when we use **local** parameters in the function — if you stick to **private**s, the relative speed of that function call will seem even more miserable). The reason for this performance gain is because a function call adds a certain amount of overhead, however slight. Having everything in-line means that the computer does not have to jump to a different function and set everything up to return the appropriate value and then jump back. Where performance is of paramount concern, having in-line code can remove the bottlenecks at run-time. Granted, these "bottlenecks" are not nearly as bad as the traffic on your average Southern California freeway at rush hour, but every little bit helps.

Pseudo-functions also give us plenty of rope with which to hang ourselves. Whenever you expand an argument list, you should be very careful of parenthetical grouping. Consider Times(), a simple pseudo-function which accepts two numerics and multiplies them together.

Original (.PRG):

```
#define TIMES(a, b)   a * b
w := 5
x := 4
y := 3
z := 2
t := TIMES(w + x, y + z)
```

Preprocessed output (.PPO):

```
t := w + x * y + z
```

As you may recall from our discussion of operator precedence in Chapter 5, multiplication will occur before addition. This outcome is not what we had in mind. Rather than 45 ((5 + 4)(3 + 2)), the variable **t** will be assigned the value of 19 (5 + (4 * 3) + 2). You are the one who left out the parentheses; the preprocessor was merely following orders. Let's fix it now!

```
#define Times(a, b) (a) * (b)
```

Demos and debugging

Have you ever included debugging code in your program?

```
// MYPROG.PRG
debug := .T.
*
* elsewhere in the program
if debug
   ? "procname() = ", procname()
   ? "procline() = ", procline()
   ? "readvar() =  ", readvar()
   ? "memory(0) =  ", memory(0)
   ? "x = ", x
   ? "y = ", y
   ? "z = ", z
endif
```

In the same manner, have you ever included code in your programs so that you could distribute a demonstration version to prospective clients?

```
if demo
   ? "This demo will access only 50 records"
   max_rec := 50
else
   max_rec := 5000000000    // mammoth file
endif
```

Even though these blocks of code will only be executed conditionally, ALL of the source code will be compiled unconditionally. Therefore, it will all end up in your object modules, and consequently, your EXE file. This is a senseless waste of memory.

Fortunately, the preprocessor provides us with the power to conditionally compile our source code. Earlier, we mentioned that you could define manifest constants without a <value> parameter, and this is exactly such an instance. By its presence alone, this type of manifest constant directs the preprocessor to compile (or not compile) sections of source code. The syntax is:

```
#define <identifier>
```

This <identifier> does not require a value. All it needs to do is exist. However, it will not be truly useful until you make use of the **#ifdef** and **#ifndef** directives. #ifdef tells the preprocessor that if a certain identifier exists, it should compile the following block. #ifndef does the opposite; it directs the preprocessor to compile the following block only if the identifier does not exist.

Let's tackle that debug example again with these new directives:

Original (.PRG):

```
#define DEBUG
#ifdef DEBUG
   ? "procname() = ", procname()
   ? "procline() = ", procline()
   ? "readvar() =  ", readvar()
   ? "memory(0) =  ", memory(0)
   ? "x = ", x
   ? "y = ", y
   ? "z = ", z
#endif
```

Preprocessed output (.PPO):

```
qout("procname() = ", procname())
qout("procline() = ", procline())
qout("readvar() =  ", readvar())
qout("memory(0) =  ", memory(0))
qout("x = ", x)
qout("y = ", y)
qout("z = ", z)
```

If we do not #define the DEBUG manifest constant, watch what happens:

Original (.PRG):

```
#ifdef DEBUG
   ? "procname() = ", procname()
   ? "procline() = ", procline()
   ? "readvar() =  ", readvar()
   ? "memory(0) =  ", memory(0)
   ? "x = ", x
   ? "y = ", y
   ? "z = ", z
#endif
```

Preprocessed output (.PPO):

```
(Space, the final frontier.)
```

Now you can safely leave in all your debugging code without fear of bulking up your EXE file. Just #define DEBUG when (or should we say if) you need to use it again!

Because you are a smart cookie, you have probably already surmised that, where there's an IF and an ENDIF, there is probably an ELSE. Sure enough, we'll use it to clean up that demo example:

Original (.PRG):

```
#define DEMO
#ifdef DEMO
   ? "This demo will access only  50 records"
   max_rec := 50
#else
   max_rec := 5000000000   // mammoth file
#endif
```

Preprocessed output(.PPO):

```
qout("This demo will access only 50 records")
max_rec := 50
```

Get rid of the DEMO definition, and...

Original (.PRG):

```
#ifdef DEMO
   ? "This demo will access only 50 records"
   max_rec := 50
#else
   max_rec := 5000000000
#endif
```

Preprocessed output (.PPO):

```
max_rec := 5000000000
```

In similar fashion, #ifndef allows conditional compilation based on the non-existence of a specific identifier:

Original (.PRG):

```
#ifndef REALTHING
   ? "This demo will access only 50 records"
   max_rec := 50
#else
   max_rec := 5000000000
#endif
```

Preprocessed output (.PPO):

```
qout("This demo will access only 50 records")
max_rec := 50
```

There is one more directive in this collection that may serve you well. **#undef** removes (undefines) an identifier. This has several purposes, the first being to restrict conditional compilation to a section of your program:

Original (.PRG):

```
#define DEMO
#ifdef DEMO
   max_rec := 50
   max_calls := 100
#else
   max_rec := 50000000
   max_calls := 100000
#endif

#undef DEMO

#ifdef DEMO
   max_times := 25
#else
   max_times := 200
#endif
```

Preprocessed output (.PPO) (most blank lines omitted):

```
max_rec := 50
max_calls := 100

max_times := 200
```

Notice what happened in the bottom #ifdef..#else..#endif block because you undefined the DEMO identifier. Because you #undefined the DEMO identifier, the preprocessor conditionally compiled as if you were not using the demo code.

Another instance would be where you would want to redefine a manifest constant. This will generate a compiler warning, unless you undefine it first:

```
#define DEMO
#ifdef DEMO
   max_recs := 50
```

```
#else
   max_recs := 10000
#endif

#undef DEMO        // remove this and watch the compiler whine!

#define DEMO .t.
```

When you #define a manifest constant, it is visible from that line until either the end of that PRG file or you #undefine it. This rule also applies to manifest constants in header files that you #include (which we will cover in greater detail very soon).

The only exception to this rule are manifest constants that have been #defined in the STD.CH header file, or an alternate standard rules file that you specify with the /U compiler option. The reason that these manifest constants are visible everywhere is because they are loaded as soon as you fire up the compiler (CLIPPER.EXE), and therefore have a scope that is not limited to any particular .PRG file.

The /D compile option

As we mentioned in Chapter 1, you can #define manifest constants at compile-time with the exceedingly clever /D compiler option. This allows you to change manifest constants without ever touching your source code. You can either create new manifest constants, or, with careful use of the #ifndef directive, override existing ones.

The syntax for the /D compiler option is:

```
clipper progname /D<ID>[=<VAL>]
```

<ID> represents the name of the identifier. You may optionally assign a value <VAL> to the identifier by following <ID> with an equal sign and the value. For example, in the last code fragment we could have removed the #define DEMO statement and compiled the program like so:

```
clipper test /dDEMO
```

This would have exactly the same effect.

You may optionally assign a value to an identifier. Suppose that you want to initialize an array to a certain size. Other things, such as FOR..NEXT loops, also rely upon the array size, and you want to be able to change all such references in one fell swoop. The easiest way to do this would be to define an identifier (or **manifest constant**) at the top of your program like so:

```
#define ELEMENTS  500
local a[ELEMENTS], total
for x := 1 to ELEMENTS
   total += (a[x] := x)
next
```

Now suppose that you want to be able to change the number of elements without changing your source code. With the /D switch, it's easy. Compiling your program with the following command-line arguments will result in an array (and loop counter) of 1000 rather than 500.

```
clipper myprog /dELEMENTS=1000
```

If you have jumped the gun and compiled this example already, you should now be complaining about a "redefinition of #define" compiler error. That makes sense — you are defining ELEMENTS twice: once when you fire up the compiler, and again within the source code where you originally #defined it. Here's a simple solution to this problem:

```
#ifndef ELEMENTS
   #define ELEMENTS  500
#endif

local a[ELEMENTS], total
for x := 1 to ELEMENTS
   total += (a[x] := x)
next
```

This tells the preprocessor to define ELEMENTS only if it has not already been defined.

The more you use manifest constants, the more time you will be able to save with the /D compile option.

Header files

Now that you are ready to build an impressive collection of your own manifest constants, you should know how to segregate them from your source code. **Header files** (also known as "include files") are the best repositories for manifest constants and user-defined commands. Clipper 5 header files generally carry the extension of ".CH".

For example, instead of putting them at the top of every source code file that uses them, like this:

```
#define CRLF            chr(13)+chr(10)
#define MAXY(a, b, c)  max(if(a > b, a, b), c)
#define NETERR_MSG     "Network error, could not add/edit" +;
                        "at this time"
#translate CENTER( <row>, <msg>) => ;
   DevPos( <row>, int((maxcol()+1 - len( <msg> )) / 2)) ;;
   DevOut( <msg> )
```

you can put them into a .CH file and then simply #include that in your programs:

```
#include "MYSTUFF.CH"
```

The #include directive is self-explanatory: It includes the contents of a header file at compile-time. You must always surround the name of the header file with quotes, and the extension must be specified. You may also optionally specify a drive and path, but if you do not, the preprocessor will search in the following three places (in order):

- The current directory.
- Directories specified by the "/i" compiler option (see Chapter 1).
- Directories listed in the INCLUDE environmental variable. (As discussed in Chapter 1, the recommended setting is SET INCLUDE=C:\CLIPPER5\INCLUDE.)

Although header files will usually contain manifest constants and user-defined commands, they may also include regular source code (except for STD.CH and any alternate standard rules file).

However, we do not necessarily advocate doing this because it will make source level debugging difficult, if not totally impossible. Another reason against putting source code in header files is that it is contrary to the purpose of such files, which exist primarily to contain preprocessor directives.

#including a header file is not the same thing as calling another program file with the DO command! When you #include a header file, the preprocessor will use only what it needs. As a result, the size of your compiled code will be kept to an absolute minimum.

You may nest #include directives up to sixteen levels deep:

```
* FILE1.PRG
#include "FILE2.CH"
*

* FILE2.CH
#include "FILE3.CH"
*

* FILE3.CH
#include "FILE4.CH"
```

and so on.

Computer Associates header files

The following files are supplied by Computer Associates with Clipper 5. These should all be in your \CLIPPER5\INCLUDE directory. Most of these header files contain manifest constants which follow a standard naming convention to make them easier to remember.

Table 7.1 Computer Associates header files

Filename	*Relevant to*	*Prefix*
ACHOICE.CH	ACHOICE() user-defined function	AC_
BOX.CH	Box-drawing commands	B_
DBEDIT.CH	DBEDIT() user-defined function	DE_
DBSTRUCT.CH	DBSTRUCT()	DBS_
DIRECTRY.CH	DIRECTORY()	F_
ERROR.CH	Clipper 5 error codes	EG_
FILEIO.CH	Low-level file functions	F_, FS_, FO_, FC_
GETEXIT.CH	get:exitState values	GE_
INKEY.CH	INKEY() values (very handy)	K_
MEMOEDIT.CH	MEMOEDIT() user-defined function	ME_
RESERVED.CH	To resolve naming conflicts	n/a
SET.CH	SET()	_SET_
SETCURS.CH	SETCURSOR()	SC_
SIMPLEIO.CH	Simplified input/output commands	n/a
STD.CH	Standard Clipper 5 language definition	n/a

Rather than list the contents of each of these files line by line, we will present a self-explanatory example that uses several of them.

Listing 7.1 Manifest constant/#include example

```
#include "BOX.CH"
#include "INKEY.CH"
#include "SET.CH"
#include "SETCURS.CH"
#define OFF .f.
#translate CENTER( <row>, <msg> ) => ;
 DevPos( <row>, int((maxcol() + 1 - len( <msg> )) / 2)) ; ;
 DevOut( <msg> )
```

```
function main
local key, oldcursor := setcursor(SC_NONE)  // turn off cursor
set(_SET_SCOREBOARD, OFF)
set(_SET_CANCEL, OFF)
cls
@ 0, 0, 24, 79 box B_DOUBLE + ' ' color 'w/b'
@ 6, 6, 18, 73 box B_SINGLE + ' ' color 'w/r'
@ 11, 18, 13, 61 box B_SINGLE_DOUBLE + ' ' color '+w/rb'
do while .t.
   center(12, "Press a key - Esc to exit")
   key := inkey(0)
   scroll(12, 19, 12, 60, 0)
   do case
       case key == K_ENTER
          center(12, "You pressed Enter")
       case key == K_F1
          center(12, "No help available")
       case key == K_SH_F1
          center(12, "Still no help available")
       case key == K_ALT_A
          center(12, "You pressed Alt-A")
       case key == K_CTRL_Y
          center(12, "You pressed Ctrl-Y")
       case key == K_ESC
          exit
       otherwise
          center(12, "Unknown keypress")
   endcase
   inkey(1)
enddo
setcursor(oldcursor)  // restore cursor
return nil
```

User-defined commands

There are several drawbacks to using #define to create preprocessor functions. The biggest is that, as mentioned above, the preprocessor treats #define directives as case-sensitive. This means that one wrong character will keep the preprocessor from translating your pseudo-function. Another drawback comes when you need to do more than a simple translation, e.g., convert a parameter to a character string or code block. This is where the #command, #translate, #xcommand, and #xtranslate directives come into play. These directives allow us to create our own user-defined commands.

The first place you should turn for excellent examples of these four directives is the STD.CH file, which contains dozens of user-defined commands. Actually, as you look closely at STD.CH, you will realize that there are no longer "commands" per se. Every single command gets preprocessed into one or more function calls. This in itself is quite an eye-opening experience.

STD.CH is provided for review purposes only. Its contents are embedded in the Clipper compiler (CLIPPER.EXE) for performance purposes. If you wish to alter any of the standard Clipper command set, we highly recommend that you make a copy of STD.CH. Then be sure to specify this modified STD.CH with the compiler /U option (see Chapter 1).

If you plan to modify only several of the commands, you may wish to put those commands in a header file and #include that in your source code. This principle will be demonstrated in later chapters.

#xcommand and #xtranslate

These directives were added with Clipper 5.01. They are identical to #command and #translate, respectively, with the exception that they require **exact** matches. #command and #translate only require a match on the first four letters of the input text.

These directives are extremely useful in situations such as the following: Suppose that you want to have a preprocessor function called DateWord(), which would return the verbose system date.

```
#translate DateWord() => ;
        cmonth(date()) + ' ' + ltrim(str(day(date()))) + ;
        ', ' + str(year(date()), 4)
function main
? dateword()
return nil
```

Unfortunately, the preprocessor will look at only the first four characters, and thus mistake your DateWord() call for DATE(). This will obviously cause you problems. In fact, this particular example will not even compile because DATE() is used as part of the output text. Therefore, a circular reference will result, closely followed by a stack overflow crash.

We highly recommend that you use #xcommand and #xtranslate rather than #command and #translate. The #command and #translate directives are useful only for compatibility with the dBASE convention of abbreviating commands. But as you have already seen, they can lead to circularity errors and general confusion, so they should be avoided at all costs.

Structure of a user-defined command

The basic syntax of a user-defined command is:

```
#xcommand <input text> => <result text>
#xtranslate <input text> => <result text>
```

A user-defined command consists of three basic parts: the input text, arrow separator ("=>"), and result text.

An important distinction between the #xcommand and #xtranslate directives is that user-defined commands specified with the #xtranslate or #translate directive may appear anywhere in a statement (as can #defines). By contrast, user-defined commands specified with #xcommand or #command MUST be the first non-whitespace characters on a line.

For example, look at the Clipper redefinition of the CLEAR command:

```
#command CLEAR => CLEAR SCREEN ; CLEAR GETS;
```

If you changed this directive to a #translate, and then attempted the following command:

```
@ 10, 12 CLEAR
```

the preprocessor would run into problems. Its first pass would produce the following:

```
@ 10, 12 CLEAR SCREEN ; CLEAR GETS ;
```

CLEAR SCREEN and CLEAR GETS are both #command directives, and therefore cannot appear within a statement in this fashion. However, a bigger problem is that the preprocessor will look at the "CLEAR" in CLEAR SCREEN and attempt to translate that **yet again** based on the #translate CLEAR directive! This will quickly lead to a circularity error that stops compilation dead in its tracks.

Here's a simple rule of thumb for you to use when deciding upon #xcommand or #xtranslate: If the translated expression returns a value, use #xtranslate. Otherwise, use #xcommand.

Input text

This is what the preprocessor will be looking for as it scans your source code. Input text can contain any or all of the following three items:

- **Literal values** — characters that must appear exactly in your input text for the preprocessor to be able to translate it. An example of a literal value is the "@" in the @..CLEAR command:

```
#command  @ <top>, <left>  CLEAR   => ;
__AtClear( <top>, <left>, MaxRow(), MaxCol())
```

- **Words** — keywords that are compared according to the time-honored dBASE tradition (case-insensitive and first four letters only). Therefore, if you write:

```
@ 0, 0 clea
```

  the preprocessor will still be able to translate it according to the #command directive given for @..CLEAR.

- **Match-Markers** — the "parameters" that vary according to the user-defined command. These are treated differently than in #define statements. In a #define, you simply specify a parameter between parentheses:

```
#define TIMES(a, b)    (a) * (b)
```

  When you use a #xtranslate or #xcommand directive, however, you must surround such parameters by "<" and ">" on both sides of the arrow:

```
#xtranslate TIMES( <a>, <b> )  =>  ( <a> ) * ( <b> )
```

Match-markers assign each parameter a name, which you can then refer to in the output (or "result") text. In the TIMES() example shown above, the match-markers mark and assign two chunks of text: **a** and **b.**

Match-markers correspond to **result-markers**, which write the text resulting from the preprocessor's translation. You can easily see from the TIMES() example how **a** and **b** are configured to appear in the resulting preprocessor output for this command. (We'll get to result-markers in more detail in the discussion of **result text**.)

Before we hurl ourselves into the match-marker discussion, let's introduce several important new terms:

- **"stringify"** — convert into a character string
- **"blockify"** — convert into a code block
- **"logify"** — convert into a logical value

We also must ask you to buckle up and put on your thinking caps, because you are about to enter a zone congested with new terminology.

Match-markers

Of the many new Clipper 5 concepts, match-markers (and result-markers) are perhaps the most difficult to grasp. There are many different types of match-markers, all of which serve particular purposes. If you do not fully understand the significance of most of these match-markers, do not spend any time worrying about it. The one that you will rely upon most often is the regular match-marker. As you become more confident with the preprocessor and more sophisticated with your user-defined commands, then you may wish to refer back to this section to learn exactly how and where to use the more specialized match-markers.

Table 7.2 Match-markers

Syntax	*Type*
`<name>`	Regular Match-marker
`<name, ...>`	List Match-marker
`<name: word list>`	Restricted Match-marker
`<*name*>`	Wild Match-marker
`<(name)>`	Extended Expression Match-marker

- The regular match-marker is the most common of the match-markers. It simply matches the next legal expression in the input text. The regular match-marker is used most often with the regular result-marker, but can also be used with the stringify result-markers, and the blockify result-marker. An example of this type of match-marker is the DO WHILE command.

```
#command DO WHILE <exp>  => while <exp>
```

- The list match-marker matches a comma-separated list of expressions. If no input text matches the match-marker, the specified marker name will contain nothing and will thus not be used in the result text. An example of the list match-marker is the ? command, which accepts a list of parameters.

```
#command ? [list, ...>]  =>  QOUT (<list>)
```

- The restricted match-marker is for processing input text that must match one of the words in a comma-separated list. If the input text is not contained in the specified list, the match will fail and the marker name contains nothing. This type of match-marker is most often used with the logify result-marker to write a logical value into the result text. Examples of this match-marker can be found in many of the SET commands, which generally accept the words "ON", "OFF", or a variable name preceded by the macro operator. If a variable is used, it must have a character value, preferably "ON" or "OFF" as you will see from the following example.

```
#command SET CENTURY <x:ON,OFF,&> =>;
__SetCentury(ONOFF( <(x)> ))
y := "on"
set century to &y    //  __SetCentury((Upper(y) == "ON"))
```

- The wild match-marker will match any input text from the current position to the end of a statement. This can be used to match input text that may not be a legal expression. A notable example of this usage is the tongue-in-cheek "compatibility" section of STD.CH, which dispenses with numerous dBASE III PLUS commands that are useless to a compiler:

```
#command SET ECHO <*x*>        =>
#command SET HEADING <*x*>     =>
#command SET MENU <*x*>        =>
#command SET STATUS <*x*>      =>
#command SET STEP <*x*>        =>
#command SET SAFETY <*x*>      =>
#command SET TALK <*x*>        =>
```

Therefore, if you included this flippant line in your source code:

```
set echo, is there an echo in here?
```

the preprocessor would output a blank line without even flinching.

The wild match-marker is also used to gather the input text to the end of the statement and write it to the result text using one of the stringify result-markers. An example of this usage is the SET PATH TO command.

```
#command SET PATH TO <*path*>  => Set(_SET_PATH, <(path)> )
```

- The extended expression match-marker will match a regular or extended expression, including filename or path specifications. This allows you to pass a specification without quotes, or in parentheses as an extended expression. You can then use the smart stringify result-marker to ensure that extended expressions will not get stringified. The SET DEFAULT command provides an example of the extended expression match-marker.

```
#xcommand SET DEFAULT TO <(path)> =>;
          set(_SET_DEFAULT, <(path)> )
SET DEFAULT TO c:\app     // set(_SET_DEFAULT, "c:\app")
SET DEFAULT TO ("c:\app") // Set(_SET_DEFAULT, ("c:\app"))
```

Optional clauses

You may specify optional match-clauses by enclosing them in brackets ("[" and "]"). Optional clauses may contain literal values, words, match-markers, and even other optional clauses. There are two types of optional match-clauses:

- A keyword followed by match-marker(s), such as @..GET:

```
#command @ <row>, <col> GET <var> [PICTURE <pic>];
           [RANGE <lo>, <hi>]
```

- A keyword by itself, such as SET KEY TO:

```
#command  set key <n> [TO]  =>  SetKey( <n>, nil)
```

Result text

Result text is the preprocessor's output after translating your source code. It can contain any or all of the following three items:

- **Literal values** — characters that are written directly to the result text. There are examples of literal values in nearly every user-defined command.

- **Words** — keywords and identifiers that are written directly to the output text. Again, there are examples of these in nearly every user-defined command.

- **Result-Markers** — references to match-marker names. As mentioned previously, input text which is matched by a match-marker is written to the result text via a result-marker. As with match-markers, result-markers must be surrounded by "<" and ">".

Result-markers

As with match-markers, there are numerous result-markers. Once again, do not fret if these do not all make sense right now. The one that will be used most often is the regular result-marker. As you write more complex user-defined commands, you can always refer back to this section to learn exactly how and where to use the more specialized result-markers.

Table 7.3 Result-Markers

Syntax	*Type*
<name>	Regular result-marker
#<name>	Dumb stringify result-marker
<"name">	Normal stringify result-marker
<(name)>	Smart stringify result-marker
<{name}>	Blockify result-marker
<.name.>	Logify result-marker

- The regular result-marker writes the matched input text to the result text. It writes nothing if no input text is matched. As with the regular match-marker, this is the most common result-marker and therefore most likely to be used. This result-marker is used most often with the regular match-marker but can be used in combination with any of them. We will rewrite our TIMES() pseudo-function to give an example of regular result-markers.

```
#xtranslate TIMES( <a> , <b> )  =>  ( <a> * <b> )
```

- The dumb stringify result-marker turns the matched input text into a character string and writes it to the result text. If no input text is matched, this result-marker will write a null string ("") to the result text. If used in conjunction with the list match-marker, the list will be converted to a character string and written to the result text. An example of this result-marker is the SET COLOR TO command, which accepts an unquoted color specification.

```
#command SET COLOR TO [<*spec*>]   =>  SetColor(#<spec> )
set color to w/b                   //  SetColor("w/b")
```

Note: the dumb stringify result-marker is not quite as dumb as you might think. It is intelligent enough to detect the presence of string delimiters in your character string and work around that.

```
#xtranslate show_msg( <message> ) => showmsg(#<message> )
show_msg(test1)                   // showmsg("test1")
show_msg("test2")                 // showmsg('"test2"')
```

- The normal stringify result-marker is very similar to the dumb stringify result-marker. The differences are that if no input text is matched, this result-marker writes nothing (rather than a null string). Also, if used with the list match-marker, each element in the list will be stringified, as opposed to the entire list as one entity. The RELEASE command provides an example of the normal stringify result-marker.

```
#command RELEASE <vars,...> =>  __MXRelease( <"vars"> )
release mvar                //  __MXRelease("mvar")
release mvar, mvar2, mvar3  //  __MXRelease("mvar",;
                            //                "mvar2","mvar3")
```

- The smart stringify result-marker converts the matched input text to a character string only if it is enclosed in parentheses. If no input text is matched, nothing is written to the result text. If used in conjunction with the list match-marker, each element in the list is stringified using this same rule and written to the result text.

  The smart stringify result-marker is designed specifically to support extended expressions for commands other than SETs. One such use is the ERASE command.

```
#command  ERASE <(file)>     =>  FErase( <(file)> )
mvar := "temp.dbf"
ERASE temp.dbf               //  FErase("temp.dbf")
ERASE (mvar)                 //  FErase((mvar))
```

- The blockify result-marker converts the matched input text to a code block. If no input text is matched, nothing is written to the result text. If used with the list match-marker, each element in the list is converted that way. Many Clipper 5 functions rely upon code blocks, which makes this result-marker a lot more important than you might imagine. An example of blockifying is the SET FILTER command.

```
#command SET FILTER TO <xpr> => dbSetFilter(<{xpr}>,<"xpr"> )
set filter to ! deleted  //  dbSetFilter({|| ! deleted()},;
                         //              "! deleted()")
```

- The logify result-market writes true (.T.) to the result text if input text is matched, or false (.F.) if it is not. The input text itself is not written to the result text. As mentioned above, this type of result-marker is best used with the restricted match-marker. An example demonstrating both of these is the SET MESSAGE TO command.

```
#command SET MESSAGE TO <n> [<cent: CENTER, CENTRE>] => ;
set(_SET_MESSAGE, <n> ) ; Set(_SET_MCENTER, <.cent.> )
set message to 24          // Set(_SET_MESSAGE, 24) ;;
                              // Set(_SET_MCENTER, .F.)
set message to 24 center   // Set(_SET_MESSAGE, 24) ;;
                              // Set(_SET_MCENTER, .T.)
```

As you have seen in these examples, the output text can contain more than one statement. Each statement must be separated by a semicolon. When you start writing more complex user-defined commands that need continuation lines, be sure not to skimp on the semicolons.

```
#xtranslate endsearch() => mrow := row() ; mcol := col() ; ;
                           searching := .f. ; searchstr := '' ; ;
                           devpos(ntop, (maxcol() + 1) / 2 - 11) ; ;
                           devout(replicate(chr(205), 22)) ; ;
                           devpos(mrow, mcol)
```

If you want to use a less than symbol ("<") or brackets ("[", "]") in the output text, you must preface them with a backward slash ("\"). The backslash is necessary because those characters all carry special meaning to the preprocessor. "<" indicates the beginning of a match-marker, and brackets indicate optional clauses.

Please feel free to use white space liberally in your #xcommand and #xtranslate constructs. The preprocessor needs it to be able to properly convert everything. In fact, the only place where you would not want white space is between the angle brackets and the match markers (i.e., use "<msg>" rather than "< msg >"). It will compile properly, but will detract from the readability of your code.

One of the benefits to writing your own user-defined commands is to minimize naming conflicts between your functions and others of the same name. Center() is a great example of this — nearly every Clipper programmer has a Center() function, and they all use slightly different syntax. This can create massive problems when you call your Center() function but link in someone else's. You will get run-time type mismatch errors and not understand why.

However, if you make Center() into a user-defined command as we did earlier, *it no longer exists as a function.* All centering is done in-line, which therefore completely eliminates any potential naming conflicts. You will never have to worry again about accidentally invoking someone else's Center() function.

Scope of user-defined commands

When you write a user-defined command with the #xcommand or #xtranslate directives, it will remain visible from that line until the end of that PRG file. It will not be visible in other PRG files. The following code fragment demonstrates this principle.

Listing 7.2 Scope of user-defined commands

```
/* MAIN.PRG */
#xcommand REDRAW => @ 0, 0, maxrow(), maxcol();
          box replicate(chr(176),9)

function main
redraw
do test
return nil
* eof: main.prg

/* TEST.PRG */
redraw
return nil
* eof: test.prg
```

The preprocessor will be unable to translate the REDRAW command in TEST.PRG, which will lead to a compile error ("statement unterminated").

The only exception to this rule of visibility are user-defined commands in STD.CH (or an alternate standard rules file that you specify with the /U compile option).

Precedence

Multiple directives per statement

The preprocessor translates the three primary directives in this order: #define; #translate; #command. As each directive is encountered, the preprocessor will translate it appropriately and then rescan that line of code for any other directives. Look at the following directives:

```
#define OFFSET   20
#define FROMBACK(a) len(a - OFFSET)
#xtranslate addem( <a> ) => aeval( <a>, { | ele | msum += ele },;
           FROMBACK( <a> ))
AddEm(myarray)
```

When the preprocessor encounters the AddEm() user-defined command, it will convert it to:

```
aeval(myarray, { | ele | msum += ele }, FROMBACK( myarray))
```

It will then make another pass at that line, which will reveal FROMBACK. Because this has been #defined as a pseudo-function, it too will be translated:

```
aeval(myarray, { | ele | msum += ele }, len(myarray - OFFSET))
```

Finally, the preprocessor will act upon the #definition of OFFSET to translate that as well:

```
aeval(myarray, { | ele | msum += ele }, len(myarray - 20))
```

Since there are no more directives to be processed for this line, the preprocessor considers this a job well done and moves on.

Most recent definition

The preprocessor will consider the most recent definition of each directive when translating your code. This means that, for example, if you #define a manifest constant in your source code and then #include a header file that redefines it, the redefinition will be used. The following example demonstrates this:

```
// TEMP.PRG
#define ELEMENTS 5
#xtranslate Center( <a> ) => ;
            space(int((80 - len( <a> ))/2))
#translate READ => readmodal(getlist) ; ;
                    aadd(mastergets, getlist)
#include "MYSTUFF.CH"

function main
memvar getlist
local a[ELEMENTS], mastergets := {}, string := space(40)
cls
@ 2, 20 get string
read
string = trim(string)
@ 3, center(string) say string
return nil
* end of file TEMP.PRG

// MYSTUFF.CH
#define ELEMENTS 100
#xtranslate Center( <row>, <msg> ) => ;
@ <row>, space(int((80 - len( <msg> )) / 2) say <msg>
```

The preprocessed output will look like this:

```
#line 1 "d:\MYSTUFF.CH"
#line 6 "d:\TEMP.PRG"
function main
memvar getlist
local a[100], mastergets := {}, string := space(40)
Scroll (); SetPos(0, 0)
SetPos(2, 20) ; AAdd(GetList, _GET_(string, "string",,,))
```

```
readmodal(getlist) ; aadd(mastergets, getlist)
string = trim(string)
DevPos(3, space(int((80 - len( string ))/2))) ; ;
DevOut(string)
return nil
```

Although the manifest constant ELEMENTS was defined in TEMP.PRG, the preprocessor used the value found in MYSTUFF.CH since that file was #included after the #define statement. In similar fashion, the user-defined command Center() gets pulled in from MYSTUFF.CH and thus overrides the original #xtranslate directive in TEMP.PRG.

Note that unlike #defines, if you redefine a #command or #translate directive you will **not** get a compiler warning.

Did you notice the redefinition of the Clipper READ command? You can override standard Clipper commands in this manner. Clipper's standard rule set (as seen in STD.CH) is loaded at the beginning of the compilation process. In accordance with the rule of most recent definition, the preprocessor will therefore use your redefinition of the READ command.

The #error directive

This directive was added with the release of Clipper 5.01. If the #error directive is encountered by the compiler, it will cause the compilation process to stop dead in its tracks.

Why might you want to do this? The best reason is that #error allows you to bullet-proof your code in situations where you absolutely, positively must depend upon certain manifest constants. There are at least two instances where this would be important:

1. If you are working with other programmers in a team environment.

2. If your code assumes that certain directives will be passed on the command-line with the /D compiler switch.

The following code fragment shows how you can ensure that the manifest constant ITERATIONS exists:

```
#ifndef ITERATIONS
  #error Missing ITERATIONS - try again, bucko
#endif
```

This directive is used extensively in the RESERVED.CH header file, which is used to preclude naming collisions between your functions and reserved Clipper function names. Please refer directly to the RESERVED.CH file for numerous examples.

The #STDOUT directive

The #STDOUT directive will cause literal text to be outputted on the default device (usually the screen) during compilation. Its syntax is as follows:

```
#STDOUT character string
```

The #STDOUT directive can be useful for displaying on the screen the fact that you are compiling a DEBUG version, (because previously you defined a DEBUG variable). If you have a large application to do, the #STDOUT can notify you that you are making the debug version instead of the production version. This will allow you to stop the compilation if you want to remove the debugging code.

Examples

Writing bilingual programs

Suppose that you have a vertical market application that will be used by both English- and French-speaking people. There are three basic ways of addressing this problem:

1. Maintain two completely separate versions of your source code. This is obviously not very practical and is hardly worth doing.

2. Strip all static (user interface) text out of the program and create text or MEM files for each language. Restructure the program to read in the variables from this file at the beginning and make use of it throughout.

This is infinitely preferable to method #1. However, it has several potential drawbacks, which include the performance penalty you must incur for the disk access, and potential simultaneous file access problems on networks. But for a single-user system running on a relatively quick CPU (for example, a 386/25 Mhz or above), this is a very adequate solution.

3. Use the preprocessor!

You can probably guess that we plan to discuss the third option, since that is the whole point of this dissertation. It's really quite easy — we rely upon the #ifdef directive, whose power we only briefly hinted at earlier. For example:

Listing 7.3 Bilingual manifest constants

```
#ifdef FRENCH
   #define M_NETERR     "Dossier entrain d'être utiliser, " +;
                        "ne pouvez pas modifier"
   #define M_CONTINUE   "Voulez-vous continuer? (O/N)"
   #define M_TOF        "Commencement de fichier!"
   #define M_BOF        "Fin de fichier!"
   #define M_PRINT      "Imprimante ou fichier?"
   #define M_CONFIRM    "Etes-vous sur?"
   #define M_NOTFOUND   "Pas Trouver!"
   #define M_ADDING     "Ajoute dossier - ^W pour sauver; "+;
                        "Esc pour sortir"
   #define M_EDITING    "Modifie dossier - ^W pour sauver; "+;
                        "Esc pour sortir"
#else
   #define M_NETERR     "Could not lock record at this time - "+;
                        "edits not saved"
   #define M_CONTINUE   "Would you like to continue? (Y/N)"
   #define M_TOF        "Top of file!"
   #define M_BOF        "Bottom of file!"
   #define M_PRINT      "Print to printer or file?"
   #define M_CONFIRM    "Are you sure?"
   #define M_NOTFOUND   "Not Found!"
   #define M_ADDING     "Add record - ^W to save; Esc to exit"
   #define M_EDITING    "Edit record- ^W to save; Esc to exit"
#endif
```

Next, you refer to these messages by the manifest constants that identify them. For example, here is the code for a failed SEEK:

```
seek whatever
if ! found()
    Center(maxrow(),M_NOTFOUND)
endif
```

Now you can switch effortlessly between the two languages by using the /D compiler option. If you want to use French, compile with the following command:

```
clipper myprog /dFRENCH
```

The preprocessor will detect the presence of the FRENCH identifier, and use only the French manifest constants.

If you want to use English, just compile without using the /D option. Because the FRENCH identifier will be undefined, the preprocessor will use the English manifest constants.

Box drawing

Are you as tired of drawing box outlines as we are? Here are some user-defined commands and a handy literal array to address this.

Before proceeding, remember that Nantucket does include a BOX.CH header file that has some useful manifest constants representing box outlines. Our main complaint with their definitions is that none of them include the ninth character (which fills the box), so you therefore have to add it yourself for the interior of your boxes to be cleared. This leads directly into our first two examples:

```
#xtranslate SINGLEBOX( <top>, <left>, <bottom>, <right> ) => ;
                 @ <top>, <left>, <bottom>, <right> BOX "┌─┐│┘─└│ "
#xtranslate DOUBLEBOX( <top>, <left>, <bottom>, <right> ) => ;
                 @ <top>, <left>, <bottom>, <right> BOX "╔═╗║╝═╚║ "
```

So if you want to draw a single box, all you need to do is:

```
singlebox(5, 0, 10, 50)
```

It does not get much easier than that! But if you want more flexibility with the box outline, here is another example that you can use:

```
#define BOXFRAMES{'╔═╗║╝═╚║', '┌─┐│┘─└│', '╒═╕│╛═╘│',;
               '╓─╖║╜─╙║', '█▀███▄██', SPACE (9) }
```

This is not an in-line function; instead, it is a literal array containing six elements. Whenever you refer to BOXFRAMES in your source code, the preprocessor will substitute this array in its place.

As you can tell, each of these six elements is a different sort of box outline. How would you use this? Let's suppose that you wanted to draw a box with a thick border. The thick border is the fifth element in the array. Here's the call:

```
@ 5, 0, 10, 50 box BOXFRAMES[5]
```

Again, this is quite easy and very clean. To make matters even simpler, you could set up manifest constants referring to each type of box outline so that you would not even have to remember the array element numbers:

```
#define B_DOUBLE          1
#define B_SINGLE          2
#define B_DOUBLESINGLE    3
#define B_SINGLEDOUBLE    4
#define B_THICK           5
#define B_NONE            6
@ 5, 0, 10, 50 box BOXFRAMES[B_THICK]
```

Date literals

This idea comes courtesy of Don Caton. Mr. Caton is a very clever fellow who actually found something to like about dBASE IV: its literal representation of dates. It is old news that to declare a date variable in Clipper (and dBASE III PLUS), you had to rely upon the CTOD() function.

```
mdate := ctod("03/01/91")
```

dBASE IV lets you declare that date like so:

```
mdate = {03/01/91}
```

Don seized the opportunity to use the #xtranslate directive and the dumb stringify result-marker to provide this functionality for Clipper 5 programmers.

Original (.PRG):

```
#xtranslate { <m> / <d> / <y> } =>;
            ctod(#<m> + "/" + #<d> + "/" + #<y> )
mdate := {03/01/91}
```

Preprocessed output (.PPO):

```
mdate := ctod("03" + "/" + "01" + "/" + "91")
```

As you can see, the month, day, and year do not need to be enclosed in quotes because the dumb stringify result-marker will do that for you. Yes, this still calls the CTOD() function, but it cleans up your code and saves you time coding. (Note that there is an infinitesimal chance of the preprocessor getting confused between a date literal and, say, a literal array, but it has not happened to any of us.)

Default

Clipper 5.2 now includes the DEFAULT .. TO command and the UPDATE command in its header files. The commands are as follows:

```
#xcommand DEFAULT <v1> TO <x1> [, <vn> TO <xn> ]  ;
=>
IF <v1> == NIL ; <
[; IF <vn> == NIL ; <vn> := <xn> ; END ]

#command UPDATE <v1> IF <exp> TO <v2> ; END
```

In addition, several other useful directives are now included in a file called COMMON.CH:

```
#define TRUE   .T.
#define FALSE  .F.
#define YES    .T.
#define NO     .F.

#translate ISNIL( <v1> )           => ( <v1> == NIL )
#translate ISARRAY( <v1> )         => ( valtype( <v1> ) == "A" )
#translate ISBLOCK( <v1> )         => ( valtype( <v1> ) == "B" )
#translate ISCHARACTER( <v1> )     => ( valtype( <v1> ) == "C" )
#translate ISDATE( <v1> )          => ( valtype( <v1> ) == "D" )
#translate ISLOGICAL( <v1> )       => ( valtype( <v1> ) == "L" )
#translate ISMEMO( <v1> )          => ( valtype( <v1> ) == "M" )
#translate ISNUMBER( <v1> )        => ( valtype( <v1> ) == "N" )
#translate ISOBJECT( <v1> )        => ( valtype( <v1> ) == "O" )
```

Free-format function parameter lists

But wait, that's not all you can do with NIL. You can also construct free-format function parameter lists. In this example, you could write a preprocessor translation directive for ShowMsg() that would allow you to pass the three parameters in any order you wanted. The only provision would be that you would have to identify the parameter.

```
#xtranslate showmsg([MSG <msg>] [BOXCOL <boxcol>];
                    [MSGCOL <msgcol>]) ;
          => showmsg( <msg>, <boxcol>, <msgcol> )
```

Each clause should be surrounded by brackets to indicate that it is optional, and there is no need to separate them with commas.

The following statements:

```
showmsg(MSGCOL 'w/b' MSG 'this is the message' BOXCOL 'w/r')
showmsg(MSGCOL 'w/b' BOXCOL 'w/r' MSG 'this is the message')
showmsg(BOXCOL 'w/r' MSGCOL 'w/b' MSG 'this is the message')
```

will all be neatly translated into:

```
showmsg("this is the message", "w/r", "w/b")
```

Omitting a parameter is no big deal, since Clipper 5 lets us skip parameters.

Original (.PRG)

```
showmsg(MSGCOL 'w/b' MSG 'this is the message')
```

Preprocessed output (.PPO)

```
showmsg('this is the message',, 'w/b')
```

With this syntax the second parameter (box color) gets passed as a NIL. Because we have already configured our logic to test each parameter against NIL, there is no possible way that anything can go wrong.

Adding extensions to filenames

Most Clipper programs prompt the user to enter a filename. They are often allowed to enter an optional extension, but if they do not, the program must add one itself. The following user-defined command fills the bill quite neatly:

Original: (.PRG)

```
#xtranslate AddExtension( <file>, <ext> ) => ;
      <file> := upper( <file> ) + if(! "." + upper( <ext> ) $ ;
                upper( <file> ), "." + upper( <ext> ), '')

AddExtension(mfile, 'dbf')
```

Preprocessed: (.PPO)

```
mfile := upper(mfile) + if(! "." + upper("dbf") $ upper(mfile), ;
               "." + upper("dbf"), "")
```

No more STRPAD()

Computer Associates should have included this directive in STD.CH. If you used the STRPAD() function in Clipper Summer '87, you may have already discovered that it does not exist in Clipper 5. However, Clipper 5 does provide the PADR() function, which does everything that STRPAD() did. Rather than having to go through your code and change each occurrence of STRPAD() to PADR(), you could write a simple translation to do it for you:

```
#xtranslate strpad( <msg>, <length> ) => padr( <msg>, <length> )
```

Alias expressions

As you may recall from Chapter 5, the alias operator ("->") allows you to refer to a field or evaluate an expression in an unselected work area. The alias operator will automatically SELECT the desired work area, perform the operation, and reselect the previous work area. This allows you to compact your code by requiring fewer explicit SELECT statements. (The ALIAS clause exists only with the SKIP command.)

These are some examples to get you started. The basic idea is to add the optional clause "[ALIAS <a>]" to the input text, and the corresponding optional clause "[<a> ->]" to the result text. You also must make sure to surround the relevant function call with parentheses.

Listing 7.4 Alias expressions

```
#command SEEK <xpr>    [ALIAS <a>] =>  [<a> ->] (dbSeek( <xpr> ))
#command GOTO <n>      [ALIAS <a>] =>  [<a> ->] (dbGoto( <n> ))
#command GO <n>        [ALIAS <a>] =>  [<a> ->] (dbGoto( <n> ))
#command GOTO TOP      [ALIAS <a>] =>  [<a> ->] (dbGoTop())
#command GO TOP        [ALIAS <a>] =>  [<a> ->] (dbGoTop())
#command GOTO BOTTOM   [ALIAS <a>] =>  [<a> ->] (dbGoBottom())
#command GO BOTTOM     [ALIAS <a>] =>  [<a> ->] (dbGoBottom())
#command CONTINUE      [ALIAS <a>] =>  [<a> ->] (dbContinue())
#command APPEND BLANK [ALIAS <a>] =>  [<a> ->] (dbAppend())
#command UNLOCK        [ALIAS <a>] =>  [<a> ->] (dbUnlock())
#command PACK          [ALIAS <a>] =>  [<a> ->] (__dbPack())
#command ZAP           [ALIAS <a>] =>  [<a> ->] (__dbZap())
#command DELETE        [ALIAS <a>] =>  [<a> ->] (dbDelete())
#command RECALL        [ALIAS <a>] =>  [<a> ->] (dbRecall())

function Main
use invoices new
set index to invoices
use customer new
seek customer->Custno alias invoices
delete alias invoices
go top alias invoices
return nil
```

As mentioned earlier, you should not modify the STD.CH file directly. If you want to use the alias clause as outlined here, make a copy of STD.CH, rename it to something else (ALIAS.CH might be appropriate), and modify the database commands accordingly. Then strip out everything except what you have changed. By #including this new header file in your source code, your database commands will override the Clipper defaults.

Throughout this book we advise you against modifying the STD.CH file. Here are the reasons:

- STD.CH is provided for reference purposes only. The rules therein are actually embedded within the compiler (CLIPPER. EXE) to enhance performance.

- If you made changes to STD.CH, you would then have to use the compiler /U option to use your modified file as the standard rules file. This will cause your compilation process to be significantly slower.

- Rather than make changes to STD.CH and use it with /U as outlined above, we recommend that if you plan to modify one or two commands, you should place those modifications in your own header file and #include that in your source code. Because the standard rules are loaded first, anything that you redefine will override the standard definition. This will allow you to use your modified commands, without sacrificing speed during compilation.

Grabbing text/color attributes

If you need to check the text and/or color attribute at a particular location on the screen, you can use SAVESCREEN() to save that element and then parse it. However, rather than clutter your code with lots of messy SAVESCREEN() calls, use these two user-defined commands, TextAt() and ColorAt().

Original: (.PRG)

```
#xtranslate TextAt( <r>, <c> ) => ;
                  substr(savescreen( <r>, <c>, <r>, <c> ), 1, 1)
#xtranslate ColorAt( <r>, <c> ) => ;
                  substr(savescreen( <r>, <c>, <r>, <c> ), 2, 1)
x := TextAt(10, 0)
```

Preprocessed: (.PPO)

```
x := substr(savescreen(10, 0, 10, 0), 1, 1)
```

Music Maestro please

Even if you scoff at the prospect of using audio feedback in your programs, it still behooves you to look at the coding techniques presented here. We have included three familiar musical themes: "Charge", "NannyBoo", and "TheFifth" (opening notes to Beethoven's Fifth). When you call one of these commands, the preprocessor will convert it to a multi-dimensional array (containing note frequency and duration), which in turn gets passed to the function Tunes(). Tunes() is not actually a function, so the preprocessor translates it into an AEVAL() statement which invokes the TONE() function to play one note for each element in the array.

Because the #xcommand directive is used, these song names must begin a statement rather than be contained within it.

Listing 7.5 Preprocessed music

```
#xcommand Charge   => tunes({ {523,2}, {698,2}, {880,2}, ;
                        {1046,4}, {880,2}, {1046,8} } )
#xcommand NannyBoo => tunes({ {196,4}, {196,4}, {164,4}, {220,4}, ;
                        {196,8}, {164,8} } )
#xcommand TheFifth => tunes({ {392,2},{392,2},{392,2},{311,10},;
                        {15,12}, {349,2}, {349,2}, {349,2},;
                        {293,10} } )
#xtranslate tunes( <a> ) => aeval( <a>,;
                         { | a | tone(a\[1], a\[2]) } )

function Music
charge
inkey(0)
nannyboo
inkey(0)
thefifth
inkey(0)
return nil
```

This should whet your appetite for AEVAL() and multi-dimensional arrays, which are covered at length in the next two chapters, respectively.

Summary

You are now ready to put the Clipper 5 preprocessor to work for you. You understand how to define manifest constants both in your source code and on the command-line. You know how to conditionally compile your source code via manifest constants.

A thorough knowledge of the preprocessor is a prerequisite for many of the topics that await you. For example, we will use the preprocessor to write a replacement for Clipper's light-bar menu system (@..PROMPT and MENU TO) in Chapter 14. We will also rely upon the preprocessor to add more clauses to the @..GET command in Chapter 26.

CHAPTER 8

Code Blocks

Code blocks are a new data type in Clipper 5. They often engender a great deal of fear and confusion at first, because they are such a radically different concept.

Therefore, this chapter will shed some much-needed light on these maligned and misunderstood creatures. When you have finished, you should be ready and willing to make the code block your ally instead of your enemy.

We will also discuss in depth the numerous Clipper functions that use code blocks, including EVAL(), AEVAL(), DBEVAL(), FIELDBLOCK(), FIELDWBLOCK(), and SETKEY().

Overview

Code blocks are an integral (and inescapable) part of Clipper 5. Even if you never explicitly write a code block, you can bet that the preprocessor will be turning many of your commands into code blocks, so you might as well learn how to use them to your advantage.

Code blocks are a data type that contain compiled Clipper code. They can be compiled either at compile-time with the rest of your Clipper code, or at run-time with the use of the "&" operator.

This is a code block in its rawest form:

```
{ | [<argument list>] | <expression list> }
```

Code blocks look quite similar to Clipper 5 literal arrays. Both code blocks and arrays begin with an open curly brace ("{") and end with a closed curly brace ("}"). But code blocks differentiate themselves by including two "pipe" characters ("|") directly after the opening brace. These pipe characters delimit an optional <argument list>, which would then be passed to the code block upon evaluation. The <argument list> must be comma-delimited (e.g., "a, b, c...").

Although the white space between the pipe characters and braces is purely optional, we highly recommend you use it for the sake of readability.

The <expression list> is, obviously enough, a comma-delimited list of any valid Clipper expressions. These can run the gamut, as you will quickly discover.

Writing a code block

There are three methods for writing a code block:

- To be compiled into a code block at compile-time, for example:

```
local myblock := { | | fname }
```

- As a character string, which can be compiled to a code block at run-time. For such compilation you can use the & operator. Yes, the same one that is used for macros. But remember that this is not the same thing as macro substitution! Suppose you wanted to set up a TBrowse() object to browse a database. You would need to establish a column for each field in the database. When setting up TBrowse() columns, you must specify a code block, which when evaluated contains the contents of that column. If you knew in advance that our database contained the fields FNAME, LNAME, and SSN, it would be a simple matter to write the code blocks so that they could be compiled at compile-time:

```
local x, browse := TBrowseDB(3, 19, 15, 60), column
use test new
column := TBColumnNew("FNAME", { | | fname } )
```

```
browse:AddColumn(column)
column := TBColumnNew("LNAME", { | | lname } )
browse:AddColumn(column)
column := TBColumnNew("SSN", { | | ssn } )
browse:AddColumn(column)
do while ! browse:stabilize()
enddo
```

However, let us further suppose that we wish this routine to be generic. We therefore cannot hard-code field names, because the structure will be unknown until run-time. Listing 8.1 shows how we could approach it.

Listing 8.1 Generic TBrowse column setup

```
local x, browse := TBrowseDB(3, 19, 15, 60), column
use test new
for x := 1 to fcount()
   column := TBColumnNew(field(x), &("{ | | " + field(x) + "}"))
   browse:AddColumn(column)
next
do while ! browse:stabilize()
enddo
```

(Note: Later in this chapter we will discuss how to accomplish this same thing with the FIELDWBLOCK() function.)

The Clipper FIELD() function returns the name of the field based at the ordinal position in the database structure. For example, FIELD(2) will return the name of the second field in the database ("LNAME" in our little example).

Caveat: If you compile a code block at run-time that refers to a static or local variable, it will crash unless you pass that variable as an argument. The following code will not run:

```
function Main
static x := 5, y, z
y := &("{ | | x * 200 }")
? eval(y)    // boom
```

This is because when you attempt to compile the code block with the "&" operator, the variable will not be resolvable because **local** and **static** memory variables do not have entries in the symbol table.

The workaround is to structure your code block to accept arguments, and then pass any static/local variables as parameters at evaluation.

```
function Main
static x := 5, y, z
y := &("{ | x | x * 200 }")
? eval(y, x)
```

Because **x** is declared as an argument to this code block, it will be treated as a variable local to that code block. All you need to do then is make sure to pass an argument when you evaluate the code block.

Note the use of **x** within the code block. This **x** will be local to the code block, and is therefore not related in any way to the variable **x**.

- Don't dirty your head with the mechanics of code blocks and let the preprocessor write them all for you. For example, if you write the following code:

```
index on fname to customer
```

the preprocessor will dedicate a code block in your honor:

```
dbCreateIndex( "customer", "fname", {|| fname},;
               if(.f., .t., nil))
```

Code blocks have much in common with inner city cockroaches: You can neither run nor hide from them. Thankfully, code blocks are a lot more fun and a million times more useful than cockroaches (which is why, if you have read this far, you should keep reading and stop playing with your pet cockroach).

Evaluating code blocks

The only operation that you can perform on a code block is *evaluation*. You can think of evaluation as being analogous to calling a function and returning a value from it. Code blocks can be evaluated by the EVAL(), AEVAL(), or DBEVAL() functions. They are also evaluated internally when you pass them as parameters to functions that can use them.

When evaluated, code blocks return the value of the rightmost expression within them. For example, if you create the following code block:

```
local myblock := { | | mvar }
```

When you evaluate this code block, it will return the current value of **mvar**. If **mvar** is undefined at the time that you evaluate the code block, you will get an undefined error.

```
local myblock := { | | mvar }
local mvar := 500
local x
x := eval(myblock)
? x                            // output: 500
```

Remember that code blocks can contain any valid Clipper expressions. This means that you can get considerably fancier with them than we have dared thus far. For example:

```
local myblock := { | | qout(var1), qqout(var2), 500 }
local var1 := "Clipper ", var2 := "5"
x := eval(myblock)                  // "Clipper 5"
? x                                 // 500
```

Look again at that last statement. How does **x** get the value of 500? When you evaluate a code block with EVAL(), it returns the value of the last (or rightmost) expression within it. Because the last expression in **myblock** is 500, the variable **x** is assigned that value.

Using code blocks without parameters

These are examples of simple code blocks that do not use parameters. The first simply outputs a value to the console:

```
local myblock := { | | qout(mvar) }, mvar := "testing"
eval(myblock)     // "testing"
```

This returns a constant (5000), which upon evaluation is assigned to the variable X.

```
local myblock := { | | 5000 }
x := eval(myblock)
? x                   // 5000
```

This crashes upon evaluation because the variable **x** has not been defined.

```
local myblock := { | | x++ }
for y := 1 to 100
   eval(myblock) // boom!
next
? x
```

This is the fixed version of the last example. X is defined, and there is joy in Mudville.

```
local myblock := { | | x++ }, x := 1  // much nicer thanks
for y := 1 to 100
   eval(myblock)
next
? x                   // output: 101
```

This is an example of calling one of your own functions from within a code block:

```
local myblock := { | | BlueFunc() }
eval(myblock)   // calls BlueFunc() which displays a message
return nil

static function BlueFunc
? "here we are in a BlueFunc() - will we ever escape?"
inkey(5)
return nil
```

Using code blocks with parameters

Just as with functions, there is far greater power to harness with code blocks when you begin passing parameters. Writing a parameter list for a code block is nearly identical to writing one for a function. However, because it is harder to conceptualize in the linear world of a code block, we'll write a simple code block and then rewrite it as a function:

```
local myblock := { | a, b, c | max(a, max(b, c)) }

function MMax(a, b, c)
return max(a, max(b, c))
```

As you can readily see, the function MMax() returns the highest of the three parameters passed to it. Evaluating the code block **myblock** will return exactly the same thing. However, we must first slip past another stumbling block: how to pass parameters to a code block. It is actually quite simple; the EVAL() function accepts optional parameters after the name of the code block. Each such optional parameter represents a parameter to be passed to the code block. For example, if you write:

```
eval(myblock, 20)
```

you are in effect passing the numeric parameter 20 to the code block defined as **myblock**. Let's have another look at our MMax() function and code block so that you can get a feel for passing parameters with EVAL():

```
local myblock := { | a, b, c | max(a, max(b, c)) }
? MMax(20, 100, 30)              // 100
? eval(myblock, 20, 100, 30)     // 100
```

Do you remember the BlueFunc() that we were just in? (Hope you're feeling better now.) Let's modify the function and the code block to accept a parameter which will dictate how long to wait for a keypress.

```
local myblock := { | x | BlueFunc(x) }
eval(myblock, 20)   // calls BlueFunc() and will wait 20 seconds
return nil
```

```
static function BlueFunc(delay)
? "we're in a BlueFunc() for " + ltrim(str(delay)) + " seconds"
inkey(delay)
return nil
```

Here is a code block that accepts up to three parameters and displays them on the screen:

```
local myblock := { | a, b, c | qout(a, b, c) }
eval(myblock, 1, 2, 3)          // 1 2 3
x := eval(myblock, 1, 2)        // 1 2 nil
? x                             // nil
```

You already know why the second EVAL() statement outputs 1, 2, and NIL, right? It is because any declared parameters that are not received are initialized to NIL. Because **myblock** expects three parameters (**a**, **b**, **c**), and we only pass two, **c** gets initialized to NIL. But here's a trick question for you: Do you know why **x** takes the value of NIL? No, it has nothing to do with the fact that we passed too few parameters. Rather, it is because the code block returns the value of the expression QOUT(**a**, **b**, **c**). The Clipper 5 QOUT() function always returns NIL. (If you already knew this, give yourself a pat on the back.)

Important Note: Any arguments that you specify in a code block are automatically given local scope. Such arguments will not be visible to any nested code blocks! This merits another example:

```
local firstblock := { | | qout(x) }
local myblock := { | x | x++, eval(firstblock) }
eval(myblock, 3)
```

This program will crash when you attempt to evaluate **firstblock**. It would seem that the argument **x** in **myblock** should be visible within **firstblock**. But do not be fooled — **x** is local to **myblock** and is therefore NOT visible to **firstblock**.

Functions that crave code blocks

EVAL(<block>, [<arg list>])

You should have already surmised that EVAL() evaluates a code block, which you pass to it as the <block> parameter. The optional parameter <arg list> is a comma-delimited list of parameters to be passed to the code block when you evaluate it.

Return value: As we mentioned previously, EVAL() returns the value of the last (rightmost) expression within the block.

AEVAL(<array>, <block>, [<start>], [<count>])

AEVAL() is similar to EVAL() but is specially designed to work with arrays. It evaluates a code block (specified by the <block> parameter) for each element in the array (specified by the <array> parameter). You may optionally specify a <start> element, and a number of elements (<count>) to process. If you do not use these optional parameters, AEVAL() will begin with the first element in the array and process all of them.

The following AEVAL() is a real workhorse; it determines the maximum, minimum, and sum of all elements in the array MYARRAY:

```
local myarray := { 75, 100, 2, 200, .25, -25, 40, 52 }, ;
        nmax, nmin, nsum := 0
nmax := nmin := myarray[1]
aeval(myarray, { | a | nmax := max(nmax, a),;
                       nmin := min(nmin, a),;
                       nsum += a } )
? "Maximum value:", nmax          // 200
? "Minimum value:", nmin          // -25
? "Total amount: ", nsum          // 444.25
```

AEVAL() automatically passes two parameters to the code block: <value> and <number>. <value> is the value of the array element being processed. <number> is the number of the array element being processed. You have already seen how <value> is used, but why should we bother with <number>? Suppose that you want to increment each element in MYARRAY. You would probably write your code block like this:

```
aeval(myarray, { | a | a++ } )
aeval(myarray, { | a | qout(a) } ) // display results
```

Surprise, surprise! This will not do a single thing to the elements of the array, because they are passed by value (not reference) to the code block. (See Chapter 9 for a thorough discussion of arrays.) Passing by value means that the code block makes a copy of the array element, and any manipulation done within the code block is performed on the copy rather than the genuine article. Let's try it again with the <number> parameter:

```
aeval(myarray, { | a, b | myarray[b]++ } )
aeval(myarray, { | a | qout(a) } )
```

Return value: AEVAL() returns a reference to the array you ask it to process.

DBEVAL(<block>, [<for>], [<while>], [<next>], [<record>], [<rest>])

DBEVAL() is similar to AEVAL(), except that it deals with databases rather than arrays. It also provides far greater control, including FOR, WHILE, NEXT, RECORD, and REST clauses. If you look at the STD.CH header file, you will see that the COUNT, SUM, and AVERAGE commands, as well as the iterator versions of DELETE, RECALL, and REPLACE, are all preprocessed into calls to DBEVAL(). For example, if you want to sum the field BALANCE for all records in your database, the following DBEVAL() would do the trick:

```
ntotal := 0
dbeval( { | | ntotal += balance} )
```

You could easily modify this to keep track of the highest balance:

```
use customer new alias cust
ntotal := nmax := 0
dbeval( { | | ntotal += cust->balance, ;
              nmax := max(nmax, cust->balance) } )
? "Total:   ", ntotal
? "Maximum:", nmax
```

<block> is the code block to evaluate for each database record. There are a plethora of optional parameters.

<for> and <while> are code blocks that correspond directly to the FOR and WHILE clauses. Basically, if you use either or both of these clauses, DBEVAL() will process records until the code blocks return false (.f.). The following code fragment expands upon the previous example, and tracks the total and highest balance for all customers in the state of California ("CA") WHILE the record pointer is less than 200.

```
use customer new alias cust
ntotal := nmax := 0

dbeval( { | | ntotal += cust->balance, ;
              nmax := max(nmax, cust->balance) } ),;
        { | | cust->state = "CA"}, { | | recno() < 200} )
? "Total:   ", ntotal
? "Maximum:", nmax
```

<next> and <record> are both numerics; <next> specifies how many records to process from the current record, and <record> specifies which record number to process. Let's take another look at that example, but this time process the next 100 records for customers in the state of Oregon.

```
use customer new alias cust
ntotal := nmax := 0
dbeval( { | | ntotal += cust->balance,;
              nmax := max(nmax, cust->balance) }, ;
         { | | cust->state == "OR"},, 100)
? "Total:   ", ntotal
? "Maximum:", nmax
```

<rest> is a logical that determines whether the DBEVAL() scope will be from the current record to the end-of-file, or all records. If you pass true (.t.), DBEVAL() will assume that you prefer the former (i.e., start from current record). If you pass false or ignore this parameter, DBEVAL() will process all records.

Return Value: DBEVAL() always returns NIL.

ASCAN(<array>, <value>, [<start>], [<count>])

As in the Summer '87 version of Clipper, ASCAN() scans an array for a given <value>. However, the big difference is that you can now pass a code block as the <value>! "Why would I want to do that?" you moan. One useful situation would be the case-insensitive ASCAN(). First, try writing it in Summer '87. Then after you give up, bask in the comfort of knowing that it takes nothing more than a well-placed code block in Clipper 5:

```
ascan(myarray, { | a | upper(a) = upper("search value")} )
```

This will scan **myarray** and test the upper-case equivalent of each array element against the upper-case search value. But before we move on, let's bulletproof this code block. Do you know what happens if you try to convert a non-character value with UPPER()? (The answer is...an unexpected DOS holiday.) So let us ensure that each element thus tested is indeed a character string:

```
ascan(array, { | a | if(valtype(a) == "C", ;
                        upper(a) == upper(value), .f.) } )
```

An ounce of prevention is worth a day of debugging.

ASORT(<array>, [<start>], [<count>], [<block>])

As in Summer '87, ASORT() sorts an array. The optional parameters <start> and <count> are the same here as in AEVAL(). However, as with ASORT(), code blocks let you dramatically change the shape of things. You could come up with any manner of arcane sorts: Put all elements containing a certain substring at the top of the array; descending order; alphabetical order based on the last letter in the word (!). Each time your code block is evaluated by ASORT(), the function passes two array elements to the block. The block is then expected to compare them in some fashion that you specify, and return either true (.t.) if the elements are in proper order or false (.f.) if they are not.

Here's a descending sort:

```
local myarray := {"CHARLES", "JUSTIN", "JENNIFER", "TRACI", "DON"}
asort(myarray,,, { | x, y | x > y } )
aeval(myarray, { | a | qout(a) } ) // so you can see it worked!
```

One situation where a code block sort would save the day is when you must sort a multi-dimensional array. Let's fill an array with information from DIRECTORY(), and then sort it by filename. Bear in mind that DIRECTORY() returns an array containing one array for each file. The structure of this array is shown in Table 8.1.

Table 8.1 Structure of directory array

Array Element	*Information*	*Manifest Constant in DIRECTRY.CH*
1	file name	F_NAME
2	file size	F_SIZE
3	file date	F_DATE
4	file time	F_TIME
5	attribute	F_ATTR

(Refer back to Chapter 7, "The Preprocessor" if you need more information about manifest constants.)

In Summer '87, you must rely upon the soon-to-be-put-out-to-pasture ADIR() function, which requires that you establish an array for each piece of information that you wish to capture. Listing 8.2 compares the Summer '87 and Clipper 5 methods for sorting a directory by filename.

Listing 8.2 Sorting a directory by filename

```
* first in Summer '87
private files_[adir("*.*")]
adir("*.*", files_)
asort(files_)

* then in Clipper 5
#include "DIRECTRY.CH'
local files_ := directory("*.*")
asort(files_,,, { | x, y | x[F_NAME] < y[F_NAME] } )
```

Now let's sort the directory by date, as shown in Listing 8.3.

Listing 8.3 Sorting a directory by date

```
* Summer '87
private files_[adir("*.*")], dates_[adir("*.*")]
adir("*.*", files_, "", dates_)
asort(dates_)

* Clipper 5
#include "DIRECTRY.CH"
local files_ := directory("*.*")
asort(files_,,, { | x, y | x[F_DATE] < y[F_DATE] } )
```

You can see that the Summer '87 code has become increasingly convoluted as you add arrays to capture the other information. Not only that, but when you sort the **dates_** array, the **files_** array (which contains the filenames) is left unchanged, thus undercutting your best efforts. By stark contrast, you only need to change two digits in the Clipper 5 code, and do not have to worry about sorting one array while leaving another untouched. Now let's sort the directory by date and name, as shown in Listing 8.4.

Listing 8.4 Sorting a directory by date and name

```
* Summer '87
* I give up!

* Clipper 5
#include "DIRECTRY.CH"
local files_ := directory("*.*")
asort(files_,,, { | x, y | if( x[F_DATE] == y[F_DATE],;
                              x[F_NAME] < y[F_NAME], ;
                              x[F_DATE] < y[F_DATE] ) } )
aeval(files_, { | a | qout(padr(a[F_NAME], 14), a[F_DATE]) } )
```

(Note the use of PADR() to ensure that all the filenames line up.)

Because of the wonderful DIRECTORY() function, you can easily determine if the dates are the same (x[F_DATE] == y[F_DATE]). If they are, then compare the file names (x[F_NAME] < y[F_NAME]). Otherwise, compare the file dates (x[F_DATE] < y[F_DATE]). This is but one small example of something that you can now do in Clipper 5 that you could not (or would not dare) do in prior versions of Clipper.

If you want to sort by file extension, Clipper 5 makes it easy, as demonstrated in Listing 8.5.

Listing 8.5 Sorting a directory by file extension

```
#include "DIRECTRY.CH"
#translate ext( <f> ) => ;
   if('.' $ <f>, substr(<f>, at('.', <f>) + 1), '')

function main
local myarray_ := directory("*.*")
asort(myarray_,,, { | x, y | ext(x[F_NAME]) < ext(y[F_NAME]) } )
aeval(myarray_, { | a | qout(padr(a[F_NAME], 14), a[F_DATE]) } )
return nil
```

For the grand finale, let's sort the directory by date, file extension, and file name in Listing 8.6.

Listing 8.6 Sorting a directory by date, extension, and name

```
#include "DIRECTRY.CH"
#translate ext( <f> ) => ;
   if('.' $ <f>, substr(<f>, at('.', <f>) + 1), '')

function main
local myarray_ := directory("*.*")
asort(myarray_,,, { | x, y | if( x[F_DATE] == y[F_DATE],;
                             if( ext(x[F_NAME]) == ext(y[F_NAME]),;
                                   x[F_NAME] < y[F_NAME],;
                                ext(x[F_NAME]) < ext(y[F_NAME])),;
                                   x[F_DATE] < y[F_DATE] ) } )
aeval(myarray_, { | a | qout(padr(a[F_NAME], 14), a[F_DATE]) } )
return nil
```

SETKEY(<key>, [<block>])

If you have ever used the Summer '87 SET KEY command to establish "hotkey" procedures, you may have been frustrated at the clumsiness of managing your hotkeys. For example, if you wanted to turn off all hot keys while the user was in a hotkey procedure, it required a certain degree of tedious coding. Hot key procedures are yet another area where Clipper 5 gives you unprecedented control. Whenever you establish a hotkey procedure with the SET KEY command, you are basically attaching a code block to that keypress with the new SETKEY() function. SETKEY() allows you to poll any INKEY() value to determine whether a code block is attached to it. Like all of the other SET() functions, it also permits you to change the current setting, i.e., attach a code block to any key.

The <key> parameter is a numeric corresponding to the INKEY() value of the keypress. (Please refer to Appendix A or the INKEY.CH header file for a complete listing of INKEY() values.)

The optional <block> parameter is the code block to be evaluated if the <key> is pressed during a wait state. Wait states include ACHOICE(), DBEDIT(), MEMOEDIT(), ACCEPT, INPUT, READ, WAIT, and MENU TO. (See below for a discussion on INKEY(), the black sheep of the wait state family.)

SETKEY() either returns a code block if one is tied to the <key>, or nil. If you pass the <block> parameter, it will attach that code block to the <key>.

The SET KEY command

Before looking at any SETKEY() examples, let us first look at how the SET KEY command is handled in Clipper 5:

```
set key 28 to helpdev
```

gets translated by the preprocessor into the following:

```
setkey( 28, {|p, l, v| helpdev(p, l, v)} )
```

The **p**, **l**, and **v** parameters correspond to PROCNAME() (procedure name), PROCLINE() (current source code line number), and READVAR() (variable name), which will automatically be passed to the code block when it is evaluated. (Yes indeed, these are the same parameters passed to hot key procedures in Summer '87.) However, you can omit these arguments in your code block declaration if you will not be using them therein. By the same token, you are completely free to pass entirely different parameters to the function. (We will use this technique to pass local variables via code blocks a bit later.)

Whenever you come to a Clipper wait state, your keypress will be evaluated in approximately this fashion to determine whether or not there is a hot-key procedure tied to it:

```
keypress := inkey(0)
if setkey(keypress) != nil
   eval(setkey(keypress))
endif
```

SETKEY() == Better Housekeeping

Here is a good example where SETKEY() makes the difference between finding a solution and a gnashing of teeth: Suppose that within a hot key procedure you wish to temporarily attach a hot key definition to the F10 keypress. However, you may have F10 activating various different procedures throughout the course of your program. In Summer '87, this presented a big problem because you were unable to determine which procedure was tied to F10. You would therefore be unable to change it and expect to reset it properly. This is no longer a problem with SETKEY(). In Listing 8.7, we redefine F10 to call BlahBlah(), and reset it when we are finished.

Listing 8.7 SETKEY() Housekeeping

```
#include "inkey.ch"      // for INKEY() constants

function Test(p, l, v)
local old_f10 := setkey(K_F10, { | p,l,v | BlahBlah(p, l, v)} )
* main code goes here
setkey(K_F10, old_f10)                // restore F10 hot key
return nil
```

old_f10 is assigned the code block (if any) that is attached to F10. F10 is then reassigned to trigger BlahBlah(). When we prepare to exit, we reset the previous code block (stored in **old_f10**) to the F10 keypress. (Once again, please remember that you can omit the **p**, **l**, **v** arguments in your code block declaration if you will not be using them in the hotkey function.)

Important Note: Before you go hog wild with hot keys, you should know that there are a limit of 32 SETKEY() (or SET KEY, same difference) procedures at any given time.

INKEY() := Wait State?

As with Summer '87, INKEY() is not a bona fide wait state. But as you have just seen, SETKEY() makes it very easy to create your own INKEY() wait state. Listing 8.8 shows the function Ginkey() from the Grumpfish Library.

You may have already noticed that there is a function similar to this in the file KEYBOARD.PRG, which is included on your Clipper 5 distribution diskettes. However, the Computer Associates function does not take into account a strange quirk of the Clipper 5 INKEY(). If you explicitly pass a NIL to INKEY(), the function will perform as though you passed it zero — it will wait indefinitely for a keypress. Therefore, the INKEY() wait state function must be smart enough to differentiate between a NIL passed to it, and a NIL that comes as a result of NOT receiving a formally declared parameter. (For more information about NIL, please review Chapter 4, "Data Types".)

Special thanks to Jeff Gruber for bringing this INKEY() idiosyncrasy to light.

Listing 8.8 INKEY() as a wait state

```
/*
      GINKEY() - INKEY() wait state
      Excerpted from GRUMPFISH LIBRARY
      Author: Greg Lief
*/
function Ginkey(waittime)
local key, cblock
do case
   /* if no WAITTIME passed, go straight through */
   case pcount() == 0
        key := inkey()
   /* if you pass inkey(nil), it is identical to INKEY(0) */
   case waittime == nil .and. pcount() == 1
        key := inkey(0)
   otherwise
        key := inkey(waittime)
endcase
cblock := setkey(key)
if cblock != nil
   // run the code block associated with this key and pass
   // name of previous procedure and previous line number
   eval(cblock, procname(1), procline(1), 'Ginkey')
endif
return key
```

As mentioned earlier, the third parameter passed to hot key procedures is the name of the variable being read. In this function, "Ginkey" is serving as a dummy variable name. Please feel free to change it to anything you desire. If you really wanted to, you could pass a variable name as a second parameter to Ginkey(), and in turn pass that to the code block if and when it was evaluated.

Notice that when the code block is evaluated, instead of passing it the current procedure name and line number, we pass it the information that is one level previous on the activation stack. Otherwise, the hot key procedure would always think that it had just come from GINKEY(). This would in turn louse things up by forcing you to have the same help screen for every GINKEY() wait state.

FIELDBLOCK(<field>)

FIELDBLOCK() is the first of three new functions that return "set-get" code blocks. One of the biggest reasons to use this trio of functions is to preclude the use of the macro operator. (As you should have already surmised from the way we carry on about them, swearing off macros will make your programs run faster and look more svelte.)

FIELDBLOCK() returns a retrieval/assignment code block for a specified field. The parameter <field> is a character string representing the field name to refer to. You can then either retrieve (get) or assign (set) the value of <field> by evaluating the code block returned by FIELDBLOCK(). If <field> does not exist in the currently active work area, FIELDBLOCK() will return NIL.

Note: if the <field> that you pass to FIELDBLOCK() exists in more than one work area, FIELDBLOCK()'s return value will correspond only to the <field> in the current area. Here's an example of retrieving the value:

```
local bblock, mfield := "FNAME"
dbcreate("customer", { { "FNAME", "C", 10, 0 } })
use customer new
append blank
customer->fname := "JOE"
```

```
bblock := fieldblock(mfield)
? eval(bblock)      // "JOE"
/* note the dreaded macro alternative */
? &mfield           // slow, and simply no longer chic
```

To assign a value to a field, you merely evaluate the code block and pass the desired value as a parameter. For example:

```
local bblock, mfield := "FNAME"
use customer new
bblock := fieldblock(mfield)
eval(fieldblock(mfield), "Craig")
? customer->fname      // "Craig"
/* note the dreaded macro alternative */
replace &mfield with "Craig"  // ugh!
```

The function Struct() loops through the structure array created by DBSTRUCT() and uses FIELDBLOCK() to retrieve the value for each field in your database. Listing 8.10 contains the source code for Struct(), and Figure 8.1 shows sample output.

Figure 8.1 Sample output from function Struct()

```
D>t articles

Field Name Type Len Dec Contents of First Record
NAME       C     20   0 Craig Yellick
TITLE      C     50   0 The Clipper Debugger
DATE       C      5   0 07/90
KEYWORDS   C     50   0 DEBUG ARRAYS
FILENAME   C     12   0 buggy.a
CODEFILE   C     12   0 buggy.p
READ       L      1   0 .F.
D>
```

Listing 8.10 Showing .DBF structure with FIELDBLOCK()

```
function Struct(dbf_file)
local struct, x
if dbf_file == NIL
   qout("Syntax: struct <dbf_name>")
elseif ! file(dbf_file) .and. ! file(dbf_file + ".dbf")
   qout("Could not open " + dbf_file)
else
   use (dbf_file) new
   struct := dbstruct()
   qout("Field Name Type Len Dec Contents of First Record")
   for x = 1 to len(struct)
       qout(padr(struct[x, 1], 10), padr(struct[x, 2], 4), ;
            str(struct[x, 3], 3), str(struct[x, 4], 3),    ;
            eval(fieldblock(struct[x, 1])) )
   next
   use
endif
return nil
```

FIELDWBLOCK(<field>, <work area>)

FIELDWBLOCK() is quite similar to FIELDBLOCK(). However, as you may have already guessed from the "W" in its name, it allows you to refer to a different work area to retrieve or assign the <field> value.

As with FIELDBLOCK(), the <field> parameter is a character string representing the field name to refer to. The new parameter <work area> is a numeric indicating which work area to search for the <field>.

Once again, you can then either retrieve or assign the value of <field> by evaluating the code block returned by FIELDWBLOCK(). If <field> does not exist in the specified <work area>, FIELDWBLOCK() will return NIL. (Note: FIELDWBLOCK() does not change the active work area.)

Here's FIELDWBLOCK() in action. Note the use of the SELECT() function to determine the work areas; this is much easier than having to hard-code (and then remember) work area numbers.

```
dbcreate("customer", { { "LNAME", "C", 10, 0 } })
dbcreate("", { { "LNAME", "C", 10, 0 } })
use customer new
append blank
customer->lname := "CUSTOMER1"
use vendor new
append blank
vendor->lname := "VENDOR1"
? eval(fieldwblock("LNAME", select("customer"))) // CUSTOMER1
? eval(fieldwblock("LNAME", select("vendor")))   // VENDOR1
? eval(fieldwblock("LNAME", select("vendor")), "Grumpfish")
? vendor->Lname                                  // Grumpfish
```

As with FIELDBLOCK(), it is quite easy to assign a value to a field. Simply evaluate the code block returned by FIELDWBLOCK() and pass the desired value as a parameter. We used this method to change the field LNAME in VENDOR.DBF in the next to last line above.

Earlier in this chapter, we showed an example of creating a generic TBrowse object to browse a database. FIELDWBLOCK() offers a different solution:

```
local x, browse := TBrowseDB(3, 19, 15, 60), column
use test new
for x := 1 to fcount()
   column := TBColumnNew(field(x),;
                         fieldwblock(field(x), select()))
   browse:AddColumn( column )
next
do while ! browse:stabilize()
enddo
```

MEMVARBLOCK(<memvar>)

MEMVARBLOCK() is also quite similar to FIELDBLOCK(), except that it operates upon memory variables rather than database fields. MEMVARBLOCK() returns a code block for a memory variable as specified by the <memvar> parameter. You can then either retrieve the value of <memvar> by evaluating the code block returned by MEMVARBLOCK(), or assign <memvar> a value by evaluating the code block and passing the value as a parameter.

If the <memvar> does not exist, MEMVARBLOCK() will return NIL.

Very Important Note: If the <memvar> is either static or local, MEMVARBLOCK() will also return NIL. This is because MEMVARBLOCK() can only operate on public and private variables. In this example, MEMVARBLOCK() retrieves the value of each of four memory variables.

```
// note PRIVATE declaration - MEMVARBLOCK() doesn't like locals

private mtot1 := 75, mtot2 := 400, mtot3 := 30, mtot4 := 205, x
for x := 1 to 4
   ? eval(memvarblock("mtot" + str(x, 1)))
next
```

FIELDGET(), FIELDPUT(), FIELDPOS()

Although these functions do not use code blocks, they are conceptually related to FIELDBLOCK(). All of these functions make it very easy for us to create generic "scatter" and "gather" routines without the use of macros. "Scatter" routines dump database fields to memory variables for editing, and "gather" routines assign values in said memory variables to database fields.

FIELDGET() and FIELDPUT() accept one numeric parameter, which corresponds to a field's ordinal position in the database structure. FIELDPUT() also accepts a second parameter, which is the value to assign to the field.

Both of these functions return the value of the field in question. If the field number parameter does not correspond with any fields in the database structure, they will return NIL.

Listing 8.11 demonstrates two scatter/gather routines, one with macros, and one with FIELDGET()/FIELDPUT().

Listing 8.11 Scatter/Gather with FIELDGET()/FIELDPUT() and macros

```
function Test
local nfields, xx, ahold := {}, mfield
memvar getlist
// first create test database
dbcreate('rolodex', { { "FNAME",   "C", 15, 0}, ;
                      { "LNAME",   "C", 15, 0}, ;
                      { "ADDRESS","C", 35, 0}, ;
                      { "CITY",    "C", 30, 0}, ;
                      { "STATE",   "C", 2,  0}, ;
                      { "ZIP",     "C", 10, 0} } )
use rolodex new
nfields := fcount()
cls
/* first let's try it with macros */
// dump all field contents to array for editing
for xx := 1 to nfields
   mfield := field(xx)
   aadd(ahold, &mfield)             // the macro, aarrgghhhh
   @ xx, 1 say padr(mfield, 11) get ahold[xx]
next
read
append blank
// now dump array contents to the fields of the blank record
for xx := 1 to nfields
   mfield := field(xx)
   replace &mfield with ahold[xx]   // the macro again, ugh!
next
```

```
/* now with FIELDGET() and FIELDPUT() */
ahold := {}    // clear out the array
// dump all field contents to array for editing
for xx := 1 to nfields
   aadd(ahold, fieldget(xx))        // look ma, no macro
   @ xx, 1 say padr(field(xx), 11) get ahold[xx]
next
read
// now dump array contents to the fields of this record
aeval(ahold, { | ele, num | FieldPut(num, ele) } )
return nil
```

This example is fairly simple, because it creates the test database each time. However, suppose that you want to be able to add a record to a database that already has records. Rather than going through gyrations to determine the initial values of each field, you can simply issue a "GO 0" command prior to loading the **ahold** array.

Any attempt to GO to a record that is out of range will position the record pointer at LASTREC() + 1, which is sometimes referred to as "the phantom record."

In the above example, we scattered and gathered all of the fields in the database. However, suppose that you only wanted to scatter/gather two of the fields. That is where the FIELDPOS() function (new with Clipper 5.01) comes into play. FIELDPOS() returns the position of a specified field within the DBF structure corresponding to the active work area.

The syntax for FIELDPOS() is:

```
FIELDPOS( <cField> )
```

<cField> is the name of the desired field in the current work area. FIELDPOS() returns the ordinal position of the specified field in the .DBF structure associated with the current work area. If the field cannot be found in the current work area, FIELDPOS() returns zero.

Listing 8.12 relies upon FIELDPOS() to scatter/gather two of the fields from our ROLODEX database.

Listing 8.12 FIELDPOS() for scatter/gather

```
function Main
local fields_ := { "LNAME", "ADDRESS" }, ahold_ := {}
use rolodex new
for x := 1 to len(fields_)
   aadd(ahold_, fieldget(fieldpos(fields_[x])) )
   @ x, 1 say padr(fields_[x] + ":", 12) get ahold_[x]
next
read
// now dump array contents to the fields of this record
aeval(ahold_, { | ele, num |;
      fieldput(fieldpos(fields_[num]), ele) } )
return nil
```

Tying local variables to code blocks

We all know that the scope of a **local** variable is the procedure or function in which it is declared. However, you can access local variables belonging to lower-level functions. To do so, you must create a code block in the lower-level function that refers to the local variable, and pass that block back to the higher-level function. The following code snippet demonstrates this principle:

```
function Test
local myblock
myblock := ClipVer()
? eval(myblock)
return nil

static function ClipVer
local xx := "Clipper 5.01"
return { | | xx }
```

The variable **xx** remains accessible via the code block even though the function ClipVer() is no longer active. The reference to **xx** remains active as long as any code blocks referring to it (such as **myblock**) remain active.

This ability has tremendous ramifications for code blocks. One problem it solves is where a code block needs long-term ownership of certain values. For example, you should only need to macro-compile a code block if the actual code to be executed isn't known until run-time, as opposed to situations where the code block must contain a value which isn't known until run-time (this would have traditionally been handled with the macro operator).

As always, each time you call a function, a unique set of local variables is generated. This rule applies even when using the aforementioned technique with code blocks. Take the following code fragment:

```
function Test
local myblock1, myblock2
myblock1 := Counter()
myblock2 := Counter()
? eval(myblock1)   // output: 1
? eval(myblock1)   // output: 2
? eval(myblock2)   // output: 1
return nil

static function Counter()
local xx := 1
return { | | xx++ }
```

myblock1 and **myblock2** both contain references to the variable **xx**, but they are completely independent of each other. This is demonstrated by evaluating **myblock1** twice, which increments its copy of **xx** to 2. However, evaluation of **myblock2** reveals that its copy of **xx** still contains the value of 1.

Passing local variables in a code block

In similar fashion, you can actually pass **local** variables to other functions via code blocks. Watch this:

```
function Main
local bblock := { | | x }, x := 500
Test1(bblock)
return nil

function Test1(b)
? eval(b)   // output: 500
return nil
```

When **bblock** is compiled in Main(), it will contain a reference to **x**, which is a variable local to Main(). However, when the block **bblock** is passed as a parameter to Test1(), and subsequently evaluated therein, **x**'s value will indeed be available.

Note: We do not advocate the unmitigated use of this technique. It does not seem to be exactly what the Clipper 5 architects had in mind for local variables. But one situation comes to mind where this method would save the day.

You need to GET a variable and wish to allow the user to press a hot key to pop up a list of valid entries. This sounds pretty simple, doesn't it? It would be, except that the GET variable in question is local and thus restricted in scope to the function in which we are getting it. What to do... what to do?

Listing 8.13 shows code that solves the problem with the clever use of a code block. Figure 8.2 shows the pop-up picklist on the screen, with the name "Neff" highlighted for selection. Figure 8.3 proves conclusively that this value gets properly assigned to the local variable in the calling routine.

Figure 8.2 Pop-up pick list of author names

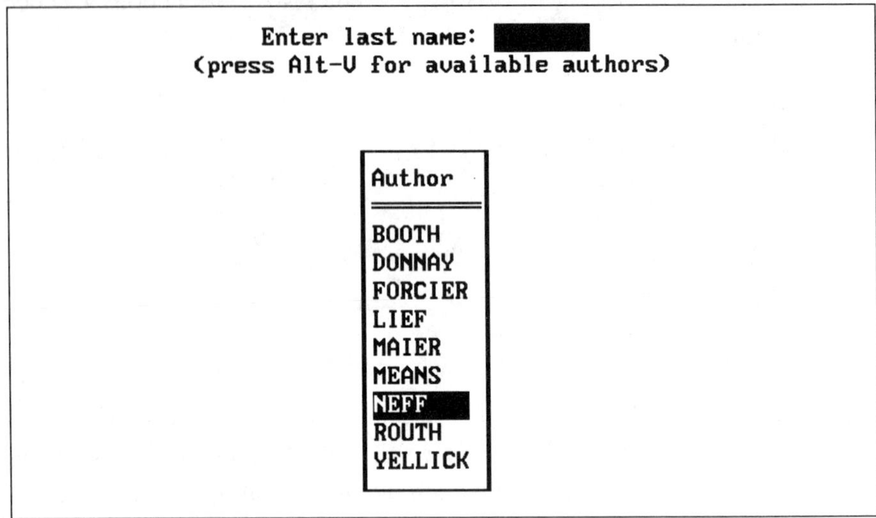

Figure 8.3 GET changed via code block

Listing 8.13 Passing local variables in a code block

```
#include "inkey.ch"
#include "box.ch"


function Test
local mvalue := space(7), oldaltv, x
memvar getlist
if ! file("lookup.dbf")
   dbcreate("lookup", { { "LNAME", "C", 7, 0 } } )
   use lookup new
   for x := 1 to 9
      append blank
      /* note use of unnamed array - it works just fine this way */
      replace lookup->lname with { "BOOTH", "DONNAY", "FORCIER", ;
                  "LIEF", "MAIER", "MEANS", "NEFF", "ROUTH", ;
                  "YELLICK" }[x]
   next
else
   use lookup new
endif
/* note that we pass MVALUE by reference to VIEW_VALS() below */
oldaltv := setkey( K_ALT_V, {| | View_Vals(@mvalue)} )
cls
@ 4, 28 say "Enter last name:" get mvalue
@ 5, 23 say '(press Alt-V for available authors)' color '+w/b'
read
quit

static function View_Vals(v)
local browse, column, key, marker := recno(), ;
      oldscrn  := savescreen(8, 35, 20, 44, 2), ;
      oldcolor := setcolor("+W/RB"), oldcursor := setcursor(0), ;
      oldblock := setkey( K_ALT_V, NIL)  // turn off ALT-V
@ 8, 35, 20, 44 box B_SINGLE + chr(32)
browse := TBrowseDB(9, 36, 19, 43)
browse:headSep := "-"
browse:colorSpec := '+W/RB, +W/N'
column := TBColumnNew( "Author", FieldBlock("lname") )
```

```
browse:addColumn(column)
go top
do while .t.
   do while ! browse:stabilize() .and. (key := inkey()) == 0
   enddo
   if browse:stable
      key := inkey(0)
   endif
   do case
   case key == K_UP
      browse:up()
   case key == K_DOWN
      browse:down()
   case key == K_ESC .or. key == K_ENTER
      exit
   endcase
enddo
if lastkey() != K_ESC
   /*
     because we passed the variable BY REFERENCE in the code
     block, any changes we make here are being made to the actual
     variable, and that is the key to this whole mess working the
     way it does!
   */
   v := eval(fieldblock('lname'))
endif
go marker
restscreen(8, 35, 20, 44, oldscrn)
setcolor(oldcolor)
setcursor(oldcursor)
setkey(K_ALT_V, oldblock)   // reset Alt-V for next time
return nil
```

Summary

Any mental blocks that you formerly had about code blocks should be lying in pieces around your chair. You should now be absolutely fearless in the presence of code blocks. In fact, you might even like them. You are now certainly able to write your own. You understand how to pass parameters to code blocks, and how to evaluate them. You are also familiar with the many Clipper 5 functions that use them.

Before you go on to any other chapters, move over to the PC and experiment with code blocks. Test out the examples in this chapter (which are all available on the accompanying source code diskette). Write a few of your own. Go wild! As with most things in Clipper 5, your imagination should be your only limit when dealing with code blocks. After you have written several dozen of your own, turn off the computer and take a break. You've earned it!

CHAPTER 9

Arrays

Arrays are a powerful feature of the Clipper language and are implemented very differently than arrays in other languages. Arrays in Clipper Summer '87 are relatively crude compared to the power and flexibility offered in Clipper 5. Additionally, arrays have become a fundamental part of the Clipper 5 language extensions rather than being a minor feature of Summer '87. To get the most out of Clipper you need to be comfortable with arrays.

This chapter starts with an introduction to arrays as they appear in Summer '87, then describes the major enhancements found in Clipper 5 and offers simple examples. We then discuss how arrays can be put to effective use in more complex situations.

After reading the first half of this chapter you should understand the major features of Clipper arrays and know how to take advantage of their flexibility. The second half should generate ideas and motivate you to use arrays for more than just simple list processing. Don't try to read this chapter straight through from beginning to end. Try to get some practical experience with Clipper 5's new array capabilities before forging ahead into the applications section.

A Summer '87 introduction

Arrays in Clipper Summer '87 are considerably more limited and are conceptually easier to understand than in Clipper 5. This section introduces arrays from the context of their implementation in Summer '87. Everything you read in this section is completely applicable to Clipper 5. To reduce confusion we will use Summer '87 syntax in the source code examples. Keep in mind that this is a simplified introduction and you should not pattern your use of arrays after the syntax shown here; wait until we discuss the substantial improvements found in Clipper 5.

Arrays are single memory variable names that can hold more than a single value, similar to the way a single database file name can hold more than a single record. Arrays must be declared as such prior to making assignments. In Summer '87 you need to specify, in advance, the maximum number of values the array name can hold. This maximum number is referred to as the array's size or length, and the individual values are called elements. The declare statement is used to create an array and establish the maximum number of elements.

```
declare aList[100]
```

In the above example an array called aList is created with a maximum of 100 elements, meaning aList can contain between zero and 100 different values.

The maximum size of any array is 4,096 elements. Each element is accessed by specifying its element number. Element numbers are like record numbers, starting with element number one. This is different from other languages which start numbering elements with zero.

The following assigns a character string to the first element in the aList array.

```
aList[1]= "The first element in the array"
```

Another difference between Clipper arrays and arrays found in other languages is that Clipper allows any combination of variable types in the same array. Array elements start out as undefined, and can be assigned and changed at any time. We'll be referring to the following example for the next several paragraphs.

```
declare aList[5]
aList[1]= "XYZ"
aList[2]= 987
aList[3]= .t.
aList[4]= date()
```

In the above example, aList has a maximum of five elements, the first four of which are assigned values of different data types. The following commands will yield the indicated results.

```
? type("aList")      &&  "A" for array
? type("aList[1]")   &&  "C" for character
? type("aList[2]")   &&  "N" for number
? type("aList[3]")   &&  "L" for logical
? type("aList[4]")   &&  "D" for date
? type("aList[5]")   &&  "U" for undefined
```

Programmers working in "pure" languages see this as a cursed abomination. We see it as a wonderful expression of the blind trust that our language places in the programmer.

Important point: Note how the TYPE() function returns an "A" when just the array name is passed, while returning the appropriate type of individual array elements when specific elements are passed. In Clipper 5 use of the VALTYPE() function is preferred over TYPE(). TYPE() uses the macro operator to determine the data type and consequently does not work with static and local variables. See Chapter 4, "Data Types," for details.

An array element can be used as a parameter for any function or procedure, just like a regular memory variable. In addition to TYPE(), the LEN() function also has a dual nature when working with arrays.

```
? len(aList)      &&  5, the number of elements in aList
? len(aList[1])   &&  3, the length of "XYZ"
? len(aList[3])   &&  run-time error, type mismatch
```

Another important point: Note the LEN() function returns the number of elements declared for the array, which is not necessarily the number of elements with useful values. When a specific array element is passed to LEN(), the expected type checking is in place. In the example, element number three contains a logical value, resulting in LEN() taking a side trip to the run-time error handler.

To refer to the entire array you simply use the array name without an element number. In this example, the entire aList array is passed as a parameter to the ACHOICE() function.

```
achoice(5,10,12,22, aList)
```

Unlike regular memory variables, arrays are always passed to functions by reference, not value. This means that any changes made to the array by the function will be reflected in the calling routine.

```
MyFunc(aList)
quit

function MyFunc
parameter a
private i
for i = 1 to len(a)
  a[i] = i
next i
return ""
```

In the above example, the **aList** array is modified by MyFunc(). There is no way to pass an entire array by value to a function. You can, however, pass *individual elements* by value to functions.

```
AnotherFunc(aList)           && Pass entire array by reference
AnotherFunc(aList[1])        && Pass element by value
```

In the above example, **aList** is passed by reference, so any changes made in AnotherFunc() will be reflected in **aList**. The reference to **aList[1]** is for only a single element, so only the value of the array element is passed to the function. Changes made within AnotherFunc() are not reflected in the **aList[1]** array element.

Summer '87 arrays cannot shrink or grow in size once they are declared to be a specific length. Memory occupied by an array is not released until the program exits the routine where the array was declared. Arrays can be declared to be **private** or **public**, with the same effect as for regular memory variables. The DECLARE statement is a synonym for **private**.

```
public acolors[15]
private adata[250]
```

If you assign a memory variable the same name as an existing array, the entire array is wiped out and replaced by the single value.

```
declare anames[10]      && Ten elements in the array
afill(anames, "abc")    && Assign "abc" to all elements
anames= 123             && Array is wiped out
```

Before they had true arrays, xBASE programmers often simulated them with macros. While such a simulation was often the only way to accomplish many goals, the use of macros exacts a heavy price in speed and memory use.

```
* Before arrays: Result is regular memory variables
* named TEST_1 through TEST_100 being created.
*
for i = 1 to 100
  c = ltrim(str(i, 3))
  test_&c. = i
next i

* With arrays: Result is single name with 100 values,
* TEST_[1] through TEST_[100].
*
declare test_[100]
for i = 1 to 100
  test_[i] = i
next i
```

In Summer '87, only two functions use arrays as parameters for more than just manipulating the array. These functions perform user-interface actions: ACHOICE() and DBEDIT(). All other array-related functions are used to manipulate the contents of existing arrays: AFILL(), AINS(), ADEL(), AFIELDS(), and ADIR().

An Alternate Naming Convention

Computer Associates' documentation uses a naming convention that indicates a variable's data type via the first letter of the variable's name.

```
iNumber := 100      // Integer
cString := "abc"    // Character
aArray := {1,2,3}   // Array
//  Etc
```

While this is very useful for keeping things straight in general, we have developed a variation on this convention that helps even more with arrays. Our convention is to place a trailing underscore character at the end of the array's variable name. The leading letter convention can then be used to indicate the contents of the array rather than the mere fact that the variable is an array.

```
iEven_     := {2,4,6,8}
cState_    := {"MN","OR","NY"}
lChosen_   := {.t., .t., .f., .f.}
```

We are not as persnickety about always using the first letter of the variable name to indicate the type. We usually only use the convention when the variable's type is not immediately obvious in the context it appears. So, in the remainder of this chapter when you see a trailing underscore you know the variable is an array. If no leading character is used it implies that the data type does not matter for the purpose of the example source code, or that the array contains a mixture of data types, or even that the contents are arbitrary.

A helpful side effect of the trailing underscore is to visually separate the name of the array from the element number in square brackets. In dense source code lines it is easier to see that a reference is being made to an array element instead of a function call with parameters.

```
A := MyFunc(str(z), this[1] + that(2))
B := MyFunc(str(z), this_[1] + that(2))
```

The assignment to **B** as compared to **A** is slightly more clear, especially when the lines are buried among hundreds of lines of similar code or when viewed on a 43-line monitor or condensed source code listing. The purpose is to help you differentiate more easily between array references and function calls, since they differ only by the shape of the delimiters. In the above example, **this[1]** looks very similar to a function called **this(1)**, while **this_[1]** is less likely to be mistaken.

What's new in Clipper 5?

Clipper 5 expands Clipper's support of arrays in so many ways that it's hard to know where to begin. In Summer '87 arrays are essentially alternatives to memory variables and macros, or "memory databases" with one field. In Clipper 5 arrays have become a fundamental part of the language, implemented in a way that makes them more than simple alternatives to memory variables or databases.

Dynamic Size

Arrays no longer need to be declared in advance with a maximum size. You can start with an array of zero elements and add (or delete) elements as needed, at any time. This is distinct from the AINS() and ADEL() functions found in Summer '87. AINS() inserts an undefined value in an array and shifts the rest of the elements down, dropping any that go beyond the original declared length. ADEL() moves all elements up, placing an undefined element at the end of the array (or specified section of the array). Neither AINS() or ADEL() alter the actual *size* of the array, only the *contents*. The functions AADD() and ASIZE(), new in Clipper 5, are used to dynamically alter the size of arrays.

```
//  Array starts out with ten elements
local this_[10]
? len(this_)  //  10

//  Array now has eleven elements
aadd(this_, "abc")
? len(this_)  //  11
? this_[11]   //  "abc"

//  Array has been reduced to seven elements
asize(this_, 7)
? len(this_)  //  7

//  Array has been increased by 20 to 27 elements
asize(this_, len(this_) +20)
? len(this_)  //  27
```

Note the AADD() function's ability to supply a value to assign to a new element.

```
//  Add new element, value is "abc"
aadd(this_, "abc")

//  Add another new element, value is 123
aadd(this_, 123)
```

ASIZE() does not assign values. It either adds or removes elements to match the specified size.

Multiple dimensions

Any element in an array can be another array, nested as deeply as you wish. One dimension isn't terribly difficult to grasp: If you declare that **this_** has ten values and number each value, **this_[5]** is the fifth value in **this_**. Additional dimensions are often confusing to beginning programmers (and not just a few "advanced" ones), so an explanation is in order.

This section introduces multidimensional arrays by using a database file as an analogy. Not everyone will find this intuitively obvious. If not, consider jumping ahead to the section on practical applications of multidimensional, variable array structures which uses a different analogy.

When you work with a database you are using what amounts to a two-dimensional array. Let's use the datebase structure in figure 9.1 as an example. The first dimension is the record number: If THIS.DBF has ten records, each record is associated with a number between one and ten. The second dimension is the field: Each record in THIS.DBF has four fields; the second field is the customer name.

Figure 9.1. A simple database structure

```
THIS.DBF:
```

Field	*Name*	*Width*
1	ID	3
2	NAME	20
3	ADDRESS	20
4	CSZ	20

For the visually oriented reader, Figure 9.2 depicts the database analogy for arrays with multiple dimensions.

Figure 9.2. Seeing a database listing as a multi-dimensional array

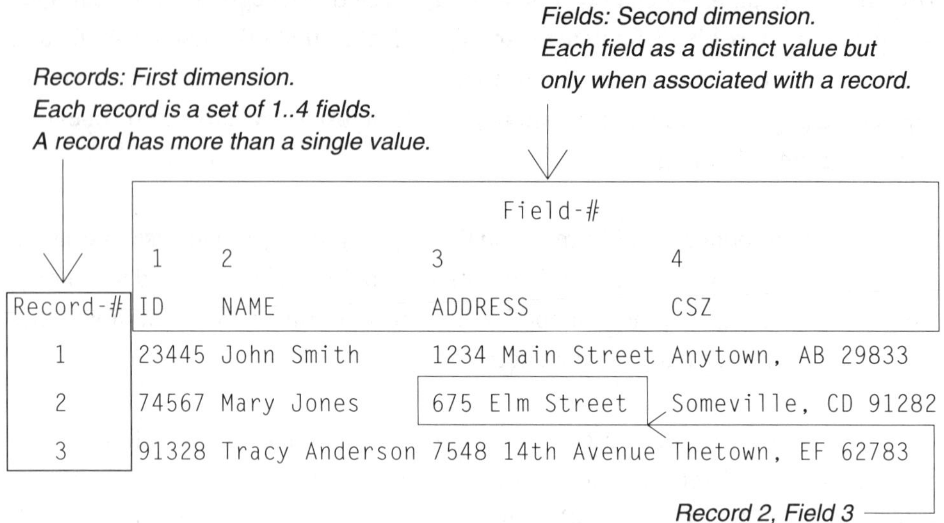

Fields: Second dimension.
Each field as a distinct value but
only when associated with a record.
Records: First dimension.
Each record is a set of 1..4 fields.
A record has more than a single value.
Field-#
1 2 3 4
Record-# ID NAME ADDRESS CSZ
1 23445 John Smith 1234 Main Street Anytown, AB 29833
2 74567 Mary Jones 675 Elm Street Someville, CD 91282
3 91328 Tracy Anderson 7548 14th Avenue Thetown, EF 62783
Record 2, Field 3

Record 2 has more than just a single value:

```
{"74567", "Mary Jones", "675 Elm Street", "Someville, CD 91282"}
```

Field 3 for record 2 has only a single value:

```
"675 Elm Street"
```

If THIS.DBF were an array named THIS, then THIS[2] refers to the entire contents of the second record. THIS[2,3] refers to the single value found in field three of the second record.

We can go to a desired record and refer to the field name of a desired field. We can, if we want to, refer to the fields by number instead of field name. We use field names because they make our code easier to read and maintain. Let's make up a user-defined function, called Go_get(), that returns a specified field from a specified record. It could look something like the following.

```
//  Record 5, field 4
cust_name := Go_get(5, 4)

function Go_get(rec, fld)
goto (rec)
return fieldget(fld)
```

An array with two dimensions can be constructed and accessed in the same way. The first dimension is an array of record numbers. When you refer to an element in the first dimension you are talking about the complete set of fields for that record. You must supply an element number in the second dimension in order to refer to a specific value in a field. The following example illustrates this concept (assume the contents of a database are loaded into a two-dimensional array called DATA_).

```
full_record := data_[5]    // An array of field values
                           // for record 5
cust_name := data_[5, 4]   // Value of field 4
```

Clipper allows two ways to refer to elements in an array with more than one dimension. You can list the element in each dimension with a pair of square brackets, or specify each individual element in its own brackets.

```
? data_[5, 4]
? data_[5][4]
```

Our preference is listing all dimensions together. All those square brackets make source code difficult to read, especially in arrays with many dimensions.

The preprocessor allows us to deal with multiple dimensions in a more understandable way by using the #define directive to assign names to the dimensions, as illustrated in the following example.

```
#define ID      1
#define NAME    2
#define ADDRESS 3
#define CSZ     4

? data_[3, NAME]    //  Field 2 in record 3
? data_[1, CSZ]     //  Field 4 in record 1
```

The manifest constants ID, NAME, ADDRESS, and CSZ make immediate sense to anyone reading the source code, compared to the more abstract numbers 1, 2, 3, and 4.

Ok, so two dimensions isn't all that hard to grasp when compared to database structures. Let's tackle a three-dimensional array. Once again, you are already familiar with a third dimension when using databases! Each field has a number of characters that form the value. It's easy to determine the seventh character of the second field of the fifth record of a database, right?

```
goto 5
? substr(THIS->Name, 7, 1)  //  "Name" is the 2nd field
```

Extending the user-defined function we discussed earlier, we could write something like the following.

```
//  Record 5, field 2, character 7
character_7 := Go_get(5, 2, 7)
```

If a database was loaded into an array called **data_**, the following references can be made.

```
full_record := data_[2]         //  Array of field arrays
                                //    for record #2
field_chars := data_[2, 3]      //  Array of characters
                                //    in field #3
a_character := data_[2, 3, 7]   //  7th character
                                //    in field #3
```

When using a multiple dimension array you must be careful to keep track of what you're referring to. The number of elements in each dimension is important, too. Use of preprocessor #define directives makes array references easier to understand. The ID and NAME fields are the first and second elements in the array.

```
#define ID     1
#define NAME   2
```

In the previous example, the ID field is three characters wide while the name is 30 characters wide. A reference to **data_[2, NAME, 25]** is legal because we are referring to the 25th element in an array of 30 elements. However, a reference to **data_[2, ID, 25]** is not legal because there are only three elements in that array. The following is an example of the ID field array being assigned "A,B,C" for record number two.

```
data_[2, ID, 1] := "A"
data_[2, ID, 2] := "B"
data_[2, ID, 3] := "C"
```

If we are using only two dimensions we write the following instead.

```
data_[2, ID] := "ABC"
```

If multiple array dimensions still isn't making sense, please hang in there. There are many more examples and explanations still to come.

Abbreviated syntax

Clipper makes array declarations and assignments considerably easier through the use of the inline assignment operator and the curly brace delimiters. The following are equivalent.

```
local iList_[3]
iList_[1] := 10
iList_[2] := 20
iList_[3] := 30
*
local iList_ := { 10, 20, 30 }
```

The array called **iList_** is termed a literal array, because it is created directly from the source code syntax and not from a run-time process.

Clipper's completely dynamic implmentation of arrays means you don't need to know the size of the array when it is first created.

```
this_ := {}
//  Many lines later
asize(this_, reccount())
```

Assignments to multiple dimensions can also be made more clear. In the following example, **iTest_** ends up as a two-dimensional array. The first dimension is controlled by the AADD() functions, and each call adds an array of three numbers which form the second dimension.

```
iTest_ := {}
aadd(iTest_, {1,2,3})
aadd(iTest_, {4,5,6})
aadd(iTest_, {7,8,9})
```

Whether you find the above technique clearer than an equivalent example, below, is a matter of personal preference.

```
iTest_ := {{1,2,3}, {4,5,6}, {7,8,9}}
```

We prefer the "all in one statement" technique when the list of elements is reasonably short and obvious in structure. The AADD() technique is better in situations where the list is too long to fit in one or two source code lines or when the structure is too convoluted to construct correctly.

An interesting side effect of the ability to create literal arrays is that the following syntax is acceptable.

```
i := 2
? {"one", "two", "three"}[i]  //  "two"
```

The curly braces delimit an array, the square braces delimit an element reference. Put them together and out pops a value.

Variable multi-dimensional structure

This section gets complicated, fast. You don't need to use or even understand variable structures to make good use of Clipper arrays. Feel free to skip this section and come back later when you feel you've mastered the intricacies of less ambitious arrays.

Using a database in the previous section to illustrate multiple dimensions obscures an important point. The dimensions of an array do not have to be uniform, consistent or symmetrical. You can make a huge mess anytime you want. However, the completely arbitrary nature of array structures allows you to do things in an efficient and elegant way that are ordinarily not even practical, much less pretty.

For a real life example, let's implement an array of family members. A family has a single surname followed by one or more given names, depending on marital status and the number of children.

Let's start by describing our motivation for wanting to use a multi-dimensional array with a variable structure. Suppose a Clipper software application needs to deal with "households" as a fundamental unit, for example, a membership system for an organization. The application needs to be able to produce standard reports based on wildly different family situations: Single individuals, married with no children, married with one or more children, single parent with one or more children.

It's preferable to pass a single array containing the complete family structure to functions in the application, rather than laboriously specifying a worst-case structure in each function call. The following are examples of calls to functions that could be written to handle the arbitrary family structure. In both cases the family information is stored in related DBF files. Here is the general structure to consider.

a FAMILY is a SURNAME
plus one or two SPOUSE-NAMES
plus zero or more CHILD-NAMES

In the first example, there's a call to LoadFamily(), which does the necessary database manipulations to create a single array that contains everything known about the family. This family array can then be passed to functions that know the structure and can act on it. For example, the purpose of the StdLetter() function could be to print a standard letter that's customized for different types of families.

```
/*
   Using a variable array structure
*/
cMember := AskMemNum()             //  Ask for member number
family_ := LoadFamily(cMember)     //  Load entire family
n := ChildCount(family_)           //  Count the kids
StdLetter(family_)                 //  Send "standard" letter
```

The next example, implemented with multiple one-dimension arrays, requires a variable for each distinct component of the family structure. Sending this structure to the StdLetter() function is more complex, requiring three parameters. If we add more details to our family structure we will have to edit the source code, possibly significantly.

```
/*
   Without the use of a single family structure
*/
cMember := AskMemNum()              //  Ask for member number
surname := LoadSurname(cMember)     //  Returns single string
spouse_ := LoadSpouses(cMember)     //  One or more names
kid_ := LoadKids(cMember)           //  Zero or more names
n := len(kid_)
StdLetter(surname, spouse_, kid_)
```

The **family_** array has the following variations.

```
{"Smith", {"John"}}                //  Single individual

{"Jones", {"Bob", "Sue"}}          //  Married, no kids

{"Davis", {"Jim"},;                //  Single parent,
   {"Mike", "Glen"}}               //  two children
```

```
{"Anders", {"Tina", "Steve"},;  //  Married,
   {"Cindy"}}                   //  one child
```

It isn't always a good idea to construct complex arrays in a single statement. The following are equivalent to the previous examples.

```
//  Single individual
family_ := {"Smith"}
aadd(family_, {"John"})

//  Married, no kids
family_ := {"Jones"}
aadd(family_, {"Bob","Sue"})

//  Single parent, two children
family_ := {"Davis"}
aadd(family_, {"Jim"})
aadd(family_, {"Mike","Glen"})

//  Married, one child
family_ := {"Anders"}
aadd(family_, {"Tina","Steve"})
aadd(family_, {"Cindy"})
```

The use of intermediate arrays can also help to clarify the creation of complex array structures.

```
surname := "Beck"
spouse := {"Gene","Jean"}
kids_ := {"Jake","Rick","Roxanne","Rita"}
family_ := {surname, spouse_, kids_}
```

The first element of the array is the family surname. The second element is an array of one or two names. One name implies a single individual, two names implies a married couple. The third and optional element is an array of names of children. Note that even when there is only a single spouse or child the name is still part of an array. A list of one is still a list. Given this structure definition we can make the following observations:

```
if len(family_) = 2          //  No children
if len(family_) = 3          //  One or more children
if len(family_[2]) = 1       //  Single individual

? family_[1]         //  Family surname
? len(family_[3])    //  Number of children in family
? family_[2,1]       //  Name of first parent or individual
? family_[2,2]       //  Name of other parent, if any
? family_[3,1]       //  Name of first child, if any
? family_[3,n]       //  Name of N'th child, if any
```

A function that displays a complete description of any given family structure looks like Listing 9.1. A series of preprocessor #define directives makes it much easier to deal with arrays.

Listing 9.1 Processing a "family" array

```
#define SURNAME  1
#define PARENT   2
#define CHILD    3
#define SPOUSE1  2,1
#define SPOUSE2  2,2

function ListFamily(f_)
local i
if len(f_[PARENT]) == 1
  ? f_[SPOUSE1] +" " +f_[SURNAME]
else
  ? f_[SURNAME] +": "
  ?? f_[SPOUSE1] +" and " +f_[SPOUSE2]
endif
if len(f_) > 2
  ? "Children:"
  for i := 1 to len(f_[CHILD])
    ?? " " +f_[CHILD, i]
  next i
endif
return nil
```

Given the family structures, listed previously, calls to ListFamily(family_) will display the following:

```
John Smith

Jones: Bob and Sue

Jim Davis
Children: Mike Glen

Anders: Steve and Tina
Children: Cindy
```

In the example we described an array containing only first and last names. This is potentially useful but not terribly so. The true power will be more apparent when we add another dimension — information specific to each name. Suppose that we also wish to keep track of a mailing address for each family, membership number and date of birth for each family member, plus occupation and employer for parents and school for each child. We won't go into details (that would make a whole chapter by itself), but here are some sample array definitions that will pique your interest if you're following the concept of variable structures. We've omitted the membership numbers and dates of birth for clarity. In practice these things can get as complex as you need to model the real world.

```
{{"Smith", "1234 Main Street", "Anytown"}, ;
    {{"Bob",   37, "ACME Corp", "Sales Manager"}, ;
     {"Sally", 36, "Ajax Systems", "Analyst"}}, ;
        {{"Mark", 14, "Park Jr High"}, ;
         {"Tom",   8, "South Elementary"}, ;
         {"Mary",  2}}}
```

Translation: Bob and Sally Smith, and their children Mark (age 14), Tom (age 8), and Mary (age 2), live at 1234 Main Street in Anytown. Bob is 37 and the sales manager at ACME Corp. Sally is 36 and an analyst at Ajax Systems. Mark attends Park Jr. High and Tom attends South Elementary. Mary does not go to school.

The incredible flexibility is apparent when you consider that the same array structure will hold Barney Taft, a 47-year old unemployed person with no known address, as well as the Parker family, with seven children and two careers. Poor Barney's array is listed below. We'll leave the fairly lengthy Parker array to your imagination.

```
{{"Taft"}, {"Barney", 47}}
```

Such complex array structures may hold "real world" data logically and efficiently, but what about accessing all that data? Is it equally complex? Not really. The trick is to eliminate most of the array from consideration and concentrate on the small segment that interests you at the moment. Trying to ingest the entire array at once is extremely difficult to do. Let's decompose the complex family array by establishing #define directives for the first dimension, as we did in the previous ListFamily() function.

```
#define SURNAME 1
#define PARENT  2
#define CHILD   3
```

So, the huge array is really just three nested arrays.

```
family_[SURNAME]   //  Array of address info
family_[PARENT]    //  Array of parent arrays
family_[CHILD]     //  Array of children arrays
```

Let's take the PARENT array and decompose it in the same manner.

```
#define SPOUSE1  2,1
#define SPOUSE2  2,2
```

This makes the somewhat complicated parent array easier to deal with — it's just a pair of arrays. PARENT is the second array inside the main family array, and SPOUSE1 is the first array within the PARENT array. Becoming more clear? Let's continue with the inner workings of the SPOUSE1 array.

```
#define SPOUSE1_NAME  2,1,1
#define SPOUSE1_AGE   2,1,2
#define SPOUSE1_EMP   2,1,3
#define SPOUSE1_JOB   2,1,4
```

This breaks the SPOUSE1, or "first spouse," array into four elements. There are no more arrays, so we are done. Since undefined array elements have the value NIL, we can quickly answer many questions.

```
if family_[SPOUSE2] = NIL       //  Single individual
if family_[SPOUSE1_EMP] = NIL   //  Spouse has no employer
```

Using #define makes the array references more clear. For example, the above looks like this after preprocessing. Not nearly so obvious.

```
if family_[2,1] = NIL
if family_[2,1,3] = NIL
```

We used single #define directives to represent repeating portions of the PARENT array, which is okay for one or two parents but not such a great idea for zero to "n" children. Here's the breakdown for the CHILD array, using a slightly different #define tactic.

```
#define    CHILD   3    //  Child is 3rd element in main family
                        //  array.
#define    NAME    1    //  Child's name is first element
#define    AGE     2    //  in a child array, age is second,
#define    SCHOOL  3    //  name of school is third.
```

This allows us to refer to a child by number, rather than having to define a set of #define directives for each possibility.

```
? family_[CHILD, 6, NAME]      //  Name of sixth child
? family_[CHILD, 2, SCHOOL]    //  Second child's school
if family_[CHILD] = NIL        //  No children
? len(family_[CHILD])          //  Number of children
```

One more blow-your-mind example and we'll leave this fascinating concept alone. Suppose we want to keep track of *all* the schools each child attends? We can add another array inside of each CHILD array containing a list of zero to "n" schools attended! There is no practical limit to the amount of data that can be tucked away into a multi-dimensional array with a variable structure.

We haven't even touched on the even more powerful technique of storing record type indicators in the array, which allows us to store different structures within the same general structure. An example is storing completely different kinds of data for members versus non-members: Members have membership details while non-members have prospect information. The same outer structure (name, address, phone and so on) is used for everyone, but the inner structure is wildly different based on the value of the "membership flag" element. If yes, the inner structure contains membership number, date joined, dues paid and so on. If no, the inner structure contains date last contacted, who supplied the lead, etc. Some members may be officers in the organization, or inactive members, or trial members, so a "membership type" element indicates which kind of inner structure to expect. Yikes. Better stop conceptualizing and get back to the basics.

Storage considerations

In Summer '87 the memory storage mechanisms of arrays are fairly simple to understand. You always have to declare a variable in advance as an array, and specify its maximum size at the same time. Since there is no such thing as a literal array (where an array can be established and filled with values independent of being assigned to a memory variable), all references to arrays and array elements can be traced back to a particular array name. The programmer always explicitly creates array names and declares sizes. The ACOPY() function merely copies values from one array to another. Other functions that fill arrays with values (like ADIR() for directory information) need an additional initialization step where the arrays are created and sized prior to being used.

When an array is passed as a parameter, it isn't hard to see that it is working on the same position in memory, but is given a different name.

```
function Main
local one_[100]
MyFunc(one_)
return nil

function MyFunc(two_)
afill(two_, "")
return nil
```

In the Main() and MyFunc() examples above, **one_** and **two_** refer to the same position in memory. In Summer '87 the concepts of *equality* and *equivalence* are usually not a big deal because the programmer is totally responsible for creating and sizing the arrays. With respect to arrays these terms have the following meanings.

Equality: All the elements in one array are equal in value to all the elements in another array.

Equivalent: The two arrays occupy the exact same place in memory, meaning the two variable names refer to the same array.

one_ is equivalent to **two_** because they are different names for the same structure in memory. Consequently, equivalent arrays are "equal" only in a degenerate sense.

```
local one_[100], two_[100]
afill(one_, 0)
acopy(one_, two_)
```

In this example, two distinct arrays are created so there are two distinct structures in memory. After the ACOPY() function is finished we can say that the two arrays are equal but not equivalent. Arrays are equal only when each element has the same value in both. You cannot compare two arrays directly with =, >, <, and so on. You must compare each element individually.

In Clipper 5 the previously unambiguous attributes of equality and equivalence are no longer so clear. Since arrays can contain other arrays, an array can be equivalent in some respects and equal in others. Consider the following.

```
//  Create and fill three arrays,
//  each containing three numbers.
a := {1,2,3}
b := {4,5,6}
c := {7,8,9}

//  Create an array filled with existing arrays.
//  Array x has three elements, each element is an
//  array of three numbers.
x := {a, b, c}

//  Create an empty array with same dimensions as the x array.
y := array(3, 3)

//  Copy contents of array x into array y.
acopy(x, y)

//  Create new array z with same dimensions as array y,
//  fill with values found in array y.
z := aclone(y)

//  Assign temp as an additional name for array z.
temp := z
```

After these array assignments have been made we can depict the resulting symbol table and memory contents (see Figure 9.3). Note that this is simplified and idealized; the actual symbol table and variable storage is considerably more complicated. If the variables being considered are **local** or **static** in scope, the symbol table becomes a non-issue.

Figure 9.3. Approximation of the symbol table and arrays in memory

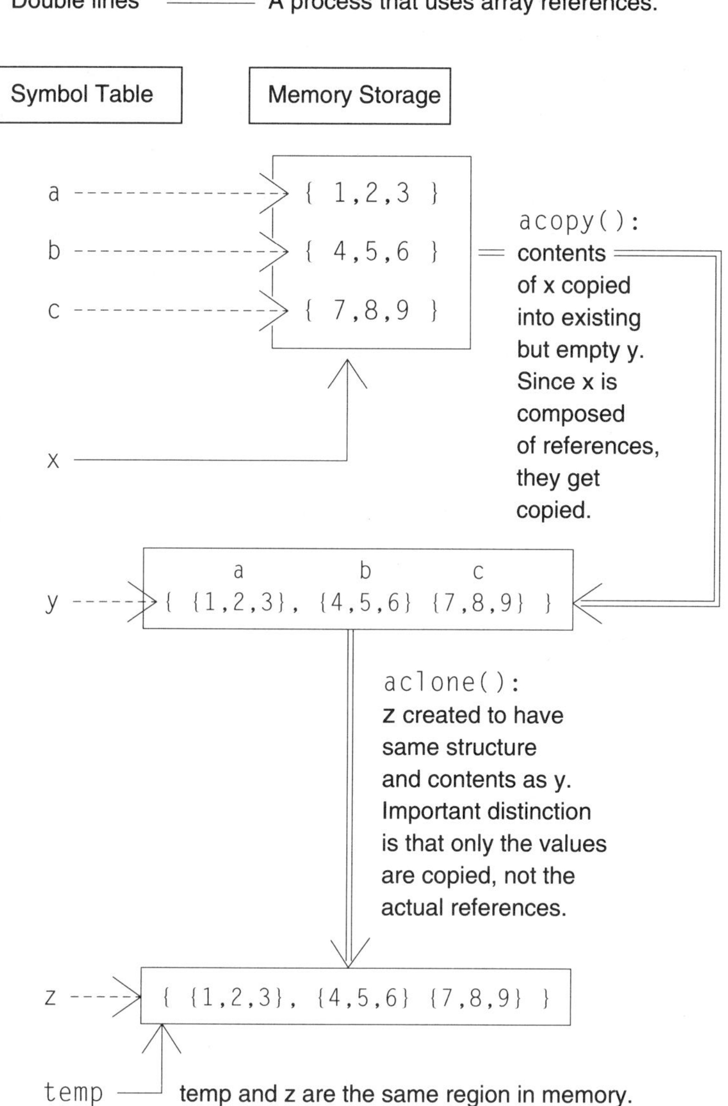
Dashed lines ------- Direct assignment to a region in memory.
Single lines A reference established to an existing region.
Double lines A process that uses array references.
Symbol Table
Memory Storage
a
b
c
{ 1,2,3 }
{ 4,5,6 }
{ 7,8,9 }
acopy():
contents of x copied into existing but empty y. Since x is composed of references, they get copied.
x
y
a b c
{ {1,2,3}, {4,5,6} {7,8,9} }
aclone():
z created to have same structure and contents as y. Important distinction is that only the values are copied, not the actual references.
z
{ {1,2,3}, {4,5,6} {7,8,9} }
temp
temp and z are the same region in memory.

In this example there are seven array names but only six distinct array structures in memory. **a, b,** and **c** are simple arrays with one dimension. **x** is an array that contains the **a,** b and **c** arrays as elements. **x[1]** is an array that is equivalent to **a,** because **x** contains references to the other arrays. The ACOPY() function fills the **y** array with the values found in **x**, but since **y** was created explicitly with the ARRAY() function to be a three-by-three array, **x** and **y** are not equivalent (since they occupy two distinct places in memory) but are considered equal since they contain equal values in all elements. Important note: **y** contains references to **a, b,** and **c** just as **x** does, since ACOPY() copies references to subarrays and not values. Despite the fact that **x** and **y** are distinct arrays, only the references to **a, b,** and **c** are stored in two different places. **x[1]** and **y[1]** still both refer to array **a**. In contrast, **z** is a completely new copy of **x**, with no references to **a, b,** or **c**. As far as the values of elements are concerned, **z** is equal to both **x** and **y**. As far as references to places in memory, **z** is not equivalent to **x** or **y** or the **a, b,** and **c** arrays. Finally, **temp** is assigned **z** in its entirety, so **temp** and **z** are equivalent, referring to the same place in memory.

The only operator that can be used directly with array references is the double equal (==), which in this context is taken to mean "are equivalent." The regular equal operator (=) and all the variations such as greater-than, less-than, and so on are not valid for entire arrays.

Given the previous list of array assignments we can make the following observations.

```
temp == z          //  True, same place in memory.

x == y             //  False, distinct structures in memory.

x[1] == y[1]       //  True, same subarray references.

z == x             //  False, different subarray references.

z[1] == x[1]       //  True, values are equal even though
                   //  the arrays are not equivalent.
```

Let's examine one more situation: Passing arrays to functions. Assume the arrays from the previous example are still available.

```
function Testing
/*
   Assume all the array assignments to a,b,c,x,y,z,
   and temp are still around, as listed previously.
   To summarize:

     Array a contains {1,2,3}
     Array b contains {4,5,6}
     Array c contains {7,8,9}

     Array x contains {a,b,c}
     which are references to arrays a, b and c.
*/

?? a[1]                  // 1
?? x[1,1]                // also 1
MyFunc(a, 0)
?? a[1]                  // now 0
?? x[1,1]                // also now 0

MyFunc(aclone(b), 999)
?? b[1]                  // still 4

return nil

function MyFunc(name, value)
afill(name, value)
return nil
```

After the call to MyFunc() the **a** array contains zeros, since **a** is passed by reference. And since **x** and **y** refer to the same position in memory as **a** does, they refer to those zeros as well. **z** was created via ACLONE() and consequently was not affected by MyFunc(). In the next call to MyFunc(), the result of ACLONE(**b**) was passed rather than **b** directly, so no values were altered outside of MyFunc(). An unnamed clone of **b** was created for the call, was altered while in MyFunc(), and was released after the call. The return value of ACLONE() was passed directly as a parameter, so as far as the rest of Testing() is concerned it never existed.

Having a firm understanding of the difference between equivalence and equality will help prevent confusion when dealing with a complex system of arrays. This is especially true when passing arrays as parameters to functions. Unless you use ACLONE(), the functions are working with equivalent arrays, referring to the same position in memory.

This brings us to one more potentially confusing aspect of array references. Based on what you know about arrays, examine the following code fragment and determine what will happen.

```
function Main()
x := {10, 20, 30}
Foobar(x)
? x[2]                  // ?
return nil

function Foobar(y)
y := {"A", "B", "C"}
return nil
```

So far we've made array references sound like simple pointers. In fact, a reference to an array name is actually a reference to yet another reference and not directly to the values in the array. In the following example we've condensed the previous call to Foobar() into the essentials we need for this discussion.

```
x := {10, 20, 30} // As established in Main()
y := x            // Upon being accepted as a parameter in Foobar()
```

The **x** and the **y** are unique names, so a reference to **x** is, at the name level, distinct from a reference to **y**. A reference to **x** points us to a particular array in memory. A reference to **y** points to the same location. We have two pointers that happen to be pointing to the same thing. If we change an element value in array **y** we'll see the same change when we refer to that element via array **x**, since the **x** and **y** pointers are pointing to the same array.

You can think of this as **x** saying "go look in box #A for the memory address of the array to which I'm pointing." **y** is saying the same thing: "See box #A." It's box #A that actually contains the address of the array, not **x** and **y**. **x** and **y** just point to box #A.

Let's return to the initial "what will happen" question. In the code fragment the Foobar() function accepted **x** as a parameter and called it **y.** The function then turns around and gives the variable name **y** an entirely new value! Instead of altering an element within the array (which we know from previous discussions would have been reflected in **x**), the function assigns **y** to a new literal array. What happens? Contrary to what you might initially think, **y**'s pointer is merely changed to the new array that Foobar() created.

Back up in function Main() the **x** array remains unchanged. Therefore, the value that gets displayed is 20, not "B". Why? Because **x** and **y** don't actually point to arrays. They started out as pointing to the same pointer, which in turn pointed to an array. **y**'s pointer got switched to a different pointer, while **x**'s pointer stayed the same.

Returning to the box analogy, **x** is still saying to look at box #A. **y**, however, is now saying "look in box #B". Box #B knows where to find the new array. Box #A still has the address of the original array. **y** did indeed get a new value, but the link to **x** (which was indirect in the first place) has been severed.

Functions using arrays as parameters

Many functions use arrays as parameters. We will discuss each one briefly. You can use arrays as parameters when writing your own functions. See a later section in this chapter for more details.

We need to take a step back for a moment and note that you can always pass individual array elements as parameters just like any other variable.

```
s := {"123", "456", "789"}
n := val( s[3] )                // 789
```

You can even @..SAY..GET an array element.

```
for i  := 1 to len(answer_)
  @ row() +1, 4 say "?"  get answer_[i]
next i
```

This section is devoted to functions that accept entire arrays as parameters. Since arrays are always passed by reference (as opposed to value), the function being called can alter the contents of the array. We can divide these functions into two broad classes: Those that are called to alter the contents of the array, and those that are called for some other effect.

Most of the functions are discussed only briefly; see your Clipper documentation or Norton Guides for syntax details and complete technical run-downs on each function.

Functions that alter the array

Many of the built-in Clipper functions designed to deal with arrays are used to alter the size or the contents of the target array.

AADD() increases the size of an array by one element. It can optionally assign a value to the new element. The new element is added to the end of the array with a NIL value. The value AADD() adds may be an array, but AADD() will add a reference to that array and not a copy of it. AADD() dynamically alters the length of the array while the array insert function, AINS(), does not.

```
a := {1,2,3}
? len(a)        //  3
aadd(a,)
? len(a)        //  4
? a[4]          //  Nil
aadd(a,"Z")
? len(a)        //  5
? a[5]          //  "Z"
```

ACLONE() makes a complete copy of any array, including multi-dimensional arrays, and places it in a new place in memory. ACLONE() creates a new array, while the array copy function, ACOPY(), does not. When ACLONE() encounters a subarray it creates a new copy of the subarray.

```
a := {1,2,3}
b := {9,8,7}
? a == b          //  False, different place in memory
x := a
? x == a          //  True, same place in memory
y := aclone(a)
? y == a          //  False, ACLONE() creates a new array
```

ACOPY() makes a copy of an array. The target array must already exist. If the source array is larger than the target, the additional elements are ignored. If the source is smaller than the target, the target elements are left as they were. When ACOPY() encounters a subarray it leaves a reference to the subarray, as opposed to a copy as ACLONE() does. ACOPY() can start copying at any point in the target array and copy only a specified number of elements. ACOPY() can also start copying at a specified point in the target array.

```
a := {1,2,3}
b := {9,8,7}
acopy(a, b)    //  b now contains {1,2,3}

c := {1,2,3,4,5,6,7,8,9}
d := {0,0,0,0,0,0,0,0,0}
acopy(c, d, 5, 2)          //  d now contains
                           //  {5,6,0,0,0,0,0,0,0}

acopy(c, d, 1, 3, 7)       //  d now contains
                           //  {5,6,0,0,0,0,1,2,3}
```

ADEL() deletes an element from an array. The size of the array is not affected. Elements below the deleted element are shifted up. The new last element has a value of NIL. If the deleted element is a subarray the entire subarray is deleted. The array sizing function, ASIZE(), is used to actually change the number of elements in the array.

```
a := {1,2,3,4}
? len(a)          //  4
adel(a, 2)        //  a now contains {1,3,4,nil}
? len(a)          //  4
? a[2]            //  3
? a[4]            //  NIL
```

ADIR() places directory information in separate arrays. The arrays must already exist. ADIR() will not increase or decrease the sizes of the target arrays. ADIR() also returns a count of the number of files in the directory that match a file specification. The count can be used to determine the optimum sizes of the target arrays. The general purpose directory loading function, DIRECTORY(), is a superior alternative. ADIR() is marked as a Summer '87 compatibility function and should be avoided.

```
file_ := {}
cnt := adir("*.DBF")  // Returns count of files matching *.DBF
asize(file_, cnt)     // Make array exactly large enough
adir("*.DBF", file_)
? file_[1]            // Name of first DBF file
```

AFIELDS() places database structure information in separate arrays. Similar to ADIR(), AFIELDS() does not alter the size of the arrays. The general purpose database structure loading function, DBSTRUCT(), is a better alternative. AFIELDS() is marked as a Summer '87 compatibility function and should be avoided.

```
use TOYS new
field_ := {}
type_ := {}
cnt := TOYS->(fcount())
asize(field_, cnt)
asize(type_, cnt)
afields(field_, type_)
? field_[1], type_[1]    //  Name and type of first field
```

AFILL() fills an array with a specified value. It does not alter the length of the array. You may specify the starting element and number of elements to process.

```
a := {1,2,3,4,5}
afill(a, 0)          //  a now contains {0,0,0,0,0}
afill(a, 9, 2, 3)    //  a now contains {0,9,9,9,0}
```

AFILL() operates on one dimension at a time, and will overwrite subarrays. Great care must be taken with multiple dimensions. The function in Listing 9.2 will safely assign the same value to every element in an array, including subarrays. It makes a recursive call to itself so there is a limit to the number of nested subarrays that can be processed.

Listing 9.2. An AFILL() for arrays with multiple dimensions

```
function M_afill(a_, value)
/*
   Multi-dimension afill()
*/
local i
for i := 1 to len(a_)
    if valtype(a_[i]) == "A"
      M_afill(a_[i], value)
```

```
    else
      a_[i] := value
    endif
next i
return nil
```

AINS() inserts an element into an array. It does not alter the size of the array. The new element has a value of NIL. Elements beneath the one inserted are shifted down and the last element value is lost. The array sizing function, ASIZE(), is used to actually change the number of elements in the array.

```
a := {1,2,3,4}
? len(a)           //  4
ains(a,3)          //  a now contains {1,2,nil,3}
? len(a)           //  4
```

ARRAY() creates an array of specified dimensions. The array is filled with NIL values for all elements.

```
a := array(3)      //  a now contains {nil, nil, nil}
b := array(3,2)    //  b now contains
                   //    {{nil,nil}, {nil,nil}, {nil,nil}}
```

ASIZE() adds or removes elements in an array. If an array is made larger, the new values will be NIL. If an array is made smaller the values will be lost.

```
a := {}
? len(a)          //  0
asize(a, 100)
? len(a)          //  100
asize(a, 5)
? len(a)          //  5
```

ASORT() sorts the contents of an array. The elements can be of any data type but must be all of the same type to sort properly. By default, ASORT() sorts only the first dimension of a multi-dimension array. You may specify the starting element and number of elements to process.

```
a := {9,8,7,1,2,3,6,5,4}
asort(a)
//  Order is now {1,2,3,4,5,6,7,8,9}

b := {8,2,1,9,4,3,7,6,5}
asort(b, 4, 3)
//  Order is now {8,2,1,3,4,9,7,6,5}
//
```

You may specify a code block which determines the sort order. The code block can be used to change the sort order from the default of ascending, or to base the sort decisions on the contents of subarrays. The code block is given two values to compare. The code block should return true if the values are considered to be in order, or false if not. For example, the following code block can be used to sort in descending order. The block will return true if the first value is greater than the second value. Written this way, the bDescend code block will sort numbers, character strings, dates and even logical values.

```
bDescend := { |a,b| a > b }
```

The code block is sent to ASORT() as the fourth parameter. If you do not want to specify the second and third parameters (the starting element and count) you must still include the commas that separate the parameters.

```
a := {9,8,7,1,2,3,6,5,4}
asort(a,,, bDescend)
//  Order is now {9,8,7,6,5,4,3,2,1}
```

The code block can get pretty fancy, doing anything it needs to determine if the two values are in sorted order, as long as it ultimately returns true or false. Here's a code block that will sort an array of full names by last name.

```
bLastName := { |a,b| LastName(a) < LastName(b) }
```

Hey — that's cheating! Not really. There's no rule that says a code block has to do everything inside the block. Here is the source code for the LastName() function.

```
function LastName(name)
return substr(name, rat(" ", name) +1)
```

Armed with a fancy code block that handles last names we can sort an array of names.

```
a := {"Mr. Alex Smith", ;
      "Heather Sue Anderson", ;
      "Tracy J. Doe"}

asort(a,,, bLastName)

//  Order is now {"Heather Sue Anderson", ;
//                "Tracy J. Doe", ;
//                "Mr. Alex Smith"}
```

Sorting within multidimensional arrays

It is possible to use a code block to help overcome ASORT()'s inability to sort on anything but the first dimension of an array. Let's take the oft-used example of ranking the members of a bowling league. After reading this chapter on arrays, a crafty programmer decided to store his team's names and scores in a multidimensional array, like so.

```
team := {}
aadd(team, {"Earl", 224, 256, 198, 202})
aadd(team, {"Bud", 290, 278, 210})
aadd(team, {"Dick", 178, 201, 199, 207, 200})
```

Each team member occupies an element in the team array. Each member element is a subarray containing the member's name and a list of scores. Pretty elegant, thought the programmer, there's no wasted space because the structure neatly accommodates the fact that not everyone plays the same number of games. But how do you sort the team by name? ASORT() code blocks come to the rescue.

```
bSort := { |a,b| a[1] < b[1] }
asort(team,,, bSort)
```

ASORT() will pass this block two elements. In the case of the team array, that's two arrays. Instead of trying to compare the two entire arrays the block will compare the first element of each array — the name. ASORT() will sort the arrays within the team array by comparing the names of team members.

Here's a challenge: Using ASORT() rank the team array by most recent score, sorting them from the highest to lowest. Remember that not all members have played the same number of games. You can assume, however, that each member has played at least one game.

Functions that don't alter the array

Other built-in Clipper functions use arrays as parameters but don't alter the contents in any way.

ACHOICE() displays array contents in a scrolling window. A second, optional array specifies which elements in the first array may be selected. ACHOICE() returns the number of the element that was selected.

```
choices := {"Add", "Change", "Delete", "Quit"}
n := achoice(1,1,4,8, choices)
```

Chapter 13, "The Art of the User Interface," goes into more detail about user interface programming.

ASCAN() searches the contents of an array. You may specify the starting element and number of elements to process. ASCAN() will stop at the first element that matches the scan value. ASCAN() returns the element number or zero if no elements match.

```
//     1 2 3 4 5 6 7 8 9
a := {1,1,1,1,2,1,1,2,1}
? ascan(a, 2)               // 5
? ascan(a, 2, 6)            // 8
? ascan(a, 2, 1, 4)         // 0
```

Instead of a value for which to scan you may specify a code block. ASCAN() will pass to the code block each element of the array, one at a time. If the code block returns true, the scan will stop. If false, the scan continues. Here's an example that scans an array for the first element value that is even.

```
//     1 2 3 4 5 6 7 8 9
a := {7,9,3,5,6,3,4,7,1}
n := ascan(a, { |n| n%2 == 0 } )
? n       //  5
? a[n]    //  6
```

ATAIL() returns the value of the last element in the array. This is a handy alternative to using the LEN() function to return the last element number. The following examples are equivalent.

```
chars_ := {"A", "B", "C"}
? chars_[len(chars_)]        //  "C"
? atail(chars_)              //  "C"
```

Note that you are able to eliminate the need for an extra reference to the array. This allows for cleaner syntax and code that's easier to understand.

DBCREATE() creates an empty database structure based on the contents of an array. The array is two dimensional. The "inner" dimension is an array of field specifications: name, type, width and decimals. The "outer" dimension is an array of these arrays, one for each field. The following creates an INVENT.DBF file containing five fields.

```
stru := {}
aadd(stru, {"id",      "C",  6, 0})
aadd(stru, {"descr",   "C", 30, 0})
aadd(stru, {"price",   "N", 10, 2})
aadd(stru, {"updated", "D",  8, 0})
aadd(stru, {"active",  "L",  1, 0})
dbcreate("INVENT", stru)

? len(stru)      // 5
use INVENT new
? fcount()       // 5
```

See the section titled **Arrays and Databases** in this chapter for a more detailed discussion of DBCREATE() and DBSTRUCT().

DBEDIT() displays records in a window, format based on a large collection of arrays. The Computer Associates manual states that DBEDIT() is a compatibility function and therefore, is no longer recommended as a programmable browse facility. The TBrowse object class is a vastly superior alternative, so don't waste any time with DBEDIT(). See Chapter 28, "Obsolete Commands and Functions," for a complete list.

LEN() determines the length (number of elements) of an array. LEN() returns the length of an individual element if you include an element reference.

```
a := {"A","B","CDEFG", "Z"}
? len(a)                    //  4
? len(a[3])                 //  5
```

TYPE() determines the type of an expression, and will return "A" if it's an array. Using TYPE() on an individual array element returns the type of the element. The VALTYPE() function is preferable to TYPE() and should be used instead. See Chapter 4, "Data Types," for more details. TYPE() can operate only on private and public variables. It cannot operate on local and static variables.

```
a := {1,2,3}
? type("a")      //  "A" for array
? type("a[1]")  //  "N" for number
```

VALTYPE() determines the type of data returned by an expression, will return "A" if an array. As with TYPE(), VALTYPE() will work with the entire array as well as an individual element. VALTYPE() is preferable to TYPE() because it can operate on local, static, private and public variables.

```
a := {1,2,3, {"A","B","C"}}
? valtype(a)                //  "A" for array
? valtype(a[4])             //  "A" for array
? valtype(a[4,1])           //  "C" for character
```

Functions that return arrays

Some functions use arrays to hold return values. We will discuss each one briefly. You can return arrays when writing user-defined functions. See a later section in this chapter for writing user-defined functions that use arrays. Three Clipper functions actually create and fill a new array. Several others don't create new arrays but return a reference to the array.

ACLONE() returns a complete copy of an array, including subarrays. ACLONE() is distinct from ACOPY(), which copies only into an existing array. See previous discussion about array storage considerations in this chapter.

```
a := {1,2,3}
b := aclone(a)
```

DBSTRUCT() creates an array containing database structure information. It is the opposite of the DBCREATE() function. DBSTRUCT() returns a two-dimensional array, one array containing field specifications (name, type, width, decimals) for each field in the database. If no database is selected the function returns an empty array. A preprocessor #include file, DBSTRUCT.CH, is supplied to make it easier to program with the database structure array.

```
#include "DBSTRUCT.CH"
use VENDOR new
stru := dbstruct()
? stru[1, DBS_NAME]         //  Name of first field
? stru[1, DBS_TYPE]         //  Type of first field
? stru[fcount(), DBS_LEN]  //  Length of last field
```

DBCREATE() can be used with DBSTRUCT() to easily make a temporary copy of a database structure.

```
dbcreate("TEMP", VENDOR->(dbstruct()))
```

See the section titled **Arrays and Databases** in this chapter for a more detailed discussion of DBCREATE() and DBSTRUCT().

DIRECTORY() creates an array containing directory information, based on an optional file specification. The array it returns is structured similar to DBSTRUCT(). The array has two dimensions, the inner array contains name, size, date, time and attributes, and the outer array contains an inner array for each file in the directory. If no files match the specification this function returns an empty array. A preprocessor #include file, DIRECTRY.CH, is supplied to make it easier to program with the directory array. This chapter contains some comprehensive examples of the DIRECTORY() function. See also Chapter 23, "Disks and Directories" for a complete discussion.

```
#include "DIRECTRY.CH"
dir := directory("*.NTX")

? dir[1, F_NAME]            // Name of first index
? dir[1, F_SIZE]            // Size in bytes
? dir[1, F_DATE]            // Date stamp
? dir[1, F_TIME]            // Time stamp
? dir[1, F_ATTR]            // File attributes

? dir[len(dir), F_NAME]     // Name of last index
```

ACOPY(), ADEL(), AEVAL(), AFILL(), AINS(), ARRAY(), ASIZE(), and ASORT() all return a reference to the array being processed. This is occasionally useful and better than returning no value at all. In the following example, an array called **q** is filled with empty strings ("") and a reference to **q** is passed to the LEN() function.

```
i := len(afill(q, ""))
```

Some programmers will find this feature irresistible, probably due to C language influence. All it does is allow you to both fill and find the length of the array and then use the length to bound a for..next loop. Obfuscation or elegance?

User-defined functions and arrays

Computer Associates' sample functions

Computer Associates supplies a collection of user-defined functions that deal with arrays. The \CLIPPER5\SOURCE\SAMPLE subdirectory contains ARRAY.PRG which includes the following functions. (This list may change over time with new releases of Clipper 5.)

```
ABROWSE()           Uses TBrowse to view contents of an array.
ABROWSEBLOCK()      Used in ABROWSE().
ABLOCK()            Used in ABROWSE().
ASKIPTEST()         Used in ABROWSE().
AMAX()              Subscript of element with highest value.
AMIN()              Subscript of element with lowest value.
ACOMP()             Compares all elements in array to a value.
DIMENSIONS()        List of dimensions in an array.
```

ABROWSE() and ABLOCK() are discussed in detail in Chapter 26 "The TBrowse Object Class". You may find the other functions in ARRAY.PRG useful as-is or as examples of general purpose user-defined functions.

Creating your own functions

You can make use of any array concepts you learn in your own user-defined functions. Your functions can accept arrays as parameters, and your functions can return arrays back to the calling routine. This opens a wide array (ahem) of possibilities for improved code efficiency and elegance.

Listing 9.3 contains an example of a user-defined function that accepts an array of strings and displays them in a box just large enough to hold them.

Listing 9.3 A function that uses an array to display messages

```
function Pugilist(r, c, msg_)
/*
   Display list of message lines in a box.
   Start display at screen coordinates r,c.
   Function will center message if r or c not specified.
   Array msg_ contains message lines.
*/
local i, width := 0

/*
   Find length of longest line
*/
for i := 1 to len(msg_)
  width := max(width, len(msg_[i]))
next i

/*
   If row or column not specified,
   calculate starting row and column
   that will center message on screen
   (maxRow() and maxCol() are supplied by the system).
*/
if r == nil
  r := (maxRow() -len(msg_)) /2
endif
if c == nil
  c := (maxCol() -width) /2
endif
```

```
/*
  Draw box large enough to contain message,
  then display each message line.
*/
@ r -1, c -1 to r +len(msg_), c +width
for i := 1 to len(msg_)
  @ r +(i -1), c say msg_[i]
next i
return nil
```

A typical call to the function looks like this.

```
Pugilist(5, 20, {"That customer number",  ;
                 "is not defined. Enter", ;
                 "another or press ESC",  ;
                 "to return to the menu."})
```

The resulting box will be just wide enough to accommodate the longest line, and will contain the four lines specified in the array. To take advantage of the function's ability to center the box in either direction you simply skip the parameter (but keep the comma!)

```
Pugilist(,, {"This","will be","in center of screen."})
Pugilist(, 60, {"Centered vertically","in column 60."})
Pugilist(7,, {"Centered","horizontally in row 7."})
```

See Chapter 13, "The Art of the User Interface," for more examples of functions that use arrays in this way.

Your user-defined functions may also return arrays. Here's an example of a function that returns an array of field values that match a given key. You pass the field value you are interested in and the field and key value the index is based upon. The function, shown in Listing 9.4, is designed to answer the request, "Give me all the parameter-1 where parameter-2 is equal to parameter-3."

Listing 9.4 A function that returns an array

```
function Gimme(what, where, when)
/*
   Returns array filled with the "what" field,
   for all records where the "where" condition is true
   when compared to the value specified by "when".
*/
local these_ := {}
seek when
do while &where. = when
  aadd(these_, &what.)
  skip
enddo
return these_
```

Here's an example of Gimme() in practice. We're looking for a list of customer names where the state is Minnesota. We assume that the customer database has name and state fields and is indexed on state.

```
who_ := CUST->(Gimme("name", "state", "MN"))
```

The names of customers in Minnesota will be in the **who_** array. **who_** can be passed on to a function that displays arrays, perhaps based on ACHOICE() or an array-based TBrowse. Advantages: The rest of the routine can mess around with the simple **who_** array rather than a database and index, and the Gimme() function can process a wide variety of similar requests. Disadvantages: **who_** will grow to be as large as the total number of matching records, which can be more than available memory can handle, or more than the 4,096 element maximum for arrays.

The listing 9.4 version of the Gimme() function uses macros to perform the logical comparison and array assignment. This was done this way to keep the basic idea easier to understand. A code block is a much better alternative because it is considerably faster and more flexible than a macro. Here's the function again, in Listing 9.5, this time using code blocks.

Listing 9.5. Same function as before, without macros

```
function Gimme(bWhat, bWhere, cStart)
/*
   Returns array filled with the result of the
   "what" code block, for all records where the
   "where" code block returns true.
   Start processing by seeking the "start" value.
*/
local these_ := {}
seek cStart
do while eval(bWhere)
  aadd(these_, eval(bWhat))
  skip
enddo
return these_
```

Here's a new Gimme() called with code block logic.

```
who_ := CUST->(Gimme( {|| name }, ;           // What to return
                      {|| state == "MN"}, ;   // Condition
                      "MN" ))                 // Where to start
```

The only obvious improvement is eliminating macros. The use of code blocks actually makes the function call look more complex. Code blocks, however, make it easier to allow flexibility in the logic and can operate using only local and static variables, something macros can't always do.

See the section called "Arrays and Databases" in this chapter for a complete discussion on this technique.

The AEVAL() function

Arrays may be processed by passing element values through a code block via the AEVAL() function. AEVAL() evaluates the specified code block for each element in an array. You may optionally specify the starting element and number of elements to process. AEVAL() does not return a value, just a reference to the array that was processed. See Chapter 8, "Code Blocks," for a complete discussion.

AEVAL() passes each array element, one at a time, to the code block. Here's an example that lists the contents of the array.

```
a := {1,2,3}
aeval(a, { |n| qout(n) } )
```

The QOUT() function is called three times, once for each element in the array. QOUT() simply displays whatever is passed to it, so the result is the contents of the array being listed to the screen. AEVAL() also sends a second parameter to the code block, the element number currently being processed. This is often very useful. Here's the previous example again, this time using the element number.

```
a := {"X","Y","Z"}
aeval(a, { |n, e| qout(e, n) } )

//  Resulting display—

    1   X
    2   Y
    3   Z
```

Here's another simple example that sums the numbers in the array.

```
a := {1,2,3,4,5,6,7,8,9}
sum := 0
aeval(a, { |n| sum += n } )
? sum                          //  45
```

The starting element parameter allows us to start processing beyond the first element. Here we start the summing process at element number six.

```
a := {1,2,3,4,5,6,7,8,9}
sum := 0
aeval(a, { |n| sum += n }, 6)
? sum                          //  30
```

The count parameter allows us to process less than the entire array. Here we sum only the first four elements.

```
a := {1,2,3,4,5,6,7,8,9}
sum := 0
aeval(a, { |n| sum += n },, 4)
? sum                               //  10
```

The following is a simple but useful user-defined function that uses AEVAL() to determine the length of the longest character string in an array.

```
function Longest(a_)
/*
   Return length of longest string in array.
*/
local n := 0
aeval(a_, { |s| n := max(len(s), n) } )
return n
```

Here's an example of a call to Longest().

```
msg_ := {"A message", ;
         "made up of several", ;
         "lines of text."}

? "Length of longest element: "
?? Longest(msg_)                        //  18
```

The Clipper manual gives some interesting but potentially confusing examples of AEVAL(). Let's take a look at each example in more detail, starting with Listing 9.6.

Listing 9.6. Example as it appears in Clipper Reference Manual

```
#include "Directry.ch"
//
local aFiles := directory("*.dbf"), nTotal := 0
aeval(aFiles, ;
  { |aDbfFile| ;
  qout(padr(aDbfFile[F_NAME], 10), aDbfFile[F_SIZE]), ;
  nTotal += aDbfFile[F_SIZE] ;
  };
)
//
?
? "Total Bytes:", nTotal
```

From the top: The #include preprocessor directive has the compiler bring in some #define directives that help make the output from the DIRECTORY() function easier to deal with. The references to F_NAME and F_SIZE come from DIRECTRY.CH.

The next line assigns the output of the DIRECTORY() function to an array called **aFiles**. The DIRECTORY() function is asked for an array of files in the current directory that match "*.DBF". Also on this line another variable, **nTotal**, is initialized to zero. **nTotal** will be used within the code block to accumulate file sizes.

The array returned from DIRECTORY() is a two-dimensional array. The inner arrays are comprised of the file name, size, date, time and attributes. For example, if there were three files matching *.DBF, DIRECTORY() will return an array with three elements, one element for each matching file. Here's an example.

```
{ {"DATA.DBF", 12654, 07/19/90, "14:25:06", "A"}, ;
  {"TEST.DBF",  3654, 06/21/87, "01:15:45", "A"}, ;
  {"ABCD.DBF", 87234, 01/12/62, "11:02:17", "A"} }
```

Note that the dates will be actual date types and not character strings or numbers. Based on this structure, the #define directive for F_NAME refers to the first element, and F_SIZE to the second.

Armed with this knowledge of what DIRECTORY() is giving us we can tackle the call to AEVAL(). The **aFiles** array is passed to the AEVAL() function, which in turn passes each element in **aFiles** through the code block. While inside the code block, the array element is called **aDbfFile**. Remember that the elements inside **aFiles** are themselves arrays, so the code block is being passed a five-element array each time it is evaluated. The first statement in the code block is a QOUT() function. QOUT() is the function equivalent of the "?" command. Code blocks can't handle direct commands. If they could, the line may have been written like the following.

```
? padr(aDbfFile[F_NAME], 10), aDbfName[F_SIZE]
```

The PADR() function pads the right side of the filename with spaces, in this case to a length of ten. This line simply displays the name and size of the current file.

The last line in the code block takes the **nTotal** variable (initialized to zero in the local statement) and adds the size of the current file. If the sample DIRECTORY() array described previously is used with the example, the following will be displayed.

```
DATA.DBF    12654
TEST.DBF     3654
ABCD.DBF    87234

Total Bytes: 103542
```

The example can be written without the use of the AEVAL() function. The following code is functionally equivalent. This will help explain what is going on inside the code block. The FOR..NEXT loop replaces the AEVAL() function. AEVAL() also made the reference to the **aFiles** array somewhat easier to manage.

```
local i
for i := 1 to len(aFiles)
  ? padr(aFiles[i, F_NAME],10)
  ?? aFiles[i, F_SIZE]
  nTotal += aFiles[i, F_SIZE]
next i
```

The second example for AEVAL() in the Clipper manual is somewhat more simple than the directory listing routine we just discussed. This example (shown below) takes the same output from DIRECTORY() and trims it down to be a single array of filenames from the more complex two-dimensional array structure.

```
#include "Directry.ch"
//
local aFiles := directory("*.dbf"), aNames := {}
aeval(aFiles, ;
  { |file| aadd(aNames, file[F_NAME]) } ;
)
```

Once again we #include the DIRECTRY.CH file which supplies the F_NAME constant. The **aFiles** array is assigned the output from DIRECTORY(), and **aNames** is initialized to be an empty array. AEVAL() is then called upon to pass each element of **aFiles** through a code block which uses AADD() to add an element to the **aNames** array, and assign it the filename. From DIRECTRY.CH, F_NAME is #defined to have a value of 1, and element one of the file array contains the filename. Remember that each element in the array returned by DIRECTORY() is a five element array. The net result is the **aName**s array contains a list of filenames.

Multi-dimensional arrays with variable structure

Clipper's ability to manipulate "ragged" arrays, where asymmetrical arrays can be nested within other arrays, allows us to perform what appear to be amazing programming feats with very little effort. This portion of the chapter provides an example of a real world use for such arrays.

Arrays with multiple dimensions are fairly easy to understand when the dimensions are uniformly and consistently structured. A good example of a two-dimensional array is the lowly database file: The overall file can be thought of as an array of records, with a record being an array of field values. Arrays with a variable structure are much more complicated. As a familiar example, consider the MS-DOS tree-structured directory.

If we want to load into memory the complete directory structure of any arbitrary drive volume, we should probably start with the directory entries in the root directory. If we load them into a single dimension array called FILES_, then FILES_[2] is the name of the second entry in the root directory. However, some of the entries will be subdirectory names which force us to load yet another set of directory entries. So, some of the FILES_ elements will have a second dimension to hold yet another array of directory entries. Since subdirectories can also contain more subdirectories this process needs to be repeated as many times as necessary. This is where the variable structure comes into play. The following example shows an array called FILES_ being filled with a simple directory structure.

```
files_[1]         := "AUTOEXEC.BAT"
files_[2]         := "CONFIG.SYS"
files_[3,1]       := "DOS"
files_[3,2,1]     := "APPEND.COM"
files_[3,2,2]     := "ASSIGN.COM"
files_[4]         := "COMMAND.COM"
```

The first two elements are simple file names. The third is a two-dimensional array, one dimension for the subdirectory name and one for an array of file names within that subdirectory. The fourth element goes back to a regular filename. This kind of notation, while “traditional” in the Summer ’87 sense, is difficult to grasp. The following code is functionally identical and does a better job of indicating the relationships among the elements.

```
files_[1] := "AUTOEXEC.BAT"
files_[2] := "CONFIG.SYS"
files_[3] := {"DOS", ;
                {"APPEND.COM", "ASSIGN.COM"} ;
             }
files_[4] := "COMMAND.COM"
```

We don't have to stop there. The following code is also functionally identical to the other examples.

```
files_ := {"AUTOEXEC.BAT", ;
           "CONFIG.SYS", ;
           {"DOS", ;
              {"APPEND.COM", "ASSIGN.COM"} ;
           }, ;
           "COMMAND.COM"}
```

We prefer the "all in one statement" technique when the list of elements is reasonably short and obvious in structure. Use of the array element adding function, AADD(), is better in situations where the list is too long to fit in one or two source code lines or when the structure is too convoluted to construct correctly. Here is the same directory structure array constructed using the AADD() function.

```
files_ := {}
aadd(files_, "AUTOEXEC.BAT")
aadd(files_, "CONFIG.SYS")
aadd(files_, {"DOS", {"APPEND.COM", "ASSIGN.COM"}})
aadd(files_, "COMMAND.COM")
```

What does another subdirectory level look like? The following example shows \DOS\UTILS containing DR.COM and ASK.COM.

```
files_ := {"AUTOEXEC.BAT", ;
           "CONFIG.SYS", ;
           {"DOS", ;
              {"APPEND.COM", ;
               "ASSIGN.COM", ;
                {"UTILS", ;
                   {"DR.COM", ;
                    "ASK.COM"} ;
                } ;
              } ;
           }, ;
           "COMMAND.COM"}
```

How do we reference elements in an array with a variable structure? You can't make a reference until you first check that you're not dealing with another array. If a reference returns a character string, you're done. If a reference returns an array, you need to dive a level deeper and start checking those array elements as well. The following is an example of a function, shown in Listing 9.7, that displays the contents of an array structured in the manner just described. To improve readability, each subdirectory gets indented three spaces. A bit further into this section we'll have a function create the necessary array automatically.

Listing 9.7. A function which lists an array with variable structure

```
function ListDir(dir_, level)
/*
   List the contents of an array containing a
   directory structure. This function uses a
   recursive call to itself.
*/
local i
if level == nil
  level := 0
endif
for i := 1 to len(dir_)
 ? space(level *3)
```

```
  if valtype(dir_[i]) == "A"
    ?? dir_[i, 1]
    ListDir(dir_[i, 2], level +1)
  else
    ?? dir_[i]
  endif
next i
return nil
```

The first time ListDir() is called it will not have a parameter, so we default the level of indentation to zero. A careful reading of the example shows a recursive call to the ListDir() function. ListDir() keeps calling itself until it runs out of array dimensions. The array was deliberately structured in such a way that any given level in the array is structured exactly like the level above it. This allows us to strip off the subdirectory name and pass the associated array of subdirectory entries along for further processing. This can go on indefinitely. The level parameter is increased by one each time ListDir() calls itself. Consequently, each subdirectory processed gets indented one level further than its parent (see Figure 9.4).

Figure 9.4. Typical output from the ListDir() function

```
CLIPPER5
  BIN
    UTILS
      LIB.EXE
      AD.EXE
    CLD.EXE
    CLIPPER.EXE
    RMAKE.EXE
    RTLINK.EXE
  INCLUDE
    ACHOICE.CH
    BOX.CH
    STD.CH
  LIB
    CLIPPER.LIB
    DBFNTX.LIB
```

So far we've been discussing how the array looks when filled and how to list its contents. But how does the subdirectory structure get loaded in the first place? The trick is in the extremely nifty DIRECTORY() function. The DIRECTORY() function is a major improvement over ADIR(). To use DIRECTORY() most effectively you should use the #include preprocessor directive to include the DIRECTRY.CH file, which contains handy constants for dealing with the arrays the function returns.

The DIRECTORY() function returns an array of arrays. Each element in the "outer" array stands for an entry in the directory. Each directory entry is described by an array of five values: name, size, date, time, and attributes. Here's an example of three files. (The dates are date-type values, not text strings or numbers.)

```
{ {"ONE.DAT",    12654, 03/09/90, "12:24:16", "A"}, ;
  {"TWO.DBF",     3654, 12/11/89, "01:25:40", "A"}, ;
  {"THREE.BAT",     24, 06/19/90, "07:12:23", "A"} }
```

Subdirectories have a "D" attribute, so we can detect them easily enough. However, each subdirectory also has those goofy "." and ".." entries, which stand for "me" and "my parent directory". These are not terribly useful in a directory listing so we can skip them.

Based on the definition of how to display the directory structure, we can write a function that creates such a structure in an array. We need to create an element for each file in the directory. Whenever we encounter a subdirectory we need to create an array instead of an element. The array contains the name of the subdirectory followed by an array of the file names within that subdirectory. Just to complicate matters further, the contents of that subdirectory may include more subdirectories! Sounds like recursion to me. See the source code in Listing 9.8.

Listing 9.8 A function that creates a variable sructure array

```
#include "DIRECTRY.CH"

function LoadDir(path)
/*
   Return array containing entire directory structure
   of drive volume. This function uses a recursive call
   to itself. You do not need to specify the path unless
   you want to load only a subset of the drive volume.

*/
local i, name, d_, r_ := {}

if path = nil
  path := "\"
endif

//  Load contents of the specified directory path,
//  including any subdirectory entries that might be there.
d_ := directory(path +"*.*", "D")

//  Loop once for each entry in directory.
for i := 1 to len(d_)
  name := d_[i, F_NAME]

   //  If the file attribute indicates this
   //  is a subdirectory entry, special handling is needed.
   if ("D" $ d_[i, F_ATTR])

   //  Skip the "." and ".." entries.
   //  (The $ operator means "contained in")
   if .not. (name $ "..")

      //  Add the subdirectory name to the array
      //  and call the directory loader function to
      //  return the array of file names.
        aadd(r_, {name, LoadDir(path +name +"\")})
      endif
```

```
  //  If the file isn't a subdirectory name,
  //  add it to the array of file names.
  else
    aadd(r_, name)
  endif
next i

return r_
```

The above code does a lot in a small number of lines. The recursion makes the whole thing possible, but at the expense of making it harder to understand. Keep in mind the general structure of the array that it builds. The repeating structure

```
{ FILE, FILE, {SUBDIR, {FILE, FILE, {SUBDIR, {...
```

represents a DOS directory structure like the following.

```
FILE
FILE
SUBDIR
  FILE
  FILE
  SUBDIR
    :
    etc
```

Multidimensional arrays with a variable structure are not trivial, but once mastered, the technique can be put to use in situations that are almost impossible to handle efficiently any other way.

Arrays and databases

Clipper 5 supplies us with the fundamental functions needed to create and manipulate databases via arrays, similar to the way the low-level file functions are implemented — just the basics, nothing fancy.

Outbound: DBCREATE(), creates an empty database file based on an array containing the structure. It writes out a database structure.

Inbound: DBSTRUCT(), returns an array containing the structure of a specified database file. It reads in a database structure.

These two functions are the inverse of one another. The following example demonstrates a new database called CLONED being created from the structure of ORIGINAL. The DBSTRUCT() function reads the structure of the currently selected database and returns an array containing that structure. The DBCREATE() function creates the specified database file with a structure based on the array.

```
//  An alternative to "copy structure to CLONED"
use ORIGINAL new
dbcreate("CLONED", dbstruct())
```

The array that these functions use has the following general structure. Each element in the array is another array, one for each field in the database. The LEN() of the array is the number of fields.

```
{field1_, field2_, .. fieldn_}
```

Each field array has the following structure.

```
{name, type, length, decimals}
```

So, an example of an array containing a database structure looks like the following. Multidimensional arrays are very handy for such things.

```
{ {"ID",     "C",  6, 0}, ;
  {"NAME",   "C", 30, 0}, ;
  {"QTY",    "N",  4, 0}, ;
  {"PRICE",  "N",  8, 2}, ;
  {"DUE",    "D",  8, 0}, ;
  {"PAID",   "L",  1, 0} }
```

Loading data from a single database

Since an array can have an arbitrary structure it is possible to mimic a database structure in memory with an array. Having the data in an array allows you to access the data at RAM speed rather than disk access speed, and allows you to close the database and release the file handle. If you need numerous small databases for control purposes you can load them once when the application first starts and not worry about the files throughout the rest of the application. For example, you may need lists of valid customer types and stock status codes.

Since we can determine any database structure with the DBSTRUCT() function, it's possible to write a general purpose function to create and fill such an array. The dbf2Array() function expects to be called in such a way that the desired database is available in the current work area.

```
//  Example of call to dbf2Array()
use SOMEDATA new
data_ := dbf2Array()

function dbf2Array
/*
   Return array containing entire contents of database,
       array := { record, record,  ... }
   where each record element is an array of the fields.
       record := { field, field, ... }
*/

local i, r_, a_ := {}

goto top
do while .not. eof()

   //  Start out with an empty record array
   r_ := {}

   //  Build a list of fields for current record
   for i := 1 to fcount()
    aadd(r_, fieldget(i))
   next i
```

```
   //  Add the resulting record to main array
   aadd(a_, r_)

    skip
enddo

return a_
```

We may not always want the value of every field to be placed in the array. Let's make the function more versatile by accepting another parameter — an array containing the field names we are interested in. No parameter means all fields.

```
//  Example of call to revised dbf2Array(),
//  load only Name and Phone fields.
data_ := dbf2Array({"Name","Phone"})

function dbf2Array(fields_)
/*
   Return array containing entire contents of database,
       array := { record, record,  ... }
   where each record element is an array of the fields.
       record := { field, field, ... }
   Array of fields may be limited to a list passed as
   a parameter.
*/
local i, r_, f_
local a_ := {}

/*
  If field list not passed,
  assume all fields are desired.
   Create a list of all field retrieval blocks.
*/
if fields_ == nil
  f_ := array(fcount())
  aeval(f_, { |n,i| f_[i] := fieldblock(field(i))})
```

```
/*
  Field list was passed,
  create a list of desired field retrieval blocks.
*/
else
  f_ := array(len(fields_))
  aeval(f_, { |n,i| f_[i] := fieldblock(fields_[i])})
endif


//  Run through all records in database
goto top
do while .not. eof()
   r_ := {}

   /*
      F_ contains a list of retrieval blocks
      for the desired fields.
      For each field in list,
      add value to record array.
   */
   aeval(f_, { |b| aadd(r_, eval(b)) } )

   //  Add record to main array
    aadd(a_, r_)

  skip
enddo
return a_
```

This version of dbf2Array() required the use of code blocks in order to best take advantage of Clipper 5's memory management and run-time speed, mainly to avoid the use of macros. See Chapter 8, "Code Blocks," for details.

To make the function even more versatile, let's add a parameter that describes which subset of records we want loaded into the array. No parameter means all records. The best way to handle this is with a code block. The code block should return .t. when we want a record, .f. when we don't.

```
//  Example of call to even fancier dbf2Array(),
//  load Names and Phones, only for the state of Minnesota.
forState := {|| State = "MN" }
data_ := dbf2Array({"Name","Phone"}, forState)

function dbf2Array(fields_, whichRecs)
local i, r_, f_
local a_ := {}

/*
   If field list not passed,
   assume all fields are desired.
  Create a list of all field retrieval blocks.
*/
if fields_ == nil
  f_ := array(fcount())
  aeval(f_, { |n,i| f_[i] := fieldblock(field(i))})

/*
   Field list was passed,
   create a list of desired field retrieval blocks.
*/
else
  f_ := array(len(fields_))
  aeval(f_, { |n,i| f_[i] := fieldblock(fields_[i])})
endif

//  If no code block specified, include all records
if whichRecs == nil
  whichRecs := {|| .t.}
endif

/*
   For each record in the database,
   check to see if it satisfies the code block.
*/
goto top
do while .not. eof()
  if eval(whichRecs)
  //  Build an array of fields
```

```
  //  and add to return array.
    r_ := {}
    aeval(f_, { |b| aadd(r_, eval(b)) } )
    aadd(a_, r_)
  endif
  skip
enddo
return a_
```

Now we have a different sort of problem. Supposedly dbf2Array() fills the **data_** array with field values, but how can we inspect it to be sure? (We're programmers after all, and know these things don't always work the way we intend! The Clipper compiler still uses DoWhatISaid logic, the elusive DoWhatIMeant version is perhaps years away). The following function is used to dump the contents of any arbitrary array to the screen. It uses recursion to doggedly track down each nested subarray. Each "level" is indented a few spaces so you can see the basic structure. DumpArray() uses the level parameter for its own internal use, and you do not need to specify anything. This function is very similar to the ListDir() function presented earlier. DumpArray() adds more documentation as an aid in identifying elements. The function in Listing 9.9 is kept simple to illustrate the basic concept.

Listing 9.9. A function which lists the contents of any array

```
function DumpArray(a_, level)
/*
   List the contents of any array.
   Listing is indented to show nesting of subarrays.
   This function uses a recursive call to itself.
   Do not specify the level parameter, it is used
   internally during the recursive calls.
*/
local i
if level == nil
  level := 0
endif
```

```
for i := 1 to len(a_)
  ? space(level *4) +str(i,4) +": "
  if valtype(a_[i]) == "A"
    ?? "{..}"
    DumpArray(a_[i], level +1)
  else
    ?? a_[i]
  endif
next i
return nil
```

The following is a sample array and what DumpArray() will display. It indicates that the third element is an array, and then goes on to list the contents of that array.

```
test_ := {1,2, {"A","B"}, "Z"}
DumpArray(test_)

//  Resulting display-

1:  1
2:  2
3:  {..}
    1:   A
    2:   B
4:  Z
```

Once loaded into an array you can use ASORT() and ASCAN() to do the same kinds of lookups and loop controlling as you do with .DBF files. Due to the complexity of the array you will need to use the new code block expression features of the ASORT() and ASCAN() functions.

Loading data from multiple databases

While it's certainly useful to load the contents of a single database into an array, we don't have to stop there. By adding more parameters to our dbf2Array() function we can have it track down fields in related databases. We can handle multiple related records by simply adding them as additional elements in an array. The true power of Clipper's arrays becomes very evident indeed.

In order to track down related records and build a single array we need to know the following information.

```
Name of parent database
Fields to include from parent database
Records to include from parent database
Name of related database
Fields to include from related database
Records to include from related database
Key to use to seek into related database
Field(s) in the related database that form the relation
```

An assumption is that the related records all have the same key value, so we can use a simple "while" loop to accumulate the records. This could be replaced by a code block which performs a more complex lookup process. Another simplification is to track down only a single related database. The parameters for the related database could be made into subarrays of a larger array, and the routine could work its way through all the related databases for each parent database record. The less ambitious specifications will allow us to see the fundamental technique without getting lost in features.

Here is an example of a call to this function. The first line indicates we want the ID, Name and City fields from the PARENT database. The double commas (,,) indicate that the "records to include" parameters have been skipped. This is permissible in Clipper 5 and is in fact a very handy feature. The next line indicates we want the Type, Name and Age fields from the CHILD database. The third and fourth lines indicate the two databases are related by the PARENT->ID field into the CHILD->Parent field. We assume both databases are open, and that the CHILD database has an index active with a key expression based on the related PARENT->ID.

```
data_ := dbf2Array("PARENT", {"ID", "Name", "City"},, ;
                   "CHILD",  {"Type", "Name", "Age"},, ;
                   { || PARENT->ID }, ;
                   { || CHILD->Parent == PARENT->ID })
DumpArray(data_)
```

The source code for the new and improved dbf2Array() follows in Listing 9.10. We have simplified the logic by assuming the function will always be used to load a related database. The logic for handling both a single database as well as two related databases obscures the technique, making it needlessly complicated to explain.

Listing 9.10. dbf2Array() revisited: load an array with records from a related database

```
function dbf2Array(parent, pFields_, pRecs, ;
                   child,  cFields_, cRecs, ;
                   key, relation)

local i, r_, rr_, rf_, fP_, fC_
local a_ := {}

/*
   If no list of fields was specified, create an array of
   field value retrieval blocks for all fields
   in database. Otherwise, create array just for
   specified fields.
*/
select (select(parent))
if pFields_ == nil
  fP_ := array(fcount())
  aeval(fP_, { |n,i| fP_[i] := fieldblock(field(i))})
else
  fP_ := array(len(pFields_))
  aeval(fP_, { |n,i| fP_[i] := fieldblock(pFields_[i])})
endif
  select (select(child))
  if cFields_ == nil
    fC_ := array(fcount())
    aeval(fC_, { |n,i| fC_[i] := fieldblock(field(i))})
  else
    fC_ := array(len(cFields_))
    aeval(fC_, { |n,i| fC_[i] := fieldblock(cFields_[i])})
  endif
```

```
// If no code block specified, include all records.
if pRecs == nil
  pRecs := {|| .t.}
endif
if cRecs = nil
  cRecs := {|| .t.}
endif

/*
   For each record in the database, check to see if it
   satisfies the code block.
*/
select (select(parent))
goto top
do while .not. eof()
  if eval(pRecs)
    /*
       Loop through the list of parent fields, building
       an array containing the values of each field for
       the current record.
    */
    r_ := {}
    aeval(fP_, { |b| aadd(r_, eval(b)) } )

    /*
       Seek the key in the child database, build
       an array containing the values for each
       related record.
    */
    rr_ := {}
    select (select(child))
    seek eval(key)
    do while eval(relation) .and. !eof()

      if eval(cRecs)
        /*
           Build array of fields in related record.
        */
        rf_ := {}
        aeval(fC_, { |b| aadd(rf_, eval(b)) } )
```

```
        /*
           Add array of fields to related record list.
        */
        aadd(rr_, rf_)
      endif
      select (select(child))
      skip
    enddo

    /*
       Add set of related records to parent record.
    */
    aadd(r_, rr_)

    /*
       Add the parent record value to the return array.
    */
    aadd(a_, r_)

  endif
  select (select(parent))
  skip
enddo

return a_
```

Here's an example of a call to dbf2Array() which uses the "which records to include" code blocks. Because we've skipped the "fields to include" array parameters, all fields will be included. The DATA_ array will be filled with records in PARENT where the state is MN, and the CHILD components of the array will be filled only by CHILD records where the value of the Age field is less than 18.

```
data_ := dbf2Array("PARENT", ,, { || State = "MN" }, ;
                   "CHILD",  ,, { || Age < 18 }, ;
                   { || PARENT->ID }, ;
                   { || CHILD->Parent == PARENT->ID })
```

Suppose we use the previous call to dbf2Array() on databases related by ID, where the databases contain family information. Using DumpArray() on the array returned by dbf2Array() displays the results depicted in Figure 9.5. These results are interpreted as "Bob Jones (who's ID is 24334) has a 14 year old son named Tom and a 6 year old daughter named Sue. Mary Smith (ID 52443) of Duluth has no children."

Figure 9.5. Sample output from the DumpArray() function

```
1:  {..}
    1:  24334
    2:  Bob Jones
    3:  Minneapolis
    4:  {..}
        1: {..}
           1:  Son
           2:  Tom
           3:  14
        2: {..}
           1:  Daughter
           2:  Sue
           3:  6
2:  {..}
    1:  52443
    2:  Mary Smith
    3:  Duluth
    4:  {..}
```

A comprehensive example

A final example implements a very complex array structure and demonstrates the use of preprocessor #define directives to make the source code easier to understand.

We've become obsessed with having our applications be completely responsible for creating the data structures they require. We like to be able to hand a client a single EXE file and have it create everything it needs. This takes care of the "oops, we forgot to send them an empty CUSTOMER.DBF file!" And it provides complete documentation for all data structures, right within the application's source code. Our goal is to create and maintain a single array that contains everything the application needs to know about databases, fields, and index keys. We've got the basic design down but are still experimenting with the details. We present here the basic idea which you can modify to suit your own needs.

Let's start from the top and work our way down through the general structure. At the outermost level, the **system_** array contains an element for each database used in the application.

```
system_ := {dbf1_, dbf2_, .. dbfn_}
```

The LEN() of system_ tells you the total number of databases. Each element is itself an array with the following structure.

```
dbf_ := {filename, comment, stru_, index_}
```

Each **dbf_** database array contains a filename, general comment, and two more arrays used to record the field structure and indexes. The **stru_** array contains an array of structure information plus some optional comments about each field. The length of **stru_** tells you the number of fields.

```
stru_ := {fieldname, type, length, decimals, comment}
```

The **index_** element contains an array of index filenames, key expressions and comments about the index.

```
index_ := {filename, key, comment}
```

In practice you establish the **system_** array during the application startup process. The LoadSystem() function is specific to each application, residing in its own source code file.

```
system_ := LoadSystem()
```

We're certain this idea isn't crystal clear when presented at such a level of abstraction, so let's take a look at an example with three databases, in Listing 9.11.

Listing 9.11. Load an aray with database structure and index key information

```
function LoadSystem
/*
    Return array containing complete information
    on all databases, fields and indexes used
    in current application.
*/
local stru_, ntx_
local dbf_ := {}

********************
*** Customer.dbf ***
********************
stru_ := {} ; ntx_ := {}

//  Fields in customer.dbf
aadd(stru_, {"id",      "C",  6, 0, "Customer ID"})
aadd(stru_, {"name",    "C", 30, 0, "Name"})
aadd(stru_, {"address", "C", 30, 0, "Street address"})
aadd(stru_, {"csz",     "C", 30, 0, "City State ZIP"})

  //  Indexes for customer.dbf
  aadd(ntx_, {"custID",   "id", ;
                "Customers by ID"})
  aadd(ntx_, {"custName", "name +ID", ;
                "Customers by Name"})

  //  Final array of info for customer.dbf
  aadd(dbf_, {"customer", "Master customer list", ;
              stru_, ntx_})

  *****************
  *** Order.dbf ***
  *****************
  stru_ := {} ; ntx_ := {}
```

```
  //  Fields for order.dbf
  aadd(stru_, {"id",        "C", 10, 0, "Order ID"})
  aadd(stru_, {"customer", "C",  6, 0, "Customer ID"})
  aadd(stru_, {"dated",    "D",  8, 0, "Date of order"})
  aadd(stru_, {"sales",    "C",  3, 0, "Salesperson"})

  //  Indexes for order.dbf
  aadd(ntx_, {"ordID",  "ID", ;
               "Orders by ID"})
  aadd(ntx_, {"ordCust", "Customer +dtos(Dated)", ;
               "Customer ID by date"})

  //  Final array of info for order.dbf
  aadd(dbf_, {"order", "Customer orders", stru_, ntx_})

  ****************
  *** Item.dbf ***
  ****************
  /*
     Just to be different this DBF_ element is
     constructed directly without using AADD() for
     individual array components. We feel this
     method is more difficult to get right the
     first time and harder to maintain.
  */
aadd(dbf_, {"item", "Customer order line items", ;
  { ;  //  Structure
    {"order",  "C", 10, 0, "Order ID"}, ;
    {"invent", "C",  8, 0, "Inventory item"}, ;
    {"qty",    "N",  4, 0, "Quantity"} ;
  },;
  { ;  //  Index
    {"itemOrd", "Order +Invent", ;
     "Order items by inventory code"} ;
  } ;
})

*** The DBF_ array now contains complete system info.

return dbf_
```

Given such an array we can create functions to perform a variety of useful services.

```
//  Create DBF structures for entire application
SysCreate(system_)

//  Create indexes just for CUSTOMER.DBF
SysIndex(system_, "Customer")

//  List everything we know about the application,
//  then just for ORDER.DBF.
ListStru(system_)
ListStru(system_, "Order")
```

Before writing these functions, let's create a preprocessor #include file that will help make the source code easier to read and understand.

```
/*
   DBFSYSTEM.CH
   The main system array has four elements
*/
#define SYS_DBFNAME    1
#define SYS_COMMENT    2
#define SYS_STRU       3
#define SYS_NTX        4

//  Each SYS_STRU element is an array of five elements
#define STRU_NAME      1
#define STRU_TYPE      2
#define STRU_LEN       3
#define STRU_DEC       4
#define STRU_COMMENT   5

//  Each SYS_NTX element is an array of three elements
#define NTX_NAME       1
#define NTX_KEY        2
#define NTX_COMMENT    3
```

These #define directives are made available to all functions in the source code file through the use of an #include directive.

```
#include "dbfsystem.ch"
```

On with the source code. We begin by writing the function that creates database structures based on the contents of the **system_** array passed to it. See Listing 9.12.

Listing 9.12. Create databases based on contents of an array.

```
function SysCreate(sys_, which)
/*
   Given a system structure array and an optional
   filename, create database(s).
*/

local n
if which <> nil
  n := ascan(sys_, ;
       { |d_| upper(d_[SYS_DBFNAME]) == upper(which)})
  if n > 0
    SysCreate1(sys_, n)
  else
    //  Error handler?
  endif

else
  for n := 1 to len(sys_)
    SysCreate1(sys_, n)
  next n
endif
return nil

static function SysCreate1(sys_, n)
local dbstru_ := {}, f
for f := 1 to len(sys_[n, SYS_STRU])
    aadd(dbstru_, {sys_[n, SYS_STRU, f, STRU_NAME],;
                   sys_[n, SYS_STRU, f, STRU_TYPE],;
                   sys_[n, SYS_STRU, f, STRU_LEN ],;
                   sys_[n, SYS_STRU, f, STRU_DEC ]})
```

```
next f
dbcreate(sys_[n, SYS_DBFNAME], dbstru_)
return nil
```

In SysCreate(), the call to ASCAN() searches the filename portion of the system array looking for the specified name. Since the system array contains only arrays we need a code block to tell ASCAN() exactly how to perform the search within the array structure. At the same time we have ASCAN() make the search insensitive to character case.

The function SysCreate1() is declared static so we can make the main SysCreate() function easier to understand. A regular function is visible to the rest of the application, so we "protect" SysCreate()'s sub-function by making it static and consequently visible only to the other functions in the source code file. This is a way to tell anyone looking at the code that they are only supposed to make calls to SysCreate() and not SysCreate1(). Listing 9.13 continues with the SysIndex() function.

Listing 9.13. Create index files based on contents of array

```
function SysIndex(sys_, which)
/*
   Given a system structure array and an optional
   database filename, create associated index(es).
*/

local n
if which <> nil
  n := ascan(sys_, ;
       { |d_| upper(d_[SYS_DBFNAME]) == upper(which)})
  if n > 0
    SysIndex1(sys_[n, SYS_DBFNAME], sys_[n, SYS_NTX])
  else
    //  Error handler?
  endif

else
  for n := 1 to len(sys_)
    SysIndex1(sys_[n, SYS_DBFNAME], sys_[n, SYS_NTX])
```

```
  next n
endif
return nil

static function SysIndex1(dbfname, ntx_)
local i, key
for i := 1 to len(ntx_)
  use (dbfname) new
  key := ntx_[i, NTX_KEY]
  index on &key. to (ntx_[i, NTX_NAME])
  use
next i
return nil
```

The code for calling the indexing routine is very similar to SysCreate(). The main difference is that in SysCreate() we passed the entire system array to SysCreate1(), and broke the array into component pieces down there. The main indexing routine took a different approach and determined the filename and isolated the array of indexes before calling Index1(). The two methods are equivalent. We used different methods for illustration only. In practice you should use a consistent method to help make maintenance easier.

The final function to write is ListStru(), which documents each database in detail. Listing 9.14 contains the source code. If you can read and understand this function you can be confident you have a very good grasp of multiple dimension arrays. If not, don't be depressed. We use such arrays all the time and we still get confused sometimes.

Listing 9.14. Print a listing of database structure and index key information based on contents of an array

```
function ListStru(sys_, which)

local n
if which <> nil
  n := ascan(sys_, ;
       { |d_| upper(d_[SYS_DBFNAME]) == upper(which)})
```

```
  if n > 0
    ListStru1(sys_, n)
  else
    //  Error handler?
  endif

else
  for n := 1 to len(sys_)
    ListStru1(sys_, n)
  next n
endif

return nil

static function ListStru1(sys_, n)
local i
?
? "Database: " +upper(rtrim(sys_[n, SYS_DBFNAME]))
?? ", " +sys_[n, SYS_COMMENT]
?

for i := 1 to len(sys_[n, SYS_STRU])
  ? str(i, 4) +space(2)
  ?? padr(sys_[n, SYS_STRU, i, STRU_NAME], 10)
  ?? space(2) +sys_[n, SYS_STRU, i, STRU_TYPE]
  ?? space(2) +str(sys_[n, SYS_STRU, i, STRU_LEN], 3)
  //  Only numeric fields need the decimals listed
  if sys_[n, SYS_STRU, i, STRU_TYPE] = "N"
    ?? "." +str(sys_[n, SYS_STRU, i, STRU_DEC], 1)
  else
    ?? space(2)
  endif
  //  Field comments are optional
  if len(sys_[n, SYS_STRU, i]) = STRU_COMMENT
    ?? space(2) +sys_[n, SYS_STRU, i, STRU_COMMENT]
  endif
next i
```

```
?
for i := 1 to len(sys_[n, SYS_NTX])
  ? space(3)
  ?? upper(rtrim(sys_[n, SYS_NTX, i, NTX_NAME]))
  ?? ", " +sys_[n, SYS_NTX, i, NTX_COMMENT]
  ? space(5) +"key: "
  ?? sys_[n, SYS_NTX, i, NTX_KEY]
next i
?
return nil
```

If the **system_** array were still around from the previous example, the result of a call to **ListStru(system_, "customer")** will look like the following.

```
Database: CUSTOMER, Master Customer List

   1  ID          C   6   Customer ID
   2  Name        C  30   Company Name
   3  Address     C  30   Street Address
   4  CSZ         C  30   City, State ZIP

   CUSTID, Customers by ID
     key: ID
   CUSTNAME, Customers by Name
     key: Name +ID
```

This concept lends itself to a variety of applications. You can pass around everything known about your application's databases and indexes using a single array. Only a single version of your general purpose maintenance routines need to be maintained if they always operate based on such a **system_** array.

Loading unknown database structures

Listing 9.15 contains a routine that creates everything (except the comments and indexes) for a **system_** array from a collection of database files, rather than requiring you to define the structure via source code. We prefer the "fresh from the source code" approach, but can see circumstances where you can't define the structure in advance.

Listing 9.15. Load an array with database structure information based on the DOS directory

```
#include "DIRECTRY.CH"
function DOS_Load
/*
   Load array containing database and field information
   directly from the contents of the DOS files, rather
   than using a source code routine.
*/
local i, name_, dbf_ := {}
name_ := directory("*.DBF")
for i := 1 to len(name_)
  use (name_[i,F_NAME]) new
  aadd(dbf_, {name_[i,F_NAME], "", dbstruct(), {}})
  use
next i
return dbf_
```

The following is an example of a call to DOS_Load().

```
function Main
system_ := DOS_Load()
//
//  Remainder of application
//
return nil
```

The DOS_Load() function takes the array of .DBF file information returned by DIRECTORY() and uses it to load an array of database filename and structure information. The description of each database (the second element of the main array), the comments about individual fields (the fifth element of the structure array), and index information (fourth element of the main array) cannot be determined from DOS directory information alone, so the ListStru() function is considerably less useful.

If you had a file-naming convention that associated indexes with databases you could also automatically load the index names and key expressions. Depending on the index key expressions and the way you name fields it may even be possible to associate an index with a database via the index key alone. This takes advance planning and rigorous attention to a naming convention that always results in a unique association of databases and index keys.

Saving and restoring arrays

Despite Clipper's almost overwhelming implementation of arrays it manages to omit one critical feature, namely, the ability to save and restore the contents of an array directly to and from disk storage. The regular Clipper storage mechanisms, database (.DBF) and memory (.MEM) files, are very inefficient and limited in the kinds of arrays they can accommodate, and even then, only after some tortuous programming.

In the final section of this ambitious chapter we provide solutions for direct array storage and retrieval: SaveArray() and RestArray(). These functions have been designed to handle any Clipper array structure and contents. A powerful programming technique, called recursion, allows us to process deeply nested arrays the same way we process simple arrays with single dimensions.

Since Clipper has a complete set of data type functions we can store any data type to a file and read it back in again. The only exception is the code block data type. A code block is really more of a reference to program code sitting in memory than an actual sequence of digits or characters or logical values, so it is not possible to transfer a code block outside of the application. You can, however, store the source code for a code block as a character string and use the macro compiler operator, &(), to produce a code block.

```
//  An array with two code blocks as elements.
//  Can't save this array outside of the application.
a_ := { { || Test1() }, { || Test2() } }

//  An array of two character strings.
//  The strings form code blocks.
//  This array can be saved outside of the application.
b_ := { "{ || Test1() }", "{ || Test2() }" }

//  Compile and run the code block defined by
//  the source code in array element number one.
c :=&(b_[1])
eval(c)
```

The SaveArray() function will write a NIL value should it encounter a code block. This is done to preserve the original structure of the array and not because NIL is a reasonable approximation of the code block.

Saving an array to a file

Saving an array to a file is accomplished by a call to the SaveArray() function. The syntax is illustrated below.

```
n_ := {1,2,3, {4,5,6, {7,8,9}}}
if SaveArray(n_, "NUMS.ARY")
  ? "Array-save process was successful."
else
  ? "An error occurred during the array-save process."
endif
```

You pass the array to save and the name of the target file. The target file will be created if it does not exist and overwritten, without warning, if it does exist. As the above example indicates, SaveArray() returns a logical value signaling the success or failure of the operation.

Restoring an array from a file

The file created by SaveArray() is of limited value unless there's a way to read it back in again, and that's done through a call to the RestArray() function. Once again an example will clearly illustrate the syntax.

```
x_ := RestArray("NUMS.ARY")
if len(x_) > 0
  ? "Array restored successfully."
else
  ? "An error occurred during the array-restore process."
endif
```

You pass the name of the file containing the array. The function returns a reference to the array it creates.

Source code

The SaveArray() and RestArray() functions are actually just the publicly visible interfaces to other functions that do all the work. (This technique is discussed in more detail in Chapter 12, "Program Design.) The source code for both sets of functions is found in Listings 9.16 through 9.19. The comments within the source code listings completely document the design and programming techniques.

Listing 9.16. The SaveArray() function. Writes an array to a disk file.

```
function SaveArray(a_, fileName)
/*
   General-purpose function for saving an array to a disk
   file. This is only the public interface. The real work is done
   by recursive calls to the ElementOut() function.

   Pass an array (or a reference to an array) and the name of the
   file to store the array.

       SaveArray({1,2,3,4}, "NUMS.ARY")
```

```
   This function returns .t. if successful, .f. if not.
*/
local cnt := len(a_)
local success := .f.
local handle := fcreate(fileName)

if handle != -1
   success := ElementOut(handle, a_)
   fclose(handle)
endif

return success
```

Listing 9.17. The ElementOut() function. Handles output for a single array dimension

```
static function ElementOut(handle, a_)
/*
   Given a file handle and an array, write the contents of the
   array to the file in the following form.

      LL T WW E... T WW E...

   Where LL is a two byte integer representing the number of
   elements in the array, T is a character representing the data
   type of the first element, WW is a two byte integer
   representing the width of the element; followed by repetitions
   of that basic pattern.

   Nested arrays are handled by calling ElementOut() whenever an
   array is encountered within the elements in the array
   currently being processed. (Known as recursion.)  The LL length
   bytes are written following an "A" data type and the process
   gets repeated. Isn't recursion wonderful?

   This is a static function and therefore not visible to any
   functions outside of the source code file containing it.
   All calls from the outside must be made to SaveArray().
*/
```

```
local success := .t.
local i, buffer
local cnt := len(a_)

//  Write the overall array size.
fwrite(handle, i2bin(cnt))

//  Process each element in the array.
for i := 1 to cnt

   /*
       Special handling for the nil and code block data types.
       Both will be labeled type "Z" and for consistency with
       the other data types, will have a width of one and an
       element value of "Z". However, a NIL will be placed in
       the array when it comes time to load it from the file.
   */
   if (a_[i] == nil) .or. (valtype(a_[i]) == "B")
        buffer := "Z" +i2bin(1) +"Z"

  else
   /*
        Each element is encoded as follows.
            Data type:  C,D,L,N.
                Width:  Number of characters needed.
        Element Value:  String version of the value.
   */

     buffer := valtype(a_[i])
     do case
     case buffer == "C"
       buffer += i2bin(len(a_[i]))    //  Width of the string
       buffer += a_[i]

     case buffer == "D"
       buffer += i2bin(8)             //  Dates are 8 wide
       buffer += dtoc(a_[i])

     case buffer == "L"
       buffer += i2bin(1)             //  Logicals are 1 wide
       buffer += if(a_[i], "T", "F")
```

```
      case buffer == "N"
        //  Convert number to string, trim spaces, and
         //  calculate width of number based on the string.
         buffer += i2bin(len(ltrim(str(a_[i]))))
         buffer += ltrim(str(a_[i]))

      otherwise
        //  Type "A" for arrays will be handled
        //  after we write the type.
      endcase
   endif

   //  Write the buffer, constructed above, to the file.
   if fwrite(handle, buffer, len(buffer)) != len(buffer)
      success := .f.
      exit
   endif

   /*
      If this is a nested array, it's recursion time!

      Call ElementOut() again, it will append a series
      of types/widths/values to the current file.
   */
   if left(buffer, 1) == "A"
      ElementOut(handle, a_[i])
   endif
next i

return success
```

Listing 9.18. The RestArray() function. Restores an array from a disk file

```
function RestArray(fileName)
/*
   General-purpose function for restoring an array from a disk
   file. This is only the public interface. The real work is done
   by recursive calls to the ElementIn() function.
```

```
   This function expects the name of a file created previously by
   the SaveArray() function. It reads the file to construct the
   array that was saved.

      n_ := RestArray("NUMS.ARY")

   This function returns a reference to the array it creates.
*/

local handle, a_ := {}

if (handle := fopen(fileName)) != -1
   ElementIn(handle, a_)
endif
fclose(handle)

return a_
```

Listing 9.19. The ElementIn() function. Handles restoring of a single array dimension

```
static function ElementIn(handle, a_)
/*
  Given a file handle and a reference to an array, read elements
  from the file and add them to the array.

  The file must be created by the SaveArray() function and be
  structured as described in the SaveArray() comments.

  Nested arrays are detected and sub-arrays stored in the main
  array as needed. The file reading for a sub-array is
  accomplished through another call to ElementIn(). This is
  known as recursion.

  This is a static function and therefore not visible to any
  functions outside of the source code file containing it.
  All calls from the outside must be made to RestArray().
*/
```

```
local buffer, i, cnt, iLen, iType

//  Read the overall array size
buffer := space(2)
if fread(handle, @buffer, 2) = 2

   //  Process each array element stored in the file.
   cnt := bin2w(buffer)
   for i := 1 to cnt

      //  Read the element's data type.
      //  If element is a nested array - recursion time!
      //
      if (iType := freadstr(handle,1)) = "A"
        aadd(a_, {})
        ElementIn( handle, a_[ len(a_) ] )

      else
        //  Read the length of the element.
        buffer := space(2)
        if fread(handle, @buffer, 2) = 2
          iLen := bin2w(buffer)

          //  Read the actual element.
          buffer := space(iLen)
          if fread(handle, @buffer, iLen) = iLen

            //  Convert from string to specified data type.
            do case
             /*
                Note that we can't save code blocks. If you
                attempted to save one from an array, we will have
                empty space and thus must add a NIL to serve
                as a placeholder.
            */
             case (iType == "B") .or. (iType == "Z")
                aadd(a_, nil)
             case iType == "C"
                aadd(a_, buffer)
```

```
             case iType == "D"
                aadd(a_, ctod(buffer))
             case iType == "L"
                aadd(a_, (buffer == "T"))
             case iType == "N"
                aadd(a_, val(buffer))
             endcase
          endif
        endif
      endif
   next i
endif
return nil
```

Summary

You have been introduced to arrays and shown the power and flexibility they offer. We've only scratched the surface of their possible uses. Based on your understanding of how arrays are constructed and manipulated you will be able to apply arrays to almost every other facet of Clipper programming.

We've seen how Clipper 5's ability to create and manipulate arrays with multiple dimensions and a mixture of data types can be put to use to solve real-world problems. The Clipper language has the features needed to perform extremely complex yet efficient list processing, all within the context of the database management capabilities we know and love. This is a powerful combination that will yield impressive applications as you begin to fully exploit these new capabilities.

CHAPTER 10

Debugging

The debugger bundled with Clipper 5 is completely new and takes a different approach from the Summer '87 version. It is a major improvement in every respect. On the whole, it makes the task of debugging less burdensome and at times — dare we say it? — even enjoyable.

This chapter is devoted to providing an overview of the new debugger's features so you know what tools you have at your command. It closes with some "classic combinations" of features that may not be immediately obvious to the first-time user. Along the way you should pick up some useful tips and techniques, including how to avoid some initial frustration.

The debugger has a number of what we feel are either obvious or at least easily learned features that are not in need of elaboration. Examples of these are loading and scrolling through files, searching for text with find-next and find-previous, and other features that any programmer who ever used a text editor will easily figure out. Also not covered are the important but conceptually simple procedures for moving and resizing windows and changing the debugger's color scheme. All these features can be learned more quickly by just plain doing rather than by reading.

Note: In the interest of brevity we use the term **user-defined function**, and more often just **function**, rather than the more accurate (but verbose) "user-defined function or procedure". The debugger works equally well with functions or procedures. It does not operate on the internal workings of Clipper itself, so in this context the word function applies only to those that you write yourself and not to Clipper's built-in functions.

Summer '87 comparison

The Summer '87 debugger is an object file, DEBUG.OBJ, that has to be linked into your application's EXE along with the rest of your code. Consequently it occupies about 40KB of EXE file space and 35KB RAM. To invoke the debugger you must load and execute your application, and then press ALT-D or make a direct call to the ALTD() function within your source code.

In Summer '87, having to link DEBUG.OBJ into your application has a number of drawbacks. In addition to the memory and file size issue, you have to make a conscious effort either to link the debugger when you need it or to always have it linked while your application is under development and suffer a constant drain on link time and execution speed. Execution speed will be degraded even if you don't use the debugger; as long as it's linked it will be demanding attention from the application.

In Clipper 5, the debugger is a stand-alone utility, CLD.EXE, that contains all the debugging tools. Every application you link, regardless whether you thought you might need the debugger or not, can be used with the CLD utility. To use the debugger you simply specify the name of your application's .EXE file as a DOS command line parameter. For example, the following DOS command runs TEST.EXE within the debugger.

```
cld test
```

The CLD.EXE utility loads your application and executes it. Since CLD was loaded into DOS first it can perform all sorts of almost magical services for you. Well, they will seem magical to Summer '87 programmers, but not to other programmers who have seen Microsoft's CodeView or Borland's Turbo Debugger. The Clipper 5 debugger is influenced by these two extremely powerful debuggers.

Note: The Clipper 5 debugger can also be linked directly into an application for situations that demand such a configuration. The nice thing is, linking is optional. For most debugging sessions the CLD utility is the most efficient method.

What the debugger needs

Before getting started with operational details let's take a brief look at what the debugger expects from you. To get the most out of the debugger you need to supply it with several important kinds of information. It can work with less than all of the information, but with varying degrees of success.

Symbols

Many of Clipper 5's internal structural changes result in your code being optimized, particularly with respect to the "symbols" you create. Symbols are anything for which you make up a name: memory variables, function names and so on. Many of these symbols are converted to direct references to actual memory locations and consequently the name you assigned disappears. The .EXE file does not always contain the symbol name. Examples of this are **local** and **static** memory variables. The CLD utility will not be of much use to you if you can't see your original symbol names. The Clipper 5 compiler can, however, be instructed to keep the original information intact so the debugger can make use of it. This is done via the /B compiler switch.

```
clipper test /b
```

Using the /B switch will slightly increase the size of the object file (since it contains additional debugging information) and consequently the size of the .EXE. Using a dynamic overlay linker like RTLink makes this a non-issue, so we have included the /B switch in our standard Clipper compiler environment command (as mentioned in Chapter 1).

```
set clippercmd=/a /b /m /n /p /v /w
```

This ensures that debugging information is always available. If space is critical you can always recompile all objects for the application and link one final time before distributing the application EXE file.

Object code

Since special debugging information is stored in the object file (when compiled with the /B switch), the debugger needs access to the object files (.OBJ) while executing your application. The debugger can get very confused if you have recompiled any object files since the last time the .EXE was linked.

Source code

The debugger is termed a "source level debugger," meaning it can follow your source code while your application is executing. Not surprisingly the debugger needs to be able to read the source code files (.PRG) while running your application. Things will be totally out of whack if you have edited the source code since the associated object file (.OBJ) was last compiled. The debugger may appear to work but will eventually lose track of the correct source code line.

Line numbers

In order to track your application's progress through the original source code the debugger needs to refer to line numbers. Clipper stores such line numbers in the object code by default. If you suppress line numbers with the /L compiler switch you will prevent the debugger from tracking the source code. Since you have a dynamic overlay linker (.RTLink) there is very little gained by compiling without line numbers. As with the /B switch you can always recompile and link after you no longer need the line numbers for the debugger.

Removing line numbers has an additional negative side effect of making run-time errors less informative, because you'll be told only the name of the function where the error occurred, and no line number.

Preprocessor output

The debugger is capable of tracing the output from the preprocessor in addition to your original source code. Since the compiler never actually sees your source code (only the preprocessor deals with source code) there are certain classes of errors that cannot be understood by viewing the original source code. The preprocessor may have introduced the error, perhaps through a bad #define, #command, or #translate directive. If you ever need to trace the preprocessed version of your source code you will need to compile with the /P switch. Creating preprocessed output files, which end with a .PPO extension, is a time- and disk space-consuming task. Depending on the speed of your computer and the amount of disk clutter you will put up with, you may not want to have this done automatically via SET CLIPPERCMD.

Starting from DOS

To use the debugger, simply run the CLD.EXE program and supply it the name of a Clipper executable file. The following line starts the debugger with TEST.EXE as the target Clipper application to work with.

```
cld test
```

The debugger has a number of DOS command line switches that control its operation. These options are presented in the order they must occur; CLD is one of the few programs where the sequence is significant.

/43	43-line mode, or
/50	50-line mode, or
/S	Split screen into two halves
@Script	Run debugger commands found in file
AppName	Name of Clipper application to debug
AppParams	Parameters to pass to Clipper application

We'll discuss the use of the script option later in this chapter. The debugger options must be specified ahead of the application name. Any parameters following the application name will be passed along to the application.

Try the split screen feature if you have a monitor capable of displaying at least 43 lines. You'll never want to go back to debugging without a split screen again. Here's an example.

```
cld /s maxibrow customer
```

Translation: Debug MAXIBROW.EXE in split screen mode. Pass "customer" as a parameter to the MAXIBROW program.

The screen mode parameters are mutually exclusive, and if you specify more than one only the last will be used. The split screen mode will use either 43 or 50 line mode, depending on what your video adapter card is capable of doing.

Linking the debugger directly

The Clipper 5 debugger can also be linked directly into the application .EXE file via the CLD.LIB library file. Even if linked this way, the debugger still requires the /B switch when compiling. All other compiling issues discussed previously apply as well.

If linked, the debugger must be invoked manually by pressing Alt-D or by calling the ALTD() function from within the application code itself. See the discussion on the ALTD() function for details.

Overview of debugger features

A complete discussion of every debugger feature could fill several chapters and still not cover everything in detail. We will highlight some of the more important features and leave the rest to your experimentation. We strongly urge you to spend as much time as you can playing with the debugger before you actually need it in a panic situation. This utility can be very frustrating until you have mastered the basic concepts. You don't want to be learning the fundamentals with a nasty UNDEFINED IDENTIFIER problem at 5:00 p.m. on the Friday your application is due!

The debugger is also an excellent environment for learning how Clipper works. Rather than always waiting for a confusing problem or run-time error, fire up the debugger and watch what happens with small programs. You'll learn more watching your code execute in the debugger than if you relied only on what the application displays on screen.

Once the debugger is finished loading it will halt at the first executable statement in your application. What happens from there is the subject of the rest of this chapter.

General navigation

You can access most of the features of the debugger three different ways. The debugger command line is universally available for almost all features and is discussed in more detail later in this chapter. The debugger main menu can be accessed via the ALT key and the letter corresponding to a menu choice, like ALT-F for File. Frequently used features have function key short-cuts, like F9 for setting or clearing a breakpoint. Some features pop up a dialog box when they need additional information.

Table 10.1 lists the function keys as they are used in the debugger.

Table 10.1. Function keys

F1	Display help screens
F2	Zoom current window (toggle)
F3	Repeat last command on command-line
F4	Application screen (toggle)
F5	Resume execution
F6	Work area information
F7	Run to cursor
F8	Step one line
F9	Set breakpoint (toggle)
F10	Step over function

When multiple windows are displayed, the Tab and Shift-Tab keys are used to select different windows. Windows can be moved, sized, and even minimized to give you a better view of the underlying application.

Unless you are in a dialog box, any typing you do will be placed in the command line window independent of which window is actually selected. This may take some getting used to. Keep in mind that the debugger displays things in the windows based on your menu choices or the commands you type. You never type directly into any window, unless it pops up a dialog box. Once you're familiar with the nature of the command window you'll appreciate how efficient it is. You do not have to tab over to the command window — just type from wherever you happen to be at the time.

Switching screens

If you are running the debugger in split screen mode (the recommended way if your video adapter card can handle it), you don't need to concern yourself with switching between the debugger screen and the application screen — both will be completely visible at all times. If you can't run the debugger in split screen mode there are a number of other features designed to make your debugging more enjoyable.

First, the F4 key is always available to switch between the debugger screen and the application screen. As you work your way through the source code you can tap F4 to see what's going on "outside." Another press of the F4 key will send you back to the debugger screen. You can bounce back and forth as often as needed, without disturbing any of the debugger settings.

A better alternative is to move and resize the various windows to give a decent view of both the debugger's and your application's screens. Being able to see both screens makes it much easier to keep track of what's going on. All windows have built-in features for making this a simple process. Once you've configured the display to your liking you can save it to a script file. Use of script files is also covered in more detail later in this chapter.

Working with source code

When you're first getting started with the debugger, its main purpose will seem to be to step through your source code a line at a time. This is indeed an important feature and a great place to get started. However, don't stop there! Once you get the hang of the other debugger features you'll find you seldom need to "walk" through your code in this way.

When the debugger first starts up, the source code window will display the first executable line of the first function in your application. Note that some statements are not considered to be executable lines. For example, **local** and **static** declarations will be skipped, along with any preprocessor directives. Comments are skipped as well. The debugger may appear to have leapt well into your application, when actually it's just stopping at the first executable line. An exception to this rule is when you combine a declaration with an assignment operation. The debugger will stop at such lines.

```
#include "inkey.ch"  //  Debugger does not stop on this line.
#define DEBUG        //  Not here, either.
static a, b, c       //  Nope.
local x := 0         //  But, it does stop here.
```

Moving through the source code

There are two kinds of source code movement. The debugger keeps track of the line that's about to be executed and highlights it in inverse video. When the source code window is selected you can scroll around through the code, but the debugger always stays parked on the line about to be executed. You move the debugger's highlight any of the following ways:

- **Stepping line by line.** Pressing the F8 key causes the debugger to execute the highlighted line and proceed to the next. If the line was a call to a user-defined function the debugger branches to that routine and highlights the first executable line there. If the function is located in a different source code file, that file is opened automatically. (A message is displayed if no source code can be located). If the line requires a code block to be evaluated, the debugger jumps to the place where the code block was either defined (if it's a literal code block) or where it was compiled via the &() macro compiler. You can turn off this code block tracing feature under the Options menu.

- **Stepping over functions.** Sometimes you are only interested in tracking the source code in a single function and don't want to trace the execution of every single line in the application. The Clipper debugger calls this "tracing", and conveniently ties it to the F10 key. Pressing F10 is similar to F8 in that the debugger will advance to the next executable line; however, it will not track function calls outside of the current function.

- **Run to cursor.** Rather than repeatedly whacking the F8 or F10 keys to advance the source code highlight to a line in which you are interested, the F7 key can be used to allow the application to run at full speed until it hits the line at which you placed the cursor. (You must move the source code cursor to an executable line before the program pointer will advance.) The following example clearly illustrates the usefulness of this feature.

```
n := 0                  //  Current debugger highlight is here...
for i := 1 to 1000
  n += Foo(i)
next i
? n          // ...run to cursor, here!
```

- **Run to next routine.** A "run to next routine" option is available in the Clipper 5.2 debugger. Next routine (Ctrl-F5), if it is invoked, causes the debugger to advance to the next function or procedure. This would be the same as creating a "PROCLINE() == 0" tracepoint.

- **Resume execution.** Frequently you'll find it much easier to just let your application run as it normally does and then stop it when it does (or is about to do) something interesting. There's a wide array of debugger features you can use to help stop the application at opportune times. Just hit the F5 key to give control back to your application. It will execute without pausing. The debugger can be invoked once again by pressing ALT-D. We'll cover other techniques, like breakpoints and tracepoints, later in this chapter.

- **Restarting.** The debugger has a Restart option (found under the Run menu) for starting your application over from scratch. This is handy if you had to run the application to the point it hit a fatal error. Simply note where the error occurred and issue a restart. This time you can use the debugger to help determine what went wrong.

Sharing screens and animation

The debugger has a mode of operation called **Animate**, where it automatically executes source code lines one at a time with an adjustable pause between each line. **Animate** is found under the Run menu, as is the animation speed control. Animation speed is measured in tenths of a second to pause between lines, with zero being no pause at all.

This screen can be very confusing. By default, the debugger will switch to the application automatically after each line is executed. You can control this behavior with the **Exchange Screens** option under the Options menu. When OFF, the debugger will only switch to the application screen when input is required. You can eliminate even this screen switch via the **Swap on Input** option, also found under the Options menu. With both these options set off the application screen will not be displayed. Of course, you can interrupt the animation with ALT-D and press the F4 key to see the application screen at any time.

Animation is useful when you want to slow down the execution of your application and monitor it as it trundles along. If you can't run in split screen, however, the constant screen switching will likely drive you crazy.

The best way to run Animation is with the source code window made small enough and moved so that the application screen is visible. The other windows can be sized and moved as well, resulting in a reasonable balance between information on the application and the debugging information covering some of it.

Likely problem areas

There are several kinds of source code that are likely to cause confusion in step-through operations.

- **Preprocessor side effects.** Any lines directed to the preprocessor are, by their very nature, not going to be dealt with very well at run-time. The compiler, and consequently the run-time application, never see these lines. Manifest constants will not be visible anywhere but in the original source code. You can't test or alter the values of manifest constants because the **names** don't really exist in the .EXE; the preprocessor swapped the name with the value and the compiler never even saw it. Directives for including header files are also potentially troublesome. You can always use the File-Open feature to view the actual header file. You can have the debugger display the preprocessed code (selected under the Options menu), in which case you'll see the source code both before and after the preprocessing.

- **Multiple statements in single line.** The preprocessor routinely sticks multiple statements on the same source code line (using a semicolon to separate them) and consequently so can you. In limited circumstances this may be desirable, but be aware that the debugger treats the entire line as a single entity and can't individually process each statement. You are much better off keeping each statement on its own line. You gain nothing as far as run-time speed is concerned but you lose debugging capabilities.

- **Code blocks**. Code blocks allow you to write code in one place and ship it off for execution somewhere else. However, code blocks are evaluated in the context of where they were *defined*, not where they are executed. To the debugger this makes code blocks look like a function call. The debugger will trace execution back to the source code line where the code block was defined. You can disable this behavior via the *Code Block Trace* choice on the Options menu. The preprocessor will convert some otherwise innocent-looking commands to include code blocks, so don't be surprised to see the code block marker, {||...}, displayed next to source code lines that don't appear to have anything to do with code blocks. Turning on the preprocessed code display option will reveal the hidden code blocks.

Figure 10.1 Code block trace

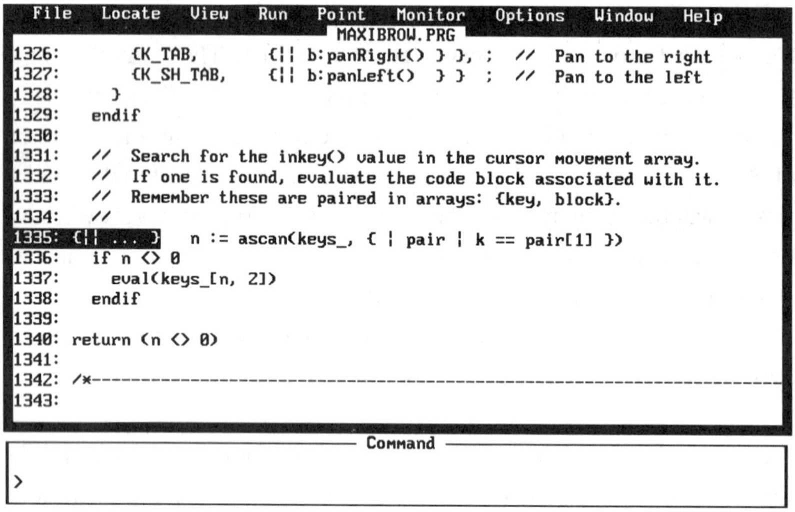
File Locate View Run Point Monitor Options Window Help
MAXIBROW.PRG
1326: {K_TAB, {|| b:panRight() } }, ; // Pan to the right
1327: {K_SH_TAB, {|| b:panLeft() } } ; // Pan to the left
1328: }
1329: endif
1330:
1331: // Search for the inkey() value in the cursor movement array.
1332: // If one is found, evaluate the code block associated with it.
1333: // Remember these are paired in arrays: {key, block}.
1334: //
1335: {|| ... } n := ascan(keys_, { | pair | k == pair[1] })
1336: if n <> 0
1337: eval(keys_[n, 2])
1338: endif
1339:
1340: return (n <> 0)
1341:
1342: /*--
1343:
Command
>

Inspecting things

Once you get over the thrill of stepping your way through your source code (which may take quite a while, it's great fun!) you should turn your attention to what is arguably the most useful feature of the debugger — its ability to inspect and alter the value of almost everything in your application.

The ? command

To see the value of any variable you can use the question mark command in the command window. The following displays the current value of x.

```
? x
```

This is best used in situations where you know the name of the variable and only want a quick peek at the value. If you don't know the name, see the later discussion on the Monitor feature. If you want to keep checking on the value, you're better off setting a watchpoint, which we will discuss in a moment.

Results of expressions

The ? command is actually displaying the results of Clipper expressions, not just simple variable names. The result of any valid Clipper expression can be displayed, providing all functions referenced have been linked into the application's .EXE. If you want to see the last 20 characters of a 1,000 character string, you can call RIGHT().

```
? right(longstring, 20)
```

You can perform mathematical calculations, data type conversions, anything at all so long as it is an acceptable Clipper expression.

```
? val(substr(data, 2, 7)) * (factor /10)
```

Since variable assignment is considered an expression in Clipper 5, you can also use the question mark command to assign values to memory variables. You can even create new variables this way. The following example either assigns **d** a new value (if it currently exists and is in scope) or creates a new variable called **d** and gives it a **private** scope (if **d** does not exist).

```
? d := date()
```

Note that you must use the inline assignment operator (:=) to make assignments. Otherwise the debugger thinks you are asking it if the variable is currently equal to the value. The following will display .T. or .F. depending on the value of **d**.

```
? d = date()
```

The ? command is capable of evaluating any legal expression, so you can do some amazing things with it. See the section "Adding Your Own Features," later in this chapter.

Watchpoints

Watchpoints open a window at the top of the screen that displays the current value of the expression you specify. Watchpoints can be set by selecting **Watchpoint** from the Point menu, or more efficiently by entering them at the command line. The following watchpoint will continuously display the current value of the **counter** variable:

```
wp counter
```

For an example that illustrates a constantly changing value, you can set a watchpoint on the PROCLINE() function. Enter the following at the command line.

```
wp procline()
```

While the program executes, the current line number will be displayed in the watch window. Any expression can be used as a watchpoint. Typically you set a watchpoint on a variable name or expression that you want to keep track of, especially when the value is independent of the function that's currently executing. A watchpoint is constantly evaluated, even when the expression is irrelevant to the function being executed.

See the "Classic Combinations" section of this chapter for some additional tips and techniques.

More efficient variable inspection

The fastest way to see the values of many variables is to use the Monitor menu and select the combination of storage classes in which you are interested. The currently active variables of each class will be displayed in the watch window. Remember that if more variables are displayed than can fit in the window you can tab over to the window and scroll around. You can also change the size of the window if you want to see large numbers of variables. A handy alternative is the F2-Zoom key, which you can use to toggle a full screen view of the Watch or Monitor windows.

See the discussion on the Callstack, and also the "classic combination" of Callstack and Monitor, later in this chapter, for some very powerful debugging tips and techniques.

Altering values

The debugger can alter the value of any variable displayed in the Watch or Monitor windows. Tab over the window, move the highlight to the desired variable, and press Enter. A dialog box will be displayed, allowing you to edit the value.

Contents of arrays

Unlike its Summer '87 predecessor, the Clipper 5 debugger can handle arrays, even those with multiple dimensions. To view and/or edit the contents of an array you must place it in either the Watch or Monitor window. Tab over to the window, move the highlight to the desired array, and press Enter. The dialog box indicates you are dealing with an array by displaying "{...}". If you type over the top of this value you replace the array with that value (be careful!). Press Enter on the {...}, and what happens next depends on the number of dimensions of the array. You may be presented with simple element values, in which case you can move the cursor to any element and edit the value. You may be presented with nested arrays, indicated as before with {...}, in which case you can highlight one and press Enter to see what it contains or type over the top of it and lose the underlying array. This process can be repeated until you run out of array dimensions. Press Esc to exit the array inspection window.

This feature is a great way to get a handle on arrays with multiple dimensions. You can walk your way deep into nested dimensions with the Enter key, and walk back out again with the Esc key.

Figure 10.2 Inspecting multi-dimensional array

```
 File  Locate  View  Run  Point  Monitor  Options  Window  Help
                              Monitor: Local
10) KEY <Local, N>:           24
11) STRU_ <Local, A>: { ... }
12) RECS_ <L
13) S <Local                  STRU_
14) N <Local
               { ... }

627:                          STRU_[1..7]
628:
629:   STRU_[1] { ... }
630:   STRU_[2] { ... }
631:
632:                          STRU_[2][1..4]
633:
634:  STRU_[2][1] "TITLE"
635:  STRU_[2][2] "C"
636:  STRU_[2][3] 50
637:  STRU_[2][4] 0
                              Command
>
```

Object instance variables

An extremely handy feature is the ability to view and alter the values of object instance variables. Similar to all the other types of variables, once placed in either a Watch or Monitor window you can press Enter when an object-variable is highlighted. Similar to arrays, the dialog box displays "Object" to indicate that the variable is an object. You can type over the top of it and lose the underlying object, or press Enter. Any of the object's instance variables that can be edited will be displayed with their current values. You can move the cursor to any instance and alter the value. Useful not only for debugging, this feature is also invaluable for learning about programming with objects in general. Press Esc to exit the object inspection window.

Figure 10.3 Inspecting object instance variables

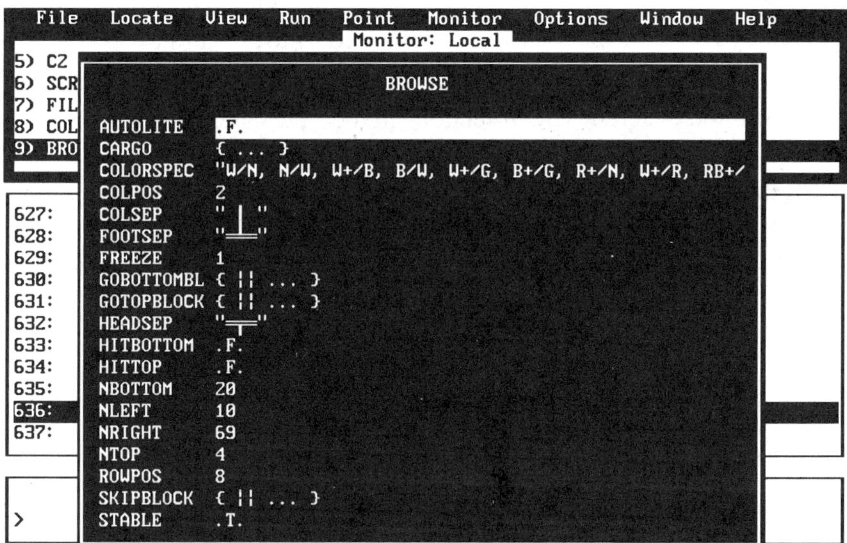

Global SET values

Clipper is controlled, perhaps to too great a degree, by dozens of application-wide settings. These include commands such as SET DELETED, SET SOFTSEEK, SET DECIMALS and so on. The current value of any of these settings can be viewed and even altered via the View Menu, Sets option. The effect of a change will occur immediately when the next source code line is executed. Press Esc to exit the SET inspection window.

Databases and work areas

Everything you would ever want to know about databases and other work area-specific information is available via the View menu's Workareas option (or, press the F6 key). Each database currently open is displayed in a list, and as you move the cursor through the database file names detailed information associated with the highlighted database is displayed. There's sometimes more than can comfortably fit in a single screen, so the information can be "collapsed" into an outline format. Use the Tab and Shift-Tab keys to move between sections of the display. Press Enter to collapse or expand the different screen sections in the status area.

The Callstack

The Callstack keeps track of the sequence of events that got your program to the current line of execution. If your Main() function called One() and One() called Two(), the callstack would look like the following:

```
two
one
main
```

You can Tab over to the Callstack window and move the highlight to any of the entries. Press Enter, and the program window is switched to the last line that was executed in that function. If you selected the One() function, above, the highlight will be sitting on the source code line that called function Two().

Function names prefixed with a "(b)" indicate that a code block is being evaluated within the context of that function.

Halting execution

While your application is running and in control there are several ways to interrupt it and return control to the debugger.

Crash!

For the sake of completeness we'll mention that when a fatal bug causes a run-time error, it's a sure way to get the debugger's attention. Your application will halt on the offending line. You can use the myriad debugger resources to determine what caused the error. Remember that the RESTART command (or select Restart from the Run menu) can be used to restart your application so testing and debugging can begin again without exiting all the way to DOS.

The ALT-D keystroke

As discussed previously, you can always press ALT-D to halt the application and display the debugger screen. The source code highlight will be on the line that would have been executed next.

The ALTD() function

You can invoke the debugger directly from within your application by calling the ALTD() function. This is equivalent to pressing ALT-D. The ALTD() function is very handy when used in conjunction with the preprocessor (see Chapter 7 for more details on the preprocessor). The following code fragment illustrates the use of the ALTD() function to trap an error condition that isn't fatal, but is serious nonetheless.

```
//  Place at top of program, or "compile it in" with
//  the /D compiler switch.
//
#define DEBUG

select vendor
seek vend_code

#ifdef DEBUG
  //  This is a serious problem - the vendor code is
  //  supposed to be found in the list. Call the debugger!
  if ! vendor->(found())
     altd()
  endif
#endif
```

Such a construction allows you to leave the debugging tests and special code in the application, permanently. When you're finished testing you can compile the source code without DEBUG being defined, and the debugging code will not be included in the resulting object code. It will still be in the source code should you need to test again. See Chapter 28, "The Error Class," for a discussion on the concept of "assertions", an additional way to trap errors of this nature. Assertions are very powerful when combined with the ALTD() function.

The ALTD() function accepts a parameter that affects both how subsequent calls to ALTD(), as well as all other debugger operations are handled. ALTD(0) disables the debugger *completely* until an ALTD(1) is encountered. While disabled, the debugger can't be invoked via the ALT-D keystroke or the ALTD() function call (with no parameter), nor are any breakpoints or tracepoints respected. ALTD(0) shuts the debugger down until the next ALTD(1).

ALTD(0) is used primarily to lock end-users out of the debugger in situations where the debugger library (CLD.LIB) is linked directly into the application. The application should default to ALTD(0) and only issue an ALTD(1) from a password-protected menu or after a special series of keystrokes. Another alternative is the use of a DOS command line parameter. Only if the parameter is specified correctly is the debugger enabled.

Another possible use is in situations where you want a section of code to run without being "caught" by tracepoints. For example, a large routine could have an ALTD(0) and ALTD(1) combination that temporarily disables the debugger whenever the routine is executed. Use of the preprocessor's conditional compilation features is important for keeping this sort of code isolated (and easily identified) from the actual function code.

Breakpoints

Breakpoints are used to halt execution when the debugger hits the specified line number in a specified function. The debugger stops before executing the line, so that you can set a breakpoint right on a line that is causing problems. The breakpoint stays active until you remove it. Setting a breakpoint on top of an existing one turns it off. You can set a breakpoint via the **Breakpoint** option on the Point menu, by issuing the BP command in the command window, or by pressing F9 on the desired line.

If you aren't sure about the line numbers for a function you can omit them. The debugger will halt on the first executable line. You can then use the F8 or F10 keys to single step through the function, or scroll through the source code and use the F7 *Run to Cursor* feature to position the debugger at the desired line.

The command line is the easiest way (short of hitting F9) to set breakpoints. You don't have to specify the name of the function when setting break points within the current source code file. The following sets a breakpoint at line 170 of the current file, at the first executable line in function ShowStat(), and at line 23 in LOADER.PRG.

```
bp 170
bp showstat
bp 23 in loader
```

Each breakpoint will be listed and associated with a sequence number. Breakpoints can be disabled by deleting them via the *Delete* option on the Point menu, or via DELETE at the command line. In either case you refer to the breakpoint by number. The following deletes the breakpoint number 2.

```
delete bp 2
```

To get rid of all breakpoints quickly you can specify ALL in the command line.

```
delete all bp
```

Tracepoints

Tracepoints are a combination watchpoint and breakpoint. You set a tracepoint on an expression just like you do with a watchpoint. The difference is that a tracepoint will halt program execution when the value of the expression changes. For example, you could set a tracepoint on a variable name. If the value of the variable changes the program will halt. In the following example, program execution will halt when the value of the **loop_count** variable changes.

```
tp loop_count
```

Tracepoints can be set on any valid Clipper expression. Keep in mind that it's not the result that matters, but a *change* in the result. Here's an amusing example. The following tracepoint will halt program execution within the next minute.

```
tp left(time(),5)
```

Note, however, that tracepoints are not evaluated during wait states in your applications. The above example will not halt execution, for example, during an INKEY(0), but the application will be halted on the very next line when the INKEY(0) is exited.

Keep in mind that tracepoints will often cause execution speed to slow down. If you have too many tracepoints, the application may slow to a crawl. Be especially frugal with tracepoints when you're using functions requiring significant amounts of processing time. All tracepoints are evaluated after each line of code is executed. Tracepoints can be deleted the same way as breakpoints.

Script files

After going to the trouble of setting up windows, monitors, watchpoints, breakpoints, tracepoints and other debugger configuration options, you can save them all to a file for later recall. The Options menu has Save and Restore choices for this purpose. When starting from DOS you can specify that a script file be used to configure the debugger immediately. In the following example a script file called MYAPP.BUG will be used in conjunction with MYAPP.EXE.

```
cld @myapp.bug myapp
```

The debugger's RESTART command also uses a script file to record all current settings, then reloads and restarts your application while retaining the previous debugger context.

The debugger will automatically load a configuration script file called INIT.CLD if one exists. INIT.CLD is an ideal way to customize the debugger. To create such a file simply save the debugger configuration as INIT.CLD.

The command line

As mentioned briefly in previous discussions, the command line can be used to perform all the major debugger functions. It's a matter of personal preference whether you find it easier to type commands or make menu selections. We find ourselves doing both. Some operations, like setting watchpoints and breakpoints, are more efficient when done from the command line. Others, like specifying which class of variable to monitor, require fewer keystrokes if selected from the menu. Table 10.2 lists the available commands.

Table 10.2 Alphabetic list of debugger commands

?	Display the value of a variable or expression
animate	Run application in animation mode
bp	Set a breakpoint
callstack	Display the callstack window
delete	Delete one, some or all "point" settings
DOS	Drop to DOS without exiting current application
find	Search for a character string in current file
go	Run the application
goto	Move cursor to specified line within file
help	Display the help screen
input	Read debugger commands from specified file
list	List some or all "point" settings
next	Search for the next occurrence of a character string
num	Toggle the display of line numbers in the code window
output	Display application screen
prev	Search for the previous occurrence of a character string
quit	Exit the debugger
restart	Reload and restart application but keep debugger settings
resume	Return to the debugger after viewing a file
speed	Specify the animation speed
step	Execute current source code line and stop
tp	Set a tracepoint
view	View the specified file
wp	Set a watchpoint

The Computer Associates documentation goes into considerable detail about the use of these commands. Remember that many of them have function key short-cuts, like F8 for STEP, and that all can be accessed from the debugger's menu.

The command line keeps a history of your entries. You can recall the most recent entry via the F3 key, or you use the Up and Down keys to scroll through previous entries, and then press Enter to execute the command.

Adding your own features

A very useful side effect of the debugger's ability to evaluate any legal Clipper expression is that you can add your own debugger features. All you need to do is make sure the functions have been linked into the current application. An easy way to do this is via the EXTERNAL command. The following example creates references to the ShowStats() and DispMem() functions, but only if the DEBUG manifest constant is currently defined (see Chapter 7, "The Preprocessor," for details).

```
#ifdef DEBUG
  external SHOWSTATS, DISPMEM, LOGGER
#endif
```

At the debugger's command line, use the ? command to cause the function to be called.

```
? ShowStats()
? Dispmem()
? Logger()
```

From inside the function you can do whatever you want. All screen activity is routed to the debugger's screen and not your application screen.

For example, Listing 10.1 shows how you can pop up a box showing memory status.

Listing 10.1 Display memory status in a pop-up box

```
function DispMem(n)
/*
   Display available memory stats.
   Return .T. if it falls below specified level (optional).
*/
local clr
if n == nil
   clr := setcolor("W+/R")
   @ 10, 40 to 16, 61 double
   @ 11, 41 say "Memory Status      KB"
   @ 12, 41 say "────────────────────"
```

```
   @ 13, 41 say "Total available " +str(memory(0),    4)
   @ 14, 41 say "Largest block   " +str(memory(1),    4)
   @ 15, 41 say "RUN area        " +str(memory(3),    4)
   inkey(0)
   setcolor(clr)
   n := 0
endif
return (memory(0) < n)
```

Note that the function returns .t. if memory falls below the optional specified value. This allows us to use the function as a tracepoint. In the following example the function will cause the application to halt when available memory falls below 125 KB.

```
tp DispMem(125)
```

To pop up the status box, use the ? command and DispMem() with no parameters.

```
? dispmem()
```

Other uses for such functions include writing key information to a log file while the application is running (a form of profiling) and displaying the status of things that are too complex to monitor via a direct tracepoint or watchpoint expression. Use your imagination! If you can link it into your Clipper application you can call it from the debugger.

Classic combinations

There are many combinations of debugger features and functions that may not immediately come to mind. In the final section of this chapter we present a few "classic combinations" of features that seem to be made for each other.

Callstack and Monitor

Combining the Callstack and Monitor windows allows you to browse through the variables in all pending functions in the calling sequence. For example, monitor **locals** and **statics** and then turn on the Callstack window. Select the Callstack window by pressing tab until the window is highlighted. As you move the cursor up and down through the callstack, note how the values of the monitored variables change. If a function has no variables of the monitored class, none are displayed. This often yields an enlightening peek into the havoc caused by private variables.

Monitor and block locals

Code blocks are hard enough to understand when you write them, much less when they are being executed at run-time. At first blush it appears impossible to see what's going on inside a code block while it is being evaluated. However, a combination of Callstack and Monitor windows allows you to peer inside a code block. Let's start with the following simple example. Once you understand the basic technique you can apply it to more complicated situations. (See Chapter 8, "Code Blocks," for more details — you must understand code blocks before you try to debug them.)

First, enter the following into a single source code file. Compile (with /B!), link, and run the resulting .EXE through the debugger. We don't care about anything being displayed on the application screen, so don't run the debugger in /S (split screen) mode. A full screen view of the debugger is easier to use.

```
function Main()
local b
b := { |x,y,z| ;
         BlockHalt(1), ;
         x := 10, y := 20, z := 30, ;
         BlockHalt(2) ;
        }
eval(b, "A", "B")
return nil

function BlockHalt(v)
return v
```

Before executing any lines of code:

1. Select Monitor:Local
2. Select View:Callstack
3. Set a breakpoint on the "return v" line in function BlockHalt(), and
4. Use the Tab key to select the Callstack window

When this is all set up, press the F5 key to begin execution. The breakpoint will cause a halt at the first call to BlockHalt() inside the code block. Since you have the Callstack window selected, move the highlight to the (b)Main line. The (b) indicates a code block is being evaluated in that function. While the (b)Main line is highlighted, the Monitor window will display any local variables that are in scope. Within the code block, variables named **x**, **y**, and **z** are in scope. The display will clearly demonstrate the relationship between the parameters specified in the EVAL() function and the parameters accepted in the code block.

Figure 10.4 Inspecting callstack and local block variables

```
 File   Locate   View   Run   Point   Monitor   Options   Window   Help
                    Monitor: Local                                  Calls
0) X <Block Local, C>: "A"                                    BLOCKHALT
1) Y <Block Local, C>: "B"                                    (b)MAIN
2) Z <Block Local, U>: NIL                                    MAIN
3) B <Local, B>: {|| ... }

                          TEMP.PRG
   function main()
      local b
      b := { | x, y, z | ;
                  BlockHalt(1), ;
                  x := 10, y := 20, z := 30, ;
                  BlockHalt(2) ;
            }
      eval(b, "A", "B")
   return nil

   function BlockHalt(v)

                          Command

>
```

3.13

```
x  "A"
y  "B"
z  nil
```

The breakpoint halted execution at the first place BlockHalt() is called within the code block, so the parameter values are displayed as they exist at the point the code block is initially evaluated. Since we didn't pass a third parameter, the value is NIL.

Press the F5 key to resume execution of the application. The breakpoint in BlockHalt() is still in effect, so the application will halt on the second call to BlockHalt() made from within the code block. Once again, move the Callstack window highlight to the (b)Main line. Note how the Monitor window reflects the local variables that are in scope with respect to the code block. The values have been changed and **z** is no longer NIL, due to the assignments made inside the code block.

You can safely add calls to BlockHalt() anywhere in any code block, since all it does is return the value passed to it. In the following example BlockHalt() will have no net effect on the code block — **num** is multiplied by 10.

```
b := { |num| BlockHalt(num) *10 }
```

In the previous example we numbered each call to BlockHalt(), making it easy to determine which occurrence of the function call is being trapped (the value of **v**, being local to BlockHalt(), is displayed in the Monitor window). Used this way, the last call to BlockHalt() will have a net effect on the code block, since the return value of BlockHalt() will be passed back to the call to EVAL().

You can even preprocess it right out of existence if you want to eliminate the wasted function call when trying for maximum run-time speed.

```
#ifndef DEBUG
  #translate BlockHalt(<v>) => <v>
#endif
```

Watchpoints on database info

There's nothing special about memory variables with respect to watchpoints. The contents of databases and the functions related to their status work just as well. You can set watchpoints on field names as well as RECCOUNT(), RECNO(), EOF(), BOF() and the rest. Use the alias operator to zero in on specific databases. The following commands establish watchpoints on the vendor database's EOF() flag and the value of the Vend_ID field in the invoice database.

```
wp vendor->(eof())
wp invoice->Vend_ID
```

Tracepoints on database info

Are you starting to get the picture? Anything that can be watched can just as easily be *traced*. Why sit and stare at the watchpoint window, waiting for the vendor database to hit end-of-file when you can have the computer do it? The following examples will cause execution to halt when either the vendor database hits end-of-file or a seek fails in the invoice file.

```
tp vendor->(eof())
tp ! invoice->(found())
```

Summary

Now that you know what the Clipper debugger needs for most effective use, and have been introduced to its basic operation, you can take full advantage of the powerful features it offers. You've also been clued in on some important tips and techniques to tap into easily overlooked capabilities. May your bugs be few and far between. Happy hunting!

CHAPTER 11

Designing Database Files

The first step in designing a computer application is to determine the data that needs to be processed and to organize this data in a meaningful way. A telephone book contains a lot of information, but if it were not organized, it wouldn't be much use. Imagine trying to look up a phone number if the phone book was in a random order.

In this chapter we will discuss how to determine the data an application needs and how to organize this data into a coherent file system using the .DBF file structure. We will also discuss data keys and the relationships among files. Finally, we will look at how Clipper can be used to create .DBF files once you've determined their structures.

There are several steps involved in designing a file system from a list of data items. These steps are:

- Systems overview
- Organize entities into logical files
- Define physical file structure
- Test your file structure

It is important during the data design phase to have interaction with and feedback from the ultimate end-users of the system. Each user will have their own view and perception of the data he or she needs to work with. The database design needs to incorporate all these views into a coherent logical structure that can be successfully modeled by the application language.

System overview

The first step in properly designing your databases is to get an overview of the system's functionality. What does the current system do? What are the goals of the new system? Should the computer provide all the functionality of the current manual system?

To get an overview of the system, you should examine the current system (if one exists). The current system might consist of a series of manual procedures or may be a computer system that the company has outgrown. It might be a combination of both. You should talk with all users about the system. Try to determine the entities and what information flows among them in the system.

Keep in mind that the computer will represent a model of the system. Your users will expect to be able to rely on the computer for information, and not on the manual procedures any more. Stock on hand will be determined by consulting the computer, not counting actual inventory.

Determining the data needs

The first step in determining the data that an application must maintain is to collect all the output that the system must be capable of producing. Output consists of printed reports, screen displays, information sent over modems, data transferred to other applications, etc.

The collection of output should not be limited to just the current system. You should strive to include anticipated future needs and changes. It is important to realize that a database is a constantly changing entity. What was extra information in last year's databases may suddenly be required to comply with new tax laws this year.

The future data needs can best be discovered by "blue-skying" with the end-users. Blue-skying means asking the users what they would like to see if there were no limits on the computer or their budgets. For example, a clerk using the A/R system might feel a wonderful feature would be a notes field to record comments while he made collection phone calls. Of course, since the clerk does not know the .DBF structure, this feature may seem like a luxury. Imagine his surprise when your finished design provides that note field.

Identify entities

The system overview will help you identify the entities that your system must work with. An entity is a person or object that the system uses in some fashion. For a payroll system, the entities would include the employee, the paycheck, the time card, etc.

Assume each piece of paper the system must track is an entity and that each organization/department/position is also an entity. Ask whether the system must track information about the entity and if the entity can be uniquely identified. If the answer to both questions is yes, the item probably should be considered an entity (which will eventually become a file) in the system.

All data in the system will belong with one entity or another. Each item in your data dictionary will belong to one file or another when the application is designed for the computer.

Determine relationships

Each entity in the system may be related to other entities. An entity is related to another entity if it owns the other entity, is created by it, etc. For example, an invoice entity belongs to a particular customer. A part might be supplied by one or more suppliers.

Each relationship must be classified as one-to-one, one-to- many, or many-to-many. A one-to-one relationship means that an entity can be related to only one other entity. These are most frequently fields in a physical file.

A one-to-many relationship means that one entity can have multiple occurrences of the second entity, but the second entity can have only one occurrence of the first. Our customer-to-invoice example is a one-to-many relationship. A customer can have many invoices, but each invoice has only one customer associated with it.

A many-to-many relationship occurs when each entity can be related to more than one record in the other entity. For example, a purchasing system which has many sources for parts contains a many-to-many relationship between vendors and parts. Each part can be supplied by many vendors and each vendor supplies many parts.

It is important during this step to classify each relationship. The design of the files will be contingent upon the types of relationships.

Obtain copies of all output the system must produce

During your system review phase, you should obtain copies of all output that the system must produce. This should include planned screen displays and printed reports. It should not, however, be limited just to visible displays/reports only. If the system must produce data to transfer to another system, this data is considered part of the output as well.

The collection of all output will be used to test your file structure later on. Since your computer system needs to produce all of the output, each item in the output must be found somewhere in the system.

Build a data dictionary

Once you've determined the data needed both for the current system and expected future use, you should organize the data into some kind of data dictionary. A data dictionary is a list of all information in the system, along with brief descriptions of its purpose and possibly information about the data type and size. Figure 11.1 illustrates a sample format for a simple data dictionary file stored in a .DBF structure.

Figure 11.1 Sample data dictionary structure

No.	*Field*	*Type*	*Size*	*Description*
1	ELEMENT	C	10	Name of this data item
2	DESC	C	50	Brief description of item
3	SIZE	N	6,2	Size of data item
4	TYPE	C	10	General classification of data
5	FILE	C	8	File name where item belongs
6	DEFAULT	C	25	Default value
7	REQUIRED	L	1	Is field required?
8	IS_KEY	L	1	Is this item a key field?
9	SOURCE	C	1	(S)torage or (D)erived

Currently, much work is being done by various xBASE vendors to define a standard data dictionary for .DBF files. The current .DBF structure is limited to name, type, and size. The future dictionary might include validations, help prompts, required flags, and so on. It is hoped that the xBASE vendors will cooperate so a common standard dictionary will result, instead of many different versions.

It is important while preparing the data dictionary to think in terms of the future. For example, one application tracked the movement of new cars to respective dealerships. A single digit was used for the number of cars that could be carried on a truck. As cars got smaller and carrier trucks got larger, it became possible to carry ten cars on a single truck. Due to the file design, many programs had to be rewritten so that X could represent 10 cars and Y 11 cars.

Once the data dictionary is created, each item needs to be reviewed to determine how the item is derived. There are five general sources from which a data item may be obtained.

Constant or hard-coded data

Some data might be hard-coded into the application program. A good example would be the prompts that appear on a menu. (You did recognize menu prompts as a screen display of output data, didn't you?) If the application is not expected ever to have different prompts, these might be candidates for data that you hard-code into the application.

Any data that's hard-coded into the program will require the program to be changed and recompiled if the data ever needs to change. Making the change might be time-consuming, but such data is very secure from the end-users, unless they happen to be programmers.

Carefully consider any data before you hard-code it. Even the menu prompts might have to be changed if the system is going to be distributed in another country. While hard-coding data also has the advantage of being easy to create, it does require a programmer to change it.

Derived data

Data can also be derived from calculations. A good example would be the total price of several items ordered on an invoice. Since this data can be readily derived from the number of items sold and the price per item, it should not be stored separately in a .DBF file.

In general, a calculation is based on other information in the system and some sort of operation. Derived data is any data which can be created by applying some sort of operation to existing data. For example, in the data dictionary in Figure 11.2, the sales tax is derived from the sales tax rate times the total amount due on the invoice.

Figure 11.2 Derived sample data dictionary

Element	*Desccription*	*Size*	*Type*	*Source*
AMOUNT	Total amount of invoice	11,2	Numeric	(S)torage
TAX_RATE	Sales tax rate	5,2	Numeric	(S)torage
SALES_TAX	Derived from AMOUNT * TAX_RATE	11,2	Numeric	(D)erived

System data

The operating system and the DOS environment maintain various pieces of information that are available to the programmer. For example:

```
? date()           // Returns the system date
? time()           // Returns the system time
```

If data can be extracted from the system, it should be treated as system data. It does not need to be stored, but can be called upon using some sort of function call.

The definition of system data should not be limited to the built-in functions provided by Clipper. For example, if you create a function that returns the full name of a state from a two-character state code, the state name from your function could be viewed as system data.

Input data

Some data will also be input and does not need to be saved. For example, a user-entered password, or the temporary holding variable for the response to the menu prompt. Input data of this sort needs to be identified, just as output data does. The input data might be necessary to control how the output is produced. While the data is not saved, it still needs to be validated and is subject to type and size considerations.

Stored data

Stored data is the basis for the file structure. All other types of data will not be included in the logical views of the file. Any data which the system will need to access repeatedly should be stored in the file structures. For example, in an accounts receivable system, the customer's billing address and phone number would be stored in the customer file.

After all the data is classified, a subset of the data dictionary should be created with just the stored fields. This subset will become the basis for our logical file views, discussed in the next session.

Eliminating redundant data

Once the list of stored fields has been created, we need to review it for redundant information. Redundant information is data that is being maintained in more than one spot. If the same information is updated in multiple programs, it is very difficult to maintain data consistency and to ensure the integrity of the information.

For example, a company might have its payroll and personnel systems computerized. As information is entered into both applications, the possibility exists that an end-user may look at a printed employee report and see different information than his or her terminal displays on that report. If such a situation arises, needless to say, it does not inspire much confidence in the computer system.

To eliminate redundancy, we must first organize our dictionary by data item. As we do this, we need to carefully review each piece of data to see if it truly is a duplicate of existing information. For example, let's assume we are computerizing an existing accounts receivable system. This system tracks customers, invoices, and payments. During our data determination step, we discover that the customer information is kept in rolodexes by the salesmen and in a box of index cards by the invoicing department. A segment of our data dictionary is shown in Figure 11.3.

Figure 11.3 Subset of Data Dictionary

Element	*Description*	*Size*	*Type*
RADDRESS	Billing address in rolodex	25	Character
IADDRESS	Billing address on index cards	25	Character
RCITY	City in rolodex	15	Character
ICITY	City on index cards	15	Character
RCOMPANY	Company name from rolodex	30	Character
ICOMPANY	Company name on index cards	30	Character
RCONTACT	Contact name from rolodex	25	Character
ICONTACT	Contact name on index cards	25	Character

At first perusal of Figure 11.3, it appears that all the data is redundant. This may very well be the case. However, upon talking to the end-users, we discover that the address, city, and company name are truly redundant, but the salesman's contact is normally the purchasing agent and the invoicing department's is usually the bookkeeper or accounts payable clerk. After we remove the redundancy, Figure 11.4 illustrates our new data dictionary.

Figure 11.4 Data dictionary with redundant data removed

Element	*Description*	*Size*	*Type*
ADDRESS	Customer billing address	25	Character
CITY	Billing city	15	Character
COMPANY	Company name	30	Character
PURCHASING	Name of purchasing agent	25	Character
BOOKKEEPER	Name of bookkeeper	25	Character

The process of removing redundant data should be done with the help of the end-users. Data that appears to be redundant on our first pass through the dictionary might not really be redundant. The dictionary should be reviewed as redundant data is removed to ensure that all output that will ever be needed can still be produced.

Redundant data can sometimes be left in the file if there is a good reason for doing so. For example, suppose in our A/R system the bookkeeping department wants an aging list of all customers with their balances due. Figure 11.5 illustrates a sample aging report.

Figure 11.5 - Sample aging report

Customer	*Current Balance*	*31-60 days*	*61-90 days*	*over 90*
ASHTON-TATE	1,000.00	500.00	250.00	100.00
COMPUTER ASSOCIATES	600.00	1,200.00	0.00	50.00
FOX	100.00	0.00	0.00	20.00

As we reviewed the data we determined that the balance field and the aging fields (31-60 days, 61-90 days, and over 90 days) are all derived fields calculated by totalling the invoices based on invoice date.

This means that whenever the aging report needs to be run, the system needs to calculate four field values for each customer. Since this will require that the invoice file be totalled each time, performance of the report could slow down for customers with many invoices.

From a theoretical standpoint, the data should be derived to eliminate the redundancy; however, this might not be practical. If the company has thousands of customers and hundreds of thousands of invoices, the bookkeeper requesting the report might kick off a computer process of two hours or more.

If we accept some redundancy in the file, we could create a separate function called Aging() which would calculate the age fields and store them in the customer file. This function might be run off-hours since it will take some time to run. Then the aging report would simply need to read stored values from the database. Obviously, this report will run much more rapidly.

Even though the report now runs more rapidly, it is only as accurate as the last aging run. The date of the last aging run should be included in the report header. This way, when a clerk displays a customer balance on a terminal that appears different on the report, they can look at the date and realize that the customer has had transactions processed since the aging report was last run.

Redundancy should be carefully considered before it is removed. First, you must make sure that the data is truly redundant, not just different data with the same element name. Second, you must weigh the performance considerations if all redundancy is removed. These should be carefully considered against the extra programming effort required in allowing redundant data.

Organize entities into files

Once you have completed your overview, you should have identified the logical entities with which the system must work. For the most part, each logical entity will represent a logical file in your finished structure. These logical files may require more than one physical .DBF file. The logical file is the end-user's view of an entity within the system. The physical file is the actual .DBF where the data is stored.

For example, a company might maintain a logical file of customers. Each customer has a bill-to address and one or more shipping addresses. To the end-user, this is one logical file, called the "CUSTOMER" file. Yet, when we write the program to work with this file, we would probably create two physical .DBF files, one to hold each customer's billing information and a second to hold the customer's shipping locations. Data normalization will help organize logical files into physical files.

Assign primary and alternate keys

Each logical file in the system should have at least one key. This key must uniquely identify the record and distinguish it from all other records in the file. This key is known as the primary key.

The primary key should be a key that has some meaning to the end-user. For an employee, a good primary key would be the social security number. It is unique and the end-user easily understands it. For other databases, a primary key might need to be created. A customer file would probably have a customer ID code created for it. These customer IDs would be unique to the customer.

Alternate keys are fields which provide alternative access into the file. These keys do not have to be unique. For example, in our customer file, the primary key is the customer ID code. A secondary key might exist for the company name, since the end-user might not remember the code but will recognize the company name when it is displayed on the screen. It is important that the end-users are aware when they use a secondary key that duplicates might exist. When displaying a list of company names, you might also display the company's city and state. This will allow the end-user to select the company they want even if two companies have the same name.

Examples of keys

In order to understand the selection of keys, let's work through an example. Assume a customer file has the structure illustrated in Figure 11.6.

Figure 11.6 Customer file structure

Field name	*Type*	*Size*	*Description*
COMPANY	Char	30	Company name
PURCHASING	Char	25	Purchasing agent
BOOKKEEPER	Char	25	Bookkeeper or A/P clerk
ADDRESS	Char	25	Billing address
CITY	Char	15	Billing city
STATE	Char	2	State
ZIPCODE	Char	10	Zip code
PHONE	Char	14	Area code and phone number
SALES_REP	Char	3	Initials of salesman
CRED_LIMIT	Num	9,2	Maximum credit limit

As we look through this list of fields, the only likely key fields are the COMPANY and PHONE fields. The company name has the potential of being duplicated and the phone number is difficult to remember. So we need to add a new field for a company ID. This field will consist of a user-assigned unique abbreviation for each company in the file. When we create a data entry screen for customers, we will prompt for a customer ID. Our program will have to make sure no duplicate customer ID codes are entered.

Now that we've defined the primary key, let's look for candidates for secondary keys. If we expect to analyze sales by territory, the STATE and ZIPCODE fields combined would probably be a good secondary key. In addition, the SALES_REP field would also likely be a secondary key. If we expect that the customer may be calling in, the phone number would be a good secondary key, since the customer knows his own phone number but probably does not know the customer ID code we've assigned as the primary key.

Assign data items to logical files

Each data item in your data dictionary should now be mapped to a particular logical file. This is done by comparing each element with the keys and determining the key with which the element is associated. For example, if our customer file has a key field of customer-id, we would expect customer name, address, billing contact, etc., to be placed into the logical customer file. The main question for each key is, "If I find this key in a database, what additional fields do I expect to find with it?" Each element in your data dictionary should end up being associated with one primary key. If your relationship shows files linked together, a foreign key will be placed in one file to refer to the primary key of the file to which it is linked.

Organize logical files into physical files

The logical files you've identified up to this point need to be represented in a way the computer can efficiently work with them. What is one file to the end-user might be several files to the computer. There are two main steps in determining your physical file requirements.

Break down many-to-many relationships

Clipper and other relational database packages cannot handle many-to-many relationships. If you have entities which share a many-to-many relationship, it's necessary to break that relationship apart. A many-to-many relationship occurs when each entry in one file can be associated with several entries in another file. The second file can also be associated with several entries from the first file. For example, Figure 11.7 shows a many-to-many relationship between checks and invoices.

Figure 11.7 Many-to-many relationship example

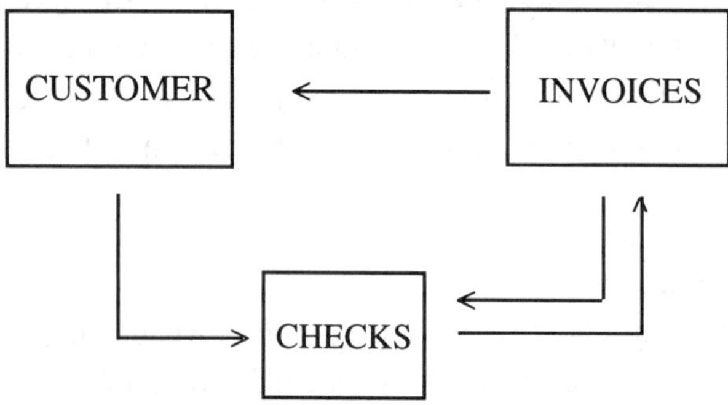

The extra set of arrows connecting INVOICES and CHECKS illustrates a many-to-many relationship. Each invoice might be paid by more than one check and each check might cover more than one invoice.

Since Clipper does not support the many-to-many relationship, we have to model it ourselves. This is done by creating a new database which sits between the two logical files. Figure 11.8 shows how to use an intermediate file to convert a many-to-many relationship into two one-to-many relationships.

Figure 11.8 Broken Many-to-many Relationship

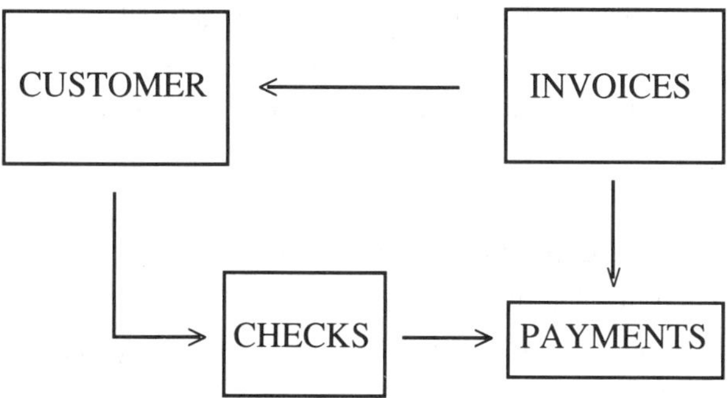

The new PAYMENTS file is used as an intermediate file to remove the many-to-many relationship between the INVOICES and CHECKS files. Now the CHECKS file has a one-to-many relationship with the check number of the PAYMENTS file. One check may have multiple payments, but each payment corresponds to only one check. Similarly, a one-to-many relationship exists between PAYMENTS and INVOICES. Each invoice may have several payments against it, but each payment corresponds to only one invoice record.

The PAYMENTS file in this example is a link file. There is no real world equivalent in the system; it is used only to allow the computer to represent a concept (many-to-many) that is permitted in the real world.

The structure of the PAYMENTS file is shown in Figure 11.9.

Figure 11.9 PAYMENTS.DBF structure

Field name	*Type*	*Size*	*Description*
CHECK_NO	Char	8	Foreign key into check file
INVOICE_NO	Char	12	Foreign key into invoice file
AMOUNT	Num	9,2	Amount of check applied to this invoice.

The PAYMENTS file would have two indexes, one on CHECK_NO and one on INVOICE_NO. These keys are known as foreign keys. A foreign key is a key in a database which is used to link to another database. The key must be the primary key in the related files.

When a check is received, it will be recorded in the check file and an entry will be made in the payment file for each invoice that the check pays. If we need a list of checks that paid a particular invoice, the PAYMENTS file will be selected and searched for all records with the INVOICE_NO number as the key.

Normalize the files

Normalization is an attempt to simplify the files and remove redundant data. Each logical file in your design should be normalized into a set of physical files that can safely model the logical file's structure.

The logical files you've derived from the data dictionary will become the basis for the actual .DBFs the system works with. Logical files represent entities that the end-user views in the system. However, these logical files might not be easily represented in a relational database. The process of data normalization can be used to convert logical files into tables which can be represented via relational data structures.

To normalize a logical file, several steps are taken to eliminate redundant data and help ensure data integrity in the system. While discussions of normalization theory can easily fill books, a brief summary of the key operations is presented here. If you need more details, refer to works by Codd and Date.

Place repeating fields into separate files

All repeating groups should be removed into a separate table or tables. For example, a logical file called INVOICE might contain a customer code, an invoice number, a sales rep, an order date, and so on. In addition, for each line item on the invoice there is a quantity, part number, and price. Figure 11.10 illustrates a logical invoice file.

Figure 11.10 Logical INVOICE file

```
CUSTOMER_ID
INVOICE_NUMBER
SALES_REP
SALESMAN_NAME
ORDER_DATE
QUANTITY      ──┐
PART_NUMBER     ├── These three fields repeat several times
PRICE         ──┘
```

We should break the INVOICE file into two files. One file will contain the heading information and the second file the information from each line item. Figure 11.11 illustrates the logical INVOICE file after the repeating fields have been moved into a separate file.

Figure 11.11 Logical INVOICE file - repeating data moved

```
Header file        Line item detail file
CUSTOMER_ID        INVOICE_NUMBER ─┐
INVOICE_NUMBER     PART_NUMBER    ─┴── Primary key
SALES_REP          QUANTITY
SALESMAN_NAME      PRICE
ORDER_DATE
```

Notice that in breaking the structure into two files we needed to duplicate the INVOICE_NUMBER field. In the line item detail file, this is known as a foreign key. A foreign key in one table must be a primary key in another. It is used to link the files together. Each entry in the line item file would be linked to the header file via the INVOICE_NUMBER field.

Remove non-dependent fields to separate files

Once all repeating groups are removed, you should review your databases for non-dependent data. Non-dependent data is data which is not solely dependent upon the primary key of the logical file.

In our line item detail file, the PRICE is not dependent upon the primary key, but it is dependent upon the PART_NUMBER. Therefore, a second file would be created which contains the part number prices. In addition, the SALESMAN_NAME field is dependent upon the SALES_REP value, not the INVOICE_NUMBER field.

Figure 11.12 illustrates the final version of the INVOICE file. Notice that it has been broken into four separate files.

Figure 11.12 INVOICE file - final version

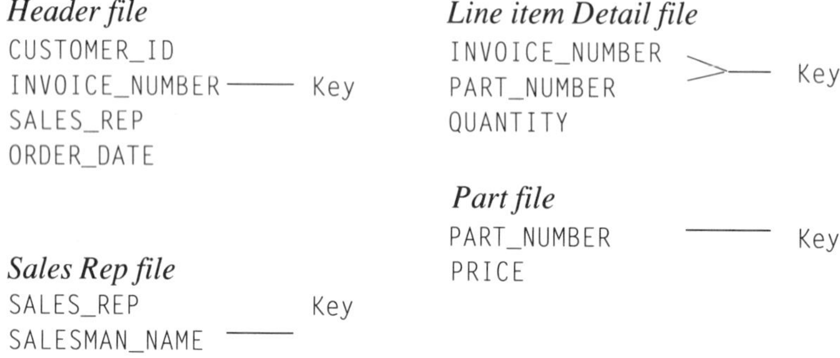

Test your file structure

Once you have finished your file structure, you should test it to see if it can do everything you need it to do. If not, plan on revising the structure in a recursive manner. Make your revision, and test again until your structure is solid. The work you do in properly designing your files will more than pay for itself when you write code.

Can all output be produced from your files?

After you've done a preliminary breakdown of logical files into physical files, you should review the sample output you've acquired during the system overview. For each output item, look at each field on the screen or report. Each data item should be either system-generated, such as the date or time, calculated such as report totals, or most importantly, capable of being extracted from the database. For example, Figure 11.13 shows a sample Customer Balance Due List.

Figure 11.13 Customer Balance Due Report

```
Report Date: Jan 22, 1991      <A>
Report Time: 4:50:00 am

                     JJ & Associates Company   <B>
                     Customer Balance Due Report

Customer     Contact      Phone #         Balance Due     <C>

XXXXXXXXXX  XXXXXXXXXX  XXX-XXX-XXXX  9,999.99
XXXXXXXXXX  XXXXXXXXXX  XXX-XXX-XXXX  9,999.99
XXXXXXXXXX  XXXXXXXXXX  XXX-XXX-XXXX  9,999.99
XXXXXXXXXX  XXXXXXXXXX  XXX-XXX-XXXX  9,999.99

   <D>          <E>          <F>          <G>

                     TOTAL BALANCE DUE   9,999.99   <H>
```

The date and time <A> are probably obtained from the system functions, while the report title <B> and column headings <C> are probably hard-coded data. The actual data items, <D> through <G> are probably pulled from the customer file, although item <G> might be calculated by totalling all the invoices the customer has open. The grand total <H> is probably a sum of all open balances as the report is produced.

By reviewing each report and screen we might identify areas where data cannot easily be obtained. For example, if no balance field exists in the customer file, the balance in the report must be derived from all open invoices. Can this easily be accomplished? If so, how many invoices will a customer typically have open? If the number is high, this report could take considerable time to produce. Will that be acceptable or will the report be run so frequently that processing time is a factor?

Referential integrity

Referential integrity means that any foreign field in any database has either a NULL value or can be found as a primary field in a different database.

Referring to our INVOICE databases in Figure 11.12, we see that the SALES_REP in the INVOICE file is a foreign field to link to the SALES REP file. To be sure that the data structure is intact, the value in the SALES_REP field of the INVOICE database must be either empty or must be a value from the SALES REP file. If any other value exists, the database is corrupt.

You should carefully review your design at this point, and throughout development, to ensure that any time a foreign field is updated it is checked against the appropriate primary key in another file. Also, any time a primary key is deleted, be sure that the deletion will not create a failure of referential integrity.

Organizing the logical structure into .DBF files

Once you've defined a normalized set of files, it is necessary to convert that logical view into a physical set of files the computer can understand.

Computers can identify data only as a bit. All computers are designed to recognize a bit as ON or OFF. As Figure 11.14 illustrates, there are quite a few groupings between the bits the computer "sees" and the "logical database" that the end-user works with.

Figure 11.14 Bits to databases

```
A computer recognizes bits being only ON or OFF.

Bit         An on/off state, such as 1/0 or Yes/No, etc.
Byte        8 bits per byte, allows for 256 different characters.
Field       A group of related characters, such as name, address,
            salary, etc.
Record      A group of fields which are related together.
File        A group of related records.
Database    A system of related files.
```

The End-user recognizes information in a text or graphic fashion.

Clipper's data management system starts at the field level. For designing applications with Clipper, we must therefore start our physical file structure at this same level. Since Clipper will enforce certain rules and restrictions on fields that we define, we can use the built-in features of Clipper's DMS (Data Management System) to our advantage.

A file definition in Clipper consists of a list of fields. Each field has a name, a type, and a size. As we look at each logical file, we can equate that file's attributes with fields in a .DBF file. Clipper supports four field types: numeric, date, logical, and character. The character type can be fixed length or variable length (as in a memo field).

Creating .DBF files

Clipper can read and write files created by dBASE and other xBASE interpreters. It can also create .DBF structures. As each version of xBASE products comes out, there is a possibility that Clipper might not be able to directly work with its files. You should include a utility in your application that creates the files you need.

DBCREATE()

The DBCREATE() function takes a two-dimensional array structure and creates a DBF according to the array's contents. Its syntax is:

```
DBCREATE( <cFilename>,<aStructure> ) [, <cDriver> ]
```

<cFilename> is the name of the .DBF file to be created. The .DBF extension is optional. <cDriver> is the name of the database driver to use when creating the file. See Chapter 18 for more information.The **<aStructure>** is the array which holds the field definitions for the file. Its structure is shown in Figure 11.15:

Figure 11.15 DBCREATE() array structure

Element	*Name*	*Manifest Constant*
1	cName	DBS_NAME
2	cType	DBS_TYPE
3	nLength	DBS_LENGTH
4	nDecimals	DBS_DECIMALS

The manifest constants for the DBCREATE() function can be found in the DBSTRUCT.CH file in the \CLIPPER5\INCLUDE directory.

Listing 11.1 illustrates a sample customer file being created using DBCREATE().

Listing 11.1 Sample DBCREATE() function call

```
local c_fld :={}

Aadd( c_fld,{ "CUSTOMER"  ,"C", 8,0})      // Customer ID
Aadd( c_fld,{ "COMPANY"   ,"C",30,0})      // Company
Aadd( c_fld,{ "PURCHASE"  ,"C",25,0})      // Purchasing
Aadd( c_fld,{ "ADDRESS"   ,"C",25,0})      // Billing address
Aadd( c_fld,{ "CITY"      ,"C",15,0})      // Billing city
Aadd( c_fld,{ "STATE"     ,"C", 2,0})      // State
Aadd( c_fld,{ "ZIPCODE"   ,"C",10,0})      // Zip code
Aadd( c_fld,{ "PHONE"     ,"C",14,0})      // Phone number
Aadd( c_fld,{ "SALES_REP" ,"C", 3,0})      // Salesman initials
Aadd( c_fld,{ "CRED_LIMIT","N", 9,2})      // Credit limit
Dbcreate( "CUSTOMER.DBF",c_fld )
return nil
```

Creating index files

An index file is used to provide rapid keyed lookup to a .DBF file. It does this by creating and maintaining a binary tree which reduces disk searching time. The INDEX ON command is used to create an index file. The SET INDEX TO command is used to associates indexes with .DBF files.

INDEX ON/DBCREATEINDEX()

Either the INDEX ON command or the DBCREATEINDEX() function can be used to create a supplemental index file. The syntax is:

```
// index on command

INDEX ON <expression> TO <cFile_name> [unique]

//  dbcreatindex() function

DBCREATEINDEX( <cFile_name>,<expression>[,<bExpr>],;
                          [lUnique] )
```

<expression> can be any valid Clipper expression, including user-defined functions. The expression must evaluate to the same length for each record in the database.

Using the ***unique*** keyword or setting **lUNIQUE** to .T. instructs Clipper to write only one entry for each occurrence of a key. If a key value returned by the index expression appears more than once, only the first occurrence will be written into the index.

SET INDEX TO/DBSETINDEX()

The SET INDEX TO command or the DBSETINDEX() function can be used to specify the list of index files that should be associated with a particular database file when it is used. It is the same as specifying an index list in the USE command. The syntax for set index is:

```
SET INDEX TO <cIndex_file(s)>
```

The syntax for DBSETINDEX() is:

```
DBSETINDEX( <cIndex_file>,<bExpression> )
```

Once the index list is set, all indexes in the list will be updated whenever a database operation is performed. If there are no index files listed, the set index command closes all open indexes in the current work area.

The list of index files can be literal names or character strings surrounded by parentheses. If the character string evaluates to spaces or a NULL, it is ignored.

See Chapter 19, "Working with Indexes" for more details about index files.

Summary

After reading this chapter you should be familiar with the steps involved in converting the data needs of an application into a physical file structure that Clipper can work with. You should also know the basics of creating .DBF files and indexes within Clipper. Chapter 18 provides more information about working with .DBF files.

CHAPTER 12

Program Design

There are as many ways to design programs as there are programmers. Some are more successful than others—programmers *and* their designs. Is there a common thread running through successful designs? Do failed designs suffer from similar defects? How can you tell success from failure? This chapter is not a step-by-step guide to guarantee good design; there isn't any such guide and hopefully never will be! As we are fond of saying, "If any idiot could program, then every idiot would and no one would pay you to do it." Program design is often a moving target, and programming is an intellectual exercise, not a word-processing task. This is a challenging environment that allows us to continually learn and grow as programmers and designers.

The issues raised and solutions presented in this chapter require a large measure of discipline and motivation to address and resolve. We don't want to come across as arrogant or unrealistic, spouting useless platitudes about programming under ideal conditions for people with lots of time on their hands. Our advice and recommendations have been hard-won over many years of doing it wrong and correcting, doing it right and remembering, and most importantly of all, doing it differently to see if it can be improved.

We will cover:

- Seeking a balance between top-down and bottom-up design.
- The vital importance of modularity.
- How to write reusable functions.
- Suggested programming standards and conventions.

This chapter is based on the premise that you design programs to meet specific real-world goals, not as purely academic exercises. We assume you've got deadlines, finite resources, and possibly even profitability to consider. From this standpoint, the definition of success is a program that meets or exceeds the expectations of the people paying for it. At the same time, we desire more out of life than a mundane grinding-out of source code that works well enough that we get paid for it. Success, then, is also defined as programs that are interesting and even enjoyable to write, easy to understand, reliable, and easy to maintain. (Did we say enjoyable? Yes!)

It's often said that you can't solve a problem until you understand it, and understanding comes from being able to describe the problem and discuss it. After reading this chapter you'll be aware of the issues involved in program design, understand the tools that Clipper provides and how best to use them, and have a set of criteria that define what we consider to be good program design.

Did you catch the "we" in the previous sentence? Good design is subjective, despite what the proponents of various techniques would have you believe. You're reading this book because you program in Clipper, and Clipper is the tool of choice for many programmers because it does not force them to fit a narrow model of the "correct" way to program. We recognize this fact and labor diligently throughout this book to explain the environment in which you're working and to provide tools to help you accomplish your goals. Program design is treated no differently.

There is, however, one section of this chapter that is not at all subjective. In fact, we go so far as to claim that it will forever change the way you program! If you read nothing else, read "Modular Programming Through Static Arrays." It will improve your programming technique and help you produce more reliable code.

Program design vs. specifications

Working definitions of some terminology are in order. There are two distinct kinds of design covered in this chapter: **program design** and **application design**. Programs are the Clipper source code routines written by a programmer, and the "designing" occurs constantly as the programmer decides how to accomplish various objectives. Applications are the final products comprised of the individual routines written by programmers. Application design usually occurs well ahead of the programming and addresses issues from the customer's perspective.

The programs you write are supposed to be based on specifications developed by someone who knows what is supposed to be accomplished. It's rare, and a likely cause for disaster, that you simply fire up your program editor and start coding. At some point someone has to design the application from the point of view of the individuals who want it developed in the first place. Once actual programming is underway, ongoing program design becomes critical to the success of the project, independent of how well the application was designed. Both types of design are discussed in this chapter.

Customers, clients, end-users?

What do you call the people who use the programs you write? What about the people who pay for it? Do you write programs for your customers, for a single company that employs you, or possibly for use in your own business? Rather than getting bogged down in terminology, we'll stick with the word *customer* when we're talking about the people who are paying for the programs you write, even though that term can mean different things to different programmers. We'll use the term end-user when we mean the individuals who literally use your software. In this sense, customers have general concerns about how long it takes you to write programs and how well the programs conform to their expectations. End-users care more about the moment-to-moment operation of your programs. This chapter concerns itself with the "big picture" of application and program design. Chapter 13, "The Art of the User Interface", is dedicated to the care and feeding of end-users.

Top down vs. bottom up

Design techniques can be divided into two broad categories: top down and bottom up. These terms are based on your approach to solving problems. Top down means starting from a global view of a problem and dividing it into smaller and smaller tasks until all design concerns have been met. In the general computer language dialect to which Clipper belongs, this is the traditional way programs are designed. Top down means you start by whipping up a main menu (the "top" of the program) and fill it with a sub-menu choice for each major group of tasks to be performed. For example, the main menu for an inventory tracking system might have choices for entering inventory and vendors and printing reports. Each of those menu choices is likely to have additional menus of their own that keep breaking down tasks into more manageable pieces. Only at the very end of the chain does something useful actually occur, for example, a list of out-of-stock inventory items rolling off the printer.

The top-down approach is favored by programmers because it models the real world as both they and their customers usually view it. As soon as you start programming you can see results. The customer immediately sees the relationship between what they said they wanted you to do and what you've done so far. A top-down design also divides the development project into more easily managed pieces. If more than one programmer is working on the project they can see where their work fits in the grand scheme. It's also easy to assign priorities and deadlines based on such a design. For example, you can decide that the six reports under the End-Of-Year main menu choice can be put off until after the critical data entry and daily reports are working to everyone's satisfaction. Top-down design is widely practiced because it accurately models the process of developing the type of software for which Clipper is ideally suited.

So what is bottom-up? As the symmetrical terms imply, bottom-up means you start out at the end of the chain, so to speak, and design the fundamental tasks that comprise the overall system. The concept is not so literally "from the bottom, up" that the main menu is thrown together only at the last possible minute before delivery to the customer. That's a far too simplistic view of the process. The principles of bottom-up design dictate that all the low-level, essential tasks that the program must perform are developed first, and only after they're proven to meet the expectations of the levels above them do you bother to write those higher levels. For example, in the inventory system example, the out-of-stock items report would not be written until the process for determining which items are out of stock has been written. And that process is not written until the mechanics of putting items into and out of inventory has been written. By the time you are ready to write the out-of-stock items report you have already written all the underlying processes that support the information on the report.

Sound difficult? It is, but no more so than top-down. The difference is in when the difficulties occur. If you started with the out-of-stock inventory report you'd soon run into the need to determine which items are out of stock, so you must "fake" it by reporting the contents of a field or memory variable that will ultimately come from somewhere else. You've simply delayed the problem of determining out-of-stock conditions by making it a task to do later.

Ah. Insightful readers have just noted the major flaw in top down design. Going from top to bottom encourages you to put off dealing with details until you have to. You can view all tasks in isolation and possibly miss important relationships between them. When writing the inventory data entry routines you may not realize you need to detect an out-of-stock condition. Only when writing the out-of-stock report do you realize you have to go back and modify the data entry routines to support the condition.

Modifications are the bane of a programmer's existence. Minor modifications are going to happen with any design technique unless the specifications are incredibly detailed and the customer is willing to leave them alone. What we're talking about here is that kicked-in-the-stomach feeling you get when your beautiful 1,000 line data entry routine has to be hacked and spliced to accommodate something for which it was not originally designed. Changes of this magnitude are more likely to occur in a top-down design.

Bottom-up design forces you to understand all the supporting concepts before you write routines that rely on them. Consequently, defects in the application design are identified while writing the supporting programs, which means before they can affect higher level program design. The difficulty most programmers have with a completely bottom-up approach is that, to the customer, nothing appears to get accomplished until the programmer is a good distance into the application. It's also easy to get lost in details and have a hard time seeing how it all must come together. Going back to the inventory application, you might spend weeks writing the fundamental routines for moving items in and out of inventory and tracking vendor shipments and never see how they all fit together, leading to different but no less troublesome design defects that the top-down approach would have identified almost immediately.

A balanced approach

What's a programmer to do? Neither design technique can be relied upon to produce perfect programs automatically. The best approach is one that draws upon the best that each technique offers. As mentioned in the previous section, design occurs at two different times during the software development process. While you're writing specifications you're doing basic *program* design. The *application* design dictates the way the programmer writes the routines that comprise the application. Poor application design is destined to yield programs that fare no better. But even with a perfect application design, flawed program design will produce a final application that does not reflect the correctness of its specifications. Top-down and bottom-up techniques should be applied to both the overall application design and individual program design.

During the initial application design process you need to go from the top and work your way down if for no other reason than to establish a framework for discussions with the customer. You're not likely to get very far into the process if you insist on ignoring their overall needs and keep asking for a detailed description of how everything works. Once you have the big picture you can start working your way down to the details. It's easy to make sweeping changes to a preliminary design should you uncover a major but previously unmentioned design concern. This happens so frequently that we're nervous about every application design until at least one major flaw is uncovered. We even have an acronym for this phenomenon: OBTW. It stands for, "Oh—by the way," the phrase uttered by a customer who's about to trash several hours of painstaking design work. If you bounce between the top, taking in the overall scope of the project, and the bottom, getting all the details necessary to support your decisions, the resulting design will stand a chance of surviving its first encounter with reality.

During the development of programs that are expected to meet the specifications, top-down and bottom-up techniques should be applied almost simultaneously. Start with a top-down design that rapidly lays the framework for the entire application. This is usually expressed in the data entry screens and report layouts developed in the specifications stage. At the same time, database structures must be constructed that support the data entry and reporting. You can't get much closer to the bottom than a list of fields in databases. As long as you keep performing "reality checks" against the database structures while you work on the topmost levels of the design you stand a better chance of avoiding monumental mistakes that require dozens of changes to propagate through existing source code.

When working on the fundamental routines that the rest of the application will rely upon, you must decide where to invest your efforts and assess how well you understand both the task at hand and the tactics needed to implement it. If you don't understand the problem, it doesn't matter how well you know Clipper—your solution will be appropriate and correct only by accident. The converse is true, too. An expert who completely understands the problem but doesn't know how to use Clipper properly is just as unlikely to write a good program. Not surprisingly, a balance must be struck. Experts are better utilized for solving problems, and programmers for programming. This is why experts who are also good at programming are always in great demand.

We can't tell you how to design and implement the many detailed and unique components of your applications. If we could, we wouldn't need programmers; instead, we could simply use program generators. But that goal is many years away. We can, however, lay the groundwork for the development of programs that are a) efficient and consequently enjoyable to write, b) reliable even through inevitable design changes, and c) easy to maintain over time.

The remainder of this chapter is dedicated to describing how to best design and implement Clipper programs that meet the goals of efficiency, reliability, and maintainability.

Modularity

While designing and programming Clipper programs and applications you should keep reminding yourself of one word: MODULAR. Stick it on your wall, write it in the dust on your monitor. In the context we are discussing, modular means:

Short A small number of lines. If the routine is more than an editor screen or two long it will be increasingly more difficult to test and maintain. As the routine approaches hundreds of lines it becomes close to impossible to understand, much less maintain. At 1,000 lines it's out of control.

Quick Written in one sitting by one programmer. If it takes a week to write there will be less continuity.

Concise Able to be understood in its entirety by someone other than the original programmer, without requiring hours or even days of intense study. This is directly related to size.

Robust Written in such a way that, once thoroughly tested and installed, the routine won't cause undesired interactions with the rest of the application. When appropriate, the routine detects errors and possibly even takes corrective action, or at least documents the problem for the end-user or the programmer.

Such routines are fit together to perform complex operations, rather than having a single routine that attempts to handle the entire operation. Any given routine should not by itself be complex. Complicated tasks are broken down until the individual subtasks can be implemented with routines that meet the above criteria for modularity.

The opposite of modular routines are huge routines written over a long period of time. We've seen thousand-line (and more!) monolithic routines that were probably never correct in the first place and were then edited and "maintained" to the point that no one, not even the original programmer, can say they understand what is happening.

Being able to design and implement the solution to a complex problem is hard enough. Adding the stipulation that the solution must also be modular makes it even more difficult. There is no substitute for the experience you gain once you've created several applications. Doing it wrong a few times is the best way to understand and appreciate the right way. Seeing a design all the way through from inception to implementation, testing, documentation, and several rounds of modification and maintenance is the only way to learn the process in a meaningful way.

Rather than ending this discussion with the somewhat depressing "take your lumps" approach, here are a number of important Clipper programming concepts you can take advantage of right from the start:

Scope Clipper provides *total control over access* to variable and function names.

Side Effects Clipper allows you to *completely eliminate the side effects* of a function call.

Errors Clipper can *detect, trap, and recover* from a wide variety of run-time errors. It can also help you *detect programming errors* through compiler switches.

Scope

Variable and function scope is the single most important addition to the structure of the Clipper language. The availability of truly "private" variables, via the **local** scope, and an alternative to the dangerous **public** variables, via the **static** scope, allow a programmer to completely control a function's run-time environment and design applications that are easier to test and more reliable. The introduction of static functions makes it possible for multiple programmers to work on the same application without the previously unavoidable naming conflicts. The preprocessor also contributes to scope-related improvements through the #include directive. Let's discuss each of these language features in the context of improved modularity. (**static** and **local** scopes are presented in considerable detail in Chapter 6, and the preprocessor in Chapter 7.)

Local variables

Simply put, the use of locally scoped variables will result in better, more reliable Clipper applications. It's not so much what the local scope does as what it absolutely forbids you to do—you cannot pass variables between functions that aren't formally specified. By declaring a variable **local** you are guaranteeing that no other function can "see" the variable, and consequently no other function can change its value. This allows a function to be written, tested, and proven to be correct, then left alone. You don't have to be concerned with bizarre interactions with other functions because:

- Every value coming into the function must be formally accepted as a local parameter.

- Every value leaving the function must be formally released as a parameter to an outside function, or as the function's return value.

- Every other variable in the function is protected from being seen and/or modified by other functions.

If you do nothing else in the way of modular programming, restricting yourself to the use of local variables will produce the most improvements. It will force you to plan ahead and completely document (by virtue of values coming in and out via function parameters) the use of each variable.

Static variables

The **static** scope is often compared to the **public** scope. Public variables suffer from the same deficiencies as private variables—other functions can "see" the variable and therefore manipulate its value. The **static** scope provides you with all the advantages of public variables without any of the problems.

The immediately obvious purpose of static variables is to allow a function to "remember" values between calls. Here's a simple function that counts how many times it's been called.

```
function Counter()
static count := 0
count++
return nil
```

You use this function in place of the following equivalent function, which uses a public variable to do the same thing.

```
function Counter()
if type("count") == "U"
  public count := 0
endif
count++
return nil
```

The problem with the second version of the function, aside from being more complicated, is that no other function in the entire application, including all libraries that might get linked in with the source code, can use the name "count" as a public variable. In a large application, especially one with more than one programmer, it's highly likely that name conflicts arise. You have to resort to special naming conventions to avoid conflicts, and even then, can't guarantee that you don't have a duplicate. With static variables, every function in the entire application can have a counter variable, and none will conflict with the others.

Our Counter() function with the static variable has one major problem: Being **static**, the count can't be seen by the rest of the application! Not much use in maintaining the counter if we can't see it. The solution is to follow the same admonition as for local variables: If you want to let the value out of the function you've got to either pass it as a parameter or return it as a value.

```
function Counter()
static count := 0
count++
return count
```

What good is such a function? Suppose you needed to generate unique numbers in several different places in the application. Each call to Counter() is guaranteed to produce such a number, because each call increments **count** by one. (The number is unique only while the application is running; the next time it starts the counter will go back to zero.)

How about values that must be assignable, not just readable? Public variables are an obvious choice, but once again we can get the same sort of effect from static variables and eliminate the previously mentioned side effects of public variables. The following function is a prototype you can copy for situations where you need to assign and read the value of a publicly available, yet static, variable.

```
function Variable(newValue)
/*
   Get/Set the value of Variable.
*/

//  Assign default value, here, if desired.
static var   //   := ?
local preVar:= var

//  If optional newValue is specified,
//  remember the old value and then assign the new.
if newValue <> nil
   var := newValue
endif
return preVar
```

This function allows you to "get" the value of the variable by calling the function with no parameter. It allows you to "set" a new value by sending it as a parameter. It returns the value that existed before the assignment is made for maximum flexibility. This is functionally equivalent to the way SETCOLOR(), SETCURSOR() and other SET functions operate.

Study the following examples of calls to the Variable() function until they make complete sense. To eliminate public variables from your applications, and thus join the ranks of completely modular Clipper programmers, you'll need to understand this technique.

```
function Main()

/*
 Application begins execution.
*/
? Variable()          //  NIL
Variable("abc")
? Variable()          //  "abc"
? Variable("xyz")     //  still "abc" - why?
? Variable()          //  now "xyz"

return nil
```

Earlier we said that public variable names can accidently be duplicated by other programmers (or even the same programmer in a huge application). We offered static variables as the solution. However, you can still accidently create another Variable() function—so what have we gained? Unlike variable names, function name duplicates are detected by the linker, so there'll be warnings long before a hapless end-user runs into the problem.

This brings us to another powerful feature of Clipper. What about those duplicate function names? Read on.

Static functions

In a large project, and even more so when more than one programmer is involved, it's possible for two functions to accidently have the same name. The linker will catch the problem, but the solution is not very clean: Someone has to go through the entire application looking for calls to the duplicate function names and change the names of some of them. This a waste of time at best, and a tedious, frustrating experience should the worst occur and the editing introduces bugs that must be tested and edited yet again.

Clipper solves much of this problem with the use of static functions, which are conceptually similar to static variables. A static function is visible only to the other functions in the same source code file. Functions in other source code files will not be able to call the static function, because as far as they are concerned the function does not exist. Because of that, the other source code files are free to have static functions with the same names. For example, suppose you have three source code files: VENDOR.PRG, CUSTOMER.PRG and INVOICE.PRG. All three could have a static function called PrintThem() and none would conflict with the others.

Static functions don't completely eliminate the duplicate name problem, but they do make it possible to restrict the visibility of certain kinds of functions. They promote the use of modular *source code files*, which have all the benefits of the modular *functions* we usually think about.

Another important use of static functions is not so much to avoid duplicate function names but to prevent other functions from calling them at all. This allows you to provide a single, "public" access point to a system of related functions in a source code file. You do not have to be concerned about other programmers making direct calls to a supporting function that you don't want used in that way.

Once you allow unrestricted access to a function, you are obligated to support the syntax in the future maintenance of the application. A static function, however, is completely off limits to anything outside of the source code file, which limits the effects of a change to just that source code file.

Another modularity-related feature of static functions is that they allow you to break down long, complex routines into smaller pieces without causing an increase in complexity as far as the "outside world" is concerned. Examples of this are the SaveArray() and RestArray() functions found in Chapter 9, "Arrays." These functions do very little; the real work is done by static functions called ElementOut() and ElementIn(). However, none but SaveArray() and RestArray() may call them. The public application interface is expressed by SaveArray() and RestArray(), which frees the lower-level functions to be implemented in the most efficient way possible. If ElementOut() or ElementIn() is perceived to be too complicated to understand or maintain, additional functions can be created without affecting the way SaveArray() and RestArray() are documented or called.

The #include directive

The preprocessor #include directive allows you to establish a standard way of doing things. Any of the preprocessor-related tips, tricks, and techniques that you see in this chapter (or anywhere else in this book) can be made a regular part of your programming tools. All you have to do is place them in a Clipper header file (.CH) and #include it in each source code file you create.

```
#include "mystd.ch"
```

What's in MYSTD.CH? Anything that you find useful: Manifest constants applicable to your industry or clients, #command and #translate directives for complicated functions, #define directives for small but handy utility functions, and so on.

An #include file can also reference other #include files, allowing you to keep groups of things separated for easy maintenance (a central tenet of modular design) rather than throwing them all together in one large file.

```
/*
   MYSTD.CH  Standard header file for my applications.
*/
//  Common manifest constants (supplied with Clipper).
#include "inkey.ch"
#include "setcurs.ch"

//  Special manifest constants for my applications.
#define MY_COMPANY  "ACME Programming, Inc."
#define MY_PHONE     "(612) 835-1080"

//  Useful commands.

#command DEFAULT <a> TO <b> ;
      =>  <a> := if(<a> = NIL, <b>, <a>)

#command SHUT DOWN ;
      =>  close databases ; setcolor("W/N") ;
          setcursor(1) ; cls ; quit
```

Side effects

Clipper 5 provides complete access to the states of all the commands and functions that have an application-wide effect. You can check the current status at the same time you change it, which gives you the option to restore it if desired.

Here's an iron-clad, no-exceptions rule in modular programming: Functions are not allowed to make permanent changes to the application environment! They can change anything they want, but must be certain to change it back before returning. What are the ramifications of leaving SOFTSEEK set ON when the following routine is finished? Or if we set it OFF again, what happens if the calling routine expects it to still be ON?

```
set softseek on
seek custName
```

The solution is to use the SET() function to save the current value, assign the new, and restore the old back again. _SET_SOFTSEEK is a manifest constant defined in STD.CH, so it is always available along with _SET constants for all the other values.

```
oldSofty := set(_SET_SOFTSEEK)
set softseek on
seek custName
set(_SET_SOFTSEEK, oldSofty)
```

If you take care never to change an application environment setting, even one as seemingly innocuous as SETCOLOR() or SETCURSOR(), you'll eliminate the possibility that one function inadvertently causes another to fail. Such bugs are the worst kind to track down, because each function, in isolation, appears to be working perfectly. The problem may occur only under the right conditions, and sometimes only after a very precise sequence of events (which will undoubtedly occur only in the branch office 1,700 miles away).

Your best bet is to call upon the services of the functions detailed in "Modular Programming Through Static Arrays," an upcoming section of this chapter. These functions make it so simple to completely save and then restore the entire application environment that it'd be a major design mistake not to implement them. Watch for the following function names, found in Listings 12.1 through 12.8:

SaveEnv()	Save the screen environment
RestEnv()	Restore the screen environment
SaveSets()	Save all of the SET values
RestSets()	Restore all of the SET values
SaveGets()	Save the pending GETs
RestGets()	Restore the pending GETs

All of these functions have been implemented using a stack-based design, so they can be called upon anytime, anywhere they are needed, with no special attention on the part of the programmer.

Programmer errors

If you make use of the /W compiler switch, so that Clipper will display a variety of warning messages concerning your source code, you'll find your applications are better structured and less prone to simple mental errors causing run-time crashes. The most common programmer error is the simple misspelled variable name. The /W switch will warn you whenever a variable name is encountered that has not been formally declared. It will detect the error in the code example below.

```
function Foo(id, qty)
local i, j, vendorName
  for i := 1 to qty
    venderName := LookUp("vendor", id)
    ShowIt()
  next i
return nul
```

Ok, so you probably noticed that "vendorName" was misspelled in the for..next loop. So will the compiler if you allow it to. The compiler can also detect that the return value of "nul" isn't defined—gotcha!

If you take care never to proceed with the linking step until all of your source code compiles "silently" with the /W switch, you will eliminate a large class of common run-time errors. If /W is not used it is entirely possible that the application containing the flawed Foo() will escape detection for months, even years, until the right conditions occur and Foo() is called upon to do its duty. You will then go through all sorts of trouble trying to get the end-user to explain the error they're experiencing, hunting down the source code, fixing the error, compiling, linking, testing, and finally mailing out a new .EXE. All that hassle can be avoided through a simple compiler switch.

Run-time errors

Even the concept of a run-time error has been made modular through the ERRORBLOCK() function. ERRORBLOCK() is used to establish a local error handler and has the ability, like all such functions, to save and later restore the previous one. See Chapter 28, "The Error Object," for a comprehensive discussion on ERRORBLOCK() and error recovery strategies. (We're limiting our comments in this chapter to design issues.)

The functions you design have the obligation to detect, avoid, and possibly recover from errors when appropriate. Not all functions should be laden with error checking. In fact, it is frequently more important that the function halt the application with a run-time error, rather than attempting to detect and recover from it.

Deciding when, and to what level, error checking is appropriate depends primarily on how difficult it is to test and verify a function's correctness, and the ramifications of an error. If an error could bring down the entire network, it's worth detecting and avoiding. If an error will show up in regular testing and is completely related to syntax or the programmer's implementation, then it is not worth the additional code. Let's look at some examples.

Suppose you write a function that accepts an array of part numbers and deletes each one from a database. What should happen if a part number isn't found in the database? The only way to determine the correct course of action is to know the context in which the function is called. If the function is supposed to be a general-purpose deletion function, then it has no business performing user-interface duties. A different function should handle the task of warning the user that one or more part numbers can't be located, and then prevent the call to the deletion function in the first place (MODULARITY!) Perhaps it doesn't even matter; it may be possible that a part number doesn't exist due to the way the application was designed. The only error checking that must be done is that the DELETE command not be issued unless the part number is found. Beyond that it depends on the application's context. Each function you design should be viewed in this way.

The primary reason the record deletion function is so difficult to design is that it relies on things outside of its control, namely, an array of part numbers and the contents of a database file. This should be your first clue that a function needs some attention regarding error checking. Functions that are completely self-contained, or that rely solely on parameters passed to them, are not likely to be in need of comprehensive error checking.

A less ambiguous example is that of simple parameter checking. The following function goes to ridiculous lengths to detect and inform the end-user about programmer mistakes.

```
function ShowMessage(r, c, msg)
/*
   Display specified message at specified coordinates.
*/
if valtype(r) <> "N"
  @ 0,0 say "Error: Row parameter isn't a number!"
elseif (r < 0) .or. (r > maxrow())
   @ 0,0 say "Error: Row parameter is outside screen " + ;
             "boundary!"
endif
if valtype(c) <> "N"
   @ 0,0 say "Error: Column parameter isn't a number!"
elseif (c < 0) .or. (c > maxcol())
```

```
   @ 0,0 say "Error: Column parameter is outside screen" + ;
             "boundary!"
endif
if valtype(msg) <> "C"
  @ 0,0 say "Error: Message parameter isn't a character " + ;
            "string!")
elseif len(msg) < 1
   @ 0,0 say "Error: Message parameter is empty!")
endif

//  Now it's safe to perform the command!
@ r, c say msg

return nil
```

Although it's patently silly, this function illustrates an important point about this kind of error checking. It's almost useless for both the programmer and the end-user to find out about the error this way, when the regular run-time error handler will document it just as well. Proper testing of all calls to the function should be sufficient to guarantee that the row and column parameters are reasonable numbers and that the message is a non-empty character string. Worst of all, the function doesn't do anything with the information it worked so hard to gather. In this example, you are better off eliminating error checking altogether. The additional code may actually serve to make the function less reliable! Even as it currently stands the function will be difficult to maintain. Imagine you add three more parameters. Think of all the work you will have to go through just to test the code that is already there.

You should be on alert whenever error checking logic is part of a function. Be careful to distinguish between errors that can be traced back to the programmer and consequently should be uncovered during reasonable testing, and those that stem from the run-time environment.

Modular programming through static arrays

If you forced us to choose just one Clipper 5 feature, the decision would be painful. But eventually we would have to admit that file-wide (or "external") static arrays are our favorite feature. File-wide static arrays are so elegantly powerful that we can't imagine programming without them. Although such a claim looks ridiculous here in print, we truly believe that this section of the chapter will forever change your approach to programming. You will learn how to use file-wide static arrays to your best advantage with stack-based functions that encapsulate both data and code into true "black boxes".

Our first stack-based function: the good housekeeper

After reading the earlier discussion regarding the absolute requirement of zero side effects, you should realize that it's good programming practice for any function to clean up after itself. Such housekeeping should include resetting the cursor position, size, color setting, screen contents, work area, and so on.

The following example shows how a Summer '87 function has to be structured to save and restore this information. Note we are unable to save and restore the cursor size, because Summer '87 does not include any functions permitting this.

```
function ewe_dee_ef

private oldcolor, oldscrn, oldrow, oldcol

oldcolor = setcolor()                  && save color setting
oldscrn = savescreen(0, 0, 24, 79)     && save screen contents
oldrow = row()                         && save current row
oldcol = col()                         && save current column
*
* body of function
*
setcolor(oldcolor)                     && restore color
restscreen(0, 0, 24, 79, oldscrn)      && restore screen
@ oldrow, oldcol say ""                && restore cursor position

return ""
```

This is as far as you can go without significant effort. However, with file-wide static arrays at our disposal, this becomes an inferior (if not obsolete) technique. There is nothing to prevent you or some other programmer on the project from inadvertently changing the contents of the **oldcolor**, **oldscrn**, **oldrow** or **oldcol** variables. Further, there is no good reason why you should carry that information around within the function, when the only time you really need it is when you are ready to exit.

Let's rewrite that function again in Clipper 5.

```
function Ewe_Dee_Ef

SaveEnv()
*
* body of function
*
RestEnv()

return whatever
```

Refer to Listings 12.1 and 12.2 for the source code to SaveEnv() and RestEnv(), which we will now discuss in detail.

First, a static array, called **envstack_**, is declared prior to the first function declaration. It starts out with zero elements, because we will add to it each time that we call SaveEnv(). When using file-wide static arrays and variables, you must declare them before the first function or procedure to guarantee that they will be visible throughout the source code file. By contrast, if you declare them within a function, they will only be visible to that particular function, which would immediately defeat their purpose.

The file containing SaveEnv() and RestEnv() must be compiled with the /N compiler switch. This option suppresses the automatic definition of a procedure with the same name as the source code (.PRG) file. If you omit the /N option, the compiler will create a start-up procedure by the same name as your source code file, which will contain only the static declaration prior to the first function call. (See Chapter 1, "Compiling", for more details on compiler switches.)

Important: If you plan to use file-wide static arrays or variables, then be sure that you are compiling with the /N switch. Failure to do so will lead to mysterious run-time errors that will drive you crazy. Get in the habit of using the /N switch. This will require that you always precede your executable code with a function or procedure declaration, but it will be worth the effort because you will certainly want to use file-wide statics to take full advantage of Clipper 5.

The next step is to define manifest constants that represent each environmental item to be saved and restored. This is purely for readability, and is therefore optional. They add absolutely no overhead to the function with respect to its operation at run-time, but are a nice aid to the programmer during design and maintenance.

The SaveEnv() function then creates a literal array as follows:

```
{ row(), col(), setcursor(), setcolor(), ;
  savescreen(0, 0, maxrow(), maxcol()) }
```

It contains the row and column position, cursor size, color setting, and current screen contents.

This array is then tacked on to the end of the **envstack_** array, thus increasing its length by one element. In other words, after the first call to SaveEnv(), **envstack_** will contain one element, which will be an array of five elements:

```
envstack_[1, 1]  // screen row
envstack_[1, 2]  // screen column
envstack_[1, 3]  // cursor size
envstack_[1, 4]  // color setting
envstack_[1, 5]  // screen contents
```

When RestEnv() is called, the length of the **envstack_** array is tested to make sure that it is not empty. (This would happen if you called RestEnv() without first calling the SaveEnv() function.) Remember that because **envstack_** is declared **static**, it retains its value for the duration of the program.

Therefore, when we re-enter the source code file that contains SaveEnv() and RestEnv(), **envstack_** will still contain whatever we put in it earlier.

If **envstack_** contains no elements, we bypass the rest of the function to avoid a bound array access error. Because Clipper arrays are one-based, there can be no such thing as **envstack_[0]**. (Other languages start numbering array elements from zero, which may cause some initial consternation if you are new to Clipper.)

Assuming that **envstack_** contains one or more nested arrays, RestEnv() plucks information from the one at the end of the array.

1. The cursor position is restored with SETPOS().
2. The cursor size is restored with SETCURSOR().
3. The color setting is restored with SETCOLOR().
4. The screen contents are restored with RESTSCREEN().

Finally, RestEnv() truncates the **envstack_** array with the ASIZE() function. This effectively lops off the last element, which has served its purpose.

Bear in mind that none of this stored information is visible in the calling function. Instead, this data is effectively "encapsulated" along with the only functions that need it, namely, SaveEnv() and RestEnv(). This is true modular programming, and obviously was but a pipe dream in Clipper Summer '87 due to the lack of the **static** scope declaration.

Listing 12.1 Save the screen environment with SaveEnv()

```
//  Stack used by both SaveEnv() and RestEnv().
static envstack_ := {}

//  Manifest constants used by RestEnv().
#define ROW     1
#define COLUMN  2
#define CURSOR  3
#define COLOR   4
```

```
#define SCREEN  5

function SaveEnv()
/*
   Save current cursor row/column/size, color, and screen.
*/

aadd(envstack_, { row(), col(), ;
                  setcursor(), ;
                  setcolor(), ;
                  savescreen(0, 0, maxrow(), maxcol()) } )
return nil
```

Listing 12.2 Restore previous screen environment with RestEnv()

```
function RestEnv()
/*
   Restore cursor row/column/size, color, and screen.
*/
local ele := len(envstack_)

//  Avoid an empty array,
//  which would cause an array access error.
if ele > 0

  //  Restore row/column position.
  setpos(envstack_[ele, ROW], envstack_[ele, COLUMN])

  //  Restore cursor state.
  setcursor(envstack_[ele, CURSOR])

  //  Restore color.
  setcolor(envstack_[ele, COLOR])

  //  Restore screen.
  restscreen(0, 0, maxrow(), maxcol(),;
                envstack_[ele, SCREEN])

  //  Truncate array by lopping off last element.
  asize(envstack_, ele - 1)
endif
return nil
```

Saving SETs with a stack

Since the new SET() function gives us access to the global SET variables, it is possible to create a stack-based function that will save and restore these as well. Refer to Listings 12.3 and 12.4 for the source code to SaveSets() and RestSets(). We'll discuss them now in detail.

As before, the static array **setstack_** is declared prior to the first function declaration. It starts out empty, to be added to each time SaveSets() is called. SaveSets() creates its own empty local array, **settings_**, that will serve later for holding all of the SET variables.

We initiate a for..next loop to process each SET variable, based on the counter _SET_COUNT, which is a manifest constant found in the standard Clipper 5 header file (STD.CH). We determine the value of each SET variable with the SET() function, and add that to the **settings_** array. When the loop is complete, we add the **settings_** array to the **setstack_** array.

As with RestEnv(), RestSets() ensures that the **setstack_** array is not empty. It initializes the local array **settings_** to the contents of the last element of **setstack_**.

We then perform another for..next loop to process each SET variable. The SET() function is passed two parameters: the loop counter (which indicates which SET variable is to be affected); and the value (from **settings_**) to be assigned. When the loop terminates, the **setstack_** array is truncated with the ASIZE() function, resulting in the last element being flung into random-access limbo.

Listing 12.3 Save all of the SET settings with SaveSets().

```
//  Stack used by both SaveSets() and RestSets().
static setstack_ := {}

function SaveSets()
/*
```

```
   Save all SET variables onto the SET stack.
*/
local i, settings_ := {}
//  Loop through all SETs to build a subarray.
//  (_SET_COUNT is found in STD.CH)
for i := 1 to _SET_COUNT
   aadd(settings_, set(i))
next
//  Add the subarray to the SET stack.
aadd(setstack_, settings_)

return nil
```

Listing 12.4 Restore previous SET settings with RestSets()

```
function RestSets()
/*
   Restore all SET variables from the SET stack.
*/

local i, settings_, ele := len(setstack_)

//  Avoid an empty array.
if ele > 0

   //  Load subarray from last elements of SET stack.
   settings_ := setstack_[ele]

   //  Loop through subarray, assigning each SET as we go.
   //  (_SET_COUNT is found in STD.CH)
   for i := 1 to _SET_COUNT
      set(i, settings_[i])
   next

   //  Truncate the SET stack.
   asize(setstack_, ele - 1)
endif
return nil
```

Saving GETs with a stack

As you may have already discovered, it is very easy to nest READs in Clipper 5. The following code demonstrates a nested READ within a VALID function.

```
memvar getlist // to squelch compiler warnings

function Main()
local x := 0, dueDate := date() + 14
cls
@ 10, 10 say "Balance: " get x ;
         picture '#####.##' valid credit(@x)
@ 11, 10 say "Due date:" get dueDate
read
return nil

function Credit(balance)
local x := 0, getlist := {}
local oldscrn := savescreen(10, 40, 10, 64)

@ 10, 40 say "Credit (if any):" get x picture '#####.##'
read
balance -= x       // subtract credit from original balance
restscreen(10, 40, 10, 64, oldscrn)

return .t.
```

However, there may be instances where you need a greater degree of control over saved GETs. For example, if you want to construct multi-screen data entry scenarios, it would certainly be handy to have the ability to push and pop active GETs at will.

We have provided a solution via the SaveGets() and RestGets() functions (see Listings 12.5 and 12.6). The methodology for these functions is very similar to that for saving the environment and SET variables.

There is, however, one significant difference. The previous functions were strictly "Last In First Out" (LIFO). That is, the last element(s) saved would be the first one(s) restored. SaveGets() and RestGets() allow you to use LIFO or random access.

SaveGets() saves the current contents of the public getlist array to the **getstack_** array. Instead of returning NIL, it returns the new length of **getstack_**, which you can save to a variable and refer to later.

RestGets() accepts an optional parameter indicating from which element to restore the getlist. If you do not pass this parameter, RestGets() assumes that you wish to use LIFO, and will therefore refer to the last element in **getstack_**. Otherwise, it will use the element that you specify. In the earlier functions, the stack array was always truncated after the restoration process. This is not the case with RestGets(), which only truncates the GET stack if you are using LIFO. If you use random access with RestGets() by passing a parameter, the function will assume that you do not want to discard the last set of GETs. (Imagine the chaos if you restored the first set of GETs, and the last set got trashed! It's not a pretty picture.)

The following code demonstrates the use of SaveGets() and RestGets() by establishing three parallel sets of GETs. Each set of GETs is "pushed" onto the GET stack with SaveGets(), and "popped" off in random order with RestGets().

```
memvar getlist   // to squelch compiler warnings

function Sets_O_Gets
local x := { 1, 2, 3, 4, 5, 6, 7, 8, 9}, y, z

// Save three sets of GETS
for z := 1 to 3
   for y := 1 to 3
      @ y * 2, 0 get x[(z - 1) * 3 + y]
   next y
   SaveGets()
next z
cls

// Restore the second set
RestGets(2)
ReGet()
read
```

```
// Restore the first set
RestGets(1)
ReGet()
read

// Restore the third set
RestGets(3)
ReGet()
read
// display all values
aeval(x, { | a | qout(a) })
return nil

static function ReGet
/*
   Redisplay all active GETs
*/
aeval(getlist, { | get | get:display() } )
return nil
```

The ReGet() function utilizes the get:display() method to redisplay all active GETs. See Chapter 26, "The Get Class," for more details on the use of the GET object class.

Listing 12.5 Save the current set of GETs

```
//  Stack used by both SaveGets() and RestGets()
static getstack_ := {}
memvar getlist

function SaveGets()
/*
   Save current GETs and clear 'em out.
   Returns the stack position where the GETs are stored.
*/

//  Add current GETs to stack.
aadd(getstack_, getlist)

//  Clear the current GETs.
```

```
getlist := {}

return len(getstack_)
```

Listing 12.6 Restore previously saved GETs

```
function RestGets(ele)
/*
   Restore GETs from stack.
   <ele>  Element number to restore, optional.
*/


// Use LIFO (last item in array) if no parameter was passed.
ele := if(ele == NIL, len(getstack_), ele)

// Avoid an empty array
if len(getstack_) > 0 .AND. ele <= len(getstack_)

   // Assign previously saved GETs to current
   getlist := getstack_[ele]

   // Truncate length of array only if using LIFO
   // i.e., no param passed.
   if ele == len(getstack_) .and. pcount() == 0
      asize(getstack_, len(getstack_) - 1)
   endif
endif

return nil
```

Making our good housekeeper great

Nice though SaveEnv() and RestEnv() are, there's room for improvement. The first area we can shore up involves saving the screen. As originally written, these functions save and restore the entire screen. There will be times when this is completely unnecessary. This is easy to address by rewriting SaveEnv() to accept an optional parameter. If you pass this parameter, SaveEnv() will save the entire screen as it presently does. If you skip this parameter, the screen will not be saved.

But what about situations where you only want to save part of the screen? With a little clever logic and type checking, that is easy to handle as well. If you pass an array of four numeric values as the optional parameter, SaveEnv() will use those numerics as coordinates for the screen region to be saved. Therefore, you have three choices for this parameter:

Nothing	The screen will not be saved and restored.
An array	It should contain four numbers, which will serve as coordinates for partial screen to be saved and restored.
Anything else	The entire screen will be saved and restored.

Here is the logic:

```
coords := if(scrn_save == NIL .or. valtype(scrn_save) == "A", ;
                   scrn_save, { 0, 0, maxrow(), maxcol() } )
```

The second area for improvement lies in the cursor and color settings. Why do you want to save these settings, anyway? Because you anticipate changing them, correct? In fact, you might already know what you are going to change them to when you call SaveEnv(), as demonstrated here:

```
SaveEnv(.t.)          //  Save entire screen.
setcursor(0)          //  Shut cursor off.
setcolor("w+/b")      //  Set color the way we like it.
```

After rewriting this scenario several dozen times, it dawned on us that we were making redundant calls to the SETCURSOR() and SETCOLOR() functions. As you may recall, SaveEnv() has to call these functions anyway to return the current settings. So what sense is there in calling them twice?

Therefore, we've modified SaveEnv() yet again (see Listing 12.7) to accept optional parameters to change the cursor and color settings at the same time that it checks their current settings.

Listing 12.7 An improved version of SaveEnv() that can assign cursor and color settings and save a specified region of the screen

```
//  Stack used by both SaveEnv() and RestEnv().
static envstack_ := {}

//  Manifest constants used by SaveEnv() and RestEnv().
#define TOP          coords[1]
#define LEFT         coords[2]
#define BOTTOM       coords[3]
#define RIGHT        coords[4]
#define NTOP         envstack_[ele, SCREEN,1]
#define NLEFT        envstack_[ele, SCREEN,2]
#define NBOTTOM      envstack_[ele, SCREEN,3]
#define NRIGHT       envstack_[ele, SCREEN,4]
#define NSCREEN      envstack_[ele, SCREEN,5]

function SaveEnv(scrn_save, curs_size, newcolor)
/*
   Save cursor row/column/size, color, and screen.

   Syntax: SaveEnv( <coords>, <cursorsize>, <color> )
           All parameters are optional

   Parameters:
     <coords> can be one of three things:
        Nil - do not save the screen.
        Array - four numeric expressions representing
                 the screen coordinates to be saved.
        Other - save the entire screen.


     <cursorsize> is a numeric representing the new cursor
       size to use. If not passed, the cursor size will
       be left unchanged. Refer to SETCURS.CH for the
       appropriate definitions. Use a comma if you want
       to skip this parameter.

     <color> is a character string representing the new color
       setting to use. If not passed, the color will be left
       unchanged.
```

```
    Examples:
    _________

    #include "setcurs.ch"

    //  Do not save screen, turn off cursor,
    //  change color to W/B.
    SaveEnv(, SC_NONE, 'w/b')

    //  Save full screen, don't change cursor,
    //  change color to R/W.
    SaveEnv(.t., , 'r/w')

    //  Save screen buffer between coordinates 10,10 and 14,69,
    //  turn off cursor, leave color unchanged.
    SaveEnv({ 10, 10, 14, 69 }, SC_NONE)
*/

local coords := ;
        if(scrn_save == NIL .or. valtype(scrn_save) =="A", ;
           scrn_save, { 0, 0, maxrow(), maxcol() })

aadd(envstack_, ;
      { row(), col(), ;
       setcursor(curs_size),
       setcolor(newcolor), ;
       if(valtype(coords) == "A",
         { TOP, LEFT, BOTTOM, RIGHT, ;
           savescreen(TOP, LEFT, BOTTOM, RIGHT) },:
         NIL) ;
      })
return nil
```

At first, we had constructed a maze of iif() logic to account for whether or not the second and third parameters were passed. This was because we were worried that passing NIL to SETCURSOR() and SETCOLOR() would be hazardous. (Remember that in Clipper 5, formal parameters are initialized to NIL if they are not actually received by the function.) However, several tests revealed that passing NIL to these functions resulted in no ill effects whatsoever, so we rewrote the logic to pass the parameters whether they were received or not.

Note that if the first optional parameter is not passed, the SAVESCREEN() call will be skipped and the fifth element of this subarray will be NIL. Otherwise, the fifth element will be an array of five elements, namely, the four screen coordinates and the contents of the screen region they encompass.

The only significant change necessary to RestEnv() is to test this fifth element against NIL. If it is not NIL, then RestEnv() knows that it is safe to call RESTSCREEN(). Because the screen coordinates have already been tucked away in the **envstack_** array, there is no need for you to pass them again to RestEnv(). See Listing 12.8.

Listing 12.8 An improved version of RestEnv() that allows for a region to be restored instead of the entire screen

```
function RestEnv()
/*
   Restore cursor row/column/size, color, and screen.
*/

local ele := len(envstack_)

//  Avoid an empty array.
if ele > 0

   //  Restore row/column position.
   setpos(envstack_[ele, ROW], envstack_[ele, COLUMN])

   //  Restore cursor state.
   setcursor(envstack_[ele, CURSOR])

   //  Restore color.
   setcolor(envstack_[ele, COLOR])

   //  Restore screen if it was saved.
   if envstack_[ele, SCREEN] != nil
      restscreen(NTOP, NLEFT, NBOTTOM, NRIGHT, NSCREEN)
   endif

   //  Truncate the array
   asize(envstack_, len(envstack_) - 1)
endif
return nil
```

Writing reusable functions: a case study

The key to the quick production of high quality, reliable Clipper source code is to write less of it. Makes sense, doesn't it? Fewer lines to write means you'll write them more quickly. Fewer lines are easier to test. Fewer lines are easier to maintain. However, we've shifted to a new problem—how to write less code and still be able to work on non-trivial applications? The answer to that question is obvious: The code you write has to do more work. Clipper has all the capabilities we need to meet that challenge.

To illustrate this notion we're going to identify a common program design problem and fix it, step by step, using the concepts discussed in the previous sections of this chapter.

A common problem

The worst waste of time for Clipper programmers occurs when they write long runs of the same code from memory. For example, every time a "Which customer number?" response is required of the end-user it's a major waste of time to write something like the following (from memory, no less):

```
cust:= space(6)
clear gets
setcolor("GR+/B")
setcursor(1)
@ 3, 10 say "Which customer #?" get cust picture "999999"
read
setcursor(0)
setcolor("W/N")
```

A few things change each time this occurs—the row and column, the prompt message, and so on—but the overall structure is exactly the same. If it occurs 20 times in an application there are 20 places that could have errors, 20 places to test and 20 places to maintain. The creation of a very simple user-defined function in Listing 12.9 solves the problem completely.

Listing 12.9 A first attempt at converting in-line code to a general-purpose user-defined function

```
function AskCust
/*
   General-purpose "Which customer #?" prompt:
      r         row,
      c         column,
      message   prompt to display at r, c

   Returns end-user's answer to the prompt.
*/
parameters r, c, message
private answer := space(6)

clear gets
setcolor("GR+/B")
setcursor(1)
@ r, c say message get answer picture "999999"
read
setcolor("W/N")
setcursor(0)

return answer
```

Instances of such a customer number prompt now look like the following.

```
cust := AskCust(3, 10, "Which Customer #?")

delCust := AskCust(17, 8, "Delete which customer #?)
```

Now we have only to worry about testing a single section of code, the AskCust() function, and are free to rely on it in the rest of the application. If the application design changes dictate that customer number prompts should be in a different color, or that a box should be drawn around the prompt, it's a simple matter to edit the source code for the single AskCust() function rather than 20 nearly identical routines scattered throughout the application.

We have successfully employed the bottom-up program design technique to produce a small, fundamental routine that can be proven correct and relied upon to perform a service for the rest of the application. AskCust() is a building block we can use again and again as part of the user-interface in other routines occurring at higher levels.

However, we can't gloat about the AskCust() function as it's currently written. We've violated almost every rule concerning good function design:

- The parameters **r**, **c**, and **message**, along with the return value, **answers**, have too broad a scope. All should be local because they have no use outside the AskCust() function call. The calling routine has its own copies of the parameters and the function returns the response. Even if AskCust() has to communicate with another function it should be obligated to formally pass parameters. Solution: Make all parameters and variables local to the function.

- As written, the AskCust() function stomps all over the general application environment by blindly clearing any pending GETs and assigning colors and cursors. It works fine under some situations, but is needlessly limited in the circumstances it can be called. The GETLIST should be local to the function and the current color and cursor should be saved before they are altered and restored before returning.

- Hard-wired colors were not a good programming practice for the original in-line code and are positively unacceptable in the user-defined function. If you ever want to change the colors for special situations you'll be out of luck because the current AskCust() function supports only one possibility.

- We could get more mileage from the function with the addition of some flexibility regarding the type of response it can solicit from the end-user. For example, if there are prompts for vendor numbers, invoice numbers, salesperson's initials, region codes, and so on scattered throughout the application, there's no reason to have a special-purpose function for each when one general- purpose function will do.

To the programmer's credit, however, the function has a satisfactory comment heading that indicates what the function is supposed to do and describes the parameters and the return value.

Each of the design and implementation deficiencies is easily remedied. We'll rewrite the flawed AskCust() function and use it to continue our discussion of writing reusable functions.

Using proper scope

Let's start by cleaning up the scope issues. Compare Listing 12.10 to the original Listing 12.9.

Listing 12.10 An improved AskCust() function with correct scope

```
function AskCust(r, c, message)
/*
   General-purpose "Which customer #?" prompt:
      r          row,
      c          column,
      message    prompt to display at r, c.

   Returns end-user's answer to the prompt.
*/
local answer := space(6)
local getlist := {}

setcolor("GR+/B")
setcursor(1)
@ r, c say message get answer picture "999999"
read
setcolor("W/N")
setcursor(0)
return answer
```

All we've done is made **r**, **c**, and **message** local by positioning them as formal function parameters and changed the return value, **answer**, from **private** to **local**. We also made the getlist array local so it has no effect on any pending GETs. This eliminates the need to clear the GETs, since as far as AskCust() is concerned there aren't any.

Limiting the side effects

AskCust() is bound to be the culprit in a number of run-time consistency problems because it blindly changes the color and cursor. Listing 12.11 takes care of this problem.

Listing 12.11 Eliminating the side-effects

```
function AskCust(r, c, message)
/*
   General-purpose "Which customer #?" prompt:
      r          row,
      c          column,
      message    prompt to display at r, c.

   Returns end-user's answer to the prompt.
*/
local answer := space(6)
local getlist := {}
local clr, crs

clr := setcolor("GR+/B")
crs := setcursor(1)
@ r, c say message get answer picture "999999"
read
setcolor(clr)
setcursor(crs)
return answer
```

We've eliminated the side-effects by saving the current color and cursor settings (in local variables, mind you!) and then restoring them before exiting the function. The routine calling AskCust() is left in exactly the same state as it was prior to the call. And best of all, we hardly changed the code. Making the new variables, **clr** and **crs**, local is the only additional line of code.

An even better alternative is to dispense with the temporary **clr** and **crs** variables and use the SaveEnv() and RestEnv() functions described earlier in this chapter.

```
SaveEnv("GR+/B", 1)
@ r, c say message get answer picture "999999"
read
RestEnv()
```

Adding flexibility

At this point the AskCust() function is "perfect" in the sense that it does its job correctly and without affecting the rest of the application in any way. A remaining design flaw is the function's very limited nature. Presently it always uses the same color for the prompt message, always presents the end-user with an empty response field, and always uses the same GET picture. Listing 12.12 has a simple solution to these limitations.

Listing 12.12 Making the function more flexible

```
function AskCust(r, c, message, msgColor, defAnswer, pict)
/*
   General-purpose "Which customer #?" prompt:
      r          row,
      c          column,
      message    prompt to display at r, c,
      msgColor   color to use for message,
      defAnswer  default answer to prompt,
      pict       picture to use with GET.

   Returns end-user's answer to the prompt.
*/
local answer := defAnswer
local getlist := {}

SaveEnv(msgColor, 1)
@ r, c say message get answer picture (pict)
read
RestEnv()

return answer
```

Making the function more flexible added only to the function parameters, no additional lines of source code were required (although several were changed). A call to the AskCust() function now looks like the following:

```
//  Regular prompt
//
cust := AskCust(3, 10, "Which customer #?", "GR+/B", ;
                space(6), "999999")

//  A prompt that remembers the previous response
//  and uses a "warning" color of bright white on red.
//
cust2 := AskCust(3, 10, "Delete customer #?", "W+/R", ;
                 cust, "999999")
```

We've added some useful features, but something is going wrong with the function—the call looks too complex. There are too many parameters to remember, especially if they'll usually be the same. We're back to having to maintain a customer number prompt in 20 different places. To be sure, the prompt is easier to maintain than the original in-line source code version, but we're rapidly losing ground by adding too many features. Fortunately there's an easy solution, read on.

Supplying default values

If the AskCust() function is going to be called the same way every time, with only an occasional deviation, we're not helping anyone by making the function call so complicated. Clipper allows us to skip parameters (they are assigned the NIL value) so we can take advantage of this fact and assign reasonable default values whenever a parameter is omitted.

Which parameters have default values? Let's go for broke and make all of them optional. See Listing 12.13 for an elegant way these can be implemented.

r	The current row as defined by row()
c	The current column as defined by col()
message	The phrase "Which customer #?"
msgColor	The color "GR+/B"
defAnswer	An empty prompt, space(6)
pict	The picture "999999"

Listing 12.13 Supplying default values for the parameters

```
function AskCust(r, c, message, msgColor, defAnswer, pict)
/*
   General-purpose "Which customer #?" prompt:
      r           row,
      c           column,
      message     prompt to display at r, c,
      msgColor    color to use for message,
      defAnswer   default answer to prompt,
      pict        picture to use with GET.

   Returns end-user's answer to the prompt.
*/
local answer := defAnswer
local getlist := {}

default r            to row()
default c            to col()
default message      to "Which Customer #?"
default msgColor     to "GR+/B"
default answer       to space(6)
default pict         to "999999"

SaveEnv("GR+/B", 1)
@ r, c say message get answer picture (pict)
read
RestEnv()
return answer
```

With the addition of default parameter values we can go back to making most of the function calls easy to understand and more likely to be written correctly, while retaining the desirable flexibility.

```
//  Back to a reasonable function call.
cust := AskCust(3, 10, "Print for which customer #?")

//  Taking advantage of the default row and column.
@ 17, 22 say "WARNING!"
delCust := AskCust(,, "Delete which customer #?", "W+/R")

//  Yes, even this is possible...
cust2 := AskCust()
```

At this point the function is a prime candidate for being freed from a final limitation. It appears to be tied to soliciting a customer number, while the code is actually capable of a broad range of such prompts. Instead of AskCust() we should give the function a name that implies greater utility, like GetString(). Calling GetString() in a wide variety of contexts brings us back to the previous problem of default values. The default values for a customer number will be different from salesperson codes. To resolve this issue we have two alternatives to consider: More function calls, or a preprocessor translation.

Let's start by making the function into a general purpose prompt. Listing 12.14 contains the new source code.

Listing 12.14 A generic "prompt for a string" function

```
function GetString(r, c, message, msgColor, defAnswer, pict)
/*
   General-purpose "Which customer #?" prompt:
      r                 row,
      c                 column,
      message           prompt to display at r, c,
      msgColor          color to use for message,
      defAnswer         default answer to prompt,
      pict              picture to use with GET.

   Returns end-user's answer to the prompt.
*/
local answer := defAnswer
local getlist := {}

default r               to row()
default c               to col()
default message         to "Your response?"
default msgColor        to "GR+/B"
default answer          to space(20)

SaveEnv("GR+/B", 1)
@ r, c say message get answer picture (pict)
read
RestEnv()

return answer
```

All we've done is change the function name and default message and answer. It's debatable whether or not the new default message and answer are truly useful or not, but they are reasonable.

Alternative 1: More function calls.

To regain the ease of use we lost by eliminating the values that are specific for the customer prompt, we can simply recreate the original user-defined function. This time, however, the function will rely on GetString() rather than reinventing the solution. This is bottom-up design technique in action! Listing 12.15 contains the reincarnation of the AskCust() function.

Listing 12.15 AskCust() returns

```
function AskCust(r, c, message, msgColor, defAnswer, pict)
/*
   General-purpose "Which customer #?" prompt:
     r                row,
     c                column,
     message          prompt to display at r, c,
     msgColor         color to use for message,
     defAnswer        default answer to prompt,
     pict             picture to use with GET.

   Returns end-user's answer to the prompt.
*/

default r            to row()
default c            to col()
default message      to "Which Customer #?"
default msgColor     to "GR+/B"
default defAnswer    to space(6)
default pict         to "999999"

return GetString(r, c, message, msgColor, defAnswer, pict)
```

Now we are free to optimize calls to GetString() by calling AskCust(), instead. Within AskCust() we can make life easy on programmers by allowing them to skip parameters with the knowledge that the default values will be reasonable. GetString(), however, remains unmodified and unaffected. If it was working correctly before it will continue to work correctly no matter how many such functions are added to our application.

This alternative is best used when each variation has a different set of default values that are also likely to be overridden on a regular basis. If the default values will be rarely (or even better, never) changed, the preprocessor is a better choice.

Alternative 2: Using the preprocessor

Rather than creating more functions you can use the preprocessor #translate directive to make GetString() appear to be more than a single function. Listing 12.16 shows the directive for the AskCust() function.

Listing 12.16 A preprocessor-based version of AskCust().

```
#translate AskCust( <r>, <c>, <msg> ) ;
       =>  GetString( <r>, <c>, <msg>, ;
              "GR+/B", space(6), "999999" )
```

With this #translate directive in effect, a call to AskCust() is converted at compile-time to GetString() with additional parameters.

```
//  Original source code
cust := AskCust(3, 10, "Which customer #?")

//  Result after preprocessing.
//  (Split into two lines here for clarity)
cust := GetString(3, 10, "Which customer #?", ;
          "GR+/B", space(6), "999999")
```

You maintain the AskCust() translation just like any other function call. If you need to override the default values you must call GetString() directly. This is why the preprocessor alternative is best taken when the parameters for AskCust() rarely change.

We can, however, make GetString() easier to use by creating another preprocessor #translate directive (Listing 12.17). This time, however, we break from traditional function call syntax where the *position* dictates the parameter.

Listing 12.17 Using the preprocessor to make GetString() easier to use

```
#translate GETSTRING( [ AT <r> [, <c> ]] ;
                      [ MESSAGE <msg> ] ;
                      [ COLOR <clr> ] ;
                      [ DEFAULT <def> ] ;
                      [ PICTURE <pict> ] ;
                          ) ;
  => GetString(<r>, <c>, <msg>, <clr>, <def>, <pict>)
```

The translation process allows the programmer to specify the parameters in any order by associating a descriptive label with each. You don't need to know much about GetString() to understand what the following function call is doing.

```
vend := GetString(message "Which vendor?" color "W+/B" ;
                  picture "@!" at 15, 2 default space(4))
```

The preprocessor translates this strange-looking syntax into the more traditional (and acceptable to the compiler!) syntax, below.

```
vend := GetString(15, 2, "Which vendor", "W+/B", space(4), "@!")
```

In one bold stroke we've satisfied both the GetString() function's requirement that each parameter appear exactly in its designated position, and the programmer's common lament that too many parameters are difficult to keep straight. Keep in mind that since GetString() supplies reasonable default values for all of the parameters we are not obligated to specify them, even when using the #translate version.

```
//  Original source code
who := GetString(default "HSY" at 6)

//  After preprocessing
who := GetString(6,,,,"HSY",)
```

See Chapter 7, "The Preprocessor," and Chapter 13, "The Art of the User Interface," for more details about the preprocessor and examples of user-defined commands.

Adding realistic error checking

Our earlier discussion on modularity stressed checking parameters for errors. This is particularly important when parameters have default values that could conflict with parameters actually passed, or with respect to other contexts, like database records.

The AskCust() and GetString() functions do not lend themselves to illustrating the parameter-error issue because there's very little that could go wrong. The addition of error checking code is not justified for what we would gain in reliability. It would be better for the application to crash with a run-time error than to attempt to identify the problem and offer recovery. The programmer can easily test the function call in the course of normal application testing.

Both functions do, however, have the potential for end-user errors. For example, what should happen if the end-user leaves the field empty? Is this acceptable? What should happen if the Escape key is pressed?

We could add yet another parameter, used to determine whether or not an empty field is acceptable, and keep displaying the prompt until they either enter something or press Escape. (You must always offer a way out, lest the end-user plan on spending the day camped out at your prompt.) No matter how the issue is resolved, the function needs to be able to return additional status to the calling routine. There's no way the GetString() function can determine what the next course of action should be if the end-user abandons the prompt.

Standards and conventions

Consistency is the single best thing you can strive for when designing applications and programs. This is especially true of the thousands of lines of source code needed to implement your designs. If nothing works out for you and the final results are bad, at least they'll be consistently bad and there's hope that you can go back and learn from your mistakes. If you jumped all over the map you're bound to make the same mistakes again. The same goes for the good results you were hoping for—if it was implemented consistently you can be certain why your design was successful.

If consistency is good for a single programmer working on a small project, it's excellent for long term projects and positively critical for multiple programmers working together on the same project.

Complete consistency is one of the hardest parts of source code management. Programming techniques evolve over time and the demands of each individual application often force you to alter your techniques. Despite the inherent difficulty, you must give it your best shot and stay with it. If you are working with multiple programmers or programs written over a long period of time, every minute spent on maintaining consistency will pay off ten times* over in debugging, maintenance, and modifications.

As we mentioned earlier, we have nothing to say about the specifics of your programming problems. It's up to you to solve problems and hopefully be consistent about it. We have plenty to say, however, on the subject of the nuts and bolts of Clipper programming. We don't need to know every little detail of your design to make observations and suggestions about the way the Clipper source code is written.

We'll start by describing the different ways Clipper programs can be consistent and then provide you with a starting point—an ad hoc list of source code conventions.

The keyword here is **conventions.** You undoubtedly follow many conventions already, but you may be hard pressed to explain why. For example, do you write language keywords, like PARAMETERS and WHILE, in all upper case letters? Do you always put an "m" in front of memory variable names? Just sometimes? Most conventions are formed when you first start programming in the language and rapidly become habits. However, your early experiences are not the best foundation for establishing habits. Part of the problem, we believe, is confusion between two very distinct kinds of conventions: educational and production.

*The figure ten times was not derived from any study or research whatsoever. We just made it up. This is one of those bogus statistical figures that 92% of the population routinely quotes with absolutely no justification.

Educational conventions

Educational conventions are used to describe and document the correct implementation of the statements, commands and functions that make up a language. They are designed to be used universally and must be as clear and unambiguous as possible. They avoid relying on prior knowledge whenever possible. Consequently, such conventions also pack as much information as possible into a few lines of code or even a small code fragment.

Computer Associates has dramatically improved the way they document Clipper. The confusing <expN>, <expC> notation of the past has been replaced with a very good naming convention. Contrast these two versions of the Clipper documentation on ACHOICE():

```
Summer '87 version:

ACHOICE(<expN1>,<expN2,<expN3>,<expN4>,<array1>
        [,<array2> [,<expC> [,<expN5> [,<expN6>]]]])

Clipper 5 version:

ACHOICE(<nTop>, <nLeft>, <nBottom>, <nRight>,
        <acMenuItems>,
        [alSelectableItems | <lSelectableItems>],
        [<cUserFunction>],
        [<cInitialItem>],
        [<nWindowRow>])
```

You don't need to read much further in the Clipper 5 Reference Manual to get a quick refresher on how to use the ACHOICE() function. The first character of each element is used to indicate its type, followed by a very brief description of what the parameter is used for. The Clipper 5 manual calls these initial characters "metasymbols." Each symbol carries information about itself. You know right away that the nTop, nLeft, nBottom and nRight parameters are numbers, and you should be able to guess what they are used for if you know even a little about ACHOICE(). Notice that some parameters have more than one metasymbol out in front. For example, the "al" indicates an array of logical values. After some experience you can read the parameter lists very quickly, yet get a significant amount of information. Clipper's reference manual has more details about metasymbols and other conventions used in documenting the language.

Another convention, which has historical roots going all the way back to the first release of dBASE-II, is the use of upper case letters for language keywords. Many, many dBASE- dialect programmers (in fact, we'd wager the vast majority) follow this convention. We do not, and in fact, discourage the practice. This doesn't mean it's not a good convention! Indeed, it's very important that Computer Associates follow the convention because they are documenting and explaining their language, not the applications written in the language. Uppercase letters alert you to the fact that you're looking at a part of the language and not a miscellaneous part of the example. Contrast the following examples of some new Clipper 5 concepts. The code is functionally the same, but which one carries more information?

```
LOCAL AFILES := DIRECTORY("*.DBF"), ANAMES := {}
AEVAL(AFILES,;
      { | FILE | AADD(ANAMES, FILE[F_NAME]) };
      )

LOCAL aFiles := DIRECTORY("*.dbf"), aNames := {}
AEVAL(aFiles,;
      { | file | AADD(aNames, file[F_NAME]) };
      )
```

If we examine the second example very carefully we can learn a great deal about how the language is being used. For example, we know that LOCAL and DIRECTORY() are Clipper keywords because they are all caps. We know that DIRECTORY() returns an array because the first letter of **aFiles** is lower case and is the metasymbol for "array". We can assume then that AEVAL() expects an array as its first parameter. The list goes on, and all from some simple conventions. When you're learning about Clipper the keywords are very important: The all caps convention alerts you to their use. Variable and parameter types are important so you are clued via the metasymbol convention.

If Computer Associates' conventions are so great shouldn't you follow them, too? Sometimes, but not always! It's appropriate to follow Computer Associates conventions when trying to explain things about Clipper to other programmers, when writing articles for publication, and when documenting general purpose library functions that you have written. You should follow Computer Associates' conventions whenever you are writing code for purposes of education or documentation. Anyone reading your code will immediately be familiar with it. They will be able to extract information from the code itself, independent of comments or other background material you supply. The conventions alone will help document your code.

This book is not a substitute for the Computer Associates reference manual. We are not obligated to carefully document each Clipper command and function each time we use one in an example. There are numerous occasions, however, where we introduce a new feature or function and need to follow the educational conventions so it's easier to understand. The net result is that we switch between conventions as we see fit rather than forcing the entire book to follow a single convention.

Those hypocrites!

Readers alert to the subject of programming conventions have noticed this book frequently doesn't follow its own advice! The efforts of three authors are represented in these pages. Each author had his own, often incompatible conventions as the project began. After a few fights over formatting and plenty of nervous handwringing by the editors, an attempt at consistency was enforced. This chapter was written primarily by one author, so his conventions "won" to that extent. The rest of the book follows them, but only to a point.

This is an example of the classic "Do as I say, not as I do" argument. If you get nothing else out of this chapter, remember this: Consistency. Three authors spread over three parts of the country, programming at different times and for different reasons, did not stay very consistent. We all have individual idiosyncracies and have already returned to them, despite the best efforts of this book's editors. Your goal is to impose as much consistency as you can; first and foremost on *yourself*, and secondly, on those with whom you are working. It really will pay off for you in the long run.

Production conventions

Production conventions are used when you are writing code for applications as opposed to education. This is where our presentation gets very subjective. The rest of this section is a list of conventions we try to follow. We attempt to enforce these conventions on all who write code for us. The more consistent the code the easier it is to read and maintain. Programmers routinely balk at first but settle down into it quite rapidly.

Many of our conventions are designed to help our source code editor search/replace functions get more "hits". If you write sloppy and inconsistent code you'll have a hard time tracking down every occurrence of a problem. If you are being rigorously consistent you will be able to trust your editor when it says "none found". Same goes for pattern searching utilities like the Norton *Text-Search* or O'Neill Software's *Text Collector*. You amplify the power of such utilities when you write consistently.

Far be it from us to develop programming rules for you to follow. As long as you're willing to do things consistently, we've successfully argued our point. This section should be used for examples of programming standards and conventions. If you follow them you'll find your code is easier to read and maintain because it is consistent, not because we received divine guidance or stumbled upon magic rules for success.

A discussion of such conventions follows. The order is not significant.

Keywords are in all lower case. We use lower case for keywords because it feels more natural to type that way. Making them all caps is time consuming and makes them STAND OUT TOO MUCH IN THE SURROUNDING CODE, IF YOU KNOW WHAT WE MEAN. The language keywords are obvious enough and there aren't that many. Keywords are not as significant as the application-specific parts of your code, so why make them stand out so much? The human eye can distinguish between lower case letters much more easily and rapidly than the uniform and sometimes nearly identical upper case letters. Code that is in ALL CAPS is very hard to read on a 43-line VGA display.

Keywords are never abbreviated. Abbreviating keywords is counterproductive and misguided. Especially worrisome is the Clipper 5 compiler's willingness to accept END to terminate control blocks of any type. Consider the following three alternatives.

```
//  #1                #2               #3
//  What?             Better            Best

    end               endif             endif   // k > 0
  end               endcase           endcase   // keystrokes
end               enddo             enddo       // .not. eof()
```

We're not advocating putting comments after every END, just when there's a large number of lines between the start of the block and the end. Even without seeing the source code preceding these three lines you can tell what is going on in alternative #3. Seeing #1 in the midst of a complex routine offers no help at all, and #2 is only a marginal improvement.

Variable names. Memory variable names are in all lower case, most of the time. They should always start with a lower case letter. Sometimes you may wish to capitalize letters in compound words to make the name more readable. They should never be all upper case.

```
foobar := 1234
vendDate := date() +30
```

Extremely short variable names imply that the scope of the variable is very limited. One-letter variables are never used to control large loops or pass global information.

```
i := 5  //  Must be used locally
```

Over the years many conventions regarding variable names have formed. The letters **i**, **j**, and **k** are used in many languages for for..next loop iterators. An **n** is usually a number, **c** a single character, and **s** a string of characters. If you adhere to these conventions your code will be easier to understand than if you deliberately go contrary and assign character strings to **i** and numbers to **c**. As you might suspect, Clipper programmers have their own special cases that run in opposition to such almost universal conventions.

Here are a list of suggested interpretations for single letter variable names. Note that several have multiple meanings and depend on the context in which they occur.

```
a     array
b     code block
b     TBrowse object
c     column
c     single character
c     TBColumn object
d     date
e     Error object
g     Get object
i     iterator in for..next loops
j     iterator in for..next loops
k     iterator in for..next loops
k     inkey() value of a keystroke
l     logical value
n     integer
o     object of an arbitrary class
r     row
s     string of one or more characters
x     floating-point number
x     implies any data type can be used
y     implies any data type can be used
z     implies any data type can be used
```

Procedure and function names that we create are made “proper” to distinguish them from language keywords. They are never all caps.

```
a := MyFunction()     //  Must be a user-defined function
b := directory()      //  Must be a Clipper function
```

References to database and alias names are in all capitals. Database manipulation is usually the purpose of our applications and the all upper case names stand out in the surrounding code, alerting you to the fact that a database is being manipulated.

```
use VNDFILE alias VENDOR new
select VENDOR
do while .not. VENDOR->(eof())
  skip alias VENDOR
enddo
```

Manifest constants are traditionally all upper case. The Clipper 5 preprocessor is sensitive to case for manifest constants so using all upper case will help prevent accidental substitutions. Since only database and other file names and aliases are in all caps it's unlikely that we'll confuse a manifest constant with anything else.

Manifest constant names follow a naming convention that places them into functional groups and hopefully clues you about which #include file they came from. Computer Associates has followed such a convention for most of the #include files that come with Clipper. The following prefixes have significant meanings in our source code.

```
CLR_  Screen color and attribute controls (also, C_)
CNF_  Default configuration parameters
LIB_  Library constants or flags
PAG_  Page margins
PRN_  Printer control codes (also, P_)
SYS_  System installation parameters
```

References to field names always use the alias prefix and are made proper (mixed upper/lower case). Since a memory variable never starts with an upper case letter, and fields always do, we can easily tell them apart.

```
//  If alias is permissible, use it.
CUSTOMER->LastName

//  If not, the convention helps even more.
c:block := fieldblock("LastName")
```

Work area numbers. We never, ever use the work area numbers or letters with the SELECT command. Database flow is hard enough to track without obscuring the intent with SELECT 1, SELECT C or other nonsense. When you see a line like SELECT VENDOR you know exactly what is going on. Always use the alias when selecting work areas. Take advantage of the NEW clause of the USE command:

```
use VENDOR new
use CUSTOMER index CUSTNAME alias CUST new
```

Alias prefix. We always use the alias prefix in front of anything that could possibly be affected by it regardless of how obvious it appears to be. This cannot be stressed enough. We routinely "audit" our staff's code in nitpicking, minute detail, red-penning any instance where the alias could have and should have been used.

```
select VENDOR
seek u_vend
if VENDOR->(found())
  //
endif
select VENDOR
goto top
do while .not. VENDOR->(eof())
  skip alias VENDOR
enddo
```

You never know when you might insert a block of code between a SELECT and a subsequent reference to EOF(), BOF(), FOUND(), RECNO() and so on. If you always include the alias you'll never have a problem. In the following example, what happens if the DoSomeThing() function selects a different work area and doesn't reselect VENDOR on exit? If you used the previous version you could add the call to DoSomeThing() and be certain that no matter what it does the main loop will work as intended.

```
//  Potential for work area trouble.
select VENDOR
goto top
dowhile .not. eof()
  DoSomeThing()
  skip
enddo
```

Use SELECT frequently. As indicated in the previous examples it's always a good idea to issue a SELECT immediately in front of anything that could possibly be affected by the work area. This means every single GOTO TOP, SEEK, LOCATE and so on should have a SELECT in extremely close proximity. It's way too easy to have the work area change on you unexpectedly. One of our worst debugging nightmares is tracing code that assumes the correct work area is selected through long chains of function calls. It doesn't slow program execution appreciably (if at all) to issue redundant SELECTs.

In fact, you can go so far as to eliminate the need for SELECT entirely. For each database-related command that does not currently have an alias option, you can add one via the preprocessor. See Chapter 7, "The Preprocessor," for a complete discussion of this topic.

We don't use the M-> alias on memory variables because we are so fanatically consistent about using aliases on field names. Additionally, using M-> gets to be a real bother and makes the code hard to read. Far better to compile with the /V switch and always make explicit scope assignments.

```
static this
local that
field SomeThing in SOMEDBF
```

Inline assignment operator (:=), use it! Always. Never use regular equals sign, ever. You'll always be able to track down assignments independent of other references. If you don't leave a space between the variable name and the operator, or just one space, or two, or whatever—that's fine. Just do it consistently.

```
//  Pick one convention and stick with it:
a :=1
b :=2
c := 3
```

Array names always end with an underscore so you can distinguish them from regular memory variables. It also makes the subscript easier to see in dense code lines. In the following example, which parameters are arrays?

```
item_[7] := "ALEX"
SomeFunc(this_, that, other_)
```

The convention of prefixing arrays with an "a", followed by data type they contain, is also helpful in some situations.

```
//  An array of characters, called Names.
acNames := {"Ralph","Carol","Robert"}
```

Local memory variables follow a less rigid naming convention that helps identify their data type or origin. Note that by "local" we mean memvar used in single functions rather than globally, not necessarily limited to the local scope. We don't intend to follow Computer Associates' metasymbol prefix. We've experimented and it doesn't feel right for production coding.

For example, we've found that data entered by the end-user is important to program flow and it helps to know when you're dealing with a user response to a prompt. You may ask for a value at the top of a long routine and start referencing it far below. We use a **u_** prefix for such information, as illustrated in the example below.

```
select ORDER
seek curDate +u_customer +u_dept
```

Use of the underscore character. We must admit we've been guilty of massive inconsistency in the past but are now reformed. We use the underscore character to indicate that the left side of the symbol name is grouping two or more of a similar kind of thing, differentiated by the right side.

```
? prn_rmar      //  PRN_ implies there are several,
? prn_lmar      //  RMAR, LMAR etc are all related
? prn_tmar      //  because they share the prefix.
? prn_bmar
x:= Ed_Cust()   // ED_ forms a set of related functions.
y:= Ed_Vend()   // CUST, VEND and ITEM are particular
z:= Ed_Item()   // editors in that set.
```

Using this convention you can look at something in isolation but know that it has related instances that may need attention. If you see a compound symbol name without an underscore you know that it's one of a kind or isn't related to anything else.

```
? prnValue      // Printer related, but a special case
t:= CalcTax()   // A calculation routine, unrelated to
                // other functions, one-of-a-kind.
```

Field values copied into memory variables. A common and highly recommended practice is to copy values from database fields into memory variables, edit the variables, and save them back to the database. Never edit the fields directly. It's a real bother to make up completely new variable names to hold the field values so many programmers have adopted the "m" convention. We always thought this makes the code hard to read, especially if you're using "m" as a prefix to other things. Our convention is to use a leading underscore. We don't use a leading underscore for anything else so we always know when we're looking at a memvar containing a copy of a field value.

```
_code      := CUST->Code
_amount    := CUST->Amount
```

Be wary of using more than a single underscore character. Computer Associates uses double-underscore prefixes to denote internal values.

Block/column structure. We spend time making our source code line up in columns whenever it looks like it might help. Well-formatted columns will actually help you find bugs! Can you see the problem in the code below?

```
//  Break "hunk" into logical pieces
id:= substr(hunk, 1, 7)
operCode:= substr(hunk, 8, 5)
marker:= substr(hunk, 3, 4)
descript:= substr(hunk, 17, 30)
notes:= substr(hunk, 47, 20)
```

Now do you see it in the columnized version?

```
//  Break "hunk" into logical pieces
id:=       substr(hunk,  1,  7)
operCode:= substr(hunk,  8,  5)
marker:=   substr(hunk,  3,  4)
descript:= substr(hunk, 17, 30)
notes:=    substr(hunk, 47, 20)
```

If you can't see it, look at the assignment to the variable named "marker". Doesn't it stick out, breaking the pattern? It's supposed to be 13, we accidently omitted the "1". Easy to spot in the columnized version. We like to line up all sorts of things, especially @..SAY..GET commands and other things that are supposed to line up on the screen.

```
@  2,  5 say "Name "           get _name
@  4, 17 say "Address  "       get _address
@ 11, 32 say "Notes/comments"  get _notes
```

Sometimes it's a waste of time, no doubt about that! You have to decide if a collection of source code lines will benefit from being lined up. In the above SAY..GET example we can scan the GET column and quickly see all the field names. In the example below we've gone all out to make the components stand out. We quickly can tell which GET has a picture or a valid clause. Formatted this way they're very difficult to miss.

```
get _name     picture "@!"        valid ValName()
get _address                      valid ValAddr()
get _notes    picture "@S 50"
```

Long source code lines. We avoid writing lines that extend beyond the visible right margin of the screen. (An exception is when defining report headings, we know they usually extend way over). The purpose is obvious—it's easy to miss what you can't see. Use the semi-colon line continuation symbol and indent multiple lines to be readable.

```
do while (VENDOR->Category == u_cat) ;
         .and. (VENDOR->State == u_state) ;
         .and. .not. VENDOR->(eof())

@ 3, 5 say "This is a long prompt for the field" ;
       get _theField picture (somePict) ;
       valid ValidFunc()
```

Continuation of expressions vs. parameter lists. We always let commas trail at the end of the current line and move operators to the beginning of the next line. This often makes it easier to determine what you're looking at in complex lines. It also imparts consistency, which never hurts.

```
if SomeFunc(  parameter1, parameter2, ;
              parameter3, parameter4  ;
            + parameter5, parameter6, ;
              parameter7)

@ 10, 5 say  this ;
           + left(that, 15) +" " ;
           + str(num, 6, 2)
```

We prefer to write FUNCTIONS over PROCEDURES. Functions are structurally compatible with the way Clipper 5 is designed. Procedures are still around for compatibility with earlier versions only. Among many deficiencies, the worst is the inability to use anything but **private** parameters. This alone banishes them from the ranks of modular programming tools. Do yourself a favor and write functions exclusively.

PRIVATE and PUBLIC. All procedures and functions must declare their scratch variables **local** to avoid conflicts. Use of **public** and especially inherited variables is avoided whenever possible.

Inherited variables (those passed down to sub-procedures in the hierarchy) are too much trouble and are to be avoided, period. If you have too many parameters to pass efficiently then develop a special naming convention and *document* them in the procedure which creates them. *Mention them in comments in every sub-procedure* which references them. And for gawd's sake don't be altering the values!

A far better solution is to tuck all the values into an array and pass the array to the functions that need them. The preprocessor can be used to retain the benefits of descriptive variable names. In the following code fragment, rather than passing 17 parameters to the FormLetter() function, we send an array with 17 elements. We give variable-like names to each of the elements to make it easier to understand the source code. This allows us to avoid the strongly discouraged practice of making the 17 variables **private** and allowing FormLetter() to inherit them.

```
#define name            param_[1]
#define address         param_[2]
//  etc.
#define paramcount      17

local param_ := array(paramcount)
```

```
name := "Heather"
address := "6340 Greenbriar Avenue"
//  etc.

FormLetter(param_)
```

LOCAL and STATIC, use them by default. Start out every variable as **local** or **static** and change it to **private** or **public** only if absolutely necessary. Don't use **private** unless you've got scads of existing Summer '87 code that isn't worth converting. Not all code will convert to **local** and **static**. If functions further down in the calling sequence need access to a value the value should be passed in the formal parameter list.

Logical levels are indented two or three spaces. We don't use tabs because in some text editors they expand and shoot everything over to the right edge of the screen and make printed source code harder to read. Two or three spaces seem to be sufficient to keep the logical nesting straight when reading the code. The default eight characters per tab is way too much space.

```
do while ...
  if ...
    for ...
      do case...
      endcase
    next
  endif
enddo
```

Very Important Note to Lazy Programmers: Don't skip adjusting the indentation when you add or remove a large logic level! We've had to clean up messes resulting from such sloth too many times. The compiler won't let you get away with really serious errors but why even tempt it?

```
do while .t.
if DBF->Amount = 0
  //
 // about 600 lines of code
  //
endif
skip
enddo
return
```

The above code is a time bomb waiting for some innocent (or even the guilty original) programmer to make a change somewhere in the middle. Buy a dedicated source code editor that can shift blocks of text by columns. Some editors can indent and adjust your source code automatically. Also, buy a code analyzer and sic it on every piece of poorly formatted code you encounter. Good analyzers will tell you where your if..endif, do..enddo, case..endcase problems are and many will even properly indent them for you.

Temporary files. Establish a file-naming convention for temporary files and stick to it. We usually use the prefix $TMP and never allow an application end-user to create file names starting with a dollar sign. That way we can ERASE $TMP*.* with wild abandon and not accidentally erase an end-user's file.

Documentation

Groan! Documentation—the necessary evil? It doesn't have to be. It's rare to find a programmer who doesn't agree that lots of documentation is good and a complete lack of documenation is bad. It's also rare to find a programmer that, despite nodding in agreement, actually does document his or her source code at an acceptable level. Here are some typical lies (or good intentions?) commonly used in justification of not commenting source code.

1. *I'll comment it after I'm finished.* Ha! As a programmer, you're never "finished" with software. The project gets wrapped up and yanked out of your hands at some point by someone interested in getting on with other things. The time to write comments is when you write the code that needs the comments.

2. *Commenting slows me down.* Good! Rapid, unstructured code cranking is second only to poor testing in the world of software development disasters. If you take the time to comment your code you're demonstrating to yourself that you understand the problem and your own solution. If it takes 200 unbroken lines of code before you know if you're on the right track, you're not on the right track.

3. *My code is self-documenting.* The key word here is "self". Comments are as much for other people as for you. What seems perfectly clear today may be unintelligible next year when you come back to maintain the code, or when the proverbial beer truck runs you down and your replacement sits down at what was formerly your keyboard. Much of what is considered self-evident actually relies heavily on the context in which it occurs. While under initial development, the database structures and relationships between various parts of the application are part of your daily life. Comments that describe these relationships are indeed unnecessary—as long as you throw away the code when you're done.

We have identified five distinct kinds of documentation and source code comments. The next five sections describe a standard format and minimum level of completeness for each.

System level

A single text file, perhaps called SYSTEM.DOC, should contain a list of all the files used by the application, both for development (PRG, CH, LNK, LIB) and run-time (DBF, NTX, MEM). Along with each filename include a brief, one sentence description of the file's purpose or what it contains. This file forms the table of contents for the rest of the documentation. If a file exists in the application or run-time directories it should have an entry in this file. See Figure 12.1.

Figure 12.1 Sample system level documentation

```
***                                                   ***
*** SYSTEM.DOC for the Acme Inventory System          ***
***                                                   ***

Programmers: John Smith, Mary Jones, Tracy Anderson,
     Ajax Programming Services.
```

```
DEVELOPMENT SECTION
===================

Source Code Files
_________________

MENU.PRG        Startup and main menu functions.
INVENT.PRG      General inventory edit and simple lists.
VENDOR.PRG      Vendor-related editor and lists.
PHYS.PRG        Physical inventory process.
CLOSE.PRG       End-of-month and end-of-year closing.
STAT.PRG        Main inventory status report.

Header Files
____________

AJAX.CH         Standard Ajax constants and commands.
ACME.CH         Acme-specific stuff.

Linker Script Files
___________________

DEBUG.LNK       Special debugging version
ACME.LNK        Regular production version

RUN-TIME SECTION
================

Database Files
______________

INVENT.DBF      Main inventory
VENDOR.DBF      Vendor list
HIST.DBF        History file
CAT.DBF         Inventory category codes

Index Files
______________

INV_ID.NTX      Main inventory by item number
INV_DESC.NTX    Main inventory by item description
INV_CAT.NTX     Main inventory by category
VENDOR.NTX      Vendors by code number
CAT.NTX         Inventory categories by category code
```

You can go to great lengths to document at the module level, but be aware that once you start you've got to keep it all up to date or it's not worth the trouble. Determine what level you and your fellow programmers are willing to support and then keep on top of it. Documentation at this level is the most difficult to maintain.

This is also the place to clearly document any static variables or note any other file-wide issues that the reader should be aware of, like preprocessor directives.

```
/*
   Static arrays to hold run-time configuration:

       colors_  Color settings
       files_   List of database files
       cats_    List of valid inventory category codes

   Preprocessor:

     CHECKCLOSE Command that combines the closing-verification
                steps so they can be called easily in several
                different places.
*/
```

Function level

Each function should have a heading that gives a brief description of what it does, plus details on what the parameters are for, which are optional, which have default values, and what the function returns. Also relevant at this level is the name of the programmer responsible for the function and possibly a revision history, if you want to track them this carefully. The /* */-style comment markers should be used due to the often lengthy nature of the comments (Figure 12.4).

Figure 12.4 Sample function level documentation

```
function CloseMonth(month, trialOnly)
/*
   Purpose: Close the specified month, optionally
     in a "trial mode" where no data is actually posted.

   Author: John Smith
           (Mods to trial close stuff by T.A.)

   Syntax:  CloseMonth( nMonth, [ lTrialMode ] )
   Returns: .t. if successful, .f. if not.

   Parameters
   ----------

   month        Month number to close.
   trialOnly    Optional flag for trial-close, default is .f.
*/
```

Don't get so caught up in carefully and completely documenting every single function that you "burn out" and stop doing it altogether. It's far more important to skip the occasional obvious functions (but still include some rudimentary header comments) so you're willing to really put the effort into the functions that desperately need clear, detailed documentation. Too often, projects start with ambitious good intentions that are abandonned before they can do anyone any good.

Another thing to keep in mind is that outdated, obsolete comments are sometimes as bad as no comments at all if they mislead the maintenance programmer.

Section level

In sufficiently large functions (which, according to the modular design recommendations in this chapter, should not occur very often), the source code should be divided into smaller sections and documented almost as if it was a separate function. (Hey, here's an idea— yank it out and make it into a static function.) If nothing else, at least insert a large, visible break where a major logical division occurs. "White space" costs your application nothing but will be appreciated by anyone who must read and understand the function.

```
/*-------------------------------------------------------------*/
/*           ESTABLISH THE DEFAULT SETTINGS                    */
/*-------------------------------------------------------------*/

blah := blahblah

//  50 lines later

/*-------------------------------------------------------------*/
/*              DISPLAY DATA ENTRY SCREEN                      */
/*-------------------------------------------------------------*/
```

In-line comments

There are two kinds of in-line comments: Those immediately preceding a line (or a small number of lines), and those that are tacked on to the end of a source code line.

The first variety are strongly encouraged. It's almost impossible to have too many, unless you go overboard and document lines that should be obvious to anyone with a reasonable amount of Clipper programming experience. A rule of thumb: If you are particularly proud of a section of code it's more than likely because it's tricky or was difficult to figure out. This is a red flag situation—you might not remember exactly why it was so nifty and the next person to maintain the code isn't likely to be impressed by undocumented tricks.

The second variety, same-line comments, are discouraged in all but a small set of circumstances. The rule is: The comment must be very brief and be strictly limited to something in the same source code line. Unless you do some fancy editing, the comment will be traveling with the source code line, so it best be relevant to, and only to, the line to which it's attached.

```
/*
   Good use of same-line comments
*/

key := inkey(0)
do case
case key = K_F7  //  Delete current record
case key = K_F8  //  Display vendor summary screen
endcase
```

The problem with the examples below is that even minor editing of the routine will likely require you to shift the comments all over the place.

```
/*
   Bad use of same-line comments
*/
for i := 1 to len(a_)  //  Process array and check status
  ListName(i)
  if CheckStat()        //  If .t., call error log and exit
    if .not. neterr()
      ErrorLog()
    endif
    exit
  endif
next
```

Clipper 5.2 has introduced the concept of INIT and EXIT procedures into the language. An INIT procedure is the first procedure called prior to your program startup and an EXIT procedure is the last procedure called after your program has finished.

INIT/EXIT procedures

INIT/EXIT procedures are usually contained in separate program files that can contain STATIC and LOCAL data variables. Each procedure can only be called by Clipper internally and is not accessible to the rest of your program. However, the ANNOUNCE statement can be used to make the INIT/EXIT set of procedures visible to your application

In order to understand the power of INIT and EXIT, create a procedure to save the screen before your program begins, and to restore it afeterwards. Call the procedure SAVEWORLD.

```
* Program..: SAVEWORLD
*
*

ANNOUNCE SaveWorld          // Name for application

#define DOS_SCREEN    1
#define DOS_ROW       2
#define DOS_COL       3

STATIC aStuff[ 3 ]

INIT PROCEDURE dosSave()
      save screen to aStuff[ DOS_SCREEN ]
      aStuff[ DOS ROW ]        := ROW()
      aStuff[ DOS_COL ]        := COL()
      return
```

This program creates a function called SAVEWORLD that is registered as an INIT/ EXIT procedure. The ANNOUNCE statement tells your application the name of this procedure.

The syntax for the ANNOUNCE statement is as follows:

```
ANNOUNCE  <cProcName>
```

The code itself merely saves the screen and cursor location to static variables fo both can be restored during the EXIT procedure.

You would compile this program and link it in as part of your application.

To have your application program call this procedure at program startup time and again at exit, merely request the ANNOUNCEd procedure name. To do so, use the REQUEST statement within your application:

```
REQUEST <cSomeAnnouncedProcedure>
```

By adding this request statement to the top of your program, you have added an entry into the INIT and EXIT lists. When the Clipper program starts, all procedures in the INIT list are performed sequentially (i.e., in the order you REQUESTed them). When you quit the program, all entries in the EXIT list are performed in the same order.

Summary

Important points made in this chapter:

- Good design techniques are best gained by experience.

- Clipper 5 provides you with all the tools you need to produce efficient, reliable routines. In a word: Modularity.

- There are simple tactics you can use that help make the goal of highly modular programming easier to maintain.

- If you aren't planning on using the SaveEnv(), SaveSets(), and SaveGets() functions, or variations of them, in your very next Clipper application, you didn't read the section on static arrays carefully enough.

- Consistency is more than just a good idea, it's central to the design and implementation of applications that can be programmed and maintained efficiently.

- And if you haven't heard it a thousand times before, we stress it once again: Document your work.

This chapter ends with the beginning—the issues raised and solutions presented require a large measure of discipline and motivation to address and resolve:

- doing it wrong and correcting
- doing it right and remembering

and most importantly of all, doing it differently to see if it can be improved.

CHAPTER 13

The Art of the User Interface

The "art" of the user interface? That's right — professional design and implementation of user interfaces is truly an art form. Few programmers are naturals. The majority must study the basics, develop skills, and learn the correct use of the tools at their disposal. When the end-user is busily making menu choices and entering data, they should hardly be aware that the interface is there. The interface should work intuitively, efficiently, and stay out of the user's way.

Another important but often neglected consideration is the fact that end-users respond far more positively to attractive interfaces than ugly ones. Therefore, it would behoove you to learn more about how to increase the face value of your programs.

This chapter will provide you with a firm understanding of the basic user interface features found in Clipper. After discussing the basics, we will proceed to create a comprehensive set of tools for getting and validating user input, and managing the contents of the screen and colors. When you are finished reading this chapter, you will find yourself demanding nothing less than a perfect user interface, because you will have the right tools.

Caveat

The opinions expressed in this chapter are admittedly subjective. Our definition of a good user interface is one that provides intuitive and efficient access to your application's features and the user's data. This definition encompasses an incredible variety of implementations. The tools provided in this chapter meet this goal in a way that we like and feel comfortable with. However, if you disagree, all is not lost. The underlying principles of user interface design do not change, and you will certainly be able to adapt our solutions to meet your specific needs.

Criteria

There are nine basic criteria for a good user interface. We'll consider each one in the following sections:

- Consistency
- Focus
- Easy to make the right response
- Difficult to damage something
- Immediate feedback
- Always keep the user posted
- Efficient keystrokes
- Easy escape hatch
- Validate the obvious

Consistency

The first rule of user interface design and screen layout is consistency. Even if you end up with a bad design, at least it will be a *consistently* bad design which can be modified in a straightforward manner. Consistency is best attained by routing all user interface activities through a small collection of functions. If you are using a library of standard user interface functions, often all you have to do is tweak the library and the actual application-specific source code does not even have to be recompiled!

Another good thing about rigorous consistency is that the end-user can suffer through a bad design if it is predictable. In fact, many users cannot tell the difference between good and bad, and will use anything you throw in front of them. This is not to say that they will like it; they may simply assume that "this is life with the computer" and not actively complain. If you have a bad design that is *also* inconsistent, you will have frustrated end-users and much more trouble identifying what is wrong with the design. If every prompt and every data entry screen needs to be examined separately, you and your users are in for a long, tedious process.

By always using standardized functions you will automatically end up with a consistent user interface. All end-user responses will be routed through a relatively small number of routines, so a modification to a library routine will affect all calls from the main application. It also reduces the size of the main application because you will not be forced to write the same blocks of code over and over again.

Focus

The second rule is focus. A well-designed user interface and screen layout makes it obvious what the end-user should do next. The screen should only contain information that is relevant to the task at hand.

Prompts and questions should stand out from the background text. If the program is waiting for an end-user response, it should be made quite obvious. Overlaid boxes and shadows can be used to draw the user's attention to prompts. Highlight colors can also be used to make something obvious. The highlight color or box should be removed immediately so the next prompt is not confused with the previous.

Compare Figures 13.1 and 13.2. Which screen is focused?

Figure 13.1 Unfocused screen

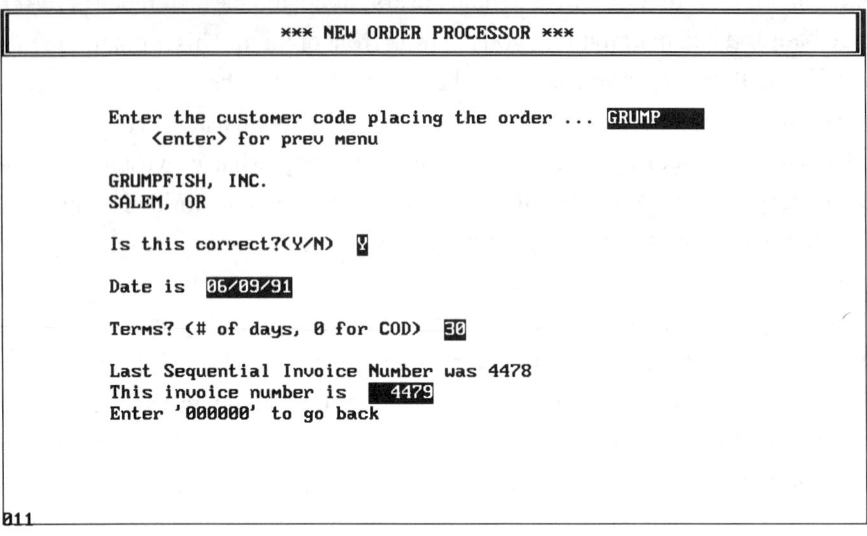

Figure 13.2 Focused screen

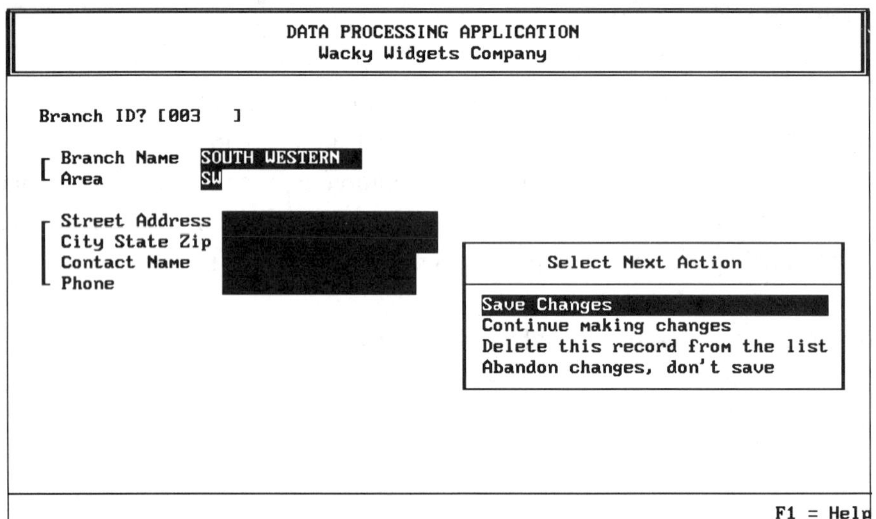

Whenever an input field is no longer pending, the fields should either be cleared from the screen or redisplayed with a color that is different from a "live" input field. The user will know exactly where the cursor can go at any time if you adhere to this convention. If you leave old, inactive input fields on the screen it is not always obvious which fields are available.

Easy to make the right response

You should strive to make it easy for the user to make the right choice or response to any prompt. Aside from reading the user's mind and making their choice first on the list (which would probably violate the consistency rule), you can anticipate what the most common or least destructive option is and make that easy to select.

This usually means phrasing all yes/no questions so that NO is the most likely or least destructive alternative. NO should always be first in the list. This is purely for consistency. If you switched YES and NO around at random depending on the question you would end up making a bad choice about 50% of the time. Keep all questions logically consistent.

Wording is also very important. Either apply the end-user's business jargon in a consistent and appropriate manner, or do not use it at all. In the same manner, never use computer and software jargon unless you are certain that all of the users are familiar with it. Avoid abbreviations and acronyms unless space limitations require it. Ambiguity and confusion is the bane of a bad user interface. Why is the following a poorly phrased prompt?

```
Happy to not save your changes? Y/N (CR = NOT)
```

If you do not want to phrase the question so NO is the proper response, then use a multiple choice prompt with the most likely and least destructive choice at the top of the list, as Figure 13.3 aptly demonstrates.

Figure 13.3 Putting the least destructive choices first

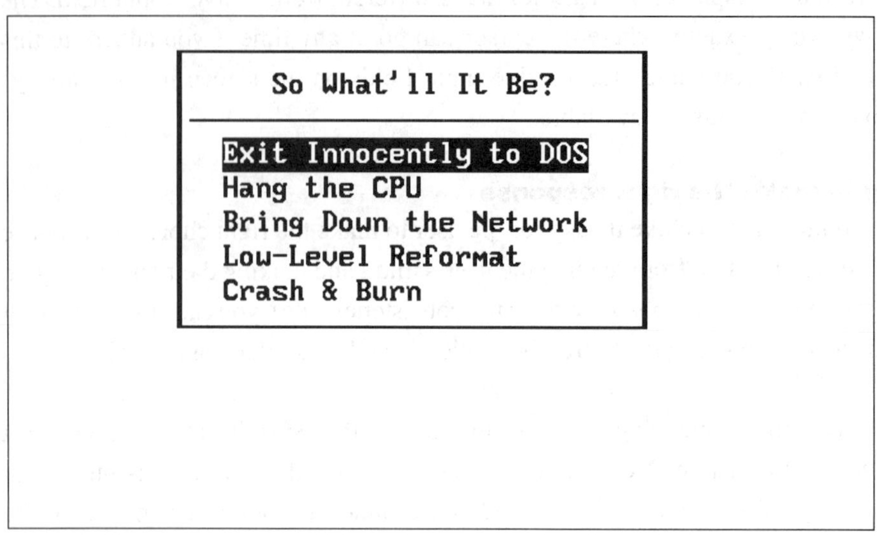

To make the right decision, you need all the information available immediately. The user manual is almost never consulted during normal program use. It is very common for user manuals to be filed and forgotten (perhaps because programmers have a bad reputation for writing ghastly instruction manuals). Some programmers counter this by providing massive on-line help systems, which make literally an entire manual available at all times. But even a context-sensitive help system such as this is almost never viewed until too late.

In the interest of immediacy, it is often better to have a brief, full-English paragraph at the bottom of the screen for every prompt in the entire system. (Later in this chapter we'll present a "describe how to do it" function to make this chore as simple as possible.) If the user has a question or concern about what their options are or what happens next, they can simply glance at the bottom of the screen. Sometimes the "how to" is simply "Press ESC to exit". Sometimes it's eight lines of detailed instructions. Either way, the users train themselves to glance at the bottom of the screen whenever they encounter something they do not immediately understand.

Difficult to damage something

Just as it is important to make the right choice easy to select, you should make the wrong choice difficult to choose accidentally. This does not mean that you have to make the choices difficult to select, but just that you prevent the user from making a devastating accidental mistake that you will pay for with hours of desperate data recovery.

Asking the same question twice or even three times with "ARE YOU REALLY, REALLY SURE?" tacked on the end is counter-productive to safety. Users just get in the habit of hitting the YES button three times whenever such a prompt is displayed! You are much better off using such devices sparingly, coupled with an out-of-the-ordinary screen display and aural feedback so they know they are at a serious prompt. If you make every prompt into an "ARE YOU SURE" sound and light show, the users quickly become immune to the shock value.

For example, some real-life users get "goose-pimples" every time they run an end-of-period process because the screen gets "so serious and foreboding." This is wonderful because it is the only time anything truly damaging to their data could occur, and everyone is careful when the "doomsday" screen is displayed. If this trick was used every time the user deleted a record, it would pass from being totally effective to merely another silly gimmick to be ignored.

Immediate feedback

It is very important to give the user immediate feedback when they make menu selections or respond to prompts. They should know immediately that their response was accepted and is being processed.

You should consider redisplaying user entries. There are circumstances, particularly when the Escape key is involved, which result in your program continuing with one value while the screen displays something completely different. When you redisplay their entry, the user knows exactly what value your program is acting upon. When applicable, you should also interpret their response. For example, after answering a series of questions about what should show up on a report, the user should see a brief summary of how they responded and what going to happen. They should know BEFORE, not AFTER.

Keep the user posted

If there is any possibility for any sort of delay following an end-user's response, you should display a "wait" graphic of some sort specific to the reason they are waiting. There is nothing worse than hitting Enter and wondering if anything is happening because the screen looks exactly the same as it did when the prompt first appeared.

Despite the extra time it takes to display a graphic, users frequently perceive an increase in speed. This happens because the appearance of a graphic, even one they see frequently and anticipate, causes them to think about it and acknowledge its presence. Although this artifice is purely subconscious, it takes so little effort and has a high enough success rate that you should consider using it.

One favorite is the "construction" graphic (Figure 13.4), which is supposed to look like a brick wall being built. It is abstract enough not to be immediately recognized, but not so obvious that it is ignored. No matter how many times you see it, you still look at it for a moment. However, if you use any graphic too often it will cease to have an effect on the user.

Figure 13.4 Construction graphic for time-consuming process

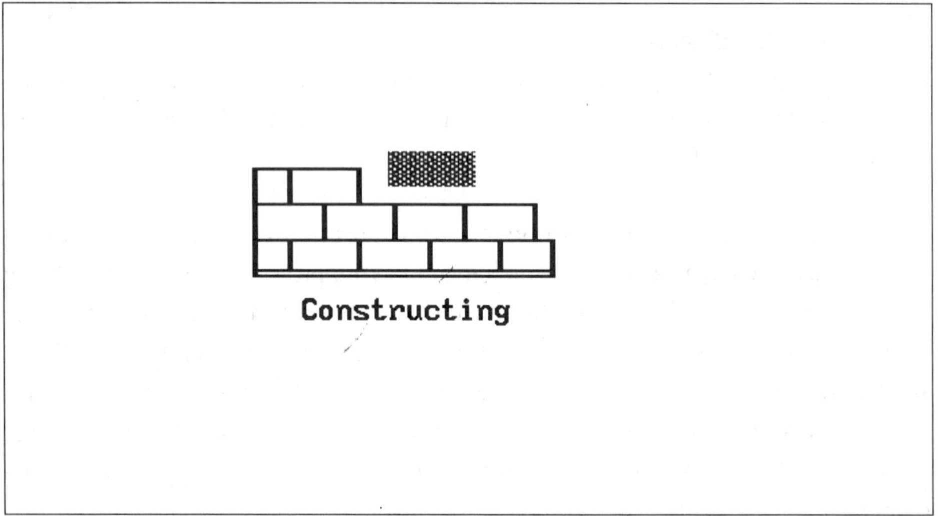

Another popular graphic is the status bar (Figure 13.5). This is perfect for the creation of large index files. The status bar provides continuous feedback, thus convincing the user that yes, the computer is hard at work and should not be rebooted.

You must judge which processes will take long enough to require a status display. Sometimes the process happens so fast the graphic flashes up and disappears too quickly, which annoys people. For this reason, you should incorporate a slight delay whenever a graphic is displayed. It should always stay on the screen for at least one half of a second, which is long enough for it to be recognized.

Figure 13.5 Status bar graphic for index file

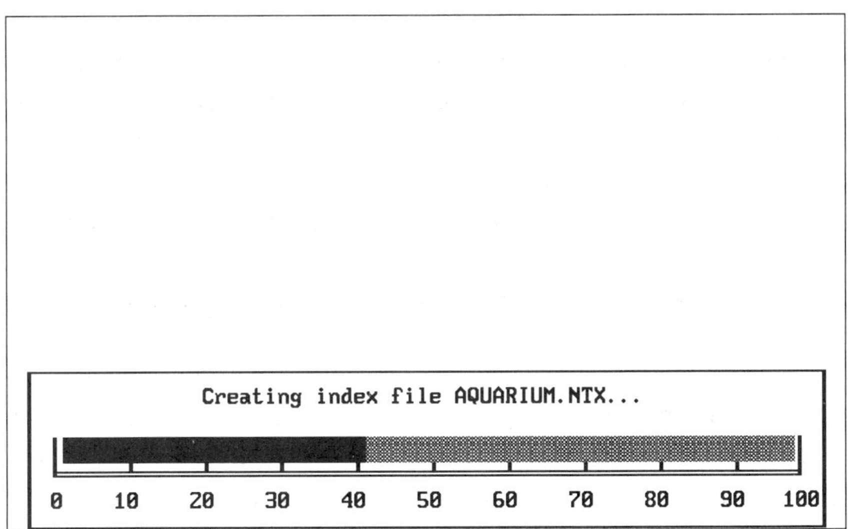

When you must ask several questions in sequence, always leave a "trail" of responses behind you. The user will appreciate knowing how they answered previous questions while they think up responses to the subsequent ones. Once finished with the prompts, leave the redisplayed versions on the screen. Do not clear the screen completely and throw up a "wait" message. There is nothing worse than a flashing WAIT in the middle of the screen while the hard disk is thrashing wildly — what's going on? What did they select? This signals many users that it is time to panic.

Finally, try not to intersperse long processes between questions that must eventually be answered. It is more efficient to get all necessary data up front, and then start the time-consuming processes.

From the Hall of Shame comes a heinous example: A huge publishing company with a staff of professional designers came up with a seemingly useful rule — before any report began printing, a standard PRESS A KEY TO BEGIN THE REPORT screen must be displayed, warning the user that the printer should be on-line with paper loaded, and so on and so forth. This rule was never to be violated, and all the programmers on the numerous projects under the publisher's supervision coded each report as specified. When it came time for the product to be used in the "real world" a major bottleneck was created. Many reports took several hours to sort and construct. Without exception each one stopped cold and waited for someone to notice and hit a key before they would finish up by printing the results. This frustrated many people who wanted to select a report and go do something productive rather than watching for the insipid PRESS A KEY screen. A common end-user practice was to put a paperweight on top of the Enter key and walk away, thus defeating the whole purpose of the warning screen. The moral of this sad but true story is that status displays are an important part of a user interface, but care must be taken in the way they are implemented.

Efficient keystrokes

Another important point to be made is efficiency. Do not confuse ease to use with efficiency. This is a very hard balance to achieve. A "friendly" system makes the users happy until they get used to it, then all the hand-holding slows them down.

Well-designed library functions can promote efficiency by providing two ways to make a selection — using the arrow keys to move a lightbar and Enter to select, or by pressing the first letter (which should be unique for each choice).

Easy escape hatch

You should offer an easy way out of every prompt in the entire application. Users appreciate this feature because they do not have to study the screen so hard to get out of something, especially if they got there by accident. They just tap the designated "I'm done with this" key and the application reacts accordingly, usually by exiting or backing up one step. The Escape key is almost universally used for such purposes.

Note that pressing Escape is different and distinct from taking a default response. Even a supposedly binary prompt like YES OR NO really has a third option: None of the above. Listing 13.1 shows an example of testing for such an escape hatch.

Listing 13.1 Checking for escape hatch

```
alphaSort := YesNo("Sort the listing alphabetically?")
if !(lastkey == K_ESC)
  if alphaSort
     // do one thing
  else
     // do something else
  endif
endif
```

Note that there are three ways the end-user's response is interpreted. They can select YES or NO as you expect, but they can also hit the Escape key and exit the entire procedure. This prevents the end-user from having to answer additional questions that are pointless because they don't want to be doing the procedure in the first place. This is particularly important if the prompt is heavily validated or difficult to answer correctly. The end-user should be able to "bail out" without having to think so hard.

This is also a good way to avoid the bad habit of using a word like DONE, QUIT, or END to indicate that the user is finished with a prompt. These types of prompts are difficult to handle for new users and are somewhat inefficient. Even worse, poorly implemented ones will prevent certain types of data from being entered. Listing 13.2 shows a condensed example of a prompt that was dredged up from an actual Clipper system.

Listing 13.2 The wrong way to write an escape hatch

```
accept "Last name or END to exit?" to lastname
lastname := upper(lastname)
if lastname = "DONE" .or. lastname = "END"
  return
endif
```

This application refused to allow names like DONECKER, DONEGAN, DONELLY, and DONER, as well as ENDER, ENDORF, ENDRES and ENDRIS. The programmer thought he was being helpful by allowing more than one way to exit. The end-users could understand why the ENDxxxx names were not working (not that they liked it), but the DONExxxx had everyone confused because it was not documented at the prompt. The major mistake was not realizing that longer strings are logically equal to shorter strings that match. Test data did not uncover the problem because they used obvious names like SMITH and JONES. What happens when a client with the last name of DONE or END (or EXIT or QUIT or...) comes along? Stranger things have happened.

Another real life example: A sports league spent a small fortune on an application for tracking players and scoring and so on. At numerous prompts throughout the system a player's jersey number was used for quick identification, since there is only one jersey number for each player on any given team. Number zero (0) was used to exit these prompts, and you can guess what happened. Jersey number zero started playing one season and the whole application and documentation had to be modified at great expense.

Validate the obvious

Your applications are in control of an extremely powerful microcomputer, capable of performing complex calculations in a fraction of a second. There is no excuse for not performing at least the most obvious error and validity checks at every prompt in your application.

Unless the application is extremely generic and broad in scope, the people who are going to use it will be able to tell you how to validate their entries. They will appreciate being warned that an entry does not appear to be correct. Untold hours are wasted tracking down simple data entry mistakes that should have been caught as soon as they were entered. The following are common things to check for.

Dates and date ranges

Dates are very easy to enter incorrectly. If you use a true date-type entry field, the Clipper run-time system will at least ensure that the date is properly formatted. If you allow dates to be entered into a character string with a "99/99/99" picture you should convert the string to a date and back to a string to see if it survived the process. Otherwise people will put 31 days in November and forget about leap years and so on. Listing 13.3 shows an easy way to validate a character string used as a date. After this process, **theDate** is still a character string. If it was invalid the string will contain " / / ".

Listing 13.3 Validating a Character-Type Date

```
theDate := "  /  /  "
@ 10, 12 say "The date " get theDate picture "99/99/99"
read
theDate := dtoc(ctod(theDate))
if theDate = "  /  /  "
  * invalid entry
else
  * valid entry
endif
```

Another common problem is with ranges of dates. It is not uncommon to reverse starting and ending dates, especially if the user is accustomed to thinking about the ending date as being more significant than the starting date. You should compare the two dates and swap them if the starting date is later than the ending. If the user enters the dates backward, an operation such as the following will lead to unexpected results.

```
copy to temp for OrderDate >= startDate ;
         .and. OrderDate <= endDate
```

Less obvious and sometimes more difficult to detect are correctly formatted dates that are not reasonable or even possible. For example, suppose you are associating line item shipment dates with the original purchase order records. It is not possible to ship an item before it was even ordered, so you should not allow a shipment date that is earlier than the original order date. These types of errors are extremely difficult to track down after the fact, but very simple to detect during data entry. It is easy to transpose two numbers in a date and have it look reasonable but still be in error.

Another similar situation is when a shipment date is too old to be reasonable for the original order. This is harder to detect because it may be possible to have items shipped, for example, 90 days beyond the order date. You cannot flag the date as an error and refuse to allow it because on a small number of occasions it may be correct. The users will probably like to have a warning that the date is suspect. They can double-check the date and be certain about it. You could provide a user-definable "maximum days old" parameter and allow them to fine-tune it themselves over the life of the application. If the range is too short the warning message pops up too frequently and gets ignored. If the range is too long it will not catch enough problems. Allowing the user to change the parameter provides an acceptable alternative.

Here is one more date problem to be aware of: When entering original documents (like purchase orders) you should establish some kind of "safety" date which no document can precede. Allow the user to move it forward periodically. For example, suppose that you install an application for use in 1991. Data prior to January 1, 1991 will not be kept in the system. If you check to be sure that no dates are prior to this you will cut down on potential data entry errors. Not all dates will be subject to the "safety date" check; for example, activity in January may reference dates in previous months. The check should be performed only on significant dates.

Another safety date could be established for the maximum allowable date. If data is to be entered for a particular fiscal year you can catch accidental entries too far into the future. If you give the user (or a system support/maintenance person) the ability to move these dates as the year progresses, you can trap a large number of data entry errors.

A common data entry error is transposing the digits in the year, entering 19 when you meant 91, or fumbling around the keyboard and producing 01, 09, and so on. A good date checking routine should catch all of these errors and at the very least pop up a warning message. Later in this chapter we will present message display functions ideally suited to this task.

Numbers

As with dates, there are a wide variety of simple checks that can be performed to catch bad numeric data. Ask your users about the kinds of data they encounter. Is zero ever a valid entry? Can an amount ever be negative? Can the sum of a set of transactions ever exceed the base amount? Should the sum of the transactions always equal the base amount? Is there an upper limit that is unlikely to be exceeded?

There is a big difference between saying that a field must accommodate five digits and saying that the maximum entry is 99,999. Your users may tell you that the maximum reasonable entry is more like 20,000, and an entry in the 50,000 range or higher should be impossible. Depending on the application, establishing some kind of floor and ceiling may help cut down on data entry errors.

Character strings

The use of PICTURE statements is encouraged, because they are your first line of defense. If you want the entry to be upper case, it's much easier to use the "@!" picture than to convert entries with the UPPER() function. Avoid using long strings of template symbols in field pictures, especially if the entry will be stored in a database. Database field widths are changed more often than we like, and every time it happens there are bound to be PICTURE templates that use the "old" width.

Here is an example. The customer name field was sworn to be 20 characters long.

```
@ 10, 15 get custName picture "!!!!!!!!!!!!!!!!!!!!"
```

Only near the end of the project did the client start encountering the really long names, so they requested it be increased to 25 characters. A clever programmer would avoid getting bitten like this again and store the picture in a variable.

```
@ 10, 15 get custName picture (pictCust)
```

This is better because changes to the width of the field need only affect the single assignment to the pictCust variable. However, there's an even easier way to accomplish the same thing.

```
@ 10, 15 get custName picture "@!"
```

Any picture template symbol can be used in this way. The picture will be as wide as the data it is associated with. It will vary on the fly, expanding and contracting to fit the data.

Screen layout

Screen layouts can cause problems at two different times: (a) when they are used at run-time; and (b) when they are originally programmed. Each problem makes the other one worse. Complex data entry screens are difficult to program, and screens that are difficult to program often look bad on the screen. This is a no-win situation.

Screen painting and code generating utilities are often a quick solution. However, they can sometimes create problems of their own by encouraging excessive use of boxes, colors, and other fancy tricks, simply because the tools are available and easy to use. Moreover, there is no time involved for laboriously typing all the complex formatting commands by hand.

This is not meant to discourage the use of screen painting and code generators; in fact, we think that with a well-designed template, you can (and usually will) generate well-designed applications. Just be sure that your templates are well-planned, and that the screens you paint with such utilities do not rely too heavily on gimmicks. A flashy, complicated screen is not a substitute for good design, and anyone with programming experience will be able to tell the difference.

Attempt to keep lines displayed on the screen to under 50 characters, and to write in complete sentences without abbreviations. Long (70+) character lines are difficult to read, especially if they wrap over several lines. If you liberally sprinkle the text with acronyms and abbreviations, the information quickly becomes unreadable, and consequently ignored.

One rule of thumb that you may wish to consider is: If you can't explain a prompt in a few short lines in a "how to" area at the bottom of the screen, then the prompt is too complicated and should be broken down. In such cases you could establish a direction (either the user wants to exit or continue) and then ask for additional information specific to the direction. In situations where there are several equally likely alternatives, a general-purpose menu function can be put to good use.

The natural way to read anything is from top to bottom and left to right, so this is how you should design your screens. Think of the screen as being divided into three zones (as shown in Figure 13.6). The topmost three lines or so almost never change. They are the "anchor", a point of reference. They establish the name of the application and the sub-module that is currently in use. This is desirable because, after all, your application is rarely the only one that runs on that particular computer. Even if it is, you should still indicate that your application is running.

Very inexperienced users often cannot distinguish between DOS and an application program, despite the seemingly obvious changes in screen formats. It is never acceptable to clear the entire screen and flash a "wait" message. The screen should always tell the user which application is making them wait, and even better, which process within the application is doing the work.

The middle zone is the obvious choice for messages and pertinent data, because the user's eyes will naturally be drawn to the center of the screen. This zone changes constantly as the user moves from prompt to prompt. It is cleared during long waits when the information on the screen is not applicable to the wait.

The bottom zone is for the instructional ("how to do it") text. It, too, changes constantly as the user moves from prompt to prompt. The changes are still uniform and consistent despite the difference in content. The "how to" text always pushes the text to the very bottom of the screen and separates itself from the middle zone of the screen, either with a line or a change in color.

The three-zone technique allows the user to concentrate on the middle portion of the screen, venturing to the top and bottom only when an unusual or unexpected situation arises.

The keyboard

Thus far we have talked only about displaying things on the screen. An equally important part of user interface design is the way you accept keystrokes from the end-user.

Figure 13.6 The Screen as Three Zones

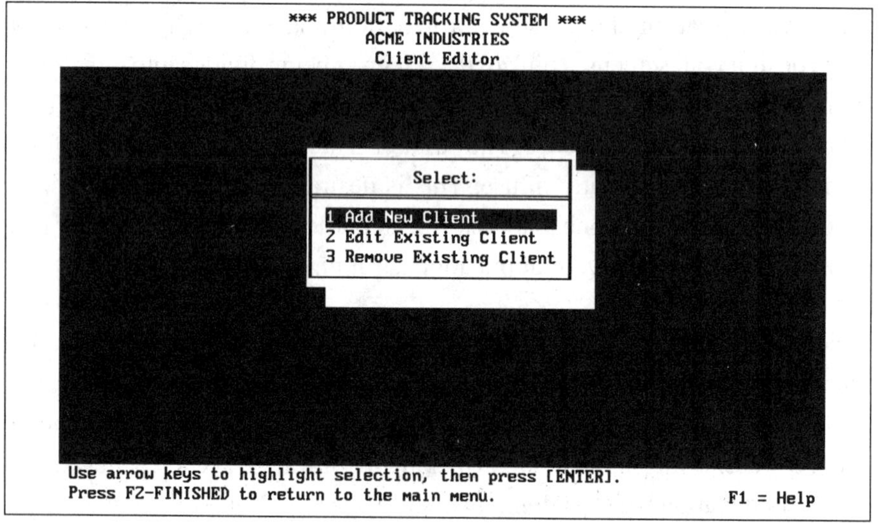

There are two major ways to handle the keyboard. One is to assign a number of keys to a number of functions and make them active almost all of the time. The "many keys" method is used by word processors and similar programs. At any given instant a huge number of keyboard combinations are available to perform different functions.

The other method is to activate a small number of keys and use them to invoke menus where the real functions are selected. Other programs have a relatively small number of active keys and use menu choices to perform functions. Most spreadsheets fall into this category. You hit a designated menu key and then start making selections from the menus.

A word processor which forces you to go through numerous menus is difficult to use, and similarly, in a complex application like a spreadsheet it is difficult to remember the hundreds of key combinations necessary to perform all the functions. Different applications require different approaches to the keyboard. Through trial and error (with heavy emphasis on the latter), we tend to use the "designated menu key" approach. Such applications are easier to use for beginning operators, and if implemented correctly, can also be efficient even for experienced users. Some programmers like to assign major functions to the ten function keys. They display a function key map at the bottom of the screen, something like the following.

```
F1      F2       F3       F4       F5      F6            F10

HELP    SEARCH   APPEND   DELETE   NEXT    PREVIOUS ... EXIT
```

Such a technique is appropriate when rapid access to the various functions is important. However, problems begin to surface when the function key assignments are not maintained exactly the same way through the entire application. If function key F3 appends a new record on one data entry screen, it should append a record on *every* data entry screen, or be disabled for that screen. Applications which assign different functions to keys depending on the screen are difficult to use efficiently, because the user can never get comfortable with the keys. They will always have to stop to check the meaning of each key on each screen, which will lead to inefficiency and general bad feelings about your application.

When you start using SHIFT and CONTROL combinations to support all your features, you are getting further and further away from a balanced approach to the keyboard. There are a small number of applications that can benefit from dozens of special purpose keystrokes, but the majority will be better served by a menu-driven approach.

Once again, our approach follows our opinion of what makes a good user interface. After trying most methods, we keep coming back to the "designated menu key" concept with a few special purpose keys. This design is easier to implement, easier to explain to the user, easier to document, and easier to modify at a later date. Most of the time, the options that are possible apply only when the user has completed the current action. For example, during a data entry screen the append, next, previous, and search operations can only be used when the current record is no longer being edited.

Think of a data entry screen containing a glaring error that cannot be ignored. If the user presses any of the function keys (append a new record, move to next, previous and so on), you would have to alert them about the error and force them to either fix the current problem or discard the edits. Therefore, having all the functions available all of the time is not necessarily going to make things easier. If a single key is used to indicate "I'm done with this operation," you can do the error checking and loop back in a more natural way — "No, fix your errors and then you can leave". Once the screen is correct, the other options are displayed. If the option menu is laid out efficiently, you are adding a single extra keystroke to the call to any function. But two keystrokes can actually be faster than one if the single keystrokes are messy and inconsistent.

Using sound

The Summer '87 version of Clipper introduced the TONE() function. TONE() allows you to manipulate the IBM speaker to play tones at specified frequencies for varying durations. It is entirely possible that many Clipper developers have dismissed TONE() as being silly or unnecessary. If you count yourself among this group, we urge you to think again about using TONE().

Sound is an important part of any professional software package. It can be used in any of the following capacities:

- To alert the user that a time-consuming procedure is completed (e.g., reindexing all files, printing a complex report). Thus the user need not remain glued to a monitor; he or she can work on something else until the theme is heard.

- In conjunction with error messages. This is particularly useful for data entry-intensive applications where the user may be watching his or her data instead of the input screen.

- In tandem with alerts or warnings, (e.g., the user tries to print a report and the printer is off-line; the user is about to delete a large number of records, etc).

- To indicate different modes or states, if your application utilizes them. The user can associate each theme with a particular mode, which will prevent confusion.

- With data as a stimulus. There is at least one commercially available software package that displays data, and plays music corresponding to the patterns thereof. For example, where the numbers increase in value, the program might play a musical progression that began with low notes and went higher. (This type of integration of music and data is very much in its infancy.)

TONE()

The syntax for the TONE() function is:

```
TONE(<frequency>, <duration>)
```

<frequency> is an integer numeric expression representing the frequency (in hertz) at which to play the speaker.

<duration> is an integer numeric expression representing the duration of the tone in eighteenth of a second intervals. For example, passing a value of 18 would sound a tone for one second. If you do not pass this parameter, the default duration is 1/18 of a second.

The TONE() function does not return a value.

Examples

Near the end of Chapter 7, "The Preprocessor," we introduced several user-defined commands that played short musical themes. We will revisit two of those in Listing 13.4.

Listing 13.4 Charge and NannyBoo musical themes

```
#xcommand Charge => ;
            tunes({ {523,2}, {698,2}, {880,2}, ;
                  {1046,4}, {880,2}, {1046,8} } )

#xcommand NannyBoo => ;
            tunes( { {196,2}, {196,2}, {164,2}, ;
                  {220,2}, {196,4}, {164,4} } )

#xtranslate tunes(<a>) => ;
            aeval(<a>, { | a | tone(a\[1], a\[2]) } )
```

The "Charge" theme is handy for multi-user applications. If users are waiting for a file or record to become available, they can work on something else until they hear "Charge!", at which time they know they can return to their terminal.

"NannyBoo" is well suited to accompany error messages.

In addition, the following simple two-note combinations can be used to accompany alert or warning messages.

```
* Example 1

TONE(440,1)
TONE(440,1)

* Example 2
TONE(880,1)
TONE(880,1)
```

If you make use of sound in your applications, you should probably also consider allowing the user to change a global SOUND parameter to mute the application. There will always be some fuddy-duddies out there who think that any PC application that emits any kind of sound can only be a game.

Using color

Color is an extremely subjective thing, and some monitors do a better job than others with different color combinations. Everyone has seen software that comes with incredibly bad color combinations (which are more often than not hard-wired). Many are almost unreadable on laptop computer monitors because of the way laptops fake color through gray scales. Even on color monitors the color schemes are sometimes ludicrous, but somewhere out there a (color-blind?) programmer is mighty proud of his innovative use of color.

In your source code it is much easier to understand the intent of a reference to blinking or inverse text than it is to a particular color. There is a danger in using too many different color combinations simultaneously. Excessive colors obscure the significance of any given color. Flashy, colorful applications that look nifty during a demo might be too difficult to follow in actual use. Another potential problem is that the more colors you use, the better your chance for hideous color clashes.

Remember the FOCUS rule — a well-designed screen should be understood at a glance. If the user gets a long phone call right in the middle of your application and comes back 30 minutes later, will he be able to figure out where he was and what is expected of him next? Consistent and thoughtful use of color will make the screen easier to understand.

Avoid using hard-coded colors in your applications. Instead, refer to the situation that demands the use of some special handling. References to color mean nothing on a monochrome monitor (and in fact may not work at all they way you intend). Additionally, it is preferable to allow the users to modify (or at the very least have you modify for them) the colors used in their application. A comprehensive color selection and installation tool follows.

Color management

In Chapter 12 ("Program Design"), you tasted the power of file-wide static arrays. Now we will apply static arrays to the management of color settings. These principles can easily be applied to any type of global variables, including printer escape sequences, company/user identification, and so on.

Summer '87

If you used the Summer '87 version of Clipper, you might have handled your color settings by declaring **public** variables at the top of your main program, as shown in Listing 13.5.

Listing 13.5 Clipper Summer '87 Color Settings

```
* MAIN.PRG
public c_normal, c_bold, c_enhanced, c_blink, c_msg, c_warning
if iscolor()
   c_normal       := 'W/B'
   c_bold         := '+W/B'
   c_enhanced     := '+GR/B'
   c_blink        := '*W/B'
   c_msg          := '+W/RB'
   c_warning      := '+W/R'
else
   c_normal       := 'W/N'
   c_bold         := '+W/N'
   c_enhanced     := '+W/N'
   c_blink        := '*W/N'
   c_msg          := 'N/W'
   c_warning      := 'N/W'
endif
```

Another alternative was to put this code in a ColorInit() function that would in turn be called upon entering the main program. In either event, the variables would be declared as **public** so as to maintain visibility everywhere throughout the program.

When it came time to change color, the developer could pass one of these **public** variables to SETCOLOR() as shown in Listing 13.6.

Listing 13.6 Passing color variables to SETCOLOR()

```
* note: this is Summer '87 code!
whoops("File not available")
*
function whoops
parameter msg
private buffer, leftcol, oldcolor, oldrow, oldcol
oldrow = row()
oldcol = col()
leftcol = int( (76 - len(msg)) / 2)
oldcolor = setcolor(c_warning)          && PUBLIC color setting
buffer = savescreen(11, leftcol, 13, 80 - leftcol)
@ 11, leftcol, 13, 80 - leftcol box "┌─┐│┘─└│ "
@ 12, leftcol + 2 say msg
inkey(0)
** restore screen, cursor position, and color
restscreen(11, leftcol, 13, 80 - leftcol)
@ oldrow, oldcol say ''
setcolor(oldcolor)
return .t.
```

Clipper 5

With the tools that we had at our disposal at that time, the **public** declarations were the best solution. However, with the availability of the **static** declaration, there is no reason to use **public** variables in this fashion.

This is not meant to imply that **public** variables should be jettisoned altogether. There will continue to be uses in Clipper 5 for the **public** declaration, particularly if you plan to convert any major Summer '87 applications to Clipper 5. It would probably be too time-consuming for you to switch any such entrenched **public** color management routines in favor of the methods shown here.

However, as you write new applications in Clipper 5, you should strongly consider abandoning the use of **public** variables to manage your color (and other global) settings. The **static** declaration reveals two inherent deficiencies of **public** variables:

- As mentioned in Chapter 6 ("Variable Scoping"), public variables require an entry in the symbol table. This means that your programs will require more memory and execute more slowly. Static variables are faster than public variables because static (and local) variables are resolved at compile-time and thus do not require a symbol table entry.

  Whenever your code refers to a **private** or **public** variable, the run-time engine must first look in the symbol table to determine that variable's actual address in memory. It then looks at that memory address to retrieve the value of the variable. Because static and local variables are already resolved, your program need only look in one place to retrieve their value.

  Therefore, each time you refer to a public or private variable you are suffering a performance hit. Granted, this still happens in the blink of an eye, but if you multiply this by the thousands of times you refer to such variables, you can see the advantages of switching to static and local variables.

- Because public variables are visible everywhere throughout your program, that also means that they are subject to change everywhere. Computers are perfect, but unfortunately the people who program them are imperfect. These hapless humans occasionally make silly mistakes (especially when facing a deadline at three o'clock in the morning).

  There is nothing to prevent you from inadvertently trashing the value of a public variable, especially if you are not using a good naming convention for your variables. By contrast, static (and local) variables are visible only within the function or procedure that created them. This means that you will be unable to accidentally change them unless you are within the function that created them.

Encapsulation

The trick, therefore, is to tuck our color variables safely out of harm's way. The best approach is to "encapsulate" the variables (or data) along with the only function(s) that need to access them. Listing 13.7 shows a simple function, C_Normal(), that demonstrates encapsulation, along with a twist.

Listing 13.7 Simple encapsulation

```
function C_Normal(newcolor)
static color := "W/B"
/* change color setting if parameter was received */
if newcolor != NIL
   color := newcolor
endif
return setcolor(color)
```

C_Normal() declares a static variable **color** to white on blue. The function accepts an optional parameter, **newcolor**. If this parameter is passed, the static variable **color** will be assigned its value. You can see now why we must declare **color** as static rather than local, because we want it to retain its value for the next time we call C_Normal(). Local variables have to "start over" each time the function is called.

Finally, C_Normal() calls SETCOLOR() to actually change the color setting. It returns the SETCOLOR() return value, namely the current color setting, so that you can save this to a variable and restore it elsewhere.

There are two ways for you to utilize C_Normal(). The first is to call it normally:

```
C_Normal()
```

In this case it will simply change the color to white on blue (assuming that we had not yet changed the default color). However, you can also change this default by passing a parameter as shown in the following code fragment:

```
C_Normal("+w/r")
cls
setcolor("w/b")
? "this will be white on blue"
C_Normal()
? "this will be hi white on red"
```

This will cause the default normal color to be changed to bright white on red. Because the variable holding that value is static, it will retain its value for any subsequent calls to C_Normal(), as this example shows.

This effectively hides the normal color setting in the only function that needs to know it! You can no longer change it by accident. You can still change it if necessary, but because you have to make a conscious effort to pass the parameter, any such changes will be far more controlled than in the past.

If you look at this approach and think "Ugh... extra work", you're half right. It *is* going to require some additional thought when you write your code. But remember that far more time is spent during the maintenance (a.k.a. "debugging") phase than the coding phase. If you adhere to this approach, you will save yourself much time and many debugging headaches in the long run. You also make it much easier to change colors by keeping everything in just one place.

Function of many colors

C_Normal() was merely intended to demonstrate the encapsulation principle. In actual practice, there is little point in having one function for each color. Take the Clipper SET() function as an example. Clipper uses this function to handle all of the global settings (38 as of the release of Clipper 5.01; see Chapter 17, table 17.3, for a complete list of the SET manifest constants). The syntax for SET() is:

```
SET(<setting> [,<newvalue>])
```

The first parameter is a numeric expression that denotes which SETTING to look at. A complete list of manifest constants for each SETTING can be found in the SET.CH header file. For example, the CONSOLE setting can be referred to with this manifest constant:

```
#define _SET_CONSOLE          17

oldcons := set(_SET_CONSOLE, .F.)    // set console off
*
set(_SET_CONSOLE, oldcons)          // restore previous value
```

(Once again, you should always refer to the SETtings by their manifest constants rather than their numeric values. Computer Associates warns that the numerics are subject to change, whereas the manifest constants will be maintained. Besides, the manifest constants are a lot easier to remember!)

Like C_Normal(), SET() accepts an optional **<newvalue>** parameter. If this parameter is passed, the global SETting is changed to the <newvalue>.

Inspired by this brevity, let's rewrite C_Normal() to handle all of our colors instead of just one (as shown in Listing 13.8). The gist of this change is to use a static array containing multiple color settings, which is easily accomplished.

Listing 13.8 ColorSet()

```
function ColorSet(colornum, newcolor)
static colors := { "W/B", "+W/B", "+GR/B", ;
                   "*W/B", "+W/RB", "+W/R" }
/* change applicable color setting if second parameter was passed
*/
if newcolor != NIL
   colors[colornum] := newcolor
endif
return setcolor(colors[colornum])
```

Let's also establish manifest constants so that we do not have to remember which array element corresponds to which color. Listing 13.9 shows these manifest constants, which will be stored in the COLOR.CH header file.

Listing 13.9 COLOR.CH: Manifest constants for color settings

```
/* COLOR.CH Header File */

#define  C_NORMAL     1
#define  C_BOLD       2
#define  C_ENHANCED   3
#define  C_BLINK      4
#define  C_MESSAGE    5
#define  C_WARNING    6
```

The Missing() function (shown in Listing 13.10) shows how you could refer to these colors.

Listing 13.10 Use of ColorSet() and Manifest Constants

```
#include "box. ch"
function Missing()
local oldcolor := ColorSet(C_BOLD)
local oldscrn := savescreen(11,30,13,49)
@ 11, 30, 13, 49 box B_SINGLE + " "
ColorSet(C_BLINK)
@ 12, 32 say "Record not found"
inkey(0)
setcolor(oldcolor)
restscreen(11, 30, 13, 49, oldscrn)
return nil
```

The Great Debate: color vs. monochrome

Actually, the answer is obvious. If God had intended for the world to be black and white, he would not have created rainbows. To our continuing dismay, even in the dawning of the age of VGA there are still numerous monochrome monitors in use. Therefore, we must devise an easy way to handle these aberrations.

We will have to follow two steps:

1. write a miniature function to initialize our color settings to either color or monochrome; and

2. expand the static array of color settings to include monochrome equivalents.

For the first step, we must declare a file-wide static variable **iscolor**. This is necessary because it will need to be visible in two functions.

The function ColorInit() will have one small but vitally important mission in life: to initialize **iscolor** to either true (yes, we are using color) or false (monochrome, yuch). If you call it without parameters, it will use the Clipper ISCOLOR() function as the basis for future colors.

However, as we have all learned by now, ISCOLOR() is not infallible. For example, ISCOLOR() will look at the everyday occurrence of a CGA video card and a monochrome monitor and return a value of true, even though the monitor obviously cannot display colors. Therefore, ColorInit() is structured to accept an optional parameter. If passed, this logical parameter will override ISCOLOR() to make the color vs. monochrome determination. Pass true for color, false for monochrome.

The second step is to modify the array in ColorSet() to hold monochrome settings for each color. This array must therefore be changed from a single-dimensional array of six elements, to an array containing six sub-arrays, each containing two elements. The first element of each sub-array will contain the color setting, and the second element will contain the monochrome setting. The static variable **iscolor** will serve as a pointer into the sub-array. See Listing 13.11 for ColorInit() and ColorSet().

Listing 13.11 ColorInit() and ColorSet()

```
static iscolor := 1

/* ColorInit(): initialize color system to color or mono */
function ColorInit(override)
iscolor := if(override == NIL, if(iscolor(), 1, 2), ;
              if(override, 1, 2))
return nil

/* ColorSet(): change colors in accordance with internal settings
*/
function ColorSet(colornum, newcolor)
static colors := {  { "W/B",    "W/N"  } , ;
                    { "+W/B",   "+W/N" } , ;
                    { "+GR/B",  "+W/N" } , ;
                    { "*W/B",   "*W/N" } , ;
                    { "+W/RB",  "N/W"  } , ;
                    { "+W/R",   "N/W"  } }

/* change color setting if second parameter was passed */
if newcolor != NIL
   colors[colornum, iscolor] := newcolor
endif
return setcolor(colors[colornum, iscolor])
```

The sample code shown in Listing 13.12 demonstrates how you can use ColorInit() and ColorSet() in your program.

Listing 13.12 Using ColorInit() and ColorSet()

```
function Main
/* verify that this is REALLY a color system */
if iscolor()
   ? "Press C for color monitor, any other key for monochrome"
   /* this looks nuts, but works perfectly - can you see why? */
   ColorInit( chr(inkey(0)) $ "cC" )
else
   ColorInit()
endif
ColorSet(C_NORMAL)
cls
ColorSet(C_BOLD)
@ 11, 24, 13, 55 box"┌─┐│┘─└│ "
ColorSet(C_ENHANCED)
@ 12, 26 say "Welcome to the Brownout Zone"
inkey(0)
return nil
```

Allowing changes

The final piece of this puzzle involves saving the color settings if they are modified. Clipper does not inherently provide for saving and restoring arrays. However, in Chapter 9 we presented two functions, SaveArray() and RestArray(), that accomplish this. We must rely upon these two functions to save and restore our color settings.

We also must make two slight changes to our functions. First, ColorInit() should be modified to accept a filename. If it receives one, it should be smart enough to attempt to load the color settings from that file.

Because the **colors** array must now be visible within ColorInit() as well as ColorSet(), we must pull it out of ColorSet() and make it file-wide (but you were expecting that anyway). To complete the scenario, we have provided the ColorMod() function, which displays samples of each color setting, and allows you to change them. You are then given the option of saving your color settings to a file.

Listing 13.13 shows ColorInit(), ColorSet() and ColorMod(), along with a test program demonstrating their use. Note that this relies upon the functions SaveEnv() and RestEnv(), which save and restore the environment. These were introduced in Chapter 12 ("Program Design"). Note that all of the color settings have been changed from the defaults to use cyan as the background.

Listing 13.13 Clipper 5 color management system

```
#include "box.ch"
#include "inkey.ch"
#define  TESTING       /* will compile stub program for testing */

#define  C_NORMAL      1
#define  C_BOLD        2
#define  C_ENHANCED    3
#define  C_BLINK       4
#define  C_MESSAGE     5
#define  C_WARNING     6
#define  COLOR_CNT     6

/* default name for color configuration file - change if you want
*/

#define  CFG_FILE      "colors.cfg"

// convert logical to numeric: 1 if .T., 2 if .F.
#translate Logic2Num( <a> ) => ( if( <a>, 1, 2) )

static iscolor :=1    //  flag for color (1) or mono (2)

/*
   The following array contains color and monochrome settings
   for each type of color. The third element describes the color
   it applies to, which makes it completely self-documenting. This
   third element is also used during the ColorMod() routine to
   identify each color.
*/
```

```
static colors := {  { "W/B",    "W/N" , "Normal"    }, ;
                    { "+W/B",   "+W/N", "Bold"      }, ;
                    { "+GR/B",  "+W/N", "Enhanced" }, ;
                    { "*W/B",   "*W/N", "Blinking" }, ;
                    { "+W/RB",  "N/W" , "Messages" }, ;
                    { "+W/R",   "N/W" , "Warnings" }  }

// stub program begins here
#ifdef TESTING

function Main
local oldcolor
do case
   case file(CFG_FILE)
       ColorInit(CFG_FILE)
   /* verify that this is REALLY a color system */
   case iscolor()
       qout("Press C for color monitor, any other key for mono")
       /* this looks nuts, but works perfectly - see why? */
       ColorInit( chr(inkey(0)) $ "cC" )
   otherwise
       ColorInit()
endcase
oldcolor := ColorSet(C_NORMAL)
cls
ColorSet(C_BOLD)
@ 11, 24, 13, 55 box "┌─┐│┘─└│ "
ColorSet(C_ENHANCED)
@ 12, 26 say "Welcome to the Brownout Zone"
inkey(3)
ColorMod()
ColorSet(C_BLINK)
@ 12, 26 say "Hope you enjoyed your visit!"
inkey(3)
setcolor(oldcolor)
cls
return nil
#endif
// stub program ends here... main functions begin

/*
```

```
     ColorInit(): initializes color management system
                  to either color or monochrome, or
                  load previously saved color settings

*/
function ColorInit(override)
local temparray
do case
   case override == NIL
        iscolor := Logic2Num(iscolor())
   case valtype(override) == 'L'
        iscolor := Logic2Num(override)
   otherwise
        if file(override)
           if len( temparray := Gloadarray(override) ) = 0
            qout("Could not load colors from " + override)
            inkey(0)
           else
            colors := temparray
           endif
           iscolor := logic2num( iscolor() )
        endif
endcase
return NIL
* end function ColorInit()
*-------------------------------------------*
/*
     ColorSet(): changes color in accordance with
                 internal settings stored in array
*/

function ColorSet(colornum, newcolor)
/* modify color setting if second parameter was passed */
if newcolor != NIL
   colors[colornum, iscolor] := newcolor
endif
return setcolor(colors[colornum, iscolor])
* end function ColorSet()
*-------------------------------------------*

/*
```

```
   ColorMod() - View/Modify all global color settings

*/
function ColorMod()
local key := 0, newcolor, ntop, xx, getlist := {}, colorfile, ;
  oldscore := set(_SET_SCOREBOARD, .f.)  // shut off scoreboard
SaveEnv(.t.)       // save entire screen for later restoration
ColorSet(C_NORMAL)
ntop := ( maxrow() - COLOR_CNT ) / 2
@ ntop, 22, ntop + COLOR_CNT + 1, 57 box B_SINGLE + ' '
setpos(ntop, 0)
/* pad each color setting to 8 characters for data entry */
aeval(colors, { | a, b | ;
      colors[b, iscolor] := padr(colors[b, iscolor], 8) } )
for xx := 1 to COLOR_CNT
   @ row() + 1, 24 say colors[xx, 3] + " Color"
   ColorSet(xx)
   @ row(), 42 say "SAMPLE" get colors[xx, iscolor];
                            valid Redraw(ntop)
   ColorSet(C_NORMAL)
next
read

/* trim each color setting */
aeval(colors,{ | a, b | ;
      colors[b, iscolor] := trim(colors[b, iscolor]) } )
setpos(ntop + COLOR_CNT + 1, 24)
dispout("Press F10 to save these settings")
if inkey(0) == K_F10
   colorfile := padr(CFG_FILE, 12)
   ColorSet(C_MESSAGE)
   @ 11, 18, 13, 61 box B_DOUBLE + ' '
   @ 12, 20 say "Enter file name to save to:"
   @ 12, 48 get colorfile picture '@!'
   setcursor(1)
   read
   setcursor(0)
   if lastkey() != K_ESC .and. ! empty(colorfile)
       Gsavearray(colors, ltrim(trim(colorfile)))
   endif
```

```
endif
RestEnv()
set(_SET_SCOREBOARD, oldscore)
return NIL

* end function ColorMod()
*------------------------------------------*


/*
   Redraw() - redraw color samples after each GET
*/
static function redraw(ntop)
local oldcolor := ColorSet(row() - ntop)
@ row(), 42 say "SAMPLE"
setcolor(oldcolor)
return .t.

* end static function Redraw()
*-------------------------------------------*
```

Primitives

In earlier versions of Clipper, it was easy to run into glitches involving output. The most frequent problem was having an @..SAY message sent to the printer when it was intended for the screen. (This occurred because Clipper blindly followed the DEVICE setting.)

Fortunately, Clipper 5 gives us a much finer degree of control with a handful of new output functions:

Function	*Description*
DEVOUT()	Write a value to the current device
DEVOUTPICT()	Write a value to the current device w/ PICTURE clause
DEVPOS()	Move the cursor or printhead to a new position dependent upon the current state of SET DEVICE
DISPBOX()	Display a box on the screen
DISPOUT()	Write a value to the display

MAXCOL()	Returns maximum column that can be displayed on screen
MAXROW()	Returns maximum row that can be displayed on screen
OUTERR()	Write a list of values to the standard error device
OUTSTD()	Write a list of values to the standard output device
QOUT()	Display a list of expressions to next screen row
QQOUT()	Display a list of expressions to current screen position
SCROLL()	Scroll region of screen up or down, or optionally clear region of screen
SETCURSOR()	Controls size and shape of the cursor
SETMODE()	Changes display mode
SETPOS()	Move the cursor to a new position
SETPRC()	Reset positions of printer row and column (not new for Clipper 5 but relevant nonetheless)

Positioning Functions

DEVPOS(), SETPOS(), and SETPRC() all move the cursor and/or printhead. DEVPOS() moves either the cursor or printhead based on the current DEVICE setting: if SCREEN, the cursor is moved; if PRINTER, the printhead is moved. By contrast, SETPOS() and SETPRC() apply only to the cursor and printhead, respectively, regardless of the current device setting.

All three of these functions accept two parameters: <row> and<col>. These are numeric expressions representing the target row and column to which the cursor/printhead should be moved.

If the cursor is moved, the values of ROW() and COL() (functions that return the current cursor position) will be updated accordingly. In the same fashion, printhead movement will update the values of PROW() and PCOL().

All three of these functions always return NIL.

The code fragment shown in Listing 13.14 demonstrates the use of these three functions, as well as how they are affected (or unaffected) by the SET DEVICE command.

Listing 13.14 Clipper 5 Primitive Output Functions

```
set device to print
setpos(10, 20)              // moves cursor
devpos(1, 2)                // moves printhead because of DEVICE
set device to screen
devpos(8, 0)                // now moves cursor because of DEVICE
setprc(10, 10)              // moves printhead
```

DEVPOS() Notes:

- If DEVPOS() is asked to move the printhead to a row less than the current PROW(), it will force a page eject.

- If DEVPOS() is requested to move the printhead to a column less than the current PCOL(), it will issue a carriage return and the required number of spaces.

- If the printer is redirected to a file using the SET PRINTER command, DEVPOS() updates the file instead of the printer.

- DEVPOS() is used in tandem with DEVOUT() to enable the @..SAY command. (See below for a discussion of @..SAY.)

Output functions

The following functions handle actual output: DEVOUT(), DEVOUTPICT(), DISPOUT(), QOUT(), QQOUT(), OUTERR(), and OUTSTD(). These functions fall neatly into logical groupings, so we will look at them in that context.

DEVOUT(), DEVOUTPICT(), and DISPOUT()

These three functions output a value. All of them ignore the current SET CONSOLE status. DEVOUT() and DEVOUTPICT() direct their output to the current device, as determined by either the SET DEVICE command or the SET() function. By contrast, DISPOUT() always writes its output to the screen, no matter what device is current. Though subtle, this distinction makes a world of difference, as we shall see shortly.

All of these functions accept two parameters: (a) the value to be displayed; and (b) a character expression representing the color in which to display the value on the screen.

The color parameter was new with release 5.01. It is optional, and (naturally) is ignored when output is directed to the printer. Being able to specify the color directly will cut down on many lines of code. If you have ever written something like this:

```
oldcolor := setcolor("+W/R")
@ 12, 20 say "WARNING!"
setcolor(oldcolor)
```

you will now be able to write it like so:

```
@ 12, 20 say "WARNING!" color "+W/R"
```

Clipper will take care of setting the color back to its previous setting.

DEVOUTPICT() also accepts a third parameter, which is a character string representing the color to use for displaying the value. Note that this applies only to screen output.

All three of these functions return a value of NIL. The code sample shown in Listing 13.15 demonstrates their use, and their relationship to the current device setting.

Listing 13.15 DEVOUT(), DEVOUTPICT() and DISPOUT()

```
function Test
cstring = "Test message"
devout(cstring)             // goes to screen
devout(cstring, "W/R")      // goes to screen in white on red
set device to print
devout(cstring)             // goes to printer
devout(cstring, "W/R")      // goes to printer, color ignored
devoutpict(cstring,"@!")    // goes to printer, all upper-case
dispout(cstring)            // goes to screen
dispout(cstring, "W/B")     // goes to screen in white on blue
return nil
```

@..SAY — to get a better idea of how these functions are used, let's review the preprocessor translations for the @..SAY command (as seen in the STD.CH header file):

```
#command @ <row>, <col> SAY <xpr> [PICTURE <pic>] ;
                                  [COLOR <color>] ;
                => DevPos( <row>, <col> )             ;;
                DevOutPict( <xpr>, <pic> [, <color>] )

#command @ <row>, <col> SAY <xpr> [COLOR <color>]     ;
                => DevPos( <row>, <col> )             ;;
                   DevOut( <xpr> [, <color>] )
```

DEVPOS() positions the cursor or printhead at the desired location. DEVOUT() outputs the desired value to the screen or printer. (If you specify a PICTURE clause, DEVOUTPICT() is used instead of DEVOUT()).

Note that DEVOUT() and DEVOUTPICT() are dependent upon the current device status, which means that your message could get misdirected to the printer. However, it is easy to ensure that your @..SAY messages always go to the screen. You can use the preprocessor to create your own user-defined command, @..SSAY, which relies upon the screen-specific SETPOS() and DISPOUT() functions. @..SSAY is shown in Listing 13.16.

Listing 13.16 @..SSAY

```
#xcommand  @ <row>, <col> SSAY <xpr> => ;
           SetPos( <row>, <col> ) ; DispOut( <xpr> )

function Main
set device to print
@ 10,10 say 'this goes to the printer'
@ row(),col() ssay 'this always goes to the screen'
return nil
```

We highly recommend that you add the @..SSAY command to your header file for future use. We also recommend that you write your user feedback functions (error messages, etc.) to make use of this command. That way, you will always be assured of having your message on the screen rather than the printer.

QOUT() and QQOUT()

These functions are the equivalent of the **?** and **??** commands. They both output a list of values to the screen. The only difference between them is that QOUT() spits out a carriage return/linefeed combination prior to the values, whereas QQOUT() outputs the values at the current position.

These functions accept a comma-delimited list of values to be displayed. These values can be of any type (excepting array and block), and you do not have to concern yourself with converting everything to character string. The following statement demonstrates this:

```
qout(date(), 5, "string", .f.)   // perfectly valid
```

(Note that these functions will output a space between each value in your list.)

These functions are both device-dependent, and thus write to either the screen or printer. If you use them to write to the screen, the values of ROW() and COL() will be updated accordingly. If they are used to write to the printer, PROW() and PCOL() will be updated.

At first glance, it would appear that QOUT() and QQOUT() are unnecessary because of the **?** and **??** commands (which by the way are now translated by the preprocessor into calls to these functions). However, QOUT() and QQOUT() do indeed have their place. One such instance would be displaying values within an expression. Suppose that you want to display all the elements of an array with AEVAL() (introduced in Chapter 8, "Code Blocks"). You cannot use **?** or **??** within an expression because the preprocessor will be unable to translate them! Listing 13.17 illustrates this principle.

Listing 13.17 QOUT() vs. the ? command

```
function Test
local a := { "qout()", "vs.", "?", "which", "will", "work" }
aeval(a, { | ele | ? ele } )          // will not compile
aeval(a, { | ele | qout(ele) } )      // much better!
return nil
```

OUTERR() and OUTSTD()

These two functions output a list of values. OUTERR() directs its output to the standard error device (**stderr**), whereas OUTSTD() writes to the standard output device (**stdout**).

As with QOUT() and QQOUT(), these two functions accept a list of values to be displayed. These values can be of any type (excluding array and block).

OUTERR() and OUTSTD() both return NIL.

Output from both of these functions bypasses the Clipper console stream. This means that you have no control over placement — functions such as DEVPOS() and SETPOS() will have absolutely no bearing.

However, you may have programs that will not require full-screen output. In those instances you can use these functions to avoid loading the terminal output subsystem, which will in turn save you approximately 25K in your executable file. To ease this process, you may wish to use the redefinitions of the **?** and **??** commands shown in Listing 13.18 (which use OUTSTD() instead of DEVOUT()).

Listing 13.18 ? and ?? commands using OUTSTD()

```
#command  ? [ <list,...> ]      => outstd(chr(13)+chr(10)) ; ;
                                      outstd( <list> )
#command  ?? [ <list,...> ]     =>  outstd( <list> )
```

(The Computer Associates-supplied SIMPLEIO.CH header file contains similar definitions.)

Unlike the other Clipper output functions, you may use DOS redirection with OUTSTD(). However, OUTERR() bypasses such redirection as well. The sample program shown in Listing 13.19 uses many of the output functions. You can readily see the destination of each function's output.

Listing 13.19 Redirection examples

```
/* TEMP.PRG */

function Main
set device to printer
qout("*to screen")
dispout("*to screen")
devout("*to printer")
outstd("*redirection")
outerr("*to screen")
return nil

D:\>temp
*to screen*to screen*redirection*to screen

D:\>temp > output
*to screen*to screen*to screen

D:\>type output
*redirection
```

DISPBOX()

DISPBOX() displays a box at specified coordinates. You can optionally specify a color parameter. The syntax is as follows:

```
DISPBOX( <t>, <l>, <b>, <r> [, <boxtype> ] [, <cColor> ] )
```

<t>, <l>, <b>, <r> are the coordinates of the box.

Optional parameter **<boxtype>** may be either a numeric or a character expression. Numeric value 1 indicates a single-line box, and 2 indicates a double-line box. Neither of these boxes will be cleared; i.e., they are the functional equivalent of the dBASE @ r,c TO r1,c1.

If you specify a character string, it will be treated as per the @..BOX command.

Optional parameter **<cColor>** is a character expression indicating the color in which to display the box. If you do not pass this, the current standard color will be used.

Examples of its use are:

```
DISPBOX(0, 0, 5, 10, 1)                  // single line
DISPBOX(10, 1, 13, 50, 2)                // double line
DISPBOX(10, 1, 13, 50, 2, 'W/R')        // double, white on red
DISPBOX(20, 20, 22, 40, B_SINGLE)       // single line
```

SCROLL()

SCROLL() is used either to scroll a portion of the screen up or down a specified number of rows, or to clear a portion (or all) of the screen. Its parameters are as follows:

```
SCROLL( <nTop>, <nLeft>, <nBottom>, <nRight>, <nRows>, <nCols>)
```

<nTop>, <nLeft>, <nBottom>, and **<nRight>** represent the box coordinates. <nRows> is the number of rows to scroll. Positive values are scrolled down, and negative values are scrolled up. If you pass zero for <nRows>, the designated screen region will be cleared.

<nCols> is the number of columns to scroll. A positive value scrolls left and a negative value scrolls right. Keep in mind that horizontal scrolling may not work on all terminals.

With the Clipper 5.01 release, all SCROLL() parameters are optional. If you do not send any coordinate parameters, the coordinates of the full visible screen is assumed. If you skip the fifth parameter (representing the number of lines to scroll), SCROLL() assumes that you want to clear the area.

If you look at the STD.CH file, you will notice that SCROLL() replaces previous internal functions __Clear() and __AtClear(). The following are excerpts from STD.CH.

```
#command @ <r>, <c> => Scroll( <r>, <c>, <r> ) ; ;
                       SetPos( <r>, <c> )

#command CLS => Scroll() ; SetPos(0,0)

#command @ <t>, <l> CLEAR ; => Scroll( <t>, <l> ) ; ;
                              SetPos( <t>, <l> )
```

Miscellaneous functions

SETMODE()

SETMODE() allows us to change the video display mode. It accepts two numeric parameters, **<rows>** and **<columns>**, and attempts to switch to the appropriate mode. **Undocumented feature**: If you pass a zero as one of these parameters, SETMODE() will *not* change that item.

SETMODE() returns a logical value: true if the mode change was successful, or false if it failed. If you have an EGA or VGA adapter, you could switch modes with the function shown in Listing 13.21.

Note that in order for a mode to be considered valid, that mode must be understood and recognized by both your hardware and the video driver.

Listing 13.21 Changing video modes

```
#define  EGA       43
#define  VGA       50
#define  REG       25
#define  SINGLE    80
#define  DOUBLE    40
#define  NOCHANGE   0
```

```
function Main
local oldrows := maxrow() + 1, oldcols := maxcol() + 1
cls
ChangeMode(VGA, SINGLE)
ChangeMode(NOCHANGE, DOUBLE)
ChangeMode(REG, 0)
ChangeMode(oldrows, oldcols)
return nil

function ChangeMode(rows, cols)
local ret_val := setmode(rows, cols)
if ! ret_val
   ? ltrim(str(rows)) + " x " + ltrim(str(cols)) + ;
      " mode not available"
else
   @ maxrow() - 2, 0 say "MAXROW(): " +str(maxrow())
   @ maxrow() - 1, 0 say "MAXCOL(): " +str(maxcol())
   @ maxrow(), 0 say "Current mode: " +ltrim(str(maxrow()+1))+;
                        " x " + ltrim(str(maxcol()+1))
endif
inkey(0)
return ret_val
```

MAXROW() and MAXCOL()

These functions return the maximum row and column positions that can be displayed.

The typical return values for these functions are 24 and 79, because most of your work will be in text mode (25 rows x 80 columns). However, as you have just seen with SETMODE(), it is now possible to use different display modes in your Clipper programs.

Although it may be awhile before you are predominantly working in graphics mode, you should expect it to be a question of “WHEN”, not “IF”. Accordingly, to save yourself a lot of drudgery later, you should adopt defensive programming techniques now. MAXROW() and MAXCOL() make it easy to do so:

- Instead of saving and restoring a screen like this:

```
oldscrn := savescreen(0, 0, 24, 79)
*
restscreen(0, 0, 24, 79, oldscrn)
```

  you should save and restore it like so:

```
oldscrn := savescreen(0, 0, maxrow(), maxcol())
*
restscreen(0, 0, maxrow(), maxcol(), oldscrn)
```

- When centering text on the screen, use MAXCOL() + 1 as the width instead of 80, because you might not always be in 80-column mode. (See the examples below for a display mode-independent CENTER() preprocessor function.)

SETCURSOR()

This function is a godsend for manipulating the size of the cursor. Prior to Clipper 5, the only way to do so was via the extremely limited SET CURSOR command. This command offered only two settings: ON and OFF. It was impossible to save the status of the cursor for restoration (as you would with screen contents and/or current color setting) without resorting to C or Assembler.

Thankfully, SETCURSOR() returns the current setting of the cursor. You can then save this to a memory variable or array element, change the cursor size, and restore it to its previous state.

That reason alone is sufficient to abandon the SET CURSOR command. But wait... there's more! You have greater flexibility with the size and shape of the cursor. Table 13.2 shows all available cursor types, along with the applicable parameter and manifest constant.

Table 13.2 Cursor types

Manifest Constant (in SETCURS.CH)	*Number*	*Description*
SC_NONE	0	No cursor
SC_NORMAL	1	Normal (underline)
SC_INSERT	2	Lower half block
SC_SPECIAL1	3	Full block
SC_SPECIAL2	4	Upper half block

Once again, we highly recommend that you refer to the manifest constants rather than the numeric values, which are subject to change. The code shown in Listing 13.22 illustrates the use of SETCURSOR() and these manifest constants.

Listing 13.22 Changing the cursor with SETCURSOR()

```
#include "setcurs.ch"  // for using the manifest constants

function Whatever
local oldcursor := setcursor(SC_NONE)  // turn off cursor
*
*
setcursor(SC_SPECIAL1)          // full block cursor
read
setcursor(SC_NONE)              // turn off cursor again
*
*
setcursor(oldcursor)            // restore to previous state
return nil
```

Examples

Centering text

Centering text on the screen is a basic need for any Clipper application. Listing 13.23 presents two user-defined commands. CENTER() centers text on either the screen or printer, dependent upon the current device. SCRNCENTER() always centers the text on the screen, thanks to SETPOS() and DISPOUT().

Listing 13.23 Centering text on screen and printer

```
#xtranslate CENTER(<row>, <msg> [,<color>] ] => ;
   DevPos( <row>, int(( maxcol()+1 - len(<msg>)) / 2)) ; ;
   DevOut( <msg> [, <color>] )

#xtranslate SCRNCENTER(<row>, <msg> [, <color>] ) => ;
   SetPos( <row>, int(( maxcol()+1 - len(<msg>)) / 2)) ; ;
   DispOut( <msg> [, <color>] )

function test
set device to print
center(1, "this goes to the printer")
scrncenter(1, "this goes to the screen")
return nil
```

As mentioned previously, note that both CENTER() and SCRNCENTER() make use of the MAXCOL() function to determine the width for centering your message. This makes them oblivious to changes in video mode, thus saving you valuable time recoding your applications should you decide to change to a graphical user interface in the future.

Saving/restoring cursor position

If you wanted to save and restore the cursor position in prior versions of Clipper, you probably used logic similar to that shown in Listing 13.24.

Listing 13.24 Saving/restoring cursor position in Summer '87

```
function MyFunc
private mrow, mcol
mrow = row()
mcol = col()
*
@ mrow, mcol say ''
return ret_val
```

There are two reasons why you would not want to do this in Clipper 5:

- The preprocessor converts the @..SAY command into calls to DEVPOS() and DEVOUT(). Because you do not want to display a value, the DEVOUT() call is completely unnecessary.

- If the device is set to PRINT, the printhead position will be changed instead of the cursor, thus undermining your housekeeping attempts.

Therefore, you should use the following command to reposition the cursor:

```
setpos(mrow, mcol)
```

This kills both birds with one line by eliminating the useless function call and forcing the cursor to be updated regardless of the current device.

In similar fashion, there is no longer any need for you to write code such as the following:

```
@ prow(), 1 say cust->lname
@ prow(), pcol(), say cust->fname
```

Because you want to print **fname** at the current printhead position, you need only call DEVOUT(). Thus you will avoid a redundant DEVPOS() function call.

User feedback on large databases

Suppose that you want to sum a numeric field on a 50,000 record database. As you probably already know, the SUM operation does not give any user feedback whatsoever. Given a large enough database (and a slow enough CPU), a timid user might think that the machine is locked up, and thus be tempted to reboot. Heaven forbid!

The COUNT, SUM, and AVERAGE commands are translated by the preprocessor into DBEVAL() calls. As discussed in Chapter 8 ("Code Blocks"), DBEVAL() evaluates a code block for a given set of records in a database. It is therefore quite easy for us to put "hooks" into this code block that will display the current record number being processed, which will give the user a clear indication that the computer is indeed clicking away.

The following command:

```
sum ITEM->quantity to temp
```

is translated to:

```
temp := 0 ; ;
DBEval( {|| temp := temp + item->quantity},,,,, .F.)
```

This is fairly straightforward. The variable **temp** is initialized to zero, and will be incremented by the value of **quantity** for each record in the database. (Note that you can easily limit the scope of this command by supplying one or more other code blocks to DBEVAL(). For more specifics, please refer back to Chapter 8.)

Two function calls are added to the code block to display the current record number and running total. SETPOS() positions the cursor where we want it, and QQOUT() displays the values. While we're at it, we will also use the compound assignment operator "+=", which should have been in there in the first place. Listing 13.25 shows the source code for this code block, and Figure 13.7 shows how it looks on the screen.

Figure 13.7 User feedback during SUM operation

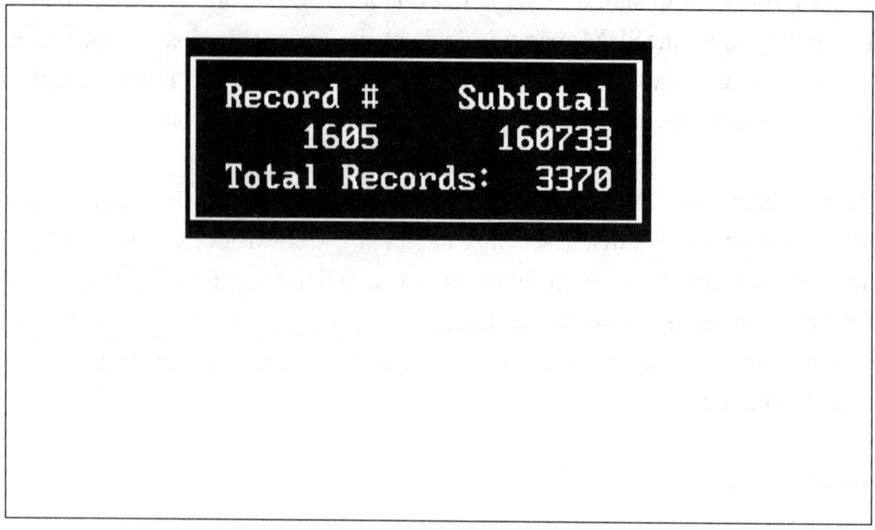

Listing 13.25 User feedback during SUM operation

```
#include "box.ch"

function Test
cls
setcolor('+w/b')
use item
dispbox(10, 28, 14, 51, B_SINGLE + ' ')
@ 11, 30 say "Record #   Subtotal"
@ 13, 30 say "Total Records: " + ltrim(str(lastrec()))
temp := 0
DBEval( {|| temp += item->quantity, ;
         setpos(12, 30), qqout(recno(), temp) },,,,, .F. )
return nil
```

Displaying page numbers while printing

Listing 13.26 demonstrates the use of SETPOS() and DISPOUT() to display page numbers on the screen while printing a report. The use of these two functions precludes you from having to switch the DEVICE setting back and forth (which can get very confusing very quickly).

Listing 13.26 Displaying page numbers while printing

```
#include "box.ch"
function Report
use customer
dispbox(11, 28, 13, 52, B_SINGLE + ' ')
@ 12, 30 say "Now printing page "
set device to print
heading(init)
do while ! eof()
   @ prow()+1, 0 say trim(customer->lname) + ', ' + ;
                     left(trim(customer->fname), 1)
   @ prow(),  25 say customer->addr1
   @ prow(),  55 say customer->city
   @ prow(),  70 say customer->state
   @ prow(),  74 say left(customer->zip, 5)
  if prow() > 57
      heading()
   endif
   skip
enddo
set device to screen
return nil

function Heading(init)
static page := 1
/*
   if parameter was passed to Heading(), we are in initialize mode
   and must reset the page counter - this is necessary if you run
   this report a second (or third) time
*/
if init != NIL
   page := 1
endif
@ 0, 0 say "Customer List - Page " + ltrim(str(page))
setpos(12, 48)
dispout(str(page++, 3))      // increment page counter
return nil
```

The function Heading() declares **page** as a static variable, which means that it will retain its value each time you re-enter the function. However, this does have its drawbacks, which become painfully obvious when you run this report a second time and start at page 20! Therefore, the first time you call Heading(), you should pass it any parameter, which instructs the function to re-initialize the page counter to 1.

Heading() moves the printhead to the top of the page and displays a brief heading along with the page number. It then displays the page number on the screen in the message box, and increments the page counter.

User interface building blocks

Now that you understand the Clipper primitives, let's create a few specialized user interface tools that cut the task of user interface programming down to size.

That darn cursor

A very simple thing you can do to spruce up your Clipper screen displays is to turn the cursor off. The only time it needs to be on is during READ and MEMOEDIT(), and those are easy enough to track down. Simply turn the cursor on right before a READ or MEMOEDIT() and then off again when they are finished. If you write a function that needs to turn the cursor on, save the current state and be sure to restore it on exit from the function. All the functions in this section either assume the cursor is already off, or they turn it off and restore it on exit. Fortunately, this is easy to do, as Listing 13.27 demonstrates.

Listing 13.27 Managing the cursor

```
//  Save existing cursor state (could be on or off)
//  and then shut it off.
curs := setcursor(0)
//  Restore original cursor state.
setcursor(curs)
```

Most of the "SET" series of functions work like this. Frequently you'll need to save more than just the cursor. If you are going to mess up the screen and change colors, your functions should clean up after themselves and restore the entire environment. See Chapter 12, "Program Design," for some excellent functions that accomplish this task via the use of static arrays.

Yes/No questions

For the amount of information you ultimately receive from them, hard-wired yes/no prompts are more trouble than they're worth. Consider the amount of code they take to implement, as shown in Listing 13.28.

Listing 13.28 Hard-wired Yes/No prompt

```
@ 10, 15 say "Are you sure (Y/N)?"
k := inkey(0)
if upper(chr(k)) == "Y"
  zap
endif
```

No Clipper programmer should have to go through all that when user-defined functions are available. Listing 13.29 shows the Yes() function, which greatly simplifies the task.

Listing 13.29 Yes() function for Yes/No prompt

```
function Yes(r, c, message)
@ r, c say message
return (upper(inkey(0)) == "Y")
```

The previous example can now be reduced to the following:

```
if Yes(10, 15, "Are you sure (Y/N)?")
  zap
endif
```

While this alone is a substantial improvement, we are now free to add more features to the basic function. YesBox() (shown in Listing 13.30) makes the message more visible to the end-user by drawing a box around it.

Listing 13.30 YesBox()

```
#include "box.ch"

function YesBox(r, c, message)
//  Draw a box that will surround the message.
dispbox(r, c, r + 2, c + len(message), B_SINGLE + ' ')
// Display the message.
@ r + 1, c + 1 say message
return (upper(inkey(0)) == "Y")
```

Note how adding such features costs us nothing — the function call stays simple while the function itself can get as complex as we need to support the features. This is the basic concept behind user interface building blocks.

There are other features that can be added to illustrate more of these building block concepts. One such feature is a "time-out," where if the user does not press a key before a certain amount of time, "no" is assumed and the function continues. Listing 13.31 adds this feature to YesBox().

Listing 13.31 YesBox() with time-out

```
#include "box.ch"

function YesBox(r, c, message, wait)
//  Draw a box that will surround the message.
dispbox(r, c, r + 2, c + len(message), B_SINGLE + ' ')
//  Display the message.
@ r +1, c +1 say message
return (upper(inkey(wait)) == "Y")
```

While a time-out feature is very handy when you need it, it gets in the way when you do not want it. As written above, YesBox() requires a time period or it will crash when it hits the INKEY() function. It would be better to make the time period parameter optional. If it is not specified, the function should wait "forever" as did the earlier versions of the function. As you saw in Chapter 4 ("Data Types"), if you do not pass a parameter, Clipper assigns it a value of NIL, so the missing parameters are easy to test.

Listing 13.33 YesBox() with DEFAULT

```
#include "box.ch"

function YesBox(r, c, message, wait)
default wait to 0
//  Draw a box that will surround the message.
dispbox(r, c, r + 2, c + len(message), B_SINGLE + ' ')
//  Display the message.
@ r +1, c +1 say message
return (upper(inkey(wait)) == "Y")
```

YesBox() can now be called with or without the time-out parameter, and it will react in a manner consistent with what you would expect from the syntax.

```
if YesBox("Take your time... Y or N?")
 if YesBox("Quick! You've got three seconds! Y/N?", 3)
  endif
endif
```

While you're at it, why not make the row and column parameters optional, too? All that is necessary are reasonable default values for each parameter. The most reasonable thing to do is center the message on the screen. If no row is specified, start the box in the middle. If no column is specified, center the message on the screen. Listing 13.34 demonstrates these additions to YesBox(). Note the use of MAXROW() and MAXCOL() to ensure video-mode independence.

Listing 13.34 YesBox() with default row and column

```
#include "box.ch"

function YesBox(r, c, message, wait)
// assign default values
default r to (maxrow() / 2) - 1
default c to (maxcol() - len(message)) / 2
default wait to 0
// Draw a box that will surround the message.
```

```
dispbox(r, c, r + 2, c + len(message), B_SINGLE + ' ')
//  Display the message.
@ r + 1, c + 1 say message
return (upper(inkey(wait)) == "Y")
```

At this point you have an extremely versatile user interface function capable of making screen position and duration assumptions based on how it is called, and you have not even worked up a sweat! Listing 13.35 shows how you could phrase your calls to YesBox() in its current configuration.

Listing 13.35 YesBox() sample calls

```
if YesBox(,, "Is this centered on the screen?")
  //  We wrote the function correctly.
endif

if .not. YesBox(17,, "Is this centered on row 17?")
  //  We screwed up somewhere – time to debug.
endif

if YesBox(, 20, "Is this starting in column 20?")
  //  Amazing, we can skip any combination.
endif
```

Let's pull out all the stops and write the ultimate in Yes/No prompts, one that uses a lightbar menu for a "dialog box" feel. You should also be able to specify a color to use. Of course, everything but the actual prompt message should be optional. Here's an example of a call that uses all the parameters.

```
answer := YesNoMenu(10, 15, "Are you sure?", C_MESSAGE)
```

This doesn't look much different than the YesBox() function. Things are starting to get more complex inside the function. However, the calls to the function remain easy to read and remember because you have laid out the parameters and given some thought to default values. Listing 13.36 contains the source code for YesNoMenu(). (Note that this function calls on the ColorSet() function, discussed previously in this chapter, for color handling.)

Listing 13.36 Lightbar menu-based Yes/No prompt

```
#include "box.ch"
#include "colors.ch"
function YesNoMenu(r, c, msg, clr)
/*
     General-purpose Yes/No prompt function.
     Parameter  Description

     r          Starting row, default is center of screen.
     c          Starting column, default is center of screen.
     msg        Message to display as a prompt.
     clr        Color number to use, default is current color.

     Note: Color selection for this function is handled by
     the ColorSet() function.

*/

local response                  //  User's response
local r2, c2, offset            //  Help with box coordinates
local pYes, pNo                 //  Prompts for "Yes" and "No"

//  Make sure all parameters have reasonable default values.
default r to (maxrow() / 2) -2
default c to (maxcol() - len(msg)) / 2
default clr to C_NORMAL
//  Prompts to display for choices.
pYes := "YES"
pNo  := "NO"
/*
     Calculate ending box coordinates. Box width must be able to
     accommodate the longest of either the prompt message or the
     YES and NO selections.
*/

r2 := r +3
c2 := c +len(msg) +1
c2 := max(c2, c +len(pYes) +2 +len(pNo))
//  Calculate how far to indent Yes/No prompts within the box.
```

```
offset := ((c2 -c) -(len(pYes) +2 +len(pNo))) /2
//  Save existing screen, color etc. (SaveEnv() is in Chapter 12)
SaveEnv()
//  Clear the area and draw a box
dispbox(r, c, r2, c2, B_SINGLE + ' ')
//  Display message and Yes/No prompts, wait for response.
@ r +1, c +1 say msg
@ r +2, c +1 +offset prompt pYes
@ r +2, col() +2  prompt pNo
menu to response
//  Restore original screen, color etc before returning.
RestEnv()
return (response ==1)
```

A careful reading of the source code shows that YesNoMenu() takes great pains not to leave any "tracks" on the screen. Everything related to the screen is left as it was before the call to the function. YesNoMenu() can pop up over a complicated screen, ask its question, and disappear without disturbing anything. This is not simply a nice convenience feature — it is the only way that general-purpose functions should be written. The amount of effort you put into the functions is paid back many times in more reliable and consistent applications.

ALERT()

ALERT() is a function added with the 5.01 release of Clipper. Although it is used primarily in the run-time error handler (ERRORSYS.PRG), you will find plenty of situations in your programs (apart from error handling) where you will be able to make excellent use of ALERT().

It is a marvelous little function that displays a message, and presents one or more options for the user to select from. The syntax is:

```
ALERT( <cMessage> [, <aOptions> ][, <cColor> ] )
```

<cMessage> is the message to be displayed.

Optional parameter **<aOptions>** is an array of options. If you do not use this, the only option will be "OK".

Undocumented optional parameter <cColor> is the color in which to display the box. The default colors are hi white on red for the box and message, and hi white on blue for the highlighted option. Bear in mind that since this parameter is undocumented, it is subject to future change.

ALERT() displays a box centered on the screen. Your message is centered on the top row within the box, and the options are centered just below that.

ALERT() returns a numeric value representing the option that was selected. For example, if the user selected "Quit" in the following code fragment, ALERT() would return 2. As with MENU TO and ACHOICE(), if the user exits with Esc ALERT() will return a zero.

```
ALERT("Something horrible has happened", ;
      { "Ignore", "Quit" })
```

NOTE: ALERT() is sensitive to the presence (or absence) of the full-screen input/output subsystem. If your program does not make use of these functions, ALERT() will display its messages using output of the standard device, as opposed to full-screen output. This means that the pleasant lightbar interface will not be used, but the idea will still be clear enough to the user.

Message boxes

Message boxes are handy user interface devices for displaying information that is kept separate from the rest of the contents of the screen. A message box is immediately visible and recognizable to the end-user. It should not get lost in the screen clutter. This is especially important if the message is displayed under a wide variety of conditions and you do not know what else might be in the vicinity.

A good message box must be flexible enough to be placed anywhere on the screen and contain any number of lines. Being able to handle an arbitrary number of lines spells trouble for the techniques covered thus far in YesBox() and YesNoMenu(). They can handle only a single line of text.

The best solution is to place the lines of message text in an array and pass it to the message box function (as shown in Listing 13.37). That way the number of parameters passed to the function remains the same whether one or a dozen lines are required.

Listing 13.37 Sample call to Message()

```
//  Draws box from 5,17 to 10,25
//  then displays the three lines inside the box.

Message(5, 17, 10, 25, {"A message","with three","lines."})
```

Although this would be a useful function in its own right, we are going to keep adding features and capabilities until we have a very powerful, general-purpose function. This is leading up to an important design technique, so please hang in there as this seemingly pedestrian message box function grows into a nearly unmanageable monster. The monster will eventually be slain with an incredibly elegant user-defined command.

The first potentially annoying thing about Message() is the need to specify all four coordinates. It is nearly impossible to whip up a few lines of text for a message on the fly and then be able to calculate the exact dimensions of the box that should surround them, so the function should be able to determine any coordinates automatically. On the other hand, there are times when the box must be exactly a certain size, at a specific place on the screen, so the function must be able to accept all coordinates as parameters (see Listing 13.38).

Listing 13.38 Sample calls to Message()

```
//  Allow the starting column and ending row/column
//  to be calculated based on the message lines.

Message(10, , , , {"Centered","in row ten."})

//  Center row, starting in column 30.

Message( , 30, , , {"Centered","at column 30."})
```

Another handy feature is the ability to control the exact dimensions of the box not by calculating the coordinates but by specifying the desired width and depth directly. However, this requires two more parameters (as shown in Listing 13.39), since the function will not be able to tell the difference between an ending column number and a width.

Listing 13.39 Width and depth parameters for Message()

```
//  msgArray contains an array of message lines.

//  Box starts at 7,21 and is 20 columns wide,
//  four rows deep, independent of what's in the array.

Message(7, 12, , , 20, 4, msgArray)
```

So far we have seven parameters: four box coordinates, desired width, desired depth, and the array of message lines. With the ending row/column and width/depth parameters being mutually exclusive, the function call is getting more difficult to write correctly. At this point it is well beyond being self-documenting and intuitive. As mentioned above, there will be an elegant solution, so let's forge ahead.

Let's add a color option so that a box can be completely described in a single function call rather than relying on the current color (see Listing 13.40). If the function restores the original color on exit, there won't be any unpleasant side effects.

Listing 13.40 MsgBox() with color parameter

```
//  Starting at 8,19, width of 15 columns,
//  automatic depth calculation, three message lines,
//  displayed in the "bold" color.

MsgBox(8, 19, , , 15, , {"A", "B", "C"}, C_BOLD)
```

Sometimes you will want the message to stay on the screen until the user presses a key, and other times it should stay permanently until we clear it on our own. This requires two more parameters: one to indicate how long we want to wait for a keystroke (zero means wait forever); and another to indicate whether or not the message should disappear after the keystroke. Listing 13.41 shows sample calls to MsgBox() utilizing these two additional parameters.

Listing 13.41 MsgBox() with wait and restore parameters

```
//  Wait for up to 7 seconds and then
//  restore the previous screen.

MsgBox(8, 19, , , 15, , ;
            {"No data found.", "Press any key to continue..."}, ;
            C_WARNING, 7, .t.)

//  Wait forever, don't restore the screen.

MsgBox(8, 19, , , 15, , ;
            {"Finished posting invoices.", ;
            "Press a key to return to the main menu."}, ;
            C_ENHANCED, 0, .f.)
```

At this point we have a very ugly function on our hands, and we're still not finished adding features! If the function is going to wait around for a keystroke, it may as well offer a list of possible selections and get more mileage out of the prompt. Therefore, we'll need a parameter for the array of possible choices and another for the color to use for the choices. These two new parameters will be inserted right after the existing message and color parameters (see Listing 13.42), so the two sets of text stay together.

Listing 13.42 MsgBox() with choices array

```
//  Now we need a return value for the selection.

dest := MsgBox(8, 19, , , 30, , ;
                    {"Select a destination for the report:"}, ;
                    C_BOLD, ;
                    {"Printer", "Screen","File"}, ;
                    C_ENHANCED, , ,)
```

If you could make such a function call correctly from memory, you have an incredibly good memory! There are two major problems with the current MsgBox() syntax. Most of the parameters are difficult to tell apart even when constants are used, and are even more confusing if each parameter is a variable.

The exact sequence is also critical. If you skip a parameter, you must be careful to count out the correct number of commas so that the next parameter is in the right position. However, user-defined commands do not have to be quite as exacting as user-defined functions, and this is where we will find an acceptable solution.

Listing 13.43 calls the same nasty "report destination" prompt as seen before, but this time using syntax from a user-defined command.

Listing 13.43 MESSAGE syntax

```
message "Select a destination for the report:" ;
              color C_MESSAGE ;
              choose "Printer", "Screen", "File" ;
              choosecolor C_BOLD ;
              at 8,19 width 30 into dest
```

The beauty of the user-defined command is that the sequence in which the parameters appear (if they indeed appear at all) is completely irrelevant. Listing 13.44 demonstrates this by rearranging nearly all of the prompts. The resulting message box, however, will be exactly the same.

Listing 13.44 MESSAGE syntax

```
message "Select a destination for the report:" ;
              into dest at 8,19 width 30 color C_MESSAGE ;
              choose "Printer", "Screen", "File" ;
              choosecolor C_BOLD
```

Listing 13.45 shows simple examples that use some of the other parameters. You should be able to guess from the syntax alone how the message box is going to behave.

Listing 13.45 Other MESSAGE examples

```
message "Can't lock the record.", "Press any key..." ;
              at 20 wait 10 restore

message "Your Choice" color C_MESSAGE at 3, 5 to 8, 20 ;
              choose "A. Edit vendors", "B. Print vendors";
              into theChoice

message msgArray at 10,25 depth 7 choose chArray into sel
```

Although it looks strange, as long as the user-defined command is constructed properly you can assign a return value as if it were a function. This is because, after all, it is nothing but a function after the preprocessor is finished with it.

The complete source code for MsgBox() is too large to insert in this chapter, and can be found in Appendix B. At this point the user-defined command definition (as shown in Listing 13.46) is more relevant to our discussion.

Listing 13.46 User interface building block: the MESSAGE command

```
#xtranslate MESSAGE <msg,...> ;
                   [ AT <r1> [, <c1>] ] ;
                   [ TO <r2> [, <c2>] ] ;
                   [ WIDTH <w> ] ;
                   [ DEPTH <d> ] ;
                   [ COLOR <clr> ] ;
                   [ CHOOSE <ch,...> ] ;
```

```
                    [ CHOOSECOLOR <chClr> ] ;
                    [ CHCOLOR <chClr> ] ;
                    [ INTO <ret> ] ;
                    [ WAIT <wait> ] ;
                    [ <rest:RESTORE,REST> ] ;

     => ;

                  [<ret> := ] MsgBox( <r1>, <c1>, <r2>, <c2>,;
                              <w>, <d>, {<msg>}, ;
                              <clr>, {<ch>}, <chClr>, ;
                              <wait>, <.rest.> )
```

Note that there are full and abbreviated words for some of the parts of the command. For example, rather than having to type CHOOSECOLOR every time you can shorten it to CHCOLOR.

Such a comprehensive user-defined command is not a trivial bit of programming. Chapter 7, “The Preprocessor”, covers the nitty-gritty of how you would construct such a command, so we won’t go into specifics here.

Listing 13.47 shows one more example of the power and flexibility of user-defined functions being combined with the ease of use of commands.

Listing 13.47 Picking a file with MESSAGE

```
//  Load an array with filenames

dir_ := {}
aeval(directory(), { |f_| aadd(dir_, f_[1]) } )
//  Allow user to select a file
message "Pick a file..." color C_ENHANCED ;
        choose dir_ choosecolor C_BOLD into sel ;
        at 8,32 depth 14

//  Show them what they selected.
message "You selected: " +if(sel == 0, "<none>", dir_[sel]), ;
        "Press any key to continue..." color C_WARNING ;
        wait 0 at 9,38
```

Yes/No prompts revisited

Let's make the YesNoMenu() discussed earlier into a user-defined command along the same lines as the MsgBox() function. Creating a YESNO command will allow you to easily add features to YesNoMenu() without sacrificing the original ease of use. Listing 13.48 shows a #xtranslate directive to get you started.

Listing 13.48 User interface building block: the YESNO command

```
#xtranslate YESNO <msg> ;
              [ AT <r> [, <c>] ] ;
              [ COLOR <clr> ] ;
              [ INTO <ret> ] ;
      => ;
      [<ret> := ] YesNoMenu( <r>, <c>, <msg>, <clr> )
```

Calls to the resulting command look like the following.

```
yesno "Are you sure?" at 17,50 color C_WARNING into doIt
if doIt
  //
endif
purge := YesNo "Purge the old data?" at 2
```

Here are some suggested improvements that you can tackle:

- Make the YES and NO prompts into optional parameters. For example, SAVE and ABANDON. YES and NO should be the default values.

  ```
  go := yesno "Shall we go?" yesPrompt "GO" noPrompt "NOGO"
  ```

- Give the menu prompts an optional color. The menu prompts will stand out better if they are colored differently.

  ```
  yesno "Continue?" color C_MESSAGE menucolor C_BOLD
  ```

- Make the message an array of lines rather than limiting it to a single line. This is a substantial but valuable modification. You can use the MsgBox() function as a guide.

```
yesno "An error has occurred.", ;
"Do you want to continue", "with the process?" ;
at 10, 5 into keepGoing
```

How-to messages

As mentioned earlier in this chapter, your users should always know what's expected of them each time that the application stops and waits for input. It does not take much analysis and design to determine that if you display instructions right on the screen, that pretty well takes care of the issue. The problem is that it's a major effort to keep displaying such instructions over and over, while at the same time keeping the screen cleaned up and looking professional. The HowTo() function is presented as a solution to this problem. Its sole purpose is to display one or more lines of text at the bottom of the screen and later clean up after itself.

```
HowTo( {"Use arrow keys to highlight your selection,", ;
        "then press ENTER. Press ESC to exit without", ;
        "making a selection."} )
```

HowTo() is based on an array of message lines. This allows you to prepackage commonly used instructions, as shown in Listing 13.49.

Listing 13.49 Array of Message Lines

```
how_EDIT := {"Make changes as needed to the", ;
             "information on this screen.", ;
             "Press Control-End when finished."}
```

HowTo() can be configured to display a small message in the lower right corner of the screen, indicating that there's a more detailed help screen available. If true (.T.) is passed as a second parameter, HowTo() will display the special help message (as shown in Listing 13.50).

Listing 13.50 Calling HowTo()

```
//  Call a function that checks to see if help
//  is available for the current screen.

helpAvailable := CheckHelp(screenID)

how_EDIT := {"Make changes as needed to the", ;
             "information on this screen.", ;
             "Press Control-End when finished."}

//  Display standard "how to edit" message
//  and notify user that more detailed help
//  is available.

HowTo(how_EDIT, helpAvailable)
```

HowTo()'s cleanup procedure is very simple, but quite effective when most of your screens have how-to messages associated with them. HowTo() maintains a static variable that keeps track of how many lines were in the last message, and clears from that point down before displaying the current message. There will be times, however, where this isn't desirable. Therefore, HowTo() can be told to "forget" about the previous call by calling it with no parameters.

```
//  Reset the internal "previous" variable.

HowTo()
```

Finally, as a convenience feature, HowTo() is implemented to accept a single character string in place of an array in the event that your how-to message is brief.

```
HowTo("Just make a selection and let's get on with it.")
```

Without further ado, Listing 13.51 contains the source code for HowTo().

Listing 13.51 User interface building block: the HowTo() function

```
function HowTo(msg_, hasHelp)

/*
     General-purpose "How To Do It" function, displays specified
lines of text at bottom of screen that describe what's happening
on the screen and what the user is expected to do next.

    Parameter         Description

    msg_              Array of message lines. (If single line, a
                      string is ok.)
    hasHelp           Logical flag, .t. indicates a help screen is
                      available.

   HowTo() called with no parameters removes the last set of mes-
sages and resets the low row variable so future calls do not mess
up the screen.
*/

#define HELP_KEY_MSG  " [ F1-Help ]"

local i

// Remember the lowest row the previous messages occupied.
static previous

//  Clear previous message lines (if any).
if previous != NIL
     scroll(previous, 0)
endif

//  No message, reset
if msg_ == NIL
     previous := NIL
     //  Displaying message lines.
else
```

```
    //  As a convenience feature if there's only one line in
    //  the message it can be passed as a single string instead
    //  of an array.

    if valtype(msg_) == "C"
       msg_ := { msg_ }
    endif


    //  Display lines to bottom of screen.
    for i := 0 to (len(msg_) - 1)
       @ maxrow() - i, 0 say ;
                   padr(msg_[ len(msg_) - i ],  maxcol())
    next i
    @ row() -1, 0 say replicate(chr(196), maxcol())
    previous := row()

    /*
         Display message regarding the help key, if applicable.
         Clipper's "short circuit logic" allows us to check for a
         valid type on the same line as we need the actual value,
        it won't even consider ".and. hasHelp" unless the
        valtype() function returns true.
    */

    if (valtype(hasHelp) == "L") .and. hasHelp
       setpos(maxrow(), maxcol() - len(HELP_KEY_MSG))
       dispout(HELP_KEY_MSG)
    endif
endif
return nil
```

Try implementing a series of well-crafted HowTo() messages in one segment of a large application. Then compare that section to other sections of your application that display complex prompts and expect the user to remember quirky little details about which keys are used for which purposes, or even (Heaven forbid), why they are being asked the question in the first place!

Your users will appreciate the HowTo(), and so will your programmers. Here's why: The same messages that guide the end-user through the application are also visible to the programmer in the source code. The same comments function as documentation both inside the source code and outside on the screen. Now is it easier to justify the effort?

There's another benefit to which we alluded in the introductory comments to this chapter. While writing a HowTo() message, if you notice it's going to take more than a few simple sentences to describe what's going on, then perhaps there's *too much* going on. Break the situation down into smaller pieces that are easier to describe. For example, you might first ask the user a yes/no question that establishes a direction. Then you can eliminate things that are not relevant to what they're trying to accomplish, thus reducing the overall complexity.

Windowing

Windowing is a technique that is used to split a computer screen into multiple smaller viewing areas. It is basically intended to mimic your desktop. Imagine that you are working at your desk and you receive a memo. You probably do not bother clearing your desk to read the memo, but instead place it on top of whatever happens to be there already. Once you have read it, you remove it from your desk and resume whatever you were doing.

A window represents this concept on a computer screen. In Figure 13.8, the memo regarding lunch is a window that appears on top of the sales report. (Chapter 17 will discuss in greater detail considerations for creating programs that pop up over other screens.)

Clipper 5 makes it easy to create your own library of windowing functions. These functions allow you to create, write to, clear, and close windows.

Figure 13.8 - Window example

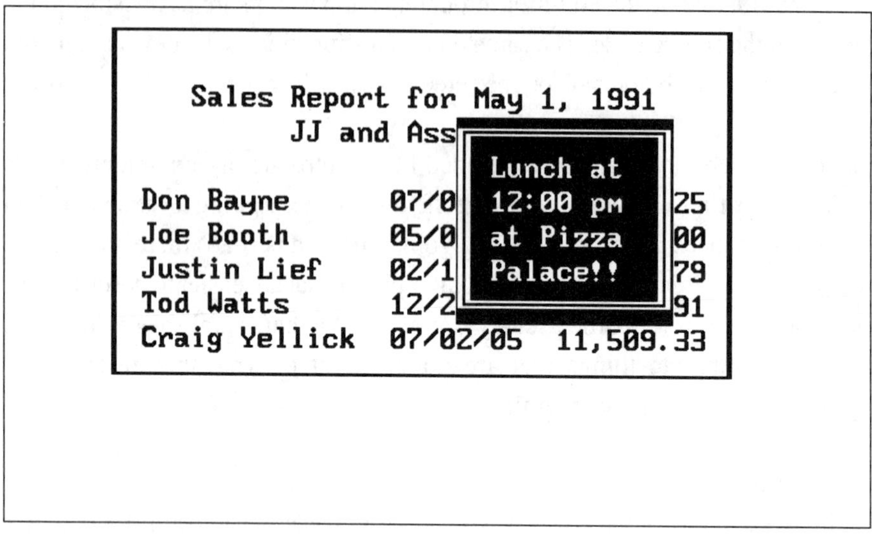

WCreate()

The WCreate() function creates a new window on the screen. It also stores the window parameters on the window stack. This window becomes the active screen for subsequent windowing functions until either it is closed or another window is created. Its syntax is:

```
WCreate( <t>, <l>, <b>, <r> [, <color>] )
```

<t>, <l>, <b>, <r> are all numeric expressions representing the coordinates to use for the window. The optional **<color>** parameter is a character string representing the color to use for drawing the window. Note that all text drawn to this window with the WSay() command will obey this color setting as well. If you do not pass <color>, the current color setting will be used.

WSay()

WSay() allows you to write text to a portion of the window without knowing the physical coordinates on the screen. Its syntax is:

```
WSay( <row>, <column>, <text> )
```

The **<row>** and **<column>** coordinates are relative to the window. The following statements demonstrate this.

```
WCreate(10, 20, 20, 60, "W+/B")    // Create a window
WSay(1, 1, "Lunch is ready")       // Will print at screen
                                   // coordinates 11,21
                                   // rather than 1,1.
```

This means that even if you change the coordinates passed to the WCreate() function, all subsequent window text will still appear in the proper screen locations.

WPrompt()

This is the same as WSay(), except that it displays a menu option (using the traditional @..PROMPT command) relative to the coordinates of the active window.

WClear()

This function erases the contents of the current active window. It does not require parameters.

WKill()

WKill() closes a previously created window and restores the text that was underneath it. It also restores the color and the cursor location. It does not require parameters.

WRow()

This function determines the absolute screen row based on the coordinates of the current active window and the offset requested.

WCol()

This function determines the absolute screen column based on the coordinates of the current active window and the offset requested.

The following module illustrates how the window functions can be used in an application program. This application implements a suggestion box screen to allow the end-users to write suggested enhancements to a log for the programmer to read.

Since all the screen positions are expressed in relative terms, the coordinates passed to WCreate() can be changed and the program responds to the new locations automatically. This approach allows you to have data-driven windows with an absolute minimum of coding.

Listing 13.52 contains the source code for these windowing functions, along with a sample program to demonstrate them. The sample program creates and displays a window over the current screen. The user can then input change order information, which is in turn written (or appended) to a file entitled CHANGE.LOG.

The preprocessor is an important player in this example. Manifest constants greatly enhance the readability of this code, particularly when referring to the attributes of the current window. User-defined commands (@..WSAY and @..WGET) allow you to continue using familiar Clipper command syntax.

Listing 13.52 Windowing functions

```
static wstack := {}
memvar getlist      // to squelch compiler warnings

#define TOP       wstack[len(wstack), 1]
#define LEFT      wstack[len(wstack), 2]
#define BOTTOM    wstack[len(wstack), 3]
#define RIGHT     wstack[len(wstack), 4]
#define CONTENTS  wstack[len(wstack), 5]

#define TESTING   // to compile test program - remove at will

// begin test program

#ifdef TESTING

/* user-defined command to allow familiar @..SAY / @..GET style
syntax */

#xcommand @ <r>, <c> WSAY <t>  =>  WSay( <r>, <c>, <t> )
```

```
#xcommand @ <r>, <c> WGET <v> [<list,...>]  => ;
            @ WRow( <r> ), WCol( <c> ) get <v> [<list>]

#include "box.ch"
#include "inkey.ch"
#include "fileio.ch"
#define LOGFILE  "change.log"       // default name for log file
#define CRLF     chr(13)+chr(10)    // self-explanatory

function Sugg_Box

local mwho := space(3), mdate := date(), mtime := time(), x
local handle, mnotes := [], lines, oldcolor := setcolor()
local oldf10
local oldscore := set(_SET_SCOREBOARD, .F.)
WCreate(5, 20, 16, 60, "B+/W")          // Display a window
/* note that all of the following @ coordinates will be
   positioned relative to the active window! */

@ 0, 2 wsay "Change Suggestions"
@ 1, 1 wsay "Who :"
@ 2, 1 wsay "Date:"
@ 3, 1 wsay "Time:"
@ 4, 1 wsay "Idea:"
@ 1, 7 wget mwho picture "!!!"
@ 2, 7 wget mdate
@ 3, 7 wget mtime
read
if lastkey() <> K_ESC
   /* enable F10 to emulate Ctrl-W keypress - see below */
   oldf10 := setkey(K_F10, { || quicksave() } )
   @ 11, 8 wsay "Press F10 to save notes"
   mnotes := memoedit(mnotes, WRow(4), WCol(7), WRow(10), ;
             WCol(38), .t.)
   if ! empty(mnotes)
      if file( LOGFILE )
         handle := fopen( LOGFILE, FO_READWRITE)
          /* move to end of file in order to append to it */
          fseek(handle, 0, FS_END)
      else
```

```
         handle := fcreate( LOGFILE, FC_NORMAL)
      endif
      Fwrite(handle, "WHO: " + mwho + " on " + dtoc(mdate) + ;
              " at " + mtime + CRLF, 34)
      lines := mlcount(mnotes, 50)
      for x := 1 to lines
        fwrite(handle, memoline(mnotes, 50, x), 50)
      next
      fwrite(handle, CRLF)
      fclose(handle)
   endif
   setkey(K_F10, oldf10)
endif
WKill()
setcolor(oldcolor)                   // reset color
set(_SET_SCOREBOARD, oldscore)       // reset SCOREBOARD status
return NIL

static function quicksave
keyboard chr(23)
return nil

#endif

// end test program — begin main windowing functions

/* WCreate() - create and open active window */

function WCreate(t, l, b, r, w_color)
/* use current color setting if color was not passed */
w_color := if(w_color = NIL, setcolor(), w_color)

/* add this information to the window stack */
aadd(wstack, { t, l, b, r, savescreen(t, l, b, r) } )
setcolor(w_color)
dispbox(t, l, b, r, B_DOUBLE + ' ')
return NIL

/* WKill() - close active window and remove from stack */
function WKill
```

```
/* make sure window stack is not empty */
if ! empty(wstack)
   /* restore previous screen under this window */
   Restscreen( TOP, LEFT, BOTTOM, RIGHT, CONTENTS)
   /* truncate window stack */
   asize(wstack, len(wstack) - 1)
endif
return NIL

/* WRow() - returns row relative to window */
function WRow(_offrow)
return if(empty(wstack), 0, TOP + _offrow)

/* WCol() - returns column relative to window */
function WCol(_offcol)
return if(empty(wstack), 0, LEFT + _offcol)

/* WClear() - clear contents of active window */
function WClear
if ! empty(wstack)
   scroll(TOP + 1, LEFT + 1, BOTTOM - 1, RIGHT - 1, 0)
endif
return NIL

/* WSay() - @..SAY redirected to current window */
function WSay(wrow, wcol, wtext)
if ! empty(wstack)
   @ WRow(wrow), WCol(wcol) say wtext
endif
return NIL

/* WPrompt() - @..PROMPT redirected to current window */
function WPrompt(wrow, wcol, wtext)
if ! empty(wstack)
   @ WRow(wrow), WCol(wcol) prompt wtext
endif
return NIL
```

Virtual screens

Virtual screens are screens which are not shown on the actual (physical) screen. A virtual windowing system would allow you to draw text and boxes to virtual screens without affecting the physical screen. You would then be able to "pop" the contents of such virtual screens onto the physical screen.

Along with all the other great features in Clipper 5, there are the rudiments of a virtual windowing system. The heart of this system are the two functions DISPBEGIN() and DISPEND(). You can use these functions to great advantage.

DISPBEGIN() and DISPEND()

These two functions form the cornerstone of Clipper 5's covert virtual windowing system. DISPBEGIN() redirects all Clipper console output from the physical screen to a virtual screen. This includes output from @..SAY, @..BOX, QOUT(), QQOUT(), DEVOUT(), and DISPOUT().

DISPEND() is vaguely reminiscent of RESTSCREEN(). Rather than restoring a previously saved screen, though, it pops the contents of your virtual screen onto the physical screen.

Listing 13.53 shows a simple example of these two functions in action.

Listing 13.53 DISPBEGIN() and DISPEND() demonstration

```
function Main
dispbegin()
setcolor('+w/r')
/* the following box will not appear on the screen until later */
dispbox(0, 0, maxrow(), maxcol(), replicate("*",9))
inkey(0)
dispend()                          // presto!
return nil
```

DISPBEGIN() calls are nested internally. If more than one DISPBEGIN() call is made, the video output will be buffered until the same number of DISPEND() calls occur.

DISPCOUNT() returns the number of DISPBEGINS() calls that have been made without corresponding DISPEND() calls.

OUTERR() and OUTSTD() Caveat

Note that DISPBEGIN() will not redirect output from OUTERR() and OUTSTD(). OUTERR() always directs output to the standard error device (usually the screen), and OUTSTD() always directs output to the standard output device (again, usually the screen). Neither of these can be redirected in any manner.

Plus, you should beware that using either of OUTERR() or OUTSTD() in conjunction with DISPBEGIN() will cause the contents of your virtual screen to be dumped immediately onto the physical screen. Therefore, we recommend that you not use them for virtual windowing.

Examples

Listing 13.54 serves as proof that although there may be nothing on the physical screen, the SAVESCREEN() function will nonetheless save the contents of the virtual screen to a memory variable for restoration later. This means that you can prepare any number of screens — unbeknownst to the user — to be popped onto the screen at various times throughout your program.

Blinkey() calls DISPBEGIN() to redirect output to the virtual screen. At that point, two tableaux with alternating blue and red boxes are drawn. Each tableau is saved with SAVESCREEN() and added to a **screens** array. DISPEND() is called, which puts the contents of the second virtual screen onto the physical screen. You then enter a DO WHILE loop which alternates between the two saved screens every 2/10 second. Press any key to escape the loop (and avoid certain insanity).

Listing 13.54 Saving and restoring virtual screens

```
#include "box.ch"
#xtranslate drawbox( <color>, <t>, <l>, <b>, <r>, <fill> ) => ;
            setcolor( <color> ) ; ;
            dispbox(<t>, <l>, <b>, <r>, B_SINGLE + <fill>)

/*
   BLINKEY() - Flashing alternate screens
*/
function Blinkey
local x, screens := {}
dispbegin()
setcursor(0)
drawbox('w/b', 0, 0, maxrow(), maxcol(), '1')
drawbox('w/r', 5, 5, 17, 74, '2')
aadd(screens, savescreen(0, 0, maxrow(), maxcol()))
drawbox('w/r', 0, 0, maxrow(), maxcol(), '1')
drawbox('w/b', 5, 5, 17, 74, '2')
aadd(screens, savescreen(0, 0, maxrow(), maxcol()))
dispend()
do while inkey(.2) = 0
   x := if(x == 1, 2, 1)
   dispbegin()
   restscreen(0, 0, maxrow(), maxcol(), screens[x])
   dispend()
enddo
return nil
```

If you are familiar with Grumpfish Library, you have probably already seen the Save_Drape() and Pull_Drape() functions. These allow you to display title screens using the popular "spreading curtains" effect. However, the methodology behind these functions is that you must first paint your screen, and then call Save_Drape(), which chops it into column-sized chunks and saves those chunks to a file. Pull_Drape() can then operate on that file to restore the screen from the center out.

The point of including these functions herein is that with DISPBEGIN() and DISPEND(), you can display your title screen and save it with Save_Drape() without the user ever seeing it! Simply call DISPBEGIN() prior to your @..BOX and @..SAY commands. Then call Save_Drape() to save the screen to a file, clear the screen, and call DISPEND() to activate the physical screen. Listing 13.55 shows the code, and Figures 13.9, 13.10, and 13.11 show the curtains unfolding.

Figure 13.9 Pull_Drape() begins to reveal screen

Figure 13.10 Pull_Drape() continues to unfold

Figure 13.11 Pull_Drape() completed -- the screen revealed

Listing 13.55 Spreading curtain effect

```
#include "box.ch"
#include "fileio.ch"
#xtranslate drawbox( <color>, <t>, <l>, <b>, <r>, <fill> ) => ;
             setcolor( <color> ) ; ;
             dispbox(<t>, <l>, <b>, <r>, B_SINGLE + <fill>)

/*
     Function: CURTAINS()
     Purpose:  Demonstrate spreading curtains effect
*/
function Curtains
local x
dispbegin()
setcursor(0)
drawbox('w/b', 0, 0, maxrow(), maxcol(), ' ')
drawbox('w/r', 5, 5, 19, 74, ' ')
drawbox('w/rb', 9, 15, 16, 64, ' ')
drawbox('n/bg', 11, 24, 14, 55, ' ')
```

```
@ 12, 32 say "The Killer App"
@ 13, 26 say "Copyright (c) 1991 Joe Blow"
save_drape('title.scr')
setcolor('w/n')
cls
dispend()
pull_drape('title.scr')
inkey(0)
return nil
/*
   Function: PULL_DRAPE()
   Purpose:  Draw title screen from specified memory file
   Excerpted from the Grumpfish Library
*/
function Pull_Drape(cfile)
local nhandle, screen_ := {}, buffer, xx, yy, midpoint, ;
      mwidth, mlength, oldcurs := setcursor(0), ndelay := 10
if file(cfile)
   if ( nhandle := fopen(cfile, FO_READ) ) != -1
      mwidth := ( maxrow() + 1 ) * 2
      buffer := space(mwidth)
   for xx := 1 to maxcol() + 1
         fread(nhandle, @buffer, mwidth)
         aadd(screen_, buffer)
      next
      fclose(nhandle)
      midpoint := int((maxcol() + 1) / 2) + 1
      for xx := midpoint to maxcol() + 1
         restscreen(0, xx - 1, maxrow(), xx - 1, screen_[xx])
         restscreen(0, maxcol() + 1 - xx, maxrow(), ;
         maxcol() + 1 - xx, screen_[maxcol() + 2 - xx])
          for yy := 1 to ndelay
          next
      next
   endif
endif
setcursor(oldcurs)
return NIL
* end function Pull_Drape()
*-----------------------------------*
```

```
/*
      Function: SAVE_DRAPE()
      Purpose:  Save title screen to specified memory file
      Excerpted from the Grumpfish Library
*/
function Save_Drape(cfile)
local buffer, nhandle := fcreate(cfile), xx, ret_val := .f.
if ferror() == 0
   ret_val := .t.
   for xx := 0 to maxcol()
       buffer := savescreen(0, xx, maxrow(), xx)
       if fwrite(nhandle, buffer) != ( maxrow() + 1) * 2
          ret_val := .f.
          exit
       endif
   next
   fclose(nhandle)
endif
return ret_val
* end function Save_Drape()
*--------------------------------------------------------------------*
```

Note the subtle yet important step of resetting the color and clearing the screen prior to calling DISPEND() with these humble statements:

```
setcolor('w/n')
cls
dispend()
```

If you did not reset the color, the screen would be cleared in the last color used to display your title screen. Moreover, if you forget to clear the screen, DISPEND() will cause the contents of your pretty title screen to leap onto the physical screen and thus completely defeat the purpose.

The third example, Movement(), presents logic for resizing a box with the arrow keys. This is a two-stage process: First you drag the top left corner of the box, then the lower right corner. The top, left, bottom, and right arrows all behave in self-explanatory fashion. Listing 13.56 contains the source code for this function.

Movement() accepts one parameter, **<noflicker>**. This can be of any data type. If you pass this parameter, Movement() will utilize DISPBEGIN() and DISPEND() to eliminate screen flicker as the screen beneath the box is restored. If you omit this parameter, you will notice the annoying flicker, particularly if you hold down the left or right arrow keys. Try it both ways and the difference will be painfully obvious.

Listing 13.56 Resizing a box

```
#include "box.ch"
#include "inkey.ch"
#define DIAMOND  chr(4)

/*
      Function: MOVEMENT()
      Purpose:  Resize a box with the arrow keys
*/

function Movement(noflicker)
local t := 10, l := 10, b := 12, r := 69, x, oldscrn, key := 0
/* if no parameter passed, allow screen flicker */
noflicker := ! (noflicker == NIL)
setcursor(0)
setcolor('w/b')
/* draw bogus backdrop to prove the point */
for x := 0 to maxrow()
   @ x, 0 say replicate(chr(x), maxcol() + 1)
next
oldscrn := savescreen(0, 0, maxrow(), maxcol())
setcolor('n/bg')
dispbox(t, l, b, r, DIAMOND + substr(B_SINGLE, 2)+ ' ')
/* first allow anchoring of top left corner */
do while key != K_ESC .and. key != K_ENTER
   key := inkey(0)
   do case
       case key == K_LEFT .and. l > 0
          l--
       case key == K_RIGHT .and. l < r + 1
          l++
       case key == K_UP .and. t > 0
          t--
```

```
        case key == K_DOWN .and. t < b - 1
           t++
   endcase
   if noflicker
     dispbegin()
   endif
   restscreen(0, 0, maxrow(), maxcol(), oldscrn)
   dispbox(t, l, b, r, DIAMOND + substr(B_SINGLE, 2)+ ' ')
   if noflicker
     dispend()
   endif
enddo
key := 0
dispbox(t, l, b, r, substr(B_SINGLE, 1,4)+ DIAMOND + ;
                     substr(B_SINGLE,6)+ ' ')
/* now allow anchoring of bottom right corner */
do while key != K_ESC .and. key != K_ENTER
   key := inkey(0)
   do case
        case key == K_LEFT .and. r > l + 1
           r--
        case key == K_RIGHT .and. r < maxcol()
           r++
        case key == K_UP .and. b > t + 1
           b--
        case key == K_DOWN .and. b < maxrow()
           b++
   endcase
   if noflicker
        dispbegin()
   endif
   restscreen(0, 0, maxrow(), maxcol(), oldscrn)
   dispbox(t, l, b, r, substr(B_SINGLE, 1,4)+ DIAMOND + ;
                     substr(B_SINGLE,6)+ ' ')
   if noflicker
     dispend()
   endif
enddo
return nil
```

Experiment with DISPBEGIN() and DISPEND(). You will undoubtedly find intriguing uses for them in your Clipper 5 applications. Bear in mind that all changes you make to the virtual screen will affect the physical screen — it's just that you will not see the changes until you call DISPEND().

Clipper's functions that work on the screen are kept in TERMINAL.LIB, which gets linked in by default. Clipper 5.2 also provides three other terminal drivers that can be used in special situations:

ANSITERM

The ANSITERM library is used for hardware that does not support either direct writes to the video hardware or BIOS calls for screen desplay such as alternative display hardware for the blind.

You can use ANSITERM by replacing the TERMINAL.LIB in your link cycle with ANSITERM.LIB. You will also need to include the line:

```
DEVICE=ANSI.SYS
```

in your CONFIG.SYS file. ANSITERM will run considerably slower than normal terminal operations.

NOVTERM

The NOVTERM library is used to allow Clipper to share resources with the file server when running on a non-dedicated fileserver rather than on a dedicated which waits until the program has idle time to perform network tasks. Since Clipper uses this idle time for housekeeping tasks, the network tasks are never allocated any time. Thus, using Clipper on dedicated servers can cause poor network performance while it is running.

You can use NOVTERM by replacing the TERMINAL.LIB in your link cycle with NOVTERM.LIB. Keep in mind that performance will suffer when using NOVTERM in place of TERMINAL.LIB.

PCBIOS

The PCBIOS library is used to force all video output to go through the PC-BIOS calls. While performance will be adversely affected, some applications must use the BIOS calls to guarantee proper behavior. Double-byte character sets are a prime example of such an application.

You can use PCBIOS by replacing the TERMINAL.LIB in your link cycle with PCBIOS.LIB.

Summary

You have absorbed a lot of information in this chapter. We discussed the basic criteria that make for good user interfaces. You also learned about the various Clipper primitives for output and positioning. You now have numerous building block functions that you can add to your programming arsenal to simplify the task of creating a consistent, easy-to-use interface. We also covered efficient color management, windowing, and virtual screens. You should be able to apply this knowledge to creating attractive, consistent user interfaces for your Clipper 5 programs.

Before moving along to the mechanics of printing and networking in the next two chapters, we would like to mention a programming tenet introduced in the *Tao of Programming* (by Geoffrey James, published by InfoBooks). This is the "Law of Least Astonishment", and states simply that your programs should always respond to the user in the way that astonishes him or her least. As you design your user interface, adhering to the Law of Least Astonishment will yield positive results.

CHAPTER 14

Menus

Clipper provides us with the tools to create menus that are far more attractive than anything dBASE III PLUS could offer. This chapter will discuss the Clipper commands and functions that can be used for menuing. Although these tools are already easy to use, we will present several generic functions to make your job of displaying menus even easier. We will also utilize the Clipper 5 preprocessor to create a special alternate menu that uses standard Clipper syntax.

Overview

We have all ordered from a menu in a restaurant. As you know, the menu provides you with a list of available selections. When you make your selection, it triggers a chain reaction that begins with the waiter directing the chef to prepare your selection, and ends when the food is delivered to your table.

The methodology for software menus is quite similar to that of restaurants. When you make a selection, the program acts upon your choice by directing the computer to take a particular course of action.

Software and restaurant menus have one thing in common: The more appealing the menu, the more likely it is that someone will want to select from it. If menus created in dBASE III PLUS were applied to a restaurant, chances are that the restaurant would go out of business! dBASE III PLUS menus were very primitive, and typically consisted of static options displayed on the screen and a GET at the bottom. The following listing demonstrates how not to write a menu.

Listing 14.1 Primitive dBASE III PLUS (or "How not to write a") menu

```
clear
sel = ' '
do while sel <> 'Q'
   @ 10, 33 say "A. Data Entry"
   @ 11, 33 say "B. Reports"
   @ 12, 33 say "C. Maintenance"
   @ 13, 33 say "D. Backup"
   @ 14, 33 say "Q. Quit"
   @ 18, 31 say "Your Selection:" get sel picture '!'
   read
   if sel = "A"
      dataentry()
   elseif sel = "B"
      reports()
   elseif sel = "C"
      maint()
   elseif sel = "D"
      backup()
   endif
enddo
```

Although it is possible to write a light-bar menuing system in dBASE III PLUS, actually doing so is akin to painting a house with a toothbrush. Rather than presenting an example of such staggering boredom, we will instead focus on how Clipper lets you do light-bar menus (and many other nice things) in just a few lines of code.

Menuing commands

Clipper has several commands that affect the creation and operation of light-bar menus. They are all quite easy to use, as you shall soon see.

@..PROMPT

This command initializes and displays a light-bar menu option. The syntax is:

```
@ <row>, <column> PROMPT <prompt> [ MESSAGE <message> ]
```

<row> and **<column>** are numeric expressions that determine where the menu option will be displayed on the screen.

<prompt> is a character expression that will be used as the text of the menu option.

The optional parameter **<message>** is a character expression that will be displayed at the message row whenever this menu option is highlighted. The message row is determined by the SET MESSAGE command, which we'll discuss in a moment. You may selectively specify a <message> for some menu options and not others.

Note that the order of your @..PROMPT commands directly affects the order of the options within the light-bar menu. This will be discussed in more detail along with MENU TO.

Cursor position

Each time that you issue an @..PROMPT command, the screen cursor position is reset to just beyond the rightmost character of the menu option.

```
@ 10, 0 prompt "Option 1"
mrow := row()       // 10
mcol := col()       //  8
```

You may act upon this by using the ROW() and COL() functions for relative positioning of subsequent menu options, as demonstrated here.

```
@ 10, 0               prompt "Option 1"
@ row(), col() + 2    prompt "Option 2"
@ row() + 1, 0        prompt "Option 3"
@ row(), col() + 2    prompt "Option 4"
```

The basic idea is to display all of your menu options with the @..PROMPT command. You then use the MENU TO command to actually trigger the light-bar menu.

MENU TO

This command sends the light-bar menu highlighting and bouncing into action. The syntax is:

```
MENU to <var>
```

<var> is the name of a memory variable or array element. This item will be assigned a numeric value based on the menu option that the user selects.

If you assign <var> a numeric value prior to the MENU TO statement, that value will be used to determine which menu option should initially be highlighted. Otherwise, the first option will be highlighted.

Table 14.1 shows all keys that are active in the light-bar menu.

Table 14.1 MENU TO active keys

Key	*Action*
UpArrow	Move to previous menu option. If at first option and WRAP is enabled, move to last menu option (see SET WRAP below).
DownArrow	Move to next menu option. If at last option and WRAP is enabled, move to first menu option (see SET WRAP below).
LeftArrow	Move to previous menu option. If at first option and WRAP is enabled, move to last menu option (see SET WRAP below).
RightArrow	Move to next menu option. If at last option and WRAP is enabled, move to first menu option (see SET WRAP below).
Home	Move to first menu option.
End	Move to last menu option.
Enter	Select current option and exit.
PgUp	Select current option and exit.
PgDn	Select current option and exit.
Esc	Return zero and exit.

You may also select an option by pressing the key corresponding to its first character. For example, the menu option "Reports" could be selected by pressing "R" or "r".

The selected (highlighted) menu option is displayed in the current enhanced color. All unselected menu options are shown in the current standard color.

Order of options

As alluded to above, the order of your menu options is determined by the order of your @..PROMPT commands. In other words, if you were to list your options in this order:

```
@ 20, 0 prompt "option 1"
@ 19, 0 prompt "option 2"
@ 18, 0 prompt "option 3"
@ 17, 0 prompt "option 4"
menu to sel
```

The bottom option would be considered the first, and the top option would be considered the last. Pressing UpArrow would move you down, and DnArrow would move you up. Your users would probably declare mutiny! However, you can make use of this information without being sadistic. For example, you can order menu options from left to right and top to bottom as shown here:

```
@ 10,  0 prompt "Option 1"
@ 10, 15 prompt "Option 2"
@ 11,  0 prompt "Option 3"
@ 11, 15 prompt "Option 4"
menu to sel
```

SET MESSAGE

As mentioned above, this command determines where messages will be placed on the screen. The syntax is:

```
SET MESSAGE TO <row> [CENTER]
```

<row> is a numeric expression representing the row at which to display the message for the highlighted menu option.

If you follow the <row> with the word CENTER (or CENTRE for our friends in the U.K.), the message will automatically be centered horizontally on the desired row.

Messages will not be displayed until you issue the SET MESSAGE command.

set(_SET_MESSAGE) and set(_SET_MCENTER)

The example below shows the clinical view of the SET MESSAGE command (as found in STD.CH).

```
#command  set message to <n> [<cent: CENTER, CENTRE>] ;
          => ;
          set( _SET_MESSAGE, <n> ) ; set( _SET_MCENTER, <.cent.> )
```

The preprocessor converts the SET MESSAGE command into two calls to the SET() function. The first uses the manifest constant _SET_MESSAGE and establishes the message row. The second uses _SET_MCENTER to determine whether or not the message will automatically be centered.

As we discussed in Chapter 12 ("Program Design"), you may use the SET() function to poll current global SETtings and/or change them. This is particularly useful if you want to change the message row and/or centering in a lower-level function and then reset it.

The example in Listing 14.2 sets the message row to the bottom row of the screen (as determined by the Clipper MAXROW() function), and ensures that the messages will be centered. Upon exit, these settings will be properly reset to their previous values.

Listing 14.2 Using SET() for message row/centering

```
function ShowMenu
local oldrow := set(_SET_MESSAGE, maxrow()),;
      oldctr := set(_SET_MCENTER, .T.)
*
*
*
/* reset prior values */
set(_SET_MESSAGE, oldrow)
set(_SET_MCENTER, oldctr)
return nil
```

SET WRAP

This command enables wrap-around from top and bottom and vice versa. By default, wrap-around is disabled unless you issue this command. The syntax is:

```
SET WRAP ON/OFF
```

You may also pass a logical expression instead of the words "ON" or "OFF." A logical True (**.T.**) equates to "ON", and False (**.F.**) is "OFF". If you choose to do so, be sure to surround the expression by parentheses, as shown here:

```
mwrap := .t.
set wrap (mwrap)
```

With wraparound enabled, pressing UpArrow or LeftArrow at the first menu option will move you to the last menu option. Pressing DownArrow or RightArrow at the last menu option will move you to the first menu option.

SET(_SET_WRAP)

Like SET MESSAGE, the SET WRAP command is also remapped to the SET() function. The example below shows a clinical view of this command.

```
#command SET WRAP <x:ON,OFF,&>  =>  Set(_SET_WRAP, ONOFF( <(x)> ))
#command SET WRAP (<x>)         =>  Set(_SET_WRAP, <x> )
```

The preprocessor converts the SET WRAP command into a call to the SET() function with the _SET_WRAP manifest constant.

Because the SET() function returns the current value of each global SETting, you can use this syntax to save and restore the WRAP status. The example below demonstrates this logic.

```
function ShowMenu
local oldwrap := set(_SET_WRAP, .T.)   // set wrap on
*
*
*
/* reset prior value */
set(_SET_WRAP, oldwrap)
return nil
```

ACHOICE()

ACHOICE() allows you to present a menu consisting of elements in an array. The syntax for this function is:

```
achoice(<top>, <left>, <bottom>, <right>, <options> ;
     [,<selectable> [,<userfunc> [, <curr_item> [,<curr_row>]]]])
```

The first five parameters are fairly basic. **<top>**, **<left>**, **<bottom>**, and **<right>** are numeric expressions representing the top, left, bottom and right window coordinates, respectively. **<options>** is the name of the array containing the character strings to be displayed.

The last four parameters are optional and you might not use them often. However, they will be crucial to an ACHOICE() shell later in this chapter, so pay close attention to them:

<selectable> is a parallel array containing logical values. This array is used to determine which elements are selectable and which are not. This is ideal for situations when you might not want the user to select specific items. You may also pass a logical expression, in which case either all (**.T.**) or none (**.F.**) of the items would be selectable.

<userfunc> is a character expression representing the name of a user-defined function that will execute when an "unrecognized" key is pressed. This user-defined function will be integral to an example later in this discussion.

<curr_item> is a numeric expression representing the initial item to highlight. If this parameter is not passed, the first selectable item in the array serves as the default.

<curr_row> is a numeric expression representing the initial relative window row (beginning with position zero). For example, if <curr_row> is five, then the top row shown in the ACHOICE() window will be the fifth row. If this parameter is not specified, the initial relative window row is the row that contains the initial current item.

The selected (highlighted) array element is displayed in the current enhanced color. Unselected elements are shown in the current standard color. Unavailable items (as determined by the <selectable> array) are displayed in the unselected color.

Active keys

ACHOICE() is actually a schizophrenic function. Its active keys depend upon whether or not you have specified a user-defined function. Table 14.2 shows the keys that are active if you have *not* specified a UDF.

Table 14.2 ACHOICE() Active keys (without UDF)

Key	*Action*
UpArrow	Move up one item
DownArrow	Move down one item
Home	Jump to first item
End	Jump to last item
Ctrl-Home	Jump to first item in window
Ctrl-End	Jump to last item in window
PgUp	Move up one screenful of elements
PgDn	Move down one screenful of elements
Ctrl-PgUp	Jump to first item
Ctrl-PgDn	Jump to last item
Return	Select current item and return position (end ACHOICE())
Esc	Abort ACHOICE(), return zero
LeftArrow	Abort ACHOICE(), return zero
RightArrow	Abort ACHOICE(), return zero
First letter	Jump to next item with same first letter

When you specify a user-defined function, however, the following keys will be processed as "keystroke exceptions": LeftArrow, RightArrow, Home, End, Return, Esc and letter keys. Therefore, you must be careful to account for these keys in your user-defined function.

Listing 14.3 shows the function Pick_a_Day(). Pick_a_Day() returns a day of the week. It uses ACHOICE() to display a menu containing the days and allow selection. Notice the DO WHILE loop. This is to preclude the possibility of an array access error, which would happen if the user pressed Esc to exit the ACHOICE(). See Figure 14.1 for a view of this function in action.

Figure 14.1 Function Pick_a_Day() in action

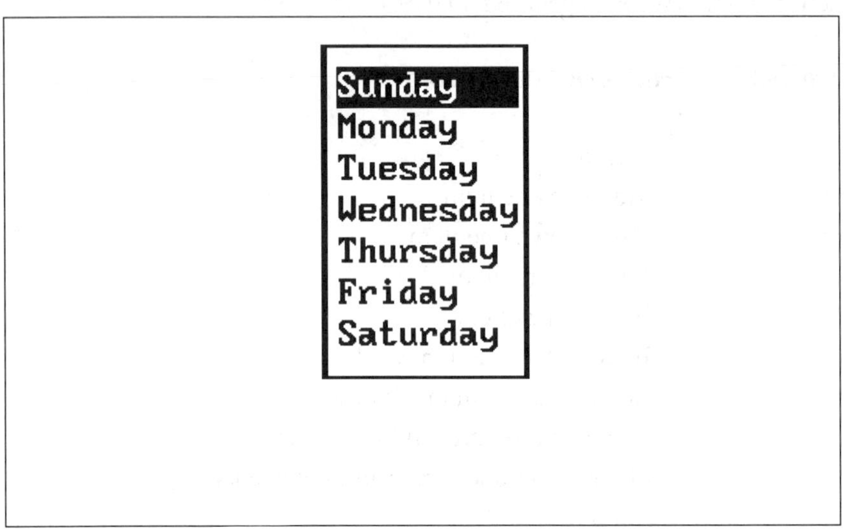

Listing 14.3 Displaying menu with ACHOICE()

```
#include "box.ch"
function Pick_a_Day
local days := { "Sunday", "Monday", "Tuesday", "Wednesday",;
                "Thursday", "Friday", "Saturday" },;
      sel := 0
```

```
local oldscrn := savescreen(8, 35, 16, 45)
@ 8, 35, 16, 45 box B_SINGLE + " " color "+W/R"
/* do not allow user to Esc out, which would cause array access
   error */
do while sel == 0
   sel := achoice(9, 36, 15, 44, days)
enddo
/* restore previous screen contents */
restscreen(8, 35, 16, 45, oldscrn)
return days[sel]
```

Now let's make use of the parallel logical array to make the current day unselectable, as shown in Listing 14.4.

Listing 14.4 ACHOICE() menu with parallel logical array

```
#include "box.ch"
function pick_a_day

local days := { "Sunday", "Monday", "Tuesday", "Wednesday",;
                "Thursday", "Friday", "Saturday" },;
      sel := 0,;
      available := array(7)
local oldscrn := savescreen(8, 35, 16, 45)
afill(available, .t.)                    /* load parallel array */
available[dow(date())] := .f.            /* toggle current day */
@ 8, 35, 16, 45 box B_SINGLE + " " color " + W/R "
/* do not allow user to Esc out, which would cause array access
   error */
do while sel == 0
   sel := achoice(9, 36, 15, 44, days, available)
enddo
/* restore previous screen contents */
restscreen(8, 35, 16, 45, oldscrn)
return days[sel]
```

Functions

Although you can undoubtedly write your own menus, the purpose of this book is to make you as productive as possible in your Clipper programming endeavors. Therefore, we will now cover some generic menu functions that handle much of the grunt work for you.

Among other things, HorizMenu() and VertMenu() apply the principles of code blocks and multi-dimensional arrays (discussed in Chapters 8 and 9, respectively). These functions neatly demonstrate that although the many new Clipper 5 features are wonderful, their sum is certainly more than the whole of its parts.

HorizMenu()

This function lets you easily paint a horizontal Lotus-style light-bar menu. The syntax is:

```
HorizMenu(<row>, <column>, <prompts>)
```

<row> and **<column>** are numeric expressions representing where to display the first menu option. Subsequent menu options will be offset by two spaces to the right, although you can easily change this. (Look for the manifest constant **SPACING**.) **<prompts>** is a multi-dimensional array. Each element of this array is an array in and of itself. The structure of these arrays is:

Element	*Contents*
1	Menu option
2	Message (optional)
3	Action block (optional)

If you include a message, it will be displayed whenever that menu option is highlighted. If you include an action block, it will be evaluated when that menu option is selected. The fact that you can include the action block will rid your code of reams of CASE or IF..ELSEIF logic.

HorizMenu() returns a numeric value representing the selected menu option. For example, if the user pressed **'D'** in the sample below, the return value would be **1**.

If you have not established a row at which to display the messages (with SET MESSAGE), HorizMenu() will use the row just below that where the menu options are displayed.

Listing 14.5 shows the code for HorizMenu(). See Figure 14.2 for a peek at this function in action.

Figure 14.2 HorizMenu() in action

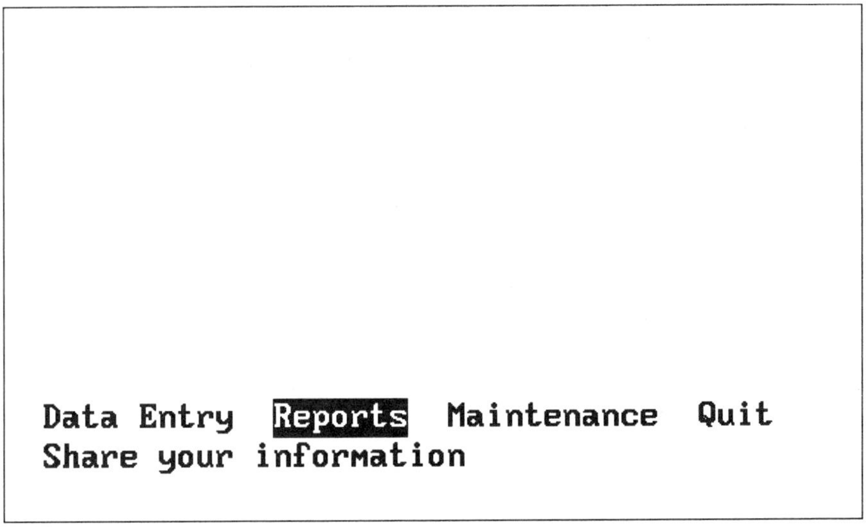

```
Data Entry  Reports  Maintenance  Quit
Share your information
```

Listing 14.5 Displaying horizontal menu with HorizMenu()

```
/* stub program */
function Main
local sel := 1
do while sel != 0 .and. sel != 4
   sel := HorizMenu(20, 0, ;
   {{"Data Entry", "Enter data, naturally", { || dataentry()}} , ;
    {"Reports", "Share your information"  , { || reports()}}   , ;
    {"Maintenance", "Reindex files etc"   , { || maint()}}     , ;
    {"Quit", "Take a siesta" }})
enddo
return nil

/*
   HorizMenu() - display horizontal menu
*/

#define SPACING  2      // 2 spaces between each menu option

function HorizMenu(nrow, ncol, prompts)
local choice := 1, x, oldwrap := set(_SET_WRAP, .T.), ;
      oldmessrow, oldcursor := setcursor(0) // turn off cursor

/* if no message row has been established, use row beneath menu
   options*/
if (oldmessrow := set(_SET_MESSAGE)) == 0
   set(_SET_MESSAGE, nrow + 1)
endif
/* loop through menu prompts array and display each */
for x := 1 to len(prompts)
   if len(prompts[x]) > 1
      @ nrow, ncol prompt prompts[x, 1];
                  message padr(prompts[x, 2], maxcol())
   else
      @ nrow, ncol prompt prompts[x, 1]
   endif
   ncol += len(prompts[x, 1]) + SPACING
next
menu to choice
```

```
/* if there is an action block for this menu option, run it now */
if choice != 0 .and. len(prompts[choice]) == 3
   eval(prompts[choice, 3])
endif
/* restore previous message and wrap settings */
set(_SET_MESSAGE, oldmessrow)
set(_SET_WRAP, oldwrap)
setcursor(oldcursor)
return(choice)
```

VertMenu()

This function displays a light-bar menu vertically on screen. Its methodology is similar to that of HorizMenu(). However, VertMenu() is designed to be entirely self-contained. There is no need to have a DO WHILE loop or any sort of CASE structure outside this function. VertMenu() also handles all cosmetics by automatically centering the menu on the screen, and framing it with a box.

The syntax is quite simple:

```
VertMenu(<prompts>)
```

<prompts> is a multi-dimensional array. As with HorizMenu(), each element of this array is also an array. The structure of these arrays is:

Element	*Contents*
1	Menu option
2	Message (optional)
3	Action block (optional)

If you include a message, it will be displayed whenever that menu option is highlighted. Because of the way that VertMenu() is designed, the action block should be included for each menu option except the last. Whenever a menu option is selected, its corresponding action block will be evaluated.

Because VertMenu() is self-contained, its NIL return value is irrelevant.

If you have not established a row at which to display the messages (with SET MESSAGE), VertMenu() will use the bottom row of the screen (as determined by the Clipper MAXROW() function).

Figure 14.3 VertMenu() in action

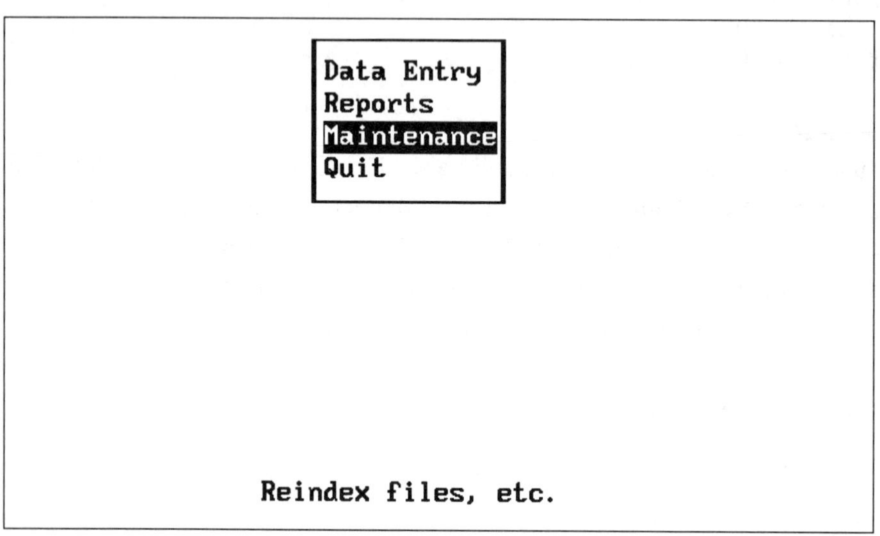

Now take a look at Listing 14.6. There is a main menu with three sub-menus attached to it. Note that there is only one executable statement in the main function!

Listing 14.6 Displaying vertical menu with VertMenu()

```
#include "box.ch"
function main
local mainmenu := ;
{{ "Data Entry", "Enter data",  {|| vertmenu(datamenu)  } },;
 { "Reports",     "Hard copy",  {|| vertmenu(repmenu)    } },;
 { "Maintenance","Reindex files, etc.",{||vertmenu(maintmenu)}},;
 { "Quit", "See ya later" }}
```

```
local datamenu := { { "Customers", , { || cust()     } }, ;
                    { "Invoices",  , { || inv()      } }, ;
                    { "Vendors",   , { || vendors() } }, ;
                    { "Exit", "Return to Main Menu" } }

local repmenu :=  { { "Customer List", , { || custrep()   } }, ;
                    { "Past Due",      , { || pastdue()   } }, ;
                    { "Weekly Sales",  , { || weeksales() } }, ;
                    { "Monthly P&L",   , { || monthpl()   } }, ;
                    { "Vendor List",   , { || vendorrep() } }, ;
                    { "Exit", "Return to Main Menu" } }

local maintmenu := { { "Reindex",  "Rebuild index files",      ;
                                     { || re_ntx()   } }, ;
                     { "Backup",   "Backup data files"  ,      ;
                                     { || backup()   } }, ;
                     { "Compress", "Compress data files",      ;
                                     { || compress() } }, ;
                     { "Exit", "Return to Main Menu" } }

VertMenu(mainmenu)
return nil

/*
   VertMenu(): display vertical menu
*/
function VertMenu(menuinfo)
local choice := 1, num_opts := len(menuinfo), maxwidth := 0,;
      nleft, x, oldscrn
local ntop, oldwrap := set(_SET_WRAP, .T.),;
      oldctr := set(_SET_MCENTER, .T.)
local oldmessrow := set(_SET_MESSAGE)

/* if no message row has been established, use bottom row */
if oldmessrow == 0
   set(_SET_MESSAGE, maxrow() )
endif

/* determine longest menu option */
aeval(menuinfo,{ | ele | maxwidth := max(maxwidth, len(ele[1])) })
```

```
/* establish top and left box coordinates */
nleft := int( maxcol() - maxwidth ) / 2
ntop  := 12 - int(num_opts / 2)
do while choice != 0 .and. choice != num_opts
   oldscrn := savescreen(ntop, nleft - 1, ntop + num_opts + 1,;
                         maxcol() - nleft)
   @ ntop, nleft - 1, ntop + num_opts + 1, maxcol() - nleft;
           box B_SINGLE + ' '
   setpos(ntop, nleft)
   for x := 1 to len(menuinfo)
     if len(menuinfo[x]) > 1 .and. menuinfo[x, 2] != NIL
        @ row() + 1, nleft prompt padr(menuinfo[x, 1], maxwidth) ;
                            message menuinfo[x, 2]
     else
        @ row() + 1, nleft prompt padr(menuinfo[x, 1], maxwidth)
     endif
   next
   menu to choice
   restscreen(ntop, nleft - 1, ntop + num_opts + 1,;
              maxcol() - nleft, oldscrn)
   /* execute action block attached to this option if there is one
   */
   if choice > 0 .and. len( menuinfo[ choice ] ) == 3
      eval( menuinfo[choice, 3] )
   endif
enddo
/* restore previous message and wrap settings */
set(_SET_MESSAGE, oldmessrow)
set(_SET_MCENTER, oldctr)
set(_SET_WRAP, oldwrap)
return nil
```

PullDown()

This function uses elements introduced in HorizMenu() and VertMenu() to manage a simplified pull-down menu system.

The top-level menu will be shown horizontally along the top row. Sub-menus will be drawn below each corresponding top-level option. When you press left or right arrow in a sub-menu, you will move to the next adjacent top-level menu option. If that top-level menu option has a corresponding sub-menu, you will immediately be placed within it.

Like VertMenu(), PullDown() is entirely self-contained. There is no need for supplemental CASE structure. The syntax is easy:

```
PullDown(<prompts>)
```

<prompts> is a multi-dimensional array. If you had any difficulty grasping the array used in VertMenu(), we recommend that you brush up on multi-dimensional arrays (Chapter 9) before going on.

Each element in the <prompts> array is an array. Each of these arrays contains the menu option, message, and optionally either an action or submenu to be executed when that option is selected. The latter is the key element in this array. Let's review the possibilities:

- Code block — Action block to be executed when the menu option is selected. The following example will display "Customers" as the menu option. "Enter customer data" will be used as the message. The custentry() function will be executed if this option is selected.

```
{ "Customers", "Enter customer data", { | | CustEntry() } }
```

- Array — Submenu to be executed when the menu option is selected. Here is an example for dissection:

```
{ "Data Entry", "Enter data", ;
{ { "Customers", , { || cust()    } }, ;
  { "Invoices",  , { || inv()     } }, ;
  { "Vendors",   , { || vendors() } }, ;
  { "Exit", "Return to Main Menu" } } }
```

This example will display "Data Entry" as the menu option. "Enter data" will be used as the message. If this option is selected, a submenu will be executed. The submenu will contain four options: "Customers", "Invoices", "Vendors", and "Exit". Each of the first three sub-options has an action block attached to it. If the fourth sub-option ("Exit") is selected, PullDown() will return you to the top-level menu because there is nothing attached to this menu option.

- Nothing — PullDown() will return you to the top-level menu when this option is selected. If you are already at the top-level menu, PullDown() will kick you out altogether.

As with VertMenu(), PullDown() returns NIL, which is probably irrelevant since it is self-contained.

If you have not established a row at which to display the messages (with SET MESSAGE), PullDown() will use the bottom row of the screen (as determined by the Clipper MAXROW() function).

Listing 14.7 shows a call to PullDown(). It uses the identical menu structure as shown in VertMenu(). Once again, note that there is only one executable statement in the calling program. See Figures 14.4 and 14.5 for PullDown() in action.

Figure 14.4 PullDown() showing Reports sub-menu

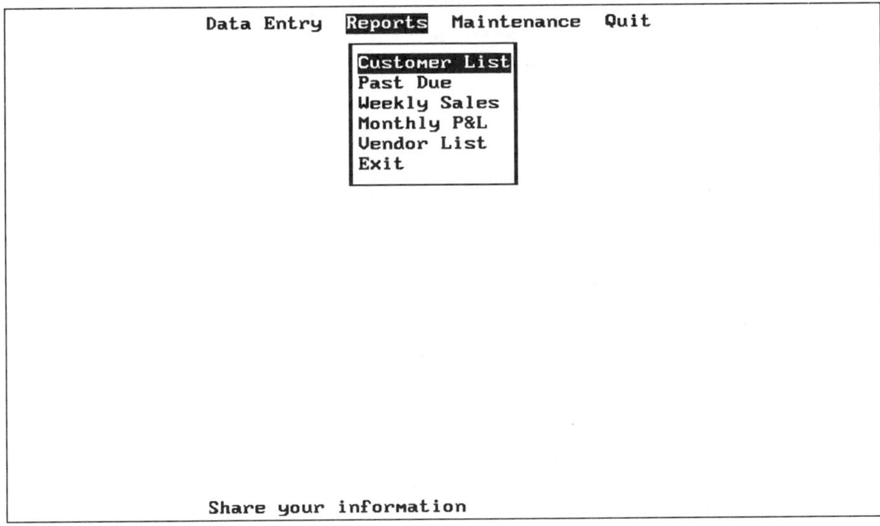

Figure 14.5 PullDown() showing Data Entry sub-menu

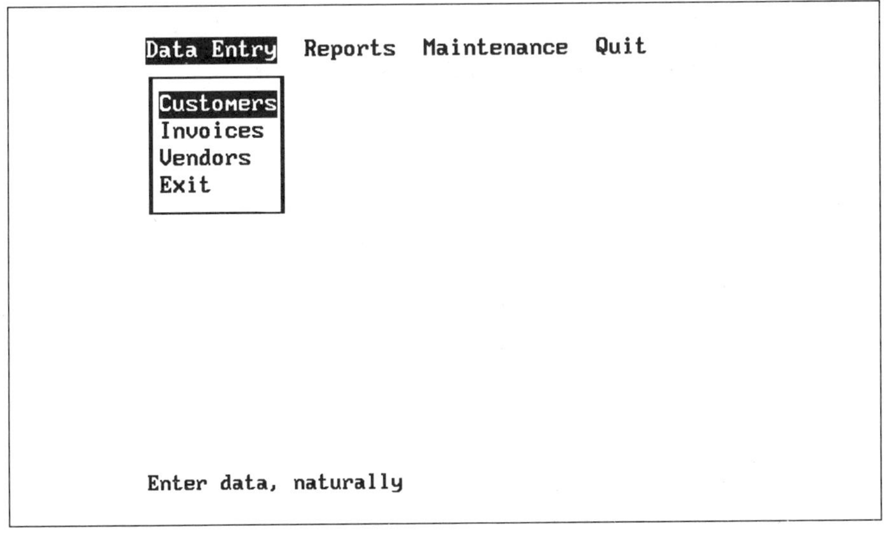

Listing 14.7 Displaying pull-down menu with PullDown()

```
static coords := {}  // must be file-wide for PullDown() to work
                     // properly

/* stub program */
function Main
PullDown({ { "Data Entry", "Enter data, naturally", ;
            { { "Customers", , { || cust()    } }, ;
              { "Invoices",  , { || inv()     } }, ;
              { "Vendors",   , { || vendors() } }, ;
              { "Exit", "Return to Main Menu" } } }, ;
          { "Reports", "Share your information"  , ;
            { { "Customer List", , { || custrep()   } }, ;
              { "Past Due",      , { || pastdue()   } }, ;
              { "Weekly Sales",  , { || weeksales() } }, ;
              { "Monthly P&L",   , { || monthpl()   } }, ;
              { "Vendor List",   , { || vendorrep() } }, ;
              { "Exit", "Return to Main Menu" } } }, ;
          { "Maintenance", "Reindex files etc"   , ;
            { { "Reindex", "Rebuild index files", ;
                                    { || re_ntx() } }, ;
              { "Backup",   "Backup data files"  , ;
                                    { || backup()   } }, ;
              { "Compress", "Compress data files", ;
                                    { || compress() } }, ;
              { "Exit", "Return to Main Menu" } } }, ;
          { "Quit", "Take a siesta" } } )
return nil

/*
   PullDown() - display pull-down menu
*/

#include "box.ch"
#include "inkey.ch"
#define TOPROW       0
#define LEFTCOL(x)  coords[x, 1]
#define BOTROW(x)   coords[x, 2]
#define RIGHTCOL(x) coords[x, 3]
```

```
#define OPTION(x)   prompts[x, 1]
#define MESSAGE(x)  prompts[x, 2]
#define ACTION(x)   prompts[x, 3]

function PullDown(prompts)
local mainsel := 1, x, oldwrap := set(_SET_WRAP, .T.),;
      oldmessrow, maxwidth
local nprompts := len(prompts), oldleft, oldright,;
      oldcursor := setcursor(0)
local ncol, subsel, buffer, tempsel

/* if no message row has been established, use bottom screen row
*/
if (oldmessrow := set(_SET_MESSAGE)) == 0
   set(_SET_MESSAGE, maxrow())
endif
/* loop through menu prompts array and determine coordinates for
   each submenu */
ncol := 0                    /* placeholder for left column */
for x := 1 to nprompts
   /* Is there a submenu for this menu option?
      If so, it would contain four elements */
   if len(prompts[x]) > 2 .and. valtype( ACTION(x) ) == "A"
      /* determine length of widest submenu option */
      maxwidth := 0
      aeval(ACTION(x), { | a | maxwidth := max(maxwidth,;
                               len(a[1])) } )
      /* add left and right columns and bottom row for the submenu
         box to COORDS array and increment left column accordingly
*/
      aadd(coords, { ncol, len(ACTION(x)) + 2,;
                     ncol + 1 + maxwidth } )
   else
      /* no submenu - add current left column to COORDS array
         and increment left column by length of this menu option
      */
      aadd(coords, { ncol } )
   endif
   ncol += len( OPTION(x) ) + 2
   /* pad all messages so that they will occupy the entire bottom
```

```
      row otherwise, messages from sub-menus might not erase
      messages from the main menu. */
   if MESSAGE(x) != NIL
      MESSAGE(x) := padr(MESSAGE(x), maxcol())
   endif
next

/* begin loop for top-level menu */
do while mainsel != 0
   /* loop through prompts array and display each top-level prompt
   */
   for x := 1 to nprompts
      /* display message only if one exists */
      if len(prompts[x]) > 1
         @ TOPROW, LEFTCOL(x) prompt OPTION(x) message MESSAGE(x)
      else
         @ TOPROW, LEFTCOL(x) prompt OPTION(x)
      endif
   next
   menu to mainsel
   if mainsel > 0
      do case
         /* no submenu or action tied to this element - force exit
         */
         case len(prompts[mainsel]) < 3
           mainsel := 0

         /* submenu */
         case valtype( ACTION(mainsel) ) == "A"
             /* we must store the main selection to a temporary
                variable because if we escape the submenu with a
                left or right arrow, we need to know which coordi-
                nates were used to draw the box around the submenu
                so that we can properly restore the screen */
            tempsel := mainsel
            subsel := 1
            /* redefine left & right arrows to exit submenu */
            oldleft  := setkey(K_LEFT,  { | | jumpleft(@mainsel,;
                              nprompts) } )
```

```
   oldright := setkey(K_RIGHT, { | | jumpright(@mainsel,;
                     nprompts) } )
   buffer := savescreen(TOPROW + 1, LEFTCOL(tempsel), ;
                      BOTROW(tempsel),RIGHTCOL(tempsel))
   @ TOPROW+1, LEFTCOL(tempsel), BOTROW(tempsel),;
     RIGHTCOL(tempsel) box B_SINGLE + chr(32)
   do while subsel != 0
      devpos(TOPROW + 1, 0)
      for x := 1 to len(ACTION(tempsel))
         /* display message only if one exists */
         if len(ACTION(tempsel)[x]) > 1
            @ row()+1, LEFTCOL(tempsel)+1;
                       prompt ACTION(tempsel)[x, 1];
                       message ACTION(tempsel)[x, 2]
         else
            @ TOPROW,  LEFTCOL(tempsel)+1;
                       prompt ACTION(tempsel)[x, 1]
         endif
      next
      menu to subsel
      if subsel > 0
         if len(ACTION(tempsel)[subsel]) > 2 .and. ;
              valtype(ACTION(tempsel)[subsel, 3]) == "B"
            eval( ACTION(tempsel)[subsel, 3])
         else
            subsel := 0
         endif
      endif
   enddo
   restscreen(TOPROW + 1, LEFTCOL(tempsel),;
             BOTROW(tempsel), RIGHTCOL(tempsel), buffer)
   setkey(K_LEFT, oldleft)
   setkey(K_RIGHT, oldright)

/* action block */
case valtype( ACTION(mainsel) ) == "B"
   eval( ACTION(mainsel) )

/* your guess is as good as mine */
otherwise
```

```
      endcase
   endif
enddo
/* restore previous message and wrap settings */
set(_SET_MESSAGE, oldmessrow)
set(_SET_WRAP, oldwrap)
setcursor(oldcursor)
return nil


/*
   JumpLeft() - make left arrow exit sub-menu
*/
static function JumpLeft(main, maxprompts)
if main == 1
   main := maxprompts
else
   main--
endif
/* peek in COORDS array to see if there is a sub-menu attached to
   the new top-level menu option - if so, stuff an Enter to jump
   right into the sub-menu - if not, leave it alone */
keyboard chr(K_ESC) + if(len(coords[main]) > 1, chr(K_ENTER), '')
return nil

/*
   JumpRight() - make left arrow exit sub-menu
*/
static function JumpRight(main, maxprompts)
if main == maxprompts
   main := 1
else
   main++
endif
/* peek in COORDS array to see if there is a sub-menu attached to
   the new top-level menu option - if so, stuff an Enter to jump
   right into the sub-menu - if not, leave it alone */
keyboard chr(K_ESC) + if(len(coords[main]) > 1, chr(K_ENTER), '')
return nil
```

ACHOICE() shell

Although ACHOICE() is a tremendous function right out of the box, its true power lies in its extendability. You may instruct ACHOICE() to call your own User-Defined Function (UDF) after each keypress. The results can be absolutely devastating, as you shall see.

When ACHOICE() executes your UDF, it will automatically pass three parameters:

- **Status**, indicating the current state of ACHOICE(). Table 14.3 lists these status codes.

Table 14.3 ACHOICE() status codes

Mode	*Description*	*Manifest Constant in ACHOICE.CH*
0	Idle	AC_IDLE
1	Cursor past top of list	AC_HITTOP
2	Cursor past end of list	AC_HITBOTTOM
3	Keystroke exception	AC_EXCEPT
4	No item selectable	AC_NOITEM

- Current element in the array
- Relative window position within the ACHOICE() window.

The UDF must return a value to ACHOICE() after it has finished working whatever magic it has been asked to perform. The possible return values are shown in Table 14.4.

Table 14.4 ACHOICE() UDF return codes

Mode	*Description*	*Manifest Constant in ACHOICE.CH*
0	Abort selection, returning zero	AC_ABORT
1	Make selection, returning element number of current item	AC_SELECT
2	Continue ACHOICE()	AC_CONT
3	Go to the next array item whose first character matches the last key pressed	AC_GOTO

As you have noticed, all status and return codes are represented by manifest constants in the ACHOICE.CH header file. We recommend that you refer to these codes by their manifest constants rather than their values.

Now that you understand the ground rules, let's devise a UDF that will add these features to ACHOICE():

- Tagging multiple array elements
- Wrapping
- Status bar showing relative position in array
- Quick-search (allowing entry of multiple letters)
- Easy determination of selectable/non-selectable items
- Additional aesthetic control

The first step to get any of these enhancements to work is to enclose the ACHOICE() in a DO WHILE loop, because we will need to keep popping in and out of it. Most of these items will return "0" (abort) to ACHOICE(), and if we did not use the DO WHILE loop, we would simply abort the ACHOICE() process and continue (blissfully unaware) through the program.

```
do while .t.
   achoice(mtop + 1, mleft + 1, mbot - 1, mright - 1, ;
           aarray, achoices, 'KeyTest', rel_elem, rel_row)
   if lastkey() == K_ENTER .or. lastkey() == K_ESC
      exit
   endif
enddo
```

Tagging multiple array elements

It's important to give users the ability to tag any or all items. We will let them do so by highlighting an item and pressing the space bar. But why stop there? Let's add three more active keys:

- F8 - Tag all items in the array
- F9 - Untag all items in the array
- F10 - Toggle each item to the opposite of what it was

ACHOICE() does not automatically redisplay the array items. For example, if we were to press F8 to tag all of the items in the array, we would be unaware that anything happened because nothing would change on the screen. For this reason, we must return zero from the UDF to force ACHOICE() to abort. Remember that because we are in the DO WHILE loop, we re-enter it so quickly that the user would have to be superhuman to know that anything out of the ordinary has transpired. See Figure 14.6 for an example of tagged array elements.

Figure 14.6 ACHOICE() display with tagged array items

As mentioned previously, the SET WRAP command can be used to enable wrap-around for MENU TO menus. However, ACHOICE() has no such provision. Fortunately, it is simple to tweak our UDF to handle this. We take advantage of the fact that ACHOICE() is kind enough to designate special status codes in the event that we attempt to move past the top or bottom of the array.

Status bar

The ubiquitous status (aka "elevator") bar shows you your current position relative to the top and bottom of the array. This is incredibly handy when your array has more elements than will fit in one window. We'll use ASCII character 176 (pattern fill) as the status bar, painted in plain-jane white on black. ASCII character 219 (solid block), done up in hot yellow, will serve as our positional indicator.

The status bar is one of the more difficult magic tricks in our UDF. It necessitates some legwork (or fingerwork) prior to calling ACHOICE(). First we must determine whether or not we actually need the status bar by testing the length of the array against the window coordinates. If necessary, we draw the elevator bar at this time using ASCII character 176.

```
#include "box.ch"
dispbox(mtop, mleft, mbottom, mright, B_SINGLE + " ")
draw_bar := (last_ele > mbottom - mtop - 1)
if draw_bar
   @ ntop + 1, nright, nbottom - 1, nright box chr(176);
   color bar_clr
endif
```

The next item is far more subtle, and took your humble author quite a while to vanquish. Clipper's MEMOEDIT(), ACHOICE(), and DBEDIT() functions all permit you to attach a key processing function. However, of these three, only

ACHOICE() does not make a call to this function upon start-up. Therefore, when you enter ACHOICE(), the status bar will be drawn, but the position indicator will not be displayed until you press a key. To get around this, we'll stuff the keyboard buffer with ASCII character 255 just prior to calling ACHOICE(). This key forces an initial keystroke exception call to the UDF, and CHR(255) is completely innocuous. We'll also use this trick when wrapping from top to bottom or vice versa.

Before calling ACHOICE(), we initialize variable **bar_line**, which will keep track of the current row position of the position indicator. We initialize it to the value of the top window row plus 2, which will force the position indicator to be drawn on the first pass through the UDF.

Inside the UDF, we test for either an ACHOICE() status code of 0 (idle), or a keypress of 255 (as just explained). If either of these conditions is met, we go through several steps:

1. Draw an **up arrow** above the status bar if there are elements beyond the top of the window.
2. Draw a **down arrow** below the status bar if there are elements below the bottom of the window.
3. Calculate our relative position in the array and determine whether the position indicator must be moved. If so, we first redraw the previous location of the position indicator with ASCII character 176, then redisplay the position indicator where it needs to be.

We then return a value of 2 to ACHOICE(), bidding it to continue its work. See Figure 14.7 for a demonstration of the status bar. As you can see, it indicates that the current highlighted element is approximately in the middle of the array.

Figure 14.7 ACHOICE() display of status bar indicating relative position in array

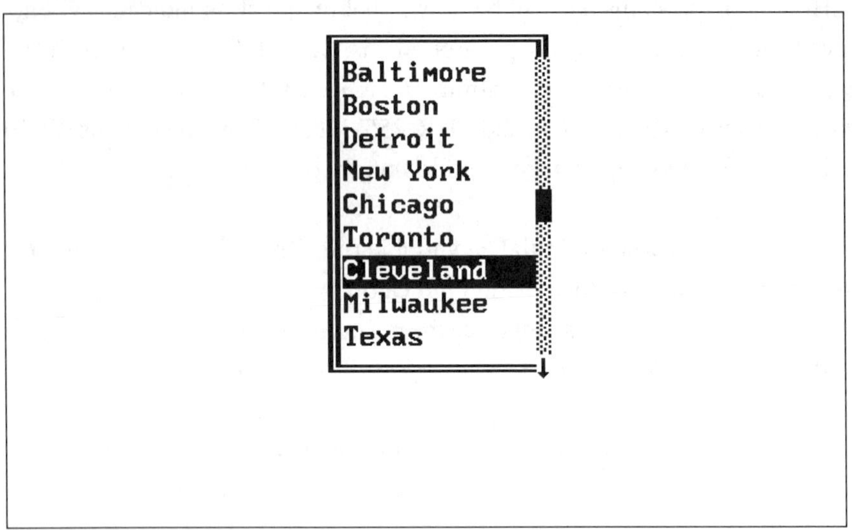

Quick-search

When you press a letter key, ACHOICE() jumps to the next array element that begins with that letter. However, this is not particularly useful. The ability to type in the entire element (or at least enough to uniquely identify it) is always preferable. That is the least we can give to our harried user.

As with the status bar, we must prepare beforehand, though not quite as stringently. We declare a variable **searchstr** and initialize it to a null string. This will contain the value to search the array for.

Meanwhile, back in the UDF, we test for a letter keypress. If one is detected, we add it to **searchstr** and search the array for it by calling ASCAN(). The syntax and parameters for ASCAN() are:

```
ASCAN(<array to search>, <value to search for>
      [,<element at which to begin search>]
      [,<number of elements to search>])
```

(The two optional parameters are not relevant to this example.)

ASCAN() returns a numeric value which represents the first find. If it is unable to find the desired value, it returns zero. Therefore, if ASCAN() returns a non-zero value, we know that our array contains the search value, and we change the current element to the element where it was found. We also display the contents of **searchstr** (up to the first six characters, which should be sufficient) centered on the bottom row of the box for easy reference.

Clipper 5 lets us pass a code block as the value to search for. This allows us to easily perform a case-insensitive search of the array:

```
return ascan(array, { | a | upper(a) = upper(value) } )
```

We should also give the user the ability to backspace if they type in the wrong letter to search for. Therefore, we perform a subsequent test in the UDF for a Backspace or LeftArrow. If either of these is detected, we will lop off the rightmost character of **searchstr**, and rescan the array for its new value. Note that if we reduce **searchstr** to a null string (length zero), we redisplay the bottom row of the box as a solid line. Attention to details such as these make for seamless applications and increased user satisfaction (even if only upon a subliminal level).

Figure 14.8 ACHOICE() quick-search in action

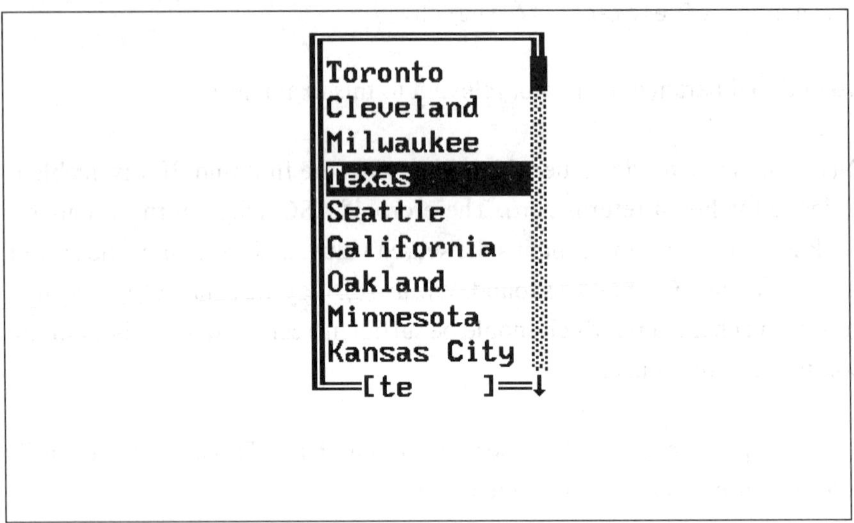

Selectable/non-selectable items

With ACHOICE(), you generally have to pass a parallel logical array to instruct ACHOICE() as to which items are selectable. However, this can grow tiresome, so we came up with a more "developer-friendly" method. If an item in the array is to be unselectable, simply precede it with a tilde ("~").

First we create **available**, a local array of zero elements, which will hold the logical values. Then we can scan through the main array looking for such items, and dynamically add to **available** either a false (unselectable) or true (selectable), depending on whether the menu item begins with a tilde or not:

```
aevaL(aarray, { | a | aadd(available, (substr(a, 1, 1) != '~') ) } )
```

Of course, this means that we have to get rid of the tilde before we display the array for selection. We'll kill two birds with one stone in the next discussion.

Additional aesthetic control

It has become fairly popular to use horizontal lines in a menu to separate similar menu options. To accommodate this, the function will test for any strings in the array that begin with a tilde and have only one other character. If such an item is found, the second character will be expanded (with the REPLICATE() function) into a horizontal line spanning the width of the ACHOICE() box. Witness the following example:

```
aarray := {"Move Box", "Size Box", "Erase Box", "~-", ;
           "Change Text", "Write Text", "Erase Text"}
```

The three box-related commands will be separated from the text-related commands by a horizontal line.

Here is how we handle not only the expansion of such horizontal lines, but adding a space to the end of each menu item in order to accommodate the checkmark.

```
for x := 1 to num_opts
   if ischar(aarray[x])
      if left(aarray[x], 1) != '~'
         aarray[x] += chr(K_SPACEBAR)
      else
         aarray := substr(aarray[x], 2)
         // see if they want to draw a horizontal line - if so,
         // trimmed length of this array element will now be one.
         if len(trim(aarray[x])) = 1
            aarray[x] := replicate(trim(aarray[x]), maxwidth)
         endif
      endif
   endif
next
```

First, we test whether the menu option begins with a tilde. If not, it is a regular selectable option and we add a space to the end of it. If it does begin with a tilde, then it is either an unselectable item or a horizontal line in the making. We can easily distinguish between the two, because the horizontal line items would be only two characters long. Therefore, if the array element is more than two characters long, we strip out the tilde and add a space. If it is two characters long, we strip out the tilde and use the REPLICATE() function to expand the horizontal line based on the second character.

There is one ACHOICE() deficiency that we must skirt around. There is no way to pass any parameters to the user-defined function (other than the three that Clipper automatically passes). Because there are many relevant items that must be visible in the user-defined function, we must declare a number of file-wide statics, including the coordinates of the ACHOICE() window and other items necessary for the elevator bar. We also must receive the array as a **private**, rather than a **local**, with the **parameter** statement. There is no way around this because the array must be visible in the user-defined function so that we can manipulate it.

Figure 14.9 does double duty by showing both an example of a horizontal line and an unselectable array element.

Figure 14.9 Horizontal line and unselectable item (Cleveland)

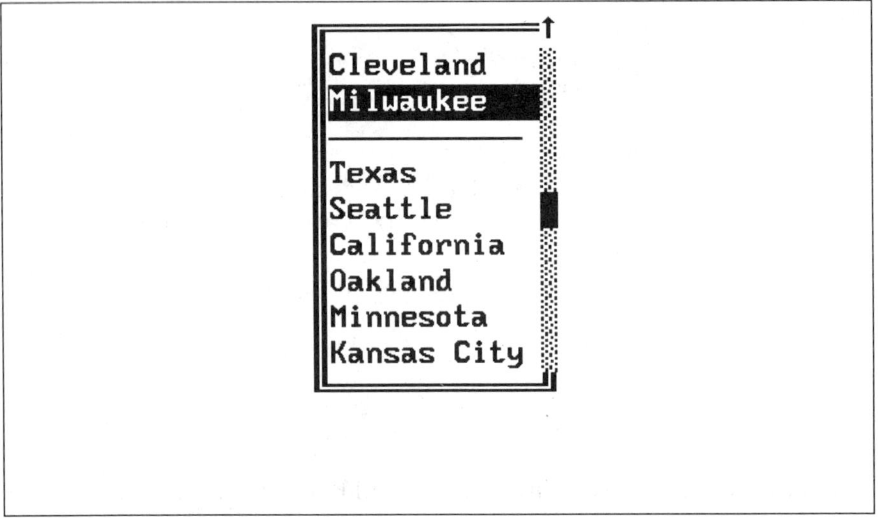

Listing 14.8 contains the entire source code for this fancy ACHOICE() shell. Figures 14.10 and 14.11 show tagged cities and the closing screen displaying those cities, respectively.

Figure 14.10 ACHOICE() displaying tagged cities

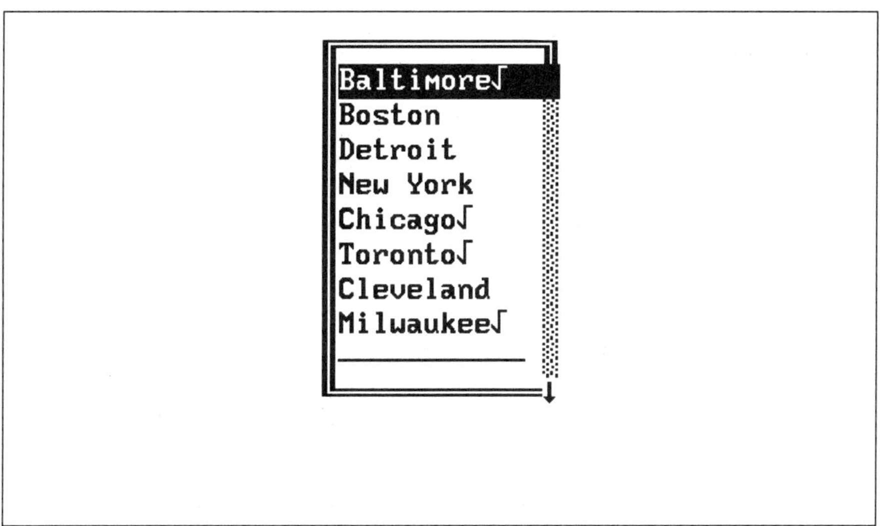

Figure 14.11 Tagged cities

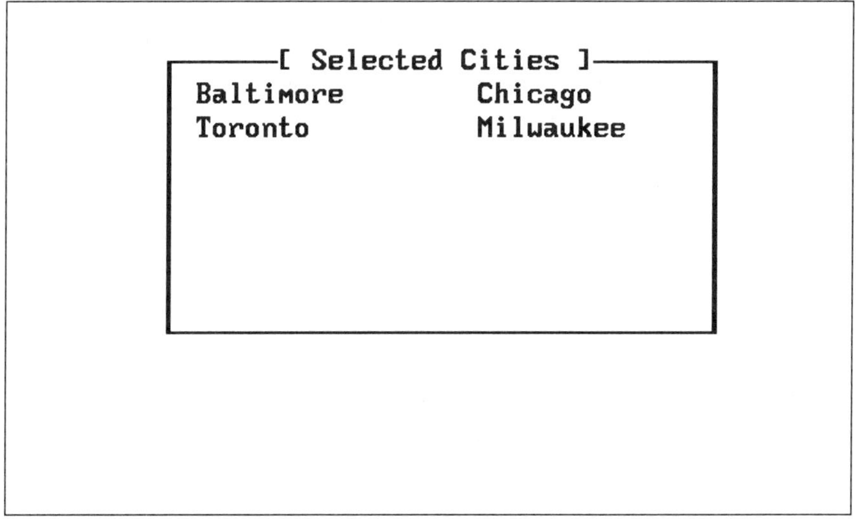

Listing 14.8 Very fancy ACHOICE() menu

```
/* compile with /N switch! */
#include "achoice.ch"
#include "box.ch"
#include "inkey.ch"

#define ISCHAR(a)        valtype(a) == "C"
#define K_SPACEBAR       32
#define CHECKMARK        chr(251)

static rel_elem     // relative element position in ACHOICE()
static rel_row      // relative row position in ACHOICE()
static num_opts     // length of array - used in ACHOICE()
static bar_line     // current position of elevator indicator
static stat_clr     // color for elevator indicator
static bar_clr      // color for status bar
static draw_bar     // flag for whether or not to draw elevator bar
static ntop, nleft, nbottom, nright  // coordinates for ACHOICE()
                                     // box

function Main
local nrow := 9, ncol := 25, x, oldcursor := setcursor(0), ;
      oldcolor, cities := {"Baltimore","Boston","Detroit", ;
      "New York","Chicago","Toronto","Cleveland","Milwaukee", ;
      "Texas","Seattle","California","Oakland","Minnesota",
      "Kansas City"}
cls
Gchoice(cities)
cls
oldcolor := setcolor("+W/RB")
@ 8, 23, 16, 56 box B_SINGLE + ' '
@ 8, 30 say "[ Selected Cities ]"
for x := 1 to len(cities)
   if right(cities[x], 1) == CHECKMARK
      @ nrow, ncol say substr(cities[x], 1, len(cities[x]) - 1)
      if ncol == 25
         ncol := 42
```

```
      else
         ncol := 25
         nrow++
      endif
   endif
next
inkey(0)
setcursor(oldcursor)
setcolor(oldcolor)
return nil

/*  GCHOICE() - shell for ACHOICE() */
function Gchoice( aarray )
local x, maxwidth := 0, oldcolor, oldscrn, available := {}, ;
      unsel_clr, box_clr, hilite_clr
num_opts := len(aarray)

/* determine widest array element and set columns accordingly */
aeval(aarray, { | a | maxwidth := max(maxwidth, len(a)) } )
nleft := int((maxcol() - 2 - maxwidth) / 2)
nright := nleft + maxwidth + 2
/* determine top and bottom rows based on length of array */
ntop  := max(7, 11 - int(num_opts / 2))
nbottom := maxrow() - ntop

/*
   build a parallel array for available choices by looping through
   the main array - unavailable selections will begin with tilde
   (~)
*/
aeval(aarray, { | a | aadd(available, ;
             if(ISCHAR(a), substr(a, 1, 1) != '~', .t.) ) } )

/*
   now we manipulate the elements in the actual array:
   1) add a space to the end of each array element,
      which will then be used for the checkmark
   2) strip out tildes
*/
```

```
for x := 1 to num_opts
   if ISCHAR(aarray[x])
      if left(aarray[x], 1) != '~'
         aarray[x] += chr(K_SPACEBAR)
      else
         aarray[x] := substr(aarray[x], 2)
         // see if they want to draw a horizontal line - if so,
         // trimmed length of this array element will now be one.
         if len(trim(aarray[x])) == 1
            aarray[x] := replicate(trim(aarray[x]), maxwidth)
         endif
      endif
   endif
next

rel_elem := rel_row := 1
box_clr  := '+W/' + if(iscolor(), 'B', 'N')
bar_clr  := 'W/N, I'
stat_clr := '+GR/N'
unsel_clr := substr(box_clr, 2)
hilite_clr := 'I'
draw_bar := (num_opts > nbottom - ntop - 1)
// force status bar to be drawn on first pass
bar_line := ntop + 2
oldcolor := setcolor(box_clr)
oldscrn := savescreen(ntop, nleft, nbottom, nright)
@ ntop, nleft, nbottom, nright box B_DOUBLE + ' '
if draw_bar
   @ ntop + 1, nright, nbottom - 1, nright box chr(176);
     color bar_clr
endif
setcolor(box_clr + ',' + hilite_clr + ',,,' + unsel_clr)
keyboard chr(255)
do while .t.
   achoice(ntop + 1, nleft + 1, nbottom - 1, nright - 1,;
           aarray, available, 'keytest', rel_elem, rel_row)
   if lastkey() == K_ENTER .or. lastkey() == K_ESC
      exit
   endif
enddo
```

```
restscreen(ntop, nleft, nbottom, nright, oldscrn)
setcolor(oldcolor)
return nil

/*  KeyTest() - Handle keystroke exceptions for ACHOICE() */
function KeyTest(status, curr_elem, curr_row)
memvar aarray
local xx, oldrow := row(), oldcol := col(), ret_val := AC_CONT, ;
      oldcolor, telem, key := lastkey()
static searchstr := []
do case

   case status == AC_HITTOP
      rel_elem := num_opts
      keyboard chr(255)        // force status bar display
      ret_val := AC_ABORT       // force ACHOICE() to restart

   case status == AC_HITBOTTOM
      rel_elem := 1
      keyboard chr(255)        // force status bar display
      ret_val := AC_ABORT       // force ACHOICE() to restart

   case status == AC_IDLE  .or. key == 255
      if draw_bar
         // draw arrows if there are elements beyond top or bottom
         // of window; first, the bottom
         @ nbottom, nright say if(num_opts - curr_elem >=;
                               nbottom - oldrow, ;
                               chr(25), chr(188))
         // then the top
         @ ntop, nright say if(oldrow - curr_elem <;
                               ntop, chr(24), chr(187))

         // if status bar position has changed, redraw it now
         if bar_line != ntop + 1 + int((curr_elem / num_opts) * ;
                        (nbottom - ntop - 2))
            // first, blank out previous status bar
            @ bar_line, nright say chr(176) color bar_clr
            // then recalculate position of status bar
```

```
            bar_line := ntop + 1 + int( (curr_elem / num_opts) * ;
                        (nbottom - ntop - 2) )
            // finally, redraw it
            @ bar_line, nright say chr(219) color stat_clr
         endif
      endif

   case key == K_SPACEBAR         // toggle this element on/off
      aArray[curr_elem] =  left(aArray[curr_elem], ;
                           len(aArray[curr_elem]) - 1) + ;
                           if(right(aArray[curr_elem], 1) = " ", ;
                           CHECKMARK, " ")
      rel_elem := curr_elem
      rel_row  := curr_row
      searchstr := []             // reset search string
      @ nbottom, 36 say replicate(chr(205), 8)
      ret_val := AC_ABORT         // Force ACHOICE redisplay

   case key == K_ENTER .or. key == K_ESC
      ret_val := AC_ABORT         // prepare to fall out

   case key == K_HOME
      keyboard chr(K_CTRL_PGUP)

   case key == K_END
      keyboard chr(K_CTRL_PGDN)

   case key == K_F8               // tag all items
      for xx := 1 to num_opts
         aArray[xx] := left(aArray[xx], len(aArray[xx]) - 1);
                       + CHECKMARK
      next
      rel_elem := curr_elem       // save current position
      rel_row  := curr_row        // and relative position
      ret_val  := AC_ABORT        // Force ACHOICE redisplay

   case key == K_F9               // clear all tags
      for xx := 1 to num_opts
         aArray[xx] = left(aArray[xx], len(aArray[xx]) - 1);
                      + chr(K_SPACEBAR)
```

```
      next
      rel_elem := curr_elem      // save current position
      rel_row  := curr_row       // and relative position
      ret_val := AC_ABORT        // Force ACHOICE redisplay

   case key == K_F10             // reverse all tags
      for xx := 1 TO num_opts
         aArray[xx] = left(aArray[xx], len(aArray[xx]) - 1) + ;
                      if(right(aArray[xx], 1) == " ", "√", " ")
      next
      rel_elem := curr_elem       // save current position
      rel_row  := curr_row        // and relative position
      ret_val  := AC_ABORT        // force ACHOICE redisplay

   case IsAlpha(chr(key))        // letter key - search
      searchstr += chr(key)
      telem := ascan2(aArray, searchstr)
      rel_elem := if(telem == 0, curr_elem, telem)
      @ nbottom, 36 say "[" + padr(searchstr, 6) + "]"
      ret_val := AC_ABORT         // Force ACHOICE redisplay

   case key == K_BS .or. key == K_LEFT
      if len(searchstr) > 0
         searchstr := substr(searchstr, 1, len(searchstr) - 1)
         telem := ascan2(aArray, searchstr)
         rel_elem := if(telem = 0, curr_elem, telem)
      endif
      @ nbottom, 36 say if(len(searchstr) == 0,;
                        replicate(chr(205), 8), ;
                        "[" + padr(searchstr, 6) + "]")
      ret_val := AC_ABORT         // Force ACHOICE redisplay

endcase
return ret_val

/* AScan2() — Case-insensitive ASCAN() */
static function AScan2(array, value)
return ascan(array, { | a | if(ISCHAR(a),;
                  upper(a) == upper(value), .F.) }, 1)
```

Lite_Menu()

Lite_Menu() is a variant on VertMenu() with three very nice twists:

- it highlights the trigger letters;
- it provides for alternate trigger letters;
- best of all, it lets you use familiar Clipper syntax by harnessing the power of the preprocessor.

Before you proceed any further, you may wish to review Chapter 7 ("The Preprocessor"). You might also want to skip ahead and peek at Chapter 27 ("The GET System"), because our use of the preprocessor here will be very similar to the manner in which it is used for the @..GET and READ commands.

The example below shows the standard Clipper @..PROMPT and MENU TO commands (as taken from the STD.CH header file).

```
#command  @ <row>, <col> PROMPT <prompt> [MESSAGE <msg>] ;
          => ;
          __AtPrompt( <row>, <col>, <prompt> , <msg> )

#command  MENU TO <v> ;
          => ;
          <v> := __MenuTo( {|_1| if(PCount() == 0, <v>,;
                                <v> := _1)}, #<v>)
```

We will direct the preprocessor to convert the standard @..PROMPT and MENU TO commands to function calls of our own design. The example below shows our modified versions of these commands.

```
#command  @ <row>, <col> PROMPT <prompt> [MESSAGE <msg>]        ;
          [ACTION <action>]                                  => ;
          if(menulist ==  NIL, menulist := {}, NIL);            ;
          aadd(menulist,{ <row>, <col>, <prompt>, <msg>,
               <{action}> })
```

```
#command  MENU TO <v> => ;
          Lite_Menu(menulist, @<v>, #<v>) ; menulist := {}
```

Again, we urge you *not* to make changes to your STD.CH file. Instead, put these modified commands into a header file named MYMENU.CH, and keep that with the rest of your Clipper 5 header files.

The syntax for our new @..PROMPT command is:

```
@ <r>,<c> PROMPT <prompt> [MESSAGE <message>] [ACTION <action>]
```

<r> and **<c>** are numeric expressions representing the starting row and column at which to display the menu item.

<prompt> is a character expression representing the menu item. To specify an alternate trigger letter, simply precede the desired letter with a tilde ("~") in the <prompt>.

The optional clause **<message>** is a character expression representing the message to be displayed when the corresponding menu option is highlighted.

The optional clause **<action>** is the name of a function to be called if the corresponding menu option is selected. It is not necessary to enclose this in quotes, because the preprocessor will convert it to a code block for evaluation.

If you look at the @..GET and READ commands, you will see that the preprocessor converts each @..GET into two primary actions: (a) Create a GET object, and (b) add it to the GETLIST array. The READ command then is translated into a call to the READMODAL() function, and passes the GETLIST array to it.

That logic serves us well here. @..PROMPT now creates a menu "object" and adds that menu object to the **menulist** array. Our menu "object" is actually an array, with structure as shown in Table 14.5.

Table 14.5 Structure of menu "object"

Element	*Contents*	*Type*
1	Row	N
2	Column	N
3	Prompt	C
4	Message	C
5	Action	B

Note the use of the blockify result-marker to convert your ACTION clause to a code block.

Our modified MENU TO command calls the function Lite_Menu() and passes it the contents of the **menulist** array. Along with this array, it passes two other parameters:

- The memory address of the variable to hold the selected option. This will allow Lite_Menu() to manipulate its value directly.

- The name of the variable. This is required in the event that a SET KEY function is triggered from within the Lite_Menu() wait state. Note the use of the dumb stringify result-marker to accomplish this.

While we're on the subject of the wait state, have you ever tried to tie context-specific help to each menu option in a MENU TO? If so, you have learned the hard way that it is virtually impossible. Fortunately, it is easy to design Lite_Menu() to allow this higher level of functionality. For example, if you are saving the menu selection to **sel**:

```
MENU TO sel
```

and you are on the third menu option, **"sel[3]"** will be passed to your hot-key procedure. (Look for the SETKEY() function call in the source code to see how easy this is to accomplish.)

There are two things that you must do in order to use Lite_Menu().

1. Be sure to include the header file containing the modified versions of the @..PROMPT and MENU TO commands.

2. Declare **menulist** at the top of your function, preferably as **local**.

Listing 14.9 contains the source code for Lite_Menu(), along with a sample program to demonstrate its use. Figure 14.12 shows Lite_Menu() in action.

Figure 14.12 Lite_Menu in action

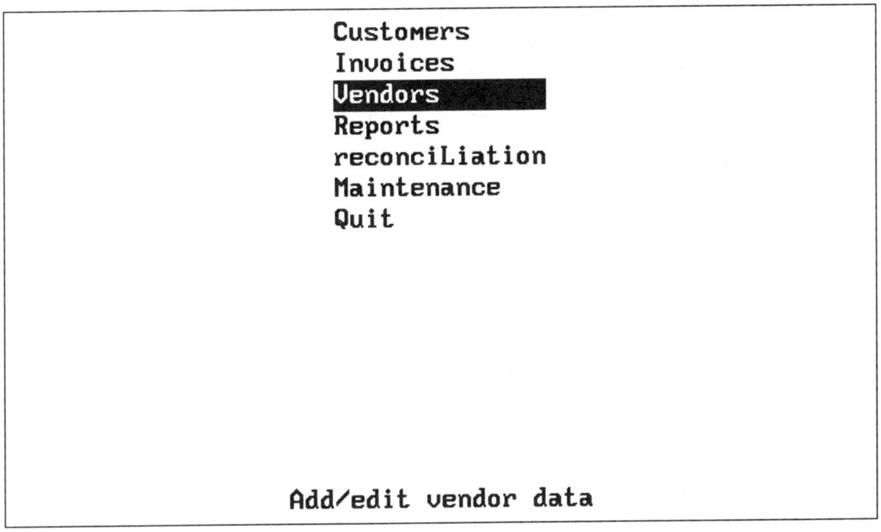

```
Customers
Invoices
Vendors
Reports
reconciLiation
Maintenance
Quit

Add/edit vendor data
```

Listing 14.9 Lite_Menu() example

```
#include "inkey.ch"
#include "mymenu.ch"  // contains modified @..PROMPT and MENU TO

function Main
local menulist, sel
cls
setcolor('w/b, n/bg')
do while sel != 0 .and. sel != 7
   @  9,33 prompt padr('Customers', 14);
           message 'Add/edit customer data' ;
           action CustFile()
   @ 10,33 prompt padr('Invoices ', 14);
           message 'Add/edit invoice data' ;
           action InvFile()
   @ 11,33 prompt padr('Vendors', 14);
           message 'Add/edit vendor data' ;
           action VendorFile()
   @ 12,33 prompt padr('Reports', 14) action Reports()
   @ 13,33 prompt 'reconci~Liation' action Reconcile()
   @ 14,33 prompt 'Maintenance   ';
           message "Rebuild indices, backup, etc." ;
           action Maint()
   @ 15,33 prompt padr('Quit', 14)
   menu to sel
enddo
return nil

static function CustFile
output("You selected the Customers option")
return nil

static function InvFile
output("You selected the Invoices option")
return nil

static function VendorFile
output("You selected the Vendors option")
return nil
```

```
static function Reports
output("You selected the Reports option")
return nil

static function Reconcile
output("You selected the Reconciliation option")
return nil

static function Maint
output("You selected the Maintenance option")
return nil

static function Output(msg)
@ maxrow(), 0 say padc(msg, maxcol() + 1) color "+gr/r"
inkey(0)
scroll(maxrow(), 0, maxrow(), maxcol(), 0)
return nil

/* these manifest constants are for easy identification
   of levels in the multi-dimensional array - they are
   not visible before this point in the .PRG file */
#define  ROW            1
#define  COL            2
#define  PROMPT         3
#define  MESSAGE        4
#define  ACTION         5

/*
   Lite_Menu() - alternate menu system
*/
function Lite_Menu(marray, selection, varname)
local num_elem := len(marray), xx, nkey := 0, triggerltr := [], ;
      fallout := .f., oldmsgctr := set(_SET_MCENTER, .T.), ptr, ;
      mess_row := set(_SET_MESSAGE), oldcursor := setcursor(0), ;
      oldcolor := setcolor(), plaincolor, hilitcolor

/* if MESSAGE row was never set, use the bottom row of screen */
if mess_row == 0
   mess_row := maxrow()
endif
```

```
/* set default colors for unselected and selected options */
xx := at(',', oldcolor)
plaincolor := substr(oldcolor, 1, xx - 1)
hilitcolor := substr(oldcolor, xx + 1)

/*
   determine initial highlighted item default to 1 — also perform
   error-checking to ensure they didn't specify an invalid
   selection
*/
if selection == NIL .or. (selection < 1 .or. selection > num_elem)
   selection := 1
endif


// build the string containing available letters for selection
for xx := 1 to num_elem
   /*
      the default is to add the first non-space character.
      However, if there is a tilde embedded in this menu
      option, use the letter directly following it.
   */
   if (ptr := at("~", marray[xx, PROMPT]) ) > 0
      triggerltr += upper(substr(marray[xx, PROMPT], ptr + 1, 1))
   else
      triggerltr += upper(left(marray[xx, PROMPT], 1))
   endif
   ShowOption(marray[xx], plaincolor)
next
// commence main key-grabbing loop
do while nkey != K_ENTER .and. nkey != K_ESC
   // display current option in highlight color
   @ marray[selection, ROW], marray[selection, COL] say ;
               strtran(marray[selection, PROMPT], "~", "") ;
               color hilitcolor
   /* display corresponding message if there is one */
   setcolor(plaincolor)
   if marray[selection, MESSAGE] == nil
      scroll(mess_row, 0, mess_row, maxcol(), 0)
   else
```

```
      @ mess_row, 0 say padc(marray[selection, MESSAGE],;
                        maxcol() + 1)
   endif
   if fallout
      exit
   else
      nkey := inkey(0)
      do case

         /* use SETKEY() to see if there's an action block at-
            tached to the last keypress - if it returns anything
            other than NIL, then you know that the answer is a
            resounding YES! */
         case setkey(nkey) != NIL
           /* pass action block the name of the previous
              procedure, along with the name of the variable
              referenced in the MENU TO statement and the current
              highlighted menu option (this means that you can tie
              a help screen to each individual menu option; try
              that with MENU TO) */
           eval(setkey(nkey),procname(1), procline(1), varname + ;
                      "[" + ltrim(str(selection)) + "]")

         /* go down one line, observing wrap-around conventions */
         case nkey == K_DOWN
            ShowOption(marray[selection], plaincolor)
            if selection == num_elem
               selection == 1
            else
               selection++
            endif

         /* go up one line, observing wrap-around conventions */
         case nkey == K_UP
            ShowOption(marray[selection], plaincolor)
            if selection == 1
               selection := num_elem
            else
               selection--
            endif
```

```
        /* jump to top option */
        case nkey == K_HOME
          /* no point in changing color if we're already there */
           if selection != 1
              ShowOption(marray[selection], plaincolor)
              selection := 1
           endif

        /* jump to bottom option */
        case nkey == K_END
          /* no point in changing color if we're already there */
           if selection != num_elem
              ShowOption(marray[selection], plaincolor)
              selection := num_elem
           endif

        /* first letter - jump to appropriate option */
        case upper(chr(nkey)) $ triggerltr
           ShowOption(marray[selection], plaincolor)
           selection := at(upper(chr(nkey)), triggerltr)
           fallout := .t.

     endcase
  endif
enddo
/* if there is an action block attached to this
  selection, run it */
if lastkey() != K_ESC
  if marray[selection, ACTION] != nil
     eval(marray[selection, ACTION])
  endif
else
  selection := 0  // since they Esc'd out, return a zero
endif
setcursor(oldcursor)
set(_SET_MCENTER, oldmsgctr)   // reset SET MESSAGE CENTER
setcolor(oldcolor)
return nil
```

```
/*
  Function: ShowOption()
  Purpose:  Display current prompt in mixed colors
*/
static function ShowOption(item, plaincolor)
local ptr := at("~", item[PROMPT])
if ptr > 0
   @ item[ROW], item[COL] say strtran(item[PROMPT], "~", "");
                          color plaincolor
   @ item[ROW], item[COL] + ptr - 1 say ;
                     substr(item[PROMPT], ptr + 1, 1);
                     color "+" + plaincolor
else
   @ item[ROW], item[COL] say left(item[PROMPT], 1);
   color "+" + plaincolor)
   DispOut(substr(item[PROMPT], 2))
endif
setcolor(plaincolor)
return nil
```

Summary

You are now ready to put an appealing face on your applications with beautiful Clipper menus. You should be able to easily prepare horizontal and vertical light-bar menus, and ACHOICE() picklists. You should also be able to prepare menus with alternate trigger letters.

CHAPTER 15

Printer Control

Although not as exciting and challenging as user interfaces, designing and implementing output routines are some of the most important things you produce when writing software. Very few applications exist for the sole purpose of entering data. At some point you are obligated to give something back to the user, and it usually takes the form of printed reports. Many applications are judged not on what happens while they are running but on the results they produce, and the people who are paying for your efforts may never see the computer, much less your program! This chapter is dedicated to making the programming of output routines as efficient, elegant, and dare we say as fun as any other part of your Clipper applications.

Output takes many forms, from the lowly 8.5" by 11" page of continuous-fed paper to cash register receipts to five-part invoice forms. Output gets directed to dot matrix printers, laser printers, text files and even to the screen. Being able to handle all these demands requires output capabilities that accommodate a wide range of page layouts, printer control codes and special device handling. Fortunately for all of us, Clipper has it all.

The REPORT and LABEL Commands

If you turned to this chapter looking for details about the REPORT FORM and LABEL FORM commands, you'll have to refer to the Clipper User's Manual, where they are covered very well. In this chapter we are dealing with programming techniques involving printers and other forms of report output, and not with the use of these relatively crude utilities.

Clipper printing essentials

Before leaping into the presentation of general purpose printer control functions, let's establish some printing essentials for those of you who just want to crank out lists or reports and don't want to make it into a major learning experience.

By default all output in Clipper goes to the screen, using the @..SAY commands or the ? and ?? commands. There are several SET commands that can alter this situation, as shown below. The options in uppercase are the default settings.

- set printer on | OFF
- set console ON | off
- set alternate on | OFF
- set alternate to [<filename>] [additive]
- set device to SCREEN | printer
- set printer to [<device> | <filename>] [additive]

See Chapter 13, "The Art of the User Interface", for other related functions like OUTSTD() and OUTERR(). In this chapter we are limiting ourselves to very basic output commands and how they relate to the printer.

The console device

Let's start with the simple ? and ?? commands. The ? command first sends a carriage return and line feed and then starts displaying information, while the ?? command starts displaying information immediately, wherever the cursor happens to be at the time. The following code displays text on the screen:

```
? "First line"
? "Second line"
?? "Still on second line"
```

This is referred to as console output, or using the console device, and is the most primitive way to send output to the screen. When you reach the end of a screen row, Clipper will wrap the output down one row and resume in column zero. In the following example 500 asterisks will be displayed, wrapping six times to fit on the screen:

```
? replicate("*", 500)
```

When you hit the last row on the screen, Clipper scrolls the screen up one line and gives you a new, clear line at the bottom. The next example displays the numbers from 1 to 100, scrolling earlier lines to make room for the new lines.

```
for i := 1 to 100
  ? i
next i
```

This example may seem crude and out of place in a product like Clipper but it's important to realize that this style of output is directly related to the way other devices, like printers and text files, work. @..SAY style output is certainly more powerful but it's meant for screens and does not transfer well to other devices.

The destination of the ? and ?? commands is controlled by combinations of the SET PRINTER, SET CONSOLE and SET ALTERNATE commands.

Following a SET PRINTER ON command, all ? and ?? commands are displayed on the screen and echoed to the printer. Output continues to go to both the screen and the printer until a SET PRINTER OFF command is issued.

```
? "On the screen."
set printer on
? "On the screen and the printer."
set printer off
? "Only on the screen."
```

When output is going to both the screen and the printer Clipper will wrap and scroll the screen. It's up to the printer to deal with its own margin boundaries. Not all printers handle boundaries in the same way. Some wrap lines for you while others ignore attempts to write beyond their physical edge.

You can turn the screen off but leave the printer on via the SET CONSOLE command.

```
? "On the screen."
set printer on
? "On the screen and the printer."
set console off
? "On the printer but not on the screen."
set printer off
? "Not on the screen, not on the printer."
set console on
? "Only on the screen."
```

Did you catch the lines where the output doesn't show up anywhere? You can set the printer and console independent of each other, so it's possible to have your application grinding out text that isn't visible anywhere. When you're experimenting with these commands and it appears your computer has hung, it's probably because both the console and printer are OFF while you're using ? and ?? commands.

Console output has one more ability we should discuss. In addition to the screen and printer you can send console output to a file name of your choice with the SET ALTERNATE command. SET ALTERNATE has two distinct variations, as the following example illustrates.

```
? "On the screen."
set alternate to MYFILE.OUT
? "Still only on the screen."
set alternate on
? "Now both on the screen and into MYFILE.OUT."
set console off
? "Only into MYFILE.OUT, not on screen."
set alternate off
? "Not on the screen, not into the file."
set console on
? "Only on the screen."

//  After the next line, MYFILE.OUT is closed
//  and has a ^Z end-of-file marker placed at the end.
set alternate to
```

When you issue a SET ALTERNATE TO <filename> command, Clipper will create the file if it doesn't exist or overwrite the file if it does exist. When you are done with an alternate console file you should always issue a SET ALTERNATE TO command with no filename. Clipper sends a ^Z end-of-file marker to the file and then closes it.

The SET ALTERNATE ON and SET ALTERNATE OFF commands can be used to suspend and resume output to the designated file without closing and reopening it.

If you specify the ADDITIVE option, new with Clipper 5.01, the file is appended to instead of overwritten. The file will be created if it does not exist.

```
set alternate to MYFILE.OUT additive
```

The ? and ?? commands are not the only ones that send output to the console. Any command that dumps text to the screen is using the console device and consequently can be routed to the printer or a text file with the same SET commands. This is where the TO PRINTER and TO FILE options for certain commands come from, for example, LIST, REPORT, and LABEL.

Listing 15.1 shows an amusing thing you can do with console commands and alternate files.

Listing 15.1 The sky's the limit with Clipper's output capabilities

```
local mystery := {235,14,67,108,105,112,112,101,114,32, ;
                  53,46,48,33,13,10,184,00,07,183,      ;
                  07,51,201,182,24,178,79,205,16,180,   ;
                  64,187,02,00,185,14,00,186,02,01,     ;
                  14,31,205,33,180,76,205,33}

? "Please wait..."
set alternate to HELLO.COM
set alternate on
set console off
```

```
aeval(mystery, { |c| qqout(chr(c)) })
set console on
set alternate off
set alternate to
?? "...done."
? "Type HELLO at the DOS command line."
quit
```

The @..SAY Command

The @..SAY command, being coordinate based, is a considerably more efficient way to put text where you want it. To get results equivalent to the example below using ? and ?? commands would take much more code and be more prone to mistakes.

```
@ 2, 4 say "Upper left..."
@ 23,60 say "...Lower right"
```

The destination of @..SAY commands is dictated by the status of the SET DEVICE command, which defaults to TO SCREEN. By changing the device to PRINTER, all @..SAY output will go to the printer instead of the screen.

```
@ 3, 4 say "On the screen."
set device to printer
@ 12, 32 say "On the printer."
set device to screen
@ 5, 25 say "Back on the screen."
```

In the above example Clipper made the printer move the printhead down twelve lines from wherever it was at the moment, and then 32 columns over. If Clipper thinks the printhead is already beyond row twelve it ejects the current page and moves twelve rows down on the new page. Note the fine distinction between Clipper thinking it knows where the printhead is and where the printer has actually parked it. Since printers don't send data back to the computer regarding the true printhead position it's possible that Clipper ejects when it doesn't really have to, or doesn't eject when it should. Keep that in mind when debugging this kind of code. The code in Listing 15.2 is guaranteed to eject a page in the wrong place every time it's run. What's wrong?

Listing 15.2 Why you should not make direct references to printhead positions

```
/*
   What's wrong with this code?
*/
set device to printer
line1 := 5
line2 := 6
@ line1, 0 say "Vendor"
@ line2, 0 say "------"
i := 0
use VENDOR new
goto top
do while .not. VENDOR->(eof())
   i ++
   @ 3 +i, 0 say VENDOR->name
   skip alias VENDOR
enddo
set device to screen
close databases
quit
```

Better yet, don't write code like Listing 15.2! There's an inherent problem with trying to address devices like printers as if they are the same as the screen. The printer has an arbitrary number of columns (depending on the model, size of the characters and the width of the paper) and an arbitrary number of rows (depending on line spacing and page length). You're not going to get very far thinking of the printed page as a special kind of screen. We'll come back to this issue in a moment, when we talk about the PROW() and PCOL() functions.

@..SAY output can also be directed to places other than the printer, using the same SET PRINTER TO command options as discussed previously for console output.

```
set device to printer
set printer to LPT2
@ 1,1 say "Out to device on LPT2 port."
set printer to COM1
```

```
@ 3,7 say "Out to device on COM1 port."
set printer to REPORT.TXT
@ 2,25 say "Out to file called REPORT.TXT."

set printer to

//  At this point REPORT.TXT is closed.
//  Unlike SET ALTERNATE, a ^Z is not added to end of file.

set device to screen
```

Similar to SET ALTERNATE TO, the SET PRINTER TO command has an ADDITIVE option new with Clipper 5.01, which provides for a way to append text to the specified file rather than overwriting it.

```
set printer to REPORT.TXT additive
```

All of these options can be confusing until you've worked with them for a while. Table 15.1 shows the print-related SET commands and the type of output with which they are associated.

Table 15.1 SET commands and where they are effective

	?,??	@..SAY
set alternate	4	
set printer on/off	4	
set printer to	4	4
set device	4	4

Printhead functions: PROW(), PCOL(), and SETPRC()

As we hinted in the @..SAY section, writing directly to specific coordinates is fine for the screen but not a very good idea for printed reports, or even reports going to a file, since the problem of page ejects occurs there as well. Our assertion is that since the printer's rows and columns are essentially arbitrary (from within our program we don't have a clue what we're connected to) and since we are obligated to start from the top and work our way down the page, we may as well do all printhead movement based on offsets from where it currently is. This way there is no possibility of accidentally getting ahead of ourselves.

Clipper provides three printhead-related functions and they're all we need to do the job right:

PCOL()	returns the current printer column,
PROW()	returns the current printer row, and
SETPRC()	sets the PROW() and PCOL() values.

Keep in mind that these values are Clipper's and not the printer's. When your application first starts, PROW() and PCOL() are both set to zero. As you send text to the printer the values are updated. The SETPRC() function is used to set these internal counters to specified values. If the printer is in the middle of the page, issuing SETPRC(0,0) has no effect on the printer but as far as Clipper is concerned it's pointing to the top of the page.

In the following code note how the PROW() and PCOL() values are updated only when the device is set to the printer:

```
set device to printer
@ 1, 6 say "abc"
? prow()                // 1
? pcol()                // 9
setprc(17, 62)
? prow()                // 17
? pcol()                // 62
set device to screen
@ 5, 23 say "xyz"
? prow()                // Still 17
? pcol()                // Still 62
```

We can take advantage of the way Clipper maintains these internal counters and use them to move the printhead around in a way guaranteed not to cause problems. What we do is express where we want to be, based in relation to where we are right now. Consider this example.

```
set device to printer
@ prow() +2, 0 say "First line"
@ prow() +5, 0 say "Second line"
@ prow(), pcol() +17 say "...further over"
set device to screen
```

The first line is printed two rows down from wherever the printhead happened to be. The second line is printed five more rows further down. The next command leaves the printhead on the current row but moves it 17 columns to the right. We never made direct references to row or column values (except for starting things off in column zero) so our code isn't sensitive to the exact position of the printhead.

If you need to start printing, for example, on the fourth line of the page, you're better off making sure that the printhead is sitting at the physical top of the page and then issuing an @..SAY with PROW() +4, rather than addressing row four directly. As we get deeper into the art of printer control you will see this is more important than it may seem now.

The EJECT command

There's one final printer-related command we need to round out our basic set of tools. The EJECT command sends the CHR(12) formfeed character to the printer and sets PROW() and PCOL() to zero. EJECT is not affected by the status of SET DEVICE or SET PRINTER ON/OFF, it always sends a formfeed to the printer or to whichever device the printer has been set.

Sending control codes

The subject of sending control codes to the printer can get amazingly involved and is covered in more detail later in this chapter. In the context of this section on basic printer control concepts, let's tackle the situation where you're writing for a single make and model of printer and know exactly what it is capable of doing. This simplifies matters and provides a number of alternatives for sending the control codes.

What are printer control codes?

Most modern printers, and certainly all the ones we're interested in dealing with in this chapter, are controlled by sending sequences of characters that have special meaning to the printer. When the printer sees the special characters it responds in the proscribed way. For example, CHR(15) is used almost universally to make dot matrix printers shift into a condensed character size and CHR(18) is used to shift the printer back into its normal character size. A CHR(15) appearing anywhere in the stream of characters going out to the printer will cause the printer to shift into condensed type at that point.

Other printer attributes are more complex and require several characters. Rather than trying to use the range of characters below ASCII 32 to identify all their attributes, most printers use escape sequences. An escape sequence requires that only a single character be given special significance, usually CHR(27), and it signals that the characters following the escape character are to be interpreted as printer commands and not as characters to be printed. At this point it's completely up to the printer manufacturer to decide what happens next. Some escape sequences are comprised of a single character, others need a dozen or more.

The most obvious thing to do is send the appropriate control codes whenever you want a particular attribute. Most dot matrix printers shift into condensed print with CHR(15) and shift back out to regular text with CHR(18), so we'll use them as an example. The code in Listing 15.3 prints a list of vendor IDs and names in regular size characters followed by the address in condensed characters.

Listing 15.3 Sending printer control codes

```
/*   List the contents of the VENDOR database,
     put address in condensed type so it fits on one line.
     Condensed on = chr(15)
     Condensed off = chr(18)
*/
```

```
use VENDOR new
goto top
set device to printer
setprc(0,0)
do while .not. VENDOR->(eof())
  @ prow() +1, 0 say VENDOR->ID
  @ prow(), pcol() +2 say VENDOR->Name
  @ prow(), pcol() say chr(15)
  @ prow(), pcol() +2 say VENDOR->Address
  @ prow(), pcol() +2 say VENDOR->City
  @ prow(), pcol() +2 say VENDOR->State
  @ prow(), pcol() +2 say VENDOR->Zip
  @ prow(), pcol() say chr(18)
  skip alias VENDOR
enddo
eject
set device to screen
quit
```

There are two problems with this approach. First, it's not a good idea to hard wire the control codes into the report: If we ever switch printers we'll have to edit the source code, and possibly in many different places if we used the control codes frequently. We can use memory variables or preprocessor #define directives to move the definition of the control codes into a single place where we can get at them easily. If we use #defines the interior of the previous do..enddo loop looks like the following:

```
#define COND_ON   chr(15)
#define COND_OFF  chr(18)

/*
   Just the interior of the do..enddo loop, from before.
*/
@ prow() +1, 0 say VENDOR->ID
@ prow(), pcol() +2 say VENDOR->Name
@ prow(), pcol() say COND_ON
@ prow(), pcol() +2 say VENDOR->Address
```

```
@ prow(), pcol() +2 say VENDOR->City
@ prow(), pcol() +2 say VENDOR->State
@ prow(), pcol() +2 say VENDOR->Zip
@ prow(), pcol() say COND_OFF
```

The other problem may not be obvious when using control codes that are only one character long, so imagine that the code sequence for condensed print was ten characters long (not at all an unusual size for laser printers). When Clipper sends the COND_ON string, it dutifully adjusts the PCOL() value to reflect the fact that it sent ten characters out on the current line. The printer, however, interpreted all ten characters internally and didn't pass anything along to the printhead, which stayed exactly where it was. Now we have a situation where our program and the printer disagree about what column we are in. Fortunately there's an easy way around the situation. The #define directives, below, route the control codes through a SendCodes() function which adjusts Clipper's internal counters, keeping them the same as they were before the control codes were sent.

```
#define COND_ON    SendCodes(chr(15))
#define COND_OFF   SendCodes(chr(18))

function SendCodes(string)
/*
   Send control codes without altering PROW() and PCOL().
*/
local r := prow(), c := pcol()
@ r, c say string
setprc(r, c)
return ""
```

Why does the function return an empty string? In the context we call SendCodes() we expect a string of control characters. The function sends the string, fixes up the internal row and column counters, and then returns the net result as far as the printhead was concerned: nothing, an empty string. This allows us to simplify the use of control codes in our example, reprinted in Listing 15.4 in it's new entirety.

Listing 15.4 The control code technique

```
#define COND_ON   sendCodes(chr(15))
#define COND_OFF  sendCodes(chr(18))

/*
   Same vendor listing as before, but this time
   using a better printer control code technique.
*/
use VENDOR new
goto top
set device to printer
setprc(0,0)
do while .not. VENDOR->(eof())
  @ prow() +1, 0 say Vendor->ID
  @ prow(), pcol() +2 say Vendor->Name
  COND_ON
  @ prow(), pcol() +2 say Vendor->Address
  @ prow(), pcol() +2 say VENDOR->City
  @ prow(), pcol() +2 say VENDOR->State
  @ prow(), pcol() +2 say VENDOR->Zip
  COND_OFF
  skip alias VENDOR
enddo
eject
set device to screen
quit
```

With this technique we can use any set of control codes and still have an accurate gauge of where the printhead is at any moment.

Top and bottom margins: when to eject?

Deciding when to eject is an important part of writing reports that might occupy more than a single page. You can ignore the page length and just plow right past the bottom, but that doesn't make for a very professional-looking report. Reports need a few blank lines at the top and bottom of each page to look their best. The exact number should really be up to the person using the application. Will they be binding the reports across the top of the page? If so, they'll need a larger top margin to accommodate the binder. Will they be stapling the reports in the corner or binding them along the side? If so, then there's no reason to waste space at the top and the margin can be made smaller.

To make the decision about when to eject we need to know how many lines are on the page and how many blank lines to leave at the top and bottom. Let's use preprocessor #define directives to record this information.

```
#define TOP_MAR   4
#define BOT_MAR   6
#define PAGE_LEN  66
```

Since the PROW() function will tell us where we are on the page at any given time, all we need to do is check the following logic before printing a line. If it's true we need to eject, advance down past the top margin, and then print the line. If false, there's room enough to print the line on the current page.

```
need_eject := (prow() +BOT_MAR) > PAGE_LEN
```

Installed in a reporting loop the logic looks like Listing 15.5.

Listing 15.5 Page eject logic

```
/*
    List vendor names, with a nice column heading.
    Eject page when we get too close to the bottom margin.
*/
use VENDOR new
goto top
set device to printer
setprc(0,0)
@1 prow() +TOP_MAR,  0 say "Vendor Name"
@ prow() +1,         0 say "-----------"
do while .not. VENDOR->(eof())
```

```
  if (prow() +BOT_MAR) > PAGE_LEN
     eject
     setprc(0,0)
     @ prow() +TOP_MAR, 0 say ""
  endif
  @ prow() +1, 0 say VENDOR->Name
  skip alias VENDOR
enddo
eject
set device to screen
quit
```

Seeing as we'll be checking for the need to eject a page on a regular basis, this is just begging to be made into a user-defined function (see Listing 15.6).

Listing 15.6 A more efficient way to detect the need for a page eject

```
function PageEject()
/*
   Check to see if it"s time to eject the page.
   If so, eject and move down beyond top margin.
   Return .t. if we ejected.
*/
local need_eject := (prow() +BOT_MAR) > PAGE_LEN
if need_eject
  eject
  setprc(0,0)
  @ prow() +TOP_MAR, 0 say ""
endif
return need_eject
```

The way our Vendor Name list is currently written it creates top and bottom margins correctly, but only the first page will have column headings. Because PageEject() as written above returns true if the page was ejected, the calling program can detect when it's time to print the column headings again. Listing 15.7 shows our reporting loop once again (Listing 15.7).

Listing 15.7 Printing column headings on every page

```
/*
   Same vendor listing as before, but this time
   print the column headings on every page and use
   the nifty PageEject() function to help out.
*/
use VENDOR new
goto top
set device to printer
setprc(0,0)
@ prow() +TOP_MAR,  0 say "Vendor Name"
@ prow() +1,        0 say "-----------"
do while .not. VENDOR->(eof())
  if PageEject()
    @ prow() +1, 0 say "Vendor Name"
    @ prow() +1, 0 say "-----------"
  endif
  @ prow() +1, 0 say VENDOR->Name
  skip alias VENDOR
enddo
eject
set device to screen
quit
```

Now we'll get column headings at the top of every page, making the report much better looking and easier to read. However, we've repeated the column heading code, once before the start of the loop and again inside it. This isn't very efficient, as we'll have to maintain the same code in two places. It would be much better if there was a single occurrence of the code. In Listing 15.8 we've modified PageEject() to detect both situations and react accordingly.

Listing 15.8 A new version of the previous page eject function

```
function PageEject()
/*
   Check to see if it"s time to eject the page.
   If so, eject and move down beyond top margin.
   Return .t. if we ejected. Correctly handles
   situation where printer is already positioned
   at the top of a page.
*/
local need_eject := ((prow() +BOT_MAR) > PAGE_LEN) ;
                    .or. (prow() == 0)
if need_eject
  if prow() > 0
    eject
    setprc(0,0)
  endif
  @ prow() +TOP_MAR, 0 say ""
endif
return need_eject
```

This is much better. Now we can write our reporting loop as illustrated in Listing 15.9.

Listing 15.9 A better way to print column headings on every page

```
/*
   One more time... THIS time we'll get column headings
   on every page without any duplication of effort.
*/
use VENDOR new
goto top
set device to printer
setprc(0,0)
do while .not. VENDOR->(eof())
  if PageEject()
```

```
    @ prow() +1, 0 say "Vendor Name"
    @ prow() +1, 0 say "-----------"
  endif
  @ prow() +1, 0 say VENDOR->Name
  skip alias VENDOR
enddo
eject
set device to screen
quit
```

Our routine now correctly handles each page, placing a column heading on the first and all subsequent pages. We can't be too proud of the report, however. This report violates a number of important design considerations, which we'll discuss next.

Page headings and pagination

Every page of every report should contain the following information.

- Name of application
- Name of report
- Date and time printed
- Page number
- Constraints in effect while printing
- Column headings

So far our Vendor Name example has only column headings. What's the big deal about the other elements? The idea is that every single page of every report should completely identify what it is and where it comes from, as well as an indication of how timely the data is and why the report contains what it does. Any page of any report should be self-contained in this respect. Figure 15.1 shows an example of a page heading containing all these elements.

Figure 15.1 Sample report heading

```
Winston Co. Inventory Tracking System          07/17/91 VLST-A
Vendor Listing                                 20:20:00 Page 3
(Active Vendors, Only)

Vendor Name           Address              YTD Total    Contracted?
------------------    ----------------     ----------   ------------
Semmer's Supply       301 Elm Street       $7,287.65    Yes
Smith Machine Corp    2763 South 42nd      $  233.34    No
Zenith Distributors   Five Mile Road       $1,356.17    No

*** End of Report ***
```

This heading tells us everything we need to know about the report. We know it was printed by Winston Co.'s Inventory Tracking System, and that it's called the Vendor Listing. The report is limited to only the active vendors (implying that the same report could be printed for inactive vendors as well), so the comment in parentheses assures there's no confusion about what the report contains. The date and time the report was printed is documented so we can tell at a glance how old it is. The page number is also printed so we know there's more prior to this page, while the last line, *** End of Report ***, makes it clear there's nothing more to follow.

The "VLST-A" tucked in the upper right corner is a short, unique identifier that is independent of the report's constraints. The programmer can use this to quickly determine the identity of a report when there are a large number of reports in the application, rather than having to remember the proper titles of dozens of reports. This eliminates tiresome phone conversations where the customer attempts to describe which report is having difficulties.

Hey, wait a minute — the report's heading isn't centered! Isn't that a violation of an age-old convention? Yes, to some people it is. We feel that unless there's a direct requirement that headings be centered, you should left-justify the report titles and right justify the page identification block. This provides for an easy way to assure consistency across a wide variety of reports, and across a wide variety of printers. Correctly centering a line text, and making it look good at the same time, is less likely to happen than left and right justification. If you disagree with this assertion, there's no problem. All of the functions we present for dealing with page headings can be altered for centering.

To provide the most flexibility we're going to need something to hold the various elements of the header. Rather than using preprocessor #define directives, let's switch to memory variables so the functions can be used throughout our applications and not rely on the way the source code is compiled. Here are the variables that describe the report.

```
/*
   Define the elements in the page heading.
*/
local sys_title := "Winston Co. Inventory Tracking"
local rpt_title :=  "Vendor Listing"
local rpt_cond  :=  "(Active Vendors, Only)"
local rpt_id    :=  "VLST-A"
local col_head1 :=  "Vendor Name                   " +;
                   "Address                          " +;
                   "YTD Total  Contracted?"
local col_head2 := "------------------- -------------------" +;
                   "--------- -----------"
```

And here are the variables that define the page. Note that we've introduced several new page parameters.

```
/*
   Define the page dimensions.
*/
local page_len   := 66
local page_width := 80
local top_mar    := 4
local bot_mar    := 3
local left_mar   := 8
local right_mar  := 2
```

These six values completely define the page and how the report should be printed on it. The length and width give the overall dimensions while the four margins define the amount of "white space" required. As discussed previously, you can't always assume the margins are constant. Some reports may get three-hole punched and kept in binders, so a large left margin is required. Other reports may need to jam as much information as possible into every line and thus can't waste the margins. If you are printing to laser printers you must leave at least one column blank on each side, and sometimes two, because laser printers can't print right up to the edge.

Assuming these variable assignments have been made we can write a page heading routine as shown in Listing 15.10.

Listing 15.10 Printing with page and column headings (a first attempt)

```
/*
   The venerable Vendor Listing again, this time with
   both page and column headings on every page.
*/
use VENDOR new
set filter to VENDOR->ytd > 0
goto top
set device to printer
setprc(0,0)
page_number := 0
do while .not. VENDOR->(eof())
  if PageEject(page_len, top_mar, bot_mar)
     page_number++
     page_id1 := dtoc(date()) +" " +rpt_id
     page_id2 := time() +" Page " +ltrim(str(page_number))
     @ prow() +1, left_mar say sys_title
     @ prow(), (page_width -(len(page_id1) +right_mar));
              say page_id1
     @ prow() +1, left_mar say rpt_title
     @ prow(), (page_width -(len(page_id2) +right_mar));
              say page_id2
     @ prow() +2, left_mar say col_head1
     @ prow() +1, left_mar say col_head2
  endif
```

```
  @ prow() +1, left_mar say VENDOR->name
  @ prow(), pcol() +2 say VENDOR->address
  @ prow(), pcol() +2 say VENDOR->ytd picture "$9,999.99"
  @ prow(), pcol() +6 say if(VENDOR->contract, "Yes", "No")
  skip alias VENDOR
enddo
@ prow() +2, left_mar say "*** End of Report ***"
eject
set device to screen
close databases
quit
```

In order to do page headings correctly we have to convert the previous version of the PageEject() function to accept parameters rather than assume the page dimensions and margins. See Listing 15.11.

Listing 15.11 Yet another version of PageEject()

```
function PageEject(length, top, bottom)
/*
   Eject page based on current printer row and
   the parameters passed.
*/
local need_eject := ((prow() +bottom) > length) ;
                    .or. (prow() == 0)
if need_eject
   if prow() > 0
   eject
   setprc(0,0)
   endif
   @ prow() +top, 0 say ""
endif
return need_eject
```

Now our report program produces page headings that completely satisfy the list of required elements. However, we paid a heavy price in convenience. It would be difficult if not impossible to write this complicated page head printing logic correctly each time we need it for a report. This is another perfect place for a user-defined function. The source code for PageHead() is found in Listing 15.12.

Listing 15.12 PageHead()

```
function PageHead(sys, rpt, id, width, left, right, page)
/*
   Print a standardized page heading
   based on the parameters passed.
*/
local a := dtoc(date()) +" " +id
local b := time() +" Page " +ltrim(str(page))
@ prow() +1, left say sys
@ prow(), (width -(len(a) +right)) say a
@ prow() +1, left say rpt
@ prow(), (width -(len(b) +right)) say b
return nil
```

Now that we can eliminate most of the page heading code our report is much easier to read. Listing 15.13 contains the new version of the do..enddo loop.

Listing 15.13 More efficient way to produce standard headings

```
/*
     The "meat" of the previous vendor listing again,
     this time handling page and column headings more
     efficiently.
*/
do while .not. VENDOR->(eof())
  if PageEject(page_len, top_mar, bot_mar)
     page_number++
     PageHead(sys_title, rpt_title, rpt_id, ;
                 page_width, left_mar, right_mar, page_number)
     @ prow() +2, left_mar say col_head1
     @ prow() +1, left_mar say col_head2
  endif
  @ prow() +1, left_mar say VENDOR->name
  @ prow(), pcol() +2 say VENDOR->address
  @ prow(), pcol() +2 say VENDOR->ytd picture "$9,999.99"
  @ prow(), pcol() +6 say if(VENDOR->contract, "Yes", "No")
  skip alias VENDOR
enddo
```

Even more refinements

Use of the PageEject() and PageHead() functions allowed us to eliminate all the source code that is usually needed for checking for page ejects and printing standard page headings. Our code is easier to read and write, which results in more reliability and programming efficiency. With the goal of tighter and more efficient code in mind, let's eliminate one more class of repetitive source code. Take a look at the sample code in Listing 15.14, taken from the previous section, and see if it makes immediate sense.

Listing 15.14 Introducing NextRow() and SameRow()

```
/*
     The same "meat" loop as before, but this time
     using two helpful mystery functions.
*/
do while .not. VENDOR->(eof())
  if PageEject(page_len, top_mar, bot_mar)
     page_number++
     PageHead(sys_title, rpt_title, rpt_id, ;
                  page_width, left_mar, right_mar, page_number)
     NextRow(2, left_mar, col_head1)
     NextRow(1, left_mar, col_head2)
  endif
  NextRow(1, left_mar, Vendor->Name)
  SameRow(2, Vendor->Address)
  SameRow(2, Vendor->YTD, "$9,999.99")
  SameRow(6, if(Vendor->Contract, "Yes", "No"))
  skip alias VENDOR
enddo
```

We've eliminated the remaining repetitive code and replaced it with two functions, one that starts printing on a new line and one that prints on the current line. Both functions handle the busy work of adding margins and skipping space between columns. Listing 15.15 and 15.16 contain the code for the two functions.

Listing 15.15 The NextRow() function

```
function NextRow(howmany, leftmar, what)
/*
     Move down specified number of rows,
     insert left margin and print specified thing.
     What to print is optional.
*/
if what == nil
    what := ""
endif
@ prow() +howMany, leftMar say what
return nil
```

Listing 15.16 The SameRow() function

```
function SameRow(colsover, what, pict)
/*
     Move over specified number of columns and
     print something, using optional picture.
*/
if what == nil
   what := ""
endif
if pict == nil
  @ prow(), pcol() +colsover say what
else
  @ prow(), pcol() +colsover say what picture (pict)
endif
return nil
```

Making the "what to print" parameters optional allows us to position the printhead without actually printing anything.

```
// Move down ten rows and over 17 columns
NextRow(10, left_mar)
SameRow(17)
```

In the above example we move 17 columns in addition to the left margin. The left margin is arbitrary, we can assign it any value at all. The SameRow(17) allows us to order the printhead to move to a specific column with respect to the rest of the report, but independent of where the printhead actually is with respect to the printed page.

The user interface

There's more to printing than just sending characters to the printer. Reports have to exist within the context of the rest of the application, and that means addressing user interface concerns. Your program is in a heap of trouble if it blindly assumes that it's attached to a perfect printer that's always plugged in, turned on, on-line, and loaded with paper. Even if it were, you can't assume that the person who requested the report wants to wait for the whole thing to print. You've got to check that the printer is ready to print before starting the report, and you've got to allow for interruptions from the user or from the printer itself.

Let's address all three of these concerns in turn, starting with checking that both the user and the printer are ready to begin the report. We've found that it's good programming practice to present a clear and consistent interface to the user of the application (for a comprehensive treatment of this subject see Chapter 13, "The Art of the User Interface").

Are both the printer and the user ready?

Even though the printer and the user are two very distinct entities it's best to check the disposition of both of them at the same time. There's nothing more frustrating than an application that asks you if you really want to print a report and then says you can't because the printer isn't ready.

Listing 15.17 contains a function that checks both and returns a go/no go signal.

Listing 15.17 The PrintReady() user interface function

```
function PrintReady(r, c)
/*
     Checks printer port to be sure printer is ready,
     then asks user if (s)he is ready to print.
     (Displays messages at specified coordinates.)
     If printer isn't ready, keeps checking until it either
     becomes available or the user hits a key.
*/
local ready := .f.
@ r, c clear to r +2, maxcol()
if .not. isprinter()
  @ r,    c say "Printer isn't responding..."
  @ r +1, c say "Check that printer is turned on and is on-line."
  @ r +2, c say "Press any key to abandon the report."
endif
do while .not. (isprinter() .or. inkey() <> 0)
enddo
@ r, c clear to r +2, maxcol()
if isprinter()
  @ r,    c say "Ready to print..."
  @ r +1, c say "Do you want to print the report?"
  @ r +2, c say "Press Y to print or any other key to abandon it."
  ready := (chr(inkey(0)) $ "Yy")
  @ r, c clear to r +2, maxcol()
endif
return ready
```

A limitation here is that Clipper's ISPRINTER() function only checks the main parallel printer port, LPT1 (also called PRN).

The companion diskette for this book contains an alternate function, isPort(), that can check any of the device ports for a printer that's ready to print. To use isPort() you must pass the DOS device name you wish to check.

```
? isPort("PRN")      //  Equivalent to ISPRINTER()
? isPort("LPT3")     //  Check parallel port #3
? isPort("COM2")     //  Check serial port #2
```

Here's an example of a call to the PrintReady() function. The idea is to verify that everything is ready to roll prior to actually trying to do anything, thus cutting down on user frustration and run-time printer errors.

```
/*
   Example of PrintReady() in the context of a report.
*/
function MyReport()

@ 8, 5 say "MY REPORT"
if .not. PrintReady(10,5)
   return .f.
endif
@ 9,0 clear
@ 10, 5 say "Printing."

//  Report goes here

return .t.
```

PrintReady() is about as ugly as they come regarding slick user interfaces, but that isn't the point of the function. You can easily customize it to look and feel like the rest of your application We've kept it simple in this chapter to make the printer-related concepts clear and uncluttered. See Chapter 13 for a collection of functions to help make PrintReady() work better.

Allowing for pauses and interruptions

Despite your PrintReady() warning that the report is ready to start spewing forth from the printer, the user may not wish to wait for the whole thing to print. Maybe they selected the wrong report, or perhaps they only need the first two pages. For whatever reason they need to be able to cleanly interrupt your reports. While we're at it we may as well deal with the related situation where they just want to pause the report and not interrupt it permanently. For example, the paper is shifting around and in danger of jamming, or the ribbon needs to be changed.

There are three distinct stages to the interrupt/pause process: Sense the keystroke, pause and wait for the end user's disposition, then either abandon or resume the report. The tricky part, believe it or not, is abandoning the report cleanly and efficiently. See Listing 15.18 for a function that checks for user interrupts.

Listing 15.18 Checking for user-requested interruptions

```
function CheckAbort(r, c)
/*
   If a keystroke is in the buffer, display prompt
   and wait for user response. Returns true if user
   wants to abort report.
*/
local abort := .f.
if inkey() <> 0
   set device to screen
   @ r, c clear to r +1, maxcol()
   @ r,    c say "Printing paused..."
   @ r +1, c say "Do you want to abort the report?"
   abort := (chr(inkey(0)) $ "Yy")
   @ r, c clear to r +1, maxcol()
   if .not. abort
    set device to printer
   endif
endif
return abort
```

For an example that uses CheckAbort(), see Listing 15.19.

Listing 15.19 Example of CheckAbort()

```
/*
   Code fragment showing how CheckAbort() is
   implemented in a reporting loop.
*/
finished_ok := .t.
```

```
do while .not. VENDOR->(eof())
   if CheckAbort(12,8)
      finished_ok := .f.
      exit
   endif
   NextRow(1, left_mar, Vendor->Name)
   SameRow(2, Vendor->Address)
   SameRow(2, Vendor->YTD, "$9,999.99")
   SameRow(6, if(Vendor->Contract, "Yes", "No"))
   skip alias VENDOR
enddo
```

Nothing happens each time the CheckAbort() is called, unless a key was pressed since the last time it was called. There's no reason to check more than once within the loop, it isn't critical to catch the keystroke and halt the report immediately. Do check frequently enough so the user is likely to get nearly immediate feedback, otherwise they'll probably start whacking keys repeatedly thinking they'll get your attention, or possibly even reboot the computer if they're sufficiently concerned about not letting the report continue (for example, when mailing labels jam the printer).

If a key was pressed, the user gets a chance to think about the situation and make a decision to either completely abandon the report or let it resume. If they chose to resume the report picks up where it left off. If they abandon the report the EXIT command drops out of the reporting loop. In the example we used a flag, **finished_ok**, to keep track of the interruption situation. We can use the flag to ask the user if they want to start the report over again, or to take other steps depending on whether or not the report was run to completion. For example, there's no reason to print grand totals or a summary page if the report was interrupted.

With this current technique CheckAbort() only works efficiently when the reporting logic is simple enough that an EXIT command will get us out of the thick of things. If there were a set of nested do..enddo loops we'd have to load our code with all sorts of additional logic to allow an interruption from any point in the report, as illustrated below.

```
/*
   CheckAbort() gets buried alive!
*/
do while .not. VENDOR->(eof())
  current_state := VENDOR->State
  do while VENDOR->State == current_state
     current_city := VENDOR->City
     do while VENDOR->City +VENDOR->state ;
           == current_city +current_state
       if CheckAbort(10,4)
         //
         //  Now What?!
         //
       endif
       skip alias VENDOR
     enddo
  enddo
enddo
```

Situations such as this are best handled with a BEGIN SEQUENCE..END block that delimits the entire report. Issuing a BREAK command at any point while the report is running causes the program to jump to the first line immediately following the END SEQUENCE command. (See Chapter 28, "The Error Object," for more details about these commands.) In the following code, even though there are three nested do..enddo loops to fight our way out of, the BREAK command leaps all the way out at once, independent of the do..enddo conditions.

```
/*
   CheckAbort() teams up with the BEGIN SEQUENCE..END
   block and BREAK to handle the situation.
*/
finished_ok := .t.
begin sequence
  do while...
     do while...
        do while...
           if CheckAbort(10,4)
              finished_ok := .f.
```

```
            break
          endif
        enddo
     enddo
   enddo
end sequence
if .not. finished_ok
  //  Report was interrupted.
endif
```

The use of a flag like **finished_ok** is the only way you should implement BEGIN SEQUENCE blocks. The report routine has no recollection of how it exited the block unless you set the flag properly. Using a flag allows you to remain in control and will help in debugging the routine.

Handling run-time printer errors

Even though ISPRINTER() returns true, it doesn't mean that it will stay true. The printer can go down at any moment while your report is printing and no amount of checking will be able to prevent a run-time error. It's not worth even trying to stick calls to ISPRINTER() all over your code, there's a much more efficient way to handle the possibility of printer errors. The same BEGIN SEQUENCE..END block that was used with CheckAbort() in the previous section can be used to handle run-time errors as well. We can take advantage of Clipper's error handling features to make it easy to catch and respond to printer errors.

This is not the place to go into details concerning the Error Class of objects now present in Clipper. See Chapter 28 for a complete discussion.

The error trapping process is accomplished in three steps: Post an error handler that's active while the report is running, display a message and get the user's disposition about any errors that occur, then either resume or abandon the report, depending on the user's response and the status of the printer. If the functions in Listings 15.20 and 15.21 don't make sense, plow through the examples as best you can, read the chapter on the Error Class, and then come back.

Listing 15.20 Sample report using a BEGIN SEQUENCE block

```
function MyReport()
/*
   Save the current error handler and
   post a new one for handling printer errors.
*/
local prevhandler := errorblock()
errorblock( {|e| PrintError(12, 10, e, prevhandler) } )

/*
        Print report as usual, but within the scope
        of a BEGIN SEQUENCE..END block.
*/
use VENDOR new
goto top
begin sequence
   set device to printer
   setprc(0,0)
   do while .not. VENDOR->(eof())
      NextRow(1, left_mar, Vendor->Name)
      SameRow(2, Vendor->Address)
      SameRow(2, Vendor->YTD, "$9,999.99")
      SameRow(6, if(Vendor->Contract, "Yes", "No"))
      skip alias VENDOR
   enddo
end sequence
/*
          Restore the previous error handler
          now that we're past the point where
          we're concerned about printer errors.
*/
errorBlock(prevHandler)
return nil
```

Listing 15.21 Printer error handling function

```
function PrintError(r, c, err, passAlong)
/*
   Error handler used during printing.

   r            Row to display messages.
   c            Column to display messages.
   err          Error object to handle.
   passAlong    Handler to pass error object along to
                if this handler can't deal with it.
*/
#include "ERROR.CH"
local tryAgain

//  If generic code indicates a printer error
if err:genCode == EG_PRINT

   /*
         Display informative message and wait for either
         the printer to come back on-line or a keystroke.
   */
   set device to screen
   @ r, c clear to r +2, maxcol()
   @ r, c    say "Printer Error!"
   @ r +1, c say "Possible problems: Out of paper," +;
                 "jammed, off-line."
   @ r +2, c say "Attempt to fix problem. Press any key " +;
                 "to continue."
   keyboard ""
   do while .not. (isprinter() .or. inkey() <> 0)
   enddo

   /*
         If the printer comes back, ask if they want to resume.
   */
```

```
   @ r, c clear to r +2, maxcol()
   if isprinter()
      @ r,     c say "Printer is back..."
      @ r +1, c say "Do you want to resume printing the report?"
      @ r +2, c say "Press Y to resume printing or any other " +;
                    "key to cancel."
      keyboard ""
      tryAgain := (chr(inkey(0)) $ "Yy")
      @ r, c clear to r +2, maxcol()
      if tryAgain
         set device to printer
         return .t.
      endif
   endif
   break

/*
    Some other kind of error occurred, pass the error
    along to the previous error handler.
*/
else
   return eval(passAlong, err)
endif
return nil
```

Note: Not all printers react the same way to the "off line" condition. It's entirely possible that it takes a minute or more for some printers to be detected. Turning the power off will usually cause the error condition to occur immediately, allowing you to test your error handling routines more efficiently. Taking the printer off line will not always result in an immediate error condition.

All together now

It took a while to get here, but now we have all the functions we need to "do it right" and program a report we can be proud of, a report that can handle everything the user or the printer throws at us. The Vendor Name report is presented one more time (Listing 15.22) with all of the printer control functions implemented.

Listing 15.22. The vendor list example with "the works"

```
#define COND_ON  SendCodes(chr(15))
#define COND_OFF SendCodes(chr(18))

function VendList()
/*
   Print the Vendor Listing once again, this time using
   every trick we've learned in this chapter.
*/

local prevhandler
local sys_title, rpt_title, rpt_cond, rpt_id, col_head1, col_head2
local page_len, page_width, top_mar, bot_mar, left_mar, right_mar
local page_number := 0

//  Let user know what's happening, get confirmation to begin.
@ 0,0 clear
@ 8, 5 say "Vendor Listing"
if .not. PrintReady(10,5)
   return nil
endif
@ 10, 5 say "Printing..."

//  Define the elements in the page heading.
sys_title := "ACME Inventory Tracking"
rpt_title := "Vendor Listing"
rpt_cond  := "(Active Vendors, Only)"
rpt_id    := "VLST-A"
col_head1 := "Vendor Name          " +;
             "Address                        " +;
             "YTD Total  Contracted?"
col_head2 := "------------------ --------------------" +;
             "--------  -----------"

//  Define the page dimensions.
page_len   := 66
page_width := 80
top_mar    := 4
```

```
bot_mar    := 3
left_mar   := 8
right_mar  := 2

//  Post the printer error handler, save the previous.
prevHandler:= errorBlock()
errorBlock( {|error| PrintError(10, 5, error, prevHandler) } )

//  Get ready to begin report
use VENDOR new
goto top
set device to printer
setprc(0,0)

//  Start the reporting loop
begin sequence
   do while .not. VENDOR->(eof())

      //  Check if user wants to interrupt the report
      if CheckAbort(10, 5)
         break
      endif

      //  Check to see if it's time to eject the page,
      //  and if so, print page and column headings.
      if PageEject(page_len, top_mar, bot_mar)
         page_number++
         PageHead(sys_title, rpt_title, rpt_id, ;
                  page_width, left_mar, right_mar, page_number)
         NextRow(2, left_mar, col_head1)
         NextRow(1, left_mar, col_head2)
      endif

      //  Print a line in the main body
      NextRow(1, left_mar, Vendor->Name)
      SameRow(2, Vendor->Address)
      SameRow(2, Vendor->YTD, "$9,999.99")
      SameRow(6, if(Vendor->Contract, "Yes", "No"))
      skip alias VENDOR
   enddo
```

```
   //  Print the last message in condensed type.
   COND_ON
   NextRow(2, left_mar, "*** End of Report ***")
   COND_OFF
   eject
end sequence

//  Restore previous error handler
errorBlock(prevHandler)

//  Close 'er down, we're done.
set device to screen
@ 10, 0 clear
@ 10, 5 say "...finished."
close databases

return nil
```

Printing essentials, Summary

We covered the small collection of Clipper commands and functions directly related to printing. We went on to show how these commands and functions are used to print lists and reports, and how to pass control codes to the printer. We discussed the elements that comprise a professional-looking report and then refined our technique by creating some user-defined functions that perform most of the repetitive tasks involved in printing. These functions are listed below.

SendCodes()	Send control codes without disturbing PCOL()
PageEject()	Check for and perform page eject if needed
PageHead()	Print standard page heading
NextRow()	Print something on a new line
SameRow()	Print something in the same line

Then we went on to cover the user interface side of printing and developed some functions that help ensure a smooth running program.

PrintReady()	Check that the user and printer are ready
CheckAbort()	Allow user to abandon the report
PrintError()	Handle printer problems

At this point we have the fundamental parts of a library of printer control functions. These functions alone make printing-related programming easier and more efficient, but there is still plenty of room for improvement. Clipper 5 provides us with the tools we need to create a comprehensive set of functions that work for a wide variety of printing needs, functions that don't fence us in with limitations. You can take the basic printer control functions presented here and adapt and enhance them to provide the kind of utility you need for your own reports.

CHAPTER 16

Networking

A network is a group of computers sharing common resources. The most commonly shared resources are hard disk drives and printers. In most networks, one (or more) computers will act as the network server. It is this computer's hard drive that is shared. In addition, the parallel and serial ports on the server are used to access the shared printers.

The server is usually connected to at least one workstation. A workstation is a computer that has access to the server's hard drive and optionally to its printers. The workstation may have its own resources (such as hard drives and printers) as well.

In this chapter, we will cover the basic components of a network, and look at some advantages and disadvantages of networks. We will also discuss programming considerations on a network. Finally, we will cover the commands and functions that Clipper provides for network programming.

Creating a network

It sometimes seems that in order to create a network, we take a mixture of hardware, software, cabling, network boards, and some technical manuals, and if we mix them together in just the right way, we have a running network. Fortunately, there is a little more organization to the process than that.

Organization

The first thing to decide when creating a network is how the components are going to be connected. The network *topology* describes the layout of cables, computers, and peripherals. There are three common network topologies.

Bus network

On a bus network, a single cable is run along the ground. Each workstation or peripheral is connected directly to this cable. Figure 16.1 illustrates a bus network.

Figure 16.1 Bus network

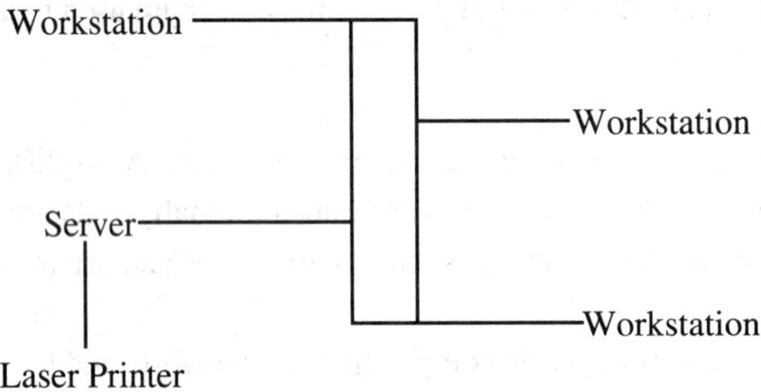

Ring network

On a ring network, the cable forms a continuous loop. Each workstation is connected to the loop at some point and will probably assist the network in sending information to the server and other devices. Figure 16.2 illustrates a ring network.

Figure 16.2 Ring network

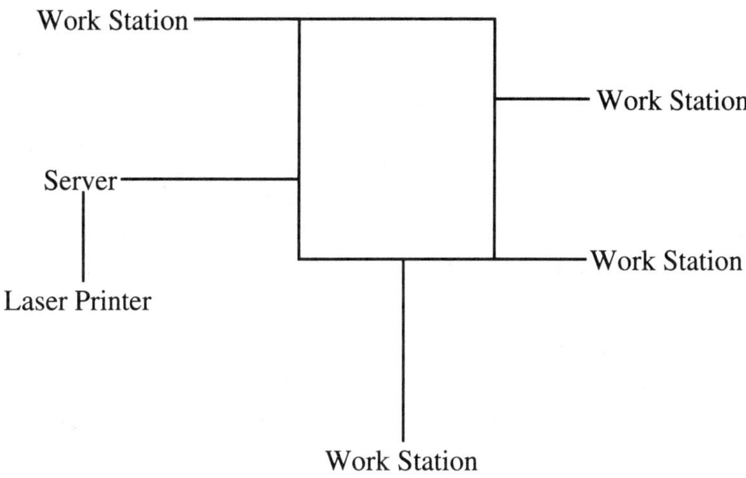

Star network

In a star network, a cable leads from the server to each individual workstation or peripheral. Figure 16.3 illustrates a star network.

Figure 16.3 Star network

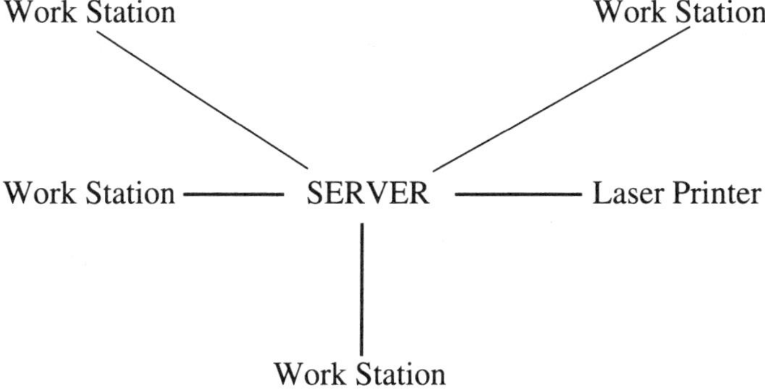

Many times in a star configuration, the cables connect into a hub. The hub generally takes a single cable from the server and splits it to multiple cables leading to other workstations.

There are two kinds of hubs available. An active hub splits the cable but also boosts the signal. As a workstation gets further from the server, the distance can become a problem in that the signal may not be strong enough when it reaches either component. An active hub strengthens the signal and sends it further along. A passive hub merely splits the signal to multiple cables and does not amplify it in any way.

The hardware components

Once the physical layout or topology is decided, the components need to be connected. This section describes those components and how they are connected.

Server

The server is the primary computer whose resources are shared and which handles the data requests. Its hard disk and printers are the resources that the network OS monitors and makes available to other computers. Most servers have large hard disks and lots of RAM. In order to keep performance good, the RAM is used to buffer disk requests.

A server may be *dedicated*, in which case only the Network OS is run on it. It may also be *non-dedicated*, which means that the server can serve a dual role as a server and a workstation. A non-dedicated server has twice the work to do and is usually used in smaller networks.

Workstations

The workstation is any computer which is connected to the server. The station is connected to the cable through a network card. This network card handles traffic between the workstation and the server.

Peripherals

Each printer or hard disk in the network can be shared or local. Local printers are attached directly to the workstations while shared devices are usually attached to the server. Some network operating systems allow workstations access to other workstation devices as well.

Network cards

The network card is usually an add-in board that occupies one slot in your computer. On the back of the card is an outlet to connect the cable. This network card contains the necessary hardware to translate disk requests from a workstation to packets of information sent along the cabling. Usually each network card will also have a physical address which can be set by switches. This allows the server to uniquely identify each workstation. A network card is also present in the server for the same purpose, converting disk activity into cable traffic.

Cabling

The cable is the thread that connects all the components together. It usually consists of two wires wrapped in some sort of protective shielding. There are three general types of cabling available.

Twisted-pair. The twisted-pair is the least expensive cabling available. It consists of two wires twisted together and wrapped in a shielding. It is similar in appearance to telephone wiring. It is also susceptible to interference and should only be used for short distances.

Coaxial. In a coaxial cable, one wire runs down the center of the cable and is shielded. The second wire is wrapped around the center cable and is also shielded. Coaxial cable offers better speed and more protection than twisted-pair cabling.

Fiber optic. Fiber optic cable transmits the data as a beam of light. This is by far the fastest transmitting cable, and the least likely to experience interference. It is also very expensive.

Software components

Once the hardware components are established and connected, the software must be installed. This section describes the necessary software components and where they are installed.

Network operating system

The Network Operating System is a program that runs on the server and handles all network activities. Its main job is to accept requests for data from other stations, check the security and availability of the data, and either process or deny the request. The Network OS also handles the printers and other system resources, allocating them to jobs as requested.

Workstation shells

In order for the workstation to communicate with the network, a program is run which intercepts calls to the hard disk and reroutes them to the network. This program is called the network shell. It is almost always a memory-resident program, using a portion of the available DOS memory. When your application program requests data from a device, the shell looks at the request and decides if it is data from the workstation's hard disk or from the network's disk. If it is from the workstation, the shell turns control back to DOS for processing. If the data is requested from the network, the shell translates the data request into a packet of information to send through the network card to the server.

DOS

DOS versions 3.1 and above are designed to allow multiple users to access files. Clipper can work with any network that utilizes standard DOS function calls. Most networks adhere to these DOS calls and Clipper only uses these function calls for network processing. This allows Clipper to be operated on a large variety of networks.

Each workstation must be running under DOS 3.1 or above to allow the application to share files.

Advantages of a network

There are many advantages to working with a network. These include:

- Sharing expensive resources, such as laser printers and fax machines.
- Concurrent update of files, allowing users to view data from other users as quickly as possible.
- Security and logging built into the network, so data can be administered and controlled properly.

Disadvantages of a network

There are also disadvantages to working with a network. These include:

- Cost of extra components, such as network cards, cabling, and software.
- Complexities in program design. As we will see later in this chapter, writing a network program is more than judicious placement of record and file locks.
- Problem tracking can be difficult, especially if the components involved come from different vendors or sources. It is the classic "hardware people blaming software" and "software people blaming hardware," on a much grander scale.

A network should be carefully considered and planned out. While the network can be a powerful tool, it can also be one of the most destructive forces known to your data. You need to decide, based on your application, if this tool is going to solve your data problems or help create new ones.

Programming on a network

Programming on a network can best be described as designing systems to circumvent Murphy's Law. One of Murphy's Laws states that if something can go wrong, it will do so at the worst possible moment. With a rule like that, we are convinced that Murphy must have spent time programming for a network.

When programming on a network, you have to make the assumption that the files and records might be in use in some other program. This means your program must be designed to wait its turn before opening or updating database files. In addition, you'll want to design the program to minimize the amount of time that your program locks a file or a record. After all, some other polite application may be waiting for your program to finish its work.

Network programming requires planning for the worst-case scenarios. A well-written network program will respond to failed record and file locks in an intelligent manner. If the program assumes that all locks are going to be successful, and does not provide for the contingency of failed locks, other problems most likely will occur. Data may become corrupt, run-time errors might occur, etc. These problems are usually very difficult to track down and correct.

For example, Listing 16.1 contains a sample program fragment to update the customer balance when a check is received. The system needs to update the balance field in the CUSTOMER database, the paid field in the INVOICE database, and the POSTED flag in the PAYMENT database.

Listing 16.1 Record customer payment

```
* Program...: Record customer payment - version 1
*
memvar chk_amount
select CUSTOMER
if rec_lock(15)          // Lock the current record
    replace CUSTOMER->Balance with ;
            CUSTOMER->Balance - chk_amount
    unlock
endif

select INVOICE
if rec_lock(15)          // Lock the current record
    replace INVOICE->Paid with ;
            INVOICE->Paid + chk_amount
```

```
    unlock
endif
select PAYMENT
if rec_lock(15)          // Lock the current record
    replace PAYMENT->posted with .t.
    unlock
endif
```

This code will compile and run successfully under Clipper and, for the most part, will not produce any problems. However, if one of the record locks fails, you could end up with very corrupt data. If the record lock on the INVOICE file were to fail, the customer's balance would be proper and the check would be marked as applied, but the invoice it was applied to would still be open.

Listing 16.2 contains the same program fragment as Listing 16.1, but makes the assumption that any record lock could fail. In this example, if one of the locks failed, the user would be warned that an out-of-balance condition exists in the CUSTOMER file.

Listing 16.2 Updated example

```
* Program...: Record customer payment – version 2
*
local ok := .f.
memvar chk_amount
begin sequence
   select CUSTOMER
   if rec_lock(15)          // Lock the current record
      replace CUSTOMER->Balance with ;
              CUSTOMER->Balance - chk_amount
      unlock
   else
      break
   endif
   select INVOICE
   if rec_lock(15)          // Lock the current record
      replace INVOICE->Paid with ;
              INVOICE->Paid + chk_amount
```

```
      unlock
   else
      break
   endif
   select PAYMENT
   if rec_lock(15)           // Lock the current record
      replace PAYMENT->Posted with .t.
      unlock
   else
      break
   endif
   ok :=.t.
end sequence
if ! ok
   ? "ERROR: Transaction not completely applied..."
endif
```

While in an actual application you would probably add code to determine which lock failed, this example illustrates the extra caution that must be taken when programming for a network.

Opening files

When programming for a single user system, the .DBF files to be worked with are going to be available. Since only one application can run at a time, that application need not be concerned about a different program simultaneously using the files.

On a networked system, there are no assurances that files are available. The operating system controls access to all files on the network. Any application on the network may request a file in either a SHARED mode or an EXCLUSIVE mode. If the operating system honors the request, it keeps track of the fact that the file is being used. If the file is being used exclusively by one application, the operating system will not allow other programs access to the file until the first application is through with it.

When opening a file on the network, you must be aware of how you plan to use that file. Your planned use will indicate how the file should be opened, either SHARED or EXCLUSIVE.

Shared mode

When a file is opened in SHARED mode, the operating system allows other programs to open the file in a SHARED mode as well. Multiple users may update records within the file. In order to keep track of portions of the file being written to, the system provides record locks. These locks give exclusive access to a portion of the file for the program obtaining the lock.

Clipper, by default, opens all files in an exclusive or non-shared mode. To override this, you should use the SHARED keyword on the USE command. The syntax to open a file in shared mode is:

```
USE <cFilename> SHARED [NEW] [READONLY]
```

The *<cFilename>* may be a character constant or a variable name enclosed in parentheses. It may be a fully qualified path and file name or just a file name. If it is a file name it is assumed to be in the current directory. If the file is not in the current directory, the directories specified in the Clipper SET PATH command are searched.

The *shared* keyword instructs Clipper to open this file in a shared mode.

The *new* keyword is optional and causes Clipper to open the file in the next available work area rather than the current one.

The *readonly* keyword is optional and allows Clipper to open a database which has been opened for read-only access. The default open mode is read-write.

Exclusive mode

When a file is opened in exclusive mode, the operating system denies other programs access to the file. Only one user may update records within the file while the user has exclusive use of it. Record and file locks are not necessary since multiple users can not access the file.

Clipper, by default, opens all files in an exclusive or non-shared mode. This means that if you don't specify a mode keyword on the USE command, it will be opened exclusively. However, you should always explicitly state the mode for future compatibility and for clarity when reading the code. The syntax to open a file in exclusive mode is:

```
USE <cFilename> EXCLUSIVE [NEW] [READONLY]
```

The *<cFilename>* may be a character constant or a variable name enclosed in parentheses. It may be a fully qualified path and file name or just a file name. If it is a file name it is assumed to be in the current directory. If not in the current directory, the directories specified in the Clipper SET PATH command are searched.

The *exclusive* keyword instructs Clipper to open this file in exclusive mode.

The *new* keyword is optional and causes Clipper to open the file in the next available work area rather than the current one.

The *readonly* keyword is optional and allows Clipper to open a database which has been opened for read-only access. The default open mode is read-write.

Keep in mind that opening a file for exclusive use prevents any other user on the system from accessing that file. Your use of exclusive files should be kept to a minimum in a network environment. The Clipper commands listed in Table 16.1 require that the file be opened exclusively. If you attempt to use any of these commands on a file opened in shared mode, a run-time error will result.

Table 16.1 Commands needing exclusive use

Command	Description
PACK	Remove deleted records
REINDEX	Recreate all indexes
ZAP	Erase all records

NETERR()

If the network OS cannot open the file in the mode you request, it sets an error flag. Clipper's NETERR() function tests this flag to see if the last network operation was successful. The syntax for NETERR() is:

```
<logical> := NETERR()
```

The *<logical>* value returned will be false unless an error occurs. On a single user system, NETERR() will always return false.

Table 16.2 lists error conditions that can set the NETERR() flag to true while attempting to open a file.

Table 16.2 Conditions which cause NETERR() to return .T.

Command	*Reason*
USE shared	File cannot be opened in shared mode if another application is using the file in exclusive mode or has the file locked.
USE exclusive	If any other application is using the file, it cannot be opened for exclusive use.

Any time you open a file, you should check to be sure that NETERR() returns false, (i.e., no error occurred). For example:

```
begin sequence
use CUSTOMER shared new
if neterr()
   *
   @ maxrow(),0 say "Someone is using the CUSTOMER file"
   inkey(500)
   break
   *
 endif
end sequence
```

Some file errors can occur which should be treated as network errors, but do not set the NETERR() flag. For example, if you use the FOPEN() function and it fails, it returns a -1 instead of a valid handle. (See Chapter 24 for more information on FOPEN() and handles.)

Clipper 5 allows you to set NETERR() to .t. or .f. if you wish to tell the error system a network error occurred. In this way a failed FOPEN() function could be passed over to the error system much the same way a failed USE command would be. The syntax to set the NETERR() return value is:

```
NETERR( <lValue> )
```

The *<lValue>* must be true (**.t.**) to turn NETERR() ON or false (**.f.**) to turn it OFF.

The example below illustrates setting NETERR() from within your application.

```
#include "FILEIO.CH"
local handle
use CUSTOMER new shared
if (handle := fopen("ERROR.LOG",FO_READWRITE))==-1
   Neterr(.t.)  // Turn on network error flag
endif
if Neterr()      // Either from CUSTOMER use or Fopen
                 // failure
   ? "FILES ARE NOT AVAILABLE ON THE NETWORK..."
endif
```

SET INDEX TO

The Clipper USE command has a keyword, INDEX, which allows you to open the index files on the same line as the DBF file. In a network environment, forget this keyword exists. You should open the index files only after you have successfully opened the .DBF file. This is done by the SET INDEX TO command. Its syntax is:

```
SET INDEX TO <cNtx_file(s)>
```

The <*cNtx_file(s)*> is the name of one or more index files that should be associated with the .DBF opened in the current work area. The following provides an example of how a .DBF file and its indexes should be opened in a network environment.

```
* Program...: Network DBF opening
*
use CUSTOMER shared new
if !neterr()
   set index to cust_1,cust_2
else
   ? "ERROR: Customer file is not available...   "
endif
```

Indexing on a network

If you need to create an index on a file in a network environment, the index file is opened exclusively. For example,

```
use CUSTOMER shared new
index on Id_code to cust_1
```

In this example, the system will attempt to open *cust_1* exclusively. If that attempt fails, a run-time error will result.

If you need to create an index that other programs can access, you should create the index, close the database, and then reopen it in a shared mode. This will release the exclusive use of the index file. The following provides an example:

```
use CUSTOMER exclusive new
if !file("cust_1.ntx")
   index on Id_code to cust_1
   use
   use CUSTOMER shared new
endif
set index to cust_1
```

Basic locking philosophy

Once the files have been opened in a shared mode, your program needs to request permission from the network to change any of its data. This is done through a locking mechanism. The network operating system builds a table that indicates which files and portions of files are currently in use. This table is known as the lock table. In Clipper, you can request entries in this table on either a file basis or on a record basis.

File locks

A file lock requests that the network does not allow any other application to update any records in the .DBF file. Other programs will be able to read the data in a locked file, but not update it until the lock is released. As a general rule, file locks are only necessary if a command will update multiple records at one time. For example:

```
replace CUSTOMER->taxable with .t.       // Record lock only
replace all CUSTOMER->taxable with .t.   // File lock required
```

If the scope of the command is ALL, REST, or NEXT, a file lock should be used.

Clipper commands which read all of the records in a file do NOT require a file lock. You may, however, wish to lock a file before issuing an operation to read multiple records. This will prevent another program from changing data you've already read. Whether this degree of protection is needed depends upon your application. Keep in mind that for the duration of the file lock, no other user may update ANY records in the locked file.

The Clipper FLOCK() function provides file-locking capabilities in a Clipper application.

Record locks

A record lock allows you to update only a portion of the file. In .DBF files, this portion is a single record. Any write to a record in a shared file will require at least a record lock. In general, the record lock should be placed just prior to the replace command or the FIELDPUT() function. If a record is to be deleted, the delete command will also require a record lock.

The Clipper RLOCK() function provides record-locking capabilities in a Clipper application.

Locking dangers

Any time you lock a record or a file in your application, you are telling the network not to let any other programs use the data until you are done with the file. This is why locks should be applied and removed as quickly as possible. In general, a lock should be applied only at the time the data is to be replaced into the .DBF and removed immediately after the **replace** statements. The longer you keep a file or record locked, the more time exists for potential problems from other applications. Let's explore some potential locking dangers.

The lunchtime lock

The lunchtime lock occurs when a record or file lock is placed on a file, and the system allows a wait state before the system unlocks the file. Under this scenario, the duration of the lock could be anywhere from a few seconds to several hours if the user walks always from his or her workstation. Don't assume all users know better than to leave a data entry screen when lunchtime comes.

For example, Listing 16.3 illustrates some sample code from an actual application.

Listing 16.3 Lunchtime lock

```
* Program...: Lunch time lock
#include "inkey.ch"
*
function Upd_Cust(cId_code)
local mname,mcontact
memvar getlist
use CUSTOMER shared new
if !neterr()
   set index to cust1,cust2
endif
seek cId_code
   if found()
```

```
   if Rec_Lock()
      mname    := CUSTOMER->Company
      mcontact := CUSTOMER->Contact
      @ 10,10 say "Company name...: " get mname
      @ 11,10 say "Billing contact: " get mcontact
      read
      if lastkey() <> K_ESC
         replace CUSTOMER->Company with mname,;
                 CUSTOMER->Contact with mcontact
      endif
      unlock
   endif
endif
return nil
```

The example function allows the end-user to update the company name and contact. It properly makes sure that no other user can access this record while the data is being changed. However, the READ command will patiently wait for the end-user to update the data. If the user gets called to a meeting during this read, the CUSTOMER record could remained locked for the duration of the meeting. While this might not be a problem, according to Murphy, this will be the one time that the president of the company wants to enter his old buddy as a contact for this customer.

The lunch time lock can be avoided by moving the Rec_Lock() function just prior to the REPLACE statements, as illustrated in Listing 16.4.

Listing 16.4 Replace statement lock

```
* Program...: Replace statement lock
*
#include "inkey.ch"
function Upd_Cust(cId_code)
local mname,mcontact
memvar getlist
use CUSTOMER shared new
```

```
if !neterr()
   set index to cust1,cust2
endif
seek cId_code
if found()
   mname    := CUSTOMER->Company
   mcontact := CUSTOMER->Contact
   @ 10,10 say "Company name...: " get mname
   @ 11,10 say "Billing contact: " get mcontact
   read
   if lastkey() <> K_ESC
      if Rec_Lock()
         replace CUSTOMER->Company with mname,;
                 CUSTOMER->Contact with mcontact
         unlock
      endif
   endif
endif
return nil
```

However, now that the lock statement has been moved, there is the potential danger that somebody else can change the very customer you are working on while you are at the meeting. This can lead to timing problems, which is another locking problem.

Timing problems

Timing problems occur when your program transfers the data into memory, and while you are working with the memory copy of the data, some other user updates the same record on the hard disk. This can particularly be a problem when the data is being displayed on the screen for the user to update. In Listing 16.3, the variables *mname* and *mcontact* are holding copies of the fields from the file at the time of the seek command. If the user goes to lunch or takes awhile to update the screen, it is very possible that another user has changed the data in the .DBF file.

There are several solutions to timing problems. The appropriate solution depends upon your application.

One-user update. If it is absolutely critical that no other user can update the record while the application is using it, you can employ the locking techniques in Listing 16.3. While this creates the opportunity for a lunchtime lock, it does prevent other users from updating the record. You would probably want to modify the GET system (see Chapter 27) to have some sort of time-out feature. (If no key is pressed within ten minutes, the GET system might force an ESCAPE key to abort the update screen and release the record lock.) Of course, you should notify the user that if a key is not pressed, the system will time-out. The user who is staring at the screen in deep thought will be in for a rude awakening when the data all of a sudden jumps off the screen.

Checking for changes. Another solution is to check the record for changes after the user has updated the screen but before the updates are applied to the record. If the record has been changed, you can notify the user and allow them to refresh their information. Listing 16.5 illustrates the concept of checking for changes using arrays.

Listing 16.5 Check for changes

```
* Program...: Check for changes
*
#include "inkey.ch"
function Upd_Cust(cId_code)
local mcust:={},oldcust:={},jj,chgd:=.f.,ok:=.t.
memvar getlist
use CUSTOMER shared new
if !neterr()
   set index to cust1,cust2
endif
seek cId_code
if found()
   for jj := 1 to fcount()
      aadd( mcust,fieldget(jj) )
   next
   oldcust := aclone(mcust)
   do while .t.
      @ 10,10 say "Company name...: " get mcust[1]
```

```
      @ 11,10 say "Billing contact: " get mcust[2]
      read
      if lastkey() <> K_ESC
         if Rec_Lock()
            for jj:=1 to fcount()
               if !(ok := fieldget(jj) == oldcust[jj])
                  jj:=fcount()+1
               endif
            next
            if !ok
               ? "WARNING: Record has been changed already"
               inkey(500)
               for jj := 1 to fcount()
                  aadd( mcust,fieldget(jj) )
               next
               unlock
               loop
            endif
            for jj:=1 to fcount()
               fieldput(jj,mcust[jj])
            next
            unlock
            exit
         endif
      endif
   enddo
endif
return ok
```

The concept illustrated in Listing 16.5 has the disadvantage of losing the user's changes if the record had been updated while he was editing the screen. Obviously, it is very important to carefully consider the application and the user's needs when attempting to deal with timing problems. You need to decide whose data is more accurate if you allow multiple users access to the same record at the same time.

Deadly embrace

A deadly embrace occurs when a process cannot continue because it is waiting for another program to release system resources, such as a file. Unfortunately, the second program is waiting for the first program to release its files before it can continue. Since the programs cannot communicate their needs to each other, each program waits patiently for the other to finish its task.

Figure 16.4 illustrates two applications that can be locked into a deadly embrace.

Figure 16.4 Deadly embrace

Application One	*Application Two*

do while !net_err()
    use CUSTOMER exclusive new
enddo
	do while !net_err()
	    use INVOICES exclusive new
	enddo

do while !net_err()
    use INVOICES exclusive new
enddo
	do while !net_err()
	    use CUSTOMER exclusive new
	enddo

If application one is successful in getting exclusive use of the CUSTOMER file, it will then attempt to get exclusive use of the INVOICES file. If application two already has obtained exclusive use of the INVOICES file, program one can not continue until program two releases the file. Unfortunately program two is attempting to get the CUSTOMER file, which program one will not release.

To avoid a deadly embrace, make sure you never have code fragments that wait forever to attempt to open a file or lock a record. If you cannot get the required access after a reasonable period of time, display an error message and let the user do something different until the file becomes available.

Clipper network functions

Clipper provides several functions to work with files on a network. There are functions for locking files and records and for checking the status of network operations.

Each work area maintains its own record and file locks, so several work areas may be locked at once by your application.

RLOCK()

This function attempts to lock the current database record in the current work area. If the lock is successful, true will be returned. If the lock fails, false will be returned. The syntax for RLOCK() is:

```
<logical> := RLOCK()
```

The RLOCK() function makes only one attempt to lock the record. If this attempt is successful, a logical true (**.t.**) will be returned. If the lock is not granted, false (**.f.**) will be returned.

DBRLOCK()

DBRLOCK() is a new function in Clipper 5.2 that allows you to lock multiple records in a single file. It takes a record number as a parameter and returns TRUE if the record has been locked or FALSE if it couldnt' be locked. If you do not specify a record number, then all current locks in the file are released and the current record is locked.

The following example illustrates how you can lock a range of records within a work area:

```
FUNCTION LockRange( nLo, nHi )
LOCAL jj
forjj := nLo TO nHi
    if ! DBRLOCK( jj )
        DBRUNLOCK()   // Failed-unlock everything
    endif
    next
    return DBRLOCKLIST()     // Return list of actual locks
```

DBRLOCKLIST()

DBRLOCKLIST() is a new function in Clipper 5.2 that returns a one-dimensional array of the locked records in the current or aliased work area.

DBRUNLOCK()

DBRUNLOCK() is a new function in Clipper 5.2 that allows you to release the lock on the specified record number in a file. It takes a record number as a parameter and always returns NIL. If no parameter is specified, all record locks in the work area are released.

FLOCK()

This function attempts to lock the entire current database file, not just a single record. If the file is successfully locked, true (**.t.**) will be returned. If the lock fails, false (**.f.**) will be returned. The syntax for FLOCK() is:

```
<logical> := FLOCK()
```

The FLOCK() function makes only one attempt to lock the file.

NETNAME()

The NETNAME() function returns a character string with the workstation identification. Its syntax is:

```
<cWork_name> := NETNAME()
```

The <*cWork_name*> is a character string which can be up to 15 characters in length. If the work station has been assigned an identification from the network, this function will return it. If no identification has been given, a null string ("") will be returned.

COMMIT

The COMMIT command instructs the network to make database updates visible to other applications. Networks generally use buffers to hold updated information before it is written to the server's disk. This is primarily done for speed reasons. The commit command requests that the network write the changes back to the disk to allow other applications to see the changed data. Its syntax is:

```
COMMIT
```

It should generally be used following a series of REPLACE operations against a work area.

While COMMIT is not required to cause the network to update the server's file, it should be used to have the update performed as quickly as possible. The Network Operating System will automatically update the databases from buffers often, but COMMIT actually requests the network to update immediately.

DBCOMMIT()

The DBCOMMIT() function performs the exact same function as the COMMIT command. (If you explore the STD.CH file, you will see that COMMIT is preprocessed into DBCOMMIT().) The function allows you to commit changes in unselected work areas as well. Its syntax is:

```
DBCOMMIT()
```

You can also commit updates in a different work area by using the extended expression syntax. For example,

```
CUSTOMER->( DBCOMMIT() )
```

would request the network to write the changes in the CUSTOMER file to the disk.

DBCOMMITALL()

The DBCOMMITALL() function performs the exact same function as the commit command, but for every work area. The function commits updates in all work areas. Its syntax is:

```
DBCOMMITALL()
```

It is the same as looping through all work areas and performing a COMMIT command or a DBCOMMIT() function.

UNLOCK

The UNLOCK command releases the file or record lock in the current work area. Its syntax is:

```
UNLOCK [ALL]
```

If the optional *[all]* keyword is specified, all locks from all work areas are released. Record and file locks will also be released in a work area if another lock is requested in the same work area.

DBUNLOCK()

The DBUNLOCK() function performs the exact same function as the unlock command. (If you explore the STD.CH file, you will see that UNLOCK is preprocessed into DBUNLOCK().) The function allows you to unlock unselected work areas as well. Its syntax is:

```
DBUNLOCK()
```

You can also release record and file locks in another work area by using the extended expression syntax. For example,

```
CUSTOMER->( DBUNLOCK() )
```

would release the lock in the CUSTOMER work area.

DBUNLOCKALL()

The DBUNLOCKALL() function performs the exact same function as the UNLOCK ALL command. The function releases locks in all work areas. Its syntax is:

```
DBUNLOCKALL()
```

NETERR()

The NETERR() function queries the network to see if the last network operation ended in a failure. It is primarily used as a logical toggle to the Clipper networking commands. The Clipper networking functions return a logical value already. The syntax for NETERR() is:

```
<logical> := NETERR()
```

The *<logical>* value returned will return false unless an error occurs. On a single-user system, NETERR() will always return false.

In addition to the USE commands, NETERR() should also be checked after you attempt to append a record into a DBF file. For example, Listing 16.6 illustrates how a record can be appended to the current work area.

Listing 16.6 Append example

```
memvar mId_code
begin sequence
   append blank
   if neterr()          // Check if append worked ok
      ? "ERROR: Cannot add a record to the file..."
      inkey(500)
      break
   endif
   if rlock()
      replace CUSTOMER->Id_code with mId_code
      unlock
   endif
end sequence
```

Network functions

The RLOCK() and FLOCK() locking functions provided by Clipper are designed to make only one attempt at the record or file lock. In some network applications, it is desirable to have the system make several attempts until the lock is successful. Computer Associates provides several user-defined functions to allow record and file locking to be a little more persistent.

AddRec()

The AddRec() function attempts to append a blank record into the selected work area. Its syntax is:

```
<logical> := AddRrec(<nSeconds>)
```

The *<nSeconds>* indicates how many seconds the system should keep trying the APPEND BLANK command. If you pass it a zero, the system will try forever. The *<logical>* will contain **.t.** if a record was successfully added. If the record was added, it will also be locked. If **.f.** is returned, a record could not be appended into the file. For example:

```
if AddRec(15)            // Try for 15 seconds
   *
   * Update data base
   *
else
   ? "Record could not be added..."
endif
```

RecLock()

The RecLock() function attempts to lock the current record. It is different from RLOCK() in that it allows you to specify how long to wait to attempt to lock the record. Its syntax is:

```
<logical> := RecLock(<nSeconds>)
```

The <*nSeconds*> indicates how many seconds the system should keep trying the RLOCK() function. If you pass it a zero, the system will try forever. The <*logical*> will contain **.t.** if a record was successfully locked. If the record could not be locked, **.f.** will be returned. For example:

```
if RecLock(15)          // Try for 15 seconds
   *
   * Update data base
   *
else
   ? "Record could not be locked.."
endif
```

FilLock()

The FilLock() function attempts to lock the file in the selected work area. Its syntax is:

```
<logical> := FilLock(<nSeconds>)
```

The <*nSeconds*> indicates how many seconds the system should keep trying to lock the file. If you pass it a zero, the system will try forever. The <*logical*> will contain **.t.** if a file was successfully locked. If **.f.** is returned, the file could not be locked. For example:

```
select CUSTOMER shared new
if FilLock(15)                    // Try for 15 seconds
   *
   replace all tax_rate with .07  // Update tax rate unlock
   *
else
   ? "Database could not be locked, tax rates are"
   ? "unchanged..."
endif
```

NetUse()

The NetUse() function is a replacement for the USE command in a network environment. Its syntax is:

```
<logical> := NetUse(<cDatabase>,<lOpenMode>,<nSeconds>)
```

The <*cDatabase*> is the name of the file you wish to open. It is assumed to be in the default directory. The <*lOpenMode*> contains **.t.** to open the file for exclusive use or **.f.** to open the file in shared mode. The <*nseconds*> indicates how many seconds the system should keep retrying the USE command.

If the file could be used in the requested mode, a **.t.** will be returned. If not **.f.** will be returned. For example:

```
if NetUse("CUSTOMER",.f.,15)    // Try for 15 seconds
   *
   set indexes to cust_1,cust_2  // Select the indexes
   *
else
   ? "CUSTOMER file could not be opened!"
endif
```

Notice that the NetUse() function does not support the NEW keyword on the USE command. If you need to open a file in a new work area, be sure to precede the NetUse() call with a SELECT 0 command.

Computer Associates includes the source code to the locking functions on the distribution diskette. You can find the source in LOCKS.PRG in the \CLIPPER5 \SOURCE\SAMPLES directory. You should carefully review your application to determine the degree of persistence you need your locking functions to use. If a record lock fails, the reason is that some other application has temporarily locked the record.

It is important to realize that throwing record locks around all REPLACE statements and checking for file opens may allow your application to run on a network. However, to create a true network application requires careful planning and design.

Maintaining compatibility with earlier programs

Prior releases of Clipper used the syntax Add_Rec(), Rec_Lock(), Net_Use() and Fil_Lock() rather than AddRec(), RecLock(), NetUse() and FilLock(). Clipper includes a preprocessor header file which translates the old function calls into the new ones. This header file is called LOCKS87.CH and should be found in the \CLIPPER5\INCLUDE directory. If you want to maintain the locking function names from earlier releases, add:

```
#include "LOCKS87.CH"
```

to the beginning of your .PRG files.

Printing on a network

The network operating system generally handles all print requests. Since network printers are attached to the server, a workstation must go through the server to use a network printer. Most network operating systems handle the print requests by capturing the printed output to a file first, and then sending the file to the printer. This process is known as spooling. Some networks allow a file to be directly placed into the spooler, while others capture all output directed to a network printer. Be sure to determine which technique is best for the network on which you are programming.

Clipper allows printed output to be redirected to any file or queue the network requires through the SET PRINTER TO command. Its syntax is:

```
SET PRINTER TO <cDevice|cFile>
```

The <*cDevice*> is the name of an output device or <*cFile*> to which the printed output should be redirected. If a device is specified, do not include the colon character.

If the network captures the output from a printer port and redirects it to the spooler automatically, you would specify the printer port, such as LPT1, and allow the network to spool the output. If the network allows a file to be spooled directly, you would set the printer to a file name. Once the file is created, you would call the network program to place the file into the print spooler.

In general, most networks will not start printing the report until you close the spooler file. This is done by specifying the SET PRINTER TO command without any parameters.

Refer to your network manual to determine how a printed file should be placed into the print spooler.

NOVTERM.LIB

Clipper 5.2 includes a screen driver that circumvents an incompatibility between some nondedicated network server software and Clipper. This incompatibility causes printers connected to the server to slow to an unusable rate. Since Clipper applications and nondedicated servers compete for resources, Clipper uses idle time to perform various system tasks. While this improves the overall performance, it creates problems because nondedicated servers use this idle time for printing. Since a Clipper application seldom makes this time available, printing slows to a crawl.

If your application needs to run on a nondedicated server, you can replace the TERMINAL.LIB in your link commands with NOVTERM.LIB. This will cause Clipper to link in the screen driver, which does not use idle time. While this will allow printing to occur, it will also slow your application's performance.

Summary

After reading this chapter you should be aware of some of the problems that can occur on a network and how to design programs to avoid them. You should know the basic networking functions and the user-defined functions for locking.

CHAPTER 17

Pop-up Programming

Early in the 1980s, Borland International released a product called Sidekick. This handy program contained a calculator, a notepad, and a calendar. What was unique about it was that all of these utilities could be called up while another program was running. Sidekick was one of the first commercially available pop-up programs. It could appear on the screen on top of the existing program, allow you to do your work, and then quietly disappear back into the depths of the computer's memory. The concept offered a new aspect of programming that had previously not been thought to be available on a DOS computer.

Pop-up programming is now an accepted part of application development. Users expect to have access to pop-up calendars, calculators, etc. while they are in the midst of their program. While early releases of Clipper allowed the programming of pop-ups, Clipper 5 provides very powerful tools to successfully implement pop-up programming. In this chapter we will discuss how Clipper can be used to assign pop-up programs to keystrokes and cover the items you must consider to write an effective pop-up program.

Pop-up background

In order to create a pop-up program in DOS, we need to understand a little about how DOS operates. The designers of DOS built the system for a large degree of flexibility. One of the things they did was use the first 1024 bytes of RAM memory in DOS to hold an interrupt table. This table consists of 256 entries, each containing an address in memory that should be executed if that interrupt occurs. The interrupts provide various services to application programs. Figure 17.1 shows some sample interrupts.

Figure 17.1 Sample interrupt table

Interrupt #	*Type*	*Action causing it*
0	Hardware	Divide by zero
5	Hardware	Print screen
9	Hardware	Key was struck
17	Software	Return equipment list
18	Software	Return BIOS memory size
28	Hardware	Clock tick (18.2 times per second)

When DOS detects a condition in the table, it calls the interrupt handler. The table is searched to find the interrupt number, and once found, the address in memory to execute is known. The program at this address is then executed.

To write a DOS program that can interrupt another program, we first need to choose the interrupt we want to use to invoke our pop-up program. Most often this will be interrupt nine, the keyboard interrupt.

Once we've chosen the interrupt, we need to change the original address to a new address somewhere within our program. Now when the interrupt occurs, control will pass to our application, rather than to the normal DOS program. In this way, we can keep control while another program is running.

Of course, since the interrupt table now points to an address in memory, we must have a way to keep our program in memory. DOS provides a special function called KEEP or **Terminate and Stay Resident** (TSR). This function instructs DOS to exit the program but save a portion of it in RAM. While this action allows our program to gain control during an interrupt, it also requires some of the 640K of RAM available in a DOS environment.

Memory

Since Clipper requires memory for its applications to operate, the use of TSR programs in RAM while a Clipper application is being executed is generally not a good idea. So how do we keep memory for our Clipper program while we keep the end users happy? The obvious answer is, we write the pop-up feature in Clipper, and link it into our application. Fortunately, Clipper recognizes this need and provides the tools to do so.

Clipper interrupts

Clipper allows a program to be interrupted during any wait state. A wait state is any function or command that gets keys from the keyboard. These functions are listed in Table 17.1

Table 17.1 Clipper WAIT states

ACHOICE()
DBEDIT()
MEMOEDIT()
ACCEPT
INPUT
READ
WAIT

The notable exception is the INKEY() function. Later in the chapter we will show how INKEY() can easily be replaced with a function that waits for keys and still processes interrupts.

Clipper has no direct provisions for providing interrupts other than at keystrokes. However, ACHOICE(), MEMOEDIT(), DBEDIT(), and the GET SYSTEM all provide the programmer with control during the keyboard input process. Code can be written in any of these functions to perform interrupts based upon other factors, such as time.

Clipper pop-ups

Clipper provides the ability for any keystroke to call a user-defined procedure. It accomplishes this by assigning a 32 element table which holds the keys and procedures to be interrupted. This table is referred to as the SET KEY table. When a key is pressed, it is checked against the SET KEY table to determine whether or not a procedure should be called.

Keystrokes are stored in the table as numeric values. The value may be either the ASCII code for the key or a number which corresponds to their INKEY codes. The ASCII codes and a Table of INKEY values are listed in Appendix A. The inkey codes are defined in the INKEY.CH header file found in the \CLIPPER5\INCLUDE subdirectory.

Assigning keys to the SET KEY table

The SET KEY table is automatically created when a Clipper application executes. Clipper provides three commands to place keys and procedures into the table.

SET KEY command

The SET KEY command is used to place a key number and a procedure name into the set key table. Its syntax is:

```
SET KEY <nInkey_code>  TO <cProcedure_name>
```

The **<nInkey_code>** is a numeric value that corresponds to either an ASCII code or one of the keys from the INKEY table. This defines the keystroke that should cause the named procedure to be executed.

The **<cProcedure_name>** is the name of the procedure or function that should be called when the key is pressed. When the function is called, it will be passed three parameters: the procedure name that called it, the current line number (if the code was compiled with line numbers), and the name of the variable awaiting input. The procedure does not have to make use of the parameters. If you do not expect to use the parameters, you do not need to declare them in a parameter statement. For example,

```
SET KEY K_F2 TO Pop_Calc
```

will cause the Pop_Calc procedure to be called whenever the user presses the F2 function key.

An entry for the F1 function key is placed into the key table automatically when the program starts. The procedure name is HELP. You can override this by explicitly assigning another procedure name to the F1 key. For example,

```
SET KEY K_F1 TO No_Help
```

will set the F1 key to a procedure called No_Help.

SET FUNCTION command

The SET FUNCTION command is a special variation of the SET KEY command. The syntax for set function is:

```
SET FUNCTION <nFunctionKey> TO <cString>
```

The **<nFunctionKey>** is the number which refers to the function key you wish to set. Table 17.2 lists the numeric codes for the function keys. Notice that these codes are not the same as the INKEY codes from Appendix A.

Table 17.2 SET FUNCTION Key Number

Key	*Alone*	*Shift+*	*Ctrl+*	*Alt+*
F1	1	11	21	31
F2	2	12	22	32
F3	3	13	23	33
F4	4	14	24	34
F5	5	15	25	35
F6	6	16	26	36
F7	7	17	27	37
F8	8	18	28	38
F9	9	19	29	39
F10	10	20	30	40

<cString> is the character string that should be placed into the keyboard buffer whenever the function key is pressed. This character string may contain control codes such as K_LEFT to allow editing while in a wait state. For example,

```
SET FUNCTION 2 TO chr(K_CTRL_Y) + "Pennsylvania"
```

will cause the the GET to be cleared and the word "Pennsylvania" to be placed into the keyboard buffer whenever the F2 key is pressed.

The SET FUNCTION command causes a code block to be written into the set key table for the particular function key. For example, the command:

```
SET FUNCTION 2 TO "Pennsylvania"+chr(K_ENTER)
```

would result in a code block, which when evaluated will perform the following action:

```
Keyboard "Pennsylvania"+chr(13)
```

Since Clipper 5 maintains only one SET KEY table, the SET FUNCTION command will overwrite any prior definition for the key. This is a change from earlier versions of Clipper which kept the SET FUNCTION table and the SET KEY table separate.

SETKEY() function

The SETKEY() function is used both to query the SET KEY table and to update entries in the table. Both the SET KEY command and the SET FUNCTION command get translated by the preprocessor into SETKEY() function calls. The syntax for the SETKEY() function is:

```
<bCodeblock>  := SETKEY( <nInkey_code>,<bNewCode> )
```

<bCodeblock> is the block of code that is assigned to the requested key code. If no code block has been assigned to this key, the function will return a NIL. The example shows a simple UDF to determine whether a function key has been assigned or not.

```
* Program...: Is_assigned()
*
function Is_assigned( nKey )
return ( setkey(nKey)==nil)
```

<nInkey_code> is either an ASCII code or an INKEY code. It indicates the key number that should be looked up in the SET KEY table.

<bNewCode> is an optional code block to assign to the selected key code. If <bNewCode> is not specified, the set key function merely returns the current code block assigned to the key or a NIL. If a code block is specified, the current code block for the specified key will be overwritten with the new code block.

If a code block is specified, it is called whenever the designated key is pressed. The code block is passed three parameters: the procedure name, the line number, and the current variable name. The code block is then evaluated using the EVAL() function. Code blocks are discussed in greater detail in Chapter 8, "Code Blocks."

The example below assigns a pop-up calendar, calculator, and message pad to function keys two through four. These pop-up programs do not need the parameter. Function key F1 gets assigned to the User_Help() function, which needs all three parameters.

```
* Program...: SETKEY()
*
#include "INKEY.CH"
setkey( K_F1, { |cProc,nLine,cVar|User_Help(cProc,nLine,cVar) })
setkey( K_F2, { || Pop_calc() } )
setkey( K_F3, { || Pop_calend() } )
setkey( K_F4, { || Pop_while() } )
```

Changing an entry in the SET KEY table

If an entry already exists in the SET KEY table for a particular key, that entry can be overwritten by calling the SET KEY command or SETKEY() function with the same key code. For example, assume the F9 key is assigned to look up either customers or vendors depending on the menu option chosen. Listing 17.1 illustrates an example of SET KEY being used to change pop-up programs.

Listing 17.1 Changing SET KEY Table Entries

```
* Program...: Example to change SET KEY table
*
#include "INKEY.CH"
local option:=1
do while !empty(option)
   @ 10,20 prompt "CUSTOMER UPDATE"
   @ 12,20 prompt "VENDOR UPDATE"
   menu to option
   if option == 1
      setkey(K_F9,{ || Cust_Look() } )
      Upd_Cust()
   elseif option == 2
      setkey(K_F9,{ || Vend_Look() } )
      Upd_Vend()
   endif
enddo
```

Removing an entry from the SET KEY table

To remove an entry from the SET KEY table you should use the SET KEY command without specifying a parameter. The syntax is:

```
SET KEY <nKeycode> [TO]
```

This will remove any procedure currently defined for the **<nKeycode>** key. The <nKeycode> may be any number from the ASCII chart or from the INKEY table (Appendix A).

Making INKEY() into a wait state

As we mentioned earlier, the INKEY() function is not a wait state that will access the SET KEY table. We can, however, write a simple UDF to be used in the place of INKEY() which will call INKEY() and test the SET KEY table. The syntax for the INKEY() function which we will replace with Ginkey() is:

```
<nKeycode>  := inkey()
```

<nKeycode> is the ASCII or INKEY code (from Appendix A) that corresponds to the key that was pressed. Our Ginkey() function appears in Chapter 8. See Listing 8.8 there for the function source code.

Writing a pop-up program

Now that we have discussed how to place entries into the SET KEY table, we need to discuss the programming considerations for the procedure that the table will invoke. It is important to remember that the procedure can be invoked anywhere a keystroke is accepted. This means that the pop-up must save the global environment and any database it might manipulate, do its work, and restore the environment and databases exactly to the way they were.

The environment consists of various global settings such as cursor, current color, etc. The global settings are defined via various SET commands. In addition, the environment also includes the current screen. The database environment consists of work areas and their status information. Only databases which the pop-up expects to manipulate need to be saved by the pop-up program. Many pop-up applications do not manipulate database files at all.

Handling the environment

With Clipper you have complete and total knowledge of the state of every SET command via the SET() function. Actually, SET commands have been eliminated completely and are replaced during the preprocessing step with calls to SET(). Here's an example:

```
SET ALTERNATE TO MYFILE.TXT       // Your source code
set(_SET_ALTFILE, "MYFILE.TXT")   // Preprocessor output
```

_SET_ALTFILE is a manifest constant defined in STD.CH along with similar constants for all the other SET commands.

The syntax for the SET() function is:

```
<current setting>  := SET( <nSet_number>,<new value> )
```

<nSet_number> is the numeric code which corresponds to the desired setting. Computer Associates stresses in the documentation that this code should never be used directly, but always through the manifest constants defined in STD.CH. The actual numbers may change over the life of the compiler. Table 17.3 contains the set manifest constants.

Table 17.3 SET manifest constants

Constant	*Value type*	*Associated Command/function*
_SET_ALTERNATE	Logical	SET ALTERNATE
_SET_ALTFILE	Character	SET ALTERNATE TO
_SET_BELL	Logical	SET BELL
_SET_CANCEL	Logical	SETCANCEL()
_SET_COLOR	Character	SETCOLOR()
_SET_CONFIRM	Logical	SET CONFIRM
_SET_CONSOLE	Logical	ET CONSOLE
_SET_CURSOR	Numeric	SETCURSOR()
_SET_DATEFORMAT	Character	SET DATE
_SET_DEBUG	Logical	ALTD()
_SET_DECIMALS	Numeric	SET DECIMALS
_SET_DEFAULT	Character	SET DEFAULT
_SET_DELETED	Logical	SET DELETED
_SET_DELIMCHARS	Character	SET DELIMITERS TO
_SET_DELIMITERS	Logical	SET DELIMITERS
_SET_DEVICE	Character	SET DEVICE
_SET_EPOCH	Numeric	SET EPOCH
_SET_ESCAPE	Logical	SET ESCAPE
_SET_EXACT	Logical	SET EXACT
_SET_EXCLUSIVE	Logical	SET EXCLUSIVE
_SET_EXIT	Logical	READEXIT()
_SET_FIXED	Logical	SET FIXED
_SET_INSERT	Logical	READINSERT()
_SET_INTENSITY	Logical	SET INTENSITY

_SET_MARGIN	Numeric	SET MARGIN
_SET_MCENTER	Logical	SET MESSAGE
_SET_MESSAGE	Numeric	SET MESSAGE
_SET_PATH	Character	SET PATH
_SET_PRINTER	Logical	SET PRINTER
_SET_PRINTFILE	Character	SET PRINTER TO
_SET_SCOREBOARD	Logical	SET SCOREBOARD
_SET_SCROLLBREAK	Logical	<varies>*
_SET_SOFTSEEK	Logical	SET SOFTSEEK
_SET_UNIQUE	Logical	SET UNIQUE
_SET_WRAP	Logical	SET WRAP

*_SET_SCROLLBREAK is a global setting which indicates how the Ctrl-S key is handled by the various keyboard commands. If set to .T., Ctrl-S is interpreted as a request to pause the program. If set to .F., Ctrl-S is treated as a cursor movement key, equivalent to the Left Arrow key.

The SET() function returns the current value of the setting.

In addition to the manifest constants in Table 17.3, Clipper also provides a constant called _SET_COUNT, which contains the number of settings currently available in the Clipper syntax.

Save the settings

SaveSets() and RestSets in Listings 12.3 and 12.4 (Chapter 12) can be used to save all global settings.

Saving the screen

Whatever portion of the screen your pop-up is going to operate in must be saved prior to any screen display. Once your pop-up is finished, the screen should be restored, leaving the user right where they were when they pressed the pop-up key.

SAVESCREEN()/RESTSCREEN()

Clipper provides functions to save the screen and restore it. The function to save the screen is SAVESCREEN(). Its syntax is:

```
<cSaved_screen> := SAVESCREEN(<nTopRow>,<TopColumn>, ;
         <nBottomRow>,<nBottomColumn>)
```

<nTopRow>,<nTopColumn> is the upper left corner of the screen to be restored. **<nBottomRow>,<nBottomColumn>** is the lower right corner. The function will return a character string which contains the screen characters and colors from the specified coordinates.

To restore a screen, Clipper provides the RESTSCREEN() function. Its syntax is:

```
RESTSCREEN(<nTopRow>,<nTopColumn>, ;
          <nBottomRow>,<nBottomColumn>, ;
          <cSaved_screen>)
```

<nTopRow>,<nTopColumn> is the upper left corner of the screen to be restored. The **<nBottomRow>,<nBottomColumn>** are the lower right corner. The **<cSaved_screen>** is a character string returned from a SAVESCREEN() function call.

Saving work areas

If your pop-up program is going to work with any .DBF files, you should save the current .DBF file in a stack as well. After all, if your user is updating a customer record and hits a pop-up in the middle, you need to ensure that when the changes are made to the customer file, they are made to the proper record number.

Pushdbf()/Popdbf()

The Pushdbf() function takes care of saving the database status. Its syntax is:

```
Pushdbf( <cAlias> )
```

<cAlias> is an optional alias name, which would default to the current work area. It saves the workarea number, the index order, the record number, and the filter condition.

Popdbf() will restore the database, reposition the record number and index order, and restore the filter command. Its syntax is:

```
Popdbf( <nCount> )
```

<nCount> is an integer indicating how many .DBFs should be restored from the stack. Since you may frequently need to save several databases, necessitating several calls to Pushdbf(), rather than making several calls to the function you can use this count. If you don't pass a number, it will pop only the most recently saved database.

The Pushdbf() and Popdbf() user-defined functions are in Listing 17.3.

Listing 17.3 Pushdbf()/Popdbf()

```
* Program ...: Pushdbf() / Popdbf()
*
static dbfstack_ :={}

function Pushdbf( cAlias )
if cAlias <> nil
   select select(cAlias)
endif
aadd(dbfstack_, Dbfarray() )
return nil
*
function Popdbf( nCount )
local i,nWork:=0,nOrder:=0,nRec:=0,cFilter:=""
local nSize := len(dbfstack_)
nCount := if(nCount=nil,1,nCount)
for i = 1 to nCount
   nWork    := dbfstack_[nSize,1]
   nOrder   := dbfstack_[nSize,2]
   nRec     := dbfstack_[nSize,3]
   cFilter  := dbfstack_[nSize,4]
   if !empty(nWork)
      select (nWork)
      set order to (nOrder)
```

```
      goto nRec
      if !empty(cFilter)
         dbsetfilter(cFilter)
      endif
   endif
   Asize(dbfstack_,nSize-1)
   nSize --
next
return nil
*
function DbfArray
local s_:={}
Aadd( s_,select() )           // Save work area number
Aadd( s_,indexord() )         // Controlling index number
Aadd( s_,recno() )            // Current record number
Aadd( s_,dbfilter() )         // Filter condition
return s_
```

Sample pop-up coding shell

Listing 17.4 illustrates a sample shell for a pop-up program. It makes the appropriate calls to various routines to save and restore the environment. It should be used as a basis for your pop-up applications.

Listing 17.4 Sample Pop-up Shell

```
* Program...: Pop-up shell
*
local back_scr := savescreen(0, 0, maxrow(), maxcol())
SaveSets()
Pushdbf()

// Pop-up program's work is done here

// End of pop-up program

Popdbf()
Rest Sets()
restscreen(0, 0, maxrow(), maxcol(),back_scr)
return nil
```

Doing the work

Once you've saved the environment and work areas, your program is free to perform its task. This can be anything from a simple calculation to writing to a log file the notes a user found during testing. Our example applications at the end of the chapter include a pop-up calculator and a calendar.

Saving/restoring GETS

If your pop-up program is going to perform any GETS or READS, it is necessary to save the current GETS. In Clipper 5, this is an extremely simple thing to do. Clipper stores the GETS in a public array called GETLIST. (The array scope is **public** unless your program declares it otherwise). When a new procedure is called, you can create an array for GET just for that procedure. The syntax to create a new GETLIST is:

```
local getlist :={}
```

By declaring GETLIST to be **local** at the beginning of your pop-up procedure, you are telling Clipper to create a new array to hold the GETS in. Any previous GETLIST array will not be overwritten, hence the original GETLIST array is intact and will be restored when your procedure finishes.

Send data back to the calling procedure

Sometimes the pop-up program will need to communicate back to the calling program. This can be accomplished through Clipper's KEYBOARD command. The syntax for the KEYBOARD command is:

```
KEYBOARD<cString>
```

<cString> contains the text of the characters to be returned. The string should also contain any necessary control codes, such as K_ENTER, to allow the GET to continue. The two most common control codes you would need are listed in Table 17.4.

Table 17.4 Common control codes

```
K_CTRL_Y   Clear the current get field
K_ENTER    Press enter or return key
```

Listing 17.5 illustrates an example of a selection from a list-box being returned to the keyboard buffer.

Listing 17.5 Keyboard example

```
* Program...: Keyboard example
*
#include "INKEY.CH"
local mcode :=space(8)
memvar getlist
set key K_F9 to Look_Cust

@ 10,10 get mcode pict "!!!!!!!!"
read
if lastkey() <> K_ESC
   *
   * Further processing ......
   *
endif
return nil

function Look_Cust(cProc,nLine,cVar)
local back_scr := savescreen( 8,20,20,60 )
local send_back
SaveSets()
Pushdbf()
select CUSTOMER
dispbox(8, 20, 20, 60, 2)
Browse(9,21,19,59)
send_back := ( lastkey() <> K_ESC )
Popdbf()
RestSets()
restscreen(8,20,20,60,back_scr)
```

```
if send_back
   keyboard chr(K_CTRL_Y)+ ;
         CUSTOMER->id_code+chr(K_ENTER)
endif
return nil
```

Data driven pop-ups

Of course, properly designing and coding a pop-up program is only part of the battle. Once the pop-ups are debugged and in your program, the requests for changes will start: "Can you move the pop-up calculator over to the left?" or "Is it possible to have a red calendar?"

Pop-ups can be coded to get their colors and positions from a .DBF or text file. Using this approach, which is called data-driven programming, you can move pop-ups all over the screen and change their colors without recompiling your program.

Pop-up database

The structure of the pop-up DBF file is shown in Figure 17.2.

Figure 17.2 POPUPS.DBF structure

File: POPUPS.DBF

Field name	*Type*	*Size*	*Description*
Pop_name	Char	12	Upper case name of pop-up
Pop_color	Char	25	Color string setting
Top_row	Numeric	2	Top row
Top_col	Numeric	2	Left column
Bottom_row	Numeric	2	Bottom row
Bottom_col	Numeric	2	Right column

This file needs not be indexed since even if all 32 set keys were assigned, the entire file would be less than 2,048 bytes. Clipper could read the entire file into memory and allow the LOCATE command to work very quickly.

Dispatch() routine

The Dispatch() user-defined function in Listing 17.7 searches the pop-up database to see if the requested pop-up can be found. If the pop-up is found, the function sets the color and returns a four-element array of screen coordinates. Its syntax is:

```
<array> := Dispatch( <cPop_up_name> )
```

The **<array>** is a four element array containing the screen coordinates corners for the requested pop-up. Table 17.5 lists the constants and array structure.

Table 17.5 Coordinates array structure

Constant	*Element*	*Contents*
TR	1	Upper top row
TC	2	Upper left corner
BR	3	Lower bottom row
BC	4	Lower right corner

Your pop-up function can then save the screen using the coordinates from the array and process its work. Listing 17.6 is an updated version of the pop-up shell from Listing 17.4.

Listing 17.6 Data driven pop-up shell

```
 * Program...: Data driven Pop-up shell
*
#include "INKEY.CH"
#define TR coords[1]
#define TC coords[2]
#define BR coords[3]
#define BC coords[4]
LOCAL back_scr,coords
SaveSets()
Pushdbf()
*
```

```
coords := Dispatch( "POPCALC" )
back_scr := savescreen(TR,TC,BR,BC)

// Pop-up program's work is done here

Popdbf()
RestSets()
restscreen(TR,TC,BR,BC,back_scr)
return nil
```

The code for the Dispatch function is in Listing 17.7.

Listing 17.7 Dispatch() Function

```
* Program...: Dispatch function
*
function Dispatch( cPop_up )
local sarr_ :={}
use POPUPS new
locate all for POPUPS->pop_name == upper(cPop_up)
if found()
   setcolor(POPUPS->pop_color)
   aadd(sarr_,POPUPS->top_row)
   aadd(sarr_,POPUPS->top_col)
   aadd(sarr_,POPUPS->bottom_row)
   aadd(sarr_,POPUPS->bottom_col)
endif
use
return sarr_
```

Pop-up examples

In this section we will provide some example pop-up programs that you might frequently need in your applications. The program can be used as written or adapted to provide additional pop-up utilities.

Pop-up calculator

Listing 17.8 illustrates a simple pop-up calculator. This program displays a calculator keypad and lets the user enter mathematical operations. The results are calculated and can be pasted back to the calling GET if desired. Figure 17.3 shows the calculator and the operations it supports.

Figure 17.3 Calculator Screen and Operations

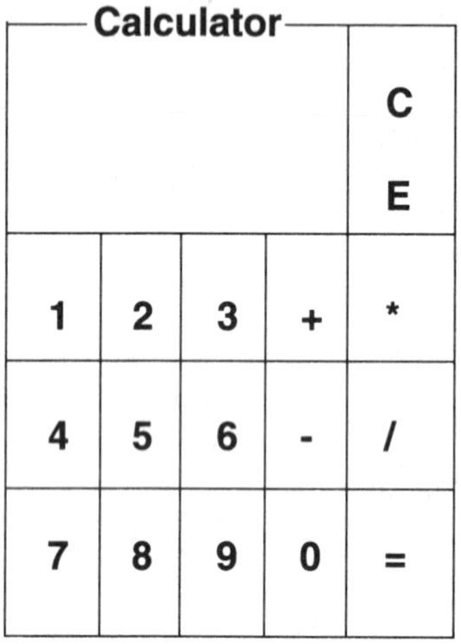

Calculator

				C E
1	2	3	+	*
4	5	6	-	/
7	8	9	0	=

C	Clear the number
+	Add number to total
-	Subtract from total
*	Multiply two numbers
/	Divide two numbers
=	Paste result to GET

Listing 17.8 Pop-up calculator

```
* Program...: Popcalc
*
#include "INKEY.CH"
#include "BOX.CH"
function Popcalc(cProc,nLine,cVar)
local back_scr := savescreen(2,5,11,25)
local adding:=.t.,first_time:=.t.
local calc_amt:=0,running:=0,calc_op:=" "
local getlist:={}                          // Protect get stack
   SaveSets()
/***********************************
*    Paint calculator on screen    *
***********************************/
```

```
@ 02,05,11,25 box B_SINGLE_DOUBLE+" "
@ 02,06 say "  Calculator "
@ 03,06 say "                | C "
@ 04,06 say "                | E "
@ 05,06 say " ________________ "
@ 06,06 say " 1 | 2 | 3 | + | * "
@ 07,06 say " ________________ "
@ 08,06 say " 4 | 5 | 6 | - | / "
@ 09,06 say " ________________ "
@ 10,06 say " 7 | 8 | 9 | 0 | = " /
****************************
*    Main calculator loop    *
****************************/
do while adding
  @ 3,9 say running picture "99999999.99"
  if !first_time
    @ 4,7 get calc_op  picture "!" valid calc_op$"+-/*=C X"
  endif
   @ 4,9 get calc_amt picture "99999999.99"
   read
   first_time := .f.
   ******************************
   *     Process key stroke     *
   ******************************
   if lastkey() <> K_ESC
      *
      do case
      case calc_op == "C"                         && Clear key
         store 0.0 to running,calc_amt
      case calc_op == " "
         running := calc_amt
      case calc_op == "+"                         && Add
         running += calc_amt
      case calc_op == "*"                         && Multiply
         running *= calc_amt
      case calc_op == "-"                         && Subtract
         running -= calc_amt
      case calc_op == "/"                         && Divide
         if calc_amt > 0
            running /=  calc_amt
```

```
         endif
      case calc_op == "X"        //  X =   Paste the result
         if valtype(cVar) = "N"
            keyboard chr(K_CTRL_Y)+str(running)+chr(K_ENTER)
         endif
      adding := .f.
   endcase
   *
   calc_amt := 0.0
   *
   else
      adding = .f.
   endif
enddo
RestSets()
restscreen(2,5,11,25,back_scr)
return NIL
```

Pop-up calendar

Listing 17.9 illustrates a simple pop-up calendar. This program displays a calendar for the current month. If the user presses the page up key, the next month's calendar will be displayed. Pressing page down will display the previous month's calendar. The home and end keys will respectively display the first and last month of the year.

Listing 17.9 Pop-up Calendar

```
* Program...: Popcalend
*
#include "INKEY.CH"
#include "BOX.CH"

function Popcalend(cProc,nLine,cVar)
local back_scr := savescreen(8,20,17,50)
local wmonth   := month(date()),nkey:=1 /
local oldcurs := setcursor (0)
*********************************
*    Paint calendar on screen    *
*********************************/
```

```
@ 08,20,17,50 box B_SINGLE_DOUBLE+" "
draw_cal( wmonth )
/****************************
*    Main calendar loop    *
****************************/
do while !empty(nKey)
   nKey := inkey()
   do case
   case nKey == K_ESC
      nKey := 0
      loop
   case nKey == K_PGUP
      if ++wmonth > 12
         wmonth :=1
      endif
      draw_cal( wmonth )
   case nKey == K_PGDN
      if --wmonth < 1
         wmonth :=12
      endif
      draw_cal( wmonth )
   case nKey == K_HOME
      wmonth :=1
      draw_cal( 1 )
   case nKey == K_END
      wmonth := 12
      draw_cal( 12 )
   endcase
enddo
restscreen(8,20,17,50,back_scr)
setcursor(oldcurs)
return nil
*
function draw_cal(nMonth)
local jj,tt,temp:=str(nMonth,2)+"/01/91"
local start := dow(ctod(temp))-1,pday:=0
local temp1 := str(if(nMonth<12, nMonth+1, 1), 2) + "01/91"
local last := day(ctod(temp1)-1)
@  9,21 clear to 16,49
@  9,21 say padc(cmonth(ctod(temp)),28)
```

```
@ 10,21 say " Sun Mon Tue Wed Thu Fri Sat"
for jj=1 to 6
   Devpos(10+jj,21)
   for tt=1 to 7
      if ((tt<start+1) .and. jj=1) .or. pday >= last
         ?? space(4)
      else
         ?? str(++pday,4)
      endif
   next
next
return nil
```

Summary

After reading this chapter you should understand how to place and remove entries from the Clipper keystroke table. You should also be aware of the considerations of coding pop-up programs. Finally, you should be comfortable with the pop-up examples in case your users need a calculator or calendar or you wish to create your own pop-up utility.

CHAPTER 18

Working with .DBF Files

Clipper was originally designed to manipulate files stored in the .DBF file format as defined by Ashton-Tate's dBASE product. The .DBF format provided a simple file structure that allowed users to define fields (discrete data elements) within a record (a collection of said elements). These fields were of various data types: character (fixed length), date, numeric, logical (yes/no, true or false), or memo (variable length character data).

This chapter explores the structure of the .DBF file, as well as the tools Clipper provides for working with .DBF files. It investigates the replaceable database drivers that were added with CA-Clipper 5.2. Finally, we will discuss data compression techniques that can be used to reduce the amount of disk storage space that a .DBF file requires.

.DBF files

DBF is an acronym for *data base file*. It is a simple file structure that consists of a header portion and a data portion. Within the header portion are a number of field definitions whose purpose is to provide the layout of each individual record. When a record is selected, the data bytes of that record are mapped into the fields and made available to the application program.

File structure of .DBF Files

Table 18.1 shows the internal structure of a .DBF file. Fields that are one byte in size are converted to numbers using the ASC() function, two-byte fields are converted using the BIN2W() function, and four-byte fields are converted using the BIN2L() function.

Table 18.1 DBF structure

Start	*Bytes*	*Contents*
1	1	Signature byte: 03 = no memo field, 131 = memo field
2	1	Year of last update
3	1	Month of last update
4	1	Day of last update
5	4	Number of records
9	2	Data offset
11	2	Record size
13	20	Filler, unused space

The field information array starts here. Each entry is 32 bytes long with the structure shown below:

Start	*Bytes*	*Contents*
1	11	Field and CHR(0) terminator
12	1	Type, (C)har, (D)ate, (L)ogical, (M)emo, (N)umeric
13	4	Not used
17	1	Field size
18	1	Field decimals
19	14	Not used

The final field definition will be followed by a CHR(13). Notice that the header portion of the structure does not keep a count of the number of fields.

Checking for memo files

If a .DBF file contains a memo field, a second file must exist that has the same name but a different extension. This second file is where the text to the memos are stored. When Clipper opens a .DBF file, it checks to see if the corresponding memo file exists. If the memo file does not exist, the following run-time error occurs:

```
Open error: <filename.ext> DOS error 2
```

DOS error 2 is Clipper's graceful way of saying that the file cannot be found. The function in Listing 18.1 uses the low-level file functions (see Chapter 25) to check if a memo is needed. If a memo file is needed and one exists, the function returns true. If one is needed, but does not exist, false is returned. This function allows your program to keep control and decide upon a course of action for missing memo files. Its syntax is:

```
<logical>  := Safe2open( <file_name> )
```

The .DBF extension is not passed as part of the file name.

Listing 18.1 Safe2open

```
* Program...: Safe2open
*
function safe2open(file_name)
LOCAL handle, retval := .t., first_byte, buffer := " "
LOCAL fn := trim(file_name)
if (handle := Fopen(fn + ".DBF" )) > -1
   fread(handle, @buffer, 1)                  // Read first byte
   if (first_byte := asc(buffer)) == 131      // Memo file ?
      retval := file( fn + ".DBT")            // Does the file exist?
   elseif(first_byte:=asc(buffer))==245 // FoxPro Memo file?
      retval := file( fn + ".FPT")            // Does the file exist?
endif
fclose(handle)                                // Close the file
endif
return retval
```

Protecting files from xBASE use

Since the .DBF file structure was designed to be used in an interpretive, interactive mode, users can easily access a .DBF file by using dBASE or another database management product. Users can also delete records or change key values easily, and when they do so the Clipper index files will not be properly updated.

To keep a casual user from accessing our .DBF files under dBASE, FoxPro, or other database management systems, we can use Clipper's low-level file functions to prevent these interpreters from recognizing the file. The first byte of a .DBF file is a signature byte identifying it as a dBASE file. If this byte is changed, dBASE will not recognize the file as a valid file. Listing 18.2 changes the first byte of the file to a different byte in order to prevent dBASE from using the file. The function syntax is:

```
Protect( <file_name> )
```

The *file_name* parameter should not include the .DBF extension. This function is not foolproof, however. A user who possesses a working knowledge of both the dBASE file format and a data recovery tool such as Norton Utilities or PC Tools could easily change the first byte back to ASCII 03 or 131.

Listing 18.2 Protect

```
* Program...: Protect
*
#include "FILEIO.CH"
function protect(file_name)
LOCAL handle, first_byte, buffer := " "
LOCAL fn := trim(file_name)
if (handle := Fopen(fn + ".DBF", FO_READWRITE)) > -1
   fread(handle, @buffer, 1)       // Read first byte first_byte :=
                                                            asc(buffer)
   fseek(handle, 0, 0)             // Go to top of file if first_byte
                                                                 == 131
                                   // If memo file field
      fwrite(handle, chr(27), 1)   // write 27 as the first
      else                         // byte, otherwise write
         fwrite(handle,chr(26),1)  // a 26.
   endif
   fclose(handle)                  // Close the file
endif
return NIL
```

Listing 18.3 provides the reverse function of the PROTECT() function. When you unprotect the file, it is available for use by Clipper and dBASE.

Listing 18.3 Unprotect

```
* Program..: Unprotect
*
#include "FILEIO.CH"
function unprotect(file_name)
LOCAL handle, first_byte, buffer := " "
LOCAL fn := trim(file_name)
if (handle := Fopen(fn + ".DBF", FO_READWRITE)) > -1
   fread(handle, @buffer, 1)          // Read first byte
   first_byte := asc(buffer)
   fseek(handle, 0, 0)                // Go to top of file
   if first_byte == 27                // Is a memo file needed?
      fwrite(handle, chr(131), 1)
   else
      fwrite(handle, chr(03), 1)
   endif
   fclose(handle)                     // Close the file
endif
return NIL
```

If keeping users away from the files is a necessity, you should use Unprotect() at the beginning of your Clipper program and Protect() at the end. You should also include code in your error-handling program to protect databases in the event of a system error. By implementing these protections, if the program aborts due to an error, the databases will still be protected from xBASE users.

If your application is running on a network, another user could alter the file with dBASE while the Clipper application is running. Unfortunately, dBASE might not recognize Clipper's file or record locks.

Work areas

To manage all the information associated with the .DBF file, Clipper creates a table in memory for storing information about open files. Each entry in this table is called a *work area*. A .DBF file must be assigned to a work area in order for Clipper to work with that file. Clipper allows as many as 250 work areas. When a program first starts, all work areas in the table are empty and the current work area is set to one.

The work area table maintains the following information for each active file.

Alias()	Work area name
Bof()	Whether the file pointer is at the beginning of the file
Dbfilter()	Whether the filter expression is active for this file
Dbstruc()	An array of field names/types/sizes
Dbrelation()	The linking expression to related files
Dbrselect()	Work area number to which this work area is related
Deleted()	Whether the current record is deleted
Eof()	Whether the file pointer is at the end of the file
Fcount()	Number of fields in the file
Field()	Field name
Found()	Result of last SEEK or LOCATE command
Header()	Size of header in bytes
Indexkey()	Key expression for an index
Indexord()	Controlling index number
Lastrec()	Number of records in the file
Lupdate()	Last date .DBF file was updated
Recno()	Current record number
Recsize()	Record size in bytes
Select()	Work area number
Used()	Whether an open file is in a work area

To open a .DBF file, you must select the work area where you wish to store the file. The SELECT command and the DBSELECTAREA() function allow you to choose a work area. The syntax is:

```
//  SELECT COMMAND
    select <nWorkarea>
    // dbSelectArea() function
    dbSelectArea( <nWorkarea> )
```

If the work area is between one and 250, that work area becomes the current work area. Clipper does not check to see if that work area is empty or not. If you select 0 as the work area, Clipper selects the next available empty work area.

The SELECT command and DBSELECTAREA() function also allow you to specify an alias name rather than a work area number. The syntax is:

```
// SELECT command using alias name
    select <cAlias>
    //  dbSelectArea() function
dbSelectArea( <cAlias> )
```

When possible, try to use the second form of the SELECT command. It produces more readable code. For example,

```
select CUSTOMER
```

instead of

```
select 5
```

Opening a file

Once you have selected a work area, you may invoke the USE command or the DBUSEAREA() function to open a .DBF file in that work area. The syntax is:

```
// USE command

USE <cDbf_file> [ INDEX <cNtx_file(s)> ]
[ALIAS <cAlias>]  [NEW]  [SHARED | EXCLUSIVE] [READONLY]
[VIA <cDriver>]

// dbUseArea() function

dbUseArea( [<lNew>], [<cDriver>], <cDbf_file>, ; [<cAlias>], [<lShared>],
                                                   [<lReadonly>]
```

cDbf_file is the name of the database file you wish to open. If another file is already in the work area, that file will be closed before the new file is opened. The cDbf_file may be a literal value or a character string enclosed in parentheses.

cNtx_file(s) is a list of index file names to open in the work area. This list may contain up to 15 index files. Although this syntax is available, in a network environment the preferred syntax is to use the SET INDEX TO command. When you are operating on a network, you need to check whether the file was successfully opened before assigning indexes to the work area. The SET INDEX command lets you separate the file opening and the index opening into two commands. This allows you to check the file's open status first.

Notice that the DBUSEAREA() function does not provide for opening of indexes. This would have to be done using the DBSETINDEX() function described later.

They *cAlias* keyword allows you to specify a different alias name for the file. If you do not specify an alias, the file name will be used as the work area alias. An alias can be up to eight characters long. It is not a good practice to use a single letter as an alias name, because doing so introduces the possibility of your alias name conflicting with Clipper's built-in alias names.

In Clipper 5.2, alias names may not be duplicated. Doing so will generate an error. Also, illegal characters in an alias name will generate an error condition.

The *New* keyword or setting *lNew* to .T. informs Clipper to open this file in the next available work area. If new is not specified, the file is opened in the current work area. *New* has the same effect as specifying select 0 before the USE command.

The *Shared* or *Exclusive* keyword determine if other users will be able to access this file on a network. The SET EXCLUSIVE command allows you to specify the default, which is normally exclusive. However, SET EXCLUSIVE is considered a compatibility command, which means it might not exist in future releases. We recommend explicitly stating the shared or exclusive mode when you open the file.

The *<lShared>* flag on the DBUSEAREA() function can be set to .T. for shared access, or .F. for exclusive file use.

If the keyword *Readonly* is specified, the file will be opened for reading only. This allows password and other key tables to be opened, but not updated. Setting *Readonly* to .T. has the same effect as specifying the *Readonly* keyword. The default is to open the file for reading and writing access.

The keyword *via<cDriver>* or the *<cDriver>* option is used to specify a *replaceable database driver* (RDD) when the file is opened. Each work area can use a different driver, which means that you can have many different types of data in your application (e.g., Paradox, FoxPro, dBASE IV, dBASE III, and of course, Clipper).

Replaceable database drivers

Replaceable database drivers were one of the most touted CA-Clipper 5.0 features. RDDs were intended to serve as "plug-and-play" back ends, allowing Clipper developers to broaden their horizons by accessing a wide variety of data formats, including dBASE III (.dbf), dBASE IV (.mdx), Paradox (.db), and FoxPro (.cdx). RDDs made users happier because they could switch back and forth between data formats instead of being tied always to the dBASE III (.dbf) standard.

CA-Clipper 5.2 allows each work area to be controlled by a different device driver. All database-related commands and functions issued in a given work area go through a database driver that actually performs the desired action. One work area might contain a dBASE III file while another area reads a Paradox file, and so on.

Having this flexibility *does not* mean you have to write different types of code for each RDD. CA-Clipper 5.2 provides many new and enhanced commands for accessing and manipulating databases. Using these commands, you can write code that for the most part will handle any RDD in a completely transparent fashion.

With the USE command or DBUSEAREA() function, you can specify a database driver when you open a database file. The database driver you specify will be used for all operations on that database (except for commands and functions that create new databases, which always use the default driver).

The promise of RDDs was not truly fulfilled until the release of CA-Clipper 5.2. The following RDDs are supplied with CA-Clipper 5.2: DBFNTX, DBFCDX, DBFMDX, DBFNDX, and DBPX. Each of these is supplied as a separate library (.LIB) file that you link into your application.

To ensure that alternate drivers are linked into your application, you must not only link in the appropriate .LIB file, but you should also use the REQUEST <cDriver> command (this command is similar to the EXTERNAL command). See Listing 18.4 in the next section for an example of how REQUEST is used.

Changing the default RDD

If you do not specify the name of a driver when you open a database, the default driver will be used. The default driver is DBFNTX, but you are free to change the default by modifying the RDDSYS.PRG file provided with CA-Clipper 5.2.

RDDSYS.PRG, located in the \CLIPPER\SOURCE\SYS directory, consists of a small INIT (start-up) PROCEDURE called RDDINIT. How to use RDDINIT is self-explanatory. If you want to use a default driver other than DBFNTX, simply replace the two occurrences of DBFNTX with the name of the driver you want. You should then compile RDDSYS.PRG and link RDDSYS.OBJ into your application. Be certain not to change anything else in the file (especially not the copyright notice!). Listing 18.4 shows how you could modify RDDSYS.PRG to use DBFNDX as the default database driver.

Listing 18.4 RDDSYS.PRG modified to use DBFNDX

```
*Copyright (c) 1993, Computer Associates International, Inc.
ANNOUNCE RDDSYS                  // This line must not change

INIT PROCEDURE RddInit
REQUEST DBFNDX                   // Causes DBFNDX RDD to be linked in
rddSetDefault("DBFNDX")          // Set up DBFNDX as default driver
RETURN
```

If you want to use RDDs besides DBFNTX, you do not need to disable the automatic DBFNTX loading. However, if you are not planning to use DBFNTX in any way, shape, or form, you can save overhead by preventing it from being loaded. Listing 18.5 demonstrates how you could modify RDDSYS.PRG to *not* use any default database driver. If you made this modification, you would have to specify a database driver each time you opened a database.

Listing 18.5 RDDSYS.PRG with no default driver

```
*Copyright (c) 1993, Computer Associates International, Inc.
ANNOUNCE RDDSYS                  // This line must not change
INIT PROCEDURE RddInit
RETURN
```

You can also use the DBSETDRIVER() function within your application to change the current default database driver. The syntax is:

```
cCurrent_driver := dbsetdriver( [<cDriver>] )
```

This function returns the name of the current default driver. If you pass the optional <*cDriver*> parameter, that will become the new default driver, assuming that you have linked that driver/library into the application.

Let's take a brief look at each of CA-Clipper 5.2's RDDs. For more details about how to use the features specific to each RDD, please refer to Chapter 19, "Advanced Indexing Techniques."

DBFNTX

DBFNTX is CA-Clipper's default database driver. It permits access to dBASE III database (.dbf) and memo (.dbt) files, as well as Clipper's index files (.ntx). Although DBFNTX is provided for backward compatibility with earlier versions of Clipper, the CA-Clipper 5.2 version also offers the following wonderful features:

- Conditional indexes based on a FOR condition
- Scoped indexes or subindexes based on a WHILE condition or other scope
- Descending indexes without using the DESCEND() function
- Hooks that allow you to provide continuous user feedback (so that nobody reboots the machine in the middle of a 90-minute reindexing process!)

DBFCDX

The DBFCDX database driver provides access to FoxPro 2 .cdx and .idx file formats. This driver provides the following features:

- FoxPro 2 file format compatibility
- Compact indexes
- Compound indexes
- Conditional indexes
- Memo files smaller than DBFNTX format

DBFMDX

The DBFMDX database driver allows you access to dBASE IV .dbf, .dbt, and .mdx file formats. DBFMDX also supports file- and record-locking that is compatible with dBASE IV's locking schemes (these schemes are different than those used by CA-Clipper).

DBFNDX

Use the DBFNDX database driver only if you need to create, access, and update dBASE III-compatible index files (.ndx). (In prior versions of Clipper, this was accomplished by linking in a separate .OBJ file.)

DBPX

The DBPX database driver allows you to access to Paradox 3.5's .db, .px, .x, and .y file formats. In addition to the ability to create, select, and modify Paradox tables, records, and fields, you can also import Paradox tables directly into CA-Clipper arrays.

ALIAS()

The ALIAS() function returns the database name for any work area. If an alias was specified in the USE command, the alias will be returned rather than the database name. The syntax is:

```
<cName> := Alias( <nWork_area> )
```

The *<nWork_area>* is a number in the range of 1 through 250. If not supplied, the current work area will be used. ALIAS() can be used to present a list of files for the user to select from. The PICKALIAS() function in Listing 18.6 returns an array of open alias names.

Listing 18.6 Pickalias()

```
* Program....: Pickalias()
*
function pickalias
LOCAL alist:={}, jj
for jj := 1 to 250
   if !empty(Alias(jj))
      Aadd(alist, Alias(jj))
   endif
next
return alist
```

USED()

The USED() function returns a logical value indicating whether a file is opened in a particular work area. Its syntax is:

```
<lUsed> := Used()
```

This function only checks the current work area. To check a different work area number, you need to first issue a SELECT command such as

```
select 20
? Used()
```

If you know the work area's alias, you can use the extended expression syntax, as shown in this example:

```
use CUSTOMER new
select 20
? CUSTOMER->( used() )
```

SELECT()

The SELECT() function returns the work area number for any alias. It is the inverse of ALIAS(). Its syntax is:

```
<nWork_area> := Select( <cAlias> )
```

<*nWork_area*> will be a number in the range of 1 through 250. If an alias is not supplied, the current work area's alias will be used. If the alias specified is not found, the function will return zero.

The SELECT() function can be used to save the current work area and restore it later. The PUSHALIAS() and POPALIAS() functions in Listing 18.7 illustrate this functionality.

Listing 18.7 PUSHALIAS() and POPALIAS()

```
* Program...: Push&pop alias
*
STATIC astack:={}

function pushalias
Aadd(astack, select())
return nil

function popalias
LOCAL x
x:= atail(astack)
Asize(astack, len(astack) - 1)
select (x)
return nil
```

This program requires the /n compiler switch because of the file-wide static array.

These two functions can be useful in designing pop-up programs. A pop-up program might change the work area. By starting the function with a Pushalias() call and ending with a Popalias() call, your pop-up program is free to move around in different work areas. The use of a stack allows pop-up programs to be called from within other pop-up programs. See Chapter 17 for more information on pop-up programming.

Using indexes

An index is a supplemental file to a .DBF file. It is used to speed access and to provide a logical order to the file. The index file consists of a list of key expressions and record pointers. The expressions are stored in a *b-tree* structure, which allows rapid lookup and transversal.

A b-tree structure is an expansion of the binary search technique. The binary search is a quick method for searching an ordered list of values. It begins by examining the value in the middle of the list. If that value is the key we are seeking, the search is done. However, if that value is greater than the key we are seeking, we compute a new midpoint in the lower half of the list, and if the value is lower than the key, we compute a new midpoint in the upper half of the list. The process is completed until the key is found. Figure 18.1 illustrates a binary search to find the value of 90 in a list of 100 records.

Figure 18.1 Binary search, seeking value 90

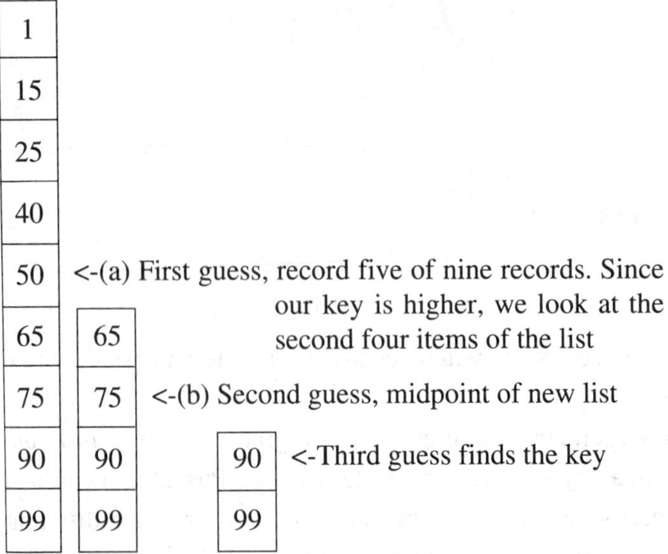
1
15
25
40
50 <-(a) First guess, record five of nine records. Since our key is higher, we look at the second four items of the list
65 65
75 75 <-(b) Second guess, midpoint of new list
90 90 90 <-Third guess finds the key
99 99 99

The b-tree expands the technique by using pages. A *page* consists of as many entries as possible. To determine the number of entries per page, Clipper takes the page size of 1024 bytes and divides it by the size of the index key plus an eight-byte pointer. Each entry in a page consists of the key value, a record number, and pointers. When a page is read into memory, all the entries are compared with the key. If an entry is found, the database is moved to that record number. If an entry is not found, Clipper uses the pointers to determine the next index page to read from the disk. The process is repeated until a key is found or until the pointer values indicate that there are no more pages.

Clipper index files cram as many pointers as possible into each page. This helps reduce the number of disk reads needed to find the record. The fewer disk accesses, the faster the lookup takes place. When designing your index keys, keep in mind that smaller keys allow more keys per page, and result in fewer disk reads. This makes for faster index lookups.

A database file can have a maximum of 15 indexes. All indexes must be specified when the file is open to ensure that they will be properly updated during database operations. One index is considered the controlling index. This index determines the order of the records and is the index against which seeks and find are checked. If the controlling index is zero, the database is ordered by record numbers.

Clipper supports a variety of index types. The first index is Clipper's own indexing scheme, which has the file extension .NTX. This is the default indexing scheme to use. The structure for a Clipper index file is listed in Table 18.2.

Table 18.2 .NTX file structure

Header 1024 Bytes long

Start	*Size*	*Contents*
1	2	Signature byte 06, signifying a Clipper index file
3	2	Count of index file updates
5	4	Offset in the file of first index page
9	4	Offset to list of unused pages
13	2	Key size plus 8 bytes for pointers
15	2	Key size
17	2	Decimal places in key, if numeric
19	2	Maximum entries per page
21	2	Minimum number of entries per page
23	256	Key expression followed by a chr(0)
279	1	1 if unique index, 0 if not
280	744	Filler

Clipper also supports dBASE-compatible indexes (.ndx) through the DBFNDX replaceable database driver. This allows your application to work with index files the user updates during an interpretive session in dBASE. The structure of a dBASE compatible index is listed in Table 18.3.

Table 18.3 .NDX file structure

Header 512 bytes long

Start	*Size*	*Contents*
1	4	Record number of root page
5	4	Number of 512 byte pages in the file
9	4	Filler
13	2	Size of index key
15	2	Maximum number of keys per page
17	2	Key type: 1 if numeric, 0 if character
19	4	Size of key records
23	1	Filler
24	1	1 if unique index, 0 otherwise
25	488	Key expression

Clipper also supports FoxPro compatible indexes (.cdx and .idx) through the DBFCDX replaceable database driver. The structures for these index formats are shown in Tables 18.4 and 18.5.

Table 18.4 .CDX file structure

Header 1024 bytes long

Start	*Size*	*Contents*
1	4	Pointer to first (root) index page
5	4	Pointer to list of free index pages; -1 if none
9	4	Reserved for future use
13	2	Length of key expression
15	1	Index options:
		1, a unique index
		8 , an index with a FOR clause
		32, compact index format
		64, compound index
		(the numbers may be combined if needed)
16	1	Reserved for future use
17	485	Reserved for internal use
503	2	0 is Ascending, 1 is Descending
505	2	Reserved for internal use
507	2	Length of FOR expressions
509	2	Reserved for internal use
511	2	Length for key expressions
513	512	Expressions (key and FOR)

Table 18.5 .IDX file structure

Header 512 bytes long

Start	*Size*	*Contents*
1	4	Pointer to first (root) index page
5	4	Pointer to list of free index pages; -1 if none
9	4	File size
13	2	Length of key expression
15	1	Index options
		1, unique index
		8, index with FOR clause
		9, unique index with a FOR clause
16	1	Reserved for future use
17	220	Key expression
237	220	FOR expression, if Index options are 8 or 9
457	56	Filler, not used

Clipper also supports DBASE IV tagged indexes (.mdx) through the DBFMDX replaceable database driver. Table 18.6 shows the format of the MDX index file.

Table 18.6 .MDX file structure

Header 512 bytes long

Start	*Size*	*Contents*
1	1	Signature byte, (2)
2	3	Last reindex date
5	16	Root name of associated DBF file
21	2	Block size value
23	2	Block size in bytes

24	1	Production MDX file? 1 if Yes
25	1	Filler, not used
26	2	Number of index tags in the file
28	2	Reserved
30	4	Page number of end of file
34	4	Page number of next free block
38	4	Number of pages in next free block
42	3	Date file was created YMD
45	1	Reserved

The MDX structure also contains information about the key values, type, page numbers, and so on.

Creating INDEX files

The INDEX command or DBCREATEINDEX() function can be used to create a supplemental index file. Their syntax is:

```
// INDEX command
INDEX ON <cKey> TO <cFile> [UNIQUE]
// DBCREATEINDEX() function
dbcreateindex( <cFile>, <cKey>, [<bIndex>], [<lUnique>] )
```

The <*key*> can be any valid Clipper expression, including user-defined functions. The expression must evaluate to the same length for each record in the database. For example, the following index command creates an index file that most likely will become corrupted very quickly:

```
index on trim(NAME) to cust001
```

Unless each name in the database is exactly the same size, indexing on the trim() will produce variable length index keys. Clipper does not support variable length index keys. This becomes even more important when using user-defined functions as index keys.

When using a user-defined function, be sure to keep the function as small as possible. The INDEX ON command processes every record in the database. If your user-defined function comprises 20 lines of code and there are 500 records in the database, 10,000 lines of Clipper code must be executed by the INDEX ON command.

The optional *<bIndex>* parameter (passed to DBCREATEINDEX()) is the code block that should be used to create the index. Contrary to what the documentation says, if you choose to call DBCREATEINDEX() directly, you *must* supply this parameter. Using the *<bIndex>* code block in conjunction with DBCREATEINDEX() function allows indexes to be created without forcing Clipper to use the macro processor.

However, even if you supply the *<bIndex>* parameter, you must also provide the *<key>* parameter. This expression needs to be written into the index file header because Clipper cannot write a code block to disk.

<cFile> is the name of the index file to be created. If it already exists on-disk, it will be overwritten. If you are using the default DBFNTX database driver, the index file name will automatically get the extension of .NTX if no extension is specified.

Both the *Unique* keyword and setting the *<lUnique>* parameter to True (.T.) instruct Clipper to write only one entry for each occurrence of a key. If a key value returned by the index expression appears more than once, only the first occurrence will be written into the index.

Unique indexes can also be created using the SET UNIQUE command. Its syntax is:

```
SET UNIQUE <ON | OFF| <lToggle>
```

The normal default for index creation is non-unique indexes. The SET UNIQUE command allows you to set the default value. However, SET UNIQUE is a compatibility command and will not necessarily be in future releases of the compiler. We encourage you to use either the UNIQUE keyword in conjunction with INDEX ON, or the *<lUnique>* parameter for DBCREATEINDEX().

CA-Clipper 5.2 provides an expanded version of the INDEX ON command. This version features optional clauses for conditional indexes, scoped indexes, descending indexes, and continuous user feedback. The syntax is as follows:

```
INDEX ON <cKey> [TAG <cOrderName>] TO <cFile> [FOR <lCondition>]
[ALL] [WHILE <lCondition>] [NEXT <nRecs>] [RECORD <nRecord>]
                                            ; [REST] [EVAL]
<lCondition>] [EVERY <nRecs>] [UNIQUE]
         [ASCENDING | DESCENDING]
```

When you use this version of the INDEX ON command, the underlying

functional equivalents are the new 5.2 ORDCONDSET() and ORDCREATE() functions (rather than DBCREATEINDEX()). For more information about these options, refer to Chapter 19.

Indexing dates

When indexing date fields, it is better to use the DTOS() function instead of the DTOC() function. DTOS() converts the date to a consistent format, YYYYMMDD, which produces sequential ordering. DTOC() is dependent upon the setting of the SET DATE command, which can vary between indexing and updating the index.

Descend()

Indexing normally occurs in ascending order, but you can create a descending index by enclosing the index expression as a parameter to the DESCEND() function. DESCEND() returns a complemented form of the expression passed, which causes the index to appear in descending order. The syntax is:

```
<expression>  := Descend( <expression> )
```

The type of the returned expression will be the same type as the type of the parameter, except if the parameter is a date. In that case, the DESCEND() function will return a numeric value that complements the date passed.

To understand how DESCEND() works, let's look at two approaches you can use to write a DESCEND() function. The purpose of DESCEND() is to switch the order of the data from low-to-high to high-to-low. One simple approach would be to multiply the data by negative one (-1). This makes the highest numbers the lowest and vice-versa. The drawback of this approach is that it only works on numbers. For numeric data, this is the approach Clipper's DESCEND() function uses.

The second approach is to substract the number from a much larger number. The larger the starting number, the smaller the result when we subtract it, as the following example illustrates.

```
big := 10000

   ? 1500, big - 1500      //     displays  1500   8500
   ? 3000, big - 3000      //               3000   7000
   ? 4500, big - 4500      //               4500   5500
```

When you apply this approach to characters, remember that the computer treats character strings as an array of ASCII numbers. To create a descending order string, Clipper subtracts each character's ASCII code from 255, and returns the CHR() of the result. This approach solves the descend problem, but also produces some strange-looking character strings.

Listing 18.8 shows some examples of the DESCEND() function.

Listing 18.8 DESCEND() examples

```
index on descend(trans_date)  to trans.ntx
seek descend( date() )

? descend("CLIPPER")     // displays +
? descend(1500)          // displays -1500
```

NOTE: You can also use the new CA-Clipper 5.2 DESCENDING option in conjunction with the INDEX ON command.

Reindexing files

The REINDEX command recreates all open indexes within a work area. The syntax is:

```
// REINDEX command

REINDEX [EVAL <lCondition>] [EVERY <nRecords>]
```

The optional *EVAL* and *EVERY* clauses enable you to provide continuous user feedback throughout the process. The *EVAL* clause discussed here is the same as the one used with the expanded INDEX ON command. Examples of using the *EVAL* clause are provided in Chapter 19.

REINDEX processes the list of open index files for a particular work area and rebuilds each one. It only rebuilds the body of the index—that is, the key values—and not the header. If the index file header has somehow become corrupted, the REINDEX command will not fix it.

The following example reindexes all open indexes in the customer work area.

```
use CUSTOMER index CUST1,CUST2 new
   reindex
```

You can also use the DBREINDEX() or ORDLISTREBUILD() function to rebuild indexes in an unselected work area, as in the following example:

```
CUSTOMER->( dbReindex() )
```

Remember that if an index file is corrupted, REINDEX will not repair it.

Specifying indexes

The SET INDEX TO command, DBSETINDEX() function, or ORDLISTADD() function can be used to specify the list of index files to associate with a particular database file when it is used. Using the command or one of the two functions is the same as specifying an index list in the USE command.

The syntax for SET INDEX is:

```
SET INDEX TO <cIndex_file(s)>
```

The syntax for the two functions are:

```
dbSetIndex( <cIndex_file> )

ordListAdd( <cIndex_file> )
```

<cIndex_file> is the name of the disk file containing the index. The SET INDEX command allows multiple files to be specified at one time, but the DBSETINDEX() and ORDLISTADD() functions allow only one index at a time to be specified. A second call to SET INDEX releases the old list of index files and establishes a new list. However, calls to DBSETINDEX() or ORDLISTADD() are additive, so you can open several indexes by calling these functions several times.

Once the index list is set, all indexes in the list will be updated whenever a database operation is performed. If no index files are listed, the SET INDEX command closes all open indexes in the current work area. You can also accomplish this using either the DBCLEARINDEX() or ORDLISTCLEAR() functions (neither of which accept any parameters).

The list of index files can be literal names or character strings surrounded by parentheses. If the character string evaluates to spaces or a NULL, it is ignored.

Listing 18.9 shows some examples of using SET INDEX and DBSETINDEX().

Listing 18.9 SET INDEX examples

```
* Program...: Set index examples
*
LOCAL mfile:="VENDOR",mfile1:="",mfile2:="",mfile3:=""
LOCAL ixarr_:={ "LINE1","LINE2" },k
```

```
use CUSTOMER new
set index to CUST1,CUST2,CUST3

mfile1 := "VEND1"
mfile2 := "VEND2"

use (mfile)
set index to (mfile1),(mfile2),(mfile3)

use INVOICES new
dbsetindex( "INV01" )
dbsetindex( "INV02" )

use LINEITEM
for k= 1 to len(ixarr_)
dbsetindex( ixarr_[k] )
next
```

SET ORDER TO

Once indexes are established for a work area, the SET ORDER TO command, or the DBSETORDER() and ORDSETFOCUS() functions, allow you to switch the controlling index. The *controlling index* is the one considered active. The database will be displayed in the order established by the controlling index, and all SEEK commands will use this index. The syntax is:

```
// SET ORDER TO command

set order to <nOrder>

// dbSetOrder() function

dbsetorder( <nOrder> )

// ordSetFocus() function

ordSetFocus( <xOrder> [, <cOrdBag>] )
```

The <*nOrder*> may be any number from zero to the number of index files for the work area, a maximum of 15. If no number is specified, the order will be set to zero, the natural order—that is, the physical order in which the file is written to disk.

For more details about the ORDSETFOCUS() function, see Chapter 19.

No matter which index is the controlling index or whether the file is in natural order, all open indexes will still be updated during database operations.

INDEXKEY()

The INDEXKEY() function returns the key expression on which the specified index was created. The index must be open either by a USE or a SET INDEX command. The syntax is:

```
<cExpression> := Indexkey(<nOrder>)
```

<*nOrder*> indicates which index file from the list the expression should be returned for. If <*nOrder*> is zero, the expression of the controlling index is returned.

INDEXKEY() can be used to present a list of sorted views of the database for a user to choose. Listing 18.10 provides a function that will return an array of currently open index expressions in a work area.

Listing 18.10 Ntxkeylist()

```
* Program...: Ntxkeylist
*
function ntxkeylist
LOCAL ixlist:={}, jj, kk := indexord()
LOCAL jj := 1
do while ! empty(indexkey(jj))
   Aadd(ixlist, indexkey(jj) + if(kk == jj,” _ “,”    “))
enddo
return ixlist
```

The controlling index is flagged with a check mark when the array is returned.

INDEXORD()

The INDEXORD() function returns an integer value that corresponds to one of the indexes specified on the USE or SET INDEX command. The value returned by INDEXORD() denotes the number of the controlling index. The controlling index is the index file that determines the database order and also the index file against which you issue SEEK commands. Clipper will automatically update all open indexes, but only one index may be in control at a time. The SET ORDER command (or DBSETORDER() and ORDSETFOCUS() functions) allows you to switch among multiple indexes.

If there is no controlling index, the INDEXORD() function returns a zero and records are accessed in natural order—that is, they are accessed in the physical order they are in the file.

The syntax for INDEXORD() is:

```
<nControl> := Indexord()
```

INDEXORD() can be used to save the current controlling index and restore it after some commands are performed. For example:

```
use CUSTOMER new index cust_id,cust_nam
   nCurrent := Indexord()        // 1 - cust_id index
   set order to 2                // switch to name order
   list id_code,name,address,city,state to print off
   set order to (nCurrent)       // restore original order
```

INDEXEXT()

The INDEXEXT() function returns a three-character code indicating the index driver currently in use for the work area. The default code is NTX, but it varies depending on which database driver is active for the given work area.

The syntax for INDEXEXT() is:

```
<cExtension> := INDEXEXT()
```

Use the INDEXEXT() function when testing for the presence of index files, like so:

```
if file("CUST1." + indexext())
   set index to custl
else
   index on id_code to custl
endif
```

Relating files

In database operations, files often need to share information. For example, a vendor's name and address, appearing in a purchase order, would also be stored in a vendor file. However, when data is stored in separate files there is the risk of data being updated in one file but not in the other. Moreover, storing the same data in different files is redundant and wastes space on the hard disk.

The best way to solve this problem in Clipper is to *relate* the two files. This is done by choosing a common key between them. For example, a common key shared by a purchase order file and the vendor file would probably be the VEND_ID code. The purchase order file would include a field for VEND_ID with no additional vendor information. When the vendor name and address is needed, the programmer would ask the system to go into the vendor file, find the vendor with the appropriate VEND_ID, and display that vendor's information.

Clipper provides commands and functions to make file relations easier.

SET RELATION and DBSETRELATION()

The SET RELATION command, or DBSETRELATION() function, is used to link two or more work areas by a common key field or by record numbers. Both work areas must be opened. The syntax is:

```
// SET RELATION command

SET RELATION TO <expression| RECNO()> INTO <cAlias
   [ADDITIVE]

//  dbSetRelation() function
dbSetRelation( <nArea|cAlias>,<bExpr>,[<expression>] )
```

<expression> is the key field or expression where the link takes place. When Clipper encounters this field, it assumes the related database was indexed on this field and that this index is the controlling index. This expression is returned by the DBRELATION() function.

If *<RECNO()* is used, the files will be linked by their record numbers. The use of record numbers to link files should be carefully considered. If the database is packed, record numbers may change, which would corrupt the relation. In addition, if two files are related by record numbers, the second file must not have any active indexes. Either no indexes are opened for that file or a SET ORDER TO 0 command has to be issued in that work area.

<bExpr> on the DBSETRELATION() call is a code block that is evaluated to determine the value used to reposition the related file. By specifying a code block instead of a character expression, macro-expansion is not performed. The *<expression>* is still used, however, to return a value from the DBRELATION() function.

The *<cAlias>* or *<nArea>* indicates the work area alias to which the current work area should be related. It may be a literal value or an extended expression enclosed by parentheses, or it may be a numeric work area reference. It cannot be the current work area.

The *ADDITIVE* keyword allows additional relations to be created in the same file. If *ADDITIVE* is not specified, a SET RELATION command will erase previous relations before creating the new link. The DBSETRELATION() function is additive—that is, it does not clear any existing relations.

SET RELATION TO with no parameters removes the link between files. You may also use the function DBCLEARRELATION() to remove the links between files. Its syntax is:

```
dbClearRelation()
```

More than one relation can be specified on a single SET RELATION command, as in this example:

```
set relation to VEND_ID into vendor, ZIP_CODE into zips
```

The code in Listing 18.11 illustrates a relation to link the purchase order file to the vendor database.

Listing 18.11 SET RELATION example

```
use PURCHORD new
use VENDOR new index VEND_ID
select PURCHORD
set relation to VEND_ID into VENDOR
```

Relations are numbered sequentially as they are applied to a file. This occurs whether the relations are established on the same line or through use of the ADDITIVE option.

DBRELATION()

DBRELATION() returns a character string indicating the link expression defined between the current work area and another. If no relationship exists, a null string ("") is returned. The DBRELATION() function expects a numeric parameter indicating which relation should be evaluated. The syntax is:

```
<cExpression> := DBRELATION( <nRelation_number> )
```

Following is an example of using DBRELATION():

```
use PURCHORD new
use VENDOR new index VEND_ID
select PURCHORD
set relation to VEND_ID into VENDOR

? dbrelation(1)      // Displays VEND_ID
? dbrelation(2)      // Displays ""
```

DBRSELECT()

The DBRSELECT() function returns the numeric work area that relates to the current work area. If no relationship exists, a zero is returned. DBRSELECT() expects a numeric parameter indicating which relation should be evaluated. The syntax is:

```
<nExpression> := DBRSELECT( <nRelation_number> )
```

Here is an example of using DBRSELECT():

```
select 1
use PURCHORD
select 2
use VENDOR new index VEND_ID
select PURCHORD
set relation to VEND_ID into VENDOR

? dbrelation(1)      // Displays VEND_ID
? dbrselect(1)       // Displays 1
```

DBRELATION() and DBRSELECT() can be used to temporarily remove a relation between files and then restore it. Listing 18.12 contains the SAVE_RELA() and REST_RELA() functions, which demonstrate this principle.

Listing 18.12 Save/restore relations

```
* Program....: SAVE/RESTORE RELATIONS
*
STATIC rstack_ := {}

function save_rela
Aadd( rstack_, { dbrelation(1), dbrselect(1) } ) return NIL

function rest_rela
LOCAL rsize := len(rstack_)
LOCAL r_exp, r_area, r_work
if rsize > 0
   r_exp  := rstack_[rsize, 1]
```

```
    r_area := rstack_[rsize, 2]
    r_work := alias(r_area)
    dbsetrelation(r_work,;
        &("{ || "+r_exp+"} "), r_exp)
        Asize(rstack_, rsize - 1)
endif
return NIL
```

Filtering files

A *subset* is a smaller set of records extracted from a larger set. For example, in a file with all students at a school, the students in a particular class would be a subset of the entire file. *Filtering* is a technique that lets you define a set of conditions and apply it to a work area. Only records meeting the conditions will be available for operations on that work area. The filter enables you to create subsets within larger files.

SET FILTER

The SET FILTER command, or DBSETFILTER() function, defines the set of conditions to be applied to a database. Each record is checked against the conditions. If the record meets the conditions in the filter statement, the record may be used by the program. If not, the program ignores the record entirely. The syntax to set a filter is:

```
// SET FILTER command

set filter to <lExpression>

// dbSetFilter() function

dbSetFilter( <bCondition> [, <cExpression> ]
```

<lExpression> indicates the conditions that must be met in order for the record to be recognized by Clipper. For example:

```
select STUDENTS
set filter to class == "ACCT 101"
```

<bCondition>, a code block, is evaluated to determine whether a record is included in the filter. It must evaluate to a logical result, .T. meaning to include the record, and .F. meaning to exclude it.

<cCondition> is a character string returned by the DBFILTER() function. It is optional to the DBSETFILTER() function.

Once a filter is set, you must move the record pointer in order to activate the filter. The most common way to do so is by issuing the GO TOP command.

Most Clipper commands will recognize the filter. Any command that moves the pointer by specifying a record number will not recognize the filter. These commands include:

```
go to  <nRecord_number>
```

Record movement commands are discussed later in this chapter.

Filtering should be done with extreme care. If the filter condition causes most records to be ignored, processing commands could spend considerable time searching the database for the next record to work on.

If the SET FILTER command is issued without a logical expression, any filter applied to the current work area is removed. You can also remove a filter by using the dbClearFilter() function. The syntax is:

```
dbClearFilter()
```

NOTE: If you are using a database driver that supports conditional indexing (e.g., DBFNTX or DBFCDX), you should strongly consider doing that rather than filtering.

DBFILTER()

The DBFILTER() function returns a string value that represents the filter condition for the current work area. If no filter has been set, a null string ("") will be returned. The syntax is:

```
<cFilter> := DBFILTER()
```

DBFILTER() can be used to save and restore database queries. The functions in Listing 18.13 can be used to save and restore filter conditions. The syntax is:

```
save_filt()    // Save current filter condition
rest_filt()    // Restore filter and apply it
```

Listing 18.13 Save/Restore filters

```
* Program....: SAVE/RESTORE FILTERS
*
STATIC fstack_ := {}

function save_filt
Aadd( fstack_, dbfilter() )
return NIL

function rest_filt
LOCAL fsize := len(fstack_)
LOCAL f_exp
if fsize > 0
   f_exp  := fstack_[fsize]
   dbsetfilter( &("{ ||"+f_exp+"} "),;
      f_exp )
   Asize(fstack_, fsize - 1)
endif
return NIL
```

Database file status

Clipper provides functions that read the database header and retrieve information from it. In order for these functions to work, the database must be opened in a work area.

HEADER()—Size of DBF header

A .DBF file contains heading information, such as record size, record count, and field lists, as well as the actual data. The HEADER() function returns the number of bytes in the header portion of the .DBF file. Its syntax is:

```
<nBytes> := Header()
```

The *<nBytes>* returned will be an integer length including the header and all the field definitions. The size of the header is most often needed to determine the .DBF file's size for backup purposes.

LASTREC()—Number of records in the file

The LASTREC() function reads the .DBF header and returns a numeric value indicating the last record number in the file. Its syntax is:

```
<nRecord_number> := Lastrec()
```

This number is read from the header, so it is not affected by any filter conditions. It always refers to the physical number of records in the file. Records deleted before a pack operation are included in the value returned by LASTREC().

LASTREC() is identical in operation to RECCOUNT(). RECCOUNT() is considered a compatibility function and may not be supported in future compiler releases.

LUPDDATE()—Date file was last updated

The LUPDATE() function reads the last update year, month, and day from the header record and returns the information as a date variable. This function is useful for checking to see whether the file should be backed up or if indexes need to be recreated. Its syntax is:

```
<dLast_update> := Lupdate()an
```

As an example, the code fragment in Listing 18.14 compares the file date of the index with the last update date of the .DBF file. If the file has been updated more recently than the index file's date stamp, the index file is recreated.

Listing 18.14 LUPDATE() example

```
#include "DIRECTRY.CH"
LOCAL ntx_array := directory("CUST.NTX")
use CUSTOMER new
if Lupdate() > ntx_array[1,F_DATE]
   index on cust_id to cust.ntx
endif
set index to cust
```

RECSIZE()—Record size

RECSIZE() sums up all the field sizes with the current work area and returns the resulting record size. If no file is opened in the current work area, RECSIZE() returns zero. The syntax is:

```
<nBytes> := Recsize()
```

For example, the code fragment in Listing 18.15 shows how to use RECSIZE() to determine whether all fields from a database can be printed on a single line.

Listing 18.15 RECSIZE() example

```
* Program...: Recsize() example
*
function can_fit
if recsize() < 132
   for jj = 1 to fcount()
      ?? fieldget(jj)
   next
   ?
elseif recsize() < 255
```

```
    ?? chr(15)          // Set printer to condensed print
    for jj = 1 to fcount()
       ?? fieldget(jj)
    next
    ? chr(18)           // Set printer to normal print
endif
return nil
```

The database status functions can be used in a backup utility to see whether a particular .DBF file will fit on a floppy disk. Listing 18.16 illustrates a simple backup system using the database status functions. The syntax for Backdbf() is:

```
<logical>  := Backdbf(<cDbf_file>,<cDrive letter>)
```

Listing 18.16 Backdbf()

```
* Program...: Backdbf
*
function backdbf(cDbf_file, cDrive)
LOCAL ndrv := asc(upper(cDrive)) - 64
LOCAL oldfile :=trim(cDbf_file) + ".DBF"
LOCAL newfile :=cDrive + ":\" + oldfile
LOCAL tarr, num_recs
if header() + (recsize() * lastrec()) > diskspace(ndrv)
   go top
   do while ! eof()
      num_recs := ( diskspace(ndrv) - header() ) / recsize()
      copy next num_recs to (newfile)
      ? "Insert a new diskette in drive " + cDrive
      inkey(500)
   enddo
else
   copy file (oldfile) to (newfile)
endif
return NIL
```

Information about fields

The .DBF file structure allows each record to be broken into a number of fields. The field names, types, and sizes are stored in the database header. When a record from the database is read into memory, the current record is transferred into a buffer area and broken into fields. The field names are then available for use by your application program.

FCOUNT()

FCOUNT() returns an integer indicating how many fields are in the current .DBF structure. FCOUNT() is useful for setting the upper boundary in a FOR..NEXT loop that will display all fields from the current record. Its syntax is:

```
<nFields>  := Fcount()
```

Listing 18.17 illustrates a simple database export utility to create a comma-delimited ASCII file from all the fields in the current work area.

Listing 18.17 Simple Export()

```
* Program...: Simple Export()
*
function sexport(cFilename)
LOCAL nFields := fcount()
LOCAL jj
set alternate to (cFilename)
set alternate on
go top
while ! eof()
   for jj := 1 to nFields
      ?? fieldget(jj),","
   next
   ?
   skip +1
enddo
close alternate
return nil
```

FIELD()

The FIELD() function returns the field name for the specified field number. Its syntax is:

```
<cFld_name>  := Field( <nField_number> )
```

The FIELD() function is useful in applications where the field names may not be known. Listing 18.18 illustrates a very simple generic data entry screen using the FIELD() function.

Listing 18.18 Generic data entry

```
* Program....:  Generic data entry example
*
#include "inkey.ch"

function GenDataEntry
LOCAL nFields := fcount(), jj
LOCAL fld_list := array(nFields)
@ 00,00 clear
for jj=1 to nFields
     fld_list[jj] := fieldget(jj)
     @ jj,01 say field(jj) get fld_list[jj]
next
read
if lastkey() <> K_ESC
   for jj := 1 to nFields
      fieldput(jj, fld_list[jj])
   next
endif
return NIL
```

This function can be used for very simple database structures because it offers no validation and does not check the screen positioning. It primarily demonstrates the use of the FIELD() function to display a prompt for the user to enter data.

FIELDPOS()

The FIELDPOS() function returns the ordinal field number for a specified field name. Its syntax is:

```
<nField_number>  := Fieldpos( <cField_name> )
```

The FIELDPOS() function can be used in conjunction with the FIELDGET() function to return the value of a field whose name is known. Following is an example:

```
use CUSTOMER new

? Fieldget(Fieldpos("CUST_ID"))
```

DBSTRUCT()

The DBSTRUCT() function returns an array that contains the field name, type, length, and decimal places for each field in the .DBF file. The syntax for DBSTRUCT() is:

```
<Array>   := DBSTRUCT()
```

The returned array has four elements per field. Its structure is listed in the following table:

Element	*Description*	*Manifest constant*
1	cField_name	DBS_NAME
2	cField_type	DBS_TYPE
3	nField_len	DBS_LEN
4	nField_dec	DBS_DEC

The manifest constants are defined in the DBSTRUCT.CH file found in the \CLIPPER5\INCLUDE directory. The structure of the returned array is the same structure that the DBCREATE() function uses to create a file. This makes it very simple to copy the structure of a .DBF file to a new file, as in the following example:

```
the_struct := dbstruct()
dbcreate("NEWFILE.DBF", the_struct)
```

Moving about the file

A record pointer is maintained for each work area. This pointer refers to a physical record number in the file. Clipper provides commands and functions to update the pointer to different record numbers. The pointer's position determines where the next read or write operation will be performed.

SEEK—Quick lookup of an indexed file

The SEEK command requires an index file to have been created and opened for the current work area. It uses the index to determine the record number, and if a match is found, positions the file at the requested record. Its syntax is:

```
SEEK <expression>
```

The DBSEEK() function can also be used to look up records in an ordered database. Its syntax is:

```
dbseek( <expression>, [<lSoftseek>]
```

The *<expression>* is the key expression for indexing the current work area's controlling index. If the expression is found within the database, the record pointer will move to the appropriate record. If not, the record pointer will be positioned after the last record in the .DBF file.

The *<lSoftseek>* is .T. if SOFTSEEK should be used, or .F. otherwise. This is preferable to using the global SET SOFTSEEK command because specifying this parameter does not actually change the global setting.

In addition to moving the pointer, each SEEK will set a logical value indicating whether the key value was actually found. This value can be determined through the FOUND() function, discussed later in this chapter. Here is an example:

```
use CUSTOMER new
index on upper(cust_id) to cust.ntx
```

```
seek "GRUMPFISH"
? found()            // will return TRUE if GRUMPFISH is
                     // in the customer file, otherwise
                     // FALSE
```

DBSEEK() can be used to seek expressions in unselected work areas, like so:

```
use CUSTOMER new index cust.ntx
use INVOICE  new
ok := CUSTOMER->( dbseek("GRUMPFISH" )
```

DBSEEK() returns a logical value indicating whether the key was found.

LOCATE—Linear search of a .DBF file

LOCATE performs a linear (top to bottom) search of the .DBF file looking for a matching condition. If the condition is found, the database is positioned at the appropriate record number and the FOUND() status is updated. If the data is not found, the record pointer is moved to one plus the end of the file, and the FOUND() status is set to FALSE. The syntax for LOCATE is:

```
LOCATE <scope> FOR <condition> [WHILE <condition> ]
```

The *<scope>* determines both the starting point and the number of records to process. The default scope is ALL, which starts at the top of the file and searches every record. The possible *<scope>* values are shown in Table 18.7.

Table 18.7 Scope values

ALL	Go to the top of the file and process every record.
NEXT <n>	Only process next <n> records from current position.
RECORD <n>	Only process record number <n>.
REST	Process all records from the current record through the end of the file.

The FOR *<condition>* indicates what we are seeking and is a required part of the command. Once the *<condition>* is met, LOCATE stops and sets FOUND() to .T. If none of the records within the scope meets the condition, the LOCATE command sets FOUND() to .F.

The WHILE *<conditions>* command is used to narrow down the records that might be returned by the LOCATE command. The condition specified after the WHILE keyword indicates how long the search should continue. As soon as a record fails to meet the WHILE condition, the LOCATE command stops and sets FOUND() to .F. The LOCATE command is discussed in more detail in Chapter 19.

GO—Go directly to a record number

GO is used to directly move to a record number in a database file. Its syntax is:

```
go[to]  <nExpression> | TOP | BOTTOM
```

The *[to]* is optional, so GO may also be written as GOTO.

The *<nExpression>* is a mathematical expression that is evaluated. The result of the expression determines which record number in the .DBF file to move the record pointer to.

The TOP keyword causes the record pointer to move to the first logical record. The BOTTOM keyword moves the pointer to the last logical record. A logical record is determined by the controlling index, and might not be the same as the physical record number.

Great care should be taken when positioning .DBF files with the GO command. If the GO command specifies a record number rather than TOP or BOTTOM, any filter condition applied to the database will be ignored. It is possible to go to a record that the SET FILTER command would otherwise ignore.

Three functions can be used to GOTO records in a database: DBGOTO(), DBTOTOP(), and DBGOBOTTOM(). Following is a description of each one.

DBGOTO()

The DBGOTO() function performs the same function as the standard GOTO command. Its syntax is:

```
dbGoTo( <nRecord> )
```

<nRecord> is the record number that the database should be positioned to. DBGOTO() always returns a NIL.

DBGOTOP()

The DBGOTOP() function performs the same function as the standard GO TOP command. Its syntax is:

```
dbGoTop()
```

DBBOTOP() moves to database pointer to the first logical record, and always returns a NIL.

DBGOBOTTOM()

The DBGOBOTTOM() function performs the same function as the standard GO BOTTOM command. Its syntax is:

```
dbGoBottom()
```

DBGOBOTTOM() moves to database pointer to the last logical record, and always returns a NIL.

SKIP—Skip to the next logical record

The SKIP command advances the record pointer incrementally to the next record. A parameter can be used to specify both the direction and number of logical records to move. Its syntax is:

```
SKIP <nExpression>
```

<nExpression> is a mathematical expression that will evaluate to a positive or negative integer value. If the expression is positive, the record pointer will be moved that many records forward (closer to the end of the file). If the expression is negative, the record pointer will be moved backward (closer to the beginning of the file).

SKIP is generally used to move through a database and process each record. For example, the code fragment in Listing 18.19 illustrates a simple report.

Listing 18.19 SKIP example

```
* Program...: SKIP example
*
use CUSTOMER new
index on upper(cust_id) to cust.ntx
set console off
set printer on
go top
while .not. eof()
   ? cust_id,cust_name,cust_city,cust_state
   skip +1
enddo
set printer off
set console on
```

NOTE: This example is intended only to illustrate the SKIP command. Refer to Chapter 15 for much more details on printing reports.

SKIP operations may also be performed using the DBSKIP() function. Its syntax is:

```
dbskip([<nRecords>])
```

<nRecords> is a mathematical expression that will evaluate to a positive or negative integer value. If the expression is positive, the record pointer will be moved that many records forward (closer to the end of the file). If the expression is negative, the record pointer will be moved backward (closer to the beginning of the file.) If you do not specify *<nRecords>*, DBSKIP() will move forward by one record.

DBSKIP() always returns a NIL.

BOF()—At beginning of work area?

The BOF() function is used to test whether the record pointer is at the beginning of the file. Its syntax is:

```
<lExpression>  := bof()
```

BOF() occurs when you try to move the .DBF backwards from the beginning of the file, as in this example:

```
use CUSTOMER new
go bottom
while ! Bof()
   ? CUSTOMER->cust_name
   skip -1   // BOF occurs when skipping   endd   endd      //
prior to the first record
```

BOF() performs a logical test rather than a physical test. If you attempt to SKIP prior to the first record in the controlling index, BOF() returns TRUE. This may or may not be the first record in the file.

EOF()—At end of work area?

The EOF() function is used to test whether the record pointer is at the end of the file. Its syntax is:

```
<lExpression>  := EOF()
```

The EOF() occurs when you try to move the .DBF forward from the end of the file. For example:

```
use CUSTOMER new
go top
while ! eof()
   ? CUSTOMER->cust_name
   skip +1              // EOF occurs when skipping
enddo                   // past the last record
```

EOF() performs a logical test rather than a physical test. If you attempt to SKIP past the last record in the controlling index, Eof() returns TRUE. This may or may not be the last record in the file.

EOF() is frequently used to control a loop for processing all records in a database. It may also be used to check the record position after a SEEK or LOCATE. Listing 18.20 illustrates some examples.

Listing 18.20 EOF() examples

```
* Program...: EOF() examples
*
LOCAL tot_due := 0, mcust
use CUSTOMER new
index on upper(cust_id) to cust.ntx
go top
while ! eof()           // Test loop for end of file
   ? CUSTOMER->custname, CUSTOMER->balance
   tot_due += CUSTOMER->balance
   skip +1
enddo

mcust = "GRUMPFISH"
seek mcust
if eof()
   ? "Customer " + mcust + " not found"
endif
```

DELETED()—Is current record flagged for deletion?

When a record is DELETED in Clipper, it is not physically removed from the file. A flag is set to indicate that the record should be considered for removal from the file. The PACK command will physically remove all records with their deleted flags set to TRUE. The DELETED() function checks the current record to see if the record has been tagged for deletion. The syntax for DELETED() is:

```
<lExpression> := DELETED()
```

Listing 18.21 counts the total number of deleted records in a file to determine if a PACK operation should be performed.

Listing 18.21 DELETED() example

```
use CUSTOMER new
count all to del_count for deleted()
if del_count > 10
   pack
endif
```

RECNO()—Current record number

The RECNO() function returns a numeric value that indicates which record number is current for the work area. Its syntax is:

```
<nRec_number> := Recno()
```

The record number is generally used by routines that process the .DBF by record number. For example, Listing 18.22 extracts every tenth record from the database for the purpose of displaying it an inventory sample report.

Listing 18.22 Inventory sample report

```
* Program...: Inventory sample report
*
use INVENT new
go top
set console off
set printer on
? Padc("INVENTORY SAMPLE REPORT",78)
while !eof()
   if recno() / 10 = int( recno()/10 )   // every tenth record
   ? part_num, desc, on_hand, "__________"
   endif
   skip +1
enddo
set printer off
set console on
```

NOTE: If you are using an alternate database driver with CA-Clipper 5.2, RECNO() may not return a numeric value. It will, however, return a unique value that represents the appropriate record. This value will differ based on what type of data file is in use.

FOUND()—Was last SEEK or LOCATE successful?

The FOUND() function is used to check if the last SEEK or LOCATE operation was successful. Clipper maintains the status for each work area of the last search command. The FOUND() function reads this status and returns it as either TRUE or FALSE. Its syntax is:

```
<lExpression>  := FOUND()
```

The FOUND() function is most commonly used after a SEEK or LOCATE to determine how to proceed. For example,

```
#include "inkey.ch"
getting := .T.
while getting
   @ 10,10 get mcust_id picture "!!!!!!!!!!"
   read
   getting := .F.
   if lastkey() <> K_ESC
      seek mcust_id
      if found()
         Edit_cust()
      else
         @ Maxrow(),02 say "CUSTOMER not found, try again."
         getting := (inkey(500) <> K_ESC)
            endif
         endif
   enddo
```

NOTE: You can use the DBSEEK() function, which returns a logical value, to replace the SEEK and FOUND() statements above with

```
if dbSeek(mcust_id)
```

Extracting data from the file

Once the record pointer is positioned, the fields in the database or table are available for use. Clipper transfers the data from the record in the database to a buffer area established for each work area. Fields may be extracted from this buffer area by using the field name as any other variable. Clipper will translate the request for a field into an appropriate position, size, and type within the buffer and return that data.

Assignment operator

The simplest way to extract data from a work area buffer is through the assignment operator. The syntax is:

```
<memory_variable> := <cField_name>
```

The field may also be treated like a regular memory variable. It is important to note that if the field is treated like a memory variable, data in the .DBF file can be updated.

If a field name and memory variable might have the same name, the field will normally take precedence. We highly recommend getting in the habit of preceding all field names with the alias identifier, as in this example:

```
? CUSTOMER->id_code   // displays ID_CODE from CUSTOMER.DBF
```

In addition, Clipper offers two statements to tell the compiler how to interpret ambiguous variable names. These are the FIELD and MEMVAR statements.

FIELD

The FIELD statement declares a list of variables to be considered as field names if they are not specifically identified as such. Its syntax is:

```
FIELD <cField_list> [IN <cAlias>]
```

For example, the code fragment in Listing 18.23 tells the compiler to consider CUST_CODE,NAME, and ADDRESS as fields and not as memory variables. VEND_CODE,VNAME, and VADDRESS are established fields from the VENDOR database file.

Listing 18.23 FIELD example

```
* Program..: FIELD Example
*
FIELD cust_code,name,address
FIELD vend_code,vname,vaddress IN vendor
```

When a FIELD statement is used, it must precede all executable statements within the function or procedure. The FIELD scope is the current procedure. The FIELD statement may be declared before any functions or procedures with a .PRG file. If the .PRG file is compiled using the /n switch, the FIELD declarations have a scope of the entire program file.

The FIELD statement also allows the compiler to check for undeclared variables when you use the /w switch.

MEMVAR

The MEMVAR statement is the opposite of the FIELD statement. It declares a list of variables to be considered memory variable names if they are not specifically identified as such. Its syntax is:

```
MEMVAR <cField_list>
```

The code fragment in Listing 18.24 tells the compiler to consider NAME, ADDRESS,CITY, and STATE to be considered memory variables and not fields.

Listing 18.24 MEMVAR example

```
* Program..: MEMVAR Example
*
MEMVAR name,address,city,state
use EMPLOYEE new
? name              // Assumed to be a memory variable
? EMPLOYEE->name    // A field from the employee database
```

When a MEMVAR statement is used, it must precede all executable statements within the function or procedure. The MEMVAR scope is the current procedure. You can change the MEMVAR scope to the entire .PRG file by declaring it before any function or procedure name, and by compiling with the /n switch.

NOTE: We encourage you *not* to rely on the FIELD and MEMVAR statements in developing Clipper 5.x. FIELD should not be necessary if you always precede field names with an alias, and MEMVAR only applies to PUBLIC and PRIVATE variables (which we sincerely hope you will abandon in lieu of LOCALs and STATICs).

FIELDGET()

The FIELDGET() function retrieves a field value from the current record for a specified field number. Its syntax is:

```
<value> := FIELDGET( <nField_no> )
```

The FIELDGET() function is very useful for extracting data from databases where the field name is not known. This allows for generic, data-independent functions to be created.

Listing 18.25 contains a scatter function that transfers all the fields from the current record into an array.

Listing 18.25 Scatter

```
* Program...: Scatter
*
function Scatter( nRec_num )
LOCAL numfld := fcount(), jj
LOCAL retarry_ := array(numfld)
if nRec_num <> NIL
   goto nRec_num
endif
for jj := 1 to numfld
   retarry_[jj] := fieldget(jj)
next
return retarry_
```

Putting data into the file

Information from Clipper's memory can be written into a database file in several ways. The information will be transferred from a memory variable into the work area's buffer. When the file pointer moves from that record, the buffer will be written back to the disk.

REPLACE

The REPLACE command allows the values of individual fields to be updated in the database. Its syntax is:

```
REPLACE <field_name> WITH <expression> [<scope>]
[FOR <lcondition> WHILE <lcondition>]
```

The *<field_name>* is the name of the field from the current work area that should be updated. If the field name is unknown, the FIELDPUT() function should be used rather than macro-expanding the field name.

The *<expression>* indicates the value that should be written into the work area buffer for a particular field. Its type must agree with the declared type of the field, or a data type mismatch run-time error will occur. The expression may be a constant, a variable, a field from another work area (preceded by that work area's alias), or a combination of these.

The *<scope>* determines both the starting point and the number of records to replace. The default scope is the current record only. Note that this is different from the default scope on other commands, such as LOCATE, SUM, and AVERAGE. On those commands the scope defaults to ALL. The possible *<scope>* values are shown earlier in this chapter in Table 18.7.

The FOR *<condition>* indicates which records should be updated with the expression. If the record meets the condition, the specified field will be updated. If the record does not meet the specified condition, the fields in that record will not be changed. Regardless of whether the field is updated, the REPLACE command continues until the scope is completed.

The WHILE <*condition*> indicates the condition that must be met in order for the REPLACE command to continue processing. As long as the condition is satisfied, the specified fields will be updated. Once a record does not meet the specified condition, the replace operation stops. The WHILE condition, if specified, overrides the scope.

Listing 18.26 illustrates several examples of the REPLACE command.

Listing 18.26 REPLACE command examples

```
* Program...: Replace examples
*
use EMPLOYEE new
index on upper(name) to employ
seek "JOE BOOTH"
if found()
   // Give the employee a 25% salary increase
   replace salary with salary*1.25
endif
// Give all employees a cost of living raise
replace all salary with salary *1.02
// All CA employees are being transferred on Dec. 15, 1993
replace all trans_date with ctod("12/15/93") ;
for EMPLOYEE->state == "CA"
```

FIELDPUT()

The FIELDPUT() function allows you to replace field contents without resorting to the use of macros to expand to the field name. The syntax is:

```
FIELDPUT( <nField_no>,<expression> )
```

The <*nField_no*> indicates which field number to replace. The expression indicates the value that should be placed into that field. If the type of the expression does not match the field type, a type mismatch run-time error will occur.

Listing 18.27 illustrates a GATHER user-defined function that writes array elements back to the .DBF file. Its syntax is:

```
Gather( <nRecord_number>,<aField_array> )
```

Listing 18.27 Gather

```
* Program...: Gather
*
function Gather( nRec_num, retarry_ )
LOCAL numfld := fcount(), jj
if nRec_num <> NIL
   goto nRec_num
endif
for jj = 1 to numfld
   fieldput( jj, retarry_ )
next
return NIL
```

Adding data to the file

Clipper can add a single record to the file by adding a record filled with spaces, or it can add a number of records from other sources. Following is an explanation of how to do both.

Adding records to the file

The APPEND BLANK command, or DBAPPEND() function, can be used to add new records to a database file. The syntax is:

```
// APPEND command

append blank

// DBAPPEND() function

dbAppend()
```

When the APPEND BLANK command or DBAPPEND() function is performed, a new empty record is added to the end of the database and the record pointer is positioned to this record.

Listing 18.28 illustrates a generic database update program that either adds a new record or updates the current record, depending on the parameter passed.

Listing 18.28 Append blank example

```
* Program...: Append blank example
*
function cust_edit( nRecord, fld_array )
LOCAL jj, fld_count := fcount()
if nRecord == NIL
   append blank
else
   goto nRecord
endif
for jj := 1 to fld_count
   Fieldput(jj, fld_array[jj] )
next
return NIL
```

Removing data from the file

Each record in a file has a flag indicating whether the record was deleted. Clipper provides commands and functions to manipulate that flag.

Flagging records for deletion

The current record may be flagged for deletion using either the DELETE command or the DBDELETE() function. The syntax is:

```
// DELETE command

DELETE

// dbDelete() function

dbDelete()
```

The current record will be flagged for deletion. The file will still be in the database until either a PACK command physically removes it or a ZAP command completely obliterates the file.

Recalling Deleted Records

If the current record is flagged for deletion, the flag may be removed using either the RECALL command or the DBRECALL() function. The syntax is:

```
// RECALL command

RECALL

//  DBRECALL() function

dbRecall()
```

The current record's deletion flag will be turned off to prevent a PACK operation from removing the record.

Physically removing the records

At some point, your application may need to reclaim the space being used by deleted records. This is done by issuing the PACK command. Its syntax is:

```
PACK
```

PACK operates on the current work area and makes a new copy of that work area without deleted records. Once a PACK is performed, the physical size of the file is reduced (if records were removed) and the records are gone.

Closing the files

After you have completed all updates of a database, you should close the file. This can be accomplished with either the USE command or the DBCLOSEAREA() function. The syntax is:

```
// USE command

USE

// dbCloseArea() function

dbCloseArea()
```

The currently selected work area will be closed. All pending updates are written to the disk and all locks are released. Be sure to select the appropriate work area to close before issuing a USE command or a DBCLOSEAREA() function.

If you need to close all work areas at once, you may use either the CLOSE DATABASES command or the DBCLOSEALL() function. The syntax is:

```
// CLOSE DATABASES command

close databases

// DBCLOSEALL() function

dbCloseAll()
```

Both the DBCLOSEAREA() and DBCLOSEALL() functions return a NIL.

Reducing storage needs

Data compression consists of a variety of techniques designed to reduce the amount of storage space required by data. Date types can be reduced to two bytes of storage, and numeric types can cut their storage requirements in half. In this section, we will explore techniques to accomplish data compression and provide some UDFs you can use to reduce disk storage requirements.

Compressing numeric information

To perform numeric compression, you have to think of numbers as strings of digits, not as numeric values. For example, the number 778,242 should be considered six one-character fields, not a value. For this particular string, the first character field is 7, the second field is 7, the third field is 8, and so on. The possible values for any of these fields can be 0 through 9, which means that ten different values are possible for each character. If we combine two fields, we have a possibility of a hundred different values. Now we use the ASCII chart (see Appendix A) to our advantage. The ASCII chart has 255 possibilities, which can be represented by a single character, and Clipper has built-in functions (CHR and ASC) that understand the ASCII chart. Now let's apply it to our advantage with the 778,242 digit string.

First, we will break the string into groups of two digits each so that 778,242 can be viewed as follows:

77 82 42

Now we use the ASCII chart to identify the characters that the ASCII chart has for each of the numbers, so that the original number can be represented as:

CHR(77) = M CHR(82) = R and CHR(42) = *

So the string MR*, which is only three characters long, contains the ASCII codes 77 82 42. Therein lies our compression ability: taking the ASCII equivalent character for each two digits in the number. By applying this technique, all numeric fields can be reduced by 50 percent. The functions in Listing 18.29 provide the capability to compress and decompress a numeric field. The syntax for the numeric compression functions are:

```
<cCompressed>  := sqz_n( <nValue>,<nSize> [,<nDecimals>] )
<nValue> := unsqz_n( <cCompressed>,<nSize> [,<nDecimals>] )
```

The *<nSize>* must be larger than the size of the string you are passing to the SQZ_N function.

Listing 18.29 Sqz functions

```
*  Program ..:  SQZ
*
function sqz_n(_number,_size,_dec)
LOCAL tmpstr,retstring:="",k
_dec   := if(_dec=NIL,0,_dec )
_number   := _number * (10**_dec)
_size  := if(_size/2<>int(_size/2),_size+1,_size)
tmpstr := str( _number,_size)
tmpstr := strtran(tmpstr," ","0")
for k = 1 to len(tmpstr) step 2
   retstring=retstring+chr(val(substr(tmpstr,k,2))+1 00)
next
return retstring
```

```
function unsqz_n(_compressed,_size,_dec)
LOCAL _tmp :="",k,multi,answer
_size     := if(_size/2<>INT(_size/2),_size+1,_size)
for k=1 to len(_compressed)
   _tmp=_tmp+str(asc(substr(_compressed,k,1))-100,2)
next
_tmp   := strtran(_tmp," ","0")
answer := substr(_tmp,1,_size-_dec)+"."+;
      substr(_tmp,_size-_dec+1)
return val(answer)
```

The SQZ functions compress a numeric value when it is stored in the database, and decompress it when it is retrieved. For example, using the SQZ functions, a REPLACE statement might be coded:

```
replace TRANS->cust_id with Sqz_n(mcust_id,8),;
   TRANS->amount  with Sqz_n(mamount,12,2)
```

To retrieve the information from the file, the code might be written as:

```
mcust_id := Unsqz_n(TRANS->cust_id,8,2)
mamount  := Unsqz_n(TRANS->amount,12,2)
```

Compressing phone numbers

A phone number, including the area code, may be compressed from 10 digits to a four-character string. This represents a savings of 60 percent on disk space. To understand how to compress a phone number, we need a little background on area codes and phone numbers. A phone number consists of three parts, as shown in Figure 18.2.

Figure 18.2: The components of a phone number

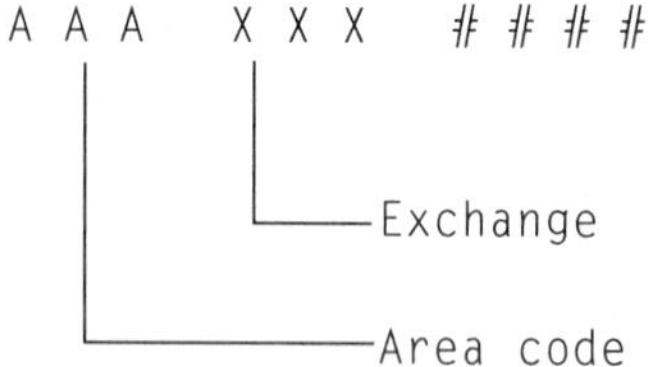

To dial a number within your area code, you dial seven digits. For a number in a different area code, you dial the three-digit area code followed by the seven digits of the number, for a total of ten digits. Phone numbers are structured such that the middle digit of all area codes must be 0 or 1. (Originally, the middle digit of exchanges was above 1, but some area codes have become so crowded that the number 1 appears in some exchanges). Once we realize that the middle digit of the area codes must be a 0 or a 1, we can reduce the number of possible phone numbers. After removing punctuation from the phone number, we have ten digits, which can range from 0 through 9,999,999,999. However, if we transpose the first and second digits, we reduce the range of possible phone numbers to zero through 1,999,999,999.

Once the range is reduced, we can use the L2BIN() function to store the number. L2BIN() has a range of 0 to 4,294,987,295, which is more than sufficient to store phone numbers. The function SQZ_P() in Listing 18.30 compresses a phone number and area code into a binary string. UNSQZ_P(), in Listing 18.31, takes the binary string and returns a punctuated phone number. The syntax for SQZ_P() is:

```
<cBinary_string> := sqz_p( <cPhone_number> )
```

The syntax for UNSQZ_P() is

```
<cPhone_numbr> := unsqz_p( <cBinary_string> )
```

Listing 18.30 SQZ_P

```
* Program...: Sqz_p
*
function sqz_p(cPhone)
LOCAL cBinary,cHold
cHold := strtran(cPhone,"(“,"")        // Remove various
cHold := strtran(cHold ,")","")        // punctation characters
cHold := strtran(cHold ,"-","")        // ( ) - and space
cHold := strtran(cHold ," “,"")
cHold := substr(cHold,2,1)+substr(cHold,1,1)+;
       substr(cHold,3,8)
cBinary := L2bin( val(cHold) )
return Cbinary
```

Listing 18.31 UNSQZ_P

```
* Program...: Unsqz_p
*
function unsqz_p(cBinary)
LOCAL cPhone,nHold,cHold
nHold  :=Bin2l(cBinary)
cHold  :=Alltrim(str(nhold,11))
cHold  :=if(len(cHold)<>10,"0"+cHold,cHold)
cPhone :="(“+substr(cHold,2,1)+substr(cHold,1,1)+;
       substr(cHold,3,1)+”) “+substr(cHold,4,3)+; “-
"+substr(cHold,7,4)
return cPhone
```

Compressing dates

You can also save room in your .DBFs by compressing dates. The eight-byte date field can be compressed to a two-byte character field. To compress dates in this way, we must first explore some tricks of the Clipper compiler. Start with the date January 22, 1989. Stored as a date, this field would contain 01/22/89. Another way of expressing the same date is to say that 01/22/89 is 3,309 days after 01/01/80 (our base date). This is where date compression can occur.

To compress a date, first convert it to an integer number of days past some base date. You must choose a base date that is older than any entries. For a transaction system, 01/01/80 is probably a good choice. Because an integer can be a number from 0 through 65,535, this allows us approximately 179 years worth of dates starting at 01/01/80. If you don't plan to still be coding in the year 2159, this range should be acceptable. If, however, you are coding a system that needs a larger range of dates, you can change the function to use the long integer format, which would allow for 2,147,418,112 days, or over five million years.

Once the date is expressed as an integer number of days, we can use the Clipper functions of I2BIN() and BIN2W() to reduce the storage requirements of the integer. I2BIN takes an integer parameter and returns a 2-character binary representation of that integer. BIN2W() does the reverse, taking the two characters and returning an integer.

Listing 18.32 provides functions to compress and uncompress dates using the 179-year window. The syntax to compress the date is:

```
<cBinary_string> := sqz_d( <dSome_date> )
```

The syntax to restore the date from the compressed string is:

```
<dSome_date> := unsqz_d( <cBinary_string> )
```

Listing 18.32 SQZ_D

```
* Program ...: Sqzdate
*
#define BASE_DATE ctod("01/01/1980")

function Sqz_d(dSquish)
return I2bin( dSquish-BASE_DATE )

function Unsqz_d(cBinary)
return BASE_DATE + Bin2w(cBinary)
```

If 179 years is not a big enough date window, you can use the functions in Listing 18.33 to compress dates down to four characters and still contain any date that Clipper accepts.

Listing 18.33 SQZ_D II

```
* Program ...: Sqzdate
*
#define BASE_DATE ctod("01/01/1980")

function Sqz_d(dSquish)
return L2bin( dSquish-BASE_DATE )

function Unsqz_d(cBinary)
return BASE_DATE + Bin2l(cBinary)
```

The BASE DATE value is the earliest date that will accurately be returned (to the specifications of the query). Change the define setting if you need to work with dates earlier than January 1, 1980.

Compressing time

While Clipper does not specifically provide a time data type, it does provide a function that returns the system time. The format for a time string is HH:MM:SS. In its formatted form, the time string requires eight characters of storage. If the seconds are not needed, a time string can be compressed to two bytes. If seconds are needed, it can be compressed to three bytes.

To compress time values, first remove the colon characters that separate the components, which leaves a string of six numbers. If seconds are not needed, the string is only four numbers. By using the numeric compression user-defined functions, we can reduce the storage requirement of a time string. The SQZ_T() function in Listing 18.34 takes a time string and returns a compressed string from it. Its syntax is:

```
<cCompressed_string> := sqz_t( <cTime>,<lSeconds> )
```

The syntax for UNSQZ_T() is:

```
<cTime> := unsqz_t( <cCompressed_string> )
```

The UNSQZ_T() function determines whether seconds are needed by the size of the string passed to it.

Listing 18.34 SZQ_T

```
* Program...: Sqz_t
*
function sqz_t(cTime,lSeconds)
LOCAL cHold,nHold
lSeconds :=if(lSeconds=NIL,.F.,lSeconds)
cHold := strtran(cTime,":","")    // Remove colons
nHold := val(cHold)               // Convert to numeric
return if(lSeconds,sqz_n(nHold,6,0),sqz_n(nHold,4,0))
*
function unsqz_t(cComp)
LOCAL nSize := len(cComp) * 2
LOCAL cHold := unsqz_n(cComp,nSize,0)
```

```
cHold := str(cHold,nSize,0)
cHold := if(nSize=4,cHold+"00",cHold)
return substr(cHold,1,2)+":"+;
   substr(cHold,3,2)+":"+;
   substr(cHold,5,2)
```

Summary

After reading this chapter you should be familiar with Clipper's primary database file structure. You should understand the basics of replaceable database driver methodology, and be excited about the possibilities these present. You should know how to create index files and how to move about the file. Getting data from the file and updating information should be clear to you. Finally, if disk space is at a premium, you should be able to use the compression techniques and functions to reduce your storage requirements.

CHAPTER 19

Advanced Indexing Techniques

Chapters 11 and 18 discuss how to create, maintain, and search indexes with Clipper 5.01. Clipper 5.2 adds a wide variety of important new indexing features. Fortunately, these indexes are implemented in such a way that what you've learned already about indexes still applies. Clipper 5.2 is also directly compatible with several other database products. With a few minor exceptions, the new features and compatibility services all fit into the syntax you already know. The replaceable data driver (RDD) concept makes this possible (see Chapter 18 for more information on RDDs). This chapter provides details on the following Clipper 5.2 indexing features:

- Conditional indexes using the FOR and WHILE clauses
- Unique index keys using the UNIQUE clause
- Descending index keys using the DESCENDING clause
- User-definable index activities using the EVAL..EVERY clauses
- Compound indexes using the TAG clause
- Compact indexes using the DBFCDX driver
- The new order management system

We will also summarize the Clipper 5.2 indexing features that are compatible with other database products. Clipper 5.2 supports file compatibility with FoxPro (.cdx and .idx files); dBASE IV (.mdx); dBASE III Plus (.ndx), and Paradox (.px).

INDEX ON command overview

Following is the full syntax of the INDEX ON command. This syntax listing is taken verbatim from the Clipper 5.2 documentation.

```
INDEX ON <expKey> [TAG <cOrderName>] TO
   <xcOrderBagName> [FOR <lCondition>] [ALL]
   [WHILE <lCondition>] [NEXT <nNumber>]
   [RECORD <nRecord>] [REST]
   [EVAL <bBlock> [EVERY <nInterval>]
   [UNIQUE] [ASCENDING|DESCENDING]
```

Changes to index terminology

The elements taken from Clipper 5.01—ON, TO, and UNIQUE—function the same way they do in that version. We'll explain the order name and order bag name references later in this chapter. In order to support the current crop of database drivers and to make room for other foreign drivers in the future, Clipper's index-related terminology has undergone many changes. What were previously simple and straightforward concepts without options are now merely alternatives in a much larger context.

Once you get over the learning curve, you'll find the new terms more concise, more accurate, and less ambiguous. You can discuss indexing and other database concepts in general terms without getting bogged down in vendor-specific syntax or terminology.

The disadvantage, however, is that until you grow comfortable with the new terms, the descriptions in the Clipper documentation and Norton Guides, which use the new terminology, may not make sense. If you are a FoxPro, dBASE, or Paradox programmer who is new to Clipper, don't worry—long-time Clipper developers are equally baffled!

This chapter gives it to you both ways. We use the familiar but abandoned terms from the past to help you make the conceptual transition. You can read our descriptions and compare them to the Clipper documentation and perhaps gain some insights that way. We also dedicate a section at the end of the chapter, "The order management system," to the new terminology.

New elements that support index features

Some elements were added to support the index features that are new in Clipper 5.2. These elements are TAG, FOR, WHILE, EVAL, EVERY, ASCENDING, and DESCENDING. A few elements—NEXT, RECORD, and REST—were added solely for conceptual compatibility with other Clipper database-related commands. These elements are not discussed in this chapter because they serve little useful purpose.

The various features of Clipper's indexes are discussed separately in this chapter, but you can combine them as needed. The features are discussed here in no particular order. You should not infer their relative importance from their order of presentation.

Reviewing INDEX ON

Before we discuss the other features, let's review the basic INDEX ON syntax. The INDEX ON command requires at least two parameters, the index key expression and the target file name. Compound indexes actually muddle the concept of a target file name, but we'll keep it simple for now and limit this overview to the default database driver as it functions in Clipper 5.01.

Consider the following source code fragment (assume the DBFNTX driver is used):

```
field Id in CUSTOMER
use CUSTOMER new
index on Id to CUSTID
```

The first line directs the compiler to treat future references to Id as a field in CUSTOMER, the second line opens the CUSTOMER.DBF database in a new work area, and the last line creates an index file called CUSTID.NTX based on the Id field. Once it has been created, the index file is associated with the database as follows:

```
// Option 1.
use CUSTOMER new index CUSTID

// Option 2.
use CUSTOMER new
set index to CUSTID
```

Once an index is associated with a database, the index controls all relative positioning commands. Consider the following example:

```
Position at the last customer Id
go bottom
// Position at the first customer Id
go top
// Move to the next Id
skip
```

By last, next and first, we mean the position based on the order of the customer ID numbers. For customer ID numbers 6536, 3487, 1928, and 2981, the first ID is 1928 and the last is 6536 when sorted. Where the "next" record is depends on where you are pointing in the list. If you are positioned at the first record, the next record is 2981 because it follows 1928. Without an index, all of the above commands would move the record pointer in the physical order of the records in the database. That is, these commands would move the record pointer to records in the order they were appended.

Besides changing the effective sort order of the database, an index provides speedy access to specified records. If the index is based on Id, the following SEEK command begins a rapid search of the index for an entry that matches the specified key. When Clipper finds the index entry, it positions the database at the associated record. The result is a relatively small amount of file activity to search a correspondingly large database.

```
seek "2981"
if found()
   ? "Customer 2981 is in record", recno()
else
   ? "There is no customer 2981"
endif
```

Without an index, the only way to find the customer with an Id of 2981 in a database that is not ordered is to use the LOCATE command. Unlike SEEK, LOCATE might need to search the entire database record by record to determine whether the specified record exists, as in the following example:

```
locate for CUSTOMER->Id == "2981"
```

Clipper indexes are based on the concept of binary trees. A *binary tree* provides a geometric yield when you search for keys. That is, each file access eliminates a large portion of the database from consideration. For example, it is possible to isolate any random index key from a list of 100,000 in a dozen index read operations, although you may need fewer accesses.

The corresponding LOCATE operation would probably require several thousand read operations. The scenario gets more complicated when you consider what it takes to determine that no record matches your request. Using the same 100,000-record example, an index SEEK yields "no matching record" in a dozen or so read operations. The equivalent LOCATE requires one read operation for every record in the database! Clearly, indexes are a necessary element of any Clipper application with large databases.

All of Clipper 5.2's database drivers support the index operations outlined so far. The rest of this chapter discusses the many ways you can augment Clipper's basic index operations. Not all database drivers support all features.

The INDEX ON..FOR clause

The FOR clause is used to create indexes that do not necessarily represent every record in the database. The FOR clause requires a logical expression that is evaluated for each record in the database. Only records that match the condition are added to the index. Later, as new records are entered in the database, the FOR condition is evaluated again and Clipper adds only the new records that meet the condition to the index. The index FOR condition is invoked whenever records are modified, and if a record no longer meets the condition, its associated index entry is removed. Likewise, records that did not previously meet the FOR condition are evaluated and may be added to the index if they now comply.

The INDEX..FOR clause is supported by drivers NTX, MDX, and CDX.

To summarize, the FOR condition is evaluated

- for every record in the database when the index is first created
- when a new record is added to the database
- when a record is modified

The effects of a FOR condition

When an index with a FOR condition is the controlling index, the database will appear to have records that meet the FOR condition only. That is, the relative record positioning commands (GO TOP, GO BOTTOM, SKIP, and SEEK) behave as if the only records present are those that meet the FOR condition. For example, GO TOP positions the database at the first record that meets the FOR condition, sorted according to the index key expression. Consider the following example:

```
field Id, Balance in CUSTOMER
use CUSTOMER new via "DBFNTX"
index on Id to CUSTBAL for Balance > 0
```

The resulting CUSTBAL.NTX index contains only the Id numbers of customers who have a balance greater than 0, which would be every record in the database if all customers have a balance. Or, if no customers have a balance, this could produce an empty index. As records are added and modified, the index is updated. The effect is a database that seems to contain only records that match the "balance greater than zero" condition, as illustrated here:

```
select CUSTOMER
go top
do while .not. CUSTOMER->( eof() )
   ?  CUSTOMER->Id, CUSTOMER->LastName
   ?? CUSTOMER->Balance
   skip alias CUSTOMER
enddo
```

The resulting display is sorted by customer ID (the index expression) and contains only the customers who currently have a balance greater than zero. It is important to remember that the FOR condition constrains even the GO TOP command when such an index is in control.

When and why to use a FOR condition

When the purpose of an index is not relevant for some portion of the database, the index will benefit from a FOR condition. For example, the CUSTBAL index lets us treat the database as if it contained only customers with a balance.

With the FOR condition, you can eliminate source code that would otherwise be required to process records. It also cuts down on the size of the resulting index file, because only keys for records that match the condition are added to the file. Finally, it promotes encapsulation by tying the FOR condition directly to the index. When the database is in use, the programmer need not know about the nature of the FOR condition, or even that a condition is present.

Keep in mind that the FOR condition is evaluated once for each record in the database, and again when users append or modify records. For this reason, keep the FOR expression as simple as possible so it can evaluate as quickly as possible. Because the FOR condition travels with the index file, you should also be mindful of relying on variables or function names that might not exist in a different application. Consider the following index command:

```
local nFactor := 2.35
field Id, ZipCode, Balance in CUSTOMER
index on ZipCode + Id to CUSTRATE ;
   for CreditRating(Balance, nFactor) == "AA"
```

The resulting index can only be opened in applications that can supply the CreditRating( ) function as well as an appropriate value for nFactor. Even then, it should be the same version of the function and same value for nFactor! Things can get tricky when you rely on user-defined functions or variables. The preceding index, for example, will not work with DBU, the Clipper database utility.

The INDEX ON..WHILE Clause

Similar to the FOR clause, the WHILE clause is used to an create index that may represent less than the entire database. It differs from the FOR clause in that Clipper does not update or maintain its indexes after they are created. Indexes created with a WHILE clause are presumed to be temporary. Moreover, the WHILE clause does not evaluate the entire database when creating an index. Clipper does not automatically start at the first record and process all the way to the last record. Rather, the WHILE operation starts at the current record position and generates only index entries that meet the WHILE condition.

Other than those two distinctions, an index with a WHILE condition operates like one with a FOR condition. The index makes the database look like it contains only the records matching the WHILE condition. The WHILE condition operates similarly to the FOR condition. For example, consider the following code fragment:

```
field Id, State, ZipCode, LastName in CUSTOMER
use CUSTOMER new via "DBFNTX"
index on State + Id to CUSTSTA
seek "MN"
index on ZipCode + LastName to TEMP ;
   while State == "MN"
```

At this point, we have two indexes. All customer records are in CUSTSTA.NTX, which will be updated if records are added or modified (and the index is open at the time). The TEMP.NTX index contains only the index entries for records of customers in the state of Minnesota, and the index is not updated if records are added or modified.

It is important to consider the SEEK command immediately preceding the INDEX ON..WHILE command. If the first record in the database does not match the WHILE condition, the resulting index will be empty. Clipper does not start processing at the first record in the database when a WHILE condition is specified; it starts wherever the record pointer is positioned. When the TEMP.NTX controls the database, it appears as though only Minnesota customers are in the database (as in the next example). The records are sorted in zip code order, and within the same zip code by last name.

```
use CUSTOMER new index TEMP via "DBFNTX":
go top
do while .not. CUSTOMER->( eof() )
   ? CUSTOMER->LastName, CUSTOMER->ZipCode
   skip alias CUSTOMER
enddo
```

You can combine the WHILE and FOR conditions. The following example illustrates such a combination. Here, the only records in the TEMP2.NTX index are Minnesotans between the age of 16 and 60 inclusive, sorted by zip code, and further sorted by last name within the same zip code. The CUSTSTA.NTX index was created in an earlier example.

```
field ZipCode, LastName, Age, State
use CUSTOMER new index CUSTSTA via "DBFNTX"
seek "MN"
index on ZipCode + LastName to TEMP2 ;
   while State == "MN" ;
   for Age >= 16 .and. Age <= 60
```

The WHILE clause is supported by drivers NTX and CDX.

When and why to use a WHILE condition

Use a WHILE condition when you want to index only a portion of a database for temporary processing or reporting. Clipper can probably build an index with a WHILE condition faster, because it does not need to read all of the database's records. Exact speed depends on how many records match the condition. The resulting index file will be smaller as well because it will only contain keys for records that match the WHILE condition. Indexes with a WHILE condition also have the same encapsulation benefits as discussed earlier in this chapter for FOR conditions.

But remember that indexes created with a WHILE condition are not updated. Keep their temporary nature in mind when naming them. Because WHILE indexes are temporary, you need not be as concerned about the presence of user-defined functions or variables in the index key expression. We recommend deleting such indexes as soon as the routine that creates them no longer needs them.

The INDEX ON..UNIQUE Clause

The UNIQUE clause lets only unique keys be added to the index. As a result, instead of one key in the index for each record in the database you get only one occurrence of each distinct key value. UNIQUE can be used successfully in conjunction with any other index clause.

Even though the results of the process do not include every index key, Clipper still must evaluate each record in the database, and—unless a WHILE condition is specified—Clipper will start at the first record in the database and process each record. Consider the following example:

```
field ZipCode in CUSTOMER
use CUSTOMER new via "DBFNTX"
index on ZipCode to TEMPZIP unique
```

The resulting TEMPZIP.NTX index has one key entry for each unique zip code in the CUSTOMER.DBF database. Suppose a database contains 5000 customer records and every customer lives in the Minneapolis-St. Paul metropolitan area. The resulting index may have only a dozen entries on the list of distinct zip codes. The process would look like this:

```
local nZips
use CUSTOMER index TEMPZIP via "DBFNTX"
count to nZips
? "Number of ZipCodes represented:", nZips
```

Ordinarily a relationship exists between an index key value and the associated database record, which is the fundamental purpose of an index. A UNIQUE index has such a pairing but should not be used. In the preceding example, an index entry for the value 55439 could be paired with record 722 in the database, but the pairing is coincidental and no more significant than any other record with the same zip code. UNIQUE indexes are similar to those with WHILE conditions because when a user adds, deletes, or modifies a record, the index may not be maintained properly. In the case of UNIQUE, many modifications may *appear* to have been handled correctly, but do not rely on this behavior.

UNIQUE is supported by drivers NTX, NDX, MDX, and CDX.

When and why to use UNIQUE

Among all the index features, UNIQUE is probably used least often. UNIQUE indexes are invaluable when you need to know the range of values present in a database. They are also useful for checking the integrity of fields that are supposed to be unique; a UNIQUE index should yield the same number of index keys as an index without UNIQUE. However, such indexes are temporary and should not be used for enforcing uniqueness. Future releases of new data drivers will probably change this behavior, but for now none of Clipper's bundled drivers can enforce uniqueness.

A UNIQUE index may be small in size when the collection of unique key values is limited compared to the number of database records. Processing a database under the control of a UNIQUE index is correspondingly faster. The only alternative to UNIQUE involves storing unique keys in an array, or pointing to another database. Neither alternative is as fast or efficient as creating a UNIQUE index.
Despite the nature of the results, Clipper still must evaluate every record while creating the UNIQUE index, and the resulting index is not guaranteed to be maintained correctly when records are added, deleted, or modified. UNIQUE indexes are considered temporary.

The INDEX ON..DESCENDING clause

The DESCENDING clause sorts the resulting index keys in reverse alphabetical order (that is, *Z* to *A*). Clipper uses the ASCII character numbering system to determine order. If your database fields contain upper- and lowercase characters, use the UPPER( ) function to ensure consistent results.

DESCENDING is supported by drivers NTX, MDX, and CDX.

The opposite of DESCENDING is ASCENDING, which is the default sort order. As a rule, you need not specify ASCENDING, but if you frequently use DESCENDING index keys it would not hurt to document the commands clearly and explicitly by including ASCENDING where appropriate.

Previous versions of Clipper required the DESCEND( ) function to create descending order indexes. Using DESCEND( ) is now recommended only in situations when you need to sort just a subset of the key expression. Use the DESCENDING clause whenever the entire key is to be sorted descending.

The effects of DESCENDING

When you use DESCENDING, Clipper creates an inverted version of the index. For example, the alphabetic string AARON is placed at the end of the spectrum, while ZYSKI is placed near the top of the list. Here's an example:

```
field LastName, Id in CUSTOMER
use CUSTOMER new via "DBFNTX"
index on left(LastName,5) + Id ;
   to CUSTNAME descending
```

If Bob Aaronson and Sue Zyskilinski are alphabetically the first and last names in the database, then the following is true:

```
go top
?  CUSTOMER->LastName // Zyskilinski
go bottom
?  CUSTOMER->LastName // Aaronson
```

The concept of a descending sort order applies to all data types. You may have to convert noncharacter field types to strings in order to combine them. Following is an example that produces an index sorted by customer balance, starting with the highest. When customers have the same balance, the index further sorts by the ID number, putting the highest ID number first.

```
field Id, Balance in CUSTOMER
use CUSTOMER new via "DBFNTX"
index on str(Balance,6) + Id ;
   to CUSTBAL descending
go top
?  "Largest balance is:", CUSTOMER->Balance
```

The SEEK command is not affected by the DESCENDING clause, which is not the case when the DESCEND( ) function is used. Assuming that SMITH exists in a LastName field, the following are true:

```
field LastName in CUSTOMER
select CUSTOMER
index on LastName to CUSTNAM1 descending
seek "SMITH"
?  found()       // .T.
index on descend(LastName) to CUSTNAM2
seek "SMITH"
?  found()       // .F.
seek descend("SMITH")
?  found()       // .T.
```

When and why to use DESCENDING

Sometimes reversing the natural (ascending) sort order produces an index better suited to your needs. This is often the case with dates and numbers. DESCENDING is useful when you need large numbers or recent dates at the top of a list.

Processing a database with a DESCENDING index is more natural than the equivalent tactic of starting at the bottom of an index and skipping backward through the list. However, be wary of combining the DESCENDING clause and an index expression that contains the DESCEND( ) function. The operation may work as you intend it to, but the results can be quite confusing when the two operations negate each other for certain parts of the key.

The INDEX ON..EVAL and EVERY clauses

EVAL and EVERY are supported by drivers NTX and CDX.

Creating an index can be a time-consuming operation. It is good practice to display a "Wait..." message on the screen to tell users that the application is busy and unavailable. Moreover, this also reassures users that the computer is not hanging! However, users do not know if the computer, for example, will be busy long enough to fetch coffee. And how much time should pass before a user suspects the computer of actually being frozen? A system can lock up tightly but still flash "Wait..." indefinitely.

The EVAL and EVERY clauses give programmers a clean way to display status information while the database is building an index. EVAL and EVERY replace many of the awkward workarounds used in versions of Clipper prior to Release 5.2. The EVAL clause also gives the end-user a way to terminate the indexing operation without interrupting and exiting the entire application.

The effects of EVAL and EVERY

While creating index keys, Clipper evaluates the code block you supply. The code block is evaluated once for each record in the database unless you specify a different frequency with the optional EVERY clause. Consider this example:

```
local nFreq
field Id in CUSTOMER
cls
use CUSTOMER new via "DBFNTX"
?  "Each dot indicates 100 records processed"
?  "out of " + ltrim(str(lastrec())) + " total."
?
index on Id to CUSTID ;
   eval {|| IndexStatus()}  every 100
?
?  "Done."
```

The INDEXSTATUS( ) function must be linked into the application, and must return a logical value. A return of .T. tells the indexing operation to continue, while .F. tells the process to terminate. Here is an example of a relatively crude but effective status function that does not allow interruptions:

```
function IndexStatus()
   ?? chr(250)
return .t.
```

In practice, the display's appearance—its color, use of boxes and menus, and other features—should conform to the rest of the application. Listing 19.1 gives an example of code that can be used for a more ambitious and self-maintaining display function. The source code comments describe the purpose of the parameters, as for example:

```
local nFreq
field Id in CUSTOMER
use CUSTOMER new via "DBFNTX" nFreq := 100
@  8,5 say "Indexing: Wait..."
index on Id to CUSTID ;
   eval {|| IndexStatus(10,5,nFreq)}  every nFreq
IndexStatus()
@  8,5 say "Indexing completed."
```

Listing 19.1 General-purpose index status function (NTXSTAT.PRG)

```
/*
   NtxStat.prg   General-purpose index status display.
*/
function IndexStatus( nRow, nCol, nFrequency, nTotal )
/*

   Display or reset an index status display.
   nRow          Row in which to display
   nCol          Column in which to display
   nFrequency    How often function will be called
   nTotal         Total record count expected
```

Returns .T. if ESC not pressed, else .F, which conforms to the requirements of an INDEX ON..EVAL clause.

Note: If no parameters are passed to it, indicates the function should clean up the screen and restore what used to be underneath.

When nCount is equal to 0, it indicates it is the first call to this function in an index creation context, and the nonchanging portion of the status display should be displayed.

```
*/
    #include "inkey.ch"
    #include "box.ch"
    #define WIDTH 18
    #define DEPTH 4
    #define COLOR_HI    "+W/R"
    #define COLOR_LOW   "N/R"
    static nCount := 0
    static aScr
    local cClr

//  No parameters passed, time to clean up,
//  providing that there is something on the screen.
//

if (pcount() == 0) .and. (aScr != nil)
    restscreen(aScr[1], aScr[2], ;
    aScr[1] + DEPTH,  ;
    aScr[2] + WIDTH,  ;
    aScr[3])
nCount := 0
     aScr := nil

    //  Update the status display
else
    //  nCount is zero only the first time called, so
    //  this is our opportunity to display background
    //  part of the status and save what's underneath.
    //
```

```
    if nCount == 0
    aScr := nRow, nCol, savescreen(nRow, nCol, ;
    nRow + DEPTH, nCol + WIDTH )
    dispbox(nRow, nCol, nRow + DEPTH, nCol + WIDTH, ;
    B_SINGLE + " ", COLOR_HI)
    @ nRow +2, nCol +2 ;
       say "% Complete:" color COLOR_LOW
    endif

    nCount += nFrequency
    @ nRow +2, nCol +14 ;
       say round((nCount / nTotal) * 100, 0) ;
       picture "999" color COLOR_HI
    endif

return inkey() != K_ESC
// eof NtxStat.prg
```

The function demonstrated can also interrupt the indexing process if a user hits the Esc key. Because the function is only called once every 100 records (in the example), it might take a few seconds to respond. If you specify an EVAL function that allows interruptions, you must check whether an interruption occurred and take the appropriate next step, because the index is incomplete.

When and why to use EVAL and EVERY

Whenever you might keep an end-user waiting while your application builds an index (or indexes), you should display enough status information for the user to decide whether to wait or do something else while the application crunches data. The benefits of a status display and an interrupt option are obvious. Professional programmers should always provide a status display.

As a caveat, remember that the function specified with EVAL will be called repeatedly, depending on the frequency of the call and the number of records to be processed. The function should work as quickly and efficiently as possible so it will not unduly burden the indexing process. A slow and complex function should be called less frequently to avoid slowing the entire operation.

The INDEX ON..TAG clause

The TAG clause is the way Clipper associates orders (indexes) with order bags (index files). (See "The order management system" section at the end of this chapter for details about this terminology.)

TAG is supported by drivers NTX, NDX, MDX, and CDX. All drivers except Paradox (DBPX) support TAG, but it is only useful when you use the dBASE IV (DBFMDX) and FoxPro (DBFCDX) drivers. This is a very slick feature of the replaceable database driver concept. RDDs let you discuss a feature in general without dealing with the physical storage details. Any RDD that supports the TAG clause is syntactically the same as the others.

TAG is used to associate multiple indexes with a single file and thereby cut down on the number of file handles required at each workstation. Reducing file handles is valuable, but an even more important benefit is no longer having to remember which indexes are associated with which database, and consequently, which indexes must be open during database modifications.

If you don't use TAG but create multiple physical index files, you have to remember which indexes go with which database. Worse, if you modify the database and neglect to open all the associated index files, you will loose data integrity. For example, if you maintain separate index files for customer Id and zip code, and add a new record without the zip code index open, the zip code index will not contain a reference to the new record and will make the database appear as if the new record is missing. Similar integrity errors occur if you modify an existing zip code without having the index open; the change is not reflected in the index.

Finally, indexes (orders) in a single index file (an order bag) can be identified by symbolic names, such as ZIPCODE, when first opened, rather than by ordinal position. Without TAG, confusion and errors may result from inconsistent index management.

Proper use of TAG should produce less source code, code that is easier to read, easier to maintain, and more reliable. Following are examples that illustrate the differences. First, an example of an operation that does not use TAG:

```
// First, create indexes
field Id, ZipCode, TypeCode in CUSTOMER
use CUSTOMER new via "DBFNTX"
index on Id to CUSTID
index on ZipCode + Id to CUSTZIP
index on TypeCode + Id to CUSTTYPE
close database
// Result: one DBF and three NTX files.

// Next, at some future time, open them
use CUSTOMER new
set index to CUSTID, CUSTZIP, CUSTTYPE

// Specify which index to apply
?  "Do we have customers in ZipCode 55439?"
select CUSTOMER
set order to 2
seek "55439"
if CUSTOMER->( found() )
   ?? " Yes."
endif
```

Next is the same example using tags. Note in this example how the individual indexes in the file are recognized automatically and are specified by TAG names rather than numbers. Also note that, because the TAG names are already associated with the CUSTOMER.DBF file, there is no need to burden the TAG name with CUST or other labels to help programmers document the association when no other context is available.

```
// First, create indexes
request DBFMDX
field Id, ZipCode, TypeCode in CUSTOMER
use CUSTOMER new via "DBFMDX"
index on Id tag ID to CUSTORD
index on ZipCode + Id tag ZIPCODE to CUSTORD
```

```
index on TypeCode + Id tag TYPECODE to CUSTORD
close database
// Result: One DBF and one MDX file.

// Next, at some future time, open them
use CUSTOMER new via "DBFMDX"
set index to CUSTORD

// Specify which index to apply
?  "Do we have customers in ZipCode 55439?"
select CUSTOMER
set order to tag ZIPCODE
seek "55439"
if CUSTOMER->( found() )
   ?? " Yes."
endif
```

Unlike these simple examples, in practice the source code that creates indexes is almost always distinct from the code that later opens and uses them. The source code that opens the database and indexes is also likely to be distant from the code that performs SEEK and other operations affected by the index order.

For example, imagine that CREATE.PRG contains the code for creating the indexes, that line 52 of EDITOR.PRG opens these indexes, and that lines 145, 298, and 451 each depend on one or more of the indexes to search or update the database.

```
/*
   CREATE.PRG: Creates indexes
*/
//... see INDEX ON examples above

/*

EDITOR.PRG: modifies the database
*/
//... line 52: open database and indexes
//...line 145: seek on Id
//... line 298: modify ZipCode
//... line 451: seek on TypeCode
```

Using "regular" separate index files, the authors of CREATE.PRG and EDITOR.PRG must remain synchronized. If CREATE.PRG adds an index, EDITOR.PRG must open the file to keep from losing integrity and becoming useless. Line 52 (where the database and indexes are opened) and the others have a direct relationship based on the order in which indexes are opened. If Index 2 is by zip code, it must remain by zip code or the lines below may not work consistently. What a terrible situation!

Using TAG indexes, the authors of CREATE.PRG and EDITOR.PRG can remain largely ignorant of each other. If CREATE.PRG adds a few indexes, EDITOR.PRG will open them correctly without any extra effort on anyone's part. Line 52 (where the database is opened) opens the index file and automatically associates all the TAG names with the database work area. Finally, the lines further down in EDITOR.PRG refer to a TAG by name, not by number, so they too are unaffected by changes to the number or position of TAGs in the index file. Finally, if someone deletes a TAG on which your routine relies, you (appropriately!) get a run-time error rather than unusual and incorrect results. If you specify index orders by number, as in SET ORDER TO 2, a second index will form in the list of orders and your routine will continue to run, but with the wrong order selected.

When and why to use TAG

If you use the MDX or CDX drivers, use TAG all the time. It offers immediate benefits without any disadvantages. If you use other drivers that support only one index per file, you gain nothing in the way of file handles but you can select orders from the list by TAG name rather than position number, so some benefit results. The highlights include:

- Fewer file handles get used
- Automatic integrity maintenance
- Use of symbolic names versus numbers

The benefits of using TAGs are worth the time it takes to become comfortable with the new terminology and syntax. However, you will need to think about what's going on and may need to change your programming tactics.

Without TAG, it is a simple matter to eliminate indexes—just delete the file and the index is gone. Using TAG, you have a single file containing 1..N index structures. If you delete this file, they all disappear. The DELETE TAG command is used to delete a specified TAG from the file without disturbing the others. Follow this procedure:

```
use CUSTOMER new via "DBFMDX"
set index to CUSTORD
delete tag TypeCode in CUSTORD
```

Compact indexes (DBFCDX)

Compact indexes are based on the premise that much of the data stored in an index file is repeated and can be compressed. The DBFCDX driver uses compression to significantly reduce the amount of space required to store an index. The space savings can range from small to incredible, depending on the nature of the data in the index. A 50 percent or greater reduction is not uncommon.

Compact indexes are supported by the CDX driver.

The effects of using CDX

When you use the DBFCDX driver, as the following example illustrates, the resulting index file is smaller than a functionally equivalent index created by any of the other drivers.

```
request DBFCDX
field Id, ZipCode in CUSTOMER
use CUSTOMER new via "DBFCDX"
index on ZipCode + Id tag ZIP to CUSTORD
```

When and why to use CDX

Obviously, you use compact indexes when space is at a premium. Smaller indexes leave more room for data, and a smaller penalty for carrying numerous special-purpose indexes. For example, maintaining indexes to support reports or queries may be difficult to justify when they occupy 25 megabytes of disk space. Reducing storage requirements to 10 megabytes could make a major difference. However, the compression process takes time, which is often a commodity more precious than disk space. Compression requires time both to create the index and, incrementally, to store new records or modify existing ones.

The order management system

Clipper employs new terminology when documenting and discussing index-related features and functions. If you are accustomed to Clipper 5.01 or earlier releases, or are used to one of the other xBase languages (FoxPro, dBASE, and the others), the new jargon can be confusing or outright frustrating. However, the new words and phrases were not intended to annoy and confuse you! In fact, the existing messy state of managing indexes is what prompted a reorganization of indexes. Clipper can now support diverse data drivers because it does not stubbornly cling to outdated and potentially misleading terminology.

This new way to think of and describe indexes is called the order management system (OMS). OMS provides a platform to expand to future data drivers that may not even exist. This is possible because OMS moves away from product- and vendor-specific terminology and employs instead a higher level of abstraction where all index features and functions are discussed using the same terms. Not surprisingly, programmers accustomed to the earlier terms cannot grasp this new jargon immediately. Let's start with the topmost index-related term and go down the list.

Term	Definition
order bag	The physical storage mechanism that contains index information. In all current data drivers, the order bag is a file. Future data drivers could use RAM or server tables for storage, rather than a specific file on a specific disk.
order	A collection of index information for a single INDEX ON operation; results are stored in an order bag. Some data drivers let more than one order be stored in the same order bag; others allow only a single order per bag. In Clipper 5.01, an order bag can contain only one order, so the concept is not very useful A single order bag (an index file) can contain as many as 50 individual orders (the result of INDEX ON) when the CDX data driver is used.
order name	(Also called a TAG.) A way to name a specific order in an order bag so you can refer to it later. The collection of orders in an order bag are not organized in any useful manner, and will not maintain an order anyway. It is much safer (and easier to write and maintain) to use the TAG name. The TAG clause of the INDEX ON command is used to assign the order name.
order list	The collection of order names associated with a database at any particular time. Multiple order bags may exist for any given database. Each order bag you open contributes its list of order names to the master list of orders for that database. The SET INDEX TO command establishes the initial list of orders. The optional ADDITIVE clause lets you add more orders to the order list.
order focus	The order controlling the database. The order focus comes from one of the orders in the current order list. If no order has focus, the database is in the “natural” order (the order in which records were appended to the database). The SET ORDER TO command changes the focus. Use the order name—for example, SET ORDER TO TAG ZIPCODE—rather than relying on the numbering sequence.

The Clipper preprocessor converts all of the index-related commands to function calls. You can mix and match functions and commands as needed. Often, the command versions of the index operations are easier to write and maintain than the function versions. For example, INDEX ON is easy to read, easy to write, and easy to understand and maintain.

Other OMS features are accessible only through function calls. The following list gives a brief overview of the functions you might want to use.

Function	**Description**
ORDBAGEXT( )	The default extension for order bag files
ORDBAGNAME( )	The order bag name that contains a specified order name
ORDCREATE( )	Create an order and put it in an order bag (INDEX ON...)
ORDDESTROY( )	Delete a specified order name from an order bag
ORDFOR( )	The FOR clause for an order (if any)
ORDKEY( )	The index key expression for an order
ORDLISTADD( )	Add specified orders to the current order list (SET INDEX TO..ADDITIVE)
ORDLISTCLEAR( )	Clear the current order list (SET INDEX TO)
ORDLISTREBUI( )	Rebuild all orders in the current order list (REINDEX)
ORDNAME( )	The name of a specified order in the current order list
ORDNUMBER( )	The position number of an order in the order list
ORDSETFOCUS( )	Set focus to an order in the current order list (SET ORDER TO...)

Summary

Table 19.1 summarizes the index features discussed in this chapter with respect to the data drivers that support them.

Table 19.1 Index features and data drivers

Feature	Clipper NTX	dBASE III+ NDX	dBASE IV MDX	FoxPro CDX	Paradox PX
FOR	Yes	No	Yes	Yes	No
WHILE	Yes	No	No	Yes	No
UNIQUE	Yes	Yes	Yes	Yes	No
DESCENDING	Yes	No	Yes	Yes	No
EVAL & EVERY	Yes	No	No	Yes	No
TAG	Yes-No*	Yes-No*	Yes	Yes	No
COMPACT INDEXES	No	No	No	Yes	No

* Although the TAG clause is supported, it is fundamentally limited by the fact that only one index (order) can be part of an index file (order bag).

Index operations have come a long way in Clipper. New features, such as the TAG clause, make indexes more reliable and easier to use. Others, such as the FOR clause, make indexes considerably more flexible. The order management system paves the way for future extensions without the associated syntax hassles.

CHAPTER 20

Searching and Querying

Searching is the process of trying to determine which record or records meet the search criteria. Querying is the process of determining information about the entire database or a subset of it. For example, a search would indicate which record contained the name Smith while a query might count how many Smiths appear in the database.

In this chapter we will explore how Clipper can be used to search the database, both with and without the benefit of index files. We will also discuss some ways to expand searching techniques. Finally, the concept of a file subset will be described, as well as Clipper techniques for creating one.

Locating your data

The easiest method to find a particular record is to perform a linear search. The primary benefit of a linear search is that the database order is unimportant. The drawback is that of speed, or lack thereof. A linear search starts at the top of the file and checks every record until a match is found. For a small database, under 100 records, this process will be performed fairly quickly. If the database is large, the linear search technique should be used only if no other options are available.

LOCATE

Clipper implements a linear search using the LOCATE command. Its syntax is:

```
LOCATE <scope> FOR <condition> [ WHILE <condition> ]
```

The <scope> determines both the starting point and the number of records to process. The default scope is ALL, which starts at the top of the file and searches every record. The possible <scope> values are shown in Table 20.1:

Table 20.1 Scope values

ALL	Go to the top of the file and process every record.
NEXT <n>	Only process the next <n> records from the current position.
RECORD <n>	Only process record number <n>.
REST	Process all records from current record through the end of the file.

The FOR <condition> indicates what we are searching for and is a required part of the command. Once the <condition> is met, LOCATE stops and sets FOUND() to true (.t.) If none of the records within the scope meets the condition, the LOCATE command will set FOUND() to false (.f.).

The WHILE <condition> is used to narrow down the records which might be returned by the LOCATE command. The condition specified after the WHILE keyword indicates how long the search should continue. As soon as a record fails to meet the WHILE condition, the LOCATE command stops and sets FOUND() to .f. Let's look at some examples:

Assume we have a database file listing all sales representatives in each state for all states. The structure of the file is shown in Figure 20.1.

Figure 20.1 Sales Rep structure

Name	*Type*	*Length*	*Decimals*
State	Char	2	0
Sales_rep	Char	3	0
Ytd_sales	Numeric	12	2

To locate the first sales rep in California, we would use

```
locate all for State == "CA"
```

If the database is ordered by state, we could use:

```
locate all for State == "CA"      // Find first CA salesman
   locate rest for Ytd_sales > 5000 while State == "CA"
```

These commands would cause the first salesman with year-to-date sales of over $5,000 to be found.

The LOCATE command can be continued from the current point by either the CONTINUE command or by changing the scope of the command.

CONTINUE

The CONTINUE command causes the LOCATE command to search for the next record which meets the condition. Its syntax is simply:

```
CONTINUE
```

For example, Listing 20.1 illustrates a function which uses a loop to list all California sales representatives within the .DBF file.

Listing 20.1 Locate/Continue loop

```
use SALESREP new
locate all for SALESREP->State == "CA"
do while found()
   ? SALESREP->Sales_rep, SALESREP->Ytd_sales
   continue
enddo
```

One problem with CONTINUE however, is that it does not maintain the scope nor the while condition of the previous LOCATE. This basically restricts the use of CONTINUE to searches where the scope is ALL and no WHILE condition is used.

Changing scope

If the CONTINUE command cannot be used, another LOCATE command should be issued with a scope of REST and the WHILE condition specified. Listing 20.2 illustrates how the California sales reps with year-to-date sales over $5,000 could be listed if the .DBF file were ordered by state.

Listing 20.2 Locate loop

```
use SALESREP new
locate all for State == "CA" .and. ;
   Ytd_sales > 5000          // First CA sales rep
do while found()
   ? SALESREP->Sales_rep, SALESREP->Ytd_sales
   locate rest for Ytd_sales > 5000 while State == "CA"
enddo
```

The use of the LOCATE command allows you to search a .DBF file regardless of how it is sorted without requiring an index file. The speed of performance however, is directly related to the number of records Clipper can read into memory at one time. For databases with many records but small record sizes or with a small number of records, LOCATE may be fast enough. For larger databases, indexes and/or sorts would probably be better.

Finding it more quickly

You can speed up searches dramatically if the database is in order by the key you are looking for. Clipper provides two ways to order the database by keys: sorting and indexing. Sorting physically rearranges the records in the database while indexing prepares a second file, called the index, which logically orders the record in the database. The functions available for searching depend upon how the database is ordered.

Sorted databases

You can create a new sorted database file from an existing .DBF by using the Clipper SORT command. Its syntax is:

```
SORT TO <cDbf> ON <cField>/<opts> ;
    <scope> WHILE <cond> FOR <cond>
```

The sort command creates a new .DBF file copied from the current work area. The new .DBF is physically sorted in the specified order.

<cDbf> specifies the name of the new file to create. If no extension is specified, it will default to .DBF.

<cField> indicates the fields that the new file should be sorted on. More than one field may be specified. The first field is the primary sort key, the second field specified is the secondary key, and so on. Clipper supports any number of sort fields.

Normally the fields will be sorted in ascending case-sensitive sequence. The <opts> can be specified to change the default. Valid options are listed in Table 20.2.

Table 20.2 Sort field options

A - Ascending order (this is the default).
D - Descending order.
C - Case insensitive, known as dictionary order.

The options are specified by putting them immediately following the field name, separated by a slash character (/). The A and D options cannot both be specified or Clipper will produce a syntax error. You can put two options together after the slash if need be. Only one slash should be used regardless of the number of options.

At least one field must be specified for the SORT command to operate. If multiple fields are used, it is possible to have one field descending and another field ascending.

The <scope> indicates which records should be sorted. The <scope> is optional and defaults to ALL records. If specified, any scope listed in Table 20.1 can be used.

The while <cond> is an optional clause which can be used to restrict the records included in the sort operation. Only records starting at the current record and ending when the condition fails will be included in the sorted database.

The for <cond> is also an optional clause which can be used to specify the records which get included in the sort operation. Only records meeting the condition will be included. If a record does not meet the condition, that record will not be included. Sort performs much of its work in memory and then writes it to a temporary disk file. The SORT operation uses at least three file handles (one each for the original .DBF, the new .DBF, and the temporary file). If the original .DBF file contains a memo field, at least two more handles will be required. A DOS error 4 on a SORT operation indicates not enough handles are available to perform the sort.

If the file being sorted is empty, a run-time error will occur when attempting to sort the file. You should include a test to establish that at least one record exists before you perform the SORT command.

Using the sorted file

Once the SORT operation is complete, you have a second .DBF file. You could erase the old file and rename the sorted version to take advantage of the speed increase offered by using a sorted file. For example:

```
use CUSTOMER new
if lastrec() > 0
   sort to New_cust on id_code/A all
   if file("New_cust.dbf")
      close databases
      rename CUSTOMER.DBF to CUSTOMER.OLD
      rename NEW_CUST.DBF to CUSTOMER.DBF
   endif
endif
use
use CUSTOMER new
```

It is important to realize that the sorted file will quickly become unsorted if you append records into the file. A sorted database should be used when you expect very little update activity to occur in the file. In one particular application file handles were at a premium and not available for indexes. The system used two files, a sorted master listing and a daily transaction log. Lookups were performed first against the sorted master using the Bsearch() UDF from Listing 20.3. If that failed, the daily transaction file was searched using LOCATE. At the end of the day, the two files were merged and a sorted database was produced for the next day.

Restricting locate

If the database is sorted on the key you are searching for, you can speed the function of the LOCATE command by restricting the records it checks by using the WHILE option. For example, assuming the database is sorted by Sales. The command

```
locate all for Sales == 1500
```

will search the entire database. However, since the database is sorted, we can restrict the LOCATE command by adding the WHILE clause. For example:

```
locate all for Sales == 1500 while Sales <= 1500
```

This command tells the LOCATE command to stop searching if the Sales field has a value above 1500. Since the database is sorted by sales, we know that once the sales amount exceeds 1500, it is impossible to find a sales value equal to 1500.

Bsearch()

Another technique to use with a sorted database is the binary find. The binary search works by cutting the search space in half repeatedly until it either finds a match or fails. Figure 20.2 illustrates how a binary search would work to find the letter F:

Figure 20.2 Binary search

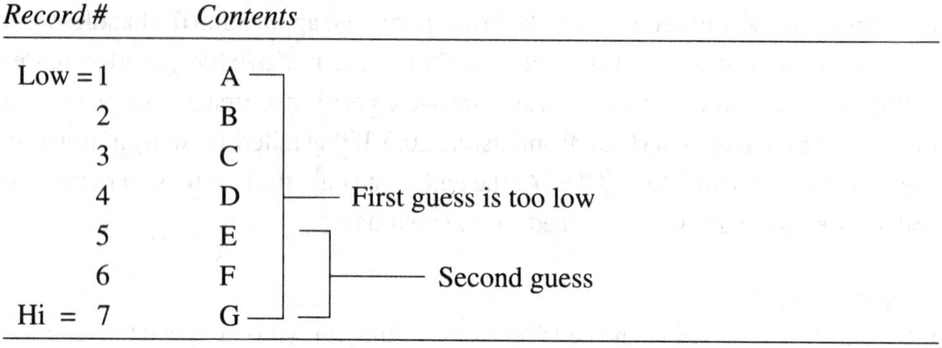

Record #	*Contents*	
Low = 1	A	
2	B	
3	C	
4	D	First guess is too low
5	E	
6	F	Second guess
Hi = 7	G	

First guess is four : low + high (1+7) divided by two
Second guess is six : new low = midpoint (four) +one or five
same high of seven
new midpoint is (low+high (5+7) / 2)

The Bsearch() user-defined function in Listing 20.3 can be used to perform a binary search on a sorted database. Its syntax is:

```
Bsearch( <field>,<key> )
```

where <field> is the numeric field number to be searched and <key> is the value to search for. If the search is successful, the database will be positioned on the proper record and the function will return true. If the search fails, a false value will be returned.

Listing 20.3 Bsearch()

```
function Bsearch( nfield,the_key )
local retval:=.f., bottom:=Lastrec(), top:=1, mid:=0
do while top <= bottom .and. !retval
   mid := int( (top+bottom)/2 )
   goto mid
   if fieldget(nfield) == the_key
    retval :=.t.
```

```
   elseif fieldget(nfield) < the_key
     bottom := mid +1
   else
      top := mid -1
   endif
enddo
return retval
```

Indexed databases

A database file may also be indexed to provide quick access to the information in the file. The index is a separate file which must be opened and updated whenever the .DBF file is opened. See Chapter 18 for more information on opening and working with index files.

An index is created by reading each record in the file and generating a key for it. That key and the record number are stored in a binary tree for rapid retrieval. An index file is created by selecting the work area and specifying the expression that should be used. The syntax to create an index is:

```
INDEX ON <expression> TO <cFilename>
```

If a database has more than one index, only one index is the controlling index at any one time. This index determines the expression that SEEK and FIND operate against. Each index is numbered ordinally by its position on the SET INDEX TO command. The default controlling index is the first one. The SET ORDER TO command can be used to switch the controlling index to another index in the list. The syntax for SET ORDER TO is:

```
SET ORDER TO <nOrder>
```

The <nOrder> must be between one and the number of indexes opened with the .DBF file. The order can be zero, which causes the database to be viewed in record number order. Regardless of the index order, all open indexes will be updated when the database is written to.

Case considerations

When indexing on character data it is important to keep in mind that indexes are case-sensitive. You should create your index using either UPPER() or LOWER() and perform the lookup based upon the proper case.

For example:

```
index on upper(emp_name) to employee
mname := "McMaster"
seek upper(mname)
```

By using the UPPER() or LOWER() function in the index expression, you can prevent the end-user from not finding his data because it was entered in a different case than the one in which it is stored.

Indexing on dates

If a date field is to be used in an index, the DTOS() function can convert the date into a string format that will properly list dates in chronological order. The format of DTOS() is YYYYMMDD. This format stays the same regardless of the setting of the SET DATE command.

For example:

```
index on dtos(hire_date) to seniority
mhired := ctod("01/22/89")
seek dtos(mhired)
```

Use of the DTOS() function is particularly important if the index is being used to display the data in date order.

DESCEND()

Indexes are normally created in ascending order. You can create a descending index by using the DESCEND() function. DESCEND() takes a parameter of any type and returns its complemented form. For example,

```
? Descend("Clipper")    // produces  ╜öùÉÉ¢Ä
? Descend(1991)         // produces  -1991.00
```

To create a descending index use:

```
INDEX ON DESCEND( <expression> ) TO <ntx_file>
```

Since DESCEND() is in EXTEND.LIB rather than CLIPPER.LIB, you will need to declare the function as external if you do not explicitly use it in your code. This would occur if DESCEND() was used in an index expression which was created by a different application, but had to be updated from within your application.

DESCEND() and its funny-looking return values are discussed in more detail in Chapter 18.

Clipper 5.2 allows you to specify descending indexes whan you create an index file. See Chapter 19 for more information.

SEEK

The SEEK command is used to search an index for a particular key. SEEK compares its parameters with all entries in the controlling index file. If a match is found, FOUND() is set to true and EOF() is set to false. The database is positioned at the found record. The syntax for SEEK is:

```
SEEK <expression>
```

The <expression> must agree with the expression that the database is currently indexed on. If the type of the expression does not agree with the type of the index, a type mismatch run-time error will occur. If the type agrees, but the expression is not the same, Clipper will SEEK the key anyway. The results probably will not be the key you are looking for.

Find

The FIND command works just like the SEEK command with a small exception. The argument to the FIND command does not require quotation marks and is considered a literal value rather than a memory variable. For example:

```
mvar := "Smith"
seek mvar        // Looks for Smith
find mvar        // Looks for mvar
find &mvar.      // Looks for Smith
```

The syntax for the FIND command is:

```
FIND <key_to_find>
```

If the key is found, FOUND() is set to .t. and EOF() is set to .f. In addition, the database is positioned on the FOUND() record.

The FIND command was designed with an interpretive environment in mind. For a user at a dot-prompt, it is more intuitive to specify the parameter without the quotation characters. Since Clipper provides no interpretive environment, FIND is considered a compatibility command and should be replaced by SEEK.

Continuing a SEEK or FIND command

It is important to understand that Clipper enforces the logical order imposed by the index on the file. Once a key is found, the way to determine the next record with the same key is by issuing a SKIP command.

For example, if the SALESREP database was indexed on state, the loop to list all salesmen in California could be coded as shown in Listing 20.4.

Listing 20.4 SEEK loop

```
use SALESREP index STATE new
seek "CA"
do while !eof() .and. State == "CA"
   ? SALESREP->Sales_rep, SALESREP->Ytd_sales
   skip +1
enddo
```

Since the index imposes a logical view, i.e. state order, on the database, the records will be read from the .DBF file in that order. Therefore the SKIP command will move to the next logical record, which might not be the next physical record in the file.

Expanding search capabilities

While the LOCATE and SEEK commands can be used to provide fast lookups of data, they both require the user to know the key they are looking up. For many applications, the user might not know the key value and will need some assistance in finding the proper record. Clipper provides commands which can be used to expand the searching capabilities of the language.

Partial searches

Many times the user knows only the first few characters of the data being sought. A partial search would allow the user to enter the characters he knew and would show a window of records from which the user could choose. Clipper supports partial lookups based on the first characters of the index expression. If a key is sought which is smaller in size than the index key, Clipper will find the first key beginning with those letters. Using a loop and array we could quickly build a picklist for the user to select the record from. Partfind() in Listing 20.5 provides a function to perform a partial search. Its syntax is:

```
<logical>  := Partfind( <seek_expr>,<field_no> )
```

The function returns a logical true if a record was selected and a false if not. It will also position the database to the found record.

Listing 20.5 Partfind()

```
function Partfind(expSeek,field_no)
local x:=0, plist:={}, y:=len(trim(expSeek)), rec:={}
seek trim(expSeek)
if found()
   do while !eof() .and. ;
     trim(expSeek)==substr(fieldget(field_no),1,y)
     Aadd(plist,fieldget(field_no))
     Aadd(rec,recno())
       skip +1
   enddo
   x :=achoice(5,20,15,45,plist,.t.)
   if !empty(x)
      goto rec[x]
     return .t.
   endif
endif
return .f.
```

SOFTSEEK

Clipper allows you to control the position of the record pointer after a SEEK command fails. Normally, if a SEEK command fails, the record pointer is positioned to the last record plus one. The EOF() function will return true and the FOUND() function returns false.

The SET SOFTSEEK command can be used to change the way the record pointer is positioned. If SOFTSEEK is set to ON and a SEEK fails, FOUND() will still return false. EOF(), however, will return false also. This indicates that the database is not positioned at the end of the file but rather is positioned at the next highest key in the .DBF file.

Figure 20.3 illustrates how SOFTSEEK operates:

Figure 20.3 Softseek

Record	*Key value*	*SEEK "Kelly"*
1	Booth	
2	Forcier	FOUND() = .f. / EOF() = .f.
3	Lief	Record number is three
4	Uchman	(Next highest key past Kelly)
5	Yellick	

The syntax for SET SOFTSEEK is:

```
SET SOFTSEEK [ ON | OFF | <logical> ]
```

The default value is OFF. The proximity search in Listing 20.6 uses SOFTSEEK to find records close to the unknown key.

In Clipper 5.2, you can specify soft seeking by adding the SOFTSEEK keyword onto your seek command. For example,

```
set softseek on
seek cKey
set softseek off
```

can be replaced in Clipper 5.2 with:

```
seek cKey softseek
```

Proximity searches

A proximity search is used to search a database for a key value and return a subset of records on either side of the key. It allows a user who does not know the key he is looking for to see keys that are close. He can then choose a key from a list. For example, suppose a customer remembers making a deposit in his bank sometime in the first couple of weeks in July, but does not remember the exact date. To perform a proximity search, the teller might enter July 7 and 7 days. The system would respond by showing a list of all transactions between July 1 and July 14. It does not matter whether a transaction occurred on July 7 or not.

Listing 20.6 contains a function called Psearch() which implements a proximity search feature. Its syntax is:

```
<array> := Psearch( <key>,<nRange>,<nField> )
```

The array returned is a list of record numbers which indicate the range of records around the specified key.

Listing 20.6 Psearch()

```
function Psearch(cKey,nRange,nField)
local arr_:={}
local oldsoft := set(_SET_SOFTSEEK, .T.)
seek cKey
skip -nRange
do while len(arr_) < (nRange*2) .and. !eof()
   aadd(arr_,fieldget(nfield))
   skip +1
enddo
set(_SET_SOFTSEEK,oldsoft)   //restore previous SOFTSEEK setting
return arr_
```

SOUNDEX()

The SOUNDEX() function returns a code that represents a phonetic spelling of a name. It is an attempt to allow names with similar sounds but different spellings to be grouped together. This increases the likelihood of finding a name even if the user is unsure of the spelling.

SOUNDEX() works by building a 4-character key based upon the consonants in the word. This key assigns the same digit to letters that have similar sounds. For example, the name Smith can be spelled as:

Smith
Smythe

The SOUNDEX() code for both spellings of Smith is S530. If the .DBF file is indexed on the SOUNDEX() code, all similar sounding words would be grouped together.

SOUNDEX() is not foolproof as it is possible to create similar SOUNDEX() codes from very different spellings and words. For example, Cajun and Cigna are pronounced differently, but both have the identical SOUNDEX() code of C250.

SOUNDEX() is useful for applications dealing with names. It should not be used as the sole lookup but should be combined with some sort of window selection. Listing 20.7 illustrates a SOUNDEX() lookup function to get a name from the database.

Listing 20.7 SOUNDEX() lookup

```
#include "inkey.ch"
local mname:=space(25), sxname:=""
use CUSTOMER new
index on soundex(CUSTOMER->Name) to cust1
@ 10,10 say "Name..: " get mname
read
if lastkey() <> K_ESC
   sxname := soundex(mname)
   seek sxname
   do while sxname == soundex(CUSTOMER->Name)
      ? CUSTOMER->Name
     skip +1
   enddo
endif
```

Multiple lookup keys

Sometimes more than one index is maintained on a .DBF file. When this occurs, the user may need to look up a key from an index other than the controlling index. To allow the user to do this, you must switch the controlling index to the one the user needs. This is done with the SET ORDER TO command. The syntax is:

```
SET ORDER TO <nOrder>
```

<nOrder> is the ordinal position of the index within the SET INDEX or USE command when the file was opened. For example:

```
#include "inkey.ch"
use CUSTOMER index By_state, By_sales, By_rep new
@ 10,10 say "Enter state ...: " get m_state
@ 11,10 say "  or Sales Rep.: " get m_rep
read
if lastkey() <> K.ESC
   if !empty(m_state)
      set order to 1
    seek m_state
   elseif !empty(m_rep)
    set order to 3
    seek m_rep
   else
    ? "Must enter a rep or a state code"
   endif
endif
```

The controlling index order can be determined by using the INDEXORD() function. Its syntax is:

```
<number> := INDEXORD()
```

The function will return the ordinal number of the controlling index. If zero is returned, the records are not in any logical order controlled by an index, but rather are in record number order.

Optimizing multiple searches

If the user is searching for records meeting two conditions that are both in index expressions, it is necessary to try to determine which expression should be sought first. Usually, whichever condition is likely to have the fewest number of records should be sought first.

For example, assume we had a database of all registered voters in the nation. The database is indexed by sex and state. The user needs to find all women in North Dakota. This problem could be solved by SEEK "F", reading those records and displaying the ones in North Dakota. Since the population of the United States is more than fifty percent women, this search would read through at least half of the database. If the search were reversed, and the state was looked for first, the number of records would be considerably smaller (since less than fifty percent of the population lives in North Dakota.)

Whenever the user needs to look up information which is available in two index files, try to make sure the index with the smaller number of entries is searched first.

Keyword files

A keyword is a word extracted from a larger string that can be used to refer to that string. For example, if you were in a library looking for books on Clipper, you would be interested in any of the titles in Figure 20.4.

Figure 20.4 Sample Clipper Books

Using Clipper
Clipper 5: A Developer's Guide
Developing Applications with Clipper

Unfortunately, there is no easy way to represent the above titles in an index file and still be able to access them by the keyword Clipper. To solve this type of lookup problem, we need to create a keyword file.

A keyword file is a separate .DBF file which contains the appropriate keyword and a pointer to the record in the primary .DBF file. The keyword file is indexed by keywords and it is searched against rather than the main .DBF.

Let's illustrate an example that might allow a video store to look up movies based upon any word from the title. Figure 20.5 contains the database structures we will use.

Figure 20.5 Keyword file .DBF structures

```
File:    VIDEOS.DBF
Index:   Upper(id_code)

 1. TITLE          Char        40   Video title
 2. RATING         Char         4   Movie rating G,PG,PG13,R,X
 3. PRICE          Numeric    6,2   Purchase price
 4. ID_CODE        Char         6   Unique code for each video

File: KEYWORDS.DBF
Index:   Upper(keyword)

 1. KEYWORD        Char        12   Single keyword
 2. ID_CODE        Char         6   Pointer into VIDEOS.DBF
```

As each video is added to the VIDEOS.DBF, an entry is made in the keyword file for each word within the title. If the movie FATAL VISION were added to the VIDEOS.DBF and assigned the code of FATVIS, the two entries added to the keyword file would be:

Keyword	*Id_code*
FATAL	FATVIS
VISION	FATVIS

When the user requests that "something VISION" movie, the system would seek "VISION" in the keyword database, and find the ID_CODE of FATVIS. This ID_CODE would be looked up in the primary database to display the movie title.

Listing 20.8 contains two functions useful for keyword files. The Keyw_Build() function writes entries into the keyword file for a title and code. Its syntax is:

```
Keyw_Build(cTitle,cId_code)
```

<cTitle> is the movie title to be added. <cId_code> is the unique code assigned to this movie.

The Keyw_Find() function returns an array of titles based on the keyword. Its syntax is:

```
<aTitles> := Keyw_Find(cWord)
```

<cWord> is the keyword that the database should be searched for.

Listing 20.8 Keyword functions

```
function Keyw_Build(cTitle,cId_code)
local skip_words:={"A","THE","OF","AND"}
local words:= Parse(upper(cTitle)," ")  // Parse() is from
local jj                                // Chapter 20.
use KEYWORD new index KEYW
for jj := 1 to len(words)
   if ascan(skip_words,words[jj]) == 0
      append blank
      replace keyword with words[jj],id_code with cId_code
   endif
next
return nil

function Keyw_Find(cWord)
local arr_ :={}
use VIDEOS new index VIDS
use KEYWORD new index KEYW
seek upper(cWord)
do while !eof() .and. upper(cWord) == KEYWORD->Keyword
   select VIDEOS
   seek KEYWORD->Id-code
   if found()
```

```
      aadd(arr_, VIDEOS->Title+' '+VIDEOS->Id-code)
   endif
   select KEYWORD
   skip +1
enddo
return arr_
```

Querying the file

Clipper provides commands that allow you to collect information about all records or a subset of records in a .DBF file. These commands process records in the database and perform the indicated operation, either counting, summing fields, or computing their average values. For more complex querying, the DBEVAL() function allows a block of code to be executed for each record in the database.

COUNT

The COUNT command is used to determine the number of records in the database which meet the specified condition. Its syntax is:

```
COUNT TO <nVar> <scope> WHILE <condition> FOR <condition>
```

<nVar> is required and indicates the numeric variable where the results of the count operation should be stored. If <nVar> has not been previously declared, COUNT will create it as a private variable. Its scope will be the current procedure and all procedures called by the current one.

<scope> is optional and indicates which records should be counted. It may be any one of the values in Table 20.1. If the <scope> is not specified, the default is ALL records.

The WHILE <condition> is optional and indicates a logical condition that each record is compared against. If the condition is true, the count operation continues. Once a false condition occurs, COUNT immediately stops.

The FOR <condition> is also optional and indicates a logical condition that each record is compared against. If the condition is true, then that record is included in the count. If false, the record is not included. Regardless of whether or not the record is included, COUNT continues to count records until the end of the scope or a failed WHILE condition.

Listing 20.9 illustrates a few examples of the COUNT command.

Listing 20.9 COUNT examples

```
use CUSTOMER new
count to how_many                 // All customers
count to ca_cust for State == "CA"  // California customers
index on State to cust1
seek "ID"
count to id_cust rest while State == "ID" // Idaho customers
```

COUNT can also be used to check for embedded EOF markers. An embedded EOF marker is a condition which can occur in a .DBF file and cause indexing problems. It usually occurs when the system crashes without properly closing all open files. The function in Listing 20.10 illustrates the use of COUNT to check for EOFs.

Listing 20.10 - Embedded EOF check

```
function CheckEof(DBF_file)
local actual_ct:=0              // Compare actual count with
use (DBF_file) new              // count stored in .DBF header.
count to actual_ct              // If they are not the same,
return (actual_ct<>Lastrec())   // probably an imbedded EOF.
```

If an embedded EOF exists, it can be corrected by following the procedures outlined in Figure 20.6.

Figure 20.6 Removing embedded EOF markers

1. Copy all records up to the EOF marker into a new file.

```
select BAD_FILE
COPY ALL TO NEW FILE1
```

2. Skip past the EOF marker.

```
skip +2
```

3. Copy the remaining records to a new file.

```
COPY REST TO NEWFILE2
```

4. Combine the two files.

```
select NEWFILE1
append from NEWFILE2
```

5. Rename the old file and replace it with the new file.

```
close databases
rename BAD_FILE.DBF to BAD_FILE.OLD
rename NEWFILE1.DBF to BAD_FILE.DBF
```

SUM

The SUM command is used to total up certain fields from the database. Its syntax is:

```
SUM <exp> TO <vars> <scope> WHILE <condition> FOR <condition>
```

<exp> is a single field expression or a list of expressions which will be summed. Each expression must have a corresponding variable in the <vars> list. If the list of expressions and the variable list do not agree in number, a compilation error will result.

<vars> is a single field variable or a list of variables which will be used to hold the results of the data summed. Each variable will hold the sum of the corresponding expression in the <exp> list.

<scope> is optional and indicates which records should be summed. It may be any one of the values in Table 20.1. If the <scope> is not specified, the default is ALL records.

The WHILE <condition> is optional and indicates a logical condition that each record is compared against. If the condition is true, the SUM operation sums this record to a variable and continues. Once a false condition occurs, SUM immediately stops.

The FOR <condition> is also optional and indicates a logical condition that each record is compared against. If the condition is true, then that record is included in the sum. If false, the record is not included. Regardless of whether or not the record is included, SUM continues to process records until the end of the scope or a failed WHILE condition.

Listing 20.11 illustrates some examples of the SUM command.

Listing 20.11 SUM examples

```
use CUSTOMER new
// Balance due for all customers
sum Balance to total_due
// Balance due for CALIFORNIA customers only
sum Balance to calif_due for State == "CA"
// Using WHILE and indexes to speed up the sum command
index on State to cust2
seek "PA"
sum rest Balance to penn_due while State == "PA"
```

AVERAGE

The AVERAGE command is used to calculate averages for numeric fields in a database. Its syntax is:

```
AVERAGE <exp> TO <vars> <scope> WHILE <condition> FOR <condition>
```

<exp> is a single field expression or a list of expressions which will be averaged. Each expression must have a corresponding variable in the <vars> list. If the expression list and variable list do not agree in count, a compilation error will be generated.

<vars> is a single field variable or a list of variables which will be used to hold the results of the data averaged. Each variable will hold the average computed by the corresponding expression in the <exp> list.

<scope> is optional and indicates which records should be averaged. It may be any one of the values in Table 20.1. If the <scope> is not specified, the default is ALL records.

The WHILE <condition> is optional and indicates a logical condition that each record is compared against. If the condition is true, the AVERAGE operation continues. Once a false condition occurs, AVERAGE immediately stops.

The FOR <condition> is also optional and indicates a logical condition that each record is compared against. If the condition is true, then that record is included in the average. If false, the record is not included. Regardless of whether or not the record is included, AVERAGE continues to average records until the end of the scope or a failed WHILE condition.

Listing 20.12 illustrates some examples of the AVERAGE command.

Listing 20.12 AVERAGE examples

```
use CUSTOMER new
// Average balance due for all customers
average balance to total_due
use INVOICES new
// Average past due balances
average inv_total to past_due for ;
      date() - inv_date > 45
```

```
// Average PA salesman over $1,000 in sales
use SALESMEN new
index on State to sale2
seek "PA"
average rest total_sales to pa_avg ;
      for total_sales > 1000 while State == "PA"
```

Efficient processing

One of the dangers of the query operations is that they can cause considerable disk activity. The functions should be used with care to prevent extra disk work. For example, consider the request to count and total all sales within the state of California. Listing 20.13 illustrates one way to approach this problem.

Listing 20.13 COUNT and TOTAL Sales

```
select SALESREP new
count to Sales_ct all for State == "CA"
sum Ytd_sales to tot_sales for State == "CA"
```

This approach will work, but also requires two passes through the database. The same effect can be accomplished as shown in Listing 20.14. Although this listing contains more lines of code, it is actually more efficient since the database is processed only once.

Listing 20.14 COUNT and TOTAL sales

```
local x, sales_ct:=0, tot_sales:=0
select SALESREP new
x:=lastrec()
for k:=1 to x
   if State == "CA"
    sales_ct++
    tot_sales += Ytd_sales
    skip
   endif
next
```

Dbeval()

The DBEVAL() function can be used to process records in a .DBF file and apply a set of code to each record. The COUNT, SUM, and AVERAGE commands are all converted to DBEVAL() function calls by the preprocessor.

The syntax for DBEVAL() is:

```
DBEVAL(<block>,<bFor>,<bWhile>,<nNext>,<nRecord>,<lRest>)
```

<block> is the code block to evaluate for each database record. This block of code is executed for each record in the .DBF file which meets the conditions set up by the other code blocks.

<bFor> and <bWhile> are code blocks that correspond directly to the FOR and WHILE clauses of the SUM, COUNT, and AVERAGE commands. Basically, if you use either or both of these clauses, DBEVAL() will process records until the code blocks return false (.f.).

<nNext> and <nRecord> are both numerics. The value of <nNext> specifies how many records to process from the current record. The <nRecord> specifies which record number to process.

<lRest> is a logical value that determines whether the DBEVAL() scope will be from the current record to the end-of-file, or all records. If you pass true (.t.), DBEVAL() will assume that you prefer the former (i.e., start from current record). If you pass false or ignore this parameter, DBEVAL() will process all records.

DBEVAL() is discussed further in Chapter 8, “Code Blocks.”

Creating subsets

Database files are collections of related records. For example, a customer .DBF file probably contains all clients for a particular company. Frequently, however, operations need to be performed on a group of records, not the entire file. This group can be referred to as a subset file.

A subset file is a smaller view of a larger file. It is used to allow a set of operations to be performed on only certain records from the file or to view only the selected records.

There are several approaches in Clipper which can be used to create subset files.

SET FILTER

The SET FILTER command allows the programmer to create a logical subset of a work area. This logical view is not a separate file, but a condition applied to a work area. The condition hides records which do not apply. This causes the database to appear to contain only a small subset of records.

The command syntax is:

```
SET FILTER TO <condition>
```

<condition> is an expression which can be evaluated to a logical result (true or false). Each record is tested against the expression. If the result is true, the record is displayed and appears to be part of the file. If the result is false, Clipper ignores the record. For example:

```
set filter to CUSTOMER->State == "PA"
```

This command creates a logical view where only the customers in the state of Pennsylvania are displayed.

The advantage of the SET FILTER command is its ease of use. The SET FILTER command automatically forces other Clipper commands to view the database as a subset of records. In addition, updates can be applied directly to the records in the database. If the subset were a separate file, any updates performed on the subset would have to be applied back to the original files.

The disadvantage is speed. SET FILTER can be very SLOW!! Most programmers avoid using SET FILTER for this very reason. When the filter creates a subset of records, all records in the dababase must be evaluated to decide whether or not to display the record. Since SET FILTER does not intelligently work with index files, a lot of extra disk reads may be necessary while trying to find a record which meets the filter condition. If the filter creates a subset of 100 records out of 5,000, then 4,900 records will be processed and ignored in order to display the 100 records.

While completely avoiding the command is a bit extreme, SET FILTER should be used with utmost caution. To the end-user, the database appears very small. This makes it difficult to explain why it takes so long to display only 50 records or so.

A filter can be used efficiently if the conditions are right. If the database contains many records which meet the filter criteria, and only a few records will be hidden, SET FILTER can be very powerful. For example, consider a voter registration database which contains a single character code for party affiliation. The possible codes are listed in Figure 20.7.

Figure 20.7 Party codes

D - Democrat

I - Independent

R - Republican

The command:

```
set filter to party $ "RD"
```

could be used to display only those voters affiliated with the Democratic or Republican parties. This filter would operate fairly efficiently (assuming most voters are Democrats or Republicans.)

The filter:

```
set filter to party == "I"
```

would probably not be a fast way to display only the independent voters.

Once a filter is created, it stays applied to the current work area until the work area is closed or a new filter is applied. The SET FILTER command can be used without any parameters to remove a filter condition from a work area. The syntax to remove a filter is:

```
SET FILTER TO
```

Saving filter queries

Once a filter is created within a work area, it can be saved as part of the work area's status information. The .DBFILTER() function returns the filter condition as a character string. Its syntax is:

```
<cFilter_expression> := .DBFILTER()
```

The <cFilter_expression> string contains the expression that was applied when the SET FILTER command was executed. This variable can be treated just like any other variable. It may be saved to a memory variable file as well. The program in Listing 20.15 illustrates a work area being closed to allow a DOS program to be run and then being reopened. Once it is reopened, the filter condition is reapplied to the database.

Listing 20.15 Saving filters

```
use CUSTOMER new
set filter to CUSTOMER->State == "OR"
*
* Some lines of code
*
cust_filt := .DBFilter()
close database
run RR    //Run external report writer
use CUSTOMER new
set filter to &cust_filt.
```

Create separate subset files

If the filter command will result in unacceptable performance, you can also create the subset file as a separate .DBF file. This will require copying the structure and the appropriate records from the primary file into the subset. Clipper provides several ways to do this.

COPY TO

The COPY TO command is used to create a new file which contains a selected set of records from the current work area. Its syntax is:

```
COPY FIELDS <flist> TO <new_DBF> <scope> ;
        WHILE <condition> FOR <condition>
```

fields <flist> specifies a list of fields from the current work area to be copied into the new file. The field names are separated by commas. If the FIELDS keyword is not specified, all fields are copied into the new file.

The WHILE <condition> is used to narrow down the records which might be returned by the COPY command. The condition specified after the WHILE keyword indicates how long the search should continue. As soon as a record fails to meet the WHILE condition, the COPY command stops.

The FOR <condition> is also optional and indicates a logical condition that each record is compared against. If the condition is true, then that record is copied to the new file. If false, the record is not copied. Regardless of whether or not the record is copied, COPY continues to transfer records until the end of the scope or until a failed WHILE condition.

Listing 20.16 illustrates some examples of the COPY TO command.

Listing 20.16 COPY TO examples

```
use CUSTOMER new
// copy all fields from CUSTOMER to drive A:
copy to a:CUSTOMER
// copy name and phone number to a .DBF file
copy fields Name,Phone to CUSTPHON

// Copy Pennsylvania customers to a separate .DBF
index on State to cust1
seek "PA"
copy rest to pa_custs while State == "PA"
```

SORT

The SORT command can also be used to create a subset database, with the added benefit of creating the subset in sorted order. The SORT command is described at the beginning of this chapter. Regardless of how the subset file is created, it is now available for processing. The biggest drawback with a separate file is that updates applied to the file must be made back to the original file as well.

To write back the information to the original file, you must determine where the original record numbers were. Listing 20.17 illustrates an example of creating a subset database and writing the changes back to the original file.

Listing 20.17 - Subset database example

```
field state, id_code
local jj, flds
use CUSTOMER new
index on State+Id_code to cust
seek "PA"
copy to PA_CUST while State == "PA"  // Create subset
use PA_CUST new                     // Use the subset file
go top
Browse()                            // Allow user to work with subset
flds := fcount()
go top
do while !eof()
   select CUSTOMER
   seek PA_CUST->State+PA_CUST->Id-code
   if eof()
      append blank
   endif
   for jj := 1 to flds
      Fieldput(jj,PA_CUST->(fieldget(jj)) )
   next
   select PA_CUST
   skip +1
enddo
```

Using arrays for subset files

If the number of records to be extracted from the database is small, they can be copied into an array in memory. This array can then be manipulated in a manner similar to a database. Since the array is in memory, the performance is very speedy. In addition, the record numbers can be stored with the array so updates can be made as each array element is processed.

To illustrate the use of arrays for file subsets, let's work through an example. An imaginary company that publishes xBASE compilers has a large file of all its employees. Each employee is assigned to a department. We need to create a program that will allow the manager to update individuals in his or her department. The pertinent fields from the employee file are shown in Figure 20.8.

Figure 20.8 Employee fields

```
Dept_id      Char      6     ACCT/TESTING/SUPPORT /
                             SALES  /PROGRAMS
Full_name    Char     25     Employee's Full Name
Hired        Date      8     Date of hire
Salary       Real   12,2     Yearly Salary
```

Figure 20.19 shows the screen the manager needs to see.

Figure 20.19 Update screen

Dept:

Employee Name	Hire Date	Salary

When the department is entered, the screen should be filled with the names, hire dates, and salaries of all employees within that department. Assuming that the employee file is indexed on DEPT_ID+FULL_NAME, the code fragment in Listing 20.19 can be used to create an array of employees.

Listing 20.19 Employee Array

```
#include "inkey.ch"
local mdept:=space(6)
private employees:={}        //Must be private to be visible in
            //ACHOICE() udf
use EMPLOYEE new index DEPT_ORD
@ 2,6 get mdept pict "!!!!!!"
setcursor(1)
read
if lastkey() <> K_ESC
   seek mdept
   do while !eof()  .and. EMPLOYEE->Dept_id == mdept
      aadd(employees,full_name+"  "+dtoc(hired)+"  "+;
      str(salary,12,2)+"  "+str(recno(),6) )
      skip +1
   enddo
endif
```

Notice that during the array add command, the record number from the employee file is included in the array. We have just created a memory structure to hold the employee information that needs to be displayed upon the screen. Now that the structure has been created, we can use ACHOICE() to display the information. Each element in the array is 56 characters long. However, we do not want to show the last 6 characters, i.e. the record number. Therefore, we call ACHOICE() with a 50 character wide window. ACHOICE() will automatically not display the last six characters, although they are still accessible in the array.

Listing 20.20 illustrates the use of ACHOICE() to perform simple data update.

Listing 20.20 ACHOICE() data update

```
#include "inkey.ch"
// The variables keepgoing, elt, and pos will be updated
// by the A_UDF called from ACHOICE. As a result, they
// must be declared as PRIVATE rather than LOCAL.

local x, mname, mdate, mamt, mrow,mrec
private keepgoing := .t., elt:=1,pos:=0, tags[len(employees)]
afill(tags,.t.)
do while keepgoing
   x :=achoice(6,15,22,65,employees,tags,"A_UDF",elt,pos)
   if x > 0
      mname := substr(employees[x],1,25)
      mdate := ctod(substr(employees[x],28,8))
      mamt  := val(substr(employees[x],37,12))
      mrec  := val(right(employees[x],6))
      mrow  := row()
      @ mrow,15 get mname
      @ mrow,42 get mdate
      @ mrow,51 get mamt
      read
      if lastkey() <> K_ESC
         select EMPLOYEE
         goto mrec
         replace EMPLOYEE->full_name with mname,;
```

```
                  EMPLOYEE->hired with mdate,;
                  EMPLOYEE->salary with mamt
            employees[x] :=mname+"   "+dtoc(mdate)+" "+;
                  str(mamt,12,2)+"   "+str(mrec,6)
      endif
   endif
enddo
```

Since the data is stored in an array, things can be done that otherwise might be too slow. The A_udf() function in Listing 20.21 illustrates a couple of simple features.

- A search feature for employee name, hire date, or salary range. If the manager wants to see all the employees who were hired during a certain year and are paid below a minimum salary, the program should be able to display only the records meeting the criteria.
- A feature to sort the array on any one of the three fields. With the code block parameter on ASORT(), positional sorts of an array are extremely easy to code.

Listing 20.21 ACHOICE() user-defined function

```
#include "ACHOICE.CH"
#include "INKEY.CH"

function A_udf(mode,element,position)
local lk:=lastkey()
memvar tags

// Private variables ELT,POS, and KEEPGOING are
// passed from the program containing the ACHOICE
// function call.

private elt, pos, keepgoing         //squelch compiler warnings
elt := element                      // update element
pos := position                     // and position
if mode == AC_EXCEPT                // Keystroke exception
   do case
```

```
   case lk == K_ESC
      keepgoing := .f.             // Tell LOOP to exit
      return AC_ABORT
   case lk == K_ENTER .or. lk == 32   // ENTER or space
      return AC_SELECT
   case chr(lk) $ "Ss"         // Sort array
      Sort_it()
      return AC_ABORT
   case chr(lk) $ "Ff"         // Find an item
      Find_it()
      return AC_ABORT
   endcase
endif
return AC_CONT
```

Sorting the array

If the user presses "S" to sort, the first thing to do is determine which field to sort on. Once we determine the field, we need to sort the array, and then return control to A_udf(), which will return a zero and cause the original routine to display the sorted records. Listing 20.22 illustrates the Sort_it() function.

Listing 20.22 Sort_it()

```
function Sort_it
local which := 1
@ 6,15 clear to 22,65
@ 6,15 prompt "Name"
@ 6,43 prompt "Date"
@ 6,52 prompt "Salary"
menu to which
do case
case which == 1
   asort(employees)
case which == 2
   asort(employees,,,{|x,y|substr(x,28,8) < substr(y,28,8)} )
case which == 3
   asort(employees,,,{|x,y|substr(x,37,12) < substr(y,37,12)} )
endcase
return nil
```

Finding a further subset

The FIND command we've described above actually reduces the subset of editable employees even further. To handle this step, we first need to determine the criteria to select on. Once we determine the criteria, we fill the tags array with .f. values, making every employee non-selectable. We then read through the array, and if the employee matches the criteria we will set the corresponding tags array element to .t. When the array is redisplayed, only the items we tagged that met the criteria will be editable. The code for Find_it() appears in Listing 20.23.

Listing 20.23 Find_it()

```
#include "inkey.ch"
function find_it
local mname:=space(25), myear:=year(date())
local mop_code :="<", mamt:=0.0, jj, tag_me, find_one:=.f.
@ 6,15 clear to 22,65
@ 6,15 get mname
@ 6,48 get myear     pict "99"
@ 6,51 get mop_code  pict "!"  ;
     valid mop_code $"<>= " .or. lastkey() == K_UP
@ 6,52 get mamt      pict "999999.99"
read
afill(tags,.f.)
for jj:=1 to len(tags)
   tag_me := .t.
   if !empty( mname )
      tag_me := (upper(mname) $ upper(substr(employees[jj],1,25)))
   endif
   if !empty( myear )
      tag_me := (year(ctod(substr(employees[jj],28,8))) == myear)
   endif
   if !empty( mamt )
      x := val(substr(employees[jj],37,12))
      do case
      case mop_code == "<"
         tag_me := (x < mamt)
      case mop_code == "="
         tag_me := (x == mamt)
```

```
      case mop_code == ">"
         tag_me := (x > mamt)
      endcase
   endif
   tags[jj] := tag_me
   if tag_me
      find_one :=.t.
   endif
next
if !find_one
   afill(tags,.t.)
endif
return nil
```

Summary

By the time you finish reading this chapter you should be able to find your data no matter how well it is hidden. You should be familar with various searching techniques and when to employ each one. You should also understand how Clipper allows data querying and be aware of the potential inefficiencies in it. Finally, you should be comfortable with various methods for handling subsets.

CHAPTER 21

Manipulating Character Strings

A string is a collection of characters stored together in memory. Both the characters and their order are maintained by the system. Clipper provides functions and operators which can specifically be used to manipulate string variables. In this chapter, we will discuss how strings are created and handled internally and the functions and operators provided for strings by Clipper. Finally, we will provide some useful user-defined functions to manipulate strings.

String variables

A string may be a single character or a group of characters. The largest string that Clipper supports is 65,519 (64K) bytes long. 64K is actually 65,536 bytes, but Clipper reserves 16 bytes for its own use and terminates the string with a null character. Clipper considers a string and the contents of a memo field to be identical for operating purposes. They are stored differently on disk, but once in memory Clipper treats them the same. This allows all functions which operate on strings to be applied to memo variables and vice versa.

Strings are a very powerful part of Clipper. Many of the commands and functions are designed to expect a character expression rather than a literal option. This allows you to use a string variable or a literal constant. This concept extends deeply into the language and contributes to its richness. A good example can be found in the picture clause of the GET command. The syntax for the command is:

```
GET <var>  PICTURE  <character string>
```

Since the picture clause is a string rather than a hard-coded literal, picture formats can be data driven. A United States zip code picture format might be "99999-9999" while the Canadian zip code format is "A9A 9A9". By creating a string variable called ZIP_FMT, we can have the same GET clause operate differently depending upon the initialization parameters specified by the user.

Creating string variables

A string is created in Clipper using the assignment operator. The assignment data may take several forms: A literal constant, a function which returns a string, a field from a database, or any combination of the three.

Literal constants

A literal constant is a string of characters surrounded by a set of delimiters, for example:

```
string := "CLIPPER is a powerful language"
```

Clipper provides three sets of delimiters. Since the delimiter character could be part of the string itself, providing three sets allows most strings to be represented. The three sets of delimiters are:

[] Left and right square brackets
"" Two double quotes, one to start and one to end
'' Two single quotes, one to start and one to end

A null string should be represented by a set of delimiters with no characters in between. For example:

```
string1  := []
string2  := ''
```

To represent a string which contains the delimiter characters, you can use an alternate delimiter set. For example, the string

```
Clipper 5: A Developer's Guide
```

could be represented as:

```
[Clipper 5: A Developer's Guide]
```

or

```
"Clipper 5: A Developer's Guide"
```

The sentence:

```
He said, "Clipper is GREAT!!!"
```

could be stored as

```
[He said, "Clipper is GREAT!!!"]
```

By using the three sets of delimiters almost any expression can be represented as a string constant. In the unlikely event that all three delimiters are needed, you can use the CHR() function instead of the literal character. The ASCII values for the delimiter characters are:

```
"     Double quote    34
'     Single quote    39
[     Left bracket    91
]     Right bracket   93
```

To represent the string:

```
He said, "Tom's code uses []."
```

in Clipper, we would write:

```
string := [He said,"Tom's code uses ]+chr(91)+chr(93)+[."]
```

Fortunately, strings containing all three delimiters do not occur very often.

Functions which return a string value

A string may also be created from a function that returns a string value. For example:

```
clip_ver := Version()       // Returns CLIPPER version
cur_proc := Procname()      // Returns current procedure name
dos_ver  := Os()            // Returns operating system name
```

(See Table 21.6 for a complete list of Clipper functions which return string values.)

A field from the database

A string may also be used to hold the contents of a character field or a memo field from a database. Assume we had the following fields in a database called CUSTOMER:

```
1. Comp_name            Char  25
2. Notes                Memo  10
```

The following assignments would transfer the company name and notes from the current record into string memory variables.

```
mcompany := CUSTOMER->Comp_name
mnotes   := CUSTOMER->Notes
```

A string may also be created by combining constants, functions, and database fields. For example, the following code fragment would produce a valid Clipper string:

```
string := "Clipper "+Version()
```

Once a string is created it can be used and manipulated by Clipper. Many functions and operators are available specifically for dealing with string variables.

String operators

Clipper provides operators to concatenate strings and to compare the sort order of strings. These operators are described in the following section.

Concatenation

Concatenation is the combining of two strings to form a new string. Clipper provides two operators for concatenating strings. These operators are the plus (+) and the minus sign (-) and are different only in the way they handle trailing spaces. The general syntax is shown below:

```
string  :=   <string1> <operator> <string2>
```

If the operator is the plus sign, the contents of **string2** are added to the end of **string1** and the result would be placed into **string**. If the operator is the minus sign, **string1** has all trailing spaces removed and appended onto the end of **string2**. Then the two strings are combined. Let's look at some examples:

```
? "Hello " + "World"
```

would display:

```
Hello World
```

while:

```
? "Hello " - "World"
```

would display:

```
HelloWorld
```

The minus operator is handy when you wish to combine first and last names. For example, assume you had a database containing the following fields:

```
1.  First       Char 12
2.  Last        Char 15
```

JOE is stored in the field FIRST and BOOTH stored in the field LAST. This is how the two concatenation operators would handle these fields

```
? FIRST + LAST      //would produce
  J O E                 B O O T H
  _ _ _ _ _ _ _ _ _ _ _ _ _ _ _ _ _ _ _ _ _ _ _ _ _ _ _
  < 12 characters       >< 15 characters          >
```

while:

```
? FIRST - LAST     //would produce
  J O E B O O T H
  _ _ _ _ _ _ _ _ _ _ _ _ _ _ _ _ _ _ _ _ _ _ _ _ _ _ _
  < 27 characters                                 >
```

Both strings would still be 27 characters long, the difference being the space characters are positioned at the end of the string.

Clipper 5 introduced a new syntax for these operators which may be used interchangeably with the plus and minus operators. The plus sign can be written as **+=** and the minus sign as **-=** . The following examples illustrate this shorthand notation.

`FIRST += LAST` is the same as `FIRST = FIRST + LAST`

`FIRST -= LAST` is the same as `FIRST = FIRST - LAST`

C programmers will immediately recognize this notation, as it is available in most C dialects.

Comparison

String variables can also be compared in a variety of ways using Clipper operators. To understand how strings are compared by Clipper, we need to first look at how a string is stored internally.

Internal string format

Strings are stored in memory (and on disk) using the ASCII character chart (see Appendix A). The ASCII chart contains a complete numerical ranking for all characters which can be represented in a string. Since a computer processes numerical information, a string can be viewed as a list of ASCII numbers. For example, the string "CLIPPER 5" and its ASCII equivalent are shown in Figure 21.1.

Figure 21.1 ASCII equivalent of string "Clipper 5"

```
C     L     I     P     P     E     R           5
67    76    73    80    80    69    82    32    53
____  ____  ____  ____  ____  ____  ____  ____  ____
```

To perform a comparison, the computer compares the numerical ranking of each character within the string. If the computer is asked if "A" is less than "B", i.e.:

```
?   "A" < "B"
```

The computer would determine that the letter **A** is the number 65 on the ASCII chart and the letter **B** is the number 66. Since 65 is less than 66, the comparison would be true, **A** is less than **B**.

Case considerations

Using the ASCII chart allows the computer to compare string variables. It also introduces some possible case confusions. For example, the ASCII code for upper case letter **B** is 66, while the code for lower case letter **A** is 97. Using these numbers, the comparison:

```
? "a" < "B"
```

would return false, since this is how they are ranked on the ASCII chart. Clipper provides case conversion functions to make comparisons of this sort more meaningful. For example, you could use:

```
? lower("a")  <  lower("B")
```

which would convert each string to lower case before comparing them. In the above case, the comparison would now produce true.

Are two strings equal?

Two operators are used to compare strings for equality. These operators are different in the way they handle strings of varying lengths. The operators are the equal sign (=) and the exactly equal sign (==). In addition, the SET EXACT command affects the way the equal sign performs.

Equal sign. The equal sign is affected by the SET EXACT command. The syntax of the SET EXACT command is:

```
SET EXACT < OFF | ON | logical >
```

The default value is OFF. SET EXACT is also considered a compatibility command that may not be supported in future releases of Clipper.

When SET EXACT is OFF, the rules in Table 21.1 are used to compare two strings:

TABLE 21.1 SET EXACT OFF

```
1. If the string on the right is null, return true.

2. If the string on the right is longer than the string on the
   left, return false.

3. For the length of the right hand string, compare each character
   with the corresponding character position in the string on the
   left. If each character is identical, return true. If not, then
   return false. It does not matter if the string on the left is
   larger than the string on the right.
```

If set exact is ON, the rules in Table 21.2 are used for comparison.

TABLE 21.2 SET EXACT ON

```
1. Remove trailing spaces from both strings.

2. If the strings are not the same length, return false.

3. Compare each character position in the two strings. If any
   characters are different return false. If all characters are the
   same, return true.
```

Let's review some examples:

```
SET EXACT OFF

? "ABC"   = "ABCDEF"      // FALSE - Table 21.1, rule 2
? "ABCDE" = "ABC"         // TRUE  - Table 21.1, rule 3
? "ABC"   = ""            // TRUE  - Table 21.1, rule 1
? ""      = "ABC"         // FALSE - Table 21.1, rule 2

SET EXACT ON

? "ABC"   = "ABCDEF"      // FALSE - Table 21.2, rule 2
? "ABCDE" = "ABC"         // FALSE - Table 21.2, rule 2
? "ABC"   = ""            // FALSE - Table 21.2, rule 2
? "ABC"   = "ABC"         // TRUE  - Table 21.2, rule 3
```

This handling of string comparisons has some subtle nuances that can cause some problems. For example, try to determine what the following comparison will yield:

```
set exact off
mvar := 50
? str(mvar,3) = " "
```

At a quick glance it appears that this equation will return false, however, the opposite will happen. The **STR(mvar,3)** function will produce a string of three characters, the first of which is a space. Since the comparison checks only one character (the length of the string on the right), both strings contain a space in the first position and hence the expression would return true.

The use of SET EXACT can make the code very confusing to read. It is best to leave SET EXACT to OFF at all times. This is the default setting, so it is not necessary to explicitly code it in your program. If you need to perform a comparison of two strings that must be the same length, use the syntax:

```
trim(<cString1>) == trim(<cString2>)
```

The exactly equal operator (==) is explained in the next section.

Exactly equal sign. The exactly equal sign is not affected by the setting of SET EXACT. It is used for a more exact comparison since the strings being compared must match exactly in both content and length. The rules in Table 21.3 describe how the double equal operator works.

TABLE 21.3 Rules of the == operator

```
1. If the lengths of the strings are not the same, then return false.

2. For the length of the strings, compare each character position
   in the right string with the corresponding character in the
   string on the left. If each character is identical, return true.
   If not, then return false.
```

Notice that trailing spaces are not removed before the comparison is performed. The strings must be identical including trailing spaces for the exactly equal operator to return TRUE.

Are strings not equal?

There are three operators which may be used to denote not equal comparison. All three operators are the same and can be used interchangeably. The not equal operators are affected by the setting of SET EXACT as well. The three operators and some examples are shown below:

```
!=    All three of these operators have the same
<>    meaning:   Are two strings not equal?
#
```

Examples:

```
if PAYROLL->Department <> "SALES"

log_out := password != "XYZ123"
```

The not equal operator is the inverse of the equal operator. It is affected by the value of SET EXACT. The rules in Tables 21.1 and 21.2 are applied in inverse fashion.

Is one string contained within another?

The **contains** (**$**)operator tests to see if one string is contained within a larger string. The smaller string is generally referred to as a substring. The syntax for **contains** is:

```
<substring> $ <string>
```

True will be returned if the substring can be found at any position in the string. If not, false will be returned. The search is case sensitive. For example:

```
?  "A"     $ "ABCDEF"    // Returns true
?  "Z"     $ "ABCDEF"    // Returns false
?  "a"     $ "ABCDEF"    // Returns false
```

The **contains** operator can be very handy when validating input to a GET variable. For example:

```
@ 10,10  say  "(P)rinter/(S)creen"
         get  choice pict "!"   valid choice $ "PS"
```

(See Chapter 27 for more details about GET validations.)

Comparing strings sort order

Strings may be compared with one another by comparing their ranking on the ASCII chart. Each character position is compared until one ranking is higher or lower than the other. Once a difference is found, the operator returns a true or false value depending on the difference. Appendix A contains an ASCII chart.

Greater Than (>). The right arrow bracket is used to designate a greater than comparison. For example,

```
? "A" > "Z"         // FALSE - A=65 , Z=90
? "JOHN" > "JOE"    // TRUE  J and O are the same, but the letter
                    // H is higher in the chart than E.
```

Greater-Than-or-Equal-to (>=). The right arrow bracket can be followed immediately by an equal sign to designate a greater-than-or-equal-to comparison.

Less-than (<). The left arrow bracket is used to designate a less-than comparison. For example,

```
? "Z" < "A"        // FALSE -  Z=90 , A=65
? "JOE" < "JOHN"   // TRUE  J and O are the same, but the
                   // letter E is lower on the chart than H.
```

Less-Than-or-Equal-to (<=). The left arrow bracket can be followed immediately by an equal sign to designate a less-than-or-equal-to comparison.

Operator summary

Clipper provides a number of different operations that can be used on strings. These operations are summarized in Table 21.4.

Table 21.4 Operator summary

```
+           Concatenate two strings.
-           Concatenate and move spaces to end.
=           Are strings equal?
==          Are strings equal and the same length?
#,!=,<>     Are strings not equal?
<           Is one string less than another?
<=          Is string less than or equal to another?
>           Is one string greater than another?
>=          Is string greater than or equal to another?
```

String functions

In addition to the operators provided, a large number of functions exist which can be used to manipulate strings. These functions can be grouped into five general categories:

TESTING	Test string size, case, contents, etc.
SPACES	Add or remove spaces from string.
EDIT	Change the contents of string characters.
SUBSTRINGS	Create and manipulate substrings.
OTHER	Clipper functions that return a string value.

Testing — test string size, etc.

The testing functions are available to test length and content of string variables.

LEN()

LEN() Determines the number of characters within a string. The size of a string may be determined using the LEN function. Its syntax is:

```
nSize := LEN( <cstring> )
```

nSize will contain an integer which is equal to the total number of characters, including all spaces (leading, trailing, and imbedded). For example:

```
?  len("Clipper 5: A Developer's Guide")      // returns 30
?  len("")                                    // returns  0
```

The LEN() function can also be used to test the size of character or memo fields from a database. In the case of character fields, LEN() will return the size defined in the database, regardless of the field's contents. In the case of a memo field, LEN() will return the number of characters, including spaces, in the memo field's contents.

EMPTY() — is a string empty?

EMPTY() is a useful function for testing variables of all types. The syntax for EMPTY() is:

```
lEmpty := EMPTY( <exp> )
```

When used with string variables, EMPTY() returns true if the variable contains spaces or is a null string. For example:

```
mpath := getenv("PATH")
if empty( mpath )
   ? "No path is specified..."
endif
```

EMPTY() can also be used to validate a GET that is required. For example, assume the account number must be entered in order for the system to continue:

```
macct := space(8)
@ 10,10 say "ACCOUNT: " get macct valid !empty(macct)
```

The user would be required to answer the account prompt in order to continue. Of course, since the user has no idea why he cannot leave the field, he might also punch the video screen.

ISALPHA() — is the first character alphabetic?
ISALPHA() will check to see if the first character of a string is an alphabetic character. It is the same as the following code:

```
? upper(left(string,1)) $ "ABCDEFGHIJKLMNOPQRSTUVWXYZ"
```

The syntax for ISALPHA() is:

```
lCheck := ISALPHA( <string> )
```

ISALPHA() could be used to check that the first character of a user-entered file name is alphabetic. For example:

```
@ 10,10 get mfile  valid isalpha(mfile)
```

ISDIGIT() — is the first character a digit?
ISDIGIT() will check to see if the first character of a string is a digit character, between 0 and 9. It is the same as the following code:

```
? left(string,1) $ "0123456789"
```

The syntax for ISDIGIT() is:

```
lCheck := ISDIGIT( <string> )
```

ISDIGIT() could be used to check that the first character of a social security number is numeric. For example:

```
@ 10,10 get mssn  valid isdigit(mssn)
```

This example would not check every character, only the first one. A more comprehensive social security check routine might be coded as illustrated in Listing 21.1.

Listing 21.1 Checkssn()

```
function Checkssn(soc_sec)
local k
for k:=1 to 11
   if .not. (k == 4 .or. k == 7)
      if .not. isdigit( substr(soc_sec,k,1) )
         return .F.
      endif
   endif
next
return .T.
```

This function checks to see that each character in the social security number (except for the dashes) is a valid digit.

ISLOWER() — is the first character a lowercase letter?

ISLOWER() will check to see if the first character of a string is a lowercase alphabetic character. It is the same as the following code:

```
? left(string,1) $ "abcdefghijklmnopqrstuvwxyz"
```

The syntax for ISLOWER() is:

```
lCheck := ISLOWER( <string> )
```

A good example of ISLOWER() is in the Formalize() user-defined function in Listing 21.2.

Listing 21.2 Formalize()

```
function Formalize(sname)
local jj, one_char,upcase:=.t.
for jj:=1 to len(sname)
   one_char := substr(sname,jj,1)
   if upcase .and. islower(one_char)
      sname := stuff(sname, jj, 1, upper(one_char))
      upcase :=.f.
   endif
   upcase := ( one_char == " " )
next
return sname
```

This function takes a string and converts the first letter of each word to uppercase. For example,

```
Formalize("clipper 5: a developer's guide")
```

would return

```
Clipper 5: A Developer's Guide
```

This function can be used to ensure that the data written to a file is consistent, regardless of how the user entered it.

ISUPPER() — is the first character an uppercase letter?

ISUPPER() will check to see if the first character of a string is an uppercase alphabetic character. It is the same as the following code:

```
? left(string,1) $ "ABCDEFGHIJKLMNOPQRSTUVWXYZ"
```

The syntax for ISUPPER() is:

```
lCheck := ISUPPER( <string> )
```

SPACES — add/remove spaces from a string

Character strings are often used for report and screen headers. Clipper provides a number of functions to manipulate the space characters within a string.

ALLTRIM() — remove leading and trailing spaces

The ALLTRIM() function removes any leading and trailing spaces from a string variable. Its syntax is:

```
<string>  := ALLTRIM( <string> )
```

For example:

```
cstring := "      CLIPPER      "

? len( cString )              // Returns 19
? len(alltrim(cString))       // Returns 7

cString := alltrim(cString)
? cString                      // Displays "CLIPPER"
```

ALLTRIM() is not an actual Clipper function, but rather a pre-processor #translate directive. (See Chapter 7 for more information on the preprocessor). The ALLTRIM() function will be converted to LTRIM(TRIM(<string>)).

LTRIM() — remove leading spaces from a string

The LTRIM() function removes any leading spaces from a string variable. Its syntax is:

```
<string>  := LTRIM( <string> )
```

For example:

```
cstring := "      CLIPPER      "

? len( cString )              // Returns 19
? len(ltrim(cString))         // Returns 13

cString := ltrim(cString)
? cString                     // Displays "CLIPPER      "
```

LTRIM() is useful when displaying STR() values. For example:

```
amount := 1000.00
? str(amount,10,2)          // Displays "   1000.00"
? ltrim(str(amount,10,2))   // Displays "1000.00"
```

RTRIM() — remove trailing spaces from a string

The RTRIM() function removes any trailing spaces from a string variable. Its syntax is:

```
<string>  := RTRIM( <string> )
```

For example:

```
cString := "      CLIPPER      "

? len( cString )             // Returns 19
? len(rtrim(cString))        // Returns 13

cString := rtrim(cString)
? cString                     // Displays "      CLIPPER"
```

RTRIM() may also be written as TRIM().

PADx() — Pad a string with spaces or other character

The PADx() functions add spaces or another pad character to various spots within a string variable. There are three PAD functions: PADC(),PADL(), and PADR(). The syntax of each is:

```
<string>  := PADX( <string>,<length> [,<character>] )
```

PADR() is the inverse to RTRIM(), PADL() to LTRIM(), and PADC() to ALLTRIM().

For example:

```
cString := "Bank Reconciliation"

? padc(cString,30)    // Displays "     Bank Reconciliation      "
? padr(cString,30)    // Displays "Bank Reconciliation           "
? padl(cString,30)    // Displays "           Bank Reconciliation"
```

The optional pad **<character>** can also be used if a character other than space is needed. For example,

```
amount := 1500
?  padl(ltrim(str(amount,10,2)),50,"*"
```

This will display

```
*******************************************1500.00
```

which is useful when the computer is printing checks.

EDIT — change a string's contents

Clipper provides four functions to change the contents of a string variable. Two of these functions are case conversions that affect the entire string. The other two allow individual characters within a string to be inserted, removed, or changed.

LOWER() — convert all characters to lower case

LOWER() will convert all alphabetic characters in a string to lower case. Its syntax is:

```
string := LOWER( <string> )
```

UPPER() — convert all characters to upper case

UPPER() will convert all alphabetic characters in a string to upper case. Its syntax is:

```
string := UPPER( <string> )
```

These two functions are very useful when searching a database. Index keys may be built in either upper or lower case. When the program seeks a key, it converts the key to the appropriate case. This way is does not matter what case the user enters, the key will still be found. For example,

```
select EMPLOYEE
index on upper(Last_name)  to employ1

mname := "Smith"
seek mname
? found()                    // Returns .F.
seek upper(mname)
? found()                    // Returns .T.
```

STRTRAN() — search and replace string characters

This function allows character patterns to be replaced with a string or memo variable. Its syntax is:

```
<cStr> :=STRTRAN(<cStr>,<cSearch>,<cReplace>,<nStart>,<nCount>)
```

The first two parameters are required. **<cStr>** is the string to search and **<cSearch>** is the pattern to search for. The optional **<cReplace>** is the pattern to replace the searched pattern with. If not supplied, it will default to a null (""), which has the effect of removing the search pattern from the string. For example:

```
mpath :=Getenv("PATH")          //  C:\DOS;C:\UTIL;C:\CLIPPER5
mpath :=strtran(mpath,";",",")
? mpath                         // C:\DOS,C:\UTIL,C:\CLIPPER5

mpath := strtran(mpath,"C:\")
? mpath                         // DOS,UTIL,CLIPPER5
```

Both the search pattern and the replace pattern can be any number of characters in length. It is possible to change the string length with STRTRAN().

The last two parameters indicate which occurrence to start the replacement at, and the number of times to perform the replacement. The default starting position is one. The default number of occurrences is all.

STUFF() — insert and remove string characters

This function allows character patterns to be inserted and removed within a string or memo variable. Its syntax is:

```
<cStr> := STUFF(<cStr>,<nStart>,<nDelete>,<cInsert>)
```

The function returns the modified string. It can be used for inserting new characters, removing characters, and replacing characters.

Inserting new characters. If the **<nDelete>** parameter is zero, then the **<cInsert>** will be inserted and the string made larger. For example,

```
? stuff("Clipper is powerful",9,0,"5 ")

// Displays "Clipper 5 is powerful"
```

Deleting characters. If the **<nDelete>** parameter is greater than zero and the **<cInsert>** string is null, characters will be removed and the string will be made shorter. For example,

```
mname := "Ms. Sandy Booth"
x := at(".",mname)
mname := stuff(mname,1,x+1)     // Produces "Sandy Booth"
x := at(" ",mname)
mname := stuff(mname,x-1,99)  //  Produces "Sandy"
```

Replacing characters. If the **<nDelete>** parameter is greater than zero, and the **<cInsert>** value is not a null, characters will be replaced in the string. The size of the new string will depend on the length of the **<cInsert>** value and the number of characters deleted. For example:

```
? stuff("DBASE III is number one!",1,9,"Clipper 5")

// Displays "Clipper 5 is number one!"
```

In this case the string size remains the same. You could also expand abbreviations using STUFF(). For example:

```
? stuff("Philadelphia, PA",15,2,"Pennsylvania")

// Displays "Philadelphia, Pennsylvania"
```

In this case the string size has increased by ten characters.

Creating and manipulating substrings

A substring is a smaller string extracted from a larger string. Clipper provides five functions to create substrings.

AT()

AT() is used to determine the starting position of a substring within a string. Its syntax is:

```
nPosition := AT(string1, string2)
```

The AT() function will search through **string2** to see if the pattern specified by **string1** occurs anywhere. If it does not appear, the function will return a zero. If the pattern does appear, the position from the beginning of the string will be returned. For example:

```
?  at( "," , "Booth, Joseph")      // returns 6
?  at( "a" , "ABCDEFG" )           // returns 0
```

AT() can be used in conjunction with the LEFT() and RIGHT() functions to produce very powerful functions. The following code illustrates how a name field can be split apart and replaced into first and last names fields. Assume the structure of the customer database has the following three fields:

```
Full_name        Char 25
First            Char 12
Last             Char 15

select CUSTOMER
go top
do while .not. eof()
   if  (x := at("," , CUSTOMER->Full_name) )  > 0
     replace CUSTOMER->First with  left(Full_name,x-1)
     replace CUSTOMER->Last  with  right(Full_name,25-x)
   endif
skip +1
enddo
```

RAT()

RAT() is used to determine the starting position of the last occurrence of a substring within a string. Its syntax is:

```
nPosition := RAT( string1, string2 )
```

The RAT() function will search through **string2** to see if the pattern specified by **string1** occurs anywhere. The search is performed in a right-to-left manner, as opposed to the left-to-right manner performed by AT(). If the substring does not appear, the function will return a zero. If the pattern does appear, the position from the beginning of the string will be returned. For example:

```
mfilename := "C:\CLIPPER5\INCLUDE\STD.CH"
x := rat("\",mfilename)
if x > 0
   ? "Path is "+left(mfilename,x-1)
endif
```

The program will display “Path is C:\CLIPPER5\INCLUDE”.

LEFT()

The LEFT() function creates a substring by extracting a number of characters from the leftmost portion of the string. Its syntax is:

```
<cSubstring> := LEFT(<cString>,<nSize>)
```

RIGHT()

The RIGHT() function creates a substring by extracting any number of characters from the rightmost portion of a string variable. Its syntax is:

```
<cSubstring>  := RIGHT( <cString>,<nSize> )
```

SUBSTR()

The SUBSTR() function creates a substring by extracting a number of characters from anywhere within the string. Its syntax is:

```
<cSubstring> := SUBSTR(<cString>,<nStart>,<nCount>)
```

The **<nStart>** parameter indicates where to start in the larger string. If **<nStart>** is positive, the starting position is relative to the beginning of the string. If **<nStart>** is negative, the starting position is relative to the end of the string.

The optional **<nCount>** parameter indicates how many characters to copy into the substring. If it's not passed, the function will extract all characters from the **<nStart>** position to the end of the string.

The example in Listing 21.3 takes a fully qualified file name and returns an array of three substrings: the drive letter, the path name, and the file name.

Listing 21.3 Split()

```
function Split(cFullname)
local x:=at(":",cFullname), y:=rat("\",cFullname)
local the_drive:="", the_path:="", the_file:=""
if x > 0
   the_drive := substr(cFullname,1,x-1)
endif
if y > 0
   the_path  := substr(cFullname,x+1,y-x)
   the_file  := substr(cFullname,y+1)
endif
return {the_drive, the_path, the_file}
```

Functions which return string values

Many of the Clipper functions return string values. Most of these functions are detailed in other chapters. Table 21.6 is a list of functions which return a string value.

Table 21.6 String functions

Function	*Description*
ALIAS()	Specified work area's alias name
CDOW()	Character day of week
CHR()	Character associated with an ASCII value
CMONTH()	Character month name
CURDIR()	The current DOS directory
DBFILTER()	Filter condition in a work area
DBRELATION()	Expression used to relate files together
DTOC()	Date in SET DATE format (MM/DD/YY)
DTOS()	Date in format YYYYMMDD
FIELD()	Name for a field number
FREAD()	Read bytes from a file using low-level function
FREADSTR()	Read a string from a file using low-level function
GETENV()	Get an environment string value
INDEXEXT()	Default index file extension, NTX or NDX
INDEXKEY()	Index key expression
I2BIN()	Integer to a binary string
L2BIN()	Long number to binary string
NETNAME()	Return the name of the network workstation
OS()	Get the operating system name
SOUNDEX()	Create a soundex code from a string
STR()	Convert a numeric variable to a string
TIME()	Current time as a string of HH:MM:SS
VERSION()	Return the Clipper version number

Useful string manipulation UDFs

To illustrate the power provided by the string tools in Clipper, we will use these tools to write some string manipulation user-defined functions.

Parse() — create an array from a string

Parse() takes a string and an optional delimiter character and returns an array which contains each token from the string. For example, the string:

```
"UPD_CUST,5,10,20,60,GR+/W"
```

would be broken into a six-element array. Each element would be of character type. The six elements are:

```
1    UPD_CUST
2    5
3    10
4    20
5    60
6    GR+/W
```

The function syntax is listed below:

```
array   := Parse( <string> [,<delimiter>] )
```

If the delimiter is not passed, it is assumed to be a comma.

Listing 21.4 contains the code for this function. It should be compiled in a separate PRG file using the /n /m compiler switches:

Listing 21.4 Parse()

```
static  def_delim := ","         // default delimiter

function Parse( pstring,pdelim )
local rlist :={}, k
pdelim := if(pdelim==nil, def_delim, pdelim)
do while len(pstring) > 0
   if (k := at(pdelim,pstring) ) > 0
      aadd(rlist,left(pstring,k-1))
```

```
      pstring := substr(pstring,k+1)
   else
      aadd(rlist,pstring)
      pstring :=""
   endif
enddo
return rlist
```

To provide an example, Listing 21.5 illustrates an application that will prompt the user for a database name to open. If the database file is not found in the current directory, the path will be searched. If found, the file will be opened, otherwise an error message will be displayed and the user will be asked to enter the file name again.

Listing 21.5 Parsedemo

```
#include "inkey.ch"
local mfile := space(8), ok := .f., k, tfile

do while ! ok
   @ 10,10 say "File Name: " get mfile pict "!!!!!!!!"
   read
   if lastkey() <> K_ESC
      tfile := trim(mfile)+".DBF"
      if ! file(tfile)
           pathlist := Parse( getenv("PATH"),";" )
           for k := 1 to len(pathlist)
              tfile := pathlist[k]+"\"+trim(mfile)+".DBF"
              if file(tfile)
                  exit
              endif
           next
      endif
      if file(tfile)
           use (tfile) new alias mfile
           ok := .t.
      else
           ? "File "+mfile-" cannot be found"
        endif
   else
        exit
   endif
enddo
```

Occurs() — count occurrences of a substring

Occurs() counts how many times a substring occurs within a larger string. Its syntax is:

```
<nCount> := Occurs(<cChar>,<cString>)
```

Here's an example of the Occurs() function:

```
function Occurs(cChar, cString)
local x:=len(cString), y:=len(strtran(cString, cChar,""))
return (x-y)/len(cChar)
```

This function illustrates a use of Clipper's STRTRAN() function. The STRTRAN() function replaces all occurrences of the sought after string with a null character. This reduces the length of the string for each occurrence. The function returns the difference in lengths between the two strings divided by the size of the string being sought.

Findany() — find first occurrence from a list

The Findany() function finds the first occurrence of a character within a character string. It is similar to the AT() function, but allows you to look for more than one possible character. Its syntax is:

```
<nPosition> := Findany(<cList>,<cSearch_string>)
```

Findany() can be used to break longer strings into tokens even if there are several possible delimiters which might be present.

Listing 21.6 Findany()

```
function Findany(chr_list, search_str)
local where:=0, k, the_char
for k:=1 to len(chr_list)
   the_char :=substr(chr_list,k,1)
   where := at(the_char,search_str)
```

```
   if where > 0
      exit
   endif
next
return where
```

Encrypt()

Data encryption is a technique to store information in a fashion that hides its meaning. It is very useful for passwords and other sensitive data in a computer file. There are many algorithms that can be used to encrypt character strings. The example listing below employs a simple substitution algorithm. While not the most secure encryption scheme, it should deter the casual user from determining the hidden information. The syntax for the function is:

```
<cEncrypted_string> := Encrypt( <cPlain_string>,<cKey> )
```

The key can be any number of characters in length. It is used to determine what letter is substituted in the password. If no key is specified the default key will be CLIPPER.

```
function Encrypt(src_word, passkey)
local pwd:="", jj, kk:=0, x
passkey:=if(passkey==nil,"CLIPPER",passkey)
for jj:=len(src_word) to 1 step -1
   kk :=if(kk>len(passkey),1,kk)
   x :=asc(substr(src_word,jj,1))+asc(substr(passkey,kk,1))
   pwd += chr(x)
next
return pwd
```

Decrypt()

Decryption is a technique that takes an encrypted string and converts it back to its original meaning. The Decrypt() function listing we show below reads the strings encrypted by the Encrypt() function as shown in the above example. Its syntax is:

```
<cPlain_string> := Decrypt( <cEncrypted_String>,<cKey> )
```

The key must be identical to the key that the password was created with. If no key is specified the default key of CLIPPER will be used.

```
function Decrypt(enc_word, passkey)
local plain:="", jj, kk:=0, x
passkey:=if(passkey==nil,"CLIPPER",passkey)
for jj:=len(enc_word) to 1 step -1
   kk  :=if(kk>len(passkey),1,kk)
   x   :=asc(substr(enc_word,jj,1))- asc(substr(passkey,kk,1))
   plain += chr(x)
next
return plain
```

Summary

After reading this chapter you should be comfortable with using character strings in Clipper. You should understand the method that is used to compare strings and you should be familiar with Clipper's string manipulation functions. The user-defined functions provided as examples should also be useful in your toolbox of Clipper functions.

CHAPTER 22

Math and Date Functions

Clipper provides a variety of operators for mathematical operations and comparison. Clipper also interprets dates as numeric values and allows mathematical operations to be performed on them as well.

In this chapter we will cover the functions provided by Clipper for mathematics and for date manipulation. In addition, we will write several user-defined functions for common business, statistical, and mathematical operations. Finally, we will look at the way that Clipper handles time variables.

Mathematical operators provided by Clipper

Clipper provides the mathematical operators listed in Figure 22.1. (See Chapter 5, "Operators", for a detailed discussion.)

Figure 22.1 Clipper mathematical operators

%	Modulus of two numbers
*	Multiplication
** ^	Exponentiation
+	Addition or positive sign
/	Division
-	Subtraction or negative sign
:=	Inline assignment
nVar++	Post-Increment operator
++nVar	Pre-Increment operator
nVar--	Post-Decrement operator
--nVar	Pre-Decrement operator

The operators can be used on Clipper variables, functions which return a numeric value, or numeric constants. For example,

```
nVar := 10
? nVar % 3              // Returns   1
? 10 * 15               // Returns 150
? nVar**2               // Returns 100
?--nVar                 // Returns   9
? int(nVar) + 5         // Returns  15
```

When coding mathematical expressions, Clipper enforces a precedence of operators as listed in Figure 22.2. This precedence can be overridden by use of parentheses. Operations surrounded by parentheses are always evaluated first, in a left-to-right order. For example:

```
? 5 * 4 + 3         //  Returns 23
? 5 * ( 4 + 3 )     //  Returns 35
```

Figure 22.2 Operator precedence

1. Functions are always evaluated first
2. Pre-increment, Pre-decrement ++nVar ,--nVar
3. Positive, Negative sign +nVar , -nVar
4. Exponentiation **, ^
5. Multiplication, division, modulus * , / , %
6. Addition, subtraction + , -
7. Inline Assignment :=
8. Post-increment, Post-decrement nVar++ , nVar--

There is tremendous flexibility in the operators that Clipper provides. This can cause some confusion. For example, what is the result of the formulas in Listing 22.1?

Listing 22.1 Formula examples

```
? "One...: ", 10 * 15 + 5 * 6
? "Two...: ", --10 * J:=5
? "Three.: ", 5++ * 8 - 9--
```

Try to determine the results based upon the precedence table in Figure 22.2. If you are unsure of the results, create a Clipper program to see how it evaluates those expressions.

You should try to use parentheses whenever possible to prevent problems when Clipper's assumptions differ from your own. This is especially important if the formula might be modified or if the code is being maintained by another programmer. The parentheses allow explicit determination of how expressions should be evaluated.

Clipper's mathematical operators are described in more detail in Chapter 5, "Operators."

Environment setting

When mathematical operations are displayed in an unformatted form, as produced with the **?** and **??** display commands, Clipper determines the appropriate number of decimal places to display. Clipper also allows the number of decimal places to be specified by the programmer using two SET commands.

SET DECIMALS

The SET DECIMALS setting determines how many decimals places should be displayed. Its syntax is:

```
SET DECIMALS TO <nValue>
```

The ***<nValue>*** is an integer value indicating number of decimal places. The default value is two. The default value is used if SET DECIMALS does not appear in your program. If you write SET DECIMALS TO without a parameter, the **<nValue>** is zero.

SET FIXED

The SET FIXED command tells the system how to display numeric values. If SET FIXED is ON or .t., the value of SET DECIMALS determines the exact number of decimal places to display. If SET FIXED is OFF or .f., the value of SET DECIMALS will return the minimum number of decimal places for the function or operation to display. The syntax for the command is:

```
SET FIXED  ON | OFF | <lFixed>
```

The default value is OFF, letting the default decimal places be displayed.

Listing 22.2 illustrates some examples of SET FIXED and SET DECIMALS.

Listing 22.2 SET FIXED/SET DECIMALS

```
? 1 / 3              // Displays  .33
SET DECIMALS TO 4
? 1 / 3              // Displays  .3333
SET FIXED ON
? 1 / 3              // Displays  .3333
SET DECIMALS TO 2
? 1 / 3              // Displays  .33
```

Neither SET DECIMALS nor SET FIXED affects the accuracy of the calculations. They only affect how the information is displayed. Numeric display can be controlled much more accurately by using the TRANSFORM() function or the PICTURE clause in the @..SAY command. TRANSFORM() is described in Chapter 4 and the @..SAY command is described in Chapter 13.

Math functions

In addition to the operators, Clipper provides a variety of mathematical functions. These functions give the programmer access to additional operations needed by some mathematical formulas.

ABS()

The ABS() function returns the absolute value of a number. The absolute value is the value without regard to its sign. If the number is negative, multiplying it by minus one will produce an absolute number. Its syntax is:

```
<nResult> := ABS( <nExpression> )
```

The algorithm to compute an absolute number is:

If the expression is less than zero, return -1 times the expression; otherwise, just return the value.

The ABS() function can be used to compare the difference between two numbers without regard to the sign. For example, if we subtract two dates we will have the number of days between the dates.

```
mdate1 := ctod("01/22/89")
mdate2 := ctod("02/15/89")
diff   := mdate1 - mdate2
? diff          //   Returns  -25
? abs(diff)     //   Returns   25
```

EXP()

The EXP() function returns the value of **e**x**. It is primarily used to estimate growth patterns. The approximate value of **e** is 2.71828. The syntax for EXP() is:

```
<nResult> := EXP( <nValue> )
```

The ***<nValue>*** represents the number which **e** should be raised to. The maximum **<nValue>** can be 45 before a numeric overflow will occur.

For example,

```
? Exp(0)       // Returns 1
? Exp(1)       // Returns 2.7182818285
? Exp(13.3)    // Returns 597,196
```

The EXP() function is the inverse of the LOG() function.

INT()

The INT() function returns the integer portion of a number. The integer portion is the value without any numbers to the right of the decimal point. Its syntax is:

```
<nResult> := INT( <nValue> )
```

The INT() function can be used to determine if a number is a multiple of another number. For example:

```
mValue := 15
? mValue/2 == int(mValue/2)    // Returns false, since 15 is
                               // not a multiple of two.
mValue := 8
? mValue/2 == int(mValue/2)    // Returns true, since 8 is a
                               // multiple of two.
```

LOG()

The LOG() function returns the natural logarithm of the number passed as a parameter. The syntax for LOG() is:

```
<nResult> := LOG( <nValue> )
```

The ***<nValue>*** represents the number for which the logarithm should be returned. It must be greater than zero or a numeric overflow condition will occur.

For example,

```
? Log(0)              // Returns **********
? Log(2.71828)        // Returns 1
? Log(10)             // Returns 2.30
```

The LOG() function is the inverse of the EXP() function.

MAX()

The MAX() function compares two values and returns the larger of the two. The parameters may be numbers or dates. Its syntax is:

```
<nLarger>   := MAX(<nFirst>,<nSecond>)
<dLarger>   := MAX(<dFirst>,<dSecond>)
```

The returned value will either be a date or a number, depending upon the types of the parameters.

The MAX() function can be used to determine the largest value in a database file. Listing 22.3 illustrates the use of MAX() within a DBEVAL() code block to find the highest salary in a payroll .DBF file.

Listing 22.3 MAX() Example

```
local biggest :=0
use PAYROLL new
dbeval( {|| biggest := Max(biggest,PAYROLL->Salary)} )
return biggest
```

MIN()

The MIN() function compares two values and returns the smaller of the two. The parameters may be numbers or dates. Its syntax is:

```
<nSmaller>   := MIN(<nFirst>,<nSecond>)
<dSmaller>   := MIN(<dFirst>,<dSecond>)
```

The returned value will either be a date or a number, depending upon the types of the parameters.

The MIN() function can be used to determine the earliest date in a database file. Listing 22.4 illustrates the use of MIN() within a DBEVAL() code block to find the earliest invoice date in a transaction file.

Listing 22.4 MIN() Example

```
local earliest := ctod("12/31/2199")
use TRANS new
dbeval( {|| earliest := min(earliest,TRANS->inv_date)} )
return earliest
```

ROUND()

The ROUND() function returns a number rounded to the specified number of digits. Its syntax is:

```
<nResult>  := ROUND( <nValue>,<nDecimals> )
```

<nValue> represents the number to be rounded. ***<nDecimals>*** indicates the number of decimal places to be retained. If **<nDecimals>** is a negative number, whole digits will be rounded.

For example:

```
? Round(100.1245,2)      // Returns   100.12
? Round(541.12965,3)     // Returns   541.130
? Round(254.691,0)       // Returns   255
? Round(256,-1)          // Returns   260
? Round(254,-1)          // Returns   250
```

If the first digit past the rounding is greater than or equal to five, the number will be rounded up. If the number is less than five, the number will be rounded down. Also keep in mind that ROUND() actually changes the value of the number. TRANSFORM() is used to display numbers without changing their values.

SQRT()

The SQRT() function returns the square root of a number. The syntax for Clipper to calculate a square root is:

```
<nRoot>  := SQRT( <nValue> )
```

<nValue> is the number of which the square root should be taken. ***<nRoot>*** is the result, the square root of the number. For example, Listing 22.5 lists the square roots of all numbers from one through ten.

Listing 22.5 Square root example

```
local jj
for jj:= 1 to 10
   ? jj, sqrt(jj)
next
```

Business user-defined functions

The world of business requires many specialized functions which do not fit in the syntax of a programming language, yet are frequently needed in many applications. In this section, we will provide functions for depreciation and interest calculations.

Depreciation

When a business invests money in capital equipment, it is generally expected to last several years. Since the benefit of using the equipment is spread out, the expense of acquiring it should be spread out over the same period of time. Depreciation is the method to attempt to spread the invested money out over several years.

To determine each period's depreciation amount, we need first to identify some terms. Table 22.1 defines common terms for depreciation.

Table 22.1 Depreciation Terms

Acquisition Cost	The purchase price, plus any shipping incurred, that the asset cost.
Useful life	A projected number of years (or months) over which the asset is expected to be useful.
Scrap value	The expected price for which the asset can be sold after it has passed its useful life.
Accumulated	Running total of all depreciation taken to depreciation date on an asset.
Book Value	The acquisition cost of the asset minus its accumulated depreciation.

Straight-line. Straight-line depreciation assumes that the asset value is evenly divided over its useful life. This method is the simplest depreciation to calculate, but also makes no provision for inflation.

The syntax for Sl() is:

```
<nArray> := Sl( <nCost>,<nScrap>,<nLife> )
```

The function will return an array filled with each period's depreciation amount.

Sum of the Year's Digits. One of the drawbacks of the straight-line method is that it makes no allowances for inflation. The sum of the year's digits depreciation method improves upon straight-line by taking more of a depreciation expense in the early years and less later.

The annual depreciation entry for sum of the year's digits is computed by summing up the digits of the year and computing a percentage based on the years of life left over total digits. For example, assume an asset has a life of five years and is worth $3000 with no scrap value. Figure 22.4 shows how the sum of the year's digits depreciation amounts would be calculated.

Figure 22.4 SYD Depreciation

(a)	Sum all years digit's...:		1+2+3+4+5	= 15	
(b)	Year one	5 years left:	5/15 = 33%	or	$1,000
	Year two	4 years left:	4/15 = 27%	or	800
	Year three	3 years left:	3/15 = 20%	or	600
	Year four	2 years left:	2/15 = 13%	or	400
	Year five	1 year left.:	1/15 = 7%	or	200

The sum of the year's digits is referred to as an accelerated depreciation formula, since more depreciation is taken in the earlier years of the asset's life.

The syntax for the Syd() function is:

```
<nArray> := Syd( <nCost>,<nScrap>,<nLife> )
```

The function will return an array filled with each period's depreciation amount.

Declining Balance. Another accelerated depreciation method is the declining balance method. This method uses a higher percentage on a progressively smaller asset value. This results in taking more depreciation expense in the early years and less later.

The annual depreciation entry for the declining balance method is computed by applying a percentage to the asset's book value, not its acquisition cost. The book value will get lower after each depreciation entry is recorded, but the percentage to depreciate remains the same. For example, assume we purchased an asset for $5,895; it has a scrap value of $1,500. Figure 22.5 shows how the declining balance depreciation amounts would be calculated.

Figure 22.5 Declining balance depreciation

	Balance	*Depreciation*	*Ending Balance*
Year one	5,895.00	1,411.62	4,483.38
Year two	4,483.38	1,073.59	3,409.78
Year three	3,409.78	816.51	2,593.27
Year four	2,593.27	620.99	1,972.29
Year five	1,972.29	472.29	1,500.00

The syntax for the Db() function is:

```
<nArray> := Db( <nCost>,<nScrap>,<nLife> )
```

The function will return an array filled with each period's depreciation amount.

Double-declining Balance. Another accelerated depreciation method is the declining balance method. This method uses a higher percentage on a progressively smaller asset value. This results in taking more depreciation expenses in the early years and less later.

The annual depreciation entry for the declining balance method is computed by applying a percentage to the asset's book value, not its acquisition cost. The book value will get lower after each depreciation entry is recorded, but the percentage to depreciate remains the same. For example, assume we purchased an asset for $1,000; it has a scrap value of $100 and a seven-year life. Figure 22.6 shows how the declining balance depreciation amounts would be calculated.

Note that during the second half of the asset's life, the formula switches over to straight-line depreciation.

Figure 22.6 Double Declining Balance Depreciation

	Balance	*Depreciation*	*Ending Balance*
Year one	1,000.00	257.14	742.86
Year two	742.86	183.67	559.18
Year three	559.18	131.20	427.99
Year four	427.99	93.72	334.27
Year five	334.27	78.09	256.18
Year six	256.18	78.09	178.09
Year seven	178.09	78.09	100.00

The syntax for the Ddb() function is:

```
<nArray> := Ddb( <nCost>,<nScrap>,<nLife> )
```

The function will return an array filled with each period's depreciation amount.

Listing 22.6 contains the four depreciation user-defined functions.

Listing 22.6 Depreciation

```
function Sl(nCost, nScrap, nLife)
local retarray[nLife],dp_amt := (nCost-nScrap)/nLife
afill(retarray,dp_amt)
return retarray
*
function Syd(nCost, nScrap, nLife)
local jj, arr_:={}
for jj:=1 to nLife
   aadd(arr_,2*(nCost-nScrap) * (nLife+1-jj)/(nLife*(nLife+1)))
next
return arr_
*
function Db(nCost, nScrap, nLife)
local accum:=0, jj, arr_:={}
for jj:=1 to nLife
   aadd(arr_,(1-(nScrap/nCost) ** (1/nLife)) * (nCost-accum))
   accum += arr_[jj]
next
return arr_
*
function Ddb(nCost, nScrap, nLife)
local accum:=0, jj, arr_:={}, factor:=2/nLife
local half:=int((nLife+1)/2)+1
for jj:=1 to nLife
   if jj < half
     aadd(arr_,factor*(nCost-nScrap-accum))
   elseif jj==half
     aadd(arr_,(nCost-nScrap-accum)/(nLife+1-half))
   else
     aadd(arr_,arr_[jj-1])
   endif
   accum += arr_[jj]
next
return arr_
```

Interest

When Benjamin Franklin said "Time is money," he seemed to be predicting the future of banking and finance. Money and time may have an adversarial or beneficial relationship, depending upon whether you are borrowing it or saving it. The functions in Listing 22.7 provide interest calculations and time value tools.

Interest calculations require the definition of several terms. These are listed in Table 22.2.

Table 22.2 Interest Terms

Principal	Initial balance or investment amount.
Rate	Percentage rate of interest payment. For purpose of these UDFs, the rate should be expressed as a decimal value (i.e. 10% = .10).
Periods	Number of periods (usually years) for calculations to use.
Payment	Regular, periodic payment.

Simple Interest. Simple interest is a payment based upon the original principal, without taking into account interest previously earned. For example, assume you opened a savings account at 6% simple interest with a $1,000 deposit. A year later that account should have $1,060 in it. (Don't forget to report the $60 to the IRS!)

The Simple() function in Listing 22.7 computes simple interest. Its syntax is:

```
<nFinal_value>  := Simple(<nPrincipal>,<nRate>,<nPeriods>)
```

The ***<nFinal_value>*** returned shows how much principal and interest will be accumulated at the end of the term of **<nPeriods>** .

Compound Interest. Compound interest is a payment based upon the original principal, plus any interest earned to date. Depending upon how frequently the interest is added to the balance, the effective interest rate will be higher than it would be under simple interest. Using our same example, assume you made that deposit in an account that compounds interest quarterly. A year later that account should have $1,060 in it. Figure 22.7 shows how this number was derived.

Figure 22.7 Compound interest on $1,000

Quarter	Interest	Balance	$1,000
1	$ 15.00	$ 1,015.00	
2	$ 15.23	$ 1,030.23	
3	$ 15.45	$ 1,045.68	
4	$ 15.68	$ 1,061.36	
		$ 1,061.36	

The Compound() function in Listing 22.7 computes compound interest. Its syntax is:

```
<nValue> := Compound(<nPrin>,<nRate>,<nPeriods>,<cFreq>)
```

The ***<nValue>*** returned shows how much principal and interest will be accumulated at the end of the term of **<nPeriods>** assuming a **<cFreq>** of one of the following: (A)nnually, (Q)uarterly, (M)onthly, or (C)ontinuously.

Present Value. Present value determines the current value today of a stream of future payments. The formula to compute present value is shown in Figure 22.8.

Figure 22.8 Present value formula

$$\text{Payment} \quad * \quad \frac{1 - (1 + \text{Rate})^{(\text{Periods}*-1)}}{\text{Rate}}$$

The Pv() user-defined function in Listing 22.7 computes present value. Its syntax is:

```
<nPresent> := Pv(<nPayment >,<nRate>,<nPeriods>)
```

<nPresent> contains the amount that represents today's value of the investment. ***<nRate>*** should be expressed as a fraction. For example, if you were to win a million dollars in the lottery and be guaranteed $50,000 a year for the next twenty years, assuming 12% yearly interest the present value of your winnings is $373,472.18.

```
? Pv(50000,.12,20)    // would display  373472.18
```

Future Value. Future value determines how much money will accumulate at the end of a period of time, assuming you make regular payments. The formula to compute future value is shown in Figure 22.9.

Figure 22.9 Future value formula

$$\text{Payment} \; * \; \frac{(1 + \text{Rate})^{\text{Periods}} - 1}{\text{Rate}}$$

The Fv() user-defined function in Listing 22.7 computes future value. Its syntax is:

```
<nFuture> := Fv(<nPayment>,<nRate>,<nPeriods>)
```

<nFuture> contains the amount that will be accumulated at the end of the period. ***<nRate>*** should be expressed as a fraction. For example, if you were to deposit $500 once a year in an investment paying 15% interest for a period of six years, you would have $4,376.87 at the end of the sixth year.

```
? Fv(500,.15,6)   // would display 4,376.87
```

Listing 22.7 Interest

```
function Simple(nPrin, nRate, nPeriods)
return nPrin * (nRate*nPeriods)
*
function Compound(nPrin, nRate, nPeriods, cFreq)
local jj,arr_ := {},multiplier := 1
cFreq := if(cFreq==nil,"Q",cFreq)
if cFreq == "C"
   multiplier := Exp(nRate)
elseif cFreq == "A"
   multiplier := (1+nRate)
elseif cFreq == "Q"
   multiplier := (1+nRate/4)**4
elseif cFreq == "M"
   multiplier := (1+nRate/12)**12
endif
aadd(arr_, nPrin * multiplier)
for jj := 2 to nPeriods
   aadd(arr_, arr_[jj-1] * multiplier)
next
return arr_
*
function Pv(payment, rate, periods)
local multi:= (1-((1+Rate)**(-1*periods))) / rate
return multi * payment
*
function Fv(payment, rate, periods)
local multi:= (((1+Rate)**periods)-1) / rate
return multi * payment
```

Statistical user-defined functions

Listing 22.8 includes several user-defined functions to calculate combinations and permutations, to calculate group statistics, and to create pseudo-random samples and normalized numbers.

Combo()

Combinations represent the number of possible groups of items that can be extracted from a larger group. The order of items in the groups is not important. A good example is to determine the number of five card poker hands in a deck of 52 cards. The Combo() function syntax is:

```
<nCombinations> := Combo( <nGroup>,<nSets> )
```

<nGroup> represents the total number of items in the larger group. ***<nSets>*** represents the number of items in each set or smaller group.

For example:

```
? Combo( 52,5 )   // Displays 259894
```

Perms()

Permutations represent the number of possible arrangements that can be extracted from a larger group. The order of items in the groups is important, since each different order represents a new arrangement. The Perms() function syntax is:

```
<nPermutations> := Perms( <nGroup>,<nArrange> )
```

<nGroup> represents the total number of items in the larger group. ***<nArrange>*** indicates the number of items in each arrangement.

For example:

```
? Combo( 10,3 )   // Displays 720
```

Mean()

The population mean is a statistical term that denotes the average value of a group of data. The Mean() function in Listing 22.8 computes the population mean for an array. Its syntax is:

```
<nMean> := Mean( <aGroups> )
```

<aGroups> is a numeric array containing the values to be averaged. For example:

```
local groups := {}, mean := 0
select PAYROLL
go top
do while !eof()
   aadd( groups, PAYROLL->salary )
   skip +1
enddo
mean := mean( groups )
```

Median()

The median is a statistical term that is used to measure central tendency in a group of data. The mean can be misleading, since it is possible that no element in the group has the mean value. For example, if two people's heights are six feet and five feet, the mean height is five foot six inches, even though no members of the group are that height. The median represents the middle value from the group, which generally means at least one member of the group is the median value. The Median() function in Listing 22.8 computes the median for an array. Its syntax is:

```
<nMedian> := Median( <aGroups> )
```

<aGroups> is a numeric array containing the values to be used. For example:

```
local groups := {}, median := 0
select PAYROLL
go top
do while !eof()
   aadd( groups, PAYROLL->salary )
   skip +1
enddo
median := Median( groups )
```

Var()

The variance is a measure of how far values are from the midpoint of the group. It is used to determine the distribution of values. The Var() function in Listing 22.8 computes the variance of an array of numbers. Its syntax is:

```
<nVariance>  := Var( <aGroups> )
```

<aGroups> is a numeric array containing the values to be computed. For example:

```
local groups := {}, variance := 0
select PAYROLL
go top
do while !eof()
   aadd( groups, PAYROLL->Salary )
   skip +1
enddo
variance := Var( groups )
```

Listing 22.8 Statistical functions

```
function Combo(nNumber,nTaken)
local nLogn := factorial(nNumber), nLogt := factorial(nTaken)
local nDiff := factorial(nNumber-nTaken)
return int(exp(nLogn-(nLogt+nDiff))+.5)

function Perms(nNumber,nTaken)
local nLogn := factorial(nNumber), nLogt := factorial(nTaken)
return int(exp(nLogn-nLogt) + .5)

static function Factorial(nX)
local appx := 1,jj
if nX <=0
   appx := 0
else
```

```
   for jj := 1 to 10
      appx *= jj
       if nX == jj
          return log(appx)
       endif
   next
   /* Sterling approximation for large integers */
   appx := log(6.283186)/2+log(nX) * (nX+.5)-nX+1/(nX*12)
endif
return appx

function Mean(aGroups)
local nSum := 0,nSize := len(aGroups),jj
for jj := 1 to nSize
   nSum =+ aGroups[jj]
next
return if(nSize==0,0,nSum/nSize)

function Median(aGroups)
local nSize := len(aGroups), nMid, nMedian
local lOdd :=  (nSize/2 <> int(nSize/2))
asort(aGroups,1,nSize)
if lOdd
   nMedian := aGroups( int(nSize/2)+1 )
else
   nMid    := int(nSize/2)
  nMedian := (aGroups(nMid)+aGroups(nMid+1))/2
endif
return nMedian

function Variance(aGroups)
local nSum := 0, nSum_Square := 0, jj, nSize := len(aGroups)
for jj := 1 to nSize
   nSum += aGroups[jj]
   nSum_Square += (aGroups[jj]**2)
next
return nSum_square/nSize-(nSum/nSize)**2
```

Mathematical user-defined functions

Listing 22.11 includes several user-defined functions to convert numbers between bases and to calculate prime numbers, greatest common divisors, and least common multiples.

Bin2Dec()/Dec2Bin()

Base two or binary numbers are representations of numbers using only the digits zero and one. The Bin2Dec() function reads a binary string and returns a decimal number. Its syntax is:

```
<nValue>  := Bin2dec( <cString_of_zeros_and_ones> )
```

A decimal number may also be converted into base two. The Dec2Bin() function reads a decimal number and returns a binary string. Its syntax is:

```
<cString_of_zeros_and_one>  := Dec2Bin(<nDecimal> )
```

These functions can be used to work with bit strings in Clipper. For example, DOS stores the computer's equipment list as a bit string as illustrated in Table 22.1. Using the FT_PEEK() function written by Ted Means, the code in Listing 22.9 returns an array containing the equipment list of the computer.

Table 22.1 DOS Equipment List Byte

Bits	*Contents*
0	1 - Disk drives are present, 0 - no disk drives
1	Not used, should be 0
2-3	System RAM 00=16K, 01=32K, 11=64K
4-5	Video mode 01=40 Columns 10=80 Color 11=80 B&W
6-7	Diskette drives 00=1, 01=2, 10=3, 11=4 drives
8	DMA installed? 1=Yes, 0=No
9-11	Number of serial ports
12	Game adapter 1=Yes, 0=No
13	Serial printer installed 1=Yes, 0=No
14-15	Number of printers

Listing 22.9 Read equipment list

```
function Equip
local eByte1 := Ft_peek(0,272)
local eByte2 := Ft_peek(0,273)
local bString1 := "", bString2 := ""
local arr_ := {}, cSport
bString1 := padl(Dec2Bin(eByte1), 8, "0")
bString2 := padl(Dec2Bin(eByte2), 8, "0")
cSport := substr(bstring2, 7, 1) +; substr(bstring2, 6, 1)
aadd(arr_, str(Bin2Dec(cSport), 2)+;" Serial Ports")
aadd(arr_, if(substr(bstring2, 4, 1) == "1", "", "No ") +;
           "Game Port")
aadd(arr_, if(substr(bstring2, 8, 1) == "1", "", "No ") +;
          "DMA Chip")
return arr_
```

Hex2Dec()/Dec2Hex()

Base sixteen or hexidecimal numbers are representations of numbers using only the digits zero through F. (A is 10, B is 11, and so on up to F is 15.) The Hex2Dec() function reads a hexidecimal string and returns a decimal number. Its syntax is:

```
<nValue>  := Hex2dec( <cHex_string> )
```

A decimal number may also be converted into hexidecimal. The Dec2Hex() function reads a decimal number and returns a hexidecimal string. Its syntax is:

```
<cHex_string>  := Dec2Hex(<nDecimal> )
```

Frequently, DOS files are viewed as hexidecimal numbers. The function in Listing 22.10 reads a DOS file and displays it as a series of hexidecimal digits. The function syntax is:

```
Hexdump( <cFilename> )
```

Listing 22.10 Hexdump

```
#define BUF_SIZE  200

function Hexdump(cFilename)
local fh := fopen(cFilename)
local buf:= space(BUF_SIZE), spot, jj, tt
if fh > -1
   do while fread(fh, @buf, BUF_SIZE) == BUF_SIZE
       for jj := 1 to 10
           ?
           for tt := 1 to 20
              spot := (jj-1) * 20 + tt
              ?? dec2hex(asc(substr(buf,spot,1)))+" "
           next
       next
   enddo
   jj := 0
   ?
  do while !empty(buf)
       jj++
       ?? Dec2Hex(asc(substr(buf,1,1))) + " "
       buf := substr(buf,2)
       if jj == 20
           jj := 0
           ?
       endif
   enddo
endif
return nil
```

Gcd()

The greatest common divisor is the largest integer that goes into two other integers. For example, the greatest common divisor of ten and fifteen is five. Euclid devised an algorithm to determine the greatest common divisor in approximately 300 B.C.

The syntax for the Gcd() function is:

```
<nGcd> := Gcd( <nFirst>,<nSecond> )
```

For example:

```
? Gcd(24,56)        // Displays 8
? Gcd(1095,155)     // Displays 5
```

Isprime()
The Isprime() function returns a logical value indicating whether or not a number is a prime number. A prime number is a number which can be evenly divided by only itself and one. The syntax for the Isprime() function is:

```
<logical>  := Isprime( <nInteger> )
```

For example,

```
local jj
for jj := 1 to 50
   if Isprime(jj)
      ? str(jj,3)," is a prime number"
   endif
next
```

Lcm()
The least common multiple is an integer value which represents the smaller number that two integers can be evenly divided into. The syntax for Lcm() is:

```
<nLeast_common_multi> := Lcm( <nInteger1>,<nInteger2> )
```

For example,

```
? Lcm( 24,56 )        // Displays 168
? Lcm( 4096,128)      // Displays 4096
```

Listing 22.11 Mathematics

```
function Bin2dec(cBinary)
local nDec := 0,jj
for jj := 1 to len(cBinary)
   nDec := nDec + nDec + val(substr(cBinary,jj,1))
next
return nDec

function Dec2Bin(nDecimal)
local nTemp := nDecimal,cBinary := ""
local nDiv  := int(nTemp/2),nRem := 0
do while nDiv <> 0
   nRem    := nTemp-(2*nDiv)
   cBinary := substr("01",nRem + 1,1) + cBinary
   nTemp   := nDiv
   nDiv    := int(nTemp/2)
enddo
return cBinary

function Hex2Dec(cHex)
LOCAL nDec := 1 to len(cHex)
     nDec := nDec * 16 + at(substr(cHex,jj,1),"123456789ABCDEF")
next
return nDec

function Dec2Hex(nDec)
LOCAL nTemp     :=nDec, cHex := ""
LOCAL nDiv      := int(nTemp/16)
LOCAL  nRem     := nTemp-(16*nDiv)
do while nDiv <> 0
     nRem := nTemp -(16*nDiv))
     cHex :=substr("0123456789ABCDEF",nRem+1,1)+cHex
     nTemp:= nDiv
     nDiv  := int(nTemp/16)
enddo
cHex := substr("0123456789ABCDEF",nRem+1,1)+cHex
return cHex
```

```
function Gcd(nX,nY)
local rmd := 1,quot := 0
do while rmd <> 0
      quot := int(nX/nY)
      rmd := nX - (nY*quot)
      if rmd <> 0
        nX := nY
       nY := rmd
      endif
enddo
return nY

function Isprime(nX)
local jj
if nX == 1
   return .F.
elseif nX < 4
   return .T.
endif
if nX == int(nX/2) * 2
   return .F.
endif
for jj := 3 to int(sqrt(nX)) step 2
   if nX == int(nX/jj) * jj
      return .F.
   endif
next
return .T.

function Lcm(nX,nY)
return nX*nY/gcd(nX,nY)
```

Clipper dates

Clipper includes very powerful date manipulation capabilities. Dates are stored internally in such a way that math operations can be performed on dates to derive other dates. Adding an integer to a date will result in a future date. Subtracting two dates will result in the number of days between the two.

Environment setting

Clipper provides three settings which control the display of dates. One controls whether or not the century is displayed, the second controls the format of the date, and the third controls which century two-digit years are placed into.

SET CENTURY

The SET CENTURY command determines whether or not the year portion of a date is display with four digits (including the century) or two digits (not including the century). The default is two digits. The syntax of the command is:

```
SET CENTURY <ON|OFF|<logical>
```

If the setting is ON or .t., then the year is displayed using four digits. If the setting is OFF or .f., only two digits are used to display the year. The default setting is OFF.

The value of the SET CENTURY setting only affects the input and display of dates and does not affect the way a date is stored in memory or on disk.

SET DATE

Clipper supports several different date display formats. The SET DATE command is used to specify which format Clipper should display dates in. The syntax is:

```
SET DATE  <literal value>
```

The literal value must be one of those formats listed in Table 22.2.

Table 22.2 SET DATE Values

American	mm/dd/yy
Ansi	yy.mm.dd
British	dd/mm/yy
French	dd/mm/yy
German	dd.mm.yy
Italian	dd-mm-yy
Japan	yy/mm/dd
USA	mm-dd-yy

You cannot use a character expression in the SET DATE command although you can macro-expand the value. For example,

```
cDformat := "AMERICAN"
set date cDformat              // Not ok
set date (cDformat)            // Still not ok!
set date &cDformat.            // This will work
```

You can also set the date format using the SET DATE FORMAT command. One benefit of the date format syntax is that it allows a character string to be used to determine the date format, rather than a literal value. The syntax for SET DATE FORMAT is:

```
SET DATE FORMAT TO <cFormat_string>
```

The format string is a combination of the following characters

YYYY	Four digit year
YY	Two digit year
MM	Month number
DD	Day number

and a separation character, such as a colon (:), a period (.), etc. The format string must be twelve or fewer characters. Clipper maps the date components onto the appropriate character, i.e. the year is mapped to YYYY, the month to MM, and the day to DD. For example:

```
set date format to "YYYY-MM-DD"
? date()                          // Displays 1991-01-22
mvar := "MM|DD/YY"
set date format to mvar
? date()                          // Displays 01|22/91
```

The SET DATE FORMAT command allows any structure of date to be used as the default date format. You may also store the date format in a memory variable to allow different users to modify their preferred date display.

SET EPOCH

The SET EPOCH command informs the system how to handle dates that use only two digits for the year. When a two-digit year is entered into a date, its year digits are compared with the year digits of the epoch setting to determine the century to place the date into. If the two digits are prior to the setting of SET EPOCH, the year is assumed to be in the next century. If the digits are greater than or equal to the SET EPOCH setting, the year is assumed to be in the current century. The setting's syntax is:

```
SET EPOCH TO <nYear>
```

The ***<nYear>*** is a four-digit year, which defaults to 1900. This default forces any date entered to be considered a date in the twentieth century.

For example,

```
set epoch to 1900
mdate := ctod("01/22/89")
? year(mdate)        // displays  1989

set epoch to 1990
mdate := ctod("01/22/89")
? year(mdate)        // displays  2089
```

A four-digit year may always be specified to explicitly determine the century that year belongs to.

Date functions

Clipper provides a large number of functions to extract components of date variables, and to convert dates to string formats. This section covers those functions.

CDOW()

The CDOW() function takes a date variable and returns the day of the week as a character string. Its syntax is:

```
<cDayname>  := CDOW( <dValue> )
```

For example, we can use the CDOW() function to display a date variable in a longer fashion.

```
mdate := ctod("01/22/89")
? cdow(mdate),mdate       // Displays  Sunday 01/22/89
```

CMONTH()

The CMONTH() function takes a date variable and returns the month of the year as a character string. Its syntax is:

```
<cMonthname>  := CMONTH( <dValue> )
```

As an example, we can use the CMONTH() function to display two dates as a range of months.

```
mdate1 := ctod("06/05/90")
mdate2 := ctod("09/15/90")
? left(cmonth(mdate1),3) + "-" + left(cmonth(mdate2),3)
```

This example will display:

```
Jun-Sep
```

CTOD()

This function reads a character string and attempts to map it into the current date format. If the string is successfully mapped, a date variable will be returned. Its syntax is:

```
<dVariable> := CTOD(<cFormatted_date_string>)
```

It is important to be aware of the current SET DATE value when using CTOD(). For example:

```
? ctod("01/05/91") // Produces 01/5/91 or January 5, 1991
                   // if SET DATE is AMERICAN and produces
                   // 05.01.91 or May 1,1991 is the SET
                   // DATE format is BRITISH or GERMAN
```

DATE()

The DATE() function returns the system date as a date variable. Its syntax is:

```
<dVariable>  := DATE()
```

For example,

```
@ 02,70 say date()
```

DAY()

The DAY() function takes a date value and returns an integer which corresponds to the day of the month. Its syntax is:

```
<nDay_of_month>  := DAY( <dValue> )
```

<dValue> must be a valid date variable. The returned value will be a number between one and thirty-one, depending upon the numbers of days in the month.

DOW()

The DOW() function takes a date value and returns a numeric value which corresponds to the day of the week. Its syntax is:

```
<nDay_number>  := DOW( <dValue> )
```

<dValue> must be a valid date variable. The returned value will be a number between one and seven. One represents Sunday and seven represents Saturday. If an empty date is passed, zero will be returned.

DTOC()

The date to character function takes a date variable as a parameter and returns a string representation of the date. The string is created in the format specified by the SET DATE or the SET DATE FORMAT command. If SET DATE has not been specified, the default date format is mm/dd/yy. The syntax for DTOC() is:

```
<cString> := DTOC( <dValue> )
```

<dValue> must be a valid date variable. If an empty date is passed, a null string will be returned.

DTOC() is frequently used to display dates. Since it formats the dates according to the SET DATE value, your program can easily work with character dates in international display formats.

DTOS()

The date to string function takes a date variable as a parameter and returns a string in the format:

YYYYMMDD

where	YYYY	represents the four digit year
	MM	represents the numeric month
	DD	represents the day of the month

The return format of the DTOS() function is not affected by the SET DATE setting. It is this string representation of the date that should be used for sorting and indexing dates, since the dates will appear in chronological order. The syntax for DTOS() is:

```
<cString> := DTOS( <dValue> )
```

<dValue> must be a valid date variable. The returned string can be used to arrange dates in chronological sequence, regardless of the date format. It is very useful when indexing databases in date order. For example, you could use DTOS() to create an index which will cause the log entries in a database to appear in chronological date sequence.

```
index on dtos(LOG_DATE) to cust01
```

The DTOS() function can also be used to create concatenated index strings. For example:

```
index on dtos(Sale_date)+state to cust01
```

MONTH()

The month function returns a two-digit month number from a date variable. Its syntax is:

```
<nMonth_no>  := MONTH( <dValue> )
```

<dValue> must be a valid date variable. The returned value will be a number between one and twelve, depending upon the month. If an empty date is passed, zero will be returned.

YEAR()

The YEAR() function takes a date value and returns a four-digit integer which corresponds to the year. Its syntax is:

```
<nYear>  := YEAR( <dValue> )
```

The YEAR() function is not affected by the SET DATE FORMAT or by the SET CENTURY setting. It will always return a four-digit year from a valid date. From an empty date, it will return a zero.

When trying to extract the year, month, or day from a date variable, it is more reliable to use the DAY(), MONTH(), and YEAR() functions rather than relying upon SUBSTR() to extract the components. Since the date format can be changed, the SUBSTR() function may not always be aware of the positioning of the components. In the AMERICAN date format, the month is the first two positions. In the GERMAN date format, the month is in positions four and five.

User-defined date functions

In addition to the standard Clipper date functions, we have included three useful user-defined functions which work with date variables.

Isleap()

The Isleap() function takes a date or a four-digit year and returns a logical value indicating whether or not the year in question is a leap year. Its syntax is:

```
<logical> := Isleap( <dValue|nYear> )
```

Isleap() works with either a four-digit numeric year or a date variable. Listing 22.12 contains the code for the function.

Listing 22.12 Isleap()

```
function Isleap(param)
local nyy := if(valtype(param) == "D", year(param),param)
local dtest := ctod("02/28/"+str(nyy,4))
return (month(dtest+1) == 2)
```

Juld()

A julian date is a three-digit integer which indicates the day of the year. The Juld() function returns a julian date for a date variable. Its syntax is:

```
<nInteger> := Juld( <dVariable> )
```

The code for the Juld date function is shown in Listing 22.13.

Listing 22.13 Juld()

```
function Juld(dVar)
local yy := str(year(dVar),4)         // Determine year
local temp := ctod("01/01/"+yy)       // Build January first of year
return (dVar-temp) +1                 // Subtract to return # of days
```

Djul()

The djul() function takes the three digit integer which indicates the day of the year and returns a date variable from it. Its syntax is:

```
<dVariable> := Dulj( <dVariable> )
```

The code for the Djul date function is shown in Listing 22.14.

Listing 22.14 Djul()

```
function Djul(nJulian)
local yy := year( date())
local temp := ctod("01/01/"+yy)     // Build January first of year
return (temp + nJulian)             // Add julian days back in
```

Making a calendar

To illustrate the date functions, Listing 22.15 contains a function which will display a calendar for the month. The syntax for the function is:

```
Disp_cal(<dVariable>)
```

The ***<dVariable>*** parameter must be a valid date.

Listing 22.15 Disp_cal()

```
function Disp_cal(param)
local jj,tt,temp :=str(month(param),2)+"/01/"+str(year(param),4)
local start := dow(ctod(temp)),pday:=0
local temp1 :=str(month(param)+1,2)+"/01/"+str(year(param),4)
local last := day(ctod(temp1)-1)

? " Sun Mon Tue Wed Thu Fri Sat"
?
for jj := 1 to 6
   for tt := 1 to 7
     if (tt < start+1) .and. jj == 1 .or. pday > last
        ?? space(4)
     else
        pday++
        ?? str(pday,4)
     endif
   next
   ?
next
return nil
```

Time functions

Clipper provides two functions to determine the system time. One function returns the time in a formatted fashion, while the other returns it as an integer number of seconds.

TIME()

The TIME() function returns the system time in the format of **hh:mm:ss**. **hh** is the hour past midnight based on a twenty-four hour clock. **mm** is minutes past the hour and **ss** is seconds past the minute. The TIME() function can be used to display the time on the screen or in a printed report. The code example below displays the date and time in the upper right-hand corner of the screen.

```
@ 1,70 say time()
@ 2,70 say date()
```

The syntax for TIME() is:

```
<cTime> := TIME()
```

<cTime> is always returned based upon a 24-hour clock. The AmPm() UDF in Listing 22.16 converts a time variable to a 12-hour clock format. Its syntax is:

```
<cTime12>  := AmPm( time() )
```

Listing 22.16 - AmPm()

```
function AmPm( cTime )
if val(cTime) < 12
   cTime += " am"
elseif val(cTime) == 12
   cTime += " pm"
else
   cTime := str(val(cTime) - 12, 2) + substr(cTime, 3) + " pm"
endif
return cTime
```

SECONDS()

The SECONDS() function returns the system time as an integer number of seconds past midnight. The range can be zero through 86,399 (the number of seconds in a day). Time returned as seconds is useful for billing calculations. The syntax of SECONDS() is:

```
<nSecs> := SECONDS()
```

The SECONDS() function could be used to track billable time spent on a project or a phone call. The start time and end time would both be stored as seconds past midnight. The Sec2hours function in Listing 22.17 takes a number of seconds and returns the hours and fractional hours the seconds represent. Its syntax is:

```
<nHours> := Sec2hours( <nSeconds> )
```

Listing 22.17 Sec2hours()

```
function Sec2hours(nSeconds)
local hh:= int(nSeconds/3600), mm := nSeconds % 3600, ss := 0
mm :=  int(mm/60)
ss :=  mm % 60
return hh+(mm/100)
```

User-defined functions

It is unfortunate that the Clipper time processing is not as robust as its capabilities with dates. Additionally, Clipper's time functions provide no methods for dealing with times across two dates. Processing time values requires some additional user-defined functions to round out the time processing functionality. The code for the following user-defined functions is presented in Listing 22.18.

In order to provide a more robust time environment, let's borrow the internal date and time representation from Lotus. In this format, the date is an integer value, some number of days past a base date. The time is the fractional portion of the number, indicating number of seconds past midnight of the specified date.

For example, assuming a base date of January 1, 1980:

```
3309.17400    - January 22, 1989 4:50am
```

The use of this format allows us to construct user-defined functions to manipulate times in a more powerful fashion.

DateTime()

This function takes a date and a time string and returns a numeric value that represents the date and time in the format used by Lotus. Its syntax is:

```
<nDateTime> := DateTime( <dVar>,<cTime> )
```

<dVar> must be a valid date variable and ***<cTime>*** must be a valid time string in 24 hour format. If either parameter is missing, the function will return a -1.

GetDate()

This function takes a numeric value created by the DateTime() function and returns a date variable. Its syntax is:

```
<dVariable> := GetDate( <nDatetime> )
```

If the ***<nDatetime>*** is an invalid date/time number, an empty date will be returned from the function.

GetTime()

This function takes a numeric value created by the DateTime() function and returns a formatted time string. Its syntax is:

```
<cTime> := GetTime( <nDatetime> )
```

If the ***<nDateTime>*** is an invalid date/time number, a null string will be returned from the function.

Elap_days()

This function takes two date/time values and returns the number of elapsed days between them. Its syntax is:

```
<nDays> := Elap_days( <nDateTime1>,<nDateTime2> )
```

If either ***<nDatetime>*** is invalid, the function will return a -1. If the number of hours remaining after all days are accounted for exceeds 12, then an extra day will be added to the return value.

Elap_hours()

This function takes two date/time values and returns the number of elapsed hours between them. Its syntax is:

```
<nHours> := Elap_hours( <nDateTime1>,<nDateTime2> )
```

If either ***<nDatetime>*** is invalid, the function will return a -1. If the number of minutes remaining after all hours are accounted for exceeds 30, then an extra hour will be added to the return value.

Elap_mins()

This function takes two date/time values and returns the number of elapsed minutes between them. Its syntax is:

```
<nMins> := Elap_mins( <nDateTime1>,<nDateTime2> )
```

If either ***<nDatetime>*** is a invalid, the function will return a -1. If the number of seconds remaining after all minutes have been accounted for exceeds 30, then an extra minute will be added to the return value.

Listing 22.18 contains the user-defined functions for working with Date/Time variables. These functions call the Sec2hours() function from Listing 22.17, so be sure to link in that function, and compile with the **/n** option.

Listing 22.18 Date/Time Functions

```
static basedate := "01/01/80"
static half_day := 43200

function DateTime(dVar,cTime)
local nDatetime := -1, nSeconds := 0
local cDate, cSeconds
if dVar == nil .OR. cTime == nil
   return -1
else
   cDate     := alltrim(str(dVar - ctod(basedate),12,0))
   nSeconds  := val(cTime)*3600 + val(substr(cTime,4,2)) * 60 ;
              + val(substr(cTime,7,2))
   cSeconds  := alltrim(str(nSeconds))
   nDatetime := val(cDate + "." + cSeconds)
endif
return nDatetime

function GetDate(nDatetime)
local dDate := ctod("")
if nDatetime <> nil
   dDate := ctod(basedate) + int(nDatetime)
endif
return dDate

function GetTime(nDatetime)
local cTemp := str(nDatetime,15,5)
local nSecs := val(substr(cTemp,11,5))
cTemp := str(Sec2hours(nSecs),5,2)
return strtran(cTemp,".",":")+":00"

function Elap_days(nDt1,nDt2)
local nDays := -1, nDiff
if nDt1 == nil .or. nDt2 == nil
   return -1
else
   nDiff := abs( nDt1-nDt2 )
   nDays := int(nDiff)
   if nDiff - nDays >  half_day
```

```
      nDays++
   endif
endif
return nDays

function Elap_hours(nDt1,nDt2)
local nHours := -1,nDiff := 0,nRest := 0,nSecs := 0
if nDt1 == nil .or. nDt2 == nil
   return -1
else
   nDiff  := abs( nDt1-nDt2 )
   nHours := int(nDiff) * 24      // Number of days * 24 hours
   nSecs  := val(substr(str(nDiff,15,5),11,5))
   nHours += (nSecs/3600)
   if nSecs % 3600 > 1800
      nHours++
   endif
endif
return nHours

function Elap_mins(nDt1,nDt2)
local nMins := -1,nDiff := 0,nRest := 0,nSecs := 0
if nDt1 == nil .or. nDt2 == nil
   return -1
else
   nDiff  := abs( nDt1-nDt2 )
   nMins  := int(nDiff) * 1440    // Number of days expressed
                                  // in minutes
   nSecs  := val(substr(str(nDiff,15,5),11,5))
   nMins  += (nSecs/3600)
   if nSecs % 60 > 30
      nMins++
   endif
endif
return nMins
```

Summary

After completing this chapter your should feel comfortable writing simple and complex formulas in Clipper. You should know the various functions Clipper provides for mathematical operations and should be able to use several user-defined functions in your applications. You should also know how Clipper handles dates and times. If you need to work with times across dates, you should be able to work with the special date/time UDFs provided at the end of the chapter.

CHAPTER 23

Disks and Directories

A computer's disk drive can be viewed as a large filing cabinet. While information can be crammed into a filing cabinet with no sense of organization, it certainly loses its value when it is. The disk operating system (DOS) provides functions to organize the hard disk much as file folders can be used to organize the file cabinet. In this chapter, we will discuss how DOS organizes its disks and how Clipper can work within DOS's structure. We will also discuss the DOS environment and the functions Clipper provides to access that environment.

DOS environment

DOS is responsible for communicating between your application program and the computer hardware. Although other operating systems are available, DOS is the only platform that Clipper currently supports. Computer Associates' future direction is to allow Clipper programs to be run on multiple platforms, such as OS/2 and Unix.

Clipper provides functions which access some of the information available from DOS. In addition, Clipper's powerful extend system allows an application to obtain status and request services from DOS using C and assembly language programs.

DOS status information

Clipper provides six functions to query DOS for various information. This information includes the operating system version, the system date and time, the current directory, the amount of space on the disk, and the environment string settings.

OS()—current operating system

The OS() function reports the current operating system and version that the application is running under. Its syntax is:

```
<cVersion>  := OS()
```

The **<cVersion>** returned will contain both the operating system name and the current version. For example, on a computer running under MS-DOS version 3.21, the OS() function would return "DOS 3.21" as a character string.

The OS() function can be useful to determine whether or not certain features in your program can be performed. For example, the DOS version must be 3.1 or above to run a Clipper network application. Here is the code for a user-defined function and an example that returns the version as a numeric value:

```
if DosVer() < 3.1
   ? "Cannot run networked application on this computer"
endif
return nil

function DosVer()
local cDos := os(), x, nVersion := 0.0
if (x := at(" ",cDos)) > 0
  nVersion := val(substr(cDos, x+1, 99))
endif
return nVersion
```

DATE()—current system date

The DATE() function returns a date variable containing the current system date. Its syntax is:

```
<dCurrent>  := DATE()
```

TIME()—current system time

The TIME() function returns a character string variable which contains the current system time. Its syntax is:

```
<cTime>  := TIME()
```

The **<cTime>** string is returned in the form of **HH:MM:SS** and is based on a 24-hour clock. The system time may also be returned as a number of seconds past midnight. The syntax for the SECONDS() function is:

```
<nSecond>   := SECONDS()
```

Dates and time are discussed in more detail in Chapter 22.

CURDIR()—current disk directory

The CURDIR() function returns the name of the current directory that the application is running in. Its syntax is:

```
<cDirectory>  := CURDIR(<cDrive>)
```

The **<cDirectory>** returned will be the directory name for the current specified drive. The directory name will not contain a leading or a trailing backslash (\) character.

<cDrive> is an optional parameter which specifies the drive letter to obtain the directory from. If not specified, the default will be the current drive. If the drive does not exist or it is not ready, a null string will be returned.

The CURDIR() function can be used to ensure that the program is running from the proper directory. Here's an example:

```
local where := curdir()
if where <> "APPL\PAYROLL"
   run cd\appl\payroll
endif
```

DISKSPACE()—free space on a disk drive

The DISKSPACE() function returns the number of bytes available on a disk drive. Its syntax is:

```
<nFreeBytes>  := DISKSPACE(<nDrive>)
```

<nFreeBytes> is an integer indicating the number of free bytes.

<nDrive> is an optional parameter which specifies the drive number to obtain the free space from. The drives are numbered starting at 1 for drive A:, 2 for B:, 3 for drive C:, and so on. If **<nDrive>** is not specified or is zero, the default will be the current drive.

The DISKSPACE() function can be used to ensure that the program has enough disk room to create needed files. The following listing checks to see if the current work area can be copied to drive A:.

```
local dbf_size
use CUSTOMER new
dbf_size := header() + (lastrec() * recsize())
if dbf_size > diskspace(1)    // Check drive A:
   ? "File too big to fit on diskette."
else
   copy to a:customer
endif
```

One caveat: The CURDIR() function and the DISKSPACE() function both accept a drive as a parameter; however CURDIR() expects the drive to be a character while DISKSPACE() expects a numeric parameter.

GETENV()—read DOS environment strings

DOS allows you to define environment strings using the SET command. Its syntax is:

```
SET <name> = <value>
```

One of the most common environment strings is the PATH setting. Clipper also makes use of DOS environment strings to control file handles, variable space, expanded memory, and so on. For example, the DOS command:

```
SET CLIPPER =E512;F35
```

instructs Clipper to restrict expanded memory usage to 512K bytes and to allow 35 file handles to be opened.

Clipper allows you to read the DOS environment strings using the GETENV() function. Its syntax is:

```
<cString>  := GETENV("cEnvironment_Variable>")
```

If the **<cEnvironment_Variable>** exists, its value will be returned in **<cString>**. If the DOS environment variable does not exist, a null string ("") will be returned. The variable name is not case-sensitive.

For example, in the listing below, the function returns the value of the **F** setting in the CLIPPER environment string. If no Clipper environment string has been specified, the function will return **20** which is the default maximum number of open files supported by Clipper.

```
function Get_F_Set()
local f_value := 20, clip_set := getenv("CLIPPER"), x
if !empty(clip_set)
   if (x := at("F", clip_set)) > 0
      f_value := val(substr(clip_set, x+1, 3))
   endif
endif
return f_value
```

Environment variables are most frequently used to pass directory and configuration information to programs. They are also very convenient ways of handling multiple configurations in a network environment.

Directories and files

When DOS formats a hard disk or a diskette, it sets aside room for a table to hold file names. This table will contain entries for any file found in the root area. In addition, DOS allows the user to create subdirectories, which allow the hard drive to be organized in an efficient manner. Each subdirectory also reserves room for a table to hold file names. These tables are called directories.

A directory is a list of all files either in the root directory or in a subdirectory. Clipper provides a function called DIRECTORY() to transfer this file list into an array. For compatibility reasons, Clipper also maintains the ADIR() function, although the stated preference is to use the newer function.

Directory entries

In order to effectively use the DIRECTORY() function, we must first explore how file names are stored within a DOS directory. Table 23.1 lists the information which is maintained for each file within a directory.

Table 23.1 File directory information

Name	*Contents*
Filename	Eight-character file name with three-character file extension. Normally, the file name and extension are separated by the period character.
File Size	The size of the file in bytes.
File Date	The date the file was last updated.
File Time	The time the file was last updated.
Attributes	A bit string indicating the type of file. It may be a combination of the following types. Normal file Hidden file System file Directory Read-only Volume label

Wildcards

The next item we need to be aware of is the wildcard. Wildcards are substitution patterns which allow functions to be performed on a select group of files. DOS uses two wildcard symbols, the asterisk and the question mark. The asterisk is used to match any files regardless of the length of the file name. The question mark is used to match any character in a particular position in the file name. For example, assume the files in Figure 23.1 exist in a directory:

Figure 23.1 Example files

```
SALES.RPT
SALESJT.RPT
SALESRA.RPT
SALESFRM.LPT
```

The pattern

*.RPT	Returns the first three files only.
*.?PT	Returns all four files.
SALES??.*	Returns the middle two files. The first file name is too short to match the pattern and the last file name is too long.

DIRECTORY()

The DIRECTORY() function allows you to select which files to place into the array by use of two parameters. The first parameter selects the pattern the file names must meet in order to be included. The second parameter specifies the attributes the file must have in order to be included. The syntax for the function is:

```
<array> := DIRECTORY( <pattern>,<attributes> )
```

<pattern> can be a single file or multiple files requested by using wildcard characters. If the **<pattern>** is not supplied, the default pattern will be *.*, which returns all files from the directory.

<attribute> can be any combination of the attribute codes listed in Table 23.2.

Table 23.2 Attribute codes

Code	*Meaning*
N	Normal files
H	Hidden files
S	System files
D	Subdirectories only
V	Volume label, excluding all other files.

The default is **Normal files**. Normal files are always included in the file list, unless the **Volume label** attribute is used.

For example, to fill the array with all normal files and all system files, the attribute would be set to "S". To get all normal files and directories, set the attribute to "D". The "V" attribute has special meaning since it excludes all files except the volume label. A function to return the volume label for any drive can be written as shown below:

```
function Vlabel( vdrive )
local test := directory( substr(vdrive,1,1) + ":\*.*", "V")
return if(empty(test),"No label found",test[1,1])
```

The function takes the drive letter specified and looks for the volume label using the directory function. If the directory function returns an empty array, then no volume label was found.

If the directory of a different subdirectory is needed, the subdirectory name can be included as part of the **<pattern>** specified to the DIRECTORY() function call.

The array that is returned is a multi-dimensional array with the structure shown in Table 23.3. The preprocessor constants are stored in DIRECTORY.CH.

Table 23.3 Directory array structure

Element #	*CONSTANT*	*Type*	*Contents*
1	F_NAME	Char	File name and extension.
2	F_SIZE	Numeric	Number of bytes in file.
3	F_DATE	Date	Date of last update.
4	F_TIME	Char	Time of last update.
5	F_ATT	Char	Attribute string

Here are a few examples of the DIRECTORY() function call.

```
#include "DIRECTRY.CH"
local  flist := directory("*.DBT")
? len(flist)                   // Displays number of .DBT files
aeval(flist,{|x| qout(x)})  // Display file names
flist := directory("CUSTOMER.DBT")
if !empty(flist)
   ?  flist[1,F_SIZE]          // Size of CUSTOMER.DBT file
endif
```

FILE()

The FILE() function is used to see if a file exists on the disk. Clipper will search the current directory and if the file is not found, will then search the Clipper path. The syntax for the function is:

```
<logical>  := FILE(<cFilespec>)
```

<cFilespec> can be any valid DOS file name or a wildcard pattern. If any file can be found that matches the file name, the function will return true. If after searching the current directory and the Clipper path, the file is not found, false will be returned.

The FILE() function will not search the DOS path, nor will it find hidden or system files. If you need to check for a hidden file, use the DIRECTORY() function.

The user-defined function in Listing 23.1 uses the Parse() UDF from Chapter 21 to search the path looking for a file. Its syntax is:

```
<logical>  := Inpath( <cFilespec> )
```

Listing 23.1 Inpath()

```
function Inpath(mfile)
local pathlist, jj, tfile
if ! file(mfile)
  pathlist := Parse( getenv("PATH"), ";" )
  for jj := 1 to len(pathlist)
     tfile := pathlist[jj] + "\" + trim(mfile)
     if file(tfile)
        return .T.
     endif
  next
else
  return .T.
endif
return .F.
```

Clipper's file searching

Clipper allows you to specify a search path that should be used when opening files. It also allows you to select the directory that Clipper should use as its default directory.

SET PATH

The SET PATH command allows you to create a list of file directories that Clipper should check if the requested file is not found in the current directory. Its syntax is:

```
SET PATH TO <cPath_list>
```

The **<cPath_list>** may be a literal constant or an expression surrounded by parentheses. The list of directories within the path can be separated by commas or semicolons. If a literal constant rather than a character expression is used, the SET PATH command line cannot be continued with the semicolon.

The path is only searched if the file is not found in the current directory and a path designation is not explicitly included in the file name. If the file is not found, Clipper will process the path list sequentially until it finds the file or the path is exhausted.

If no parameter is specified, the path list is released and Clipper will search only the current directory.

The listing below contains a user-defined function to set Clipper's internal path to the contents of the DOS path environment setting.

```
local dos_path := getenv("PATH")
if !empty(dos_path)
  set path to (dos_path)
endif
return nil
```

SET DEFAULT

When an application is started, DOS sets the current directory to the directory that the application is being run from. This is where Clipper will first look for its files. Clipper provides the SET DEFAULT command to instruct Clipper to look elsewhere for its files. Its syntax is:

```
SET DEFAULT TO <cPathspec>
```

The **<cPathspec>** may be a literal constant or an expression surrounded by parentheses. If the ***<cPathspec>*** includes a drive designation, it must be separated from the directory by a colon. If no parameter is specified the default directory will be the current DOS directory.

This command does NOT change the current directory, only where Clipper searches first for files. All temporary and low-level files will be put into the current DOS directory regardless of the setting of the SET DEFAULT command. The RUN command also accesses the current directory rather than the directory specified with SET DEFAULT.

Below is an example of a database being searched by company ID to determine the location of that company's files. Once the record is found, the SET DEFAULT value is set to the subdirectory specified in the DBF files.

```
function comp_def( comp_id )
use CONFIG.DBF new
locate all for CONFIG->id_code == comp_id
if found()
   set default to (CONFIG->directory)
endif
use
return nil
```

The low-level file functions are not affected by either the SET PATH or the SET DEFAULT settings. These functions are discussed in Chapter 24.

Running DOS programs

Clipper allows you to run a DOS application from within a compiled program. It also allows you to communicate with DOS through the ERRORLEVEL setting which DOS batch files can access. However, running an external DOS program requires memory, which is something that Clipper has an appetite for as well. For practical purposes, only small DOS utilities and commands, such as MD or FORMAT, should be run from within a Clipper application.

RUN

The RUN command executes a program or a DOS command. Its syntax is:

```
RUN <cCommand_or_program>
```

<cCommand_or_program> may either be a literal string or a character expression enclosed in parentheses. The command may be a DOS internal command, such as CLS or DIR, it may be an external DOS command, such as CHKDSK or PRINT, or it may be another application.

In order to shell out to DOS, Clipper executes another copy of COMMAND.COM and passes the requested command to it. This requires at least enough memory for COMMAND.COM (about 28K depending upon the DOS version) and for the application being run. If you expect to need memory for a DOS program, you should set the R Clipper environment string to reserve enough memory. This is done at the DOS prompt before loading the Clipper application. The DOS syntax is:

```
SET CLIPPER=R32
```

In addition to the memory requirements, Clipper must be able to find a copy of COMMAND.COM. Normally this file will reside in the root directory of the drive you booted your application from. If it is not there or the drive has been changed, a run-time error will occur. You can specify COMMAND.COM's location using the DOS environment string COMSPEC. The syntax is:

```
SET COMSPEC =<cDirectory name>
```

You can also use the RUN command to allow the user direct access to DOS. This is done by using the word COMMAND following the run command. When the user is done working in DOS, they should type in EXIT to return to the Clipper application. The DOS prompt can be changed to a message which reminds the user to type in EXIT when they are done in DOS.

You should never execute a memory-resident program using the RUN command. Doing so will almost guarantee memory problems on your return to the Clipper application.

Use RUN with extreme care. Its memory needs prevent it from being used for anything other than small commands and programs. There are several third-party libraries which take a different approach to RUNning DOS applications. If you frequently need to call DOS programs from within your Clipper application, you should investigate these libraries.

ERRORLEVEL()

The ERRORLEVEL() function is used to query and/or set the value of the DOS error level. This error level can be detected in a DOS batch file using the syntax:

```
IF ERRORLEVEL  <n>
```

By setting the error level, a Clipper program can direct a batch file's processing when the Clipper application terminates. The Clipper syntax for setting an error level is:

```
<nCurrent_setting> := ERRORLEVEL( <nNew_setting> )
```

The default error level at start-up is zero, indicating that no errors have occurred. If a Clipper application terminates with a fatal error, error level is set to one. If the program terminates normally, the error level is set to zero or the last value it was set to in the Clipper application.

Listing 23.2 illustrates a Clipper application setting the error level if the application does not complete processing. Presumably the batch file which called the Clipper application will respond by logging the problem somewhere. The batch file side of the application can best be understood by reading a DOS manual or user guide.

Listing 23.2 ERRORLEVEL() Example

```
begin sequence
   use CUSTOMER new
   if  ( header()+recsize()*lastrec() ) > diskspace(1)
      errorlevel(1)   // Couldn't fit CUSTOMER on backup disk
      break
   endif
   use VENDOR new
   if  ( header()+recsize()*lastrec() ) > diskspace(1)
      errorlevel(2)   // Couldn't fit VENDOR on backup disk
      break
   endif
   errorlevel(0)      // Everything ok, set ok errorlevel
end
quit
```

Summary

After reading this chapter you should know the functions that Clipper provides to access information from DOS. You should also know how to create a directory array and its structure. In addition, you should be able to establish paths and default directories for your Clipper commands. Finally, you should know how to execute DOS programs and commands from with a Clipper application.

CHAPTER 24

Memo Files

The xBASE file structure supports two types of fields to handle character data. The character field is used for fixed length data. The memo field is used to handle variable length data. The actual memo contents are stored in a different file from the database. The database memo field contains a numeric pointer into the second file indicating where the text is written. The memo allows comments and notes to be written and associated with a particular record.

In this chapter we will discuss how memo fields are stored on the disk and the functionality Clipper provides for memo fields. We will also discuss how to correct some of the problems memo fields have, and present an alternative to using memo fields. Finally, we will present a text editing application to illustrate the power that is available in Clipper memo facilities.

Memo fields

A memo field sounds like a programmer's panacea: A method to store character data in a variable length record. Unfortunately, that is not quite the case. While the memo field provides variable length structure, its storage and update techniques in a .DBF file are very inefficient. This inefficiency is inherent in the .DBF file structure. While Clipper's implementation improves the problem a little bit, it would be difficult to correct the inefficiencies and maintain .DBF file compatibility.

How memos are stored in .DBF files

The technique used for storing memos on disk was inherited from the original implementation for dBASE files from Ashton-Tate.

When Clipper was first introduced, it was described as a dBASE compiler. The language had to support all xBASE file formats. While the language has grown above and beyond the scope of the original dBASE language, the need to support dBASE files is still there.

When a database is created with a memo field in it, a file with the same name as the database, but with the .DBT extension, is also created. This file is where the text of the memos will be stored. The database itself has a 10-character numeric field, which holds the offset into the .DBT file.

The .DBT file consists of a series of 512-byte blocks. Each block can contain only one memo. If the memo is small, then much of this 512-byte block is unused. When a memo field is requested, Clipper's database engine looks up the offset into the .DBT file, and starts reading from the offset until the end-of-file character is reached. (A memo file may have several end-of-file characters.) This value is returned as the memo field requested. When the memo is replaced into the database this mechanism works in reverse, using the offset and rewriting the memo into the .DBT file. (This is an improvement over dBASE, which appends edited memos to the end of the .DBT file instead of back where they were read from.)

If the above were a complete description of how the memo file was handled, then the growing .DBT file problem would not exist. Unfortunately, a problem occurs. If the new memo is larger than the original memo, and this additional size will cause a 512-byte boundary to be overwritten, then the edited memo will be appended to the end of the .DBT, using however many 512-byte blocks are needed. The problem occurs because the original block is now unused, and unavailable. Figure 24.1 indicates just how the problem occurs:

Figure 24.1 Memo growth

Block # the DBF
points to

1

Block 1	Original memo contents 490 bytes long........ ....<EOF>
Block 2	Unused

After editing the memo, changing it to 520 bytes, and writing it back into the .DBT file, it looks like this:

Block # the DBF
points to

2

1

Block 1	Original memo contents 490 bytes long......... ....<EOF>
Block 2 Block 3	Contents of first 512 bytes of the new memo This memo is over the 512 bytes, so it needs two blocks in the file to store it ....<EOF>

Notice that block one in the .DBT is now unused, and it never will be used. The only solution in Clipper is to copy the database to a new file, which creates a new .DBT file. The problem is now free to start all over again.

Why use memo fields?

If memo fields are inefficient in disk storage, why use them? The concept of the memo field can have some benefits. It allows the attachment of a note field to a particular record in the database. Memo fields can be used in many applications to provide the end-users with a method of writing notes or comments about the current record in a database file. Here are some examples:

An accounts receivable system might use a memo field for the collection agent to write notes about each customer contact. During the development of a new system, the users are given a pop-up utility to write notes and bugs to the programmer. These notes are stored in a memo field in a data file.

A legal time-billing system allows the lawyers to provide detailed descriptions for the clients as to the services they provided. The timeslip information is stored in a file with a memo field.

FoxPro FPT files

The FoxPro memo system operates more efficiently than Clipper's or DBASE's, but is not compatible with DBASE DBT files. If compatibility is not important, you can use FoxPro memo files rather than the DBASE DBT files. See Chapter 19 for information about the FoxPro Datsabase driver.

Character fields vs. memo fields?

Of course, since Clipper allows character fields in a database to be up to 1024 bytes long, you could use long character fields to store notes and comments. The decision between character and memo fields is based upon your application. Each character field will take up the maximum number of characters whether or not there is data in the field. Each memo field will take up ten bytes at a minimum. Records with no data in the memo field only need the ten bytes to save the pointer information. Fields with data will take up ten bytes plus the size of the memo field in 512-byte increments.

To determine which field type to use, examine the intent of your application. If your application expects only a few records to have data in them, the extra space used by character fields is wasted and a memo field would be worth considering. If you expect that most every record is going to contain information, then very little wasted space will be used in the file if you use character fields.

You also need to consider whether or not you expect frequent updates to the memos. If the memo data is constantly changing, you run the risk of having a lot of unusable space in the memo's .DBT file. If the file exceeds 16 megabytes, no more data can be put into the memo file. (16 megabytes is room for 32,000 512-byte blocks.) In this case, you would need to periodically reorganize the .DBT file through some utility operation in the application.

How memo variables are stored in memory

Once Clipper brings a memo field into memory it is treated just like any other character field. Clipper imposes a restriction that a memo field, or any string data, cannot be longer than 64K bytes. In most applications this maximum size is more than enough.

Working with memo field variables

Clipper provides a number of functions which are specifically intended for use with memo variables. These functions will work equally well on character variables. In addition, all string functions will work on memo variables (see Chapter 21).

Reading memo variables

There are two ways to read data into a memo variable. The method you use depends on where the memo's contents are stored. Clipper can read data into a memo variable from either a memo field in a database file or from a text file.

Memo field from database

If the database has a memo field, Clipper may access that memo field by an assignment operator. The syntax is:

```
<cMemo_variable> := <cAlias> -> <cMemofield>
```

If the ***<cAlias>*** is not supplied, the memo field is assumed to be in the current work area. You can also use the FIELDGET() function to assign the memo field to a memory variable. Its syntax is:

```
<cMemo_variable> := FIELDGET( <nField_no> )
```

Clipper's database drivers automatically translate the request for a memo field into a block reference to be read from the .DBT file.

For example, Listing 24.1 shows a function to search all memo fields in a .DBF file for a particular character string. The function returns an array of record numbers which contain memos where the text was found. The syntax is:

```
<array>  := Find_memos(<cString>,<nField_no>)
```

Listing 24.1 Find_memos()

```
function Find_memos(cString,nField)
local arr_ := {}
go top
do while !eof()
   if cString $ fieldget(nField)
      aadd(arr_,recno())
   endif
   skip +1
enddo
return arr_
```

MEMOREAD()

The MEMOREAD() function is used to read a file from the disk into a memo variable. Its syntax is:

```
<cMemo>  :=  MEMOREAD( <cFilename> )
```

If ***<cFilename>*** is not in the current directory, Clipper will search the DOS path for the file. It will not search the path specified by Clipper's SET DEFAULT TO command nor by Clipper's SET PATH command. If the file cannot be found in either the current directory or the DOS path, an empty string ("") will be returned.

The maximum file size which can be read by MEMOREAD() is 65,519 (64K) bytes.

If **<cFilename>** is on a network, Clipper will attempt to open the file in a shared, read-only mode. If the file cannot be opened in that mode, Clipper returns an empty string ("").

The function in Listing 24.2 shows how a text file can be read into a variable and then edited by MEMOEDIT().

Listing 24.2 MEMOREAD()

```
function Miniedit( cFile )
local mText := memoread( cFile )
return memowrit( cFile,memoedit(mText) )
```

Editing memo fields

Clipper provides a tool for complete edit capabilities of memo and large character string variables. The MEMOEDIT() tool provides text-editing capabilities in a single function. In addition, the function allows the programmer to gain control during the middle of editing.

MEMOEDIT()

The MEMOEDIT() function is used to edit a memo variable. It can also be used to display the contents of a memo variable. Its syntax is:

```
<mString> := memoedit(<mString>, ;
<nTop_row>,<nTop_column>,<nBottom_row>, <nBottom_col>, ;
<lEdit?>,<cmemo_udf>, <nLinelength>,<nTabsize>, ;
<nTextRow>,<nTextCol>,<nWindowRow>,<WindowCol> )
```

The ***<mString>*** is the string to be edited. This string gets transferred into the memory buffer that MEMOEDIT() works on. The function will return either the original string (if the user presses the Esc key) or the modified string if the user presses the Ctrl-W combination. Depending upon the size of the string, MEMOEDIT() can be quite memory hungry, since it must hold a copy of the original string as well a copy of the edited string. If you choose to run MEMOEDIT() on a 16K character string, the function will require at least 32K of memory.

You should add a call to the MEMORY() function to determine if sufficient memory is present to run MEMOEDIT(). For example, the Mem_chk() function in Listing 24.3 returns true if there is more than three times the amount of memory than the length of the memo to be edited. Three times is an estimated factor to allow two copies of the string and some growth room in the memo buffer.

Listing 24.3 Mem_chk()

```
function Mem_chk(param)
param := if(valtype(param)=="C",len(param),param)
// Check largest contiguous block of storage //
return ( param * 3 < memory(1)*1024 )
```

The ***<nTop_row>***,***<nTop_column>***,***<nBottom_row>***, and ***<nBottom_col>*** parameters represent the coordinates in which the memo is edited. The rows can range from zero to MAXROW() and the columns for zero to MAXCOL(). If the coordinates are not supplied, the entire screen will be used. The coordinates are not framed by the MEMOEDIT() function. If you wish to create a box around the MEMOEDIT() window, you can use the @ BOX command or the @...TO syntax.

<lEdit?> is a logical value which indicates if the memo may be updated or is simply being displayed. If the value is true, the memo may be edited. A false value causes the memo to be displayed and allows the user to browse through it. The default is true.

<cMemo_udf> is an optional user-defined function name. If this parameter is specified, control is passed to this UDF during the editing of the memo. This allows your program to provide extra features and options during MEMOEDIT(). The example program at the end of this chapter includes a MEMOEDIT() UDF.

You can also specify **.f.** instead of a UDF. If false is specified, the memo is displayed and MEMOEDIT() immediately terminates. For example, Listing 24.4 displays a memo on the screen and waits for the user to press any key.

Listing 24.4 - MEMOEDIT() display only

```
function Memodisp(cMemo)
local oldscrn := savescreen(10, 10, 20, 60)
@ 10,10 to 20,60 double                    // Draw a box
memoedit( cMemo,11,11,19,59,.f.,.f. )      // Display the memo
inkey(500)                                 // Wait for any key
restscreen(10, 10, 20, 60, oldscrn)
return nil
```

<nLinelength> indicates the length of lines within the text of the memo. If a line of text is longer than this length, it will be word-wrapped to the next line. If the width of the window is smaller than the line length, horizontal scrolling will work. If you do not specify the line length, Clipper will subtract the left column coordinate from the right, and use this result as the length.

The ***<nTabsize>*** determines how many spaces tab characters should be converted to. The default is four spaces. When the user presses the tab key, this number of spaces will be inserted into the memo. If the memo contains a tab character while being displayed, Clipper will convert that tab character to the appropriate number of spaces.

<nTextRow> and ***<nTextCol>*** determine where the cursor should be positioned initially within the memo. The default location is the first memo character (i.e. row one, column zero).

<nWindowRow> and ***<nWindowCol>*** determine where the cursor should be positioned initially within the window. The default location is row zero and the current cursor column.

The sample application at the end of this chapter employs several techniques in the MEMOEDIT() user-defined function to perform macro substitution and search and replace operations.

Memoedit user-defined function

The MEMOEDIT() UDF allows the programmer to control processing while the user is in MEMOEDIT(). This UDF is a black-box process to the function. It merely passes it three parameters and expects a single parameter to be returned. As long as your function returns what Clipper expects, the internals of your function are invisible to MEMOEDIT().

To write a MEMOEDIT() UDF, we need first to understand when Clipper will call the function and what information it will pass to it. Clipper calls the function at three times. These times are designated by a mode parameter that Clipper sends the UDF. In addition to the mode parameter, Clipper also sends the current line and column of the memo.

MODE 3 - Initialization Mode. Before MEMOEDIT() starts processing, a call will be made to the user-defined function. This call is made to allow your function to specify the formatting modes. The formatting modes are listed in Table 24.1. The value your function returns instructs MEMOEDIT() what to do next. MEMOEDIT() will continue to call your function in initialization mode until your function returns a zero. The example code fragment in Listing 24.5 shows a portion of the memo UDF to toggle word wrap OFF and insert mode ON before instructing MEMOEDIT() to leave initialization mode.

Table 24.1 Formatting modes

Mode	*Default*	*Return value to toggle mode*	
word-wrap	ON	34	ME_TOGGLEWRAP
scroll	ON	35	ME_TOGGLESCROLL
insert	OFF	22	K_INS (in INKEY.CH)

Listing 24.5 Sample UDF

```
#include "MEMOEDIT.CH"
#include "INKEY.CH"
function ME_UDF( me_mode, me_row, me_col )
```

```
static me_loop :=0
if me_mode == ME_INIT      // MEMOEDIT.CH  (Mode 3)
   me_loop++
   do case
   case me_loop == 1
      return ME_TOGGLEWRAP
   case me_loop == 2
      return K_INS
   otherwise
      return 0
   endcase
endif
```

MODE 0 - Idle Mode. If MEMOEDIT() has no pending keystrokes to process, it will call your function with an idle mode. This mode is most frequently used to update the screen display of row and column. You could also use this mode to display the time on the screen, or any other background processing that needs to be performed. The example in Listing 24.6 shows a sample UDF to update the screen display during idle mode.

Listing 24.6 Idle mode example

```
#include "MEMOEDIT.CH"
#include "INKEY.CH"
function ME_UDF( me_mode, me_row, me_col )
if me_mode == ME_IDLE      // MEMOEDIT.CH  (Mode 0)
   @ 2,50 say me_row   pict "9999"
   @ 2,60 say me_col+1 pict "9999"  // Columns start at 0
   @ 2,70 say time()
endif
```

MODES 1/2 keystroke exception modes. When MEMOEDIT() detects a keystroke that it does not handle, it hands control over to your user-defined function. This call is made to allow your function to specify what you want MEMOEDIT() to do. You do this by returning a numeric value instructing MEMOEDIT() what to do. The possible return values that MEMOEDIT() can be sent are listed in Table 24.2.

Table 24.2 MEMOEDIT() UDF return values

VALUE	*MEMOEDIT.CH or INKEY.CH*	*Action to perform*
0	ME_DEFAULT	Perform default action for key
1	K_CTRL_A	Move left one word
2	K_CTRL_B	Reformat the memo's contents
3	K_PGDN	Move to next block in memo
4	K_RIGHT	Move right one character
5	K_UP	Move up one line
6	K_END	Move right one word
7	K_DEL	Delete character at cursor
8	K_BS	Delete character to left of cursor
9	K_TAB	Insert TAB or spaces
13	K_ENTER	Move to beginning of next line
18	K_PGUP	Move to previous block
19	K_LEFT	Move left one character
20	K_CTRL_T	Delete word to right
22	K_INS	Toggle insert on or off
23	K_CTRL_END	Finish editing and save memo
24	K_DOWN	Move down one line
25	K_CTRL_Y	Delete the current line
27	K_ESC	Abort edit and return original
29	K_CTRL_HOME	Move to beginning of window
30	K_CTRL_PGDN	Move to bottom of memo
31	K_CTRL_PGUP	Move to beginning of memo
32	ME_IGNORE	Ignore the keystroke
33	ME_DATA	Treat the keystroke as data
34	ME_TOGGLEWRAP	Toggle word-wrap mode
35	ME_TOGGLESCROLL	Toggle scroll mode
100	ME_WORDRIGHT	Move right one word
101	ME_BOTTOMRIGHT	Move to bottom right

When the user function is called, mode 1 will be passed if the memo has not been altered, mode 2 is passed once the memo is changed. This allows you to display a warning if the user wishes to abort an updated memo without saving it.

To handle the keystroke exceptions, you would first capture the value from the LASTKEY() function. This value would then be tested in a DO CASE sequence to determine what return value should be sent back to MEMOEDIT(). In addition to returning a value to MEMOEDIT(), your function may contain additional code as well. Listing 24.7 illustrates a code fragment which will toggle insert mode and also change the cursor shape if the user presses the INSERT key during the editing of the memo. The example program at the end of this chapter also illustrates some keystrokes that can be handled in the MEMOEDIT() user-defined function.

Listing 24.7 Keystroke exception UDF

```
#include "MEMOEDIT.CH"
#include "INKEY.CH"
#include "SETCURS.CH"

function ME_UDF( me_mode,me_row,me_col )
local keypress
if me_mode == ME_UNKEY .or. ;      // MEMOEDIT.CH (Mode 1)
   me_mode == ME_UNKEYX            // (Mode 2)
   keypress := lastkey()           // Determine key pressed
   do case
   case keypress == K_INS          // Insert key
      if readinsert()              // Is insert currently on?
         setcursor(SC_NORMAL)      // Underline cursor
      else
         setcursor(SC_SPECIAL1) // Full block cursor
      endif
      return K_INS                 // Toggle cursor ON/OFF
   case keypress == K_F5           // F5 - insert date
      keyboard dtoc(date())        // Insert system date
      return ME_DEFAULT
   otherwise
      return ME_DEFAULT          // Zero - default action
   endcase
endif
return ME_DEFAULT
```

Displaying/printing memo fields

While MEMOEDIT() can be used to display memo variables, there are times when more control over the display is needed. A good example is printing. Since printing occurs a line at a time, MEMOEDIT() cannot be used to print individual lines from the memo. The MLCOUNT(), MLPOS(), and MEMOLINE() functions provide this degree of control.

MLCOUNT()

MLCOUNT() returns an integer indicating how many lines are found in the memo field. Its syntax is:

```
<nCount> := MLCOUNT(<mString>,<nWide>,<nTabsize>,<lWrap>)
```

<nCount> will receive the total number of lines in the memo. The contents of **<nWide>**, **<nTabsize>**, and **<lWrap>** are all taken into consideration in determining the number of lines the memo will take to display.

<mString> is the memo variable to be analyzed. It may also be a character string rather than a memo field.

<nWide> is the width of each line. It can be in the range of 4 to 254. If not specified, the default value is 79 characters wide.

<nTabsize> indicates how many spaces tabs should be expanded to. The tab size defaults to four if not specified. If the tab size is larger than or equal to the **<nWide>** value, it will automatically be converted to **<nWide>** minus one.

<lWrap> is a logical setting, where **.t.** indicates that the lines should be word-wrapped and **.f.** indicates they should not. If not specified, the default is true.

MEMOLINE()

Memoline extracts a line from a memo variable. Its syntax is:

```
<cVariable> :=MEMOLINE(<cMemo>,<nLength>,;
            <nLine>,<nTab>,<lWrap>)
```

<cVariable> will contain the extracted line from the memo variable. If the line contains fewer characters than specified by **<nLength>**, it will be padded with spaces to fill the line. If the **<nLine>** is greater than the number of lines in the memo, an empty string ("") will be returned.

<cMemo> is the memo variable to be analyzed. It may also be a character string rather than a memo field.

<nLength> is the width of each line. It can be in the range of 4 to 254. If not specified, the default value is 79 characters wide.

<nLine> indicates which line to extract from the memo. If not specified, the default will be line one. If the value of **<nLine>** is larger than the number of lines in the memo, the function will return a null string.

<nTab> indicates how many spaces tabs should be expanded to. The tab size defaults to four if not specified. If the tab size is larger than or equal to the **<nWide>** value, it will automatically be converted to **<nWide>** minus one.

<lWrap> is a logical setting, where **.t.** indicates that the lines should be word-wrapped and **.f.** indicates they should not. If not specified, the default is true.

MEMOLINE() and MLCOUNT() are frequently used together to display a memo's contents to the printer. For example, Listing 24.8 shows a sample program to print a form letter from a memo field and the customer database file.

Listing 24.8 Form letter

```
STATIC nWide := 60

function Form_Lett( mText )
local num_lines := mlcount(mText,nWide), jj
use CUSTOMER new
go top
do while !eof()
  ? CUSTOMER->Name
  ? CUSTOMER->Address
  ? trim(CUSTOMER->City)+", "+CUSTOMER->State
  ?? "  "+CUSTOMER->Zip
  ?
  for jj := 1 to num_lines
     ? memoline(mText,nWide,jj)
  next
  ?? chr(12)            // eject page
  skip +1
enddo
return nil
```

MLPOS()

The MLPOS() function is used to determine the character position that a line of a memo starts at. Its syntax is:

```
<nPosition> :=mlpos(<cMemo>,<nLength>,;
                <nLine>,<nTab>,<lWrap>)
```

<nPosition> will contain an integer value indicating where the requested line is offset into the string. If the **<nLine>** value is larger than the number of lines in the string, MLPOS() will return the length of the string.

<cMemo> is the memo variable to be analyzed. It may also be a character string rather than a memo field.

<nLength> is the width of each line. It can be in the range of 4 to 254. **<nLength>** is a required parameter.

The ***<nLine>*** indicates which line to look for. The **<nLine>** parameter is required. If the value of **<nLine>** is larger than the number of lines in the memo, the function will return the length of the string.

<nTab> indicates how many spaces tabs should be expanded to. The tab size defaults to four if not specified. If the tab size is larger than or equal to the **<nWide>** value, it will automatically be converted to **<nWide>** minus one.

<lWrap> is a logical setting where **.t.** indicates that the lines should be word-wrapped and **.f.** indicates they should not. If not specified, the default is true.

MLPOS() could be used to extract a section from a memo. For example, Listing 24.9 finds the fifth line within a memo and creates a new string starting at that line.

Listing 24.9 MLPOS() example

```
nStart     := mlpos(cMemo,79,1,4,.t.)
cNew_memo  := substr(cMemo,nStart,9999)
```

Positioning memo fields

Clipper 5 provides functions to determine the byte position of a row/column coordinate within a memo field or the row/column coordinates a given byte would be displayed at.

MLCTOPOS()

The MLCTOPOS() function takes a memo field and formatting information and returns an offset byte into the memo field. The offset is the byte position that corresponds to a particular row and column coordinate. Its syntax is:

```
nByte := MLCTOPOS(<cText>, <nWide>, <nLine>,;
         <nCol>, <nTab>, <lWrap>)
```

<nByte> is an integer value representing the offset position in the memo string.

<cText> is the actual memo string to be examined.

<nWide> is the memo display width.

<nLine> is the row number and ***<nCol>*** is the column position to look for. The row number starts at one, the column number is based from zero.

<nTab> is the number of spaces between tab stops. If not supplied, it defaults to four.

<lWrap> is a logical value indicating whether or not word-wrapping should be performed. If true, which is the default, word-wrapping is considered on.

For example, assume your help system uses MEMOEDIT() to display help text on the screen. If the user moves to a word within the help text and presses the F6 key, the HELP system will extract the word at the cursor and look for HELP text about the selected word. MEMOEDIT() will handle the cursor position and pass to the MEMOEDIT() user-defined function the current screen row and column. The MLCTOPOS() function is used to take these coordinates and extract the appropriate word from the HELP text. Listing 24.10 illustrates an example.

Listing 24.10 MLCTOPOS() example

```
#include "MEMOEDIT.CH"
#include "INKEY.CH"

function ME_UDF( me_mode,me_row,me_col )
local keypress, nByte, cWord, cScr
field cHelp
if me_mode == ME_UNKEY .or. ;   // MEMOEDIT.CH (Mode 1)
   me_mode == ME_UNKEYX         // (Mode 2)
   keypress := lastkey()        // Determine key pressed
   do case
```

```
   case keypress == K_F6          // F6 - Hyper lookup
      nByte := mlctopos(cHelp,60,me_row,me_col)
      cWord := substr(cHelp,nByte,12)
      select HELP
      seek upper(cWord)
      if found()
         *
         * Display a second box to describe the word found
         *
         cScr :=savescreen(8,20,15,60)
         @ 8,20 to 15,60 double
         @ 8,21 say " "+trim(cWord)+" "
         memoedit( HELP->Text,9,21,14,59,.f.,.f.)
         inkey(500)
         restscreen(8,20,15,60,cScr)
         *
      endif
      return ME_DEFAULT
   otherwise
      return ME_DEFAULT          // Zero - default action
   endcase
endif
return ME_DEFAULT
```

MPOSTOLC()

The MPOSTOLC() function takes a memo field and formatting information and returns an array containing the row and column that a particular offset byte would be displayed at. Its syntax is:

```
<aBytes> := MPOSTOLC(<cText>, <nWide>, <nPos>, <nTab>, <lWrap>)
```

<aBytes> is a two-element array of integer values representing the row and column positions that the specified byte position would be displayed at.

<cText> is the actual memo string to be examined.

<nWide> is the memo display width.

<nPos> is the byte position within the memo string to be displayed. It starts at one, i.e. the first character of the string is offset one, not zero.

<nTab> is the number of spaces between tab stops. If not supplied, it defaults to four.

<lWrap> is a logical value indicating whether or not word-wrapping should be performed. If it's true, which is the default, word-wrapping is considered ON.

The MPOSTOLC() function is the inverse to the MLCTOPOS() function.

For example, Listing 24.11 will search all memo fields on a disk for a requested string. If the string is found, the memo will be brought up for editing, with the cursor positioned on the found word.

Listing 24.11 MPOSTOLC() example

```
function FindMemo(cWord)
local found_one := .f.,arr_ := {}, x := 0
select BOOKS
go top
do while !eof()
   if !empty(BOOKS->Desc)         // Memo field
      if (x := at(cWord,BOOKS->Desc)) > 0
         arr_ := mpostolc( BOOKS->Desc,44,x,4)
         found_one := .t.
         exit
      endif
   endif
   skip +1
enddo
if found_one
   replace BOOKS->Desc with  ;
             memoedit(BOOKS->Desc,8,20,19,65,.t.,,44,4,;
                      arr_[1],arr_[2])
endif
return nil
```

Saving memos to disk

The contents of a memo variable may be saved to either a memo field in a .DBF file or a text file in DOS.

REPLACE Command

If the database has a memo field, Clipper uses the REPLACE command to update that memo field. The syntax is:

```
REPLACE <cAlias> -> <cMemofield>  WITH <cMemo_string>
```

If ***<cAlias>*** is not supplied, the memo field is assumed to be in the current work area. You can also use the FIELDPUT() function to write the memo variable into the DBF file. Its syntax is:

```
FIELDPUT( <nField_no>,<cMemo> )
```

Clipper's database drivers automatically translate the request to write the memo field into a block reference to be written to the .DBT file.

MEMOWRIT()

The MEMOWRIT() function takes a memo variable and creates a text file with its contents. Its syntax is:

```
<logical> := MEMOWRIT(<cFile>,<cMemo_variable>)
```

If ***<cFile>*** is successfully created, a logical true value is returned. If not, false will be returned. The created file will contain soft carriage returns if any were present in the memo variable. The MEMOTRAN() function described in the next section can be used to convert the soft carriage returns to hard carriage returns.

Memo file maintenance

Memo fields are, unfortunately, not self-maintaining structures. If your system makes use of memo fields, your end-users will occasionally need to optimize the memo and reclaim unused space. If you are converting an application to Clipper 5 from earlier versions, you'll need to fix the memo files before Clipper 5 can update the field. The steps for accomplishing this uplate are described in this chapter. See section entitled "Converting Summer '87 memos to Clipper 5".

Packing the memo file

When a .DBF file is packed, all deleted records are removed and the file is rewritten to the disk. This process reduces the physical storage space the .DBF file uses. Unfortunately, it does not reorganize the corresponding .DBT. To reclaim unusable space in a memo file, you need to create a copy of the .DBF. This new copy will contain a packed .DBT file.

The procedure to create a new file, hence packing the DBT is:

```
use MEMOS new
copy to NEW_MEMO
close databases
rename MEMOS.DBF to MEMOS.BAK     // Back up the old DBF
rename MEMOS.DBT to MEMOS.TBK     //    and DBT files
rename NEW_MEMO.DBF TO MEMOS.DBF
rename NEW_MEMO.DBT TO MEMOS.DBT
```

If your application program uses memos, be sure to include a menu option to allow the user to "pack" their memo files.

Changing carriage returns

Clipper uses the ASCII code of 141 to designate a soft carriage return in a memo field. A soft carriage return is a return created when Clipper cannot fit the word on the current line and wraps it to the next line. A hard carriage return occurs when the user actually presses the enter key. The ASCII code for a hard carriage return is the number 13.

Some applications, notably Clipper's own REPORT FORM command, do not recognize carriage returns. In REPORT FORM, a semi-colon is used to designate text that should appear on the next line. In order to work with other applications and report form, Clipper provides the MEMOTRAN() function to convert carriage returns. Its syntax is:

```
<cString> := MEMOTRAN( <cString>,<cRepl_hard>,<cRepl_soft> )
```

<cString> is the memo string that should be changed. This is a required parameter; it can be a character string as well as a memo field.

<cRepl_hard> is the character that all occurrences of hard carriage returns should be replaced with. If not specified, the default is a semi-colon, which allows REPORT FORM to work with the memo's contents.

<cRepl_soft> is the character that all occurrences of soft carriage returns should be replaced with. If not specified, the default is a space character.

For example, this function call replaces all soft carriage returns with a semicolon. By changing the soft return to a semicolon, various dBASE dialects could read this string and insert a new line at each occurrence of the semicolon.

```
memowrit( "NEWFILE.TXT", memotran(cMemo,,";") )
```

Converting Summer '87 Memos To Clipper 5

In Clipper, word-wrapping occurs when a line of text is too wide to fit within the line width specified in the call to MEMOEDIT(). The line is broken into two lines by inserting a soft carriage return/line feed after the rightmost word that will fit within the specified line width.

In earlier versions of Clipper, when a soft carriage return is inserted, a single space character is removed from the text at the point where the soft carriage return is inserted. If the text is later reformatted using a different line width, each soft carriage return is replaced by a single space. This generally results in equivalent text, regardless of the formatting width. A problem arises, however, if a single word is too long to fit within the specified line width. In this case, a soft carriage return is inserted in the middle of the word. If the text is later reformatted with a greater line width, the word will appear as two words because the soft carriage return is replaced with a space.

In Clipper 5, the insertion of soft carriage returns has been enhanced so that changes in the content of the text are never permitted. When a soft carriage return is inserted between two words, the space characters between the two words are preserved. When text is reformatted, any soft carriage returns are simply removed. This leaves the text in its original form and properly handles the case where a soft carriage return has been inserted in the middle of a word.

If a text string formatted using Summer '87 MEMOEDIT() is reformatted using any of the Clipper 5 text handling functions, words that were separated by a soft carriage return will be run together because the soft carriage return is not replaced with a space.

You can use the STRTRAN() function to adjust memo fields from earlier versions of Clipper. The syntax is:

```
STRTRAN( <text>, chr(141)+chr(10), " " )
```

To convert memo values in an existing .DBF file, the following two-line program can be used:

```
use <cDatabase>
replace all <idMemo> with ;
        strtran(<idMemo>,chr(141)+chr(10), " ")
```

The memo translation process should be performed before any text in the .DBF file is reformatted and written using the Clipper 5 MEMOEDIT() function. As with any operation of this kind, be sure to back up your databases before you run the conversion program.

Sample memo application programs

To illustrate the power of memo handling, our example program will contain a complete text editor. The editor will be able to select a disk file to read, edit the contents, and write the file back to disk. During the edit mode, you will be able to search and replace strings, insert the system date, and create macros.

The code to the text editor is in Listing 24.12. We've commented it to illustrate points we've covered in the chapter. While this editor is not going to replace WordPerfect or Microsoft Word, it is a handy tool which can be included within your Clipper application. It could easily be customized to allow the end-user to store the memos in a .DBF file and search the .DBF for which memo to edit.

The main screen for our editor is illustrated in Figure 24.2.

Figure 24.2 Editor main screen

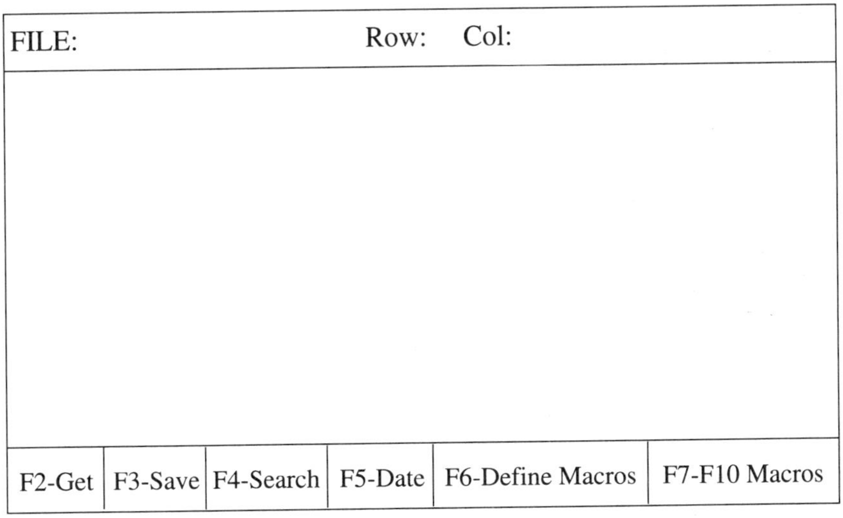

FILE: Row: Col:

F2-Get	F3-Save	F4-Search	F5-Date	F6-Define Macros	F7-F10 Macros

The function keys listed in Table 24.3 are used to control the editing process.

Table 24.3 Edit function keys

F2	Get a file from the disk
F3	Save the text to the disk
F4	Search and replace strings
F5	Insert current date
F6	Define macro keys F6 through F10
F7	Macro number one
F8	Macro number two
F9	Macro number three
F10	Macro number four

Listing 24.12 Text editor

```
// Pre-processor settings //

#define DEF_SIZE 2048
#define LINE_LNG 255
#include "MEMOEDIT.CH"
#include "INKEY.CH"
#include "BOX.CH"
#include "SETCURS.CH"
MEMVAR getlist

function Cdg_Edit
local mx := Maxrow(),mc := Maxcol()
local backscr := savescreen(0,0,mx,mc)
local msearch := space(8),mreplace := space(8)
local mcount := 1,msave

private keepgoing := .t.,memo_buff := space(DEF_SIZE)
private me_file := space(12),me_command := 0
private me_macros := {space(15),space(15),space(15),space(15)}

//  Set the colors and draw the screen  //
setcolor('W+/B')
cls
```

```
dispbox(01, 00, mx, mc, 2)
@ 02,03 say "FILE:"
@ 02,60 say "Row:      Col:"
@ 03,01 say replicate( chr(196),mc-1)
@ mx-2,01 say " ────────┬─────────┬─────────────┬────────── "+ ;
              "┌────────────────────────────────────────"
@ mx-1,01 say "  F2-Get | F3-Save | F4-Replace | F5-Date "+;
              "| F6-Define Macros | F7-F10 Macros  "
@ mx,  01 say "└════════╧═════════╧═════════════╧══════════ "+ ;
              "╘══════════════════╧═══════════════════"
setcolor ('W/B')

do while keepgoing
   memo_buff :=memoedit(memo_buff, 4, 1, mx-3,;
            mc-1, .t., "ME_UDF", LINE_LNG)
   if !empty(me_command)
      do case
      case me_command == 1
         keepgoing := .f.
         loop
      case me_command == 2        // Get a new file
         memo_buff := memoread(me_file)
      case me_command == 3        // Save existing file
         memowrit(me_file,memo_buff)
      case me_command == 4        // Search/replace a string
         msave := savescreen(2,24,2,79)
         @ 2,60 say space(18)
         @ 2,24 say "SEARCH:"  get msearch
         @ 2,42 say "REPLACE:" get mreplace
         @ 2,62 say "COUNT:"   get mcount   ;
                pict "99999" valid mcount>=0
         read
         if lastkey() <> K_ESC
            mcount := if(mcount=0,99999,mcount)
            memo_buff := strtran(memo_buff,trim(msearch),;
                         trim(mreplace),1,mcount)
         endif
         restscreen(2,24,2,79,msave)
      endcase
      me_command := 0
```

```
   endif
enddo
restscreen(0,0,mx,mc,backscr)
return nil

function ME_UDF(me_mode,me_row,me_col)
local me_key := lastkey(),me_save
MEMVAR me_macros,me_file,me_command

if me_mode == ME_INIT          // Initialization mode
   return ME_DEFAULT           // Tell memoedit to start
elseif me_mode == ME_IDLE      // Idle mode, update row/column
   @ 02,10 say me_file
   @ 02,65 say me_row    pict "9999"
   @ 02,74 say me_col+1  pict "9999"  // Starts at zero
else
   do case
   case me_key == K_INS              // Insert key
      if readinsert()                // Is insert on?
         setcursor(SC_NORMAL)        // Underline cursor
      else
         setcursor(SC_SPECIAL1)      // Full block cursor
      endif
      return K_INS      // Toggle cursor ON/OFF
   case me_key == K_ESC .or. me_key == K_CTRL_END
      me_command := 1
      return me_key
   case me_key == K_F2
      @ 2,10 get me_file pict "!!!!!!!!!!!!"  ;
             valid file(me_file) .or. lastkey() == K_UP
      read
      if lastkey() <> K_ESC
         me_command :=2
         return K_ESC
      endif
   case me_key == K_F3           // Get a file name to save
      @ 2,10 get me_file pict "!!!!!!!!!!!!" ;
             valid !empty(me_file)
      read
      if lastkey() <> K_ESC
```

```
         me_command := 3     // Set command to save contents
         return K_CTRL_END
      endif
   case me_key == K_F4
      me_command :=4        // Set command to search/replace
      return K_CTRL_END      // Save the memo's contents
   case me_key == K_F5
      keyboard dtoc(date()) // Insert a date into the memo
   case me_key == K_F6
      me_save := savescreen(9,29,14,53)
      @ 9,29,14,52 box B_DOUBLE_SINGLE + " "
      @ 10,30 say "F7  -" get me_macros[1]
      @ 11,30 say "F8  -" get me_macros[2]
      @ 12,30 say "F9  -" get me_macros[3]
      @ 13,30 say "F10 -" get me_macros[4]
      read
      restscreen(9,29,14,53,me_save)
   case me_key == K_F7
      keyboard trim(me_macros[1])  // Insert first macro
   case me_key == K_F8
      keyboard trim(me_macros[2])  // Insert second macro
   case me_key == K_F9
      keyboard trim(me_macros[3])  // Insert third macro
   case me_key == K_F10
      keyboard trim(me_macros[4])  // Insert fourth macro
   endcase
endif
return ME_DEFAULT      // Process key's default value
```

Summary

After reading this chapter and working through the example, you should feel comfortable with the power available in Clipper's memo handling. You should know how to create memo variables, how to edit them, and how to write them back to disk. If you need to create a word processor in Clipper, you should be comfortable expanding the example application to meet your needs.

CHAPTER 25

Low-level File Access

A disk file may be viewed as a series of bytes stored together on the disk. The meaning and relationship of these bytes is determined by the application that uses the file. The file is interpreted according to the structure that a program imposes on it. Database files have their own structure, as do spreadsheet files, index files, word processing files, and so on.

Clipper provides a set of functions to allow access to any file in an unstructured, low-level manner. Data from the file can be read or written on a byte level. In this chapter we will cover these functions and provide some examples. We will also review the user-defined functions found in the FILEIO.PRG included in the CLIPPER5\SOURCE\SAMPLE directory.

DOS and Files

In earlier versions of DOS, information about disk files was passed to the operating system through a File Control Block. A File Control Block (FCB) is a 44-byte area of memory which contains descriptive information about the files. This information includes the file name and extension, the record size, the current record, the current block, and other data needed for the operating system to process the file.

In order to access files, your program had to change values in the FCB and create an area, called the Data Transfer Area, to hold information from the file. This buffer area was always the size of a single record from the file, allowing one record to be in memory at a time.

DOS versions 2.0 and above relegated the file information to the control of the operating system. The operating system creates a table, called the file handle table, which holds information needed to access files. All information in this table is hidden from us and maintained by DOS. When we open or create a file, DOS allocates an entry in the table to hold the new file's information. It returns to our program a numeric pointer indicating the entry in the table where the file information is located. This pointer is referred to as a file handle.

File handles

Any file opened by an application is assigned a file handle. A file handle is a sixteen-bit integer value used to point to an entry in a file table created by DOS. This value can range from zero through 65,535. When the FOPEN() or FCREATE() function is called successfully, a handle will be returned. This handle is then used for all subsequent access to the file. If either function call fails, a **-1** will be returned instead of a valid file handle.

Expanding the file handle table

DOS sets aside an area of memory for the file handle table. Each time a file is opened, its handle is added to this table. When the file is closed, the slot it occupied in the table becomes available again. The size of this table is determined by the operating system. Versions of DOS below 3.3 provide for a maximum of 20 file handles in the table. DOS versions 3.3 and above allow 255 entries in the table, although the default value is 20. You can increase the number of handles available. The method for doing so varies depending upon the version of DOS you are using.

DOS 3.3 and above. For DOS versions 3.3 and above, a statement may be included in the system configuration file (CONFIG.SYS) which indicates the size of the file handle table. Its syntax is:

```
FILES = <nHandles>
```

Adding this statement to the CONFIG.SYS file and rebooting will cause DOS to create a larger file handle table, making room for **<nHandles>** number of files. This new number becomes the maximum number of open files DOS will allow.

In addition, the Clipper application must be informed of the number of file handles. This is done through the use of the Clipper environment string. Its syntax is:

```
SET CLIPPER=F<nHandles>
```

Whichever value is lower will determine the number of handles available to the Clipper application. For example, the following environment will make 45 file handles available to the Clipper program.

```
CONFIG.SYS
FILES = 49

SET CLIPPER=F45
```

It is always better to use an odd number for the file handle setting in the CONFIG.SYS file. A bug in some DOS versions causes an extra 60K bytes of memory to be wasted if an even number is used.

DOS 3.2 and Below. Clipper does not provide direct support for more than twenty open files under DOS versions 3.2 and below. The distribution disk which accompanies this book contains a utility function that can be used to increase the number of open handles. This utility contains a UDF called Handles(). The syntax for the function is:

```
Handles( <nHandles_needed> )
```

A Clipper program is assigned a location in memory for the file handle table when it starts. The Handles() function increases the size of the file handle table by redirecting where DOS looks for it to a different, larger section of memory.

Handles used by DOS (the first five)

The first five entries in the handles table are used by the operating system. DOS automatically opens these five handles whenever a program starts. The five standard handles are listed in table 25.1.

Table 25.1 Standard DOS file handles

Handle	*Description*	*Default Device*
0	Std Input	(CON:) - Keyboard
1	Std Output	(CON:) - Screen
2	Std error output	(CON:) - Screen
3	Std auxiliary device	(AUX:) - Serial port (COM1)
4	Std printer	(PRN:) - Parallel port (LPT1)

If you are very tight on file handles, your program could close the fourth and fifth handles. The first three handles should never be closed.

Counting file handles

To determine the number of handles a program needs, we need to understand how file handles are assigned. Each database file opened during a program occupies at least one handle. If the file contains a memo field, a second handle is used for the DBT file. Each index file also uses one handle. It is easy to see that a large program can quite quickly exceed the available handles.

For example, assume a customer file has the following structure and two indexes:

CUSTOMER.DBF

```
Id_code      Char     10
Company      Char     25
City         Char     15
State        Char      2
Zip_code     Char     10
Notes      Memo       10
```

The first index is on **Id_code** and the second is on **Company**. The command

```
use CUSTOMER index cust_01,cust_02
```

will require four handles: one for the .DBF, one for the .DBT, and one for each index.

Opening files

To open any file in an unstructured or low-level mode, two functions are available. FCREATE() is used to create a new file and FOPEN() will open an existing file. Extreme care should be used with all low-level file functions. While the lack of an imposed structure provides tremendous flexibility, it also has potential dangers. If FCREATE() is called on an existing file, the file will be truncated. FCREATE() does not care that the file it just erased contained the last two years' worth of payroll data.

FCREATE()

FCREATE() opens a file for writing. If the file does not exist, it will be created. If the file already exists, it will be truncated to zero bytes with no error or warning given. The syntax is:

```
nhandle := FCREATE( <cFile_name>[,<nAttributes>] )
```

Always assign the output from FCREATE() to a variable, since this is the only way to refer to the file's handle.

The file specified will be created in the current DOS directory unless a path is specified in the file name. In addition, the file is assigned an attribute. The attribute indicates the type of file. The **<nAttributes>** may be one of the values in Table 25.2.

Table 25.2 File opening attributes

Value	*FILEIO.CH*	*Description*
0	FC_NORMAL	Read/write file, the default value
1	FC_READONLY	Read-only
2	FC_HIDDEN	Hidden, not seen by DOS commands
4	FC_SYSTEM	System, will also be hidden from DOS

The attributes may also be combined. For example, to create a file that is both hidden and read-only, we could set the attribute to:

```
FC_READONLY + FC_HIDDEN      =   1 + 2    =  3
```

A hidden system file would be:

```
FC_HIDDEN + FC_SYSTEM         =   2 + 4   = 6
```

The file is created in read-write mode, regardless of the attributes. The attributes are not applied to the file until the file is closed. This allows your program to create a read-only file and write data to it. When your program closes the file, it will be written to the directory as a read-only file if so specified.

The example function in listing 25.1 creates a CONFIG.SYS file if one does not exist. The parameter to the function indicates the number of file handles CONFIG.SYS should have.

Listing 25.1 NewCfgSys()

```
#include "FILEIO.CH"
#define CRLF chr(13)+chr(10)

function NewCfgSys(nHandles)
local fh
if !file("CONFIG.SYS")
   fh := fcreate( "config.sys",FC_NORMAL )
   if fh > -1
      fwrite(fh,"FILES="+str(nHandles,3)+CRLF )
      fclose(fh)
   else
      ? "DOS error occurred, ",ferror()
      return .f.
   endif
endif
return .t.
```

If the handle returned by FCREATE() is a **-1**, then a DOS error occurred when attempting to create the file. The FERROR() function will return the error number. The probable error codes that FCREATE() might return are: 3 (path not found), 4 (no more handles), or 5 (access denied). Access denied occurs if you are trying to create an existing read-only file or if there is no more room in the current directory for a file. See the error handling section of this chapter for more information.

FOPEN()

FOPEN() is used to open an existing file and provide low-level access to it. Its syntax is:

```
nHandle := FOPEN( <cFile_name> [,<nOpen_mode>] )
```

Be sure to assign the output from FOPEN() to a variable, since this is the only way to refer to the file's handle.

The file specified must be in the current DOS directory unless a path is specified in the file name. FOPEN() will not search the DOS path nor the Clipper SET DEFAULT setting.

The **<nOpen_mode>** may be one of the numbers in table 25.3. If the file cannot be opened in the requested mode, FOPEN() will return a **-1** error value. If you created a read-only file and later try to open it for read-write, the FOPEN() function will fail to open the file.

Table 25.3 File open modes

Value	*FILEIO.CH*	*Description*
0	FO_READ	Read-only mode, the default value
1	FO_WRITE	Write-only mode
2	FO_READWRITE	Open for reading/writing

For safety reasons, the default open mode is **0** — read only access. Other modes are possible although they are not documented in the user's guide. Any undocumented feature is subject to change, so use these modes at your own risk. These modes are present in earlier versions of Clipper as well. The additional modes are used when opening files on a network. The modes are listed in table 25.4.

Table 25.4 File sharing modes

Value	*Description*
0	Compatibility mode, the default
16	Deny read access/write access to others
32	Deny write mode to others
48	Deny read mode to others
64	Allow read/write access from others

The value should be added to the desired open mode from Table 25.3 to get the actual mode to use. For example, to open a file for write access and deny read mode, you would use an open mode of 49 (1 from Table 25.3 plus 48 from Table 25.4). The most common mode on a network would be 66, an open file for read/write access that allows others to read and write as well.

If you need to work with network files, you should use manifest constants instead of hard coding the modes. This will make changes easier if Computer Associates changes the open modes in the future. Here are the manifest constants for the network open modes.

```
#define FS_DENY_ALL      16
#define FS_DENY_WRITE    32
#define FS_DENY_READ     48
#define FS_ALLOW_ALL     64
```

If the handle returned by FOPEN() is a **-1**, then a DOS error occurred when attempting to open the file. The FERROR() function will return the error number. The probable error codes that FOPEN() might return are: 2 file not found, 4 no more handles, 5 access denied or 12 invalid access. Invalid access occurs if you are trying to open a file on a network while someone else is using it and the file cannot be opened as shared. See the error handling section of this chapter for more information.

Moving about the file

The system maintains a file pointer for each file handle in the file table. The pointer is used to determine where the next read or write operation will occur.

FSEEK()

The FSEEK() function is the primary method used to move the file pointer. Its syntax is:

```
nPosition := FSEEK( <nHandle>,<nOffset>,<nOrigin> )
```

<nHandle> represents the entry in the file handle table you wish to move. **<nOffset>** indicates how many bytes the pointer should be moved. **<nOrigin>** indicates the starting position for the movement. It can be one of the three choices in Table 25.5.

Table 25.5 File origins

Value	*FILEIO.CH*	*Description*
0	FS_SET	Beginning of file
1	FS_RELATIVE	Current file pointer position
2	FS_END	End of file

The default value is zero or FS_SET, the beginning of the file.

For example, to open a file and append data to it, you could use this code fragment:

```
#include "FILEIO.CH"
fh := fopen("TEST.DAT",FO_READWRITE)
if fh > -1
   fseek(fh,0,FS_END)        // Position pointer at
endif                        // end of the file
```

FSEEK() returns the file position after the pointer is moved. The return value from the function call

```
fseek(fh,0,2)
```

would be the last byte in the file, or the file's size. Be sure to keep the pointer in mind when writing data to the file. The lack of automatic error checking by the low-level file functions provides great flexibility but requires careful use of the functions.

The file reading and writing functions will also move the file pointer. The pointer will be moved from its current position to the current position plus the number of bytes read or written.

The example in Figure 25.1 shows the file pointer starting at zero, the beginning of the file, and being moved ten bytes after the call to FREAD().

Figure 25.1 File pointer movement

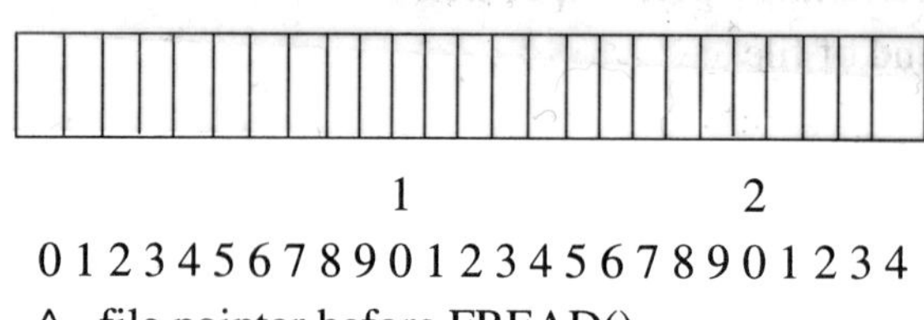

^ - file pointer before FREAD()

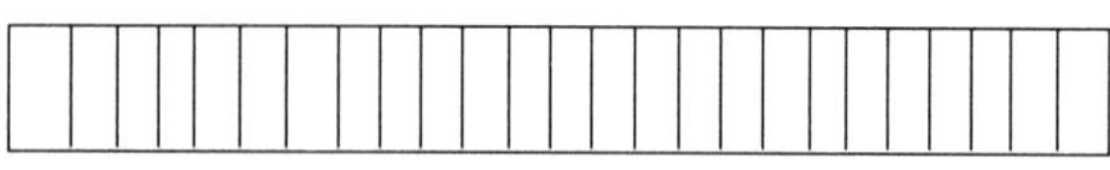

1 2
0 1 2 3 4 5 6 7 8 9 0 1 2 3 4 5 6 7 8 9 0 1 2 3 4
^ - after FREAD(handle,@buf,10)

Reading information from files

There are two functions available to extract data from a file using a handle. These functions are FREAD() and FREADSTR(). The difference between the two is that FREADSTR() will only read up to a character zero (CHR(0)) while FREAD() will read any character, including CHR(0).

FREAD()

For more low-level files, FREAD() is preferable because many files use CHR(0) as a data byte. While it requires a bit more setup to use, it will return all the data from the file. The syntax for FREAD() is:

```
cbuffer      := space(<nBytes>)
nBytes_read := FREAD(<nHandle>,<@cBuffer>,<nBytes>)
```

The character variable to hold the bytes must be filled with spaces before FREAD() is called. It must be passed to the function by reference, hence the @ is required.

The return value is the number of bytes that were read. If this number does not agree with the number of bytes that were requested then either you've attempted to read past the end of the file or a DOS error occurred. You can check FERROR() to determine what error, if any, occurred.

The function in Listing 25.2 illustrates a file copy which creates a new file from the original file converted to uppercase.

Listing 25.2 Uppercase file copy

```
#include "FILEIO.CH"
#define   BUFSIZE 2048

function Ucopy(old_file, new_file)
local in_handle, out_handle, buffer := space(BUFSIZE),nbytes
in_handle := fopen(old_file,FO_READ)
if in_handle > -1
```

```
   out_handle := fcreate(new_file,FC_NORMAL)
   if out_handle > -1
      do while (nBytes := fread(in_handle, @buffer, BUFSIZE)) > 0
         fwrite(out_handle,upper(buffer),nBytes)
         buffer := space(BUFSIZE)
      enddo
      fwrite(out_handle, upper(buffer), nBytes)
      fclose(in_handle)
      fclose(out_handle)
   else
      ? "Error ",ferror()," creating file ",new_file
   endif
else
   ? "Error ",ferror()," opening file ",old_file
endif
return nil
```

FREADSTR()

The FREADSTR() function reads bytes from a file into a memory variable. Since a Clipper string is terminated by a NULL character, CHR(0), the function will read either the requested number of bytes or up to an occurrence of a CHR(0). Its syntax is:

```
<cBuffer> := FREADSTR(<nHandle>,<nBytes>)
```

Regardless of which reading function you use, reading should be done into larger memory variables rather than into just a few bytes. Most hard disks have sector sizes of 2048 bytes (2K) which means that 2048 bytes will be read into memory by the operating system regardless of the number of bytes you specify. If you perform your reads in smaller byte sizes, the program will be forced to do extra disk reads. A disk read slows the performance down dramatically and so should be limited to the minimal number needed to get the job done. See the section in this chapter on speeding up low-level access for more information on buffering your read operations.

Writing bytes into files

The FWRITE() function is used to write information into a file identified by its handle. All information to be written to the file must be converted to character form before writing. If a line of text is to be written, a delimiter such as a carriage return/ line feed pair should be written to the file as well.

FWRITE()

The FWRITE() function is used to write a character string into a file at the current file position. Its syntax is:

```
nBytes_out := FWRITE(<nHandle>,<cBuffer>,<nWritebytes>)
```

The **<nHandle>** refers to a file which must be opened for writing or in read/write mode. The **<cBuffer>** contains the actual characters to be written, and the **<nWritebytes>** represents the number of characters to write. If the number is not specified, it will default to the length of the **<cBuffer>** string.

The function will return the number of bytes written into the file. If this return value does not agree with the number of bytes then some sort of error occurred during the write process. FERROR() will return a code indicating why the write failed. The most likely reason for a failure during the FWRITE() would be lack of sufficient disk space.

The function in listing 25.3 illustrates using FWRITE() to create a log of information about users. It might be called after the user logs on to the program or performs a particular module or function.

Listing 25.3 Writelog()

```
#define USERLOG "USER.LOG"
#include "FILEIO.CH"

function Writelog(cUserid,cMessage)
local fh,buf,retval:=.t.
if file("USER.LOG")
```

```
   fh:= fopen(USERLOG,FO_WRITE)
   if fh > -1
      fseek(fh,0,FS_END)        // Move to end of file
   else
      retval := .f.
   endif
else
   fh := fcreate(USERLOG,FC_NORMAL)
endif
if fh > -1
   buf := cUserid +" "+ ;
          dtoc( date() )+" "+;
          time()+" "+cMessage+chr(13)+chr(10)
   if fwrite(fh,buf,len(buf)) <> len(buf)
      retval :=.f.
   endif
   fclose(fh)
else
   retval:=.f.
endif

return retval
```

Closing the file

Once a file handle is no longer needed by the program, the program should close that handle. If the file was created with FCREATE(), the file attribute designated by FCREATE() (see Table 25.2) will be applied to the file by the FCLOSE() function. The syntax to close the file is:

```
<logical> := FCLOSE( <nHandle> )
```

<nHandle> represents the handle number returned from a previous FCREATE() or FOPEN() function call. FCLOSE() will first flush the DOS buffers to disk and then attempt to close the file. It returns a logical true if the buffers were flushed and the file was closed. If a problem occurred, a false will be returned.

Error handling

If an error occurs using one of the low-level functions, the function will return an error indicator. In addition, FERROR() will contain a non-zero number. Table 25.6 lists the return values that the low-level functions use to indicate an error was detected.

Table 25.6 Low-level error return values

Function	*Error return value*
FCLOSE()	.F.
FOPEN()	-1
FCREATE()	-1
FREAD()	Bytes read <> Bytes requested
FREADSTR()	Bytes read <> Bytes requested
FWRITE()	Bytes written <> Bytes requested

FERROR()

Once an error has been detected, the FERROR() function will return a numeric code indicating what error has occurred. Its syntax is simply:

```
<nErrorno>   := FERROR()
```

If no error was encountered, FERROR() will return an error code of zero. Table 25.7 lists possible FERROR() values and the course of action to recover from them.

Table 25.7 DOS errors

Error	*Meaning*	*Possible solutions*
0	Successful	
2	File not found	Check spelling of file name.
3	Path not found	Check spelling of path name, also test to see if the path exists.
4	Too many files	Increase your file handles size.
5	Access denied	Make sure the file is not set to read-only. On a network, check that you have access rights to the file.

Error	*Meaning*	*Possible Solutions*
6	Invalid handle	Check the value of the variable to be sure a handle was opened or created properly.
15	Invalid drive	The drive designated does not exist.
19	Write protected	The diskette is write protected.
21	Drive not ready	Usually because the drive door is open.
29	Write fault	Probably the disk is full or, on a network, the user doesn't have write privileges to the directory.
32	Share violation	The file is currently being used by another user and your attempt to access the file is not permitted.

The most common FERROR() error return values are two through five, since your program may not be able to check the DOS environment of all the files to which it needs access.

FERROR() can be useful to determine the status of various directories and drives. For example, the code below uses DOS's NUL: device to check a drive status. The NUL: device is a standard DOS device that can be used much like any other device, but will not be saved anywhere. It is most frequently used to redirect output from DOS operations to never-never land. The function attempts to open a NUL: device on a particular drive. This will always fail when using the low-level functions. If FERROR() returns a three, the function failed because the drive is not valid. The Isdrive() function will return true if the drive letter specified appears to be valid or false if the drive is not available or ready. The function can easily be adapted to handle subdirectories as well.

```
function Isdrive(drv_letter)
local fh := Fopen(drv_letter+":\NUL:")
return( ferror() <> 3 )
```

FERROR() can also be used to check if a file can be written to. The Ok2write() function shown below returns true if the file can be opened in a read-write mode and false if not. By checking for write access, your program can detect that a memory variable file cannot be saved. Hopefully, you will check it before your user has changed all the values and wants to save them to disk.

```
#include "FILEIO.CH"

function Ok2write(cFile)
local retval:=.f.,fh
if file( cFile )
   fh     := fopen( cFile,FO_READWRITE )
   retval := (fh >= 0 .and. ferror()== 0 )
   fclose(fh)
endif
return retval
```

Error recovery

If your program detects an error, it should provide some guidance to assist the user in recovering from the error. The program in listing 25.4 illustrates a program to be called if the value of FERROR() is not zero. It will present a message to the end-user advising him or her how to correct the problem.

Listing 25.4 - Errmsg()

```
Function Errmsg(nErr)
do case
case nErr == 2
   ? "Check the spelling of the file name...."
case nErr == 3
   ? "Check that the proper path is designated..."
case nErr == 4
   ? "Need to increase CONFIG.SYS files statement..."
case nErr == 5
   ? "The file is probably set to read-only...."
case nErr == 6
   ? "Programming problem - contact the programmmer..."
```

```
case nErr == 15
   ? "You've specified an invalid drive letter...."
case nErr == 19
   ? "Remove the write-protect tab from the diskette..."
case nErr == 21
   ? "Try shutting the drive door..."
case nErr == 29
   ? "The disk is full....."
case nErr == 32
   ? "Someone else is using the file..."
case nErr <> 0
   ? "CONTACT the programmer immediately!!!!"
endcase
return nil
```

Extending the file functions, FILEIO.PRG

The Clipper disks include a set of user-defined functions to enhance the low-level file tools. These functions are found in FILEIO.PRG which can be found in the \CLIPPER5\SOURCE\SAMPLE directory. The program should be compiled with the following switches:

/n - No default procedure name
/w - Enable warnings
/m - Compile module only
/a - Automatic **memvar** declaration

The sample functions in FILEIO.PRG can be grouped into two sections: text-file functions and file status functions.

Text file functions

A text file is a file that is broken down into lines. A line is a series of characters terminated by some delimiter, usually a carriage return or a carriage return/line feed pair. Your Clipper .PRG files, CONFIG.SYS, and AUTOEXEC.BAT files are a few examples of text files.

Freadln()

Freadln() reads a single line or multiple lines from a text file into a character buffer. Its syntax is:

```
cString := Fradln(<nHandle>,<nLines>,<nLength>,<cDelimiter>)
```

A line is usually delimited by the carriage return/line feed pair. This will be the default delimiter if none is supplied. The default number of lines is 1 and the default line length is 80 characters.

The Fgets() function included in FILEIO.PRG is identical to the Freadln() function. The Fgets() syntax is based upon a similar function available in FoxPro. You could create a preprocessor #xtranslate definition if you wanted to eliminate the Fgets() overhead from the FILEIO program. See Chapter 7 for more information about the preprocessor.

Fwriteln()

The Fwriteln() function is used to write a line of text to a file. The text is written, followed by a carriage return/line feed pair. Its syntax is:

```
nBytes :=FWRITELN(<nHandle>, <cString>, <nLength> )
```

There is no default line length in this function, so be sure to pass a value. The string will have a carriage return/line feed pair written to the file after it, so the **<nLength>** should include two extra bytes to accommodate the delimiter.

The Fputs() function included in FILEIO.PRG is identical to the Fwriteln() function. (It is also a function from FoxPro.) You could create a preprocessor #xtranslate definition if you wanted to eliminate the Fputs() overhead from the FILEIO program. See Chapter 7 for more information about the preprocessor.

Example program

The text file functions can be used to update any text file. In this example, a function called Fix_cfg() will update the values in the CONFIG.SYS file to the proper number of files and buffers. Its syntax is:

```
<logical>  := Fix_cfg( <nFiles>,<nBuffers> )
```

The **<nFiles>** indicates the number of file handles the CONFIG.SYS file should have. **<nBuffers>** indicates the number of buffers. If the CONFIG.SYS file has at least these numbers, a true value will be returned. If not, the file will be corrected and a value of false will be returned. Presumably your application program will then ask the user to reboot the computer and run the program again.

The Fix_cfg() function is shown in listing 25.5.

Listing 25.5 Fix_cfg()

```
*
* Be sure program has access to FILEIO.PRG functions
*
#include "FILEIO.CH"
#define  CRLF chr(13)+chr(10)

function Fix_cfg(nFiles, nBuffers)
local fh, retval := .t., cfg_array := {},buf := "", x, k, x2
local numfiles := 0, numBufs := 0
if file("CONFIG.SYS")
   fh := fopen("CONFIG.SYS",FO_READWRITE)
   if fh > -1
      buf := upper(Freadln(fh,1,80))
     do  while !empty(buf)
         x := at("FILES",buf)
         if x > 0
            x2        := at("=",buf)
            numFiles  := val(substr(buf,x2+1,25))
         endif
         x := at("BUFFERS",buf)
         if x > 0
            x2        := at("=",buf)
```

```
            numBufs  := val(substr(buf,x2+1,25))
         endif
         aadd(cfg_array,buf)
         buf := Freadln(fh,1,80)
      enddo
      if numFiles < nFiles .or. numBufs < nBuffers
         fclose(fh)
         frename('config.sys', 'config.old')
         fh :=fcreate("CONFIG.SYS",FC_NORMAL)
         for k := 1 to len(cfg_array)
             x := at("FILES=",cfg_array[k])
             if x > 0
                cfg_array[k] := trim("FILES="+str(nFiles,3))
             endif
             x := at("BUFFERS=",cfg_array[k])
             if x > 0
                cfg_array[k] := trim("BUFFERS="+str(nBuffers,3))
             endif
             Fwriteln(fh,cfg_array[k],len(cfg_array[k])+2)
         next
         retval :=.f.
      endif
      fclose(fh)
   endif
else
   fh := fcreate( "CONFIG.SYS",FC_NORMAL )
   if fh > -1
      fwrite(fh,"FILES="+str(nFiles,3)+CRLF+;
               "BUFFERS="+str(nBuffers,3)+CRLF)
      fclose(fh)
   endif
   retval :=.f.
endif
return retval
```

File status functions

The file status functions return information about the file size and location as well as positioning the file.

Filetop()

The Filetop() function moves the file pointer to the first byte in the file. Its syntax is:

```
< nPosition> := FileTop( <nHandle> )
```

The **<nPosition>** that is returned indicates the new file pointer position, which will always be zero. Filetop() is equivalent to writing

```
Fseek(<nHandle>,0,0)
```

FileBottom()

The Filebottom() function moves the file pointer to the last byte in the file. Its syntax is:

```
<nPosition> := Filebottom( <nHandle> )
```

The **<nPosition>** that is returned indicates the new file pointer position, which will always be the size of the file. Filebottom() is equivalent to writing

```
Fseek(<nHandle>,0,2)
```

FilePos()

The FilePos() function returns the current value of the file pointer. Its syntax is:

```
<nPosition> := FilePos( <nHandle> )
```

The **<nPosition>** that is returned indicates the current file pointer position. FilePos() is equivalent to writing

```
Fseek(<nHandle>,0,1)
```

Preprocessor #xtranslate

The functions Filetop(), Filebottom(), and Filepos() can also be written as preprocessor commands using the #xtranslate syntax. The listing in 25.10 shows a .CH header file that could be used to replace these three functions.

Listing 25.10 Preprocessor

```
#xtranslate FILETOP( <n> )    => Fseek( <n>,0,0 )
#xtranslate FILEBOTTOM( <n> ) => Fseek( <n>,0,2 )
#xtranslate FILEPOS( <n> )    => Fseek( <n>,0,1 )
```

FileSize()

The Filesize() function returns the number of bytes in the file and keeps the file pointer where it is positioned. Its syntax is:

```
<nBytes> := FileSize( <nHandle> )
```

The file size can be determined using the FSEEK() function. This function saves the current file pointer, determines the file size, and then returns to the same spot in the file. An example of its use could be:

```
if filesize(fh) > Diskspace(1)
  ? "Cannot fit file onto drive A:"
endif
```

Feof()

Feof() returns a logical value of true if the file pointer is positioned at the end of the file or false if it is not. Its syntax is:

```
<logical> := Feof( <nHandle> )
```

The function works by comparing the file pointer with the value returned from the Filesize() function. It is useful when reading a file to determine if the end of the file has been reached or not. For example:

```
do while !feof(fh)
   ? freadln(fh,1,80)
enddo
```

Conversion functions

When using the database drivers provided in Clipper's libraries, all data extracted from the .DBF file is converted by Clipper into its internal memory variable format. The low-level file functions do not have this conversion done for them. Clipper considers all data read from a low-level file to be character data. In many files, this is not the case. For example, Lotus spreadsheets store real numbers as illustrated in Figure 25.2.

Figure 25.2 - Lotus real number format

Format Info	Column Number	Row Number	Numeric value stored in IEEE long real format
1-Byte	2-Bytes	2-Bytes	8-Bytes

For Clipper to provide meaningful access to this data, it has to convert it from the character format to its numeric meaning. The conversion function to use depends upon the number of bytes the number occupies.

One byte

If one byte is extracted from a file, Clipper will return the character that the byte corresponds to on the ASCII chart. If that one byte should be treated as a number, the ASC() function can be used to perform the conversion. If a single byte number in the range of zero through 255 needs to be written to a file, you may use the CHR() function to convert the number to a character string for FWRITE() to use.

ASC()

The ASC() function takes a single character and returns its ranking on the ASCII chart. Its syntax is:

```
<nByte> := ASC( <cChar> )
```

For example, ASC("A") would return the number 65. See the ASCII chart in Appendix A for more examples.

CHR()

The CHR() function takes a single byte integer and returns its character equivalent from the ASCII chart. Its syntax is:

```
<cChar> := CHR( <nByte> )
```

For example, CHR(65) would return the character A. See the ASCII chart in Appendix A for more examples. The application program will probably view this byte as the number 65, but Clipper must convert it to a character format to write it to the low-level file.

Two bytes

If a two byte integer is to be extracted from a file, you may use the BIN2I() or the BIN2W() function. The BIN2I() function handles signed integers and the BIN2W() handles unsigned integers. In C, this two byte integer is referred to as **int** or **short**.

A two-byte integer consists of sixteen bits. For a signed integer, the first bit indicates a positive (bit=0) or negative (bit=1) value. This, in effect, reduces the number of bits from sixteen to fifteen. In an unsigned integer, all sixteen bits are used to represent the number. The BIN2I() function instructs Clipper to interpret the first bit as a sign-bit. The BIN2W() function causes the bit to be considered part of the numeric value.

BIN2I()

The BIN2I() function takes a two-character string and returns the integer equivalent of the string. This function is used for signed integers in the range of -32,768 to +32,767. Its syntax is:

```
<nInteger> := BIN2I( <cSigned_int> )
```

BIN2W()

The BIN2W() function takes a two-character string and returns the integer equivalent of the string. Unlike the BIN2I() function, BIN2W() will not return a negative number. Its range of numbers is zero through 65,535. The syntax for the function is:

```
<nInteger> := BIN2W( <cUnsigned> )
```

I2BIN()

The integer to binary function works in reverse of the BIN2x() functions. It will take an integer and convert it to a binary representation. Its syntax is:

```
<cShort> := I2BIN( <nInteger> )
```

In addition to being used for reading information from non-DBF files, these functions can be used to compress integer storage space. If the integer is in the ranges above, 2-3 bytes of storage can be saved per integer through use of these functions.

Four bytes

Some programs store large integers in a four-byte format. Clipper provides conversion features to handle this double integer format. In C, this format is called the **long integer**. Although the long integer may be signed or unsigned, the Clipper functions work with **signed long integers** only.

BIN2L()

The BIN2L() function takes a long integer represented as a four-character string and returns the integer equivalent of the string. Its range of values is -2,147,483,648 to +2,147,483,647. The syntax for the function is:

```
<nInteger> := BIN2L( <cLong_int> )
```

Bin2ul()

The Bin2ul() user-defined function takes a long integer represented as a four-character string and returns the integer equivalent of the string. Its range of values is zero to +4,294,967,294. The syntax for the function is:

```
<nInteger> := Bin2ul( <cLong_int> )
```

Listing 25.11 shows the the Bin2ul() user-defined function.

Listing 25.11 Bin2ul()

```
function Bin2ul(cLong)
local jj:=Bin2l(cLong)
if jj < 0
   jj := abs(jj)+ 2147483647
endif
return jj
```

L2BIN()

The long integer to binary function works in reverse of the BIN2L() function. It will take an integer and convert it to a long integer binary representation. Its syntax is:

```
<cLong_int> := L2BIN( <nInteger> )
```

The long integer format can also be used to compress data storage for very large integers. The equivalent of ten numeric spaces can be represented in a four-byte string, for a 60% savings in storage space.

IEEE long real format

Some programs, such as Lotus and Btrieve, store real numbers in the IEEE long real format. This is a 64-bit (8 bytes) format as shown in Figure 25.3. This format is referred to as a **double** in C.

Figure 25.3 IEEE long real number format

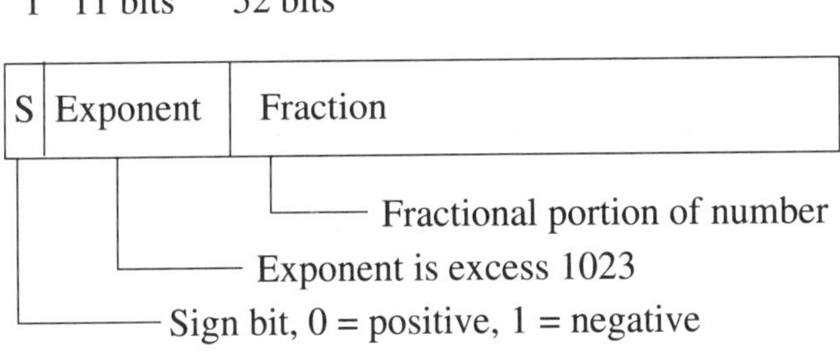

sign = if first bit is set, -1 else 1
exponent = bits 2-11 after string is built
fraction = bits 13-52 after string,
plus an implied 1 bit at the front

For Clipper to work with an IEEE real number, you must convert it from an 8-byte string into a Clipper numeric. Clipper does not provide any built-in functions to perform this conversion.

Real2iee

Listing 25.6 contains a function that will take a real number and convert it to the IEEE long real format expressed as a string variable. Its syntax is:

```
<cIeeereal> := Real2iee( <nReal_number> )
```

Listing 25.6 Real2iee()

```
function Real2iee(nReal)
local retval:=replicate(chr(0),8), exponent, sign, j
if nReal<>0                                // If non-zero
   sign     := if(nReal<0,128,0)           // Set the sign bit
   exponent:= 1075                  // Offset of 1023 + 52 bits max
   nReal    := abs(nReal)           // We already know the sign
   do while nReal < 2**52           // 2 raised to 52 power
      nReal *= 2                    // Multiply number by 2
      exponent--                    // Subtract one from exponent
   enddo
   do while nReal > 2*4503599627370496-1
      nReal /= 2
      exponent++
   enddo
   nReal   := int(nReal)     // Number is now an integer
   retval  := ''             // Build the first 48 bits in reverse
   for j   := 1 to 6         // by dividing by 256 and writing
```

```
      retval += chr(nReal%256)
      nReal := int(nReal/256) // remainder to string nReal
   next
   nReal -= 16                    // Strip out four high end bits
   retval += chr(nReal +16 * (exponent%16))+;
             chr(sign+int(exponent/16))
endif
return retval
```

Iee2real

Listing 25.7 contains a function that will take a character string and convert it to a real number. Its syntax is:

```
<nReal_number> := Iee2real( <cIeeereal> )
```

Listing 25.7 Iee2real()

```
function Iee2real(cIee)
local retval:=0, k, x1 := "", sign, exponent, fraction
if cIee <> repl(chr(0),8)       // Are all bits set to zero?
   for k:=len(cIee) to 1 step -1
      x1 += Dec2bin(asc(substr(cIee,k,1)))
   next
   sign     := (substr(x1,1,1)=="1")
   exponent := Bin2dec(substr(x1,2,11)) - 1022
   fraction := Bin2dec("1"+substr(x1,13),.t.)
   retval   := if(sign,-1,1)* (fraction * (2**exponent))
endif
return retval

function Bin2dec(_string)
local retval :=0 ,k
for k:=1 to len(_string)
   retval := if(substr(_string,k,1)=="0",0,1)+retval+retval
next
return retval
```

```
function Dec2bin(_number)
local tmp := _number, retval := "", remd, quot
do while .t.
   quot  := int(tmp/2)
   remd  := abs(tmp)-2*abs(quot)
   retval:= substr("01",remd+1,1)+retval
   if quot== 0
      exit
   endif
   tmp := quot
enddo
do while len(retval) <16
   retval := "0"+retval
enddo
return retval
```

Both of these functions can be sped up dramatically through the use of C functions. The C equivalent for these functions is illustrated in listing 25.8.

Listing 25.8 Ieereal.c

```
 * syntax:    ieereal( nIEEVar )
 * returns:   char string of length 8. each char in string
 *            represents the appropriate byte of nIEEVar.
 *
 * syntax:    realiee( cIEEStr )
 * returns:   double. converts cIEEStr to its double equivalent
 *
 * compile:   msc 5.1 – cl /W3 /Ox /AL /Gs /c /FPa /Zl ieereal.c
 *
 */

#include "extend.h"

CLIPPER ieereal(void);
CLIPPER realiee(void);
```

```
union {
          double n;
          char   s[8];
        } v;

CLIPPER ieereal()
{
    double n;

    n = _parnd(1);

    _retclen( (char far *) &n, 8);
}

CLIPPER realiee()
{
    char i;
    char far *t;

    t = _parc(1);

    for (i = 0; i < 8; i++)
        v.s[i] = *t++;

    _retnd( v.n );
}
```

Special thanks to Mike Taylor who provided these functions.

Speeding up low-level access

The low-level file functions work directly with disk files. You can improve speed dramatically by creating a buffer and doing read and write operations only when the buffer is full. Since disk operations are among the slowest the computer performs, the fewer we use, the better.

Listing 25.9 illustrates the low-level functions extracting information from a .DBF file header. (See the .DBF structure in Chapter 18). This function extracts the information one byte at a time. The result is seven disk reads.

Listing 25.9 Readdbf1

```
* Program...: Readdbf1
*
parameter dbf_file
local fh, one_byte := " ", vers_id, yy, mm, dd
local num_recs, hdr_size, rec_size

fh := fopen(dbf_file,0)        // Open the file for read only
if fh > -1                     // File opened ok?
   fread(fh,@one_byte,1)
   vers_id := asc(one_byte)
   fread(fh,@one_byte,1)
   yy      := asc(one_byte)
   fread(fh,@one_byte,1)
   mm      := asc(one_byte)
   fread(fh,@one_byte,1)
   dd      := asc(one_byte)
   one_byte:= space(4)
   fread(fh,@one_byte,4)
   num_recs:= bin2l(one_byte)
   one_byte:= space(2)
   fread(fh,@one_byte,2)
   hdr_size:= bin2w(one_byte)
   fread(fh,@one_byte,2)
   rec_size:= bin2w(one_byte)
   fclose(fh)
endif
```

Note also the use of the ASC(), BIN2L(), and BIN2W() functions to convert the character data read into numeric information.

Listing 25.10 performs the same function as Listing 25.9 but uses only one disk read. While the savings on this small example will not appear to be dramatic, they will add up on any large amounts of file I/O.

Listing 25.10 - Readdbf2

```
* Program...: Readdbf2
*
parameter dbf_file
local fh, buffer := space(12), vers_id, yy, mm, dd
local num_recs, hdr_size, rec_size

fh := fopen(dbf_file,0)       // Open the file for read only
if fh > -1                    // File opened ok?
   buffer   := fread(fh,@buffer,12)
   vers_id := asc(substr(buffer,1,1))
   yy       := asc(substr(buffer,2,1))
   mm       := asc(substr(buffer,3,1))
   dd       := asc(substr(buffer,4,1))
   num_recs:= bin2l(substr(buffer,5,4))
   hdr_size:= bin2w(substr(buffer,9,2))
   rec_size:= bin2w(substr(buffer,11,2))
   fclose(fh)
endif
```

By using a buffer we can reduce the number of disk reads and/or disk writes. This is the same technique to improve speed that many disk cache programs utilitize. If your program is going to spend a lot of time reading from a file, you should read the file in large buffers and parse it out as needed.

If you plan on reading large amounts of data from a file, the functions in listing 25.11 can be used to buffer your read and write operations, substantially speeding up the application. Be sure to specify the /N switch when you compile the functions. The two functions are Bread() and Bwrite().

Bread() — buffered read

This function takes a numeric parameter and returns that number of bytes from the buffer. If there are not enough bytes in the buffer to fulfill the read request, a new buffer will be read in from the disk. Its syntax is:

```
<cString>  := Bread(<nHandle>,<nBytes>)
```

Bwrite() — buffered write

This function takes a character string and adds it to the buffer. If the buffer size exceeds some constant number, the buffer is written to the disk and cleared out for the next set of data. Its syntax is:

```
<logical> := Bwrite(<nHandle>,<cString>)
```

Bwrite() will return false if the disk write failed. In this case, check FERROR() to determine why the write failed. All other times, Bwrite() will return a true value.

Listing 25.11 Buffered Read/Write

```
#define BUFFER_SIZE  4096
static buffer := ""

function Bread(nHandle,nBytes)
local tmp
if nBytes > len(buffer)
   tmp := buffer
   buffer := space(BUFFER_SIZE)
   fread(nHandle,@buffer,BUFFER_SIZE)
   buffer += tmp
endif
tmp := substr(buffer,1,nBytes)
buffer := substr(buffer,nBytes+1,BUFFER_SIZE)
return tmp

function Bwrite(nHandle,cString)
local x := .t.
buffer += cString
if len(buffer) >= BUFFER_SIZE
   x := (fwrite(nHandle,buffer)==len(buffer))
   buffer :=""
endif
return x
```

Sample programs

The sample programs illustrate how the low-level functions can be used to work with a variety of files.

ZipDir()

The Zipdir() function in listing 25.12 can be used to read the file directory table from a zipped file. Zip is a data compression program created by Phil Katz and is a common tool on many systems. Zip can compress database files as much as 90% which reduces disk storage space and file transfer time. A single zip file can also hold many individual files in their compressed form. It does this by maintaining a directory of files. The Zipdir() function in listing 25.12 uses the low-level functions to search for this directory and returns an array containing the file names it finds there.

Listing 25.12 ZipDir()

```
#include "FILEIO.CH"

function ZipDir(zip_file)
local zip := fopen(zip_file,FO_READ), tmp :=space(4)
local method, orig_date, fn_date, comp_size, uncomp
local fn_size, extra, junk, _array:={}, file_name
do while .t.
   tmp :== space(4)
   if fread(zip,@tmp,4) <> 4     // End of file
      exit
   endif
   if tmp = "PK"+chr(1)+chr(2)  // Central dir
      exit
   elseif tmp <> "PK"+chr(3)+chr(4)
      exit
   endif
   tmp := space(26)
   fread(zip,@tmp,26)
   method    := bin2i(substr(tmp,5,2))
   orig_date := bin2i(substr(tmp,9,2))
   fn_date   := Dos_date(orig_date)
   comp_size := bin2l(substr(tmp,15,4))
```

```
   uncomp    := bin2l(substr(tmp,19,4))
   fn_size   := bin2i(substr(tmp,23,2))
   extra     := bin2i(substr(tmp,25,2))
   file_name := freadstr(zip,fn_size)
   tmp       := space(extra)
   junk      := if(extra==0,"",fread(zip,@tmp,extra))
   fseek(zip,comp_size,1)
   aadd(_array,{file_name,comp_size,uncomp,fn_date})
enddo
fclose(zip)
return _array

function Dos_date(_datestamp)
local temp :=Dec2bin(_datestamp), yy, mm, dd
yy := Bin2dec(substr(temp,1,7)) +1980
mm := Bin2dec(substr(temp,8,4))
dd := Bin2dec(substr(temp,12,5))
return ctod(str(mm,2)+"/"+str(dd,2)+"/"+str(yy,4))

function Bin2dec(_string)
local retval :=0 ,k
for k :=1 to len(_string)
    retval := if(substr(_string,k,1) == "0",0,1)+retval+retval
next
return retval

function Dec2bin(_number)
local tmp := _number,retval:="",remd,quot
do while .t.
   quot  := int(tmp/2)
   remd  := abs(tmp)-2*abs(quot)
   retval:= substr("01",remd+1,1)+retval
   if quot == 0
      exit
   endif
   tmp := quot
enddo
do while len(retval)<16
   retval := "0"+retval
enddo
return retval
```

Zipdir() will return an array of arrays. Each file within the zip directory will contain a four element array with the structure shown in Table 25.8.

Table 25.8 Zipdir() directory structure

Element	*Contents*
1	DOS file name
2	Size of compressed file
3	Original DOS file size
4	DOS file date stamp

DBF2DIF()

DIF (Data Interchange Format) is a program-independent method of storing disk information. A .DIF file contains a header indicating the file name, number of fields, and number of records. It is followed by a data section which contains the actual data. Table 25.9 illustrates the format for a .DIF file.

Table 25.9 DIF file format

Record	*Contents*
1	TABLE <cr/lf> 0,1 <cr/lf> DIF name <cr/lf>
2	VECTORS <cr/lf> 0,<columns> <cr/lf> “” <cr/lf>
3	TUPLES <cr/lf> 0,<rows> <cr/lf> “” <cr/lf>
4	DATA <cr/lf> 0,0 <cr/lf> “” <cr/lf>

Data section starts here

Each new row	-1,0 <cr/lf> “BOT” <cr/lf>
End of file	-1,0 <cr/lf> “EOD” <cr/lf>

The program in Listing 25.13 reads a .DBF file and converts it into a .DIF file by using the low level file functions. The parameters to the function are the name of the .DBF file to be read and the name of the .DIF file to be created. Its syntax is:

```
DBF2DIF( <cDbf_file>,<cDIF_file> )
```

The function will return a zero if the file was successfully created or will return the DOS error code if an error occurred.

Listing 25.13 DBF2DIF()

```
#define SQ chr(34)
#define DQ chr(34)+chr(34)
#define CRLF chr(13)+chr(10)

function DBF2DIF(cDbf,cDif)
local retval := 0, buffer, ctr := 0,k,mfld
local how_many, fh, nbytes

use (cDBF) new ALIAS input
go top
fh := Fcreate(Cdif,0)
if fh > -1
   buffer :='TABLE'+CRLF+'0,1'+CRLF+SQ+cDBF+SQ+CRLF +;
            'VECTORS'+CRLF+'0,'+str(fcount(),2)+CRLF+DQ+CRLF+;
            'TUPLES'+CRLF+'0,'+str(lastrec(),6)+CRLF+DQ+CRLF+;
            'DATA'+CRLF+'0,0'+CRLF+DQ+CRLF
   nbytes := fwrite(fh,buffer,len(buffer))      // DIF header
   if nbytes <> len(buffer)
      retval :=ferror()
      fclose(fh)
      return retval
   endif
   how_many := fcount()
   do while !eof()
      ctr++
      buffer := '-1,0'+CRLF+'BOT'+CRLF
      for k := 1 to how_many
        mfld   :=Fieldget(k)
```

```
         buffer += DIFPUT(mfld)
      next
      Fwrite(fh,buffer)
      skip +1
   enddo
   fwrite(fh,'-1,0'+CRLF+'EOD'+CRLF,11)
   retval := ferror()
   fclose(fh)
else
   retval := ferror()
endif
return retval

function DIFPUT(fld_data)
local fld_type := valtype(fld_data), retval := ""
if fld_type == "C"
   retval := '1,0'+CRLF+SQ+trim(fld_data)+SQ+CRLF
elseif fld_type == "L"
   retval := '0,'+if(fld_data,'1','0')+CRLF+;
             SQ+if(fld_data,'true','false')+SQ+CRLF
elseif fld_type == "N"
   retval := '0,'+ltrim(trim(str(fld_data)))+CRLF+SQ+'V'+SQ+CRLF
elseif type("fld_data") == "D"
   retval := '1,0'+CRLF+SQ+dtoc(fld_data)+SQ+CRLF
endif
return retval
```

The .DIF file was the file format used by Dan Bricklan's VisiCalc program (the first spreadsheet program on a personal computer). Spreadsheet programs have since defined their own formats, but many programs still can create and read .DIF files.

Summary

After reading this chapter you should feel comfortable working with the low-level file functions and you should be familiar with the terminology describing low-level files. You should have a healthy respect for the potential of these functions, in terms of both use and abuse. Based upon our example, you should be eager to try to create various files from within a Clipper program. If you can determine the structure of a file, Clipper's functions can make that file available to you.

CHAPTER 26

The TBrowse Object Class

With the release of Clipper 5, Computer Associates has adopted a new programming paradigm, the object class. Relative to other languages derived from dBASE, Clipper 5 has leapt ahead into the "modern" world of object-oriented programming (OOP). With respect to languages like C++, Clipper is only just starting down the road. Clipper 5 is not an OOP language in the strictest definition of the term, but it is a major step in that direction and an indication of what will be the future of the language. Clipper 5's implementation of objects presents new terminology and demands a new way of thinking.

Introduction to the Object Classes

The next chapters introduce the current Clipper object classes: Get, Error, TBrowse, and TBColumn. More classes are promised in the future. Object classes are a dramatic change from the traditional dBASE way of thinking, and unfortunately they've been implemented in Clipper 5 with woefully inadequate documentation and needlessly complex examples. Lest you get the wrong impression, we think Computer Associates should be commended for taking our beloved language in this encouraging direction. Object-oriented programming is definitely the wave of the future and Computer Associates is giving us an early opportunity to get comfortable with the jargon and concepts slowly rather than being completely overwhelmed with one giant leap. The following chapters explain the object classes using concepts with which you are already familiar, allowing you to make productive use of the object classes in your everyday programming.

We will learn about OOP backwards from the way most books and magazine articles approach it: We're going to completely ignore the OOP jargon and conceptual issues and plow right into the TBrowse class as if it were a traditional Clipper programmer's tool. The new jargon and concepts will be considerably easier to digest once you know how to use the tools because you'll be thinking about them in the context of living, breathing Clipper applications that you have created, not as abstract ideas.

Once you are comfortable with the concepts you can delve more deeply into these chapters and take advantage of features and functions far more powerful than could be accomplished with traditional programming techniques. Objects will without a doubt become one of your favorite features of Clipper 5.

Introducing Objects via the TBrowse Class

TBrowse is significantly easier to understand when stripped of all the fancy new terminology and exposed for what it really is: an outstanding browse utility! As you will see as this chapter progresses, TBrowse has more power and flexibility than the equivalents in dBASE-IV and FoxPro with a significantly better programming interface. The traditional dBASE-dialect way of doing things is to keep adding parameters and options to an already overburdened command. Take a look at the BROWSE syntax in dBASE IV or FoxPro. Yikes. Not that Clipper 5 is any less ambitious; the key difference is the way all those options and parameters are specified. Rather than passing 32 parameters and issuing a dozen application-wide SET commands to establish the browse, Clipper breaks the potentially complex situation into smaller and more manageable pieces. Consider what it takes in Summer '87 to get the much-maligned DBEDIT() up and running. We shudder to think what super_DBEDIT() would have looked like if Computer Associates had copped out and just added more parameters.

We will start our introduction to the TBrowse object class by foregoing your indoctrination into the mysteries of object-oriented programming and instead just diving into the use of TBrowse as a tool for viewing database fields. Then, once you have a firm grasp of what TBrowse is all about, we will go back and see how OOP terminology and concepts help to describe and unify the new extensions of the Clipper language. We are of the opinion that most of us use Clipper to get production programming out the door, and the faster we get up to speed with its powerful new features, the better. OOP-speak, while important, should wait in line behind our employers or customers!

Although we face the risk of being branded as heretics, we are throwing back the curtain and exposing a "TBrowse Object" as a multi-dimensional array structure. When you create a TBrowse object you give it a name, and that name becomes the name of the array. When you "send messages" to the object you are assigning values to various array elements or calling a function that uses element values as data. The syntax for doing this has been adapted from OOP and is consequently a less painful introduction to such concepts. As you will see when you get more familiar with TBrowse, OOP concepts make this kind of programming much easier.

With that said, don't go overboard thinking about objects and arrays as being the same thing. They're not. In many respects they are similar, and for the purposes of introduction we're taking advantage of the similarities so we don't get bogged down in terminology.

On a fast track to our first TBrowse

Let's walk through the minimum steps for getting a TBrowse object up and running. The goal is to write the smallest possible program that browses any arbitrary database. This will form an easy-to-understand platform you can use for further experimentation. At the end of this section you'll have your first generic database browsing program.

Since a TBrowse object "lives" in what amounts to an array, the first step is to think up a name and assign it the basic TBrowse object structure.

```
browse := TBrowseDB()
```

We chose BROWSE as the name of the array. There's nothing special about the name; "RALPH" will work just as well.

We have skipped the four parameters that define the screen dimensions of the TBrowse; they default to the entire screen. TBrowseDB() is the same as TBrowseNew() except that it assigns database handling code blocks in the appropriate places in the object, which we will discuss in detail later. TBrowseDB() returns a mostly empty object. The "T" in TBrowse stands for table: TBrowse = Table-Browse. Some elements in the object deal with the entire browse, some deal with the columns that comprise a browse. At this point our browse object is a mostly empty shell with no columns and consequently nothing to display.

Each column in the browse screen is defined by a column object. Similar to a browse object, each column object is essentially an array that's eventually stored within the main browse object. The function used to return such an object is TBColumnNew().

```
column := TBColumnNew()
```

TBColumnNew() returns an object, so "column" is the name we have chosen for that object. At this point the column object is an empty shell. The minimum thing this object needs to be useful in a TBrowse object is a code block used to retrieve data for display. If you're confused by code blocks, don't despair. Most of the code blocks associated with TBrowse are easy to understand.

```
column:block := { || recno() }
```

The above line supplies a code block that returns the current record number. Our column object now "knows" how to retrieve data for the column, in this case the record number. The colon used to separate the object name from the word "block" is a completely new form of syntax in Clipper 5. In more traditional Clipper syntax this might have been written like so:

```
columnBlock(@column, { || recno() } )
```

The implication here is that the columnBlock() function is working with a parameter called column and a parameter that's a code block. Both of the previous column block lines are very different and distinct from the following, where the variable called column is being assigned a new value.

```
column := columnBlock( {|| recno()} )
```

Using the new syntax (which provides a level of power and efficiency that we're not even hinting at, yet), we are saying that of all the different values that a column object stores within itself, at this point we are providing just one of them — the code block used to retrieve data for the column.

```
column:block := { || recno() }
```

We still need to add the column we just defined to the currently column-less browse object.

```
browse:addColumn(column)
```

The addColumn() function knows precisely how to find an open spot in the main browse object and add the column object to it. Similar to the discussion about column:block, when you see browse:addColumn() you should think of addColumn() as one of several functions that know how to work with a browse object. In this case the addColumn() function adds a column object to the browse object and consequently needs a column object as a parameter.

Since we are going to browse records in a database it wasn't hard to assign a column for the record number, since all databases have record numbers. What do you do for fields? The next four lines assign all of the fields in a database as columns in the browse. Despite our original claim that this example would demonstrate only the "minimum necessary," this is a very important technique that you should understand early in the game. We could have written a few more TBColumnNew() functions, one for each field. But that would limit the resulting test routine to a single database. The following slightly more complex version will work with any database structure.

```
for n := 1 to fcount()
  column := TBColumnNew()
  column:block := fieldblock(field(n))
  browse:addColumn(column)
next n
```

We are looping through the fields, from the first to the last. The FIELDBLOCK() function returns a "get-set" code block for the field name returned by the FIELD() function. The term get-set denotes that the code block will retrieve, or get, the specified field value from the database, and can save, or set, a value back to the database. In this example we are interested only in the code block's ability to retrieve a value for display during the browse. We then use addColumn() to add the resulting column to the main browse object. If we were working with a database with name, address and city fields, the above loop could have been replaced by the following:

```
column := TBColumnNew()
column:block := fieldblock("Name")
browse:addColumn(column)

column := TBColumnNew()
column:block := fieldblock("Address")
browse:addColumn(column)

column := TBColumnNew()
column:block := fieldblock("City")
browse:addColumn(column)
```

A common question at this point is how does the browse object distinguish between column objects when in the example they all used "column" as a variable name? It's important to note that addColumn() does indeed add a column object to the browse object, but does not maintain any sort of relation between them. This will be more obvious in the next example.

If you want to eliminate the temporary variables you can use TBColumnNew()'s parameters which allow three lines of code to be combined into a single statement. TBColumnNew() takes two parameters: First, the heading for the column, and second, the code block used to retrieve the value. Since we're going for the absolute minimum in this initial example we'll skip the first parameter.

```
browse:addColumn(TBColumnNew(,    fieldblock("Name")))
browse:addColumn(TBColumnNew(,    fieldblock("Address")))
browse:addColumn(TBColumnNew(,    fieldblock("City")))
```

At this point we have the main browse structure defined with default database handling capabilities via a call to TBrowseDB() and several columns via calls to

TBColumnNew() and addColumn(). So where is the browse? How do you get this wonder of modern programming technique on the screen? This is the really neat part of TBrowse, where the Computer Associates developers demonstrate their considerable design talents. Using OOP-speak, you send the "stabilize()" message to your browse object. The stabilizing routine updates one portion of the display (usually one line of the table) and returns true if there is nothing more to update on the display. The easiest way to handle this is to wrap a "while loop" around it, as follows.

```
do while .not. browse:stabilize()
enddo
```

In rough terms, the loop will run once for each line visible in the table. The simple browse we established so far did not have any table dimensions so it fills the entire screen. On a 24-line screen browse:stabilize() would have to be called about 24 times. Why not just update the whole display? There are many reasons which we will not get into right now. Basically you can do whatever you want between each line displayed, for example, interrupting the entire process at line two rather than having to wait for all 24 lines. In this minimal example there is no way to take advantage of the feature, but it is easy to add. In the following example, any keystroke during the screen update will exit the loop.

```
do while .not. browse:stabilize()
  if nextkey() <> 0
    exit
  endif
enddo
```

The last minimum thing to do is allow the program operator to move around in the database. There are many different kinds of movement—up, down, left, or right; all the way to the top, bottom, left, or right; one screenful up or down; one column shifted to the left or right. TBrowse will do all the required scrolling in both directions. The following set of case statements will handle the minimum up/down and left/right movements. You need such a structure to associate each keystroke with a movement. (The items starting with K_ are manifest constants defined in the INKEY.CH include file).

```
#include "inkey.ch"
key := inkey(0)
do case
case key == K_UP          // up one row
  browse:up()
case key == K_DOWN        // down one row
  browse:down()
case key == K_LEFT        // left one column
  browse:left()
case key == K_RIGHT       // right one column
  browse:right()
endcase
```

All together now

We've covered all the steps required to use a TBrowse object to browse through any database.

1. Create a browse object and give it a name.
2. Create one or more column objects and add them to the browse object.
3. Display the browse window by calling the stabilizing function until there's nothing more to display.
4. Accept a movement keystroke and act on it.

Let's take a look at the final program, found in Listing 26.1. We have added the ability to pass a database filename in from the DOS command line, allowing you to more easily experiment with a variety of databases. If you have never programmed with TBrowse before you should take a break and experiment with this program. See Listing 26.1 for a sample screen generated by the MiniBrow program.

Listing 26.1 A complete TBrowse-based database browser

```
/*
   MiniBrow.Prg:  A database browser implemented with a minimum
   amount of code.
   Usage (from DOS):  minibrow datafile
   Compile with: /n /m
*/
#include "inkey.ch"

function Main(filename)
local column, browse, key, n

  //  Check for a DOS command line parameter
  if filename == nil
    ? "Must specify a database filename."
  //  Check that file exists.
  elseif .not. (file(filename) .or. file(filename +".DBF"))
    ? "File does not exist."

  //  Database checks out, clear screen and get down to it.
  else
    @ 0,0 clear
    //  Open the specified database.
    use (filename) new

    //  Create a TBrowse object that knows how to deal with data
    // bases.
    browse := TBrowseDB()

    //  Create a TBColumn object.
    column := TBColumnNew()
    //  Assign a data retrieval code block to the column object.
    column:block := { || recno() }

    //  Add the record number column to the browse.
    browse:addColumn(column)

    //  For each field in the current database...
    for n := 1 to fcount()
```

```
      //  Create a column object.
      column := TBColumnNew()
      //  Assign the column a code block that retrieves
      //  the field's value.
      column:block := fieldblock(field(n))
      //  Add the column to the browse.
      browse:addColumn(column)
    next n

    //  Keep looping as long as user wants to browse.
    do while .t.
      //  Keep looping until all rows in window have been
      // displayed.
      do while .not. browse:stabilize()
        //  Allow user to interrupt by pressing a key.
        if nextkey() <> 0
          exit
        endif
      enddo

      //  Wait for a keystroke.
      key := inkey(0)
      //  Move the pointer based on user's keystroke.
      do case
      case key == K_UP        //  Up one row
        browse:up()
      case key == K_DOWN      //  Down one row
        browse:down()
      case key K_LEFT         //  Left one column
       browse:left()
      case key == K_RIGHT     //  Right one column
        browse:right()
      case key == K_ESC       //  Done browsing
        exit
      endcase
    enddo //  While browsing
    close database
  endif //  File exists
return nil
* eof MiniBrow.Prg
```

Figure 26.1 Sample screen generated by MiniBrow.Prg.

```
126 Greg Lief             5.0 FOCUS: TBrowse, Part 2
127 Greg Lief             Ask The Grumps (8)
128 Joe Booth             MAKE and RMAKE, Part 2
129 Greg Lief             5.0 FOCUS: FIELD and MEMVAR Declarations
130 Darren Forcier        REVIEW: Scrimage
131 Greg Lief             5.0 FOCUS: Controlling Screen/Printer Output
132 Greg Lief             5.0 FOCUS: Static Arrays I - Stack-Based Functions
133 Ted Means             Assembler for Clipper Programmers: Part VII
134 Darren Forcier        REVIEW: Memory Overlay Manager for Clipper
135 Craig Yellick         5.0 FOCUS: Error Handling, Part 2
136 Greg Lief             5.0 FOCUS: Virtual Screens
137                       Clipper 5.0 Anomalies (3/91 revisions)
138                       5.0 FOCUS: /X Compiler Switch
139 Joe Booth             Low-Level File Access, Part 1
140 Greg Lief             5.0 FOCUS: TBrowse, Part 3
141 Greg Lief             Ask The Grumps (9)
142 Greg Lief             5.0 FOCUS: PROCNAME() and PROCLINE()
143 Greg Lief             5.0 FOCUS: Menus, Part 1
144 Greg Lief             5.0 FOCUS: Static Arrays II - Handling Globals
145 Greg Lief             5.0 FOCUS: Still Not Using Pre-Linked Libraries?
146 Darren Forcier        REVIEW: Desqview Clipper API
147 Kathy Uchman          TBrowse FOCUS: A Few Cosmetics
148 Joe Booth             Low-Level File Access, Part 2
149 Clayton Neff          Data Driven Data Setup for Clipper 5.0
150 Roger Donnay          5.0 FOCUS: Memory Management, Overlay Reloading #2
```

What about the OOP jargon?

Now that you understand TBrowse from a more traditional Clipper language standpoint, we will go back and associate the OOP terminology with the appropriate features. We feel this is a better way to introduce a new way of thinking and programming. You can get only so far ignoring the OOP concepts, so it is time to introduce them.

We've seen only one small example of the power of objects in Clipper 5, but it should be enough to show you why they're so important. There are two aspects to the major new step toward object-oriented programming in Clipper: ENCAPSULATION, which allows an object to wrap up some very useful and flexible functionality into one easily-handled package, and CLASSES, which allow you to create as many versions of any type of Clipper object as you may need.

- CLASSES: A class is not an object, it's the specifications for one type of object. TBrowse is one type object class just as date is one type of variable, and character is another. As we'll see next, no object can be created except as an instance of some pre-defined class. The main difference between Clipper 5 and true OOP languages resides in the current limitations of the Clipper classes (Get, Error, TBrowse and TBColumn). In a true-OOP Clipper we would have the full specification of the whole collection of variables and methods in each class, whether part of the interface or not. We could also define new classes and create modified versions of the existing ones. Such capabilities are slated as future enhancements to the Clipper language.

- INSTANCES: An instance is an object and an object is an instance. What the term "instance" emphasizes is that the object belongs to a class. "An instance of a class" is any object belonging to that class. A class may have zero, one or even one hundred instances. Each instance is a completely separate collection of variables (including exported instance variables, which we'll get to in a moment), all conforming to the same class specification.

- ENCAPSULATION: An object or instance is simply a collection of memory variables, with the one difference that the rest of the program (and the programmer) have absolutely no access to most, or even all, of this collection. "Encapsulation" means first that the collection of variables that we call an object works as a black box to the rest of the program. But then, how does the program use the object at all? This is the second aspect of encapsulation: An object has a well-defined interface that allows you, indirectly, to change or read its collection of variables, and, even more importantly, to command them to do something useful, the way the stabilize() function incrementally updates the window of a TBrowse object. Most of the interface to a normal object or instance is made up of functions, called methods. But some of the variables forming an object may also be directly accessible. In that case, they're called "exported instance variables". We'll cover both aspects of the object interface later on.

- INSTANCES: We created a single instance of a browse object and a variable number of column object instances depending on the number of fields in a database. Each instance has all the "rights and privileges" of a member of its class.

- MESSAGES: We sent a flurry of messages to the objects we created, describing exactly what each column should contain and how to react to various keystrokes.

- EXPORTED INSTANCE VARIABLES: These variables form the interface to an instance of an object. We used one of them to assign data retrieval code blocks to each of the columns.

- METHODS: We used the addColumn() method to add columns to the browse object, and several of the many navigation methods, like up() and down(), to provide services to the person using the browse.

Compiler and linker details

We should point out some technical issues regarding the way that objects, with their methods and instance variables, are implemented differently from the regular variable and function names to which they are frequently equated. Method names and instance variables are symbols just like function names and memory variables, with the important exception that they are created dynamically at run-time. The ramifications of this are important. Neither the compiler nor linker "sees" the method or instance variable names, so you will not get any compiler or linker warnings on obviously incorrect statements like

```
browse:iJustMadeThisUp := column:ObviousError(n)
```

or more subtle but equally incorrect statements like

```
browse:gotoTopBlock := { || RecPosition("top") }
```

where we accidentally misspelled browse:goTopBlock. You'll pay for your errors at run-time, at the moment Clipper encounters the incorrect method or instance variable name. Such is life with dynamic binding, a key component of object-oriented design. Only after your application calls TBrowseNew() or TBrowseDB(), the TBrowse class constructor functions, do the "correct" names become known. And even then, Clipper only knows about a problem when it is told to search a class's dictionary for a name and can't find it.

The implications for the programmer are staggering: You must vigorously test your code to ensure that every single line of object-oriented code is executed at least once at run-time. If in your testing you manage to avoid a section of code, you may never know it's a potential time-bomb waiting for the right logical conditions. This is not to imply that regular code should be any less subject to rigorous testing, only that object-oriented code merits special attention.

At run-time, Clipper will create an error with a generic error code of EG_NOVARMETHOD, or "no exported variable method", allowing you to detect the situation and possibly handle it rather than terminating the application. See Chapter 28, "The Error Class," for details on generic error codes and error handling.

What can objects do for me?

So far we have only scratched the surface of what TBrowse can do and we haven't even hinted at the other object classes. The remainder of this chapter is dedicated to a complete discussion of all the TBrowse features and functions. Then the following chapters discuss the Get and Error classes. You can use your understanding of the TBrowse object as a base to learn about the other object classes.

The TBrowse Object Class

The TBrowse class forms a general purpose table browsing utility that can be used with any form of data that is row and column oriented. Unlike the Summer '87 DBEDIT() function, TBrowse can be used to browse arrays and many other data structures, not just database files. TBrowse is perhaps the most accessible of the Clipper 5 object classes and an ideal way to introduce yourself to object-oriented programming (OOP).

This discussion explores the many features and functions of the TBrowse class and demonstrates ways you can use TBrowse objects in your everyday programming. To get the most out of TBrowse you must understand the basics of code blocks. Fortunately most of the code blocks associated with TBrowse are straightforward and don't require more than a passing familiarity with the syntax.

After reading this chapter you'll be able to create general-purpose database browsers as well as write functions for a variety of special browsing purposes. You'll also have all the tools you need to browse arrays and memo fields.

TBrowse overview

The Introduction to the Object Classes covers the basic concepts behind objects in general and TBrowse in particular.

Let's start by taking a look at the various things you can do with TBrowse and TBColumn objects as specified by the interface Computer Associates provides. The process of getting a TBrowse up and running can be broken into four general steps:

1. Create a browse object and change browse-wide values as needed. Such values include, for example, the window coordinates and color scheme.

2. Create one or more column objects and change column-specific values as needed, then add the column objects to the browse object. For example, you can assign column headings and separators.

3. Display the browse on the screen.

4. Wait for a keystroke and then possibly take action on it. Loop back to step 3 to display the effect of the action. The action may affect things established in steps 1 and 2. Examples of actions are changing the color scheme, a column heading, or reacting to an attempt to scroll past the last record in the database.

All of the features of the TBrowse and TBColumn object classes can be divided into four broad categories defined by these steps. Many features are applicable to more than a single step. We've created these divisions purely as an aid in remembering how a feature is usually used. All instance variables and methods for both TBrowse and TBColumn will be covered in the course of these four categories.

We use the term "feature" to be deliberately vague. Your interface to Clipper's objects are the exported methods and instance variables described in the documentation. Some features are tied to a method, some to an instance variable, and others appear only when several different methods and/or instance variables are used in combination. If your view of the TBrowse object class is limited to an alphabetic list of methods and instance variables you will never see the incredible potential TBrowse offers, because a TBrowse object is a dynamic, run-time event and not just another complex function call like DBEDIT().

For the remainder of this chapter we will use the object name **b** when referring to methods and instance variables that are browse-related, and **c** for those that are column-related. To keep this overview section as concise as possible we will not supply comprehensive examples of how the methods and instance variables are used. After this overview we'll examine examples that cover all features in the context of a real browsing routine.

Step 1: Changing browse-wide values

The first step entails creating a new TBrowse object and possibly changing values that affect the entire browse. Most values have defaults that we find unacceptable, for example, the browse window occupying the entire screen. The following will be discussed:

Constructors
TBrowseNew()
TBrowseDB()

Instance Variables

b:autoLite

b:cargo

b:colorSpec

b:colSep

b:footSep

b:freeze

b:goBottomBlock

b:goTopBlock

b:headSep

b:nBottom

b:nTop

b:nLeft

b:nRight

b:skipBlock

There is a timing issue involved with respect to when an instance variable or method can legitimately be called. A good rule of thumb is that anything that deals with column-related information can't be referenced until at least one column has been added to the browse object. For example, don't assign anything to b:freeze until the column to be frozen has been added to the browse object. Since it usually doesn't matter what order things are done prior to the first b:stabilize() call, it's always safe to delay making assignments until after the general browse structure has been established. Create the browse object, fill it with columns, and *then* start making assignments to instance variables that affect the appearance or operation of the browse window.

TBrowseNew (nTop, nLeft, nBottom, nRight)
TBrowseDB(nTop, nLeft, nBottom, nRight)

TBrowseNew() is the main object constructor for the TBrowse class. It returns a new TBrowse object which is devoid of any knowledge about what you intend to browse and how you want it to look, essentially an empty shell. TBrowseDB() returns the exact same thing as TBrowseNew() except it defines the three database positioning code blocks (goTopBlock, goBottomBlock and skipBlock, discussed next). The following assign a new TBrowse object to brow1 and an object with basic database handling code blocks to brow2.

```
 //  Create two TBrowse objects.
brow1 := TBrowseNew()
brow2 := TBrowseDB()
```

Both constructor functions allow you to optionally specify the browse window coordinates. If you specify any of the window coordinate parameters they will be stored in the appropriate instance variables (discussed in a moment). The following creates brow3 as a new TBrowse object and assigns the indicated window coordinates.

```
 //  Create a TBrowse object and assign window coordinates.
brow3 := TBrowseNew(4, 5, 14, 75)
```

b:goTopBlock
b:go BottomBlock
b:skipBlock

These three instance variables store code blocks that are used to manipulate the source of the data being browsed. The variable names correspond to their Clipper database counterparts: GOTO TOP, GOTO BOTTOM, and SKIP. As previously described, the TBrowseDB() object constructor initializes all three variables with code blocks that will correctly handle a standard Clipper database. TBrowseNew() leaves the variables uninitialized.

b:goTopBlock and b:goBottomBlock are very simple code blocks. All they need to do is position the data source at the first or last position and return. Here are functionally equivalent versions of the TBrowseDB()-supplied code blocks.

```
b:goTopBlock    := { || dbGoTop() }
b:goBottomBlock := { || dbGoBottom() }
```

The code block simply calls the specified function and returns.

You may notice later that when we describe these code blocks we often use terms like data source positioning and avoid using database-specific terms like record and field. This is because one of TBrowse's most powerful features, and by extension part of the beauty and elegance of Clipper 5, is that TBrowse doesn't know or care about the source of the data. We can browse databases, arrays, text files, even data files created by other non-Clipper applications, simply by supplying code blocks that perform the required actions.

So much for the simple code blocks. b:skipBlock is a different matter entirely. This code block must be able to skip forwards or backwards through the data source, must be able to skip a specified number of positions, and must return the number it was actually able to skip. If the code block returns zero or a number less than was requested it assumes the data source hit the beginning or end of data during the skip operation.

Writing b:skipBlock functions will doubtless become an art form, as Clipper programmers strive for speed, flexibility and efficiency. The function in Listing 26.2 is a general-purpose database b:skipBlock function that you can use as basis for further experiments. It is the functional equivalent of the code block installed by TBrowseDB().

Listing 26.2 General-purpose database b:skipBlock function

```
function SkipRec(howMany)
/*
   General-purpose record skipping function for use with
   TBrowse skipBlocks. TBrowse will indicate how many records
   it wants to skip, and in what direction. Positive number
   indicates skip forward, negative indicates backwards. This
   function must return the number of records it was able to skip.
*/
local actual := 0
```

```
//  Negative = Move backward.
do case
case howMany < 0

//  Keep skipping backward until we skip the number
//  requested, or run out of records to skip.
do while (actual > howMany) .and. (.not. bof())
    skip -1
    //  Can't count the skip if we hit beginning-of-file.
    if .not. bof()
      actual--
    endif
enddo

//  Positive = Move forward.
case howMany > 0

//  Keep skipping forward until we skip the number
//  requested, or run out of records to skip.
do while (actual < howMany) .and. (.not. eof())
    skip +1
    //  Can't count the skip if we hit end-of-file.
    if .not. eof()
        actual++
    endif
enddo

//  Don't leave database parked on the
//  phantom end-of-file record.
if eof()
    skip -1
endif

//  No movement requested, re-read current record.
otherwise
    skip 0
endcase

return actual
```

The assignment for the code block that calls this function looks like the following.

```
browse := TBrowseNew()
browse:skipBlock := { |n| SkipRec(n) }
```

In later sections of this chapter we'll tackle the functions necessary for performing the same data source positioning operations for arrays and text files.

b:nBottom
b:nTop
b:nLeft
b:nRight

These four instance variables establish the coordinates of the window. They can optionally be assigned via parameters in the TBrowseNew() and TBrowseDB() constructor functions. They default to a value of NIL, which causes the window to occupy the entire screen, so they are not optional for most applications. The following lines assign a browse window that is 11 rows long and 70 columns wide.

```
//  Assign TBrowse window coordinates.
b:nTop    := 4
b:nLeft   := 5
b:nBottom := 14
b:nRight  := 75
```

It's important to point out that these define the overall window, not just the scrollable region. If you define column headings, footings and separators they will consume rows in the interior of the window. So, the 11 by 70 window could display as few as seven rows if all headings, footings and separators are used.

b:colSep
b:headSep
b:footSep

The column, heading, and footing separator variables contain the characters used to separate columns from each other and the column headings (if any) from the first row of data. The default column separator is a single space. There is no default heading or footing separator. The following illustrate some common values for these variables.

```
//  Narrow column spacing, single lines.
b:headSep :=  "╤"
b:colSep  :=  "│"
b:footSep :=  "╧"

//  Wider columns, mixed single and double lines.
b:headSep :=  "═╦═"
b:colSep  :=  " ║ "
b:footSep :=  "═╩═"

//  Separators that can be output to any printer.
b:headSep :=  "---"
b:colSep  :=  " | "
b:footSep :=  "==="
```

It's convenient always to specify these values together, and to line up the values so you can visually inspect them for accuracy. These browse-wide values are used only when individual columns do not specify their own values.

b:colorSpec

Next to b:skipBlock, the b:colorSpec variable and associated color selection methods are often the most difficult TBrowse features to grasp, at least initially. TBrowse thinks of each cell (row/column intersection) as having one of two possible colors: highlighted and unhighlighted. The cell value gets displayed using the highlighted color when the browse cursor is in the cell, and the unhighlighted color when not.

TBrowse is compatible with the color setting scheme used by the rest of the Clipper commands and functions. This scheme is based on the SETCOLOR() function. (SETCOLOR() in turn is based on the SET COLOR TO command, which should have been ditched long ago along with other examples of crusty old dBASE-style syntax. We're stuck with it for the time being. But we digress.) TBrowse copies the current SETCOLOR() string into the b:colorSpec variable when a new object is created. Unless you change b:colorSpec your browse will use the same colors as appear in @..SAY..GET/READ situations.

```
set color to
? setcolor()            //  "W/N, N/W, N/N, N/N, N/W"

browse := TBrowseNew()
? browse:colorSpec      //  "W/N, N/W, N/N, N/N, N/W"
```

When presented with a b:colorSpec, TBrowse sees it as a list of possible cell colors. In the above example TBrowse thinks of the color string as having five possible cell colors. As we'll see later on when discussing c:defColor, c:colorBlock and b:colorRect(), TBrowse always deals with pairs of colors. By default TBrowse will display unhighlighted cells in the first color in the b:colorSpec list, and highlighted cells in the second color. We can assign b:colorSpec any number of colors; we are not limited to the five that the SETCOLOR() function uses. The following example illustrates a b:colorSpec with seven possible colors.

```
//  Assign TBrowse color scheme:
//
//                      1     2      3     4    5     6    7
brow:colorSpec := "BG/W, W+/B, GR+/R, R/W, W/RB, B/G, N/W"
```

We recommend always putting a comment line immediately above a b:colorSpec assignment when using literal color strings. The numbers will help you keep things straight. We'll come back to b:colorSpec in more detail when we cover the other color-related instance variables and methods.

b:autoLite

This variable controls whether or not the current cell is highlighted automatically. It defaults to .t., meaning TBrowse will call the b:hilite() and b:deHilite() methods automatically as you move the browse cursor. If you set b:autoLite to .f. you'll have to call the methods on your own. Most of the time you may as well leave b:autoLite set at .t. unless you have special highlighting needs. It's nice to have the control if you need it.

```
//  Turn automatic highlighting off.
brow:autoLite := .f.
```

b:freeze

The b:freeze instance variable is used to "freeze" one or more columns. Frozen columns will not be scrolled off the screen should you move the browse cursor into columns not currently visible. Without any columns frozen, the leftmost column would be scrolled out of the window to make room for the new column on the right of the window. b:freeze defaults to zero, meaning no columns will be frozen.

```
//  Freeze the first two columns
brow:freeze := 2
```

Column freezing is good user-interface design. The leftmost column should always be some kind of identifier that helps the user keep track of where they are in a wide set of columns.

Note: Do not assign a value to b:freeze until after columns have been defined and added to the main browse object. It gets ignored until there are columns to freeze.

b:cargo

This is a user-definable instance variable. b:cargo can be assigned any type of data and TBrowse will carry the value around for as long as the object exists.

b:cargo allows you to keep track of additional browse-related data and easily pass it along to functions that accept browse objects as parameters, as illustrated below.

```
brow:cargo := date()
? MyFunc(brow)           //  02/15/91

function MyFunc(obj)
return obj:cargo
```

b:cargo defaults to NIL and can contain any data type, including arrays with multiple dimensions. With an array you can maintain any arbitrary amount of data in a b:cargo variable.

Step 2: Changing column-specific values

After the main browse object has been established the next step is to create column objects and assign required values, and possibly change the optional values if we don't like the defaults. The finished column objects are then added to the browse object. We will discuss the following topics:

Constructor
TBColumnNew()

Method
b:addColumn()

Instance Variables
c:block
c:cargo
c:colorBlock
c:colSep
c:defColor
c:footing
c:footSep
c:heading
c:headSep
c:width

TBColumnNew(cHeading, bBlock)

TBColumnNew() is the only object constructor function for the TBColumn class. It returns a new TBColumn object with no useful default values unless the optional parameters are supplied.

```
//  Create a new TBColumn object.
col := TBColumnNew()
```

The TBColumnNew() function accepts two parameters: the column's heading and data retrieval code block. We'll discuss both instance variables next.

c:block

The data retrieval code block is the only required TBColumn object instance variable. The others can be left in their default states. The data retrieval code block is used primarily to read data from the data source, but it can refer to memory variables and expressions as well. When evaluated, the code block must return a value to display in the column. Each column's code block is evaluated repeatedly, once for each row in the browse window.

To create such a code block all you need to do is reference the database field name (or memory variable, as the case may be). A code block returns the value of the last expression evaluated, so in the case of a reference to a single field or variable name you get the current value.

```
//  Create a new TBColumn object.
col := TBColumnNew()

//  Assign a code block that retrieves
//  the current value of the LastName field.
col:block := { || LastName }
```

The value for the c:block instance variable can be passed as the second parameter to the TBColumnNew() constructor function. Since the retrieval block is never optional this is a handy place to assign it. The first parameter, as you might well guess from this example, is the column heading.

```
col2 := TBColumnNew("YTD Sales $", { || YTD_Sales } )
```

We recommend using TBColumnNew() to assign the heading and data retrieval code block at the same time. This helps keep the two items related and promotes the concept of self-documenting source code.

Since all the code block is concerned about is returning a value to display, you can do all sorts of interesting things. Here's an example of a calculation.

```
price := TBColumnNew("Item Price",   { || ItemPrice } )
qty   := TBColumnNew("Qty Ordered",  { || OrderQty } )
total := TBColumnNew("Total Cost",   { || ItemPrice * OrderQty } )
```

You can also do a better job of interpreting the raw data values for your users. Here's an example that clarifies the meaning of a logical field.

```
taxStat := TBColumnNew("Tax Status", ;
           { || if(Taxable, "Add Tax", "Exempt ") } )
```

It's important to keep the two alternatives the same length, otherwise TBrowse will produce unpredictable results, unless you assign the column width directly via the c:width instance variable. Even then it's better design to return consistent lengths.

Here's an example that adds commas to a potentially large number. You can use the transform() function on any data type to produce a wide variety of special formatting.

```
c := TBColumnNew("1970 Population", ;
                 { || transform(Pop1970, "9,999,999,999") } )
```

You can even call a user-defined function to retrieve the data. Keep in mind that the function will be called repeatedly and should perform its duty as quickly as possible.

```
col := TBColumnNew("Calc'd Result", ;
                   { || CUST->(Results()) } )

function results()
local default := 2.319
select TABLE
seek CUST->Id
if TABLE->(found())
  return (CUST->Amount * ((default /TABLE->Factor) +1))
endif
return (CUST->Amount* default)
```

If you call a user-defined function from inside a data retrieval block, pay meticulous attention to work areas and the currently selected alias. If the function call leaves the wrong work area selected TBrowse will use the wrong database to do subsequent positioning operations.

This is as deep as we'll go regarding data retrieval code blocks for now. See the discussion on b:addColumn(), later in this section, for more details and a very important column definition technique using the FIELD(), FIELDBLOCK() and FIELDWBLOCK() functions.

c:heading
c:footing

A column's heading and footing are assigned via the c:heading and c:footing instance variables. As the names imply, the heading is displayed above the column and the footing, below. In the following example we use the footing to indicate the column number, 17, which will help the user keep track of where he is in a browse with many columns.

```
col:heading := "YTD Sales"
col:footing := "(17)"
```

The semicolon character (;) is used to indicate multiple lines within a heading or footing. The size of the heading or footing area in the window is determined by the column with the most lines.

```
//  Heading area in window will be three rows deep.
col1:heading := "One Line"
col2:heading := "Two;Lines"
col3:heading := "Three;Lines;Long"
```

As mentioned previously, the TBColumnNew() function accepts the column's heading as a parameter along with the column's data retrieval code block.

```
col := TBrowseNew("YTD Sales", { || YTD_Sales })
```

c:colSep
c:headSep
c:footSep

Any column may optionally replace the default values for the column and heading separators. Any column may also have an optional footing separator character. There are no default values for these instance variables. Here are some common values for these variables:

```
//  Narrow column spacing, single lines.
c:headSep := "╤"
c:colSep  := "│"
c:footSep := "╧"

//  Wider columns, mixed single and double lines.
c:headSep := "═╦═"
c:colSep  := " ║ "
c:footSep := "═╩═"

//  Separators that can be output to any printer..
c:headSep := "---"
c:colSep  := " | "
c:footSep := "==="
```

As we suggested with the browse-wide default values, it's convenient always to specify these values together and lined up for easy visual inspection.

c:defColor

This instance variable dictates which pair of colors from the b:colorSpec string will be used to display data in the column. The pair of colors is stored in c:defColor as an array with two elements. The default value is {1,2}, meaning the first color in b:colorSpec will be used for unhighlighted cells and the second color for the highlighted cell. Keep in mind that b:colorSpec is a character string, not an array, but is treated similarly to an array.

```
//  This column will use color #3 for unselected cells
//  and color #4 for the currently selected cell.
col:defColor := {3,4}
```

Earlier, when discussing b:colorSpec, we recommended always placing a set of comment lines immediately above the color specifications. Listed below is the previous example with some c:defColor-related additions.

```
/*
   Assign TBrowse color scheme:

   1:  Unselected, regular
   2:  Selected, regular
   3:  Unselected, numeric columns
   4:  Selected, numeric
   5:  Unselected, negative numbers
   6:  Selected, negative numbers
   7:  Used when highlighting a range of cells.
*/
//                        1     2     3      4     5    6    7
brow:colorSpec := "BG/W, W+/B, W/RB, RB/W, R/N, R/W, G/W"

#define CLR_REGULAR    {1,2}
#define CLR_NUMBERS    {3,4}
#define CLR_NEGATIVE   {5,6}
#define CLR_RANGE      {7,7}
```

Since almost all TBrowse color schemes are based on pairs of numbers, it's best always to assign them consistently. Odd numbers are unselected and even numbers selected: Each pair has a distinct meaning in the scheme. The above color scheme uses preprocessor #defines to make it easier to specify color pairs correctly and consistently, as illustrated below.

```
//  Create three columns.
col1 := TBColumnNew("Customer ID", { || Cust_ID } )
col2 := TBColumnNew("Name", { || CustName } )
col3 := TBColumnNew("Balance", { || CurBal } )

//  First two columns use "regular" colors,
//  third column contains numbers so use "numeric" colors.
col1:defColor := CLR_REGULAR
col2:defColor := CLR_REGULAR
col3:defColor := CLR_NUMBERS
```

The Customer ID column and the Balance column are both comprised of numbers, but the Balance column will be in a different color and thus more difficult to mistake for something else.

Using a block of comments above b:colorSpec and a set of #defines for the c:defColor pairs allows you to establish the entire color scheme in one place, which is a great way to keep it all straight.

c:colorBlock

c:colorBlock is a fascinating feature of the column object. Based on a code block that you supply, you can have a column display its values in different colors. In the color scheme listed previously we alluded to a "negative numbers" color pair. How do we tell when a number is negative and which color to use?

Each time the column's data retrieval code block fetches a field from the data source it passes the value to c:colorBlock, if one is defined. The c:colorBlock code block is expected to return a color pair array based on the value. If you don't specify c:colorBlock, then c:defColor is used (defColor stands for "default color pair"). Here's the previous example for the customer balance column, this time using c:colorBlock.

```
col3:colorBlock := { |n| if(n < 0, CLR_NEGATIVE, CLR_NUMBERS) }
```

For each row in the window, a value is passed to the code block. If the number is negative, the CLR_NEGATIVE color pair array (#defined previously as {5,6}) is used. If the number is positive, CLR_NUMBERS is used. Very simple but very powerful.

c:width

The c:width instance variable controls the width of the column when displayed on the screen. However, TBrowse uses the larger width of the heading or footing (if any) as the absolute minimum, independent of the c:width value. On the other hand, the highlighted browse cursor is based strictly on the c:width value and not on the actual width of the column as seen on the screen.

The c:width value defaults to the width from the first field read from the data source. If you use a fancy c:block that returns something other than the direct contents of a field, be careful always to return the same length.

```
//  Create column for the State field.
col := TBColumnNew("State", { || State } )

? col:width  //  2, because State field is two char wide.

//  Fancy block for logical values
col:block := { || if(IsMember, "Member", "Non-Member") }

? col:width  //  ?, depends on first value from data source!
```

In the above example the actual width of the column as it appears on screen will be at least five columns wide, due to the column heading. The column may actually be wider than five columns if, for example, the column separator characters include spaces on either side of a line. TBrowse centers the data within the column.

TBrowse left-justifies character data, right-justifies numbers, and centers logical values within each column.

c:cargo

This is another user-definable instance variable, similar to the browse object's b:cargo. The column object's c:cargo can be assigned any type of data and TBrowse will carry the value around for as long as the object exists. A common use for c:cargo is for help messages specific to each column.

```
col7 := TBColumnNew("Due", { || InvAmt } )
col7:cargo := "Total amount due on current invoice."

col8 := TBColumnNew("Balance", { || CurBal } )
col8:cargo := "Customer's current balance as of last statement."
```

c:cargo defaults to NIL and can contain any data type, including arrays with multiple dimensions. c:cargo can contain an arbitrary amount of data if you use an array.

b:addColumn(oColumnObject)

b:addColumn() is a browse method and not a column method, but we're covering it here because it operates on column objects. You call b:addColumn() once for each column you want in the browse. The columns will be displayed in the browse window in the order they are added to the browse object.

```
//  Create a browse with three columns:
//  Record #, First Name, Last Name.
//
brow := TBrowseDB(10, 25, 19, 55)
c1 := TBColumnNew("Record #", { || recno() } )
c2 := TBColumnNew("First Name", { || First } )
c3 := TBColumnNew("Last Name", { || Last } )
brow:addColumn(c1)
brow:addColumn(c2)
brow:addColumn(c3)
```

Creating columns more efficiently

It's tedious to have to type code blocks over and over each time you create a column that's based on a database field name, which is the case for most browsing situations. This is especially true when you need a dozen (or more!) columns. Even worse, there are situations when you don't know the field names in advance.

Fortunately there are several Clipper functions that make this process considerably easier: FIELD(), FIELDBLOCK() and FIELDWBLOCK().

FIELD() returns the name of the field specified by number. If there are ten fields, FIELD(7) is the name of the seventh field. You can use FCOUNT(), the database field count function, to tell you how many fields a database contains. Here's an example that lists all the field names in the SALES database.

```
use SALES new
for i := 1 to fcount()
  ? field(i)
next i
```

FIELDBLOCK() and FIELDWBLOCK() return a code block that can be used with c:block, based on the field name you send as a character string parameter. Don't pass the actual field, these functions will attempt to use the current value of the field rather than the field's name. The FIELDBLOCK() function returns a code block that will work in any work area, while FIELDWBLOCK() returns a code block that is tied to a specific work area. The following shows FIELDBLOCK() being used to return a code block for the ZipCode field.

```
column:block := fieldblock("ZipCode")
```

The problem here is that we are referencing a symbol (the ZipCode field name) that the compiler never sees. This is not good programming practice and is likely to cause confusion in complex applications with many databases open at the same time. Use the FIELD statement to unambiguously declare ZipCode to be a field name found in a specific database.

```
//  At top of routine, tell compiler that ZipCode
//  is a field name found in the CUST database.
field ZipCode in CUST

//  Later, in body of routine...
column:block := fieldblock("ZipCode")
```

FIELDWBLOCK() is used when you might have more than a single work area in use and want to guarantee that the column displays data from only a specific work area, not the work area that happens to be selected at the moment.

```
column:block := fieldWblock("City", 3)
```

Listed below are code blocks functionally equivalent to the ones that FIELDBLOCK() and FIELDWBLOCK() return.

```
//  Code block returned from fieldblock().
{ | x | if(x == nil, ZipCode, ZipCode := x) }

//  Code block returned from fieldWblock().
{ | x | if(x == nil, 3->City, 3->City := x) }
```

in contrast, only a single row gets updated. Rather than making a call to a function that attempts to update the entire browse window at once, each call to b:stabilize() results in the update of one small portion of the window. This corresponds roughly to one row of data. To display a window with, for example, ten rows of data, b:stabilize() would need to be called at least ten times.

Sometimes only a single row in the window needs to be updated, sometimes it's the entire display. Rather than hardwiring a specific number of calls you instead take advantage of b:stabilize()'s return value. It will return .f. if TBrowse has more to do, or .t. if the window is finished being updated. The following will keep looping until the window is completely updated, or to use TBrowse terminology, is completely stable.

```
do while .not. browse:stabilize()
enddo
```

While the above loop does indeed handle the stabilizing process correctly it isn't taking advantage of the real reason the updating is done incrementally in the first place. Here's a better version:

```
do while .not. browse:stabilize()
  if nextkey() <> 0
    exit
  endif
enddo
```

This loop will exit before the window is fully stabilized if a keystroke is detected in the keyboard buffer. This allows the user to hit additional navigation or other keys without having to wait for the entire browse window to be updated. You can see this effect by hitting PageDown several times in rapid succession — rather than filling the entire screen with data, the browse will leap ahead another page and attempt to display it instead of the previous one. If you hit the key fast enough only a single row of data will be displayed before the loop is exited. The b:stabilize() method is not responsible for moving the record pointer (or whatever it's called in the data source you are browsing), only for displaying the data. When you call a navigation method,

TBrowse handles the data source positioning independent of the display. The positioning methods communicate with the b:stabilize() method via the b:stable instance variable. This is not too shabby for what appears to be a simple little method.

There's a certain type of reader who wondered if the previous example could have been written with fewer lines. Here's what he was thinking.

```
do while (!browse:stabilize()) .and. (nextkey() # 0)
enddo
```

A common question at this point is, why use NEXTKEY() instead of INKEY()? The INKEY() function actually removes the keystroke from the keyboard buffer, while NEXTKEY() takes a peek but leaves the keystroke right where it is. We'll need the value of the keystroke in order to interpret it for navigation and whatnot, so if we used INKEY() we'd need to store the value to a variable. Some programmers prefer this method. Here's an example:

```
do while .not. browse:stabilize()
  if (key := inkey()) <> 0
    exit
  endif
enddo
```

This example takes advantage of Clipper's handy ability to store a value to a variable as part of an expression, saving us the trouble of assigning INKEY() to key on one line and then testing it on the next. Some find this hard to follow, and not without justification. Still others would go even further and write the same loop like so:

```
do while (!browse:stabilize()) .and. ((key := inkey()) # 0)
enddo
```

Earlier we mentioned that b:stabilize() is not directly linked to data source positioning or navigation operations (although it is affected by them), so it really has no need for the actual value of the keystroke. Just knowing one is pending is all you have to be concerned about during the stabilizing process. It's better that the source code related to keystroke handling be responsible for retrieving keystrokes from the keyboard buffer. Has this point been sufficiently run into the ground? Good. Let's continue.

b:ForceStable()

A new method has been added in Clipper 5.2 calledForceStable(). It performs a full stabilization of the TBrowse. It realizes the same function as the following code, only slightly faster:

```
do while ! b:stabilize()
enddo
```

b:stable

This instance variable simply reflects the status of the window. If b:stable returns .f. the window needs to be updated. If it returns .t. the window is stable. Any call to a navigation method, like b:Down(), causes b:stable to return .f. According to the Computer Associates documentation, a browse window is stable when the following conditions are met: All data has been retrieved and displayed, the data source is positioned to match the placement of the browse cursor, and the current cell is highlighted.

```
do while .not. browse:stabilize()
enddo
? browse:stable     // .t.
browse:goBottom()
? browse:stable     // .f.
```

b:refreshAll()
b:refreshCurrent()

These two methods mark either the current row, or all rows, as being in need of updating. The b:stable variable will be set to .f. and the rows affected will be updated during the next stabilizing loop.

```
//  Mark current row as needing an update.
browse:refreshCurrent()

//  Mark all rows as needing an update.
browse:refreshAll()
```

Since TBrowse maintains such internal status on its own in order to automatically handle navigation calls like b:goTop() and so on, it may not be immediately obvious why you would want to mark a row (much less all the rows) for updating. As was touched upon briefly in the discussion of the c:block variable, TBrowse does not maintain a constant link between the data source and the values currently displayed on the screen. A non-TBrowse event may cause one or more rows in the data source to be changed. By calling the b:refreshAll() method you assure that the entire display will reflect the values in the data source. An example of such an event follows:

```
//  Display browse window with inventory prices.
do while .not. browse:stabilize()
enddo

//  Increase all prices by 25%.
replace all invent->price with invent->price * 1.25

? browse:stable  //  .t., as far as TBrowse knows.

browse:refreshAll()
? browse:stable  //  .f., due to refreshAll().

//  Update browse window with new inventory prices.
do while .not. browse:stabilize()
enddo
```

Unless a call is made to b:refreshAll(), the browse in the above example would still reflect the prices before the REPLACE command occurred. However, any navigation method that requires the entire window to be updated would end up using the correct prices, because data is read from the data source via the data retrieval code blocks during the stabilization process.

TBrowse works this way so you can take complete control over the timing of screen updates. It'd be pointless for TBrowse to slow down data manipulation operations just so the screen stays accurate at every instant. You can do all the manipulation you need and then request a browse window update when you want it. If you actually do want the browse window to be constantly up to date you can call the b:refreshCurrent() or b:refreshAll() methods and then stabilize the display. The point is, you are in control of the timing.

b:invalidate()

The b:invalidate() method is similar to b:refreshAll() in that b:invalidate() forces TBrowse to redisplay the entire window, including headings and footings, during the next stabilization process. The difference is that with b:invalidate() data is not read from the data source. This may result in significantly faster window updates if there's lots of data or a slow data source. b:invalidate() should be used in situations where you've changed something on the screen that isn't related to the values in the data source and need to have the window displayed again.

```
//  Display complex browse window with lots of data.
do while .not. browse:stabilize()
enddo

//  Call function that messes up the screen.
@ 0,0 clear
MessyFunc()

? browse:stable  //  .t., as far as TBrowse knows.

browse:invalidate()
? browse:stable  //  .f., due to invalidate().

//  Now window is quickly and completely redrawn.
do while .not. browse:stabilize()
enddo
```

In the above example the next time the stabilization process is performed, the browse window will be drawn completely, but faster than if TBrowse had to read all the data from the data source.

b:configure()

This browse method is similar to b:refreshAll() in that it causes TBrowse to react to changes in the browse environment. A call to b:configure() is very "expensive" with respect to processing time. It has TBrowse perform a complete reexamination of all of the instance variables for the overall browse and all of the individual columns, then make any internal adjustments needed to react to changes. The window will not be updated, however, until the next stabilizing process.

The configuration process is automatic in most circumstances. Calling b:configure() on your browse is normally required only when making direct changes to column object instance variables. TBrowse does not maintain permanent links between a browse object and the set of column objects of which it is comprised: If you alter a column's instance variables the browse object does not "see" the changes until you issue a b:configure().

This process of changing a browse or column instance variable, calling b:configure(), and then seeing the results during stabilization is broken into three distinct steps for a very good reason. It allows you to alter any number of values but have the actual changes performed all at once. If changes were reflected immediately, the display might jump around or do other disconcerting things.

Step 4: Taking action on keystrokes

The browse stabilizing process fills the window with as much data as can fit, then stops. However, a browse is a user-interface tool and is expected to do considerably more than just display one screen's worth of data. Like any other user-interface tool, a browse is manipulated by keystrokes, so the final step in the process is to accept keystrokes and take action on them. Actions take the form of navigation (moving the browse cursor around within the confines of the browse), configuration (altering column-specific or browse-wide values), and status (checking on things the browse keeps track of). We'll divide the remaining methods and instances into three categories: Navigation, configuration, and status.

Keep in mind that, as was mentioned in the previous steps, most of the browse-wide and column-specific values can be changed at any time and not just when the object is first created.

Navigation Methods

b:down()
b:end()
b:goBottom()
b:goTop()
b:home()
b:left()
b:pageDown()
b:pageUp()
b:panEnd()
b:panHome()
b:panLeft()
b:panRight()
b:right()
b:up()

Status Instance Variables

b:colCount
b:colPos
b:hitBottom
b:hitTop
b:leftVisible
b:rightVisible
b:rowCount
b:rowPos

Configuration Methods

b:colorRect()

b:delColumn()

b:deHilite()

b:getColumn()

b:hilite()

b:insColumn()

b:setColumn()

Navigation in general

TBrowse maintains an internal browse cursor. This cursor always remains within the boundaries of the browse window. A unique cursor is associated with the browse object, and is completely distinct from the common screen cursor which is controlled via the SETCURSOR() function and tracked via the ROW() and COL() functions. The navigation methods do not actually move the browse cursor on the screen; the effects of navigation calls are seen only after a stabilization process is complete. The navigation methods will cause the browse to need stabilization on their own; as a rule you do not have to worry about it unless you manipulate the screen directly or move the data source position on your own.

```
//  Jump to left-most column in browse.
b:panHome()

//  Move down one row.
b:down()

//  Browse cursor does not move on screen until
//  this stabilization loop is complete.
do while .not. b:stabilize()
enddo
```

We have a very efficient technique for dealing with the majority of your TBrowse navigation needs. See the later section in this chapter entitled "A TBrowse Toolbox."

b:up()
b:down()
b:left()
b:right()

These four navigation methods move the browse cursor in the indicated direction. If you move past a window boundary and more rows or columns are available, the window will scroll one row or column in the indicated direction.

b:end()
b:home()

These methods jump the browse cursor to the right-most or left-most visible column in the browse window. Neither method scrolls the window, if the cursor is already in the first or last visible column it is not moved.

b:pageDown()
b:pageUp()

A "page" is defined as the number of rows that fill the browse window. If ten rows are visible then b:pageUp() causes the browse window to scroll ten records backward through the data.

b:goBottom()
b:goTop()

These two methods jump the browse cursor to the very first or very last record in the data source, as processed by the b:goTopBlock and b:goBottomBlock data positioning code blocks. If the browse object is using the standard DBF database code blocks, these methods correspond to the GOTO TOP and GOTO BOTTOM commands. However, it is completely up to the data positioning blocks to determine how to satisfy the navigation request. For example, the illusive "browse while" that was such a pain to accomplish with the much maligned and now obsolete DBEDIT() function can be implemented very easily with TBrowse. See the later section entitled "A TBrowse Toolbox" for complete details.

b:panEnd()
b:panHome()

b:panEnd and b:panHome jump the browse cursor to the very first or very last column. This is in contrast to the "plain" b:home and b:end methods which only jump within the currently visible set of columns. The browse window will be scrolled as needed to accommodate the jump. After a b:panHome, for example, you are certain to be positioned in column number 1. Be aware that this includes "frozen" columns, so after a b:panHome be sure to move the column position back to the right, past the frozen columns if you don't want the browse cursor to stop there.

```
//  Check to see if a recent navigation method
//  caused browse cursor to enter the frozen columns.
//  If so, move it back out.
if brow:colPos < brow:freeze
  brow:colPos := brow:freeze +1
endif

//  Stabilize the current window.
do while (.not. brow:stabilize()) .and. (nextkey() == 0)
enddo
```

b:panLeft()
b:panRight()

These two methods scroll the browse window left or right but leave the browse cursor in the same relative column position. Sort of handy if you have lots of columns and want to stay in one spot within the window while you scroll columns left or right. Note that it's not always possible to do this, so there's no guarantee that the cursor stays in exactly the same place.

Status in general

The browse object instance variables covered in this section are used to inquire about various parts of the browse object. Most of the time these variables should not be relied upon until immediately following a stabilization process. Exceptions are b:colCount and b:rowCount.

b:colPos
b:rowPos

b:colPos and b:rowPos return the current position of the browse cursor within the browse window, not the position on the screen. Column headings, footings, and separator rows are not considered in the row position. b:rowPos refers only to visible rows and has nothing to do with the number of records in the data source. b:colPos, however, keeps track of the actual column within the entire browse, not just the ones visible on the screen.

```
//  A status message that's helpful when experimenting.
@ 0,0 say "Browse cursor is at row " +ltrim(str(brow:rowPos))
?? ", column " +ltrim(str(brow:colPos))
```

It may surprise you that both b:colPos and b:rowPos are assignable. You can position the browse cursor directly where you want it. Most of the browse status variables are assignable.

```
//  Put browse cursor in last column in center row.
brow:colPos := brow:colCount
brow:rowPos := (brow:rowCount / 2)
```

It is good practice to call on b:invalidate() to force a screen update in the event that you placed the browse cursor in a column that isn't currently visible. If you rely on the side effects of some of the other regular browse navigation methods you may frequently find the browse window left in a messed-up state.

b:colCount
b:rowCount

These two instance variables, which return the number of rows or columns defined in the browse, are based on the way the browse was created and will remain accurate unless rows or columns are added. A call to b:configure() will guarantee that these values are correct. b:configure() was discussed in a previous section.

```
//  Helpful message to display while experimenting.
@ 1,0 say "Row count: " +ltrim(str(brow:rowCount))
?? ", Column count: " +ltrim(str(brow:colCount))
```

Unlike many of the other browse status variables, the row and column counts are not assignable.

b:hitBottom
b:hitTop

b:hitTop and b:hitBottom are logical flags updated by the stabilization process and indicate whether or not the most recent navigation method attempted to read past the beginning-of-file or end-of-file. For example, calling b:up() or b:pageUp() when you are already positioned at the first record in the data source will cause b:hitTop to be .t. after the next stabilization process.

```
//  Stabilize the browse window display.
do while (.not. brow:stabilize()) .and. (nextkey() == 0)
enddo

//  Another helpful status message to display while experimenting.
@ 2,0 say "Hit top: " +if(brow:hitTop, "Yes","No ")
?? ", Hit Bottom: " +if(brow:hitBottom, "Yes","No ")
```

b:leftVisible
b:rightVisible

These instance variables are used to determine what portion of the browse columns are currently visible. b:leftVisible returns the left-most visible column number, excluding any "frozen" columns. b:rightVisible returns the number of the right-most visible column. These two values are useful for displaying "more" indicators in conjunction with the browse window, for example, displaying an arrow on the right when the last column isn't currently visible, alerting the end-user that there's more information available. The following logic illustrates how to detect such situations:

```
//  This expression is true if the left-most column
//  is not currently visible.
//
if b:leftVisible > (b:frozen +1)
  //  More columns to the left
endif
```

```
//  This expression is true if the right-most column
//  is not currently visible.
//
if b:rightVisible < b:colCount
  //  More columns to the right
endif
```

If frozen columns are not being used, the b:leftVisible logic can be simplified to the following.

```
if b:leftVisible > 1
  //  More columns to the left
endif
```

Configuration in general

This final group is a catch-all for TBrowse methods that don't fit well anywhere else. This by no means diminishes their importance! In fact, b:getColumn() and b:setColumn() are indispensable methods for the construction of dynamic browse windows that can react to the user at run-time. They are grouped here because they usually can't be called with any useful effect until after the browse window is constructed and displayed.

It's also important to point out that all the browse or column methods and instance variables that have been discussed so far can also be changed at any time, not just the few methods listed here. TBrowse is a complete dynamic user-interface tool. Everything is available to you for changes, additions or deletions at any time.

b:getColumn(nColumn)
b:setColumn(nColumn, objColumn)

b:getColumn() and b:setColumn() are the workhorses of any dynamic browse where you do more than just allow the user to scroll around the window. b:getColumn() returns the complete column object for the specified browse column. b:setColumn() reverses the process and replaces a column with the specified column object. TBrowse will not react to changes made via b:setColumn() unless you use b:configure() to force it to examine all of its internals. Then you must perform a stabilization process to actually see any results on the screen.

The example in Listing 26.3 increases or decreases all column widths in a browse object, using both the b:getColumn() and b:setColumn() methods.

Listing 26.3 Function that makes all columns in a browse more wide or more narrow by a specified amount

```
function Widen(objBrow, nHowMuch)
/*
   Given a browse object, make all columns wider
   by specified amount. (Negative = more narrow).
   Prevents column from being smaller than 1 or
   larger than the width of the window. Note: Browse
   object must have window coordinates defined.
*/
local i, objCol, wid

//  Loop once for each column in the browse.
for i := 1 to objBrow:colCount

   //  Extract a column object.
   objCol := objBrow:getColumn(i)

   //  Add the amount to widen or narrow
   //  to the column's current width.
   wid := objCol:width + nHowMuch

   //  Trap for extremes, less than 1 or
   //  greater than width of browse window.
   objCol:width := min(max(wid, 1), ;
       (objBrow:nRight - objBrow:nLeft) +1)

   //  Replace modified column object.
   objBrow:setColumn(i, objCol)
next i
return nil
```

It's often not necessary to extract a column to a temporary variable just to manipulate an instance variable. Listing 26.4 is a function that will remove footings from all columns in a browse, without having to store the columns in a temporary variable.

Listing 26.4 Remove all column footings from a browse object

```
function NoFeet(objBrow)
/*
   Remove all column footings in a browse object.
*/
local i
for i := 1 to objBrow:colCount
    objBrow:getColumn(i):footing := nil
next i
return nil
```

Whoa. What is that monstrosity? Let's take it one piece at a time. The following code fragment is functionally equivalent to the single line in the FOR..NEXT loop in Listing 26.4, which should be more clear.

```
col := objBrow:getColumn(i)
col:footing := nil
objBrow:setColumn(i, col)
```

These three lines extract a column, assign NIL to the footing, and replace the old column with the modified column. However, since the getColumn() method returns an object, we can immediately reference its footing instance variable and assign it a value.

b:delColumn(nColumn)
b:insColumn(nColumn, objColumn)

As the names imply, these methods delete and insert columns in browse objects. As with b:setColumn() you must call b:configure() and then stabilize the browse window to see the effects in the browse window.

The following example illustrates the timing between column insertions and TBrowse updating the related instance variables.

```
/*
   Insert a new column between columns 2 and 3.
*/
? brow:colCount              //  5
brow:insColumn(3, objCol)
```

```
? brow:colCount                // Still 5
brow:configure()
? brow:colCount                // Now 6
```

The next example shows that deleting columns has the same timing issue.

```
/*
   Delete last column.
*/
? brow:colCount                    // 6
brow:delColumn(brow:colCount)
? brow:colCount                    // Still 6
brow:configure()
? brow:colCount                    // Now 5
```

The following example allows the user to navigate around the browse window and press the Del key to delete the current column.

```
#include "inkey.ch"

do while .t.
  do while .not. brow:stabilize()
  enddo
  key := inkey(0)
  do case
  case key == K_ESC
    exit
  case key == K_UP
    brow:up()
  case key == K_DOWN
    brow:down()
  case key == K_LEFT
    brow:left()
  case key == K_RIGHT
    brow:right()
  case key == K_DEL
    brow:delColumn(brow:colPos)
    brow:configure()
  endcase
enddo
```

b:hilite()
b:deHilite()

b:hilite() turns the browse cursor highlight on, b:deHilite() turns the highlight off. Stated more accurately, b:hilite() causes TBrowse to display the current value in the first color in the column's color pair while b:deHilite() causes the second color to be used. Exactly which color pair is used depends on how the column was defined. See the previous discussion on b:colorSpec, b:defColor, and b:colorBlock for details, as well as the b:colorRect() method discussed below.

TBrowse reacts immediately to b:hilite() and b:deHilite(); you do not have to do any stabilization to see the effects.

If b:autoLite is true, TBrowse will automatically highlight the value where the browse cursor is currently sitting. If b:autoLite is false the browse cursor will still be accurate with respect to the row and column position within the browse window, but the current value will not be highlighted. It's up to you to call b:hilite() and b:deHilite() to manage the highlighting yourself if b:autoLite is false. The example in Listing 26.5 shows direct calls to the highlighting methods used to create a slowly flashing cursor.

Listing 26.5 A browse cursor that flashes slowly

```
function SlowFlash(browse)
/*
   A browse cursor that flashes slowly.
   On for half a second, off for a quarter second.
*/
local key
do while .t.
  brow:hilite()
  if (key := inkey(0.5)) <> 0
    exit
  endif
  brow:deHilite()
  if (key := inkey(0.25)) <> 0
    exit
  endif
enddo
return key
```

You don't have to keep turning the highlight on and off. You can turn it on and leave it on or turn it off and leave it off. That's the whole point of giving you control over the highlight.

b:colorRect(aCoords, aColors)

This method name is short for "color rectangle". It is used to establish a special color scheme for a rectangular region in the browse window. The region may include all columns but is confined to only the rows currently visible, which somewhat limits its usefulness. Still it's a handy method that allows you to quickly and easily alter row and column colors that otherwise would not be possible (or at least, not elegantly done) using the other color-related methods.

b:colorRect() takes two arrays as parameters. The first consists of the four browse window coordinates (not screen coordinates), the second is a color pair. See the discussion about b:colorSpec and b:defColor for details about color pairs.

TBrowse reacts immediately to b:colorRect(), you do not need to stabilize the window to see the results. All values within the region are displayed in the unhighlighted color, which is the first color in the color pair. When the browse cursor is moved into the region defined by b:colorRect(), the current value is displayed in the highlight color, which is the second color in the pair.

```
//  Using colors #5 and #6, display values in rows and columns
//  from row 3, column 2 through row 10, column 7.
brow:colorRect({3,2,10,7}, {5,6})
```

A comprehensive example

Is it safe to assume you didn't memorize the huge assortment of methods and instance variables just discussed? Can you picture how they all fit together at run-time? Only after considerable experimentation and practice will all these concepts come together. To demonstrate the power and versatility of TBrowse we've included a program that manages to use all of the features we've discussed in this chapter: MAXIBROW. (So named because it stands in contrast to the as-simple-as-possible MINIBROW program presented previously in the introduction to objects.)

MAXIBROW is not intended to be a routine you actually implement in your applications. It goes to sometimes ridiculous lengths to incorporate all the TBrowse features. It's intended to be a TBrowse playground of sorts where you can see various instance variables and methods in action and in the context of a large application rather than in small, isolated examples. Use it to experiment — make code changes, add new features, change constants, do whatever you find interesting. The more time you spend playing with TBrowse, the better you'll understand it.

To get the most out of MAXIBROW you should have a copy of the source code handy (either printed or available at the touch of a key with a TSR editor like Borland's SideKick or even within Clipper's source-level debugger). Trace the program flow as the program executes on the screen. Use your editor's search functions to track down instance variable and method names to see how they are used.

The use of color and the formatting of the various status messages is deliberately spartan. We didn't want fancy, colorful things to get in the way of the underlying concepts. There's enough code as it is! The screen is by design very blah until you start fiddling around with the highlighting and selection functions, or supply a database with dates, negative numbers, logical values, or memo fields. Then you'll probably wish there weren't so many colors. We predict the incredibly flexible TBrowse color scheme will be responsible for a whole new generation of garish application screens.

All the features of MAXIBROW are tied to various keystrokes. The source code comments surrounding the features describe the techniques being used. The next four sections summarize what MAXIBROW can do. Figure 26.2 shows a sample screen generated by the MaxiBrow program.

Figure 26.2 Sample screen displayed by MaxiBrow.Prg

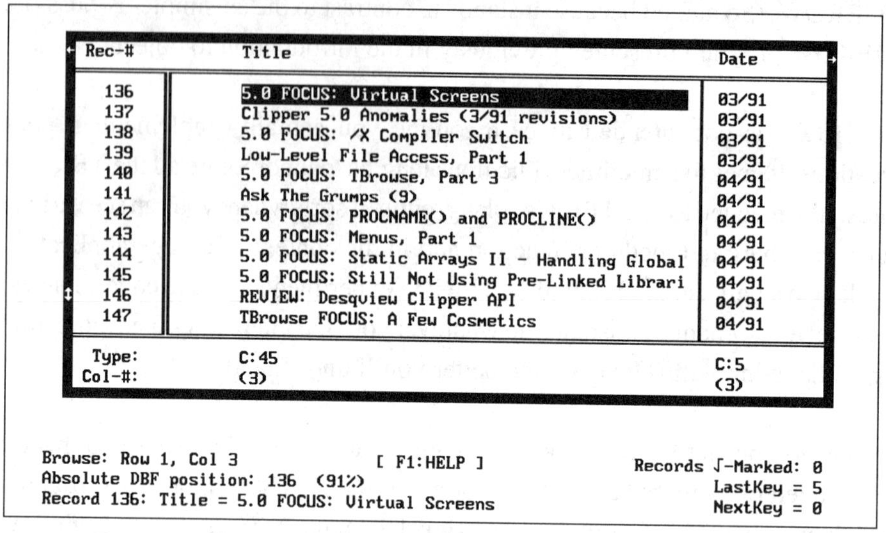

```
 Rec-#          Title                                                Date

  136           5.0 FOCUS: Virtual Screens                           03/91
  137           Clipper 5.0 Anomalies (3/91 revisions)               03/91
  138           5.0 FOCUS: /X Compiler Switch                        03/91
  139           Low-Level File Access, Part 1                        03/91
  140           5.0 FOCUS: TBrowse, Part 3                           04/91
  141           Ask The Grumps (9)                                   04/91
  142           5.0 FOCUS: PROCNAME() and PROCLINE()                 04/91
  143           5.0 FOCUS: Menus, Part 1                             04/91
  144           5.0 FOCUS: Static Arrays II - Handling Global        04/91
  145           5.0 FOCUS: Still Not Using Pre-Linked Librari        04/91
  146           REVIEW: Desqview Clipper API                         04/91
  147           TBrowse FOCUS: A Few Cosmetics                       04/91

  Type:         C:45                                                 C:5
 Col-#:         (3)                                                  (3)

Browse: Row 1, Col 3            [ F1:HELP ]          Records √-Marked: 0
Absolute DBF position: 136  (91%)                            LastKey = 5
Record 136: Title = 5.0 FOCUS: Virtual Screens               NextKey = 0
```

Navigation keys

All of the browse navigation methods are supported:

- Up, Down, Left, Right: Move one cell in any direction, will scroll rows up/down and pan columns left/right as needed.
- Home, End: Jump to first or last visible column.
- Ctrl-Home, Ctrl-End: Jump to very first or very last column.
- PageUp, PageDown: Scroll one screenful up or down.
- Ctrl-PageUp, Ctrl-PageDown: Jump to very top or very bottom of database.
- Tab, Shift-Tab: Pan the screen left or right to see more columns.

Function keys

F1 Display record numbers/columns visited during "help". Each time you press F1 the current record number is added to a list. A column-based counter is also incremented. Press F1 periodically as you move through the database. F1 also displays a brief summary of what other keystrokes do.

F2 Toggle between color and monochrome color schemes.

F3 Insert a copy of current column. Watch how changes to the original column are reflected in the copies. This is due to the referential, array-based nature of Clipper objects.

F4 Delete current column. Can't delete the last non-frozen column.

F5 Move the browse window. The Up/Down/Left/Right keys work as expected. Press any other key to finish the move. Built-in logic will prevent you from moving the window completely off the screen. Press backspace to restore coordinates to initial settings.

F6 Resize the browse window. The Up and Left keys make the window larger, Down and Right make it smaller. Press any other key to finish the resizing. Built-in logic will prevent you from making window too small to be useful. Press backspace to restore coordinates to initial settings.

F7 Rotate column positions. Non-frozen columns are shifted to the left, first column is moved to the far right. You can press F7 repeatedly to cycle through as many columns as you wish. Press Shift-F7 to rotate columns in the other direction.

F8 Toggle between drag-highlight regular navigation modes. After pressing F8 all cursor movements will enlarge a highlight box on the screen. Due to limitations inherent in TBrowse's colorRect() method the highlighted box is for the visible screen rows, only.

F9 Highlight current column. Due to aforementioned colorRect() limitation the highlight extends only for the rows currently visible.

F10	Highlight the current row. Entire row is highlighted, including columns that are not currently visible.
ESC	Finished browsing, you'll be asked to confirm that you want to exit. Press Y to exit or any other key to remain in the browse.

Editing keys

Alt-U	Toggle the global SET DELETED flag on and off.
Ctrl-U	Toggle the individual record deletion flag on and off.
Enter	Edit current cell, including a full-window editor for memo fields.
Ctrl-Enter	Clear contents of current cell and then start editing, except for memo fields.
!..chr(255)	Edit current cell, starting with the keystroke.

Other miscellaneous keys

Ctrl-Left	Make current column more narrow. Can't make column smaller than one character.
Ctrl-Right	Make current column more wide. Can't make column wider than width of original field in database.
Backspace	Clear all highlights and selections, reset all cargo instance variables, refresh entire screen. Used primarily to recover after making a mess.
Spacebar	Toggle record selection check-mark on and off. Counter at bottom of screen indicates how many have been selected. Unlike the F8, F9, and F10 highlighting functions, the check-marks are not limited to the currently visible screen. Backspace clears all selections.

Other automatic things

Other things will happen automatically depending on the contents of the database being browsed:

- Negative numbers will be in red.
- Logically false values will also be in red.
- All date columns will be in magenta, including headings and footings.
- "Thud" sounds will be heard when you attempt to scroll or pan beyond the physical boundaries of the database.
- A relative position indicator, or "elevator", will be displayed on the left side of the window if the database contains more records than can fit in the window. Important note: The indicator is maintained independent of the index, if one is being used. This is implemented very elegantly thanks to the wonderful concept of TBrowse "skipBlocks".

The source code

There's a tremendous amount of fancy browsing going on in MAXIBROW.PRG, and to help keep it all straight we've included lots of comments. Block-style comments, delimited with /* and */, are used to describe large sections of code and also are used as headers to functions.

Single line comments, //, are used when the comments are directed at the next line (or small group of lines). Two blank lines separate logical groups of source code, single blank lines separate small runs of related source code within a major group.

Other helpful conventions: If a function name is in all lowercase letters then it's part of the built-in Clipper functions. If a function name is in "proper" case it's a user-defined function and can be found in this source code file. Array names end with a trailing underscore. Manifest constants are in all upper case.

The MAXIBROW.PRG source code file contains the following functions.

- **Main(cFilename [, cIndexname])**
  Main browsing program. From DOS, send database filename and optional index filename.

- **Proper(cString)**
  Given string, returns "properized" string where first character is made uppercase. Used in this program to make the database field names look better.

- **YesNo(cMsg [, nSeconds])**
  Given a message to display an optional maximum number of seconds to wait, return .t. if "Y" or "y" is pressed, .f. if not.

- **HelpStat(oBrowse)**
  Given a browse object, use browse and current column cargo variables to display stats about how often the F1-HELP key was pressed and which records were visited.

- **FitInBox(nTop, nLeft, nBottom, nRight, aMessage)**
  Draw a box at specified coordinates and display an array of message lines within the boundaries of the box. Trim the number and width of lines to fit inside the box.

- **RecPosition([cHow] [, nHowmany])**
  This is a single function used for all three TBrowse data positioning blocks. Given the type of movement required (top, bottom or skip) and how many records to skip, function performs all the necessary database movements. If called without any parameters the function returns the current record's position within the database. The position is maintained independent of the index, if any.

- **RecDisplay(nRec, aList)**
  This function is used by the record-# column data retrieval block to format the record number for display. It handles the check-mark. The current record number is passed along with an array containing record numbers that should be displayed with check-marks.

- **aCount(aX, bCountBlock [, nStart] [, nCount])**
Given an array, use the supplied code block to count the number of elements that match a condition. Optional starting element number and number of elements to evaluate. Returns count.

- **aInsert(aX, nPos [, xValue])**
Increase size of array by inserting new value in specified position. This function combines the effects of the AINS() and ASIZE() functions.

- **aDelete(aX, nPos)**
Decrease size of array by deleting element in specified position. This function combines the effects of the ADEL() and ASIZE() functions.

- **aRotate(aX [, lDir])**
Rotates elements in array passed as parameter. Elements are shifted up one. First element is shifted to last element. Optional direction to shift, default is .t. and implies shift up, .f. is down. Returns nil.

- **ColumnColor(xValue)**
Given a value of any type, returns a color-selection array based on the type and value. Used to install logic for displaying certain data types or values in special colors. For example, negative numbers in red. Any number of additional cases can be installed as you need them.

- **Navigate(oBrowse, nKey)**
Given a browse object and a potential cursor navigation key, this function searches an internal list of keystrokes and associated browse navigation methods. If the key is found the navigation method message is sent to the browse object and the function returns .t.; if not found, function returns .f. and no action is taken.

- **EditCell(oBrowse, cFieldname, cColor)**
This is a general-purpose browse cell content editor. It works with all database field types including memo fields. All editing occurs within the boundaries of the browse window regardless of its size or position on the screen. On exit from the cell the function passes along any browse cursor navigation that occurred.

A TBrowse toolbox

MAXIBROW.PRG provides you with examples of uses for every TBrowse and TBColumn feature. You can lift some of the source code verbatim if it fills a need, or better yet, use the code to generate ideas. Let's discuss some select portions of the MAXIBROW source code in more detail. We'll cover the following points of interest:

Browse Cursor Navigation
Color Scheme Technique
Data Source Positioning
Data Source Structure
Editing the Data Source

Browse cursor navigation

All browse cursor navigation in MAXIBROW is routed through a general-purpose function called Navigate(). The following loop forms a complete window navigation routine for any browse object.

```
#include "inkey.ch"

//  Assuming browse object "brow" has been constructed.
do while .t.
  do while (.not. brow:stabilize()) .and. (nextkey() == 0)
  enddo
  key := inkey(0)
  do case
  case Navigate(brow, key)
  case key = K_ESC
    exit
  endcase
enddo
```

Exactly which keystrokes are assigned to which browse navigation methods is up to you. Navigate() provides a handy place to store them and lends a high degree of consistency to your applications. If all browse cursor navigation is handled by Navigate() then all your browse windows will behave the same way. This is a mark of professionalism and your end-users will like the consistency.

The Navigate() function returns .t. if it can handle the key, .f. if not. This allows you to call the function when it's possible that a keystroke might be intended for browse cursor movement and then handle exceptions on your own. You can install support for as many or few keystrokes as you desire. If you want to change the behavior of a key that Navigate() handles, simply check for the key and react to it prior to calling Navigate(). Listing 26.6 contains the source code.

Listing 26.6 A general-purpose browse cursor navigation function

```
function Navigate(br, k)
/*
  Establish standard navigation keystrokes and the cursor movement
  method to associate with each key.

  This function gets passed a browse object and a potential navi
  gation key. If the key is defined it's associated navigation
  message is sent to the browse.

  Function returns .t. if navigation was handled, .f. if not.
*/
local did := .t.

  if k == K_UP
    br:up()
  elseif k == K_DOWN
    br:down()
  elseif k == K_LEFT
    br:left()
  elseif k == K_RIGHT
    br:right()
  elseif k == K_PGUP
    br:pageUp()
  elseif k == K_PGDN
    br:pageDown()
  elseif k == K_CTRL_PGUP
    br:goTop()
  elseif k == K_CTRL_PGDN
    br:goBottom()
```

```
  elseif k == K_HOME
    br:home()
  elseif k == K_END
    br:end()
  elseif k == K_CTRL_HOME
    br:panHome()
  elseif k == K_CTRL_END
    br:panEnd()
  elseif k == K_TAB
    br:panRight()
  elseif k == K_SH_TAB
    br:panLeft()
  else
    did := .f.
  endif

return did
```

Color scheme technique

MAXIBROW uses a fairly complex color scheme comprised of ten different color combinations. It also supports the ability to switch on the fly between color and monochrome schemes, a very handy feature when you're trying to program for a variety of monitors. This complexity is not evident in the actual source code, however, because we've taken care to separate and isolate the color configuration from the rest of the routines.

Here's a block of preprocessor #define directives that completely describe the MAXIBROW color scheme. Note how the names associated with the various components are not directly related to a particular color. They are driven by the situation and not the desired color. The colors can be changed to suit someone's whims without any adverse effects on the rest of the application. Since TBrowse always deals with colors in pairs — the currently highlighted cell is in one color, other cells in another — we've established the colors in a way that makes it clear exactly how the color scheme works.

```
/*
    Default color scheme for all columns.
    (Used with instance variable browse:colorSpec.)

    1: Regular cell
    2: Highlighted regular cell
    3: Block-selection cell
    4: Highlighted block-selection cell
    5: Checked record-#
    6: Highlighted, checked record-#
    7: Regular negative numbers and .F. values
    8: Highlighted negative numbers and .F. values
    9: Regular dates
   10: Highlighted dates


                     1     2    3     4     5     6     7     8     9      10
*/

#define COL_COLOR "W/N,  N/W, W+/B, B/W,  W+/G, B+/G,  R+/N, W+/R,  RB+/N, W+/RB"
#define COL_MONO  "W/N,  N/W, N/W,  W*/N, W/N,  W+/N,  W+/N, N/W,   W+/N,  N/W"
```

Later, the color scheme is assigned to the browse based on the type of adapter card present at run-time.

```
useColor := iscolor()
browse:colorSpec := if(useColor, COL_COLOR, COL_MONO)
```

Although the #defines help with b:colorSpec, they don't address the actual colors, which is potentially the most confusing aspect of the way you program TBrowse colors. Color-related functions expect an array containing a color pair. If you don't assign the color pairs correctly the browse won't look and feel as logical and consistent as it should. The following preprocessor #defines, which should appear immediately following the color scheme comments and #defines listed previously, associate the color pairs with more descriptive names.

```
/*   The following make it easier to use the browse:colorSpec.
     They correspond to the color scheme defined above.
*/
#define REGULAR_CELL  {1,2}
#define BLOCKED_CELL  {3,4}
#define CHECKED_CELL  {5,6}
#define NEGVAL_CELL   {7,8}
#define DATE_CELL     {9,10}
```

Based on these #defines we can write color-related code that is immediately clear in its intent.

```
//  Date columns get special color treatment.
if type(field(n)) = "D"
  column:defColor := DATE_CELL
else
  column:defColor := REGULAR_CELL
endif

//  We want negative numbers to be in a different color.
column:colorBlock := { |n| if(n < 0, NEGVAL_CELL, REGULAR_CELL) }
//  Highlight current row.
browse:colorRect({browse:rowPos, browse:freeze +1, ;
                  browse:rowPos, browse:colCount},  ;
                  BLOCKED_CELL)
```

Data source positioning

All data source positioning in MAXIBROW is done through calls to a single function, rather than having three separate functions. Besides being easier to maintain, the use of a single function allows for some additional tricks we'll discuss in a moment. Here are the code blocks for the three data source positioning services each TBrowse object requires.

```
browse:goTopBlock    := { | | RecPosition("top")      }
browse:goBottomBlock := { | | RecPosition("bottom")   }
browse:skipBlock     := { |n| RecPosition("skip", n) }
```

Listing 26.7 contains the source code for the RecPosition() function. Note that it performs two distinct services: Record position movement and position reporting. The bulk of the code comes directly from the SkipRec() function. See Listing 26.2 for detailed source code comments.

Listing 26.7 RecPosition(), a general-purpose record positioning and status function

```
function RecPosition(how, howMany)
/*
   General-purpose record positioning function, called by TBrowse
   goTop, goBottom and skip blocks. Returns number of records
   actually skipped if in "skip" mode.

   Also can be called with no parameters to get record position
   within database, independent of presence of index.
*/
//  Assume no movement was possible
local actual := 0

static where := 1

do case
case how = "top"
   where := 1
   goto top

case how = "bottom"
   where := lastrec()
   goto bottom

case how = "skip"
   do case
      //  Moving backwards
   case howMany < 0
      do while (actual > howMany) .and. (.not. bof())
        skip -1
        if .not. bof()
          actual--
        endif
      enddo
```

```
    //  Moving forwards
    case howMany > 0
       do while (actual < howMany) .and. (.not. eof())
         skip +1
         if .not. eof()
            actual++
         endif
       enddo
    if eof()
         skip -1
       endif

    //  No movement requested, re-read current record
    otherwise
         skip 0
    endcase

   //  No parameters passed, return current position.
otherwise
    return where
endcase

//  Update position tracker and prevent boundary wrap.
where += actual
where := min(max(where, 1), lastrec())

return actual
```

One major advantage of this technique is that it keeps all data source positioning activities in one place. We'll take advantage of this later when we see how easy it is to browse a subset of a data source without resulting to a slow and inefficient SET FILTER function.

More immediately, we see that we can maintain a static data source position variable, called "where" in the function's source code. This variable starts off with a value of one, meaning we're positioned at the top of the file. As RecPosition() gets requests for record movements, we can update the variable with the new position. If we are not using an index file, all we've accomplished is a very convoluted way to determine the record number. However, this technique works just as well with an index active, and that's the reason it's being used. A call to RecPosition() with no parameters causes it to return the current value of the position tracking variable. The main browsing routine in MAXIBROW displays the current record number at the bottom of the screen along with an the absolute position. Based on comparing the position with the total record count we can display an indicator in the browse window that helps the user keep track of the relative position in the database.

```
//  Before getting started, initialize a variable used
//  as local copy of the position indicator. This is done
//  once, outside of the main browsing loop.
local relPos := 1

do while .t.
  //
  //  Update relative position indicator, but only if there
  //  are more records in database than can fit on the screen.
  //
  if lastrec() > browse:rowCount

    //  Erase previous indicator by re-displaying
    //  the section of the left edge of the window.
    //  (Adjust the +2 to accommodate more than a single
    //  row of column headings.)
    @ browse:nTop +2 +relPos, browse:nLeft -1 say chr(219)

    //  Calculate a new screen row to display the indicator,
    //  based on a percentage of the width of the window.
    relPos := min((RecPosition()/lastrec()) *browse:rowCount, ;
                  browse:rowCount -1)

    //  Save the current color, invert it, display the
    //  indicator character, then restore the original color.
    clr := setcolor("I")
    @ browse:nTop +2 +relPos, browse:nLeft -1 say chr(18)
    setcolor(clr)
  endif
  //
  //  The rest of your browse routine...
  //
enddo
```

There are several tricks present in this technique. First, we've taken care of the situation where no indicator is needed by skipping the whole process if we can already see all the records. An indicator is nice but not if it confuses the user.

Second, we update the indicator by first replacing its current position with the hunk of window border that it obscures, calculating a new position, and displaying the indicator again. Sometimes the indicator may stay right where it is if the database is so huge that it takes several screenfuls of data to make it budge.

Third, calculating where exactly to display the indicator is actually quite simple. Dividing the current position by the record count gives you a percentage to apply against the number of screen rows visible in the browse window. Suppose there are 600 records in the database and ten rows to display them in. If we're positioned at the 200th record, the indicator should be placed 33% of the way down the screen, starting from the first row of the browse window. 33% of ten lines is a hair over 3 lines, so we move the indicator down three rows. This is accurate enough for the purpose served by the indicator.

A final trick is very handy in situations where you want something to be in a different but compatible color than its surroundings. Setting the color to "I" does exactly that — it swaps the current foreground and background colors. If you were previously in "BG+/W", setting the color to "I" yields "W/BG+". The letter I is for inverse, it's not really a color but a color operator of sorts.

Let's step back for a moment and cover a limitation inherent in this technique: You must route 100% of the data source positioning through the RecDisplay() function. If you move the record pointer outside of the function the "where" variable won't get updated and the indicator will stray. This means you can't jump to a record via GOTO or SEEK; only the regular browse navigation methods are supported. Aside from that, you can use RecPosition() and a relative position indicator to spruce up any browse window.

Data source structure

If you read the source code carefully you may notice that we've gone to great lengths to load an array with database structure information and then maintain that array as the browse and column objects go through various gyrations. This was done in an attempt to make MAXIBROW, and any browse routines you create based on this design, more independent of the structure of the actual data source. If you were browsing an array with two dimensions, very little of the MAXIBROW source code needs to be changed. Follow these steps.

1. Build a stru_ array that has the same general structure as the array returned by DBSTRUCT() for database structures. (See Chapter 9, "Arrays," for details on how to manipulate arrays with multiple dimensions.) That is, the stru_ array should describe the array containing the data you wish to browse — names for the fields, data types, widths and so on.

2. Create c:block column blocks that reference array elements rather than database field names.

3. Create b:goTopBlock, b:goBottomBlock, and c:skipBlock functions that operate on arrays rather than databases.

And that is all there is to it. Once MAXIBROW is up and running almost all of its features will work with arrays. Of course, arrays don't have record numbers, deleted flags, and such so those features won't translate automatically (although all are possible with additional editing).

See the section on Browsing Arrays, later in this chapter, for details on how to perform steps 1 and 2.

Editing the data source

Allowing the user to scroll through a database with a tool as wonderful as TBrowse is sometimes a tease — you can look but you can't touch! Fortunately it's a simple matter to provide complete editing capabilities to any TBrowse window. MAXIBROW contains a complete function, called EditCell(), that handles the entire process. It even pops up a special editor for memo fields. You'll be surprised by the relatively small amount of source code it takes to pull this off. Here's what a call to EditCell() looks like within the body of the MAXIBROW browsing loop. The cell editor gets invoked whenever the user presses the Enter or Ctrl-Enter keys, or when a key within the normal keyboard range is pressed.

Note: This technique asumes *exclusive use* of the data source. Minor modifications are needed for use in shared (multi-user) situations.

```
case (key == K_ENTER) ;          //  Open current cell for editing.
.or. (key == K_CTRL_ENTER) ;     //  Clear cell contents and edit.
.or. (key > K_SPACE)             //  Edit by starting to type.
//
  EditCell(browse, ;
           stru_[browse:colPos -1, DBS_NAME], ;  //  Field name
           EDIT_COLOR)
```

The simplicity of the call to EditCell() is obscured by MAXIBROW's need to be completely generic so it can be used with any database structure. It also uses a manifest constant for the color string, defined previously (see the earlier discussion on the MAXIBROW color scheme). Here's the call written as it would look for editing the LastName field in bright white letters on a blue background.

```
EditCell(browse, "LastName", "B+/W")
```

That's all there is to it. The browse object carries with it everything we need to know to perform the edit. You may be wondering, doesn't the browse object know about the field name as well? It does, but there's no guarantee that we'll be able to pull the actual field name out of it. The column's data retrieval block is a code block and we can't reverse-engineer the field name. We could use the column's cargo variable to store the field name but it's just as easy to send it as a parameter since we have to know it to create the column, anyway.

One other important point to be aware of before you implement this function. The column field blocks must be capable of storing values back to the data source, not just retrieving values. The edit will appear to work just fine, but nothing will actually be saved. Here are three data retrieval blocks. The first won't work because it doesn't have the ability to store values back to the data source. The next two do because FIELDBLOCK() and it's cousin, FIELDWBLOCK(), return the proper kind of code block, and the way the third one is defined gives it the same capability.

```
//  Won't work if data storage is needed.
col1:block := { || CUST->FirstName }

//  These both will work.
col2:block := fieldblock("LastName")
col3:block := { |x| if(x == nil, Phone, Phone := x) }
```

The third example works the way it does because whenever Clipper wants to store something to such a code block it passes a parameter when EVALuating it. If no parameter is passed it means Clipper only wants the current value. Complete source code for EditCell() is found in Listing 26.8.

Listing 26.8 EditCell(), a general-purpose browse cell editing function

```
function EditCell(b, fieldName, editColor)
/*
   General-purpose browse cell editing function, can handle all
   database field types including memo fields. If you want the
   edits to "stick" you must assign fieldblock()-style
   column:block instance variables. All editing, including memo-
   edit, is done within the boundaries of the browse window. On
   exit, any appropriate browse cursor navigation messages are
   passed along.
```

```
   Note: In order to browse a memo field the column heading must
   be defined. This function uses the heading to display a mes-
   sage.
*/
#include "inkey.ch"

#define K_SPACE       32
#define K_CTRL_ENTER  10
#define lstr(n)       ltrim(str(n))

local c, k, clr, crs, rex, block, cell

//  Retrieve the column object for the current cell.
c := b:getColumn(b:colPos)

//  Create a field block used to check for a memo field
//  and later used to store the edited memo back. It's
//  done this way so you can have the browse window display
//  a notation like "memo" rather than displaying a small
//  hunk of the real memo field.
//
block := fieldblock(fieldName)

  //  Can't just "get" a memo, need a memoedit.
  if valtype(eval(block)) == "M"

    //  Tell the user what's going on.
    @ b:nTop, b:nLeft clear to b:nBottom, b:nRight
    @ b:nTop, b:nLeft say ;
      padc("Memo Edit: Record " +lstr(recno()) ;
          +', "'+ c:heading +'" Field', b:nRight -b:nLeft)
    @ row() +1, b:nLeft say replicate("-", b:nRight -b:nLeft +1)

    //  Turn cursor on and perform the memo edit
    //  using the specified color.
    crs := setcursor(1)
    clr := setcolor(editColor)
    cell := memoedit(eval(block), b:nTop +2, b:nLeft, b:nBottom,
            b:nRight)
    setcursor(crs)
```

```
    setcolor(clr)

    //  If they didn't abandon the edit, save changes.
    //  When passed a parameter, fieldblock-style code
    //  blocks store the value back to the database.
    //  Handiest darn thing they ever stuck in this language.
    if lastkey() <> K_ESC
      eval(block, cell)
    endif

    //  We mussed up the entire window, tell TBrowse to clean it
    // up.
    b:configure()

  //  Regular data type, do a GET/READ.
  else

    //  Pass along any additional keystrokes.
    if lastkey() == K_CTRL_ENTER
      keyboard(chr(K_CTRL_Y))
    elseif (lastkey() > K_SPACE) .and. (lastkey() < 256)
      keyboard(chr(lastkey()))
    endif

    //  Create a get object for the field.
    cell := getnew(row(), col(), ;
                   c:block, fieldName,, "W/N,"+editColor)

    //  Allow up/down to exit the read, and turn the cursor off.
    rex := readexit(.t.)
    crs := setcursor(1)

    //  Perform the read.
    readmodal({cell})

    //  Restore original cursor and read-exit states.
    setcursor(crs)
    readexit(rex)

    //  If user hit a navigation key to exit, do it.
    if Navigate(b, lastkey())
```

```
    //  If they pressed Enter, advance to next column.
    elseif lastkey() = K_ENTER
      if b:colPos < b:colCount
        b:right()
      else
        b:down()
        b:colPos := b:freeze +1
      endif
    endif

    //  We changed the field value and TBrowse doesn't know it.
    //  So we must force a re-read for the current row.
    b:refreshCurrent()
  endif

return nil
```

EditCell() first distinguishes between memo fields and other data types. Memo fields are processed with a call to the MEMOEDIT() function while all other data types use the GETSYS system for @..GET-style editing. EditCell() can be implemented in any browse routine, triggered by any keystroke you desire.

If working with something other than a memo field, EditCell() next fetches the last keystroke to see how it should react to the user. Pressing Enter simply causes the current cell to be opened for editing. Ctrl-Enter first clears the field by stuffing a Ctrl-Y into the keyboard buffer. Keys within the normal keyboard range are placed back into the keyboard buffer so they are treated as part of the cell edit. This allows the user to simply start typing when they want to enter data, rather than having to remember to first type a special "I want to edit" keystroke. You don't have to give the user such easy access to the data, sometimes it's preferable to require a special keystroke.

TBrowse versus SEEK and GOTO

If you move the record pointer directly, instead of indirectly through the data source positioning blocks, you may find TBrowse does not maintain the row position correctly. This is not due to an error in TBrowse but rather a lack of communication between TBrowse's internal tracking of the record position and your direct manipulation.

Also troublesome at times is not always staying on the same row following a call to b:refreshAll(). Fortunately there's a simple solution to both problems in Listing 26.9.

Listing 26.9 A replacement for b:refreshAll() which keeps the current row highlighted

```
function dbRefresh(browse)
/*
   A replacement for b:refreshAll() that will keep the
   current row highlighted, used primarily when you've
   moved the record pointer via SEEK or GOTO such that
   the record is still on the screen. If the entire screen
   has to be redrawn with new data, this function will
   have no net effect beyond the actual b:refreshAll()
   and won't cause any delays.
*/

//  Remember where we ended up.
local rec := recno()

  //  Perform the initial stabilizing process.
  browse:refreshAll()
  do while .not. browse:stabilize() ; enddo

  //  Most of the time this will be false,
  //  so no work will be done.
  do while recno() <> rec
    browse:up()
    //  Need to stabilize again.
    do while .not. browse:stabilize() ; enddo
  enddo

return nil
```

Here are some examples of how dbRefresh() is used.

```
goto marked_rec
VENDOR->(dbRefresh(brow))
seek someValue
ITEMS->(dbRefresh(brow))
```

Browsing within a WHILE condition

Sometimes all of the records in a database are not relevant for the task at hand, for example, viewing product orders placed by a single customer. A simple solution is the SET FILTER command. It eliminates from consideration all records not matching a condition.

```
select ORDERS
set filter to ORDERS->Customer == CUSTOMER->ID
goto top
//
//  Display a browse window.
//  ...
```

This is an acceptable solution only when dealing with a database with a small number of records, or when a majority of the records match the filter condition. Problems surface when the GOTO TOP operation has to evaluate hundreds or even thousands of records to find the first one that satisfies the condition. And for the very same reason, pressing PageDown may send the filter on a fruitless search for another screenful of data even if there isn't any. The filter will continue to evaluate records until it hits the end of the database, even if it means the user has to wait five minutes or more! Clearly, there must be a better way.

A preferable way to handle the situation is to have an index key based on the condition we want to browse. For the customer orders example it means having an index on at least the customer ID for each order. More than likely the database already has such an index as an aid in creating and maintaining the data.

```
//  Create an index on customer ID and purchase order number.
select ORDERS
index on Customer +PO to ORDCUST
```

Having TBrowse operate on a single customer's orders is a simple matter of adding some additional logic to the RecPosition() function listed previously. We'll need to pass the function two additional parameters: the value of the first index key that matches the condition and a code block that evaluates a record and returns .t. if it matches the condition.

Let's do the easiest ones first: the GOTO TOP and GOTO BOTTOM functions needed for servicing the b:goTop() and b:goBottom() navigation methods. Since we've got an index, it's trivial to go to the first record that matches our condition, just SEEK it.

```
//  GOTO TOP
seek firstKey
```

At this point the database is either pointing to the first record that matches the condition, or to end-of-file. We can handle the EOF() situation easily enough on our own before trying to browse the data so there's no reason to make it more complex than it needs to be in RecPosition().

GOTO BOTTOM is more troublesome. How do we quickly locate the last record that matches the condition? A brute-force method is simply skipping through records that match the condition until you find one that doesn't. Back up one record and there you have it. While this is certainly an improvement over the SET FILTER command's need to run through the entire database, it still requires that potentially thousands upon thousands of records be processed. Hardly a productive use of your user's time.

```
// GOTO BOTTOM
lastKey := firstKey +chr(255)
set softseek on
seek lastKey
skip -1
```

This relies on the fact that with SOFTSEEK on, the SEEK command will find the index key value that either matches or is greater than the one we're looking for. We constructed a key value that differs only minutely from the correct key by adding a chr(255), which is a value that is guaranteed to be sorted last in the index. It's very unlikely that chr(255) exists in your database files, or if it does, even more unlikely that it's part of an index key. Since SOFTSEEK makes SEEK find the first key greater than the one we specify, we'll end up positioned one record past the range we are interested in, so we back up one record.

In practice, we'll need to save the current status of SET SOFTSEEK and restore it when we're done. A general-purpose function must not have any side effects to cause problems in other parts of the application.

All that's left is the SKIP service. There are no tricks involved, just some additional conditions in the logic. While skipping forward or backward we have to check to see that we haven't left the range of records that match the condition. That's where the code block parameter comes in. When evaluated it should return .t. only when the record in question is within the range of records we wish to see. Here's an example of the code block needed in our customer order example.

```
condition := { |cust| ORDERS->Customer == cust }
```

The "skip forward" portion of the RecPosition() function then looks like the following.

```
do while (actual < howMany) .and. (.not. eof()) ;
        .and. eval(condition, firstKey)
  skip +1
  if (.not. eof()) .and. eval(condition, firstKey)
    actual++
  endif
enddo
if eof() .or. (.not. eval(condition, firstKey))
  skip -1
endif
```

Skipping backwards requires the exact same kind of logic. See Listing 26.10 for the complete function.

Listing 26.10 Record positioning function for browsing with a while condition

```
function PosWhile(how, firstKey, condition, howMany)
/*
   General-purpose record positioning function, called by
   TBrowse goTop, goBottom and skip blocks. Returns number
   of records actually skipped if in "skip" mode.
```

```
   Note: It's assumed the database is already positioned at
   the first matching key (for example, after a SEEK).
*/
// Assume no movement was possible
local actual := 0
local softStat

do case
case how == "top"
  seek firstKey

case how == "bottom"
  softStat := set(_SET_SOFTSEEK, .t.)
  seek (left(firstKey, len(firstKey) -1) +chr(255))
  skip -1
  set(_SET_SOFTSEEK, softStat)

case how == "skip"
    do case
    // Moving backwards
    case howMany < 0
      do while (actual > howMany) .and. (.not. bof()) ;
               .and. eval(condition, firstKey)
      skip -1
      if (.not. bof()) .and. eval(condition, firstKey)
        actual--
      endif
    enddo
    if (.not. eval(condition, firstKey))
      skip +1
    endif

    // Moving forwards
    case howMany > 0
      do while (actual < howMany) .and. (.not. eof()) ;
               .and. eval(condition, firstKey)
      skip +1
      if (.not. eof()) .and. eval(condition, firstKey)
        actual++
      endif
```

```
    enddo
    if eof() .or. (.not. eval(condition, firstKey))
      skip -1
    endif

    //  No movement requested, re-read current record
    otherwise
      skip 0
    endcase
  endcase
return actual
```

To use PosWhile() in your browse operations you need only assign values to the two additional parameters.

```
//  WhichCust is assigned by the user.
//
whichCust := AskWhichOne()

browse:goTopBlock    := { | | PosWhile("top",    whichCust) }
browse:goBottomBlock := { | | PosWhile("bottom", whichCust) }
browse:skipBlock     := { |n| PosWhile("skip",   whichCust, ;
                          { |x| ORDERS->Customer == x }, n) }
```

All three positioning blocks need to know the value of the first index key. Only the SKIP block has to be concerned with the "while" condition.

Keep in mind that if you alter the value of an index key you'll need to issue a b:refreshAll() to make certain TBrowse sees the change.

Browsing arrays

TBrowse can be used to view any form of data that occurs in predictable rows and columns. It is not limited to database browsing in any way. This flexibility comes from the very same browse instance variables that allow us to browse for a WHILE condition as discussed in the preceding section: b:goTopBlock, b:goBottomBlock, and b:skipBlock. All you need to do is supply code blocks that perform these services and TBrowse will never know the difference.

With this in mind we can use TBrowse to view the contents of arrays. We'll take a look at two varieties: arrays with one dimension and symmetrical arrays with two dimensions. By symmetrical we mean arrays that have a consistent and predictable structure. Examples of symmetrical arrays with two dimensions are the arrays returned by the DIRECTORY() and DBSTRUCT() functions. We'll write TBrowse routines to view both of these arrays. But first, let's start with something easier.

Arrays with one dimension

The easiest kind of arrays to browse are those with only a single dimension. The first order of business is quickly building an array to browse, and a list of files in the current subdirectory can be made into an array in a few simple lines of code. (See Chapter 9, "Arrays," for a detailed discussion of arrays and the DIRECTORY() function).

```
//  Load the files_ array with filenames
//  found in current subdirectory.
files_ := {}
aeval(directory(), { |f_| aadd(files_, f_[1]) } )
```

The TBrowse data source positioning blocks want to be able to send us to the top and bottom of the array. An array does not have a built-in pointer like database files do, so we'll have to supply one.

```
//  This will be our "element pointer".
element := 1
```

Setting up a browse object is straightforward. Just create a browse object and a single column object since the array has only one dimension.

```
//  General browse setup.
list := TBrowseNew(10, 30, 18, 50)
list:headSep := " "
list:footSep := "="

//  The file name column.
filename := TBColumnNew("File Name", { || files_[element] } )
```

Now we need some data positioning code blocks. Based on our element pointer we can reference the first and last elements very easily.

```
list:goTopBlock    := { || element := 1 }
list:goBottomBlock := { || element := len(files_) }
```

Skipping forwards and backwards for b:skipBlock would be just as easy were it not for the fact that TBrowse will often request that we skip further than the limits of the array. This in itself is not a problem because TBrowse doesn't expect every single position request to succeed completely. It does demand, however, that we inform it how many elements we were able to skip so it can adjust the display accordingly. Listing 26.11 is a function that will do the job. You pass it the array, current element position and how many elements to skip.

Listing 26.11 ArraySkip(), a b:skipBlock function for arrays

```
function ArraySkip(aLen, curPos, howMany)
/*
   General purpose array skipping function intended for
   use with TBrowse b:skipBlocks. You must pass the curPos
   parameter by reference (use the @ operator) for this
   function to work correctly with TBrowse.
*/
local actual

if howMany >= 0                    // Moving forward?
  if (curPos +howMany) > aLen // Can't go that far!
    actual := aLen - curPos   // Actual is whatever is left
    curPos := aLen            // Put pointer at end
  else                        // Can move the whole distance...
    actual := howMany         // Actual is number requested
    curPos += howMany         // Move pointer forward
  endif
else                          // Moving backward?
  if (curPos +howMany) < 1    // Can't go that far!
    actual := 1 -curPos       // Actual is whatever was left
    curPos := 1               // Put pointer at top
```

```
  else                          // Can move the whole distance...
    actual := howMany           // Actual is number requested
    curPos += howMany           // Move pointer backward
  endif
endif
return actual
```

Used in our file listing, example the b:skipBlock looks like this:

```
list:skipBlock := { |n| ArraySkip(len(files_), @element, n) }
```

The "pass by reference" symbol, @, is required because we want the ArraySkip() function to alter the value of the element pointer to our routine and return the actual skip count to TBrowse. The only way to do both in the same function is to pass a reference to the element pointer so ArraySkip() can alter it.

At this point we have the browse and column objects ready to go, so let's combine them and get the window up on the screen. We'll call upon MAXIBROW's Navigate() function (discussed earlier in this chapter) to provide a set of browse navigation keys.

```
//  Add the file name column object to the browse object.
list:addColumn(filename)

//  Display the window and process navigation keystrokes.
do while .t.
  do while .not. list:stabilize()
  enddo
  if .not. Navigate(list, inkey(0))
    exit
  endif
enddo
```

Listing 26.12 contains source code for the complete file name browsing routine, including the housekeeping code we omitted for clarity in the previous examples.

Listing 26.12 Browsing an array of file names

```
function BrowArray()
/*
   Load an array of file names and browse it.
*/
local files_, element, list, key

  //  Load the files_ array with filenames
  //  found in current subdirectory.
  files_ := {}
  aeval(directory(), { |f_| aadd(files_, f_[1]) } )

  //  This will be our "element pointer".
  element := 1

  //  General browse setup.
  list := TBrowseNew(10, 30, 18, 50)
  list:headSep := " "
  list:footSep := "="

  //  Assign the positioning blocks.
  list:goTopBlock    := { || element := 1 }
  list:goBottomBlock := { || element := len(files_) }
  list:skipBlock := { |n| ArraySkip(len(files_), @element, n) }

  //  Add a file name column object to the browse object.
  list:addColumn(TBColumnNew("File Name", ;
                { || padr(files_[element], 12) } ))

  //  Display the window and process navigation keystrokes.
  do while .t.
    do while .not. list:stabilize()
    enddo
    if .not. Navigate(list, inkey(0))
      exit
    endif
  enddo
return nil
```

The thing to keep in mind about this example is not the few things that are different about browsing an array, but that most of the source code would be exactly the same if the file listing was stored in a database instead of an array. Everything you've learned so far about browse and column objects is applicable to arrays.

Arrays with two dimensions

Browsing an array with two dimensions is done the same way as with one dimension, the only exception being the column object data retrieval blocks must refer to the additional dimension in order to extract values from the array. Let's return to the previous example and browse a complete set of directory information instead of just the file names. Compare Listing 26.12 with 26.13 to see how few changes are needed to support the additional dimension.

Listing 26.13 Browsing an array of directory information

```
function BrowArray2()

local dir_, element, list, key

  //  Load the dir_ array with a complete set of
  //  directory information for the current subdirectory.
  dir_ := directory()

  //  This will be our "element pointer".
  element := 1

  //  General browse setup.
  @ 9, 19 to 20, 61 double
  list := TBrowseNew(10, 20, 20, 60)
  list:headSep := "═╤═"
  list:colSep  := " │ "
  list:footSep := "═╧═"

  //  Assign the positioning blocks.
  list:goTopBlock    := { || element := 1 }
  list:goBottomBlock := { || element := len(dir_) }
  list:skipBlock := { |n| ArraySkip(len(dir_), @element, n) }
```

```
  //  File name is first element in array.
  list:addColumn(TBColumnNew("File Name", ;
       { || padr(dir_[element, 1], 12) } ))

  //  Size is second element.
  list:addColumn(TBColumnNew("Size", ;
       { || transform(dir_[element, 2], "999,999,999") } ))

  //  Date and time are third and fourth elements.
  //  We'll skip the file attributes in the fifth element.
  list:addColumn(TBColumnNew("Date", { || dir_[element, 3] } ))
  list:addColumn(TBColumnNew("Time", { || dir_[element, 4] } ))

  //  Display the window and process navigation keystrokes.
  do while .t.
    do while .not. list:stabilize()
    enddo
    if .not. Navigate(list, inkey(0))
      exit
    endif
  enddo
return nil
```

Browsing text files

Browsing the contents of text files is as easy as browsing arrays providing you have enough memory to load the file. Once in memory we can use Clipper memo processing functions to do most of the work for us.

MEMOREAD()	Read the file into memory.
MLCOUNT()	Count the number of lines.
MEMOLINE()	Return the specified line number.

Let's use the MEMOREAD() function to load a file into a memory variable.

```
//  Load the contents of the specified file.
textfile := memoread("TEST.TXT")
```

You can think of the text file as an array with one dimension. The length of the file in this sense is the number of lines it contains.

```
//  Determine how many lines are in the file.
lastLine := mlcount(textfile)
```

As with arrays we also need to maintain a pointer that keeps track of our position in the file.

```
//  A pointer used to keep track of which line we're on.
line := 1
```

Creating the browse and column objects should look familiar. The only wrinkle is the use of the memoline() function to retrieve a line of text for TBrowse to display.

```
txt := TBrowseNew(10, 20, 18, 60)
txt:addColumn(TBColumnNew( , ;
    { || memoline(textfile, 254, line)} ))
```

We've used a line length of 254, which is the maximum MEMOLINE() can handle. This is done so that the lines in the text file do not wrap to fit the window, which could make some files very difficult to read. Other files, however, might benefit from the automatic line wrapping. Here's an alternate way to call MEMOLINE() such that the text will wrap to fit the browse window.

```
txt:addColumn(TBColumnNew( , ;
    { || memoline(textfile, txt:nRight -txt:nLeft, line)} ))
```

As with arrays, the tricky part is establishing the data source positioning code blocks. The way text file lines are organized is so similar to that of arrays that we can use the ArraySkip() function found in Listing 26.10.

```
//  The data positioning blocks.
browse:goTopBlock     := { || line := 1 }
browse:goBottomBlock  := { || line := lastLine }
browse:skipBlock      := { |n| ArraySkip(lastLine, @line, n) }
```

Since you've seen the rest of the technique so many times by now we'll dispense with the details and just list the final version of the function in Listing 26.14.

Listing 26.14 A file browser for small text files

```
function BrowText(filename)
/*
   A general-purpose file browser for small text files.
   Pass a file name from DOS.
*/
local textfile, lastLine, line, txt

  if filename == nil
    ? "Must specify a file name."
    return nil
  endif

  //  Load the contents of the specified file.
  textfile := memoread(filename)

  //  Determine how many lines are in the file.
  lastLine := mlcount(textfile)

  //  A pointer used to keep track of which line we're on.
  line := 1

  @ 8, 19 say "File: " +filename
  @ 9, 19 to 21, 61

  //  Create the browse object.
  txt := TBrowseNew(10, 20, 20, 60)

  //  Add a column that displays a line of text.
  txt:addColumn(TBColumnNew(, ;
    { || memoline(textfile, 254, line)} ))

  //  The data positioning blocks.
  txt:goTopBlock      := { || line := 1 }
  txt:goBottomBlock   := { || line := lastLine }
  txt:skipBlock := { |n| ArraySkip(lastLine, @line, n) }
```

```
  // Display the window and process navigation keystrokes.
  do while .t.
    do while .not. txt:stabilize()
    enddo
    if .not. Navigate(txt, inkey(0))
      exit
    endif
  enddo
return nil
```

Multiple simultaneous browses

Throughout this chapter we've always been working with a single browse object at a time. While it's debatable whether or not there's a conceptual limit on how many browses we want to consider at a time, there's no practical limit. All of the browse methods and instance variables we've discussed can be applied to any arbitrary browse object, the same way a single set of column instance variables can be applied to any number of columns.

As a final example in this chapter, let's close with a function that browses a list of database files in one window and their structures in another. Both windows will be on the screen, processing navigation keystrokes and updating their respective windows, simultaneously—see Listing 26.15 Does this sound like a juggler's final, audience-dazzling trick before the curtain falls? Start spinning the plates and a let's have a drum roll, please!

Listing 26.15 Two simultaneous browse windows, one with a listing of database file names and the other with corresponding field structures

```
function DBFdirect(fileSpec)
/*
   Call this function from DOS. It will display
   two browse windows, one with database file name
   information and one with the field structure of
   the currently highlighted database.

   If you think this routine would form an excellent
   base for a general purpose database utility and are
```

```
   already dreaming up specifications and features...
   you've been bitten by that Clipper 5 bug and we
   wish you well! Turn off the lights when you leave
   and try to get some sleep once in a while.
*/
#include "inkey.ch"
#include "directry.ch"
#include "dbstruct.ch"

local dir_, stru_
local dbf, dirPos
local stru, struPos
local i, bytes, col, key

  //  Default filespec if none specified.
  if fileSpec = nil
    fileSpec := "*.dbf"
  elseif .not. ("." $ fileSpec)
    fileSpec += ".dbf"
  endif

  setcursor(0)
  @ 0,0 clear
  @ 1,0 say padc("Database Directory & Structure Viewer: " ;
                +fileSpec, 80)
  @ 2,0 say "Loading..."

  //  Load directory entries.
  dir_ := directory(fileSpec)
  if len(dir_) = 0
    @ 2,0
    @ 2,0 say "No files found."
    return nil
  endif

  //  This array will hold database structures.
  stru_ := {}

  //  For each database file in the directory...
  for i := 1 to len(dir_)
```

```
  @ 2,11 say i
  use (dir_[i, DBS_NAME]) shared

  //  Add record and field counts to the directory array.
  aadd(dir_[i], lastrec())
  aadd(dir_[i], fcount())

  //  Add current database's structure to the array.
  aadd(stru_, DBSTRUCT())
  use
next i

//  Sum the file sizes.
bytes := 0
aeval(dir_, { |f_| bytes += f_[F_SIZE] } )

//  Clear the "loading" message.
@ 2,0

//  Draw the static portions of the screen.
@  4,1 say "Up/Down, PgUp/PgDn"
@  5,0 to 15,52
@ 16,1 say ltrim(transform(bytes, "999,999,999")) ;
          +" bytes in " ;
          +ltrim(str(len(dir_))) +" files."

@ 4,54 say "Left/Right, Tab/ShiftTab"
@ 5,53 to 15,79

//  Construct a browse object for the directory array.
//
dirPos := 1
dbf := TBrowseNew(6,1,14,51)
dbf:headSep := "═╤═"
dbf:colSep  := " │ "
dbf:goTopBlock     := { | | dirPos := 1 }
dbf:goBottomBlock  := { | | dirPos := len(dir_) }
dbf:skipBlock      := { |n| ArraySkip(len(dir_), @dirPos, n) }

//  Directory window columns.
```

```
dbf:addcolumn(TBColumnNew("File Name", ;
    { || padr(dir_[dirPos, F_NAME], 12) } ))
dbf:addcolumn(TBColumnNew("Size",       ;
    { || transform(dir_[dirPos, F_SIZE], "99,999,999 ") } ))
dbf:addcolumn(TBColumnNew("Date",       ;
    { || dir_[dirPos, F_DATE] } ))
dbf:addcolumn(TBColumnNew("Records",    ;
    { || transform(dir_[dirPos, 6], "999,999 ") } ))
dbf:addcolumn(TBColumnNew("Fields",     ;
    { || transform(dir_[dirPos, 7], "999") } ))

//  Construct a browse object for the structure array.
//
struPos := 1
stru := TBrowseNew(6,54,14,78)
stru:headSep := "┬-"
stru:colSep  := "|"
stru:goTopBlock    := { | | struPos := 1 }
stru:goBottomBlock := { | | struPos := len(stru_) }
stru:skipBlock     := ;
     { |n| ArraySkip(len(stru_[dirPos]), @struPos, n) }

//  Structure window columns.
stru:addcolumn(TBColumnNew("Field", ;
     { || padr(stru_[dirPos, struPos, DBS_NAME], 10) } ))
stru:addcolumn(TBColumnNew("Type",  ;
     { || padc(stru_[dirPos, struPos, DBS_TYPE],  4) } ))
stru:addcolumn(TBColumnNew("Width", ;
     { || str(stru_[dirPos, struPos,  DBS_LEN],    5) } ))
stru:addcolumn(TBColumnNew("Dec",   ;
     { || str(stru_[dirPos, struPos,  DBS_DEC],    3) } ))

do while .t.

  //  If the directory window position was altered,
  //  we must update the structure window to match it.
  if .not. dbf:stable
    stru:rowPos := 1
    stru:goTop()
    stru:refreshAll()
  endif
```

```
    //  Stabilize both windows.
    do while (.not. dbf:stabilize()) .and. (nextkey() == 0)
    enddo
    do while (.not. stru:stabilize()) .and. (nextkey() == 0)
    enddo

    //  Update the structure summary lines.
    @ 16,54
    @ 17,54
    bytes := 0
    aeval(stru_[dirPos], { |s_| bytes += s_[DBS_LEN] } )
    @ 16,54 say ltrim(str(bytes)) +" bytes per record,"
    @ 17,54 say ltrim(str(len(stru_[dirPos]))) +" fields."

    key := inkey(0)

    //  Database window navigation keys
    do case
    case key == K_UP
      dbf:up()
    case key == K_DOWN
      dbf:down()
    case key == K_PGUP
      dbf:pageUp()
    case key == K_PGDN
      dbf:pageDown()

    //  Structure window navigation keys.
    case key == K_LEFT
      stru:up()
    case key == K_RIGHT
      stru:down()
    case key == K_TAB
      stru:pageDown()
    case key == K_SH_TAB
      stru:pageUp()
    case key == K_ESC
      exit
    endcase
  enddo
  setcursor(1)
return nil
```

Try this out in a directory full of dozens of database files with large numbers of fields. You'll be amazed how well TBrowse can handle such things. Figure 26.3 shows a sample screen generated by DBFdirect().

Figure 26.3 Typical display from DBFdirect()

```
                 Database Directory & Structure Viewer: *.dbf

 Up/Down, PgUp/PgDn                                        Left/Right, Tab/ShiftTab

 File Name     Size        Date      Records  Fields    Field        Type Width Dec

 ARTICLES.DBF     22,909 |05/06/91|     150 |  7        DATE        | D |     8| 0
 OUTBOX.DBF          673 |05/25/91|       2 | 11        SENDER      | C |    25| 0
 INCOMING.DBF      2,532 |05/25/91|      15 | 11        RECEIVER    | C |    25| 0
 OUTGOING.DBF        619 |05/25/91|       4 |  7        SUBJECT     | C |    25| 0
 USERS.DBF        46,391 |04/10/91|     771 |  3        CONF        | C |    27| 0
 CONFS.DBF           256 |03/13/91|       9 |  1        TEXT        | M |    10| 0
 FILES.DBF           259 |11/15/90|       0 |  7        READ        | L |     1| 0

 73,639 bytes in 7 files.                                  142 bytes per record,
                                                           11 fields.
```

Summary

Had enough yet? We've covered all the features of the TBrowse and TBColumn object classes, seen examples of how they are implemented, breezed through a number of handy TBrowse tool box functions, and saw how you can browse far more than just database fields, like arrays and text files. But even after all that we've barely scratched the surface! An entire book could be dedicated to the subject.

We sincerely hope this lengthy chapter inspires you not only to dive into TBrowse and create wonderful browse windows, but also to dig more deeply into the way Clipper's object-oriented design helps make the process so elegant. The Get System, which handles all the @..GET/READ-style data entry, and the Error System, which deals with run-time errors, are both implemented with this same object technology. Getting experience in one makes it easier to understand the others. Plus, we guarantee that you'll be seeing considerably more objects in the future as Computer Associates expands the Clipper language.

CHAPTER 27

The GET Object Class

The basic point of every database management application is to store data in database files. But that data must first be entered (usually by a hapless data entry clerk who could not care less what language the software is written in). In the dBASE species (of which Clipper is a part), this data capturing mechanism is known as a **GET**. Briefly, programming data entry is a two-step process: The programmer displays one or more GETs upon the screen, each representing a data item that must be entered, and then issues a READ command, which activates the GETs and allows the user to enter various forms of data.

No development platform gives you more flexibility for GETs than Clipper 5. This unprecedented degree of control is due largely to Clipper 5's new GET object and the configurable GET system. In this chapter we will explore the inner workings of the GET object. We'll also demonstrate several creative ways to use the new WHEN clause, as well as add a MESSAGE to the @..GET command.

Overview

In prior versions of Clipper, issuing a READ statement was tantamount to handing over the reins to Clipper. We could occasionally resurface to execute VALID functions or hot key procedures, but for the most part we were stuck in the bowels of the READ command, completely at Clipper's mercy.

With the GET object and the reconfigurable GET system, the rules have changed. Clipper 5 lets us configure the GETs any way our heart desires. Unlike the "old way" (i.e., vanishing into READ limbo), we now maintain complete control at all times. With earlier versions of Clipper we had no access to the READ mechanism. However, not only does Clipper 5 give us access in the form of READMODAL() and supporting functions, but *it is written entirely in Clipper* (and thus very easy to modify if necessary). The source code for READMODAL() can be found in the file GETSYS.PRG, which is supplied with Clipper 5. (A discussion of the other functions in GETSYS.PRG can be found later in this chapter.)

The WHEN clause

Before we plunge into the brave new world of GET objects, let's talk about another less glamorous but tremendously useful Clipper 5 addition: the WHEN clause. In the same fashion as the VALID clause provides *post-validation* for each GET, the WHEN clause serves as *pre-validation*. If you specify a WHEN clause, it will be evaluated before you actually enter the GET, and if it returns false, it will prevent the GET from being edited.

In the example shown below, the user will not be able to enter the credit card number unless the **credit** variable is set true.

```
local fname := space(15), lname := space(15), credit := .f.
local cardno := space(20), custno := space(6)
@ 10, 20 say "First Name: " get fname
@ 11, 20 say "Last Name:  " get lname
@ 12, 20 say "Credit?     " get credit
@ 13, 20 say "Card Number:" get cardno when credit
@ 14, 20 say "Customer No:" get custno
read
```

The WHEN clause opens up a world of possibilities. Something as rudimentary as skipping a GET is really just the tip of the iceberg. The fun begins when you start calling functions from the WHEN clause. As with the VALID clause, all you need do is ensure that your WHEN clause evaluates to a logical value (which should be true (.T.) if you want the user to be able to enter that particular GET).

Listing 27.1 applies this simple principle to provide a message for each GET. Figure 27.1 shows this code in action.

Listing 27.1 Displaying messages with WHEN

```
function Main
memvar name, address, city
dbcreate('temp', { { 'name', 'C', 20, 0 } , ;
                   { 'address', 'C', 25, 0 } , ;
                   { 'city', 'C', 20, 0 } } )
use temp new
append blank
cls
name := temp->name
address := temp->address
city := temp->city
@ 10,0 get name    when FieldHelp(24, 1, "Please enter a name")
@ 11,0 get address when FieldHelp(24, 1,;
                             "Please enter an address")
@ 12,0 get city    when FieldHelp(24, 1, "Please enter a city")
read
replace temp->name with name, temp->address with address,;
        temp->city with city
return nil

function FieldHelp(row, col, msg)
@ row, col say padr(msg, 50)
return .t.
```

Figure 27.1 GET using WHEN clause to display a message

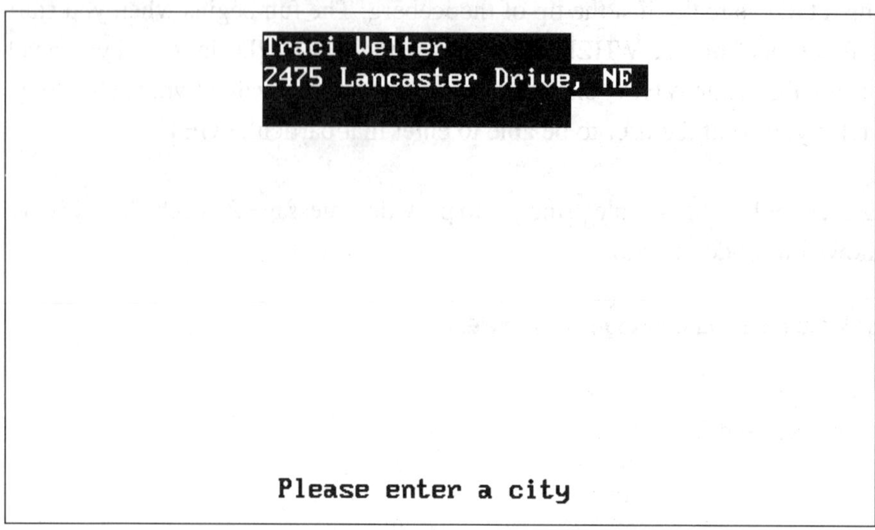

If you are using the Grumpfish Library, you probably already know about its APICK() function. APICK() makes selection from an array of available choices a breeze. Coupled with WHEN, APICK() becomes a devastating tool by which you let the user pick a value instead of typing it in. Listing 27.2 demonstrates this principle.

Listing 27.2 Displaying pop-up picklists with WHEN

```
function Main
local days := { "Monday", "Tuesday", "Wednesday", "Thursday",;
                "Friday"}
local mday := space(9), mmonth := space(9)
local months := {"January","February", "March", "April", "May",;
                "June","July","August", "September", "October",;
                "November", "December" }
cls
@ 0, 10 say "Day:  " get mday when ;
      ! empty(mday := days[ max(apick(9, 34, 15, 44, days), 1) ])
@ 1, 10 say "Month:" get mmonth when ;
      ! empty(mmonth := ;
              months[ max(apick(8, 34, 16, 44, months), 1) ] )
read
```

If you are not using Grumpfish Library, feel free to substitute ACHOICE() for APICK(). However, you may instead want to write your own user-defined function that calls ACHOICE() and handles all screen cleanup (as does APICK()). Figure 27.2 shows this code in action.

Figure 27.2 GET using WHEN to call a pop-up picklist

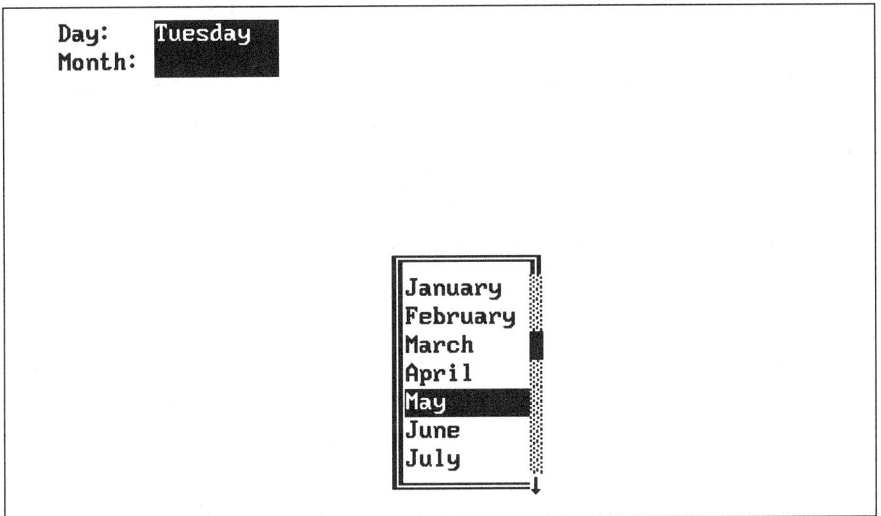

Note the careful construction of the WHEN clause. APICK() returns a numeric value that corresponds to the array element that was selected. If the user pressed the Esc key to leave APICK(), it will return 0. Because Clipper arrays are one-based rather than zero-based, a reference to array element 0 is a one-way ticket to DOS. Therefore, this possibility must be eliminated with the MAX() function, which in effect ensures that the minimum array element referred to will be one. We then assign the value of the appropriate array element to the variable and test it for emptiness. Since it will not be empty, the WHEN clause will return True, thus permitting the user to further edit the GET if required.

GETLIST

If you are compiling your Clipper 5 programs with the **/w** compiler option we discussed in Chapter 1, you have undoubtedly already made the acquaintance of the omnipresent GETLIST. This is a public array that Clipper 5 utilizes to maintain compatibility with earlier versions of Clipper. Whenever a @..GET command is issued, the preprocessor translates it into logic which creates a new GET object and adds it to the GETLIST array. When we issue the subsequent READ command, the contents of GETLIST are passed to the Clipper READMODAL() function, which then initiates the traditional full-screen edit. Thus, each GET object is an element in the GETLIST array, and the Clipper GET system moves between them as we press navigation keys (which you can completely redefine if you wish). When the READ process ends (i.e., when READMODAL() transfers control back to the calling program), the GETLIST array is cleaned out for next time (unless you specified the READ SAVE option).

Nested READs

Having access to the GETLIST array means that you will never again suffer a migraine trying to finesse nested READs. One easy way to nest READs is to declare a GETLIST array as **local** to each procedure that issues a READ command.

The source code in Listing 27.3 demonstrates this logic by nesting a READ in a VALID clause.

Listing 27.3 Example of nested READ

```
memvar getlist // to squelch compiler warnings

function Main
local x := 0, mdate := date() + 14
cls
@ 10, 10 say "Balance: " get x picture '#####.##' valid Credit(@x)
@ 11, 10 say "Due date:" get mdate
read
return nil

function Credit(balance)
local x := 0, getlist := {}, oldscrn := savescreen(10, 40, 10, 64)
```

```
@ 10, 40 say "Credit (if any):" get x picture '#####.##'
read
balance -= x          // subtract credit from original balance
restscreen(10, 40, 10, 64, oldscrn)
return .t.
```

You should already have a good grasp on the concept of file-wide statics (previously discussed in Chapter 6, "Variable Scoping", and Chapter 12, "Program Design").

The functions shown in Listing 27.4 make use of a file-wide static array (or "stack") to save and restore GETs. These are also included on the source code diskette for this book.

Listing 27.4 Stack-based functions to save/restore GETs

```
/* GFGETS.PRG — stack-based functions to save/restore GETs */
static getstack_ := {}
memvar getlist

// GFSaveGets(): save current gets
function GFSaveGets()
aadd(getstack_, getlist)
getlist := {}   /* clear out current gets */
return len(getstack_)

// GFRestGets(): restore last-saved gets
function GFRestGets(ele)
/* use LIFO (last item in array) if no parameter was passed */
ele := if(ele == nil, len(getstack_), ele)
/* preclude empty array */
if len(getstack_) > 0
  /* pull GETs from last element in array */
  getlist := getstack_[ele]
  /* truncate length of array only if using LIFO, i.e.,
     no param passed)*/
  if ele == len(getstack_) .and. pcount() == 0
     asize(getstack_, len(getstack_) - 1)
  endif
endif
return nil
```

These functions are most useful if you want to construct multi-screen data entry scenarios. They allow you to push and pop active GETs at will.

Notice that the getstack array will only be truncated if we are using Last In First Out (LIFO). If you use random access with GFRestGets() by passing a parameter, the function will assume that you do not want to lop off the last set of GETs. (Imagine the chaos if you restored the first set of GETs, and the last set got trashed! Not a pretty picture.)

The code shown in Listing 27.5 demonstrates this by establishing three parallel sets of GETs, pushing each of those onto our GET stack with GFSaveGets(), and popping them off in random order with GFRestGets().

Listing 27.5 Parallel GETs with stack-based functions

```
memvar getlist

function SetsOGets
local x := { 1, 2, 3, 4, 5, 6, 7, 8, 9}, y, z
for z := 1 to 3
   for y := 1 to 3
      @ y * 2, 0 get x[(z - 1) * 3 + y]
   next
   GFSaveGets()
next
cls

GFRestGets(2)
ReGet()
read

GFRestGets(1)
ReGet()
read

GFRestGets(3)
ReGet()
read
```

```
aeval(x, { | a | qout(a) } )
return nil

//  ReGet(): redisplay all active GETs
static function ReGet
aeval(getlist, { | get | get:display() } )
return nil
```

If you are scratching your head about that ReGet() function, it is used to redisplay all active GETs. It makes use of the Display() method, which we will discuss in more detail later.

Creating GET objects

There are two ways to create Clipper 5 GET objects. The first and most common method is to let the preprocessor do the work for you in the form of the @..GET command. The second is to use the Clipper GETNEW() function.

@..GET

The best way to fully understand this critical process is to review the syntax of the @..GET user-defined command.

```
/* STD.CH */
#command @ <row>, <col> GET <var> [PICTURE <pic>];
                [VALID <valid>] [WHEN <when>] =>      ;
              SetPos( <row>, <col>) ; ;
              aadd(GetList, _GET_( <var>, <(var)>, <pic>, ;
             <{valid}>, <{when}>) )
```

Now let's write a short sample program that calls this command. We can then examine each clause of the @..GET command to see how the preprocessor acts upon it. If you are not already familiar with the various preprocessor result-markers and their actions, now would be a good time for you to brush up on them. (See Chapter 7, "The Preprocessor.")

Original (PRG)

```
@ 20,0 get x picture '###' valid ! empty(x) when y > 5
```

Preprocessed (PPO)

```
SetPos(20, 0) ; ;
aadd(GetList, _GET_(x, "x", "###", {|| ! empty(x)}, {|| y > 5}) )
```

First, the row and column positions are output using the normal result-marker into a call to the SetPos() function. This will position the cursor at row 20, column 0. This is crucial because the current cursor position will be used to determine the position of the GET object at the instant it is created. Therefore, the cursor must be moved to the desired position before the GET object is created.

The preprocessor then acts upon all of the other clauses in order to create a call to the internal Clipper function _GET_(). First, the name of the GET variable is output twice, once with the normal result-marker and again with the smart stringify result-marker:

```
_GET_( x, "x", ...)
```

The PICTURE clause is output with the normal result-marker since it is already in the form of a character string:

```
_GET_(x, "x", "###", ...)
```

The VALID (post-validation) clause is output with the blockify result-marker, because the GET system will expect this to be in the form of a code block so that it can evaluate it if necessary.

```
_GET_(x, "x", "###", {|| ! empty(x)}, ...)
```

Finally, the WHEN (pre-validation) clause is output with the blockify result-marker. Like the VALID clause, the GET system expects this to be in the form of a code block so that it can evaluate it if necessary.

```
_GET_(x, "x", "###", {|| ! empty(x)}, {|| y > 5})
```

The final step is to add this new GET object to the end of the GETLIST array, and thus increase GETLIST's length by one element.

Something that's not readily obvious here is that _GET_() also creates a code block that will be used to manipulate the variable. GET objects change the values of the variables by evaluating this code block, rather than manipulating the variables directly. (An example of the structure of such a code block can be found below under the discussion of the block instance variable.)

As with the current cursor position, the current color setting is taken into account when creating a GET object. The current unselected and enhanced color settings will be used when the GET object is unselected and selected, respectively. For example, if this is our current color setting:

```
setcolor("w/n, +w/r, , , w/b")
```

the GET object will be displayed in white on blue when unselected and high white on red when selected. You can also change the colorSpec instance variable tied to the GET object after it is created. With the 5.01 release of Clipper, you can use the optional COLOR clause to change colorSpec at the same time that the GET object is created (see below). We will discuss this in greater detail below.

Warning: _GET_() should never be called directly! All Clipper functions that begin with an underscore are for internal use only, and are always subject to change. If you need to create a GET object without using @..GET, use GETNEW().

New Clipper 5.01 @..GET clauses

As mentioned above, you can now specify a color for the GET using the optional COLOR clause. If you wish to use this clause, your color setting should be in the form of <standard>,<enhanced>. The <enhanced> color will be used when the GET is highlighted, and the <standard> color will be used when it is not. For example, if you wanted your GET to be white on red when highlighted, and white on blue when not highlighted, you could use syntax such as the following:

```
@ 20,0 get x color "w/b,w/r"
```

You can use the SEND clause to "send" methods to GET objects. For example, the STD.CH header file uses SEND as an intermediate step for implementing the @..GET..COLOR clause, as shown in Listing 27.6:

Listing 27.6 Extract from STD. CH @ ..GET..COLOR clause using SEND

First Step:

```
#command @ <row>, <col> GET <var>                ;
                        [<clauses,...>]          ;
                        COLOR <color>            ;
                        [<moreClauses,...>]    ; ;
      => @ <row>, <col> GET <var>                ;
                        [<clauses>]              ;
                        SEND colorDisp( <color>) ;
                        [<moreClauses>]
```

Second Step:

```
#command @ <row>, <col> GET <var>                ;
                        [PICTURE <pic>]          ;
                        [VALID <valid>]          ;
                        [WHEN <when>]            ;
                        [SEND <msg>]           ; ;
                     => SetPos( <row>, <col> ) ; ;
   aadd(GetList, ;
   _GET_( <var>, <(var)>, <pic>, <{valid}>, <{when}> ) ) ;
      [; atail(GetList):<msg>]
```

Do not feel compelled to use this if you do not fully understand its significance. Just know that it is there if/when you need it.

GETNEW()

GETNEW() creates a GET object without using the @..GET command. The syntax for GETNEW() is similar, but not identical, to what the preprocessor sends to the internal _GET_() function:

```
GetNew([<row>], [<column>], [<block>], [<var>],;
                    [<picture>], [<color>])
```

<row> and **<column>** are numeric expressions that represent the starting row and column position of the GET on the screen.

<block> is a "get..set" code block for the variable to be gotten. As mentioned above, the value of the variable will be manipulated via this code block.

<var> is a character expression representing the name of the GET variable. (At press time, this parameter is not in the Clipper documentation.)

<picture> is a character expression representing the PICTURE clause to use for the GET. If you do not pass this, it will be initialized to nil.

<color> is a character expression representing the color setting to use for the GET. If you do not pass this, the current unselected and enhanced color settings will be used as previously mentioned.

All of these parameters are optional. You may supply any or all of them to GETNEW(), or you may wait to assign them later.

The major differences between GETNEW() and _GET_() are:

GETNEW()	Lets you pass the color setting as a parameter, whereas _GET_() merely uses the current color setting.
GET()	Creates the code block for the GET variable automatically, and GETNEW() does not.

GET() accepts the code blocks for pre-validation (WHEN) and post-validation (VALID) as parameters. If you want to use these with a GET object created by GETNEW(), you must manipulate the instance variables after the fact.

However, once again we urge you never to call _GET_() directly! These differences are listed for illustrative purposes only.

Instance variables

Occasionally you will need to peek into the GET object. For example, is there a WHEN (pre-validation) or VALID (post-validation) clause tied to a specific GET? Do you want to change the PICTURE clause, COLOR setting, or even the row and column position of a GET? For the answers to these, and many other questions, you would refer to an Exported Instance Variable. Instance variables can be considered as global settings that each GET object lugs around. They may be polled as often as necessary to retrieve their values.

Table 27.1 lists all instance variables associated with GET objects. The values of instance variables marked by an asterisk ("*") can be re-assigned.

Table 27.1 GET Instance Variables

Name	*Purpose*	*Type*
badDate	Checks editing buffer for an invalid date	L
block*	Code block to associate GET with a variable	B
buffer*	Character string that contains the editing buffer	C
cargo*	User-definable variable (a real jumping-off point!)	?
changed	Checks if Get:buffer was changed	L
col*	GET column number	N
colorSpec*	Color for a GET	C
decPos	Decimal point position within the editing buffer	N
exitState*	Tracks the means by which a specified GET was exited	N
hasFocus	Is this GET highlighted? (does it have "input focus"?)	L
name*	GET variable name	C
original	Character string containing original value of the GET	C
picture*	PICTURE string	C
pos*	Current cursor position within the editing buffer	N
postBlock*	Code block to validate a newly entered value (VALID)	B

Name	*Purpose*	*Type*
preBlock*	Code block to decide if editing is permitted (WHEN)	B
reader*	Custom codeblock that determines how GET is edited	B
rejected	Was last insert/overStrike character rejected?	L
row*	GET row number	N
subscript	Returns subscript(s) if GET variable is an array element	A
type	GET variable data type	C
typeOut	Did user try to move cursor out of editing buffer?	L

C = character
N = numeric
L = logical
B = code block
A = array

To refer to any of these instance variables, you first specify the GET object in question, followed by a colon and the instance variable. We will use **g:** as the GET object identifier.

g:badDate

This instance variable contains a logical value. Its value will be false (.F.) unless you are GETting a date variable and have entered an invalid date in the editing buffer.

g:block (assignable)

This is the retrieval/assignment code block that the GET object uses as an intermediary to manipulate the value of the variable. It is created automatically by the internal Clipper _GET_() function, and you must create it yourself if you are using GETNEW(). The following example provides a good template for such a code block.

```
local x := space(20)
devpos(20, 10)
theget := getnew(row(),col(),;
                  { | val | if(pcount() > 0, x := val,x) })
```

Your code block must be constructed to accept an argument (in this case, **val**). It then must test whether or not the argument was passed using either PCOUNT() > 0 or **val** = NIL. If the argument is passed, its value should be assigned to the GET variable. If not, use the value of the GET variable.

Therefore, the code block can be EVALuated with or without arguments to either assign or retrieve, respectively, the value of the GET.

```
EVAL(block)      // retrieve value of GET variable
EVAL(block, 5)  // assign 5 to GET variable
```

g:buffer

As you edit a GET, you are making changes neither to the GET variable nor the code block. Rather, you are changing the editing buffer, which is a character string no matter what type of variable you are GETting. The type conversion is done internally at the time that the buffer contents are assigned to the GET variable with the Assign() method (which we will discuss below).

g:cargo (assignable)

This is an entirely user-defined instance variable. It may be used for various and sundry things, such as a message to be displayed whenever the GET is highlighted. (In fact, we will demonstrate this usage a bit later in this chapter.)

The code snippets shown in Listing 27.7 assign a message to **g:cargo**.

Listing 27.7 Storing messages in g:cargo

```
local x := date()
@ 20, 0 get x
getlist[1]:cargo := "Enter employee's birthdate"
read
```

As you become more bold and creative with the GET objects and GETSYS, you will discover that the best thing to put in **g:cargo** is an array, because it can then hold multiple values and thus be used for multiple purposes.

g:changed

This instance variable contains a logical value based on whether the GET editing buffer has been changed. Its value will be true if the buffer has been changed, or false if it has not.

g:col (assignable)

This contains a numeric that represents the column at which the GET will be displayed on the screen. When a GET object is created with @..GET the current screen column position is used to initialize this instance variable. You may change it after the fact, as the following code fragment demonstrates.

```
local x := 0
@ 20,10 get x          //  initially displays GET at @ 20,10
getlist[1]:col := 50 // GET will be redisplayed at @ 20,50
read
```

The code shown in Listing 27.8 uses the **g:col** instance variable to move each GET into the Debit or Credit column, dependent upon its value. Figure 27.3 shows sample output from this code.

Listing 27.8 Using g:col instance variable to move GETs

```
function Main
local a := { 0, 0, 0, 0, 0 }
cls
@ 8, 30 say "Debits"
@ 8, 50 say "Credits"
@ 10,10 get a[1] valid DebitCredit()
@ 11,10 get a[2] valid DebitCredit()
@ 12,10 get a[3] valid DebitCredit()
@ 13,10 get a[4] valid DebitCredit()
@ 14,10 get a[5] valid DebitCredit()
read
return nil

function DebitCredit
if getactive():varGet() > 0
   getactive():col := 50
```

```
else
   getactive():col := 30
endif
return .t.
```

Figure 27.3 Changing g:col instance variable

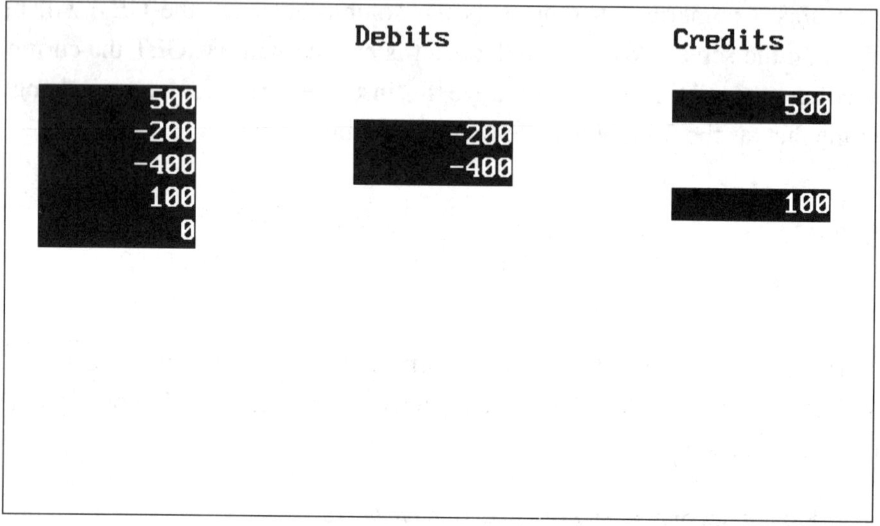

g:colorSpec (assignable)

This instance variable is a character string that dictates the color in which the GET will be displayed. The format for **g:colorSpec** is <unselected>,<selected>. When a GET object is created with @..GET, the current unselected and enhanced color settings are concatenated and used to initialize **g:colorSpec**. However, you may change it after the fact.

The sample code in Listing 27.9 illustrates how you could change the color of a GET within a VALID clause using the **g:colorSpec** instance variable. This principle could be used to call special attention to certain pieces of data.

Listing 27.9 Changing GET color in VALID clause

```
function ColorGet()
local x := 0
setcolor("w/n, w/r, , , w/b")
@ 20,10 get x valid Test()
? getlist[1]:colorSpec    // W/B,W/R
read
return nil

static function Test()
local ret_val := .t.
if getactive():varGet() == 0
   // make GET white on cyan when highlighted,
   // black on cyan when not
   getactive():colorDisp("N/BG, +W/BG")
   ret_val := .f.
endif
return ret_val
```

g:decPos

This instance variable contains a numeric value representing the position of the decimal point in the GET buffer. In the following code fragment **g:decPos** will have a value of 4.

```
local x := 0
@ 20,0 get x picture '###.##'
read
```

g:exitState (assignable)

This instance variable was added with the 5.01 release. It contains a numeric value that indicates how a GET was exited. It is used extensively within GETSYS.PRG.

Table 27.2 lists the possible **g:exitState** values, along with their manifest constants and the key(s) responsible for setting these values. Note that these are contained in the GETEXIT.CH header file. Always refer to the manifest constants rather than the numeric values, because the numerics are subject to change.

Table 27.2 g:exitState values

Value	*Manifest Constant contained in GETEXIT.CH*	*Responsible Key(s)*
0	GE_NOEXIT	Ha ha! There is no exit!!!
1	GE_UP	UpArrow
2	GE_DOWN	DnArrow
3	GE_TOP	Ctrl-Home
4	GE_BOTTOM	Ctrl-End
5	GE_ENTER	Enter
6	GE_WRITE	PgUp, PgDn, Ctrl-W
7	GE_ESCAPE	Esc
8	GE_WHEN	(WHEN clause tested False)

When you begin constructing your alternate GetReader() functions, remember to #include “getexit.ch” because you will need it.

g:hasFocus

This instance variable contains a logical value. It will be true when the GET object is highlighted (has input focus), and false if it’s not. Input focus is assigned via the **g:setFocus()** method, which is called from within GetReader(). The following code fragment demonstrates how **g:hasFocus** changes value.

```
local x := 0
@ 20,10 get x
? getlist[1]:hasFocus // .F.
inkey(0)
getlist[1]:setFocus()
? getlist[1]:hasFocus // .T.
```

g:name (assignable)

This is a character string containing the name of the GET variable. It is initialized automatically when creating GET objects with @..GET, and must be passed as a parameter to GETNEW(). The name is used for identification purposes. It is assigned to READVAR() when the GET is given input focus.

Before you get any crazy ideas in that head of yours, you should know that changing the name of a GET variable will not affect which variable is manipulated. The previously-created code block attached to the GET object has the last word in this matter. The following fragment demonstrates this principle — although the **g:name** instance variable is changed to **y**, the variable that you manipulate will still be **x**. Press F1 while in the GET to test the current value of READVAR().

```
function Main
local x := 0, y := 5
set key 28 to TestReadVar
@ 20,10 get x
getlist[1]:name := 'y'
read
? x      // whatever you changed it to
? y      // still 5
return nil

function TestReadVar
@ 0,0 say "READVAR() := " + readvar()    // Y, not X
return nil
```

g:original

This instance variable is a character string that contains a copy of the original value of the GET buffer. If necessary, the contents of the GET buffer can be reset to their original contents with the Undo() method. This occurs in the GetApplyKey() function of GETSYS.PRG when you press Esc to exit a GET.

```
/* excerpted from GetApplyKey() */
   case (key == K_ESC )
   if (Set(_SET_ESCAPE) )
      get:undo()
      get:exitState := GE_ESCAPE
   endif
```

g:picture (assignable)

This is a character string that specifies which PICTURE clause, if any, to use for displaying the GET buffer. It will be assigned if you specify a PICTURE clause with @..GET or if you pass the appropriate parameter to GETNEW(). If not assigned, it will hold the value of NIL. You may always change it after the fact, as the following fragment demonstrates. Note that because the PICTURE clause is shortened from the default nine characters for numerics, the first GET must be erased to avoid screen sloppiness.

```
local x := 0
@ 20,10 get x
? getlist[1]:picture        // NIL
inkey(0)
scroll(20, 10, 20, 20, 0)  // clear old GET
getlist[1]:picture := '###.##'
read
```

g:pos (assignable)

This instance variable contains a numeric value representing the current cursor position in the editing buffer. The following example allows you to test this for yourself by pressing F1 while in the GET.

```
local x := "Press F1 to see where you are"
set key 28 to TestPos
@ 20,0 get x
read
return nil

function TestPos
@ 0,0 say "Current cursor position: " + str(getlist[1]:pos)
return nil
```

The example shown in Listing 27.10 is a bit more ambitious. It allows you to insert a name in the GET at the current cursor position. Move the cursor to the comma position, then press F2 to pop up the picklist of names. After you have selected a name from the picklist, we rely upon the **g:right()** method to move the cursor to the right (in exact correspondence with the length of the name that was inserted). This ensures that the cursor will be restored to its original position prior to the insert.

Listing 27.9 Inserting data into a GET

```
function Main
local m_var := "Mr. , Director of Communications"
set key -1 to ShowFields
cls
@ 1, 20 get m_var
@ 2, 22 say "Press F2 to select from list of names"
read
? m_var
return nil

static function ShowFields(a, b, c)
local position := getactive():pos, val := getactive():varGet()
local names := { "Bayne", "Creagh", "Lief", "Yellick", "Welter" }
local ele := 0, xx, oldscrn := savescreen(9, 35, 15, 44)
@ 9, 35 to 15, 44
/* don't allow Esc, which would cause array access error */
do while ele == 0
   ele := achoice(10, 36, 14, 43, names)
enddo
/* drop selected name into GET at current position */
getactive():varPut(substr(val, 1, position - 1) + names[ele] + ;
                   substr(val, position))
/* move cursor to original location in GET buffer, based on
   length of the name we just inserted */
for xx := 1 to len(names[ele] )
   getactive():right()
next
restscreen(9, 35, 15, 44, oldscrn)
return nil
```

Figures 27.4 and 27.5 show the picklist of names, and the modified original GET, respectively.

Figure 27.4 Using g:pos instance variable to paste into a GET

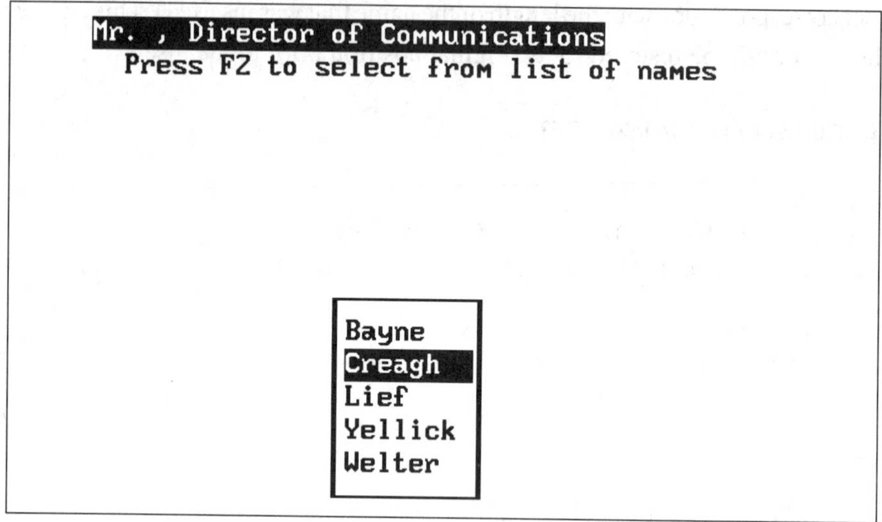

Figures 27.5 GET displaying selected name at g:pos

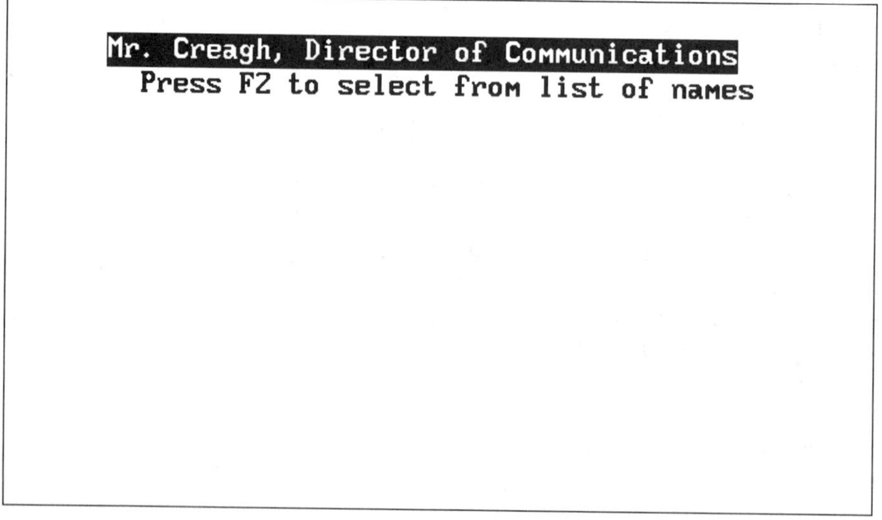

g:postBlock (assignable)

This contains a code block used to "post-validate" the entry of a get. If you specify a valid clause with @..GET, it will be converted to a code block and stored in the **g:postBlock** instance variable. If you do not use a VALID clause, **g:postBlock** will contain the valid of a NIL. After exiting a GET, GetPostValidate() tests **g:postBlock** to see if a post-validation clause has been specified, and if so, evaluates the code block (passing the current GET object as a parameter). You may change **g:postBlock** after the fact if you wish.

In the following example we initialize **g:postBlock** with the VALID clause. It will initially evaluate to true because **x** is greater than 50. But **g:postBlock** is then changed so that **x** will not satisfy its condition.

```
local x := 100
@ 20, 0 get x valid x > 50
? eval(getlist[1]:postBlock)    // .T.
inkey (0)
*/ change to the equilvalent of VALID x > 200 */
get list[1]:postBlock := { | | x > 200 */
? eval(getlist[1]:postBlock)    // .F.
inkey(0)
read
```

g:preBlock (assignable)

This instance variable is similar to **g:postBlock**, except that it is evaluated before you enter a GET instead of after you exit. If you specify a WHEN clause with @..GET, it will be converted to a code block and stored in **g:preBlock**. If you do not use a WHEN clause, **g:preBlock** will contain the value of NIL. Before you enter a GET, GetPreValidate() tests **g:preBlock** to see if a pre-validation clause exists, and if so, evaluates the code block to determine whether the GET can be entered (passing the current GET object as a parameter). As with **g:postBlock**, you may alter **g:preBlock** at will.

In the following example, **g:preBlock** begins life as a NIL (didn't we all?). We then change it to a condition that tests false, and thus the GET is bypassed when we enter READMODAL().

```
local x := 100, y := .f.
@ 20, 0 get x
@ 21, 0 get y
? getlist[1]:preBlock    // NIL
inkey(0)
/* change to the equivalent of WHEN y */
getlist[1]:preBlock := { | | y }
? eval(getlist[1]:preBlock)    // .F.
inkey(0)
read
```

g:reader (assignable)

This instance variable was added with release 5.01. You can use it to implement special READ behaviors for any GET.

If **g:reader** contains a code block, READMODAL() will evaluate that block in order to read the GET (the GET object is passed as a parameter to the block). The block may in turn call any desired function to provide custom editing of the GET. If **g:reader** does not contain a code block, READMODAL() uses a default READ procedure for the GET.

g:Reader allows individual GETs to have specialized READ behaviors without requiring you to modify the standard READMODAL() function. This maintains compatibility for GETs which are to be handled in the customary fashion, as well as eliminating potential conflicts between different extensions to the GET/READ system.

Later in this chapter we will present an alternative GetReader() function that you can address via the **g:reader** instance variable. We will also discuss all of the supporting functions contained in GETSYS.PRG. These will assist you in creating your own alternate GET reading mechanisms.

g:rejected

This contains a logical value that indicates whether the last character specified by either the **g:insert()** or **g:overstrike()** method actually went into the editing buffer.

It will contain false if the character was placed into the buffer, or true if it was rejected. Any subsequent text entry message resets this instance variable.

g:row (assignable)

The **g:row** instance variable contains a numeric that represents the row at which the GET will be displayed on the screen. When a GET object is created with @..GET, the current screen row position is used to initialize this instance variable. You may change it at any time, as shown in the following code fragment.

```
local x := 0
@ 20,10 get x           //  initially displays GET at @ 20,10
getlist[1]:row := 11  // GET will be redisplayed at @ 11,10
read
```

g:subscript

This instance variable (added with release 5.01) rectifies a long-standing problem with Clipper, namely the inability to identify which array element you were GETting. This caused great problems when you were attempting to tie context-specific help screens to each GET. If you are GETing an array element, **g:subscript** will contain an array of numeric values. This array will contain one element for each necessary subscript. (Please see the example below for more illumination.) If the GET is not an array element, **g:subscript** will contain NIL.

The following snippet demonstrates the three possible return values of the **g:subscript** instance variable.

```
local x := 0, y := { 1, 2, 3 }, z := { { 1, 2 }, { 3, 4} }
cls
@ 10, 10 get x
@ 11, 10 get y[3]
@ 12, 10 get z[1, 2]
? getlist[1]:subscript      // nil
? getlist[2]:subscript[1]   // 3
? getlist[3]:subscript[1]   // 1
? getlist[3]:subscript[2]   // 2
inkey(0)
read
```

The example below uses **g:subscript** to determine which GET you are on, and displays a help message accordingly. Although these help messages are hard-coded, this principle can easily be applied to a data-driven context-specific help system.

```
function Main
local a := {padr("John",20),padr("Doe",20),;
            padr("123 Main Street",30), ;
            padr("Anytown", 25), "MD", padr("21157", 10) }
set key 28 to HelpMe
cls
@ 10,0 get a[1]
@ 11,0 get a[2]
@ 12,0 get a[3]
@ 13,0 get a[4]
@ 14,0 get a[5]
read
return nil

static function HelpMe(p, l, v)
local helpmsg := {"first name","last name",;
                  "address","city","state","zip"}
if ! empty(getactive():subscript)
   @ maxrow(), 0 say "This is the " +
                     helpmsg[ getactive():subscript[1] ] + ;
                     "... press a key"
   inkey(0)
   scroll(maxrow(), 0, maxrow(), maxcol(), 0)
endif
return nil
```

g:type

This instance variable is a character string denoting the type of the GET variable. This information can be useful to know if you want to act upon certain keypresses only for certain data types. For example, if you were to redefine the plus and minus keys to increment and decrement a GET variable, this would only be appropriate to dates and numerics. You could therefore test **g:type** before attempting to increment a character string (with predictably disastrous results).

The sample shown in Listing 27.11 establishes four GET objects and allows you to test each one for **g:type** by pressing F1. The TestType() function calls the Clipper GETACTIVE() function, which returns the currently active GET object. (See below for an interesting alternative.)

Listing 27.11 Testing GET types

```
function Main
local w := "Press F1 to test type of each GET",x :=0, y:=.t.,
z:=date()
set key 28 to TestType
cls
@ 11, 0 get w
@ 12, 0 get x
@ 13, 0 get y
@ 14, 0 get z
read
return nil

function TestType(p, l, v)
local type := { "Character", "Numeric", "Date", "Logical" } ;
                    [at(getactive():type, "CNDL")]
@ 0,0 say "Current variable is " + padr(type, 9)
return nil
```

If someone put a gun to your head and forced you to recode this function without using GETACTIVE(), you could actually survive! Do you remember the **g:name** instance variable? Because it is always part of the GET object, it gets assigned to the READVAR() function. The return value of READVAR() is then always passed as the third parameter to hot-key procedures. Therefore, this parameter can be used to perform an ASCAN() against the GETLIST array. When a match is found for the **g:name** instance variable, then we have found the current GET object.

```
function TestType(p, l, v)
local ele := ascan(getlist, { | get | upper(get:name) == v } )
local type := { "Character", "Numeric", "Date", "Logical" } ;
                    [at(getlist[ele]:type, "CNDL")]
```

This is further proof that, no matter what the problem, Clipper 5 gives you several different ways to solve it.

g:typeout

This instance variable contains a logical value. It will contain true if you attempt to move the cursor out of the editing buffer or if there are no editable positions in the editing buffer. Its value will be reset by any of the methods that move the cursor in the GET buffer.

The source code in Listing 27.12 thoroughly demonstrates manipulation of instance variables. It initializes a GET object with the @..GET statement, which can be referred to directly because we know its position in the GETLIST array (namely, numero uno). The instance variables are then manipulated to change the screen position, color, PICTURE, and VALID clause.

Listing 27.12 Manipulating instance variables

```
function Main
memvar getlist
local x := "this is a test"
cls
@ 10,30 get x picture '@!'
devpos(16, 0)                // move cursor to row 16, column 0
qout("GET row:    ", getlist[1]:row)          // output: 10
qout("GET column:", getlist[1]:col)           // output: 30
qout("GET color:", getlist[1]:colorSpec)      // output: N/W,N/W
qout("VALID clause:   ", getlist[1]:postBlock) // output: nil
qout("PICTURE clause:", getlist[1]:picture)   // output: @!
qout()
qout('***Press any key to continue this example***')
inkey(0)
getlist[1]:row -= 5    /* change row position to 5 */
getlist[1]:col -= 20   /* change column position to 10 */
/* make GET white on blue when highlighted, white on red when not
*/
getlist[1]:colorSpec := "+W/R, +W/B"
/* add to the PICTURE clause */
```

```
getlist[1]:picture += "@K"
/* attach a VALID clause on-the-fly to prevent an empty field */
getlist[1]:postBlock := { | val | ! empty(val) }
read
```

Now you should have a better understanding of instance variables, so let's review three different ways to create the same GET object (shown in Listing 27.13).

Listing 27.13 Creating GET objects

```
/* this is common to all three examples */
local x := space(20), theget

// first example: GETNEW with all applicable parameters
theget := getnew(20, 10, { | val | if(pcount() > 0, ;
                 x := val, x) }, "x", "@!", "N/BG, +W/BG")
readmodal( {theget} )   // must be passed as an array!

// second example: GETNEW with no parameters - this also
// reinforces the relationship between the parameters
// shown above and the instance variables.
theget := getnew()
theget:row := 20
theget:col := 10
theget:block := { | val | if(pcount() > 0, x := val, x) }
theget:name := "x"
theget:picture := "@!"
theget:colorSpec := "N/BG, +W/BG"
readmodal({theget} )  // again, must be passed as an array!

// third example: @..GET
@ 20, 10 get x picture '@!' color "N/BG, +W/BG"
read
```

After looking at the code involved, you might wonder why you would ever want to use GETNEW() over @..GET. There are two good situations. First, if you want absolute control over when the GET is actually displayed, you must use GETNEW() instead of @..GET. The second situation would be in conjunction with TBrowse.

Listing 27.14 demonstrates code for a generic database browser. A multi-dimensional array is created to hold customary keypresses and corresponding code blocks. Each of the keypresses triggers the expected action, except for Enter which is reserved for editing fields via the function GrabThatVar().

Listing 27.14 GETNEW() and TBrowse

```
#include "inkey.ch"

function main
local x, browse := TBrowseDB(3, 0, 15, 79), column, key, ele
local browseaction := { { K_LEFT, { | | browse:left() } } , ;
                      { K_RIGHT, { | | browse:right() } } , ;
                      { K_UP, { | | browse:up() } } , ;
                      { K_DOWN, { | | browse:down() } } , ;
                      { K_HOME, { | | browse:home() } } , ;
                      { K_END, { | | browse:end() } } , ;
                      { K_PGUP, { | | browse:pageUp() } } , ;
                      { K_PGDN, { | | browse:pageDown() } } , ;
                      { K_CTRL_LEFT, { | | browse:panLeft() } } , ;
                      { K_CTRL_RIGHT, { | | browse:panRight() } }, ;
                      { K_CTRL_HOME, { | | browse:panHome() } } , ;
                      { K_CTRL_END, { | | browse:panEnd() } } , ;
                      { K_CTRL_PGUP, { | | browse:goTop() } } , ;
                      { K_CTRL_PGDN, { | | browse:goBottom() } } }
setcursor(0)
use articles new
for x := 1 to fcount()
   column := TBColumnNew(field(x),;
                         fieldwblock(field(x), select()))
   browse:AddColumn(column)
next
do while key != K_ESC
   dispbegin()
   do while ! browse:stabilize() .and. (key := inkey() ) == 0
   enddo
   dispend()
```

```
   if browse:stable
      key := inkey(0)
   endif
   if key == K_ENTER and browse:stable
   GrabThatVar(browse)
   elseif (ele := ascan(browseaction, { | a | key == a[1] }) ) > 0
      eval(browseaction[ele, 2])
   endif
enddo
return nil

function GrabThatVar(b)
// determine current column object out of the browse object
local column := b:getColumn(b:colPos), mget,;
      oldcurs := setcursor(2)
// create a corresponding GET
mget := getnew(row(), col(), column:block, column:heading, ;
               b:colorSpec)
readmodal({mget} )  // must pass as an array!
setcursor(oldcurs)   // restore previous cursor
b:refreshCurrent()
return nil
```

As mentioned earlier, GETNEW() requires that you create the code block corresponding to the GET variable. GrabThatVar() does this by first working backwards from the TBrowse object to determine the current column. This is easy by polling the TBrowse **b:colPos** instance variable, and then passing that result to the TBrowse **b:getColumn** method. This leaves us with a TBrowse column object, which as you should remember from Chapter 26, has a code block attached to it telling it what to display. This code block will serve as the basis for our new GET object.

IMPORTANT NOTE: If you want to give your user the ability to edit cells on-the-fly in this manner, be sure to load your TBrowse columns with retrieval/assignment code blocks. The Clipper FIELDBLOCK() and FIELDWBLOCK() functions are your best choice. If you have a simple code block such as "{| |customer->fname}" you will NOT be able to properly create a GET object from it!

Once the GET object is in hand, it is passed (as an element in a literal array) to READMODAL(). Are you wondering why we did not simply issue a READ command? Have a look and the answer should be obvious.

```
/* from STD.CH */
#command READ     => ;
                ReadModal(GetList) ; GetList := {}
```

READ is predefined to pass GETLIST as a parameter. Because GETLIST is not being used in this situation, this would do no good at all. This also demonstrates that you do not always have to pass GETLIST to READMODAL(). You can pass any array containing one or more GET objects, which is why **mget** had to be passed as an element in an array. If **mget** was passed by itself (as opposed to being an element in an array), READMODAL() would pout and sulk.

Methods

GET objects are created and then passed to READMODAL(), which processes them using various *methods*. (For simplicity you can consider methods to be functions that are tied to GET objects.) These methods handle everything from moving the cursor within a GET to highlighting and unhighlighting GETs. (By the way, the acts of highlighting and unhighlighting a GET are known in Clipper 5-speak as "setting focus" and "killing focus," respectively.)

Table 27.3 lists methods that change the status of the GET object.

Table 27.3 GET status methods

Name	*Purpose*
assign()	Assigns editing buffer contents to GET variable
colorDisp()	Changes GET color and redisplays GET on screen
display()	Displays GETon the screen
killFocus()	De-highlights GET object
reset()	Resets internal state information of the GET

setFocus()	Highlights (gives input focus to) GET object
undo()	Sets the GET variable back to **g:original**
updateBuffer()	Updates editing buffer and redisplays the GET
varGet()	Returns the current value of the GET variable
varPut()	Sets the GET variable to the passed value

Table 27.4 lists methods that move the cursor within the get:buffer.

Table 27.4 GET cursor methods

Name	*Purpose*
end()	Move cursor to rightmost position in GET
home()	Move cursor to leftmost position in GET
left()	Move cursor left one character
right()	Move cursor right one character
toDecPos()	Move cursor to immediate right of decimal position (**g:decPos**)
wordLeft()	Move cursor left one word
wordRight()	Move cursor right one word

Table 27.5 lists methods used for editing the **g:buffer**.

Table 27.5 GET editing methods

Name	*Purpose*
backspace()	Moves cursor left and deletes one character
delLeft()	Deletes character to the left of the cursor
delRight()	Deletes character to the right of the cursor
delWordLeft()	Deletes word to the left of the cursor
delWordRight()	Deletes word to the right of the cursor
insert()	Inserts characters into the editing buffer
overStrike()	Overwrites characters in the editing buffer

To refer to any of these methods, you specify the GET object in question, followed by a colon and the method. For example, the following code would highlight the get object, i.e. "g", and move the cursor to the rightmost position within it:

```
g:setfocus()
g:end()
```

The best way to learn about each of these methods is to carefully scrutinize the source code in GETSYS.PRG.

g:colorDisp() note: This method was added with the 5.01 release of Clipper. It changes a GET object's colors and redisplays it. It is functionally equivalent to assigning the **g:colorSpec** instance variable and issuing the **g:display()** method. **g:colorDisp()** means that you can specify special colors for your GETs and have them take effect immediately (instead of only after the GET has been activated).

The optional @..GET..COLOR clause gets translated by the preprocessor into a call to **g:colorDisp()**, as shown below.

Original (.PRG):

```
@ 21,0 get y color "n/bg,+w/bg"
```

Preprocessed Output (PPO):

```
SetPos(21, 0) ; ;
aadd(GetList, _GET_(y, "y",,, ) ); ;
atail(GetList):colorDisp("n/bg,+w/bg")
```

Enhancements

During the preprocessor discussion in Chapter 7, much time was spent on the esoteric match-markers and result-markers, which are confusing. However, situations like the GET system will make that tribulation worthwhile. A thorough knowledge of the preprocessor's nuances are vital to performing the following feats of magic.

As already discussed, the @..GET command is preprocessed into several function calls that create the GET object and add it to the GETLIST array. This unprecedented degree of open architecture means that we can further benefit from the preprocessor to add enhancements to the @..GET command.

Structure of GETSYS.PRG

The 5.01 release of Clipper introduced a completely overhauled GETSYS.PRG. A number of the core functions used in the standard GET handler have been made **public** so that they can be used by your customized GET readers (which you could then implement via the **g:reader** instance variable described above). These functions are as follows:

GetReader(<oGet>)

GetReader() implements the standard read behavior for GETs. By default, ReadModal() uses the GetReader() function to read GET objects. GetReader() then calls other functions in GETSYS.PRG to do the work of reading the GET. Those functions are described below.

(Note that you can supersede GetReader() by assigning a code block to the **g:reader** instance variable, which was discussed above. This code block can be configured to call your own replacement GetReader()-type function. We will show an example of this below when we address the MESSAGE clause.)

GetApplyKey(<oGet>, <nKey>)

GetApplyKey() applies an INKEY() value to a GET object. Cursor movement keys change the cursor position within the GET, data keys are entered into the GET, and so on. If you want to implement special key handling (e.g., password or calculator-style data entry), you can write your own version of this function.

GetApplyKey() properly handles keystrokes that have "hot-key" procedures attached to them.

The GET object must be highlighted ("focused") before keys are applied.

Note: If CLEAR GETS is executed by a SET KEY, **g:exitState** will be set to GE_ESCAPE. In the standard system, this cancels the current GET without assigning the edited value and terminates ReadModal().

GetPreValidate(<oGet>)
GetPreValidate() validates the GET object for editing, including evaluating **g:preBlock** (WHEN clause) if present.

GetPreValidate() returns a logical return value: true (.T.) if the GET has been successfully pre-validated, or false (.F.) if not. The **g:exitState** instance variable is also set to reflect the outcome of the prevalidation:

Setting	*Description*
GE_NOEXIT	indicates pre-validation success, ok to edit
GE_WHEN	indicates pre-validation failure
GE_ESCAPE	indicates that a CLEAR GETS was issued

In the default GET system, a **g:exitState** of GE_ESCAPE cancels the current GET and terminates ReadModal().

GetPostValidate(<oGet>)
GetPostValidate() validates a GET after editing, including evaluating **g:postBlock** (VALID clause) if present. It returns a logical value indicating whether or not the GET has been successfully post-validated. If a CLEAR GETS is issued during post-validation, **g:exitState** is set to GE_ESCAPE and GetPostValidate() returns true (.t.).

GetDoSetKey(<oGet>)
This function executes a SET KEY block, preserving the context of the passed GET object. The procedure name and line number passed to the SET KEY block are based on the most recent call to ReadModal().

@..GET..MESSAGE

You have already seen how to tie messages to each GET with the WHEN clause and the **g:cargo** instance variable. The latter method is more succinct and more in line with the intended purpose of the WHEN clause (namely, pre-validation). However, when we showed this earlier, we had to manipulate the **g:cargo** instance variable directly, which was hardly an elegant solution. The preprocessor will make this much cleaner.

```
#xcommand @ <row>, <col> GET <var> [PICTURE <pic>] ;
         [VALID <valid>] [WHEN <when>] ;
         [MESSAGE <message>] => ;
            SetPos( <row>, <col>) ; ;
            aadd(GetList, _GET_( <var>, <(var)>, <pic>, ;
                  <{valid}>, <{when}>) ) ; ;
            Atail(getlist):reader := { | g | MyReader(g) } ;
            [; Atail(getlist):cargo := <message> ]
```

We have added two additional statements to this user-defined command. The first assigns the **g:reader** instance variable to call an alternate GetReader() function. This is necessary because GetReader() is where you would want to insert the code to display the messages. However, rather than hack up Computer Associates' GetReader(), you should write your own version. That's where the reader instance variable comes into play.

The ATAIL() function (new with 5.01) refers to the last element in an array. Because this GET was just added to the GETLIST array, ATAIL() will be pointing to the new GET.

The second statement, which gets preprocessed only if you actually specify the MESSAGE clause, actually assigns the message to the **g:cargo** instance variable.

Listing 27.15 demonstrates the @..MESSAGE clause in action. It includes MyReader(), which serves as an alternative to the standard GetReader() function.

Listing 27.15 @..MESSAGE with g:cargo/g:reader instance variables

```
#xcommand @ <row>, <col> GET <var> [PICTURE <pic>] ;
         [VALID <valid>] [WHEN <when>] ;
         [MESSAGE <message>] => ;
            SetPos( <row>, <col>) ; ;
            aadd(GetList, _GET_( <var>, <(var)>, <pic>, ;
                  <{valid}>, <{when}>) ) ; ;
            atail(getlist):reader := { | g | MyReader(g) } ;
            [; atail(getlist):cargo := <message> ]

#include "getexit.ch"

function Test
local x := 0, y := 1, getlist := {}
set message to maxrow()
cls
@ 20,0 get x message "This is the first GET"
@ 21,0 get y
read
return nil

/*
     MyReader()
     Alternate modal read of a single GET.
*/
function MyReader(get)
local mess_row
// read the GET if the WHEN condition is satisfied
if (GetPreValidate(get))
   // activate the GET for reading
   mess_row := set(_SET_MESSAGE)
   if ! empty(get:cargo)
      @ mess_row, 0 say padc(get:cargo, maxcol() + 1)
   else
      scroll(mess_row, 0, mess_row, maxcol(), 0)
   endif
   get:SetFocus()
   do while (get:exitState == GE_NOEXIT)
      // check for initial typeout (no editable positions)
```

```
      if (get:typeOut)
         get:exitState := GE_ENTER
      endif

      // apply keystrokes until exit
      do while (get:exitState == GE_NOEXIT)
         GetApplyKey(get, Inkey(0))
      enddo

      // disallow exit if VALID condition is not satisfied
      if (!GetPostValidate(get))
         get:exitState := GE_NOEXIT
      endif
   enddo

   // de-activate the GET
   get:KillFocus()

endif
return nil
```

Our alternate GetReader() function calls many of the core functions in Computer Associates's GETSYS.PRG. However, it would be a relatively simple matter for you to write your own replacements for these functions. For example, the following is an alternative GetApplyKey() function that enables step entry for dates and numerics. The user can simply press "+" to increment the value, or "-" to decrement. Note that this function respects any VALID clause to limit the range of values.

Listing 27.16 Alternate GetApplyKey() function for step entry

```
/*
        Function: GKeyStep()
        Purpose: Alternate GetApplyKey() function that allows
                 step entry for dates and numerics
        Excerpted from Grumpfish Library
        Author: Greg Lief
        Copyright (c) 1991 Greg Lief
        Dialect: Clipper 5.01
*/
```

```
#include "inkey.ch"
#include "getexit.ch"
procedure GKeyStep(get, key)
local cKey
local oldvalue
local bKeyBlock

// check for SET KEY first
if bKeyBlock != NIL
   GetDoSetKey(bKeyBlock, get)
else
   do case

      case ( key == K_UP )
         get:exitState := GE_UP

      case ( key == K_SH_TAB )
         get:exitState := GE_UP

      case ( key == K_DOWN )
         get:exitState := GE_DOWN

      case ( key == K_TAB )
         get:exitState := GE_DOWN

      case ( key == K_ENTER )
         get:exitState := GE_ENTER

      case ( key == K_ESC )
         if ( Set(_SET_ESCAPE) )
            get:undo()
            get:exitState := GE_ESCAPE
         endif

      case ( key == K_PGUP )
         get:exitState := GE_WRITE

      case ( key == K_PGDN )
         get:exitState := GE_WRITE
```

```
      case ( key == K_CTRL_HOME )
         get:exitState := GE_TOP

// both ^W and ^End terminate the READ (the default)
      case (key == K_CTRL_W)
         get:exitState := GE_WRITE

      case (key == K_INS)
         Set( _SET_INSERT, ! Set(_SET_INSERT) )
         setcursor( if(set(_SET_INSERT), 3, 1) )

      case (key == K_CTRL_U)
         get:Undo()

      case (key == K_HOME)
         get:Home()

      case (key == K_END)
         get:End()

      case (key == K_RIGHT)
         get:Right()

      case (key == K_LEFT)
         get:Left()

      case (key == K_CTRL_RIGHT)
         get:WordRight()

      case (key == K_CTRL_LEFT)
         get:WordLeft()

      case (key == K_BS)
         get:BackSpace()

      case (key == K_DEL)
         get:Delete()

      case (key == K_CTRL_T)
         get:DelWordRight()
```

```
case (key == K_CTRL_Y)
   get:DelEnd()

case (key == K_CTRL_BS)
   get:DelWordLeft()

otherwise

   if (key >= 32 .and. key <= 255)
      cKey := chr(key)
      // test for step entry on numerics and dates
      if cKey $ '-+' .and. get:type $ "ND"
         oldvalue := get:varGet()
      if cKey == "-"
         get:varPut(get:varGet() - 1)
      else
         get:varPut(get:varGet() + 1)
      endif
      // make sure we are still within valid range!
      if get:postBlock != NIL .and. ;
            ! eval(get:postBlock, get)
         get:varPut(oldvalue)
      endif
      get:updateBuffer()
   else
      if (get:type == "N" .and. ;
            (cKey == "." .or. cKey == ","))
         get:ToDecPos()
         else
         if ( Set(_SET_INSERT) )
            get:Insert(cKey)
         else
            get:Overstrike(cKey)
         endif
         if (get:typeOut .and. !Set(_SET_CONFIRM) )
            if ( Set(_SET_BELL) )
               ?? Chr(7)
```

```
                    endif
                    get:exitState := GE_ENTER
                endif
            endif
        endif
    endif
  endcase
endif
return
```

Summary

We covered a lot of uncharted territory in this chapter. You are now comfortable with GET objects and the GETLIST array. You can now use the WHEN clause (and not just for skipping GETs). You should understand how to create GET objects with the GETNEW() function. You should be able to query and change instance variables with the greatest of ease. Calling methods to change the status of the cursor or GET should be child's play to you.

Finally, if you think of something that you want your GETs to do but Clipper doesn't provide, you should now have both the courage and chutzpah to do it yourself! The sky is indeed the limit with the Clipper 5 GET system.

CHAPTER 28

The Error Object Class

Clipper 5 provides programmers with precise control over run-time error handling and a way to construct otherwise impractical program logic. This chapter covers the use of the Error class of objects and other components used to control the run-time environment.

We'll start by laying the groundwork with BEGIN SEQUENCE/BREAK and the use of assertions. Then we'll move into the actual error object class and programming techniques. After reading this chapter you'll be able to construct programs that can recover efficiently from errors. You will be able to control completely what happens when errors occur.

Before jumping into error objects, see "Introduction to the Object Classes" that begins Chapter 25 for an overview of object oriented programming concepts.

Summer '87 review

In Clipper Summer '87, error handling is directed by a small collection of functions in ERRORSYS.PRG. You change the way Clipper handles run-time errors by altering these functions. When a run-time error occurs Clipper S'87 categorizes it and makes a call to one of the ERRORSYS functions along with a small number of parameters relevant to the error. There can be only one ERRORSYS.OBJ per application and consequently one version of each function. You must handle special cases by adding code to the ERRORSYS functions or by branching out of them into functions specific to your application.

```
Expr_Error(name, line, info, model, _1, _2, _3)
Undef_Error(name, line, info, model, _1)
Misc_Error(name, line, info, model)
Open_Error(name, line, info, model, _1)
Db_Error(name, line, info)
Print_Error(name, line)
```

Clipper 5 greatly improves on this concept of run-time error handling. Errors are now considered to be an instance of the error object class and can be manipulated in much the same way as other objects such as Get and TBrowse.

Starting simple with BEGIN SEQUENCE..END

The BEGIN SEQUENCE block structure is a two-edged sword that can cause a great deal of trouble. With it you can both solve and create a wide variety of problems. BEGIN SEQUENCE..END is used to delimit a block of source code that might cause trouble at run-time. The BREAK command will exit the current BEGIN SEQUENCE block (they can be nested) from anywhere in the application. Structured programming purists are shaking their heads and muttering, "that's almost as bad as a GOTO," and their paranoia should be taken into consideration. You can make a terrible mess of your program logic by misusing BEGIN SEQUENCE and BREAK. But if you promise to be careful we'll describe some situations where it solves problems in an elegant and efficient way.

To get the flavor of the programming technique, here is a common problem. Suppose you have a complex block of logical code, and deep into it you discover a situation which requires the whole thing to be shut down and exited. If you had known of the problem from the start you could have coded the logic differently, but now you're stuck. The code works perfectly except for the "exit all the way out" problem. Listing 28.1 gives a solution:

Listing 28.1 A very simple form of assertion function

```
major_error := .f.
begin sequence
  do while .t.
    if this .or. that
      for i := j to k
        do while foo > bar
          result := SomeCalc(i,j,k)
          if result = "ERROR"
            major_error= .t.
            break
          else
            DoSomeMoreWith(result)
          endif
        enddo
      next i
    else
      OtherStuff()
    endif
  enddo
end sequence
if major_error
  CleanUp("And Complain to User")
endif
```

When the BREAK is encountered the code branches execution to the next statement after the END SEQUENCE. In the above example it allowed us to cleanly exit all of the loops without complex signalling using loop control variables, like so:

```
while (foo > bar) .and. no_errors
```

Note the attempt to redeem ourselves by flagging the BREAK condition so it can be more easily tracked and debugged. The references to **major_error** are not at all necessary to use BREAK but from past experience debugging other people's code we assure you it's well worth the trouble.

So far we have not violated too many programming rules, mostly because we flagged the BREAK condition and kept the effects limited and local. Unlike other block-type commands (like IF..ENDIF and DO..ENDDO), the BREAK command can be issued against a BEGIN SEQUENCE..END block outside of the procedure or function that contains it. This can definitely lead to a debugging nightmare, but it can also be put to good use for controlling otherwise uncontrollable run-time errors.

Breaking a Bad Habit with Compiler Error C2086
Both Clipper Summer '87 and the initial release of Clipper 5 allowed a serious structural error to slip past the compiler and into your final application: a RETURN from within a BEGIN SEQUENCE..END block. By allowing the application to jump out of the block, the block is left unterminated, setting the stage for a dreaded "internal error". Clipper 5.01 properly flags this as a fatal error while compiling.

Trapping problems via assertions

The BEGIN SEQUENCE block is put to better use when you design it into complex logical blocks right from the start. A technique known as an "assertion" is used to check the success of important processes or the validity of vital assumptions. An example will help explain this technique better than a long-winded technical description. This example checks for valid results the old way, without assertions:

```
result1 := calc1()
if result1 > 0

  result2 := calc2(result1)
  if result2 == "ABC" .and. result1 < 100

    result3 := calc3(result2)

    if result3
      // etc
    endif
  endif
endif
```

In the above example you can imagine how deeply nested the logic can get if a long chain of statements must all meet special criteria. Let's create a new user-defined function to help simplify this common programming problem:

```
function Assert(expr)
if .not. expr
  break
endif
return nil
```

The above function expects as a parameter an expression that returns a logical value. If the expression is false it issues a BREAK. Using Assert(), we can rewrite the previous example.

```
/*
   Check for valid results more efficiently with assertions.
*/
begin sequence
  result1 := calc1()
  Assert(result1 > 0)

  result2 := calc2(result1)
  Assert(result2 == "ABC" .and. result1 < 100)

  result3 := calc3(result2)
  Assert(result3)
end sequence
```

If any of the assertions fails, the BEGIN SEQUENCE block is exited immediately and none of the statements following the failed assertion is executed. The BREAK sends the program to the first statement after END SEQUENCE. The very simple Assert() function can be made much more useful with the addition of a few features. As discussed previously, blindly leaping out of a block is not very good programming practice. To counter this problem we'll add another parameter that allows us to flag assertion failures:

```
function Assert(expr, flag)
if .not. expr
  flag := .f.
  break
endif
return nil
```

Note that in the next example the flag parameter must be passed by reference via the @ operator. Otherwise the flag value will not be affected by the Assert() function.

```
ok := .t.
begin sequence
  result1 := calc1()
  Assert(result1 > 0, @ok)
  result2 := calc2(result1)
  Assert(result2 == "ABC" .and. result1 < 100, @ok)
  result3 := calc3(result2)
  Assert(result3, @ok)
end sequence
if .not. ok
  ErrorMessage("Calculation Error")
endif
```

The RECOVER statement

So far the techniques we've discussed use features already available in Summer '87. Clipper 5 has added a new twist to BEGIN SEQUENCE via the RECOVER statement. RECOVER is used to create a kind of "else" for the BEGIN SEQUENCE block. Let's return to our Assert() example one more time to illustrate this feature in Listing 28.2. We can eliminate the somewhat pesky flag variable using a RECOVER statement.

Listing 28.2 An improved assertion function which flags failures

```
begin sequence
  result1 := calc1()
  Assert(result1 > 0)
  result2 := calc2()
```

```
   Assert(result2 == "ABC")
   result3 := calc3()
   Assert(result3)

recover
  ErrorMessage("Calculation Error")
end sequence

function Assert(expr)
if .not. expr
   break
endif
return nil
```

In the above example if any of the assertions fails the program will branch to the first statement after the RECOVER statement. No need for flags and other special handling. If no BREAK occurs the code in the recovery area is not executed.

The RECOVER statement with the USING clause

Before moving on to the run-time error handling system let's add one more feature to our Assert() function. Sometimes it may be important to know which assertion failed. The only completely foolproof way is to assign a unique flag to each assertion and then test each one within the RECOVER block. Not only does this defeat the purpose of Assert() in the first place, it's also far too much work if all we want is some help when debugging. The RECOVER statement has an option clause called USING. The clause allows the BREAK command to pass information back to the BEGIN SEQUENCE block. The source code below illustrates adding a counter to Assert().

```
function Assert(expr)
static counter := 0
counter++
if .not. expr
   break counter
endif
return nil
```

The counter is incremented every time an assertion is made. When an assertion fails in Assert() the current counter value is passed to the RECOVER USING statement (via the BREAK command in Assert()), as illustrated below. In this example the variable named **which** receives the current value of **counter**, as passed from the BREAK statement.

```
//  This variable will be used later as the recipient of
//  a BREAK value. Assigning a default value is not required.

local which := 0
begin sequence
  Assert(1 == 1)
  Assert(2 == 2)
  Assert(3 == 999)
recover using which
  ? "Assertion failed: "
  ?? which
end sequence
```

In the above example the third assertion will fail so the counter will equal three. Note that the variable used as the target of the USING clause must be defined, just like any other variable. The USING clause does not create it from scratch: You should give it a scope and even a default value if you will be referencing it outside of the BEGIN SEQUENCE block.

One last improvement and we promise to leave this subject alone! The problem with a **static** counter is that it never resets itself to zero. As currently written it will get less and less useful as more assertions are made. Knowing assertion number 7,287 failed isn't very useful if you can't trace the program logic back that far. Let's have the **counter** reset to zero if no parameter is passed to Assert(). This allows us to rely on the **counter** for local recovery strategies. Note that this particular implementation (see listing 28.3) prevents nested sets of BEGIN SEQUENCE because all assertions are using the same counter regardless which block they are called from.

Listing 28.3 A final version of Assert(), this one with the ability to reset the internal counter

```
function Assert(expr)
static counter := 0
if expr == nil
  counter := 0
else
  counter++
  if .not. expr
    break counter
  endif
endif
return nil
```

To reset the assertion **counter** simply call Assert() with no parameter. The example in Listing 28.4 demonstrates two distinct sets of assertions. The failure of the third assertion in the second set results in the assertion **counter** being left at three rather than five.

Listing 28.4 An example using Assert(), this one resets the internal counter

```
local which := 0

Assert()  //  Reset assertion counter to zero
begin sequence
  Assert(1 == 1)
  Assert(2 == 2)
recover using which
  ? "First set of assertions failed at: "
  ?? which
end sequence

Assert()  //  Reset assertion counter to zero
begin sequence
  Assert("A" == "A")
  Assert("B" == "B")
  Assert("C" == "ZZZ")
recover using which
  ? "Second set of assertions failed at: "
  ?? which
end sequence
```

Armed with a good grasp of BEGIN SEQUENCE..END, BREAK, RECOVER, and USING we can now discuss Clipper 5's wonderful new error handling capabilities.

Error objects and the error block function

The method for handling run-time errors in Clipper 5 touches on several wildly new concepts. It's hard even to introduce the subject without running into unfamiliar jargon and strange new techniques. Let's just jump right in; by the end of the discussion everything should be more clear.

All run-time errors in Clipper 5 are packaged up as an "error object" and passed along to the current error handler. There can be any number of error handlers defined. The most recent one gets first crack at handling the error but can pass the error object on to another handler if one is available. The error object contains all the information known about the error. The error handler contains all the code for dealing with the error. The following "exported instance variables" (as they are referred to in object-oriented jargon) are available from the error object. Detailed descriptions of each will be presented later in this chapter.

args	An array of function or operator arguments.
canDefault	Is default recovery available?
canRetry	Is retry possible after the error?
canSubstitute	Can a new result be substituted after the error?
cargo	Assignable, general-purpose variable.
description	Character description of the error condition.
filename	Name of the file associated with the error.
genCode	Generic Clipper error code number.
operation	Character description of the failed operation.
osCode	Operating system error code number.
severity	Describes the severity of the error on a numeric scale.
subCode	Subsystem-specific error code number.
subSystem	Character description of the subsystem generating the error.
tries	Number of times the failed operation has been attempted.

An error handler refers to these variables to determine its course of action. Each error produces a distinct combination of values. Figures 28.1 through 28.3 show some examples.

Figure 28.1 Example of error object values when a database USE operation fails because the file does not exist

```
use MISSING  // When MISSING.DBF does not exist

args           NIL
canDefault     .T.
canRetry       .T.
canSubstitute  .F.
description    Open error
filename       MISSING.DBF
genCode        21
operation      ""
osCode         2
severity       2
subCode        1001
subSystem      DBFNTX
tries          2
```

Figure 28.2 Error object values when an operation fails due to improper arguments

```
? "ABC" + 123  // Attempt to add string and number

args           ABC    123
canDefault     .F.
canRetry       .F.
canSubstitute  .T.
description    Argument error
filename        ""
genCode        1
operation      +
osCode         0
severity       0
subCode        1081
subSystem      BASE
tries          0
```

Figure 28.3 Error object values when a call is made to a non-existent function

```
s := "FooBar()"  // Function does not exist
? &s.

args            NIL
canDefault      .F.
canRetry        .F.
canSubstitute   .T.
description     Undefined function
filename        ""
genCode         12
operation       FOOBAR
osCode          0
severity        2
subCode         1001
subSystem       BASE
tries           0
```

The error object, as we have seen, isn't very complicated at all. But what of the error handler? So far we've mentioned it as something that reacts to the contents of an error object. Where does it come from? What does it do?

Inside ERRORSYS.PRG

Take a look at the top portion of the ERRORSYS.PRG source code file. As in Summer '87, Clipper 5 includes the contents of ERRORSYS.PRG in all of your applications. And as before, you can supply your own ERRORSYS.PRG if you desire. ERRORSYS.PRG contains a small procedure called ErrorSys(), listed below.

```
procedure ErrorSys()
ErrorBlock( { | e | DefError(e) } )
return
```

ErrorSys() is called as the first statement executed when your application starts running. Its job is to establish the first error handler. As you can infer from the source code, should an error occur control will be transferred immediately to a function called DefError(). Let's look more closely at ErrorBlock(). ErrorBlock() expects a code block as a parameter. When an error occurs the error information is collected and placed in an error object, then the specified code block will be passed the error object as a parameter. Under most circumstances the error handling code block merely passes the error object along to a user-defined function. The user-defined function is then responsible for taking action and reacting to the error. What does an error handling function look like?

The standard error handler

Reprinted here for more convenient reference is the source code for the standard error handler that comes with Clipper 5.01. The source code is found in ERRORSYS.PRG. This code forms DefError(), which ErrorSys() establishes as the function the code block will call via the error block defined with ErrorBlock(). That's a mouthful! Keep thinking about it until you get it straight. Here's a step-by-step description of how Clipper handles errors by default.

1. When Clipper starts executing your application it first calls the function named ErrorSys().

2. ErrorSys() uses the ErrorBlock() function to "post" an error handling code block.

3. The code block receives an error object as a parameter when an error occurs. The code block immediately calls DefError() with the error object as a parameter.

4. The DefError() function actually does all the error handling, based on the contents of the error object it received as a parameter from ErrorSys().

The DefError() source code (Listing 28.5) makes use of the manifest constants defined in ERROR.CH. We'll talk more about ERROR.CH later in this discussion.

Listing 28.5 Source code for Clipper's DefError() function, located in ERRORSYS.PRG

```
/* Copyright (c) 1990 Computer Associates Corp. All rights
reserved.(Reprinted here for reference. The format has been edited
slightly.) */

static func DefError(e)
local i, cMessage, aOptions, nChoice

// by default, division by zero yields zero
if ( e:genCode == EG_ZERODIV )
  return (0)
endif

// for network open error, set NETERR() and subsystem default
if ( e:genCode == EG_OPEN .and.;
    e:osCode == 32 .and. e:canDefault )
  NetErr(.t.)
  return (.f.)
endif

  // for lock error during APPEND BLANK, set NETERR()
  // and subsystem default

  if ( e:genCode == EG_APPENDLOCK .and. e:canDefault )
    NetErr(.t.)
    return (.f.)
  endif

  // build error message
  cMessage := ErrorMessage(e)

  // build options array
  // aOptions := {"Break", "Quit"}
  aOptions := {"Quit"}

  if (e:canRetry)
    aadd(aOptions, "Retry")
  endif
```

```
  if (e:canDefault)
    AAdd(aOptions, "Default")
  endif

  // put up alert box
  nChoice := 0
  do while ( nChoice == 0 )

    if ( Empty(e:osCode) )
      nChoice := Alert( cMessage, aOptions )
    else
      nChoice := Alert( cMessage + ;
             ";(DOS Error " + NTRIM(e:osCode) + ")", ;
              aOptions )
    endif

    if ( nChoice == NIL )
      exit
    endif
  enddo

if ( !Empty(nChoice) )
  // do as instructed
  if ( aOptions[nChoice] == "Break" )
    Break(e)

  elseif ( aOptions[nChoice] == "Retry" )
    return (.t.)

  elseif ( aOptions[nChoice] == "Default" )
    return (.f.)
  endif
endif

// display message and traceback
if ( !Empty(e:osCode) )
  cMessage += " (DOS Error " + NTRIM(e:osCode) + ") "
endif
```

```
? cMessage
i := 2
do while ( !Empty(ProcName(i)) )
  ? "Called from", Trim(ProcName(i)) + ;
    "(" + NTRIM(ProcLine(i)) + ")  "
  i++
enddo

// give up
ErrorLevel(1)
QUIT

return (.f.)
```

Note how every aspect of the way Clipper handles a run-time error is programmed using Clipper statements and functions. All the handling assumptions, like dividing by zero and network errors, are laid out clearly in the DefError() function. Of particular interest is the "traceback" loop. Note how easy it is to document the current calling sequence for the entire application.

Take a look at the source code in Listing 28.6. If you read it carefully you can see each element of a Clipper run-time error message being built. This function, ErrorMessage(), is found in ERRORSYS.PRG and is used by DefError() to construct the run-time error messages. The function has been declared static, so only DefError() (and other functions within the ERRORSYS.PRG source code file) can call it. If you want to use the function in your own routines you'll have to snag a copy and incorporate separately.

Listing 28.6 Source code for Clipper's ErrorMessage() function, located in ERRORSYS.PRG, reprinted here for reference

```
/* Copyright (c) 1990 Computer Associates Corp.  All rights
reserved. */
static func ErrorMessage(e)
local cMessage
```

```
// start error message
cMessage := if( e:severity > ES_WARNING, "Error ", "Warning " )

// add subsystem name if available
if ( ValType(e:subsystem) == "C" )
  cMessage += e:subsystem()
else
  cMessage += "???"
endif

// add subsystem's error code if available
if ( ValType(e:subCode) == "N" )
  cMessage += ("/" + NTRIM(e:subCode))
else
  cMessage += "/???"
endif

// add error description if available
if ( ValType(e:description) == "C" )
  cMessage += ("  " + e:description)
endif

// add either filename or operation
if ( !Empty(e:filename) )
  cMessage += (": " + e:filename)
elseif ( !Empty(e:operation) )
  cMessage += (": " + e:operation)
endif

return (cMessage)
```

If you want to alter the way Clipper handles run-time errors you could modify DefError() or even change the code block in ErrorSys(). However, you'd be back to the Summer '87 problem of needing to handle special cases by adding more code to the standard error handler or by calling special-purpose functions from inside the standard error handler. This is messy and creates maintenance problems. Clipper 5 provides us with a much better alternative, which we will now discuss.

Run-time Warnings

Clipper 5.01 adds an interesting new kind of error handling, the run-time warning. Presently only one such warning is available, concerning a low memory situation. Hopefully this trend will continue and many more such warnings will be provided. These warnings are exactly that, just a warning and not an outright error condition. The Clipper run-time engine is informing you of a situation that potentially could cause real errors. Examples of other such warnings are low disk space and keyboard buffer overflows—things you may or may not be concerned about, depending on the situation. The usual default action is to ignore the warning. However, you can install your own error handler that instead pops-up a warning box or takes other actions.

A chain of error handlers

As described previously, ErrorBlock() is used to "post" a code block as the function to call when an error occurs. You can post as many code blocks as often as you wish. The ErrorSys() function posted DefError() as the first error handler when your application started running. You can replace it with a different error handler just as easily.

```
errorblock( { | errorObject |  NewErrorHandler(errorObject) } )
```

From this point on, all error objects will be sent to NewErrorHandler() rather than DefError(). It's unlikely that you will want to completely replace the entire error handling system. It is more appropriate to establish a special error handler to deal with a specific problem. If the error turns out to be something other than the one your handler is prepared to deal with you simply pass the error to the main error handling routine. This "pass it along" technique is possible because ErrorBlock() returns the error block that currently exists. You save the current error block, post your special version, and restore the original one when the special one is no longer needed.

Listing 28.7 gives an example. We want to handle a missing database on our own and pass all other errors on to the main error handler, DefError(). Furthermore, we want to handle missing databases only in a small section of code, not for the entire application.

Remember that DefError() is already posted as the main error handler, and that the default way to handle missing databases is to report the problem and exit to DOS.

Listing 28.7 An alternative error handler

```
/*
   oldErr will hold the current error handler.
   Errorblock() posts MissingDBF() as the new error handler.
*/
oldErr := errorblock()
errorblock( { | e | MissingDBF(e, oldErr) } )

/*
   We must delimit the section of code where we want
   to use our own local error handler. If the MISSING.DBF
   file does not exist the MissingDBF() function will be
   called as the error handler.
*/
begin sequence
  use VENDOR new
  use INVOICE new
  use INVENT new
  use MISSING new
end sequence

/*
   We're beyond the section where we want to handle
   missing databases on our own, so we restore the original
   error handler.
*/
errorblock(oldErr)

/*
   If this file doesn't exist the standard error handler
   will deal with the error.
*/
use ANOTHER new

return nil
```

Note how we can open a large number of databases in rapid succession without having to check for the existence of each one individually. Without a local error handler we would need a long series like the following.

```
err := .f.
if file("VENDOR.DBF")
  use VENDOR new
else
  err := .t.
endif
// etc for the other files: INVOICE, INVENT and MISSING

if err
  @ 0,0 say "Error: All database files were not opened."
endif
```

Listing 28.8 contains the source code for the MissingDBF() function that we posted as a local error handler.

Listing 28.8 An error handler for dealing with missing databases

```
function MissingDBF(errObj, origBlock)
/*
    Special-purpose error handler for missing databases.
*/
#include "ERROR.CH"
local result

/*
   Check to see if the error is an Open Error.
   If so, report the error and BREAK back to the
   local section of code.
*/
if errObj:genCode == EG_OPEN
  @ 0,0 say "Error: All database files were not opened."
  break
/*
```

```
   Error isn't what this function is designed to handle, so
   pass the error along to the original error handler.
   Before passing it along we use the cargo instance variable
   to tack on a reminder of where the error has been. This
   might be useful in debugging. If several error handlers pass
   along the error they can all tack on a message to the cargo
   string.

*/
else
  if valtype(errObj:cargo) <> "C"
    errObj:cargo := ""
  endif
  errObj:cargo += "(Passed along from MissingDBF)"
  result := eval(origBlock, errObj)
endif

return result
```

The code for your error handler should be tested thoroughly because a run-time error within the error handler will likely result in recursive calls to the error handler. Eventually Clipper will run out of memory and crash to DOS (if you are lucky!).

We can take advantage of the RECOVER USING statement to pass the error object back to the local error handler for use in a local attempt at recovery. If we substitute the break in MissingDBF() with "break errObj", like so:

```
if errObj:genCode == EG_OPEN
  @ 0,0 say "Error: All database files were not opened."
  break errObj
```

Then we can do something like the following.

```
#define OS_ERR_NOTFOUND  2
#define OS_ERR_HANDLES   4
local the_error
```

```
begin sequence
  use ONE new
  use TWO new
  use THREE new

recover using the_error
  if the_error:osCode == OS_ERR_HANDLES
    @ 1,0 say "Too many files open."
  elseif the_error:osCode == OS_ERR_NOTFOUND
    @ 1,0 say "File not found."
  endif
end sequence
```

When MissingDBF() issues a BREAK it passes the object containing the error to the variable specified by USING, in this case, **the_error**. You can then use the **the_error** object to determine more specifically what happened to cause the error condition.

The ERROR.CH file

To make error handling code easier to follow and able to withstand future additions and modifications to the error object class, the code in ERRORSYS.PRG and our examples in this chapter make references to manifest constants defined in ERROR.CH (see Figure 28.4). You should always refer to the manifest constants and never to the actual error code numbers. The numbers may change in future versions of Clipper. If you stick to the manifest constants you'll need only to recompile your error handler functions and the codes will be adjusted.

Figure 28.4 The contents of ERROR.CH reprinted for more convenient reference

```
/* Copyright (c) 1990 Computer Associates Corp. All rights
reserved */

// Severity levels (e:severity)
#define ES_WHOCARES        0
#define ES_WARNING         1
#define ES_ERROR           2
#define ES_CATASTROPHIC    3
```

```
// Generic error codes (e:genCode)
#define EG_ARG                1
#define EG_BOUND              2
#define EG_STROVERFLOW        3
#define EG_NUMOVERFLOW        4
#define EG_ZERODIV            5
#define EG_NUMERR             6
#define EG_SYNTAX             7
#define EG_COMPLEXITY         8

#define EG_MEM               11
#define EG_NOFUNC            12
#define EG_NOMETHOD          13
#define EG_NOVAR             14
#define EG_NOALIAS           15
#define EG_NOVARMETHOD       16

#define EG_CREATE            20
#define EG_OPEN              21
#define EG_CLOSE             22
#define EG_READ              23
#define EG_WRITE             24
#define EG_PRINT             25

#define EG_UNSUPPORTED       30
#define EG_LIMIT             31
#define EG_CORRUPTION        32
#define EG_DATATYPE          33
#define EG_DATAWIDTH         34
#define EG_NOTABLE           35
#define EG_NOORDER           36
#define EG_SHARED            37
#define EG_UNLOCKED          38
#define EG_READONLY          39
#define EG_APPENDLOCK        40
```

The error object in detail

Now that we've been introduced to all the pieces of Clipper 5's error handling strategy it's time to discuss the exported instance variables supplied by an error object. Each variable has a distinct role to play in helping you understand and possibly recover from errors. (For the purpose of keeping the instance variables straight we're assuming an error object named "e" is being evaluated in the following discussions.)

e:args

e:args is an array of function or operator arguments and is not always used. **e:args** is undefined (NIL) if not used.

e:canDefault

e:canDefault indicates whether or not default recovery is available. You request default recovery by returning **.F.** from the error handling function. Exactly what happens when default recovery is requested depends on the subsystem (see **e:genCode**,below) that was responsible for the error.

e:canRetry

e:canRetry indicates whether or not it's possible to retry the operation that caused the error. You request a retry by returning **.T.** from the error handling function. As with **e:canDefault**, the ability to retry a failed operation depends on the subsystem that generated the error.

e:canSubstitute

e:canSubstitute indicates whether or not a different result can be substituted for the error. You make a substitution by returning the value from the error handling function. Because of this, **e:canSubstitute** is not an option when either **e:canDefault** or **e:canRetry** is true.

e:cargo

e:cargo is a variable you can assign on your own, useful for recording information about the error. In this chapter, the MissingDBF() function uses **e:cargo** to pass along a note that it received the error but passed it back to the error handler that preceded it. (See Listing 28.8 for an example use of **e:cargo**.)

e:description

e:description is a description of the error condition, based on the generic error code, **e:genCode**, or supplied by the subsystem if **e:genCode** is zero. Not all subsystems produce error descriptions.

e:filename

e:filename is the name of the file associated with the error. If the **e:filename** is an empty string it means that either the operation doesn't use a filename or the subsystem doesn't keep filenames.

e:genCode

e:genCode is the generic Clipper error code number. See ERROR.CH for a list of codes. If **e:genCode** is zero it means the error is unique to the subsystem and no generic code has been assigned. Generic codes allow different subsystems to share the same error strategy, for example, an "open error" is applicable to .DBF files as well as SET ALTERNATE TO.

e:operation

e:operation is a description of the failed operation. Operations are function names, like STR() or VAL(), or operators like + or -. Undefined functions or variables are also reported via **e:operations**.

e:osCode

e:osCode is the operating system's error code number, if one is applicable to the error, otherwise **e:osCode** will be zero. **e:osCode** and DOSERROR() report the same number, and if **e:osCode** is changed DOSERROR() will also get the new value.

e:severity

e:severity describes the severity of the error on a numeric scale. See ERROR.CH for manifest constants that associate descriptions with the scale. The levels of severity have the following interpretations.

Who Cares: The error condition was raised to supply information, it isn't really an error.

Warning: The error condition isn't fatal...yet. Operations may continue but a more serious error could occur in the future.

Error: This is an honest-to-goodness error, meaning the operation did not succeed. Something has to be corrected before operations can safely continue.

Catastrophic: The error condition is serious enough that operations must halt immediately and the application is terminated.

Presently Clipper will only generate errors with severity levels of **Warning** or **Error**. The other severity levels are likely to be used by add-on product vendors, especially those for replaceable database drivers (RDDs). Computer Associates may also use the other extremes in future releases of Clipper.

e:subCode

e:subCode is a subsystem-specific error code number. Every error gets a unique subsystem error code. If zero it means the subsystem does not assign error codes.

e:subSystem

e:subSystem is a description of the subsystem that generated the error. Clipper functions and operators are part of the "BASE" subsystem. Errors generated by the database driver will contain the name of the database driver. If you are using the default Clipper database driver, **e:subsystem** will be "DBFNTX". Future database drivers (known as RDDs or replaceable database drivers) will supply different subsystem names and subsystem error codes.

e:tries

e:tries is a counter that indicates the number of times the failed operation has been attempted. Not all subsystems track this number so it may be zero. You can use **e:tries** to limit the number of additional attempts that are made.

Error object inspection and recording

As an aid in identifying what different error objects contain, this book includes a function, ErrorSaver(), that can be installed as a replacement to DefError(). It displays all information about the error, including memory status, DOS information, and procedure traceback, and then optionally appends a copy to a text file. You can use the results for learning about different types of errors and developing strategies to recover from them or even avoid them in the first place.

After application development is complete, ErrorSaver() is still useful for keeping an accurate log of all run-time errors rather than relying on the end-user to print screens or copy down vital information.

To install this function as the default error handler all you need to do is add the following as the first line of code in your application. It specifies that errors will be recorded in a file called ERR.TXT. You can omit the filename parameter if you don't want the information recorded.

```
errorblock( { |e| ErrorSaver(e, "ERR.TXT") } )
```

Figure 28.5 shows the ErrorSaver() screen in action, and Figure 28.6, the resulting error log file entry.

Figure 28.5. A sample ErrorSaver() screen

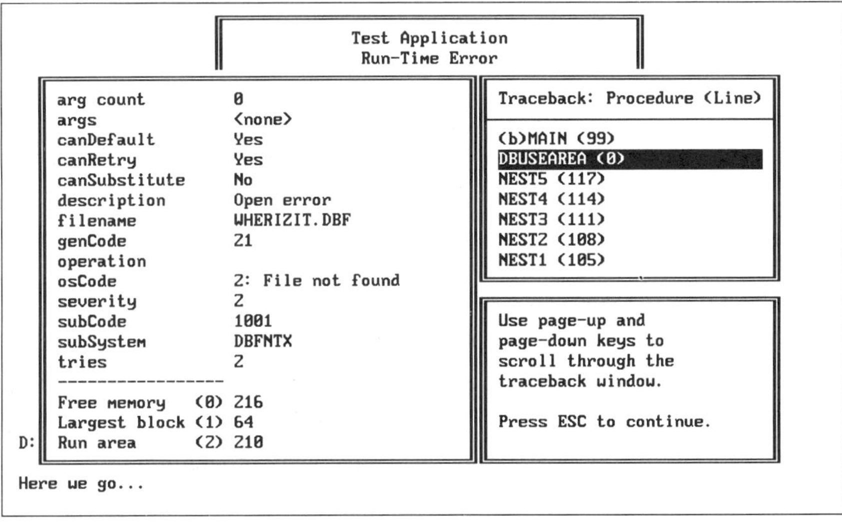

Figure 28.6 A sample entry in the error log file.

```
=============================================================================
ErrorSaver: This run-time error logged on 03/05/91 at 15:10:30
Application: Test Application
Operating system = DOS 3.20, network = <none>
Available diskspace = 1,349,632 in C:\TEST
PATH     = c:\clipper5\bin;c:\dos;c:\norton;c:\utils;c:\bat
COMSPEC = C:\COMMAND.COM
CLIPPER = F51
____________________________________

Traceback: Proc (Line)   Error Information
~~~~~~~~~~~~~~~~~~~~~~   ~~~~~~~~~~~~~~~~~~~~~~~~~~~~~~~~~~~~~~~~~
  DBUSE (0)               arg count          0
  NEST5 (114)             args               <none>
  NEST4 (111)             canDefault         Yes
  NEST3 (108)             canRetry           Yes
  NEST2 (105)             canSubstitute      No
  NEST1 (102)             description        Open error
  MAIN (98)               filename           WHERIZIT.DBF
                          genCode            21
                          operation
                          osCode             2: File not found
                          severity           2
                          subCode            1001
                          subSystem          DBFNTX
                          tries              2
                          ________

                          Free memory    (0) 185
                          Largest block  (1) 64
                          Run area       (2) 178
```

Functions related to error handling

Clipper 5 provides a variety of functions used in error detection and handling. We've covered several of them already. Most are quite simple but are still vitally important to a comprehensive error handling strategy. The following list can serve as a reference when searching for tools in your error detection and recovery programming.

Alert()	A general-purpose user-interface function used in ERRORSYS.PRG to report errors and optionally solicit a response from the user. You can call Alert() for your own purposes; it can be used outside of ERRORSYS.PRG.
DefError()	The default error handler. Found in ERRORSYS.PRG, it can be altered or, preferably, superseded by another call to ErrorBlock() that installs a new error handler.
DosError()	The error number of the most recent DOS-related error. Zero indicates no error. Keep in mind that DosError() can be assigned a new value, which allows your error handler to decide if the original error number (or even zero) should be returned to the main application.
ErrorBlock()	Returns current error handling code block and optionally posts a new one.
ErrorLevel()	Returns current DOS ERRORLEVEL number and optionally assigns a new value.
ErrorSys()	Always called as first executed statement when your application starts running. Found in ERRORSYS.PRG, it can be altered or, preferably, superseded by another call to ErrorBlock() that installs a different error handler.
Ferror()	Result of most recent low-level file operation. Returns 0 if the operation was successful or a positive number if an error occurred.
NetErr()	Returns result of most recent USE or APPEND BLANK command: true if it succeeded, false if it failed. Keep in mind that NetErr(), like DosError(), can be assigned a new value, which allows your error handler to decide if it should be true or not when returned to the main application.

Alert() in more detail

The Alert() function is an important addition to your programming tools and should not be associated only with runtime errors. First, Alert() can detect the absence of Clipper's full-screen terminal I/O and reverts to standard TTY-style I/O. TTY-style means the lowest common denominator among video adapter cards and monitors, allowing only simple output capabilities. This is essential for having a generic error-handling system that does not depend in any way on the functions linked into an application. Using Alert() allows you to develop routines that are more device-independent than regular Clipper routines using MENU TO and @..SAY. Second, Alert() packs a very powerful pop-up message box and menu selection routine into a simple function call.

Alert() accepts two parameters, a message and an array of options. It returns the number of the option selected or zero if no selection was made.

```
nChoice := alert(cMessage [, aOptions])
```

If an array of options is not passed, Alert() displays a single "OK" choice. The message string accommodates multiple-line messages by using the semicolon as a line separator. The following example produces a box with the two message lines centered above the three options.

```
now_what := alert("Something terrible;has happened!", ;
                  {"Abort","Retry","Ignore"})
```

You are free to use Alert() in your own error handling routines as well as anywhere else in your application you see fit.

Note that Alert() is actually a preprocessor translation directive. See the file ASSERT.CH for more details. As of this writing, ASSERT.CH can be found in the \CLIPPER5\SOURCE\SAMPLE subdirectory, and not in \CLIPPER5\INCLUDE as you might expect. This may change in subsequent releases.

Creating your own errors

Who needs help creating errors? You say you do fine on your own, thank you? The error class, like all object classes, has a constructor function that returns an error object. You can use this newly created object to produce run-time errors that are difficult (and often tedious) to generate "naturally". Who wants to fill up a hard disk or trash DOS's memory control blocks just to see if an error handler works correctly for that situation? The error doesn't really occur, but the error handler doesn't know that. This also means that error recovery operations may not work correctly since the error condition doesn't really exist, so it's not perfect.

To create a new error object you simply call ErrorNew(), of all things, and receive one.

```
test := errorNew()
```

Then you can construct any nasty errors you can think of by simply making assignments to the object's instance variables. The following sets up a "file not found" situation for the USE command.

```
test:filename   := "TEST.DBF"
test:genCode    := EG_OPEN
test:osCode     := 2
test:subCode    := 1001
test:subSystem  := "DBFNTX"
```

Don't bother assigning a description if you use **e:genCode**, because as soon as you assign the **e:genCode** variable the associated description is placed in the description variable. Once the error is defined as much as you need it to be for testing, pass it as a parameter to an error handling function.

```
eval(errorblock(), test)
```

The error handler will react to the error object as if the error it represents had actually happened. Feels nice to be in the driver's seat of an error condition for a change, doesn't it? Go ahead, torture DefError() all you want.

Summary

Error detection, reporting and recovery have been made considerably more powerful, and at the same time, more easy to implement in Clipper 5. You've seen how the BEGIN SEQUENCE block, coupled with BREAK and RECOVER USING, can be used to construct bullet-proof program logic. We tackled the error object class and found it to be very simple to understand. You know how ERRORSYS.PRG works and how to install our own error handlers. Now all you need to do is put all this knowledge to work keeping your applications running smoothly even when errors occur.

CHAPTER 29

Obsolete Commands and Functions

Change is inevitable in anything related to computers, and the evolution of Clipper is no exception. Up through the release of Clipper 5 Computer Associates followed an often twisting path, managing to stay relatively compatible with other DBASE dialects while at the same time extending the language in powerful and unique ways. Clipper 5 is the first release that takes a more dramatic departure from the existing standards. On the whole, this departure makes Clipper a better, more stable platform for software developers and signals Computer Associates' intention to make Clipper a distinct alternative to other languages, not just an alternative to the other DBASE dialects.

Not surprisingly, to accomplish this transformation Clipper programmers are going to have to alter their styles and techniques to take advantage of what future versions of Clipper will offer. Clipper 5 can be treated to a certain extent like an improved Summer '87; you will likely see some improvements in speed and memory management simply by recompiling existing applications and linking them with RTLink. However, an attitude of "it's the same, but better" isn't going to get you very far. In fact, Computer Associates has made some very broad hints about the direction in which they are headed. These hints take the form of a notation in the Clipper documentation regarding certain "compatibility" commands and functions. All such commands and functions are indicated with an asterisk next to their entries in the printed documentation and in the Norton Guides. The book you are reading has taken these notations to heart and consciously avoids the commands, functions, and techniques that don't fit with Computer Associates' vision of Clipper's future. We think you'll agree that in all cases a switch from the old to the new will improve your programming technique and produce better, more reliable applications. If you do not take heed and alter your techniques you may find it difficult to work with future versions of Clipper.

This chapter is dedicated to identifying these commands and functions, explaining their deficiencies and offering reasonable alternatives. By following the advice offered here you'll be in a better position to make a smooth transition to Clipper 5 as well as future versions of Clipper.

Obsolete statements

Statements form the fundamental control features of Clipper. They are used to divide your applications into modules, to indicate the storage class of variables, and to control logical flow at run-time. There are a few new statements that are covered in detail in other chapters of this book: **field**, **local**, **memvar** and **static**. There are two that have been marked as obsolete: DECLARE and DO. There are four that aren't considered obsolete but should, in our opinion, be avoided to make best use of the language: **parameters**, **private**, **procedure**, and **public**.

DECLARE

DECLARE is used to create **private** arrays and variables.

Deficiency: Because it has the exact same effect as the **private** statement, DECLARE is not required under any circumstances.

Remedy: You can replace all occurrences of DECLARE with **private** without causing any side-effects. However, we recommend avoiding **private** as well. See Chapter 6, "Variable Scoping," for details.

DO

DO is used to invoke a procedure. When used with parameters, DO passes them by reference instead of by value.

Deficiency: Clipper functions can be called on lines by themselves, so they function identically to commands in that respect.

```
do MyRoutine  //  These have the identical effect
MyRoutine()   //  of executing "MyRoutine."
```

The most troublesome feature of commands is that they pass parameters by reference, meaning the values of any variables used as parameters can be altered by the procedure. This can cause unintended side-effects and reduces the reliability of your applications.

```
x := 123
y := 789
do MyProc with x
MyFunc(y)
? x                    //  "abc", the value was altered
? y                    //  789, the value was not altered

procedure MyProc
parameter p
p := "abc"
return

function MyFunc
parameter p
p := "xyz"
return nil
```

Remedy: Design all new routines as functions and stop using procedures. Edit existing procedures into functions in situations where it's an easy change; however, you may introduce errors in complex applications by blindly converting every procedure to a function.

If you need to take advantage of a procedure's ability to directly alter the contents of its parameters, use the "pass by reference" operator, **@**, instead. The **@** operator makes it obvious to anyone reading your source code that you are passing the parameter by reference and they should anticipate potential changes to the value. Use of **@** also has the desirable effect of allowing you to pass some parameters by reference and others by value, whereas with a procedure all parameters are passed by reference. See Chapter 5, "Operators", for a detailed discussion of passing variables by reference.

```
x := 123
y := 789
MyFunc(@x, y)
? x                 // "abc"
? y                 // 789

function MyFunc
parameters a, b
a := "abc"
b := "xyz"
return nil
```

If you have a large number of procedures in existing applications but still want to eliminate the potential side effects of passing parameters by reference, note that by simply enclosing each parameter in parentheses you make it an *expression*.

```
// The value of x will remain unchanged
// no matter what happens in the procedure
x := 123
do MyProc with (x)
```

Many Clipper programmers use procedures to indicate that the routine is called for the effect it produces and not for any value it might return. While this is a reasonable use for procedures, the same effect can be gained with a preprocessor #xcommand directive.

```
#xcommand do MyProc  =>  MyProc()
```

Although all functions return values, you do not have to acknowledge the value when the function is called. We recommend returning NIL when the function is not designed to return a useful value. Some programmers use the C language convention of using the keyword VOID to indicate a function has no return value.

```
#define VOID nil

function Nothing
return VOID
```

PROCEDURE

PROCEDURE is used to mark the start of a routine.

Deficiency: The PROCEDURE statement is tied to the DO statement, which was discussed in detail in the previous section.

Remedy: Try to use FUNCTION exclusively.

PRIVATE and PUBLIC

The PRIVATE and PUBLIC statements create and declare the scope of variables.

Deficiency: The variables are dangerously visible to too much of the rest of the application

Remedy: PRIVATE and PUBLIC should be replaced with LOCAL and STATIC when possible. See Chapter 6, "Variable Scoping," for details.

PARAMETERS

The PARAMETERS statement establishes a list of variable names used as parameters within procedures and functions.

Deficiency: The PARAMETERS statement creates **private** variables.

Remedy: Parameters should be defined via syntax that creates local variables. Again, see Chapter 6 for details.

```
function One
parameters a, b, c
  //  a, b, and c are PRIVATE variables
return nil

function Two(x, y, z)
  //  x, y and z are local variables
return nil
```

Note that when you make the switch to LOCAL parameters you will no longer be able to use the TYPE() function to test them. You must instead us VALTYPE(). See Chapter 6 for a detailed discussion of TYPE() and VALTYPE().

Obsolete commands

Although it isn't apparent unless you study the contents of STD.CH — the main preprocessor header file — Clipper 5 doesn't really have any commands! Strange but true, the language has been divided into statements, functions, and preprocessor directives, with no commands. What we traditionally consider commands, like GOTO TOP and READ, are actually converted to function calls by the preprocessor. However, though implemented differently, commands are still an important part of the language. Using commands has always made the dBASE dialects easier to understand and more accessible for novices than other languages like C or Pascal. This remains true in Clipper 5, and in fact it's now possible to write your own commands via the incredible preprocessor.

With that said, there are some commands which have outlived their usefulness in Clipper. Some probably never should have made it as far as Summer '87, much less Clipper 5, and others are only now made obsolete by new capabilities. Either way, the sooner you leave them behind, the better. However, with the advent of user-defined commands it is now possible to recover from future changes by adding commands you need right back into the language.

CALL

CALL executes procedures external to your Clipper application, written in C or assembler.

Deficiency: CALL is a crude way to execute external procedures and does not lend itself to seamless integration with the rest of the Clipper language. It exists primarily for compatibility with routines originally meant for use with dBASE III Plus.

Remedy: Clipper's Extend System is a considerably more elegant and efficient way to accomplish the same thing.

CANCEL

CANCEL stops program execution, closes all open files and exits to the operating system.

Deficiency: CANCEL is a synonym for QUIT and has the exact same effect. CANCEL in interpreted dialects exits only to the "dot prompt", which is unavailable in Clipper.

Remedy: Replace all occurrences of CANCEL with QUIT, there are no side-effects.

CLEAR ALL

CLEAR ALL releases all **private** and **public** variables and closes all open files.

Deficiency: This command has effects more wide ranging than is considered appropriate in an application while it is executing. Computer Associates sometimes refers to CLEAR ALL as "the command that knew too much."

Remedy: CLEAR ALL should be replaced with a combination of other CLEAR commands that have the desired effect. CLEAR ALL (as well as CLEAR MEMORY) has no effect on **local** and **static** variables, so if you follow our advice regarding avoiding the use of **private** and **public** variables, CLEAR ALL will have no more effect than CLOSE ALL. With that said, CLEAR ALL isn't that big of a deal and can be easily recreated with a user-defined command.

DIR

DIR displays a directory listing.

Deficiency: In this the age of modern user interfaces and careful control of the screen, DIR is an anachronism which lobs text to the screen in an almost uncontrolled manner.

Remedy: The awkward DIR should be replaced by a call to DIRECTORY() to load the desired directory information into an array, followed by a simple array-based TBrowse that will allow the user to view the results. The only side effect is the addition of a DIR replacement function and a new user-defined command that converts the bumbling DIR to the new function call.

```
#command DIR [<filespec>] => DirBrowse([<filespec>])

function DirBrowse(spec)
  //  Emulation of DIR's output in a TBrowse.
return nil
```

FIND

FIND searches the current index for a matching key value.

Deficiency: FIND was originally intended for use with literal values at a "dot prompt" command line. Clipper has no such prompt and is almost always working with variable names and expressions, rendering FIND almost useless.

Remedy: FIND can be replaced with SEEK with no side effects as long as the search key is made into an expression.

```
find MN
seek "MN"   //  Same effect as FIND MN.
seek MN     //  Assumes a variable called MN is available,
            //  will likely cause a run-time error.
```

NOTE

Note makes a single-line comment in a source code file.

Deficiency: As if there weren't enough options for comments. You have //, *, &&, and /* */. The use of NOTE is just begging to be confused with real commands that actually do something.

Remedy: Replace all occurrences of NOTE with //. If you really prefer to do all that typing you can always create a user-defined command.

```
#command COMMENTARY <*x*> =>
#command DO NOT COMPILE THIS <*x*> =>
```

SAVE and RESTORE SCREEN

SAVE SCREEN and RESTORE SCREEN are used to save a copy of the current screen and then restore it.

Deficiency: These commands work on the entire screen, and can even be used to save and restore without specifying a variable to hold the screen image. There are better ways to handle screen saves, and you should always store the screens explicitly to a variable name to prevent collisions with other functions that also need to save or restore the screen.

Remedy: Replace SAVE SCREEN and RESTORE SCREEN with calls to the SAVESCREEN() and RESTSCREEN() functions, which can operate on partial screens and must be used with a variable name.

```
//  These are equivalent, entire screen is stored to TEMP.
save screen to temp
temp := savescreen(0,0, maxRow(), maxCol())

// These are also equivalent, entire screen is restored from
// TEMP.
restore screen from temp
restscreen(0,0, maxRow(), maxCol(), temp)
```

Admittedly, when you simply want to save and later restore the entire screen with a minimum of fuss, using the verbose SAVESCREEN() and RESTSCREEN() functions is a bit of a pain. The following reduces the process to a single function call.

```
temp := ScreenShot()
//
//  Do something that messes up the screen.
//
ScreenShot(temp)  // Screen is now restored.
quit

function ScreenShot(scr)
/*
```

```
   Return a screen save, or restore from screen passed as param-
eter.
*/
if scr == nil
  scr := savescreen(0,0,maxRow(),maxCol())
else
  restscreen(0,0,maxRow(),maxCol(), scr)
endif
return scr
```

SET COLOR

The SET COLOR command establishes screen colors.

Deficiency: This command blindly sets the colors and offers no way to save the current color settings.

Remedy: SET COLOR can be completely replaced by the SETCOLOR() function. SETCOLOR() returns the current color setting string before establishing the new string. Saving the existing color string allows you to restore the original colors if necessary. This is an important consideration when writing general-purpose functions.

```
setcolor("G/N")
@ 10, 15 say "Status: "
if ferror()
  Warning("There's an Error!")
endif
@ 12, 15 say "Still using G/N color."
quit

function Warning(message)
local clr
//  Flashing red on white for a warning message.
clr := setcolor("R*/W")
@ row(), col() say message
//  Restore colors to what they were previously.
setcolor(clr)
return nil
```

When it comes right down to it, even the use of SETCOLOR() as demonstrated above can be eliminated via the new COLOR clause available with @...SAY and other commands. This example should serve only to illustrate the use of SETCOLOR() to save and restore the current color.

SET EXACT

SET EXACT specifies whether character strings must match exactly when comparing them.

Deficiency: SET EXACT is an application-wide setting and may have far-reaching consequences that you do not intend.

Remedy: Write expressions that yield precisely the type of match you wish to make, don't rely on the setting of SET EXACT. The double equal (==) operator is better used to compare two strings for an exact match.

```
? "abc" = "a"    //  True if EXACT is OFF, False if ON.
? "abc" == "a"   //  False no matter what the status of EXACT.
```

See Chapter 21, Tables 21-1, and 21-2 for the the rules of using SET EXACT.

SET EXCLUSIVE

SET EXCLUSIVE specifies whether all database files should be opened as shared or as exclusive.

Deficiency: SET EXCLUSIVE is an application-wide setting that is better handled on a file-by-file basis.

Remedy: Use the EXCLUSIVE and SHARED options of the USE command rather than relying on the status of SET EXCLUSIVE. The programmer should make an explicit reference to EXCLUSIVE when opening a database file. This eliminates toggling SET EXCLUSIVE ON and OFF all over your application and the resulting potential for mistakes.

```
use MYFILE exclusive
use OURFILE shared
```

SET FORMAT

SET FORMAT specifies a format file to be used when a READ is executed.

Deficiency: Clipper doesn't really use format files the way they are implemented in interpreted dBASE dialects. Clipper treats SET FORMAT TO **<name>** the same as DO **<name>**. Even when implemented as intended, SET FORMAT TO is pretty useless in the other dBASE dialects.

Remedy: Eliminate SET FORMAT TO by calling an equivalent function that displays prompts and establishes GETs.

SET PROCEDURE

SET PROCEDURE instructs the compiler to locate the specified source code file and incorporate the contents into the current object file being created.

Deficiency: SET PROCEDURE is still around as a compatibility function. It serves no purpose in Clipper other than to obscure the structure and relationships of source code files. You must compile without the /**M** switch for a SET PROCEDURE to be effective. The rationale for using SET PROCEDURE is related to product design flaws never present in Clipper in the first place.

Remedy: If you want a particular object file to be included in your application you should make an explicit reference to it when linking. Or, if you want several source code files to be combined into a single object file you can create a .CLP file and compile it, instead.

SET UNIQUE

SET UNIQUE determines whether non-unique keys are included in index files.

Deficiency: SET UNIQUE is an application-wide setting and may introduce unintended side effects.

Remedy: Rather than using SET UNIQUE, take advantage of the INDEX command's UNIQUE clause so the creation of a unique index is limited to a single line, rather than the entire application. This eliminates toggling SET UNIQUE on and off all over your application and the resulting potential for mistakes.

```
index on Name to temp1
index on Zip to temp2 unique
```

STORE

STORE assigns a value to one or more variables.

Deficiency: Aside from being longer to type than the equivalent assignment operator, :=, using STORE brands you as a hopelessly old-fashioned dBASE bumbler.

Remedy: Use the assignment operators, := or =, wherever a STORE is encountered. The := operator is preferable to =, which should be reserved for use in logical comparisons.

```
store 0 to n     //  Your colleagues will snicker.
t := 0           //  Much better.
```

Prior to Clipper 5, programmers were required to use STORE to efficiently assign the same value to multiple variables. There is no harm in leaving existing code this way because the STORE command is preprocessed into a series of := operators, anyway. Converting a STORE command is easy. When writing new code you should get in the habit of using the := operator, just in case it becomes fashionable to laugh at even the previously legitimate use of the STORE command.

```
store 0 to a, b, c, d, e, f      //  These are equivalent.
a := b:= c := d := e := f := 0
```

TEXT..ENDTEXT

TEXT..ENDTEXT delimits a block of text to display.

Deficiency: Similar to DIR, TEXT..ENDTEXT is a chain saw in the toolbox of Clipper display capabilities. It offers almost no control over formatting and has no place in modern user interface design.

Remedy: There are numerous alternatives to TEXT..ENDTEXT, like using @..SAY or even storing the text to be displayed in a long string and displaying it via MEMOLINE(). Almost any solution is preferable to the unwieldy TEXT..ENDTEXT block.

With that said, there are indeed situations where it is useful to just dump a large amount of text to the screen or printer, but perhaps the question is not "should I use TEXT..ENDTEXT" but rather, "why is all this static text sitting in my source code in the first place?" What appears between TEXT and ENDTEXT is actually data, and good application design dictates that it be treated as such.

WAIT

WAIT pauses program execution and displays an optional message, keeps waiting until a key is pressed, and optionally stores a keypress to a variable.

Deficiency: WAIT is in the same boat as DIR and TEXT..ENDTEXT with respect to modern user interfaces. It isn't very pretty and has some major limitations on how it reacts to Ctrl and Alt keys (all return CHR(0)). Function keys are ignored unless they are assigned with a SET FUNCTION or SET KEY command. WAIT advances down one screen row regardless of whether a message is specified or not.

Remedy: A simple INKEY(0) is equivalent to WAIT, without any limitations on keystrokes. and it doesn't disturb the screen. You can store the result of INKEY(0) just as easily as with WAIT TO and gain access to the entire keyboard rather than the limited set of keys that WAIT will recognize. You can use the ?, ??, and @..SAY commands to display messages with more accuracy and flexibility.

```
wait "Your choice?" to c
                              // These two are equivalent
? "Your choice?"
c := chr(inkey(0))
```

Obsolete functions

Ah, user-defined functions. Pioneered by Computer Associates and even now not implemented as completely or successfully in other DBASE dialects, user-defined functions make it unlikely that you'll suffer very long should Computer Associates drop a function you need. The functions currently considered obsolete will not be missed by most Clipper programmers. New programmers should not use them at all.

ADIR()

The ADIR() function fills a set of arrays with DOS directory information.

Deficiency: Saddled with a two-pass calling procedure and cursed with the need for up to five individual arrays, ADIR() is a needlessly clumsy way to get directory information.

Remedy: The DIRECTORY() function does everything ADIR() does, without requiring more than a single array.

AFIELDS()

The AFIELDS() function fills a series of arrays with database structure information.

Deficiency: Similar to ADIR(), AFIELDS() demands that a set of predefined arrays be available to receive various pieces of a database structure. Up to four individual arrays are required.

Remedy: The DBSTRUCT() function does everything AFIELDS() does, and needs only a single array to do it.

DBEDIT()

DBEDIT() displays database records in a table layout.

Deficiency: Don't even get us started — DBEDIT() is so pathetic in comparison to the TBrowse object class that it's not worth the time it takes to describe all the DBEDIT() deficiencies. Let's just say that DBEDIT() was a feeble attempt to answer the question, "Why can't Clipper support the BROWSE command?" Contrary to what the name DBEDIT() implies, it can't edit anything without loads of additional programming. Even the act of simply browsing through a database is an exercise in source code gymnastics.

Remedy: Gratefully abandon DBEDIT(), or don't get started in the first place. It isn't trivial but you can, without much effort, convert any DBEDIT() into a TBrowse. Along the way you'll discover how easy it is to implement fancy browsing features. Even TBrowse doesn't offer edit capabilities without some additional programming, but compared to DBEDIT() it's a walk in the park. See Chapter 26, "The TBrowse Object Class," for details.

DBF()

Returns name of current alias.

Deficiency: There's nothing inherently bad about DBF(), it's just superseded by the more flexible ALIAS() function.

Remedy: Use the ALIAS() function instead. ALIAS() is preferable because you can specify a work area while DBF() only operates on the current work area.

FKLABEL()

FKLABEL() returns the "name" of a function key.

Deficiency: FKLABEL()'s sole purpose is to make a very small percentage of DBASE applications compile under Clipper. All it does is stick an "F" on the front of the number you pass to it.

Remedy: If you actually manage to find a use for FKLABEL() we'd like to hear about it.

FKMAX()

FKMAX() returns the number of function keys present.

Deficiency: In Clipper this value is hard-wired at 40. Precious little is gained by that. Using 40 implies that there are 10 function keys and you can press them alone or in combination with the Shift, Ctrl and Alt keys.

Remedy: This is one function that could find some utility in Clipper if it returned the number of function keys actually present on the keyboard, allowing you to sense the F11 and F12 keys or who knows what else IBM will jam into the keyboards of the future. As it stands now you should disregard FKMAX() entirely; it's as close to a useless function as you're likely to encounter in Clipper.

MOD()

MOD() returns the modulus of two numbers and attempts to repeat some of the mistakes made in the dBASE III Plus implementation.

Deficiency: MOD() does mathematically incorrect things when presented with a zero divisor or negative numbers.

Remedy: Use Clipper's modulus operator, %, instead, and review all source code where MOD() is relied upon for correct results. (See Chapter 5, "Operators", for a detailed discussion of the modules operator and a comparison of "%", Clipper MOD(), and dBASE III MOD().)

READKEY()

READKEY() returns an indication of which key was used to exit a READ.

Deficiency: READKEY() emulates the function as it is implemented in dBASE III Plus. For whatever reason, it is designed to take what should be a simple READ exit status situation and make it incompatible with other keyboard events.

Remedy: Use a combination of LASTKEY() and UPDATED() to get the same information that's returned by READKEY(), but in a more standard manner that is compatible with other keyboard events.

RECCOUNT()

RECCOUNT() returns the number of records in a database file.

Deficiency: RECCOUNT() is identical in all respects to LASTREC(). Why we ever needed two functions for the same thing escapes logic, and evidently someone within Computer Associates decided that the intuitive name RECCOUNT() had to go in favor of the more ambiguous LASTREC().

Remedy: RECCOUNT() can be replaced by LASTREC() in all situations with no side effects.

WORD()

WORD() converts numerics from type double to type int, but only in the context of a CALL command.

Deficiency: Because the CALL command is slated for obsolescence, it's not surprising that any functions related to it are also headed for the bit bucket.

Remedy: Convert routines currently used with the CALL command to use with the Clipper Extend System. Once the CALL is gone all occurrences of WORD() will be gone as well.

The End?

There will no doubt be more obsolete commands and functions in future releases of Clipper, as Computer Associates attempts to wean us from our dBASE heritage and moves us into more efficient and more reliable programming techniques. If you eliminate the current list from your applications you stand a better chance of weathering future changes. Even if they weren't considered obsolete, many of the commands and functions aren't very well designed or implemented in the first place and you'll lose nothing by changing your programming habits.

Appendix A

STANDARD INKEY() KEY-CODE DEFINITIONS

```
// Cursor movement keys
#define K_UP            5
#define K_DOWN          24
#define K_LEFT          19
#define K_RIGHT         4
#define K_HOME          1
#define K_END           6
#define K_PGUP          18
#define K_PGDN          3
#define K_CTRL_LEFT     26
#define K_CTRL_RIGHT    2
#define K_CTRL_HOME     29
#define K_CTRL_END      23
#define K_CTRL_PGUP     31
#define K_CTRL_PGDN     30
#define K_CTRL_RET      10

#define K_ESC           27
#define K_RETURN        13
#define K_ENTER         13

// Editing keys
#define K_INS           22
#define K_DEL           7
#define K_BS            8
#define K_CTRL_BS       127
#define K_TAB           9
#define K_SH_TAB        271

// Control keys
#define K_CTRL_A        1
#define K_CTRL_B        2
#define K_CTRL_C        3
#define K_CTRL_D        4
#define K_CTRL_E        5
#define K_CTRL_F        6
#define K_CTRL_G        7
#define K_CTRL_H        8
#define K_CTRL_I        9
#define K_CTRL_J        10
#define K_CTRL_K        11
#define K_CTRL_L        12
#define K_CTRL_M        13
#define K_CTRL_N        14
#define K_CTRL_O        15
#define K_CTRL_P        16
#define K_CTRL_Q        17
#define K_CTRL_R        18
#define K_CTRL_S *      19
#define K_CTRL_T        20
#define K_CTRL_U        21
#define K_CTRL_V        22
#define K_CTRL_W        23
#define K_CTRL_X        24
#define K_CTRL_Y        25
#define K_CTRL_Z        26

// Alt keys
#define K_ALT_A         286
#define K_ALT_B         304
#define K_ALT_C       * 302
#define K_ALT_D       * 288
#define K_ALT_E         274
#define K_ALT_F         289
#define K_ALT_G         290
#define K_ALT_H         291
#define K_ALT_I         279
#define K_ALT_J         292
#define K_ALT_K         293
#define K_ALT_L         294
#define K_ALT_M         306
#define K_ALT_N         305
#define K_ALT_O         280
#define K_ALT_P         281
#define K_ALT_Q         272
#define K_ALT_R         275
#define K_ALT_S         287
#define K_ALT_T         276
#define K_ALT_U         278
#define K_ALT_V         303
#define K_ALT_W         273
#define K_ALT_X         301
#define K_ALT_Y         277
#define K_ALT_Z         300

// Function keys
#define K_F1            28
#define K_F2            -1
#define K_F3            -2
#define K_F4            -3
#define K_F5            -4
#define K_F6            -5
#define K_F7            -6
#define K_F8            -7
#define K_F9            -8
#define K_F10           -9

// Control-function keys
#define K_CTRL_F1       -20
#define K_CTRL_F2       -21
#define K_CTRL_F3       -22
#define K_CTRL_F4       -23
#define K_CTRL_F5       -24
#define K_CTRL_F6       -25
#define K_CTRL_F7       -26
#define K_CTRL_F8       -27
#define K_CTRL_F9       -28
#define K_CTRL_F10      -29

// Alt-function keys
#define K_ALT_F1        -30
#define K_ALT_F2        -31
#define K_ALT_F3        -32
#define K_ALT_F4        -33
#define K_ALT_F5        -34
#define K_ALT_F6        -35
#define K_ALT_F7        -36
#define K_ALT_F8        -37
#define K_ALT_F9        -38
#define K_ALT_F10       -39

// Shift-function keys
#define K_SH_F1         -10
#define K_SH_F2         -11
#define K_SH_F3         -12
#define K_SH_F4         -13
#define K_SH_F5         -14
#define K_SH_F6         -15
#define K_SH_F7         -16
#define K_SH_F8         -17
#define K_SH_F9         -18
#define K_SH_F10        -19
```

**** WARNING: Before You Turn CTRL-S, ALT-C, or ALT-D Into Hot Keys***

These keys have previously defined meaning to a Clipper application:

CTRL-S pauses execution and removes key from buffer unless SCROLLBREAK is set off

ALT-C interrupts execution

ALT-D invokes debugger if present; otherwise it is ignored

While it is possible to change the definition of these keys, it is best not to do so unless you must, and then be wary of potential side effects.

THE "IRRATIONAL" ASCII CHART

Val.	Char.	Val.	Char.	Val.	Char.	Val.	Char.	Val.	Char.
0		26		52	4	78	N	104	h
1	☺	27	←	53	5	79	O	105	i
2	☻	28	∟	54	6	80	P	106	j
3	♥	29	↔	55	7	81	Q	107	k
4	♦	30	▲	56	8	82	R	108	l
5	♣	31	▼	57	9	83	S	109	m
6	♠	32		58	:	84	T	110	n
7	•	33	!	59	;	85	U	111	o
8	◘	34	"	60	<	86	V	112	p
9	○	35	#	61	=	87	W	113	q
10		36	$	62	>	88	X	114	r
11	♂	37	%	63	?	89	Y	115	s
12	♀	38	&	64	@	90	Z	116	t
13	♪	39	'	65	A	91	[	117	u
14	♫	40	(	66	B	92	\	118	v
15	☼	41	)	67	C	93	]	119	w
16	►	42	*	68	D	94	^	120	x
17	◄	43	+	69	E	95	_	121	y
18	↕	44	,	70	F	96	`	122	z
19	‼	45	-	71	G	97	a	123	{
20	¶	46	.	72	H	98	b	124	¦
21	§	47	/	73	I	99	c	125	}
22	▬	48	0	74	J	100	d	126	~
23	↨	49	1	75	K	101	e	127	⌂
24	↑	50	2	76	L	102	f		
25	↓	51	3	77	M	103	g		

Val.	Char.	Val.	Char.	Val.	Char.	Val.	Char.	Val.	Char.
128	Ç	154	Ü	180	┤	206	╬	232	Φ
129	ü	155	¢	181	╡	207	╧	233	Θ
130	é	156	£	182	╢	208	╨	234	Ω
131	â	157	¥	183	╖	209	╤	235	δ
132	ä	158	₧	184	╕	210	╥	236	∞
133	à	159	ƒ	185	╣	211	╙	237	φ
134	å	160	á	186	║	212	╘	238	∈
135	ç	161	í	187	╗	213	╒	239	∩
136	ê	162	ó	188	╝	214	╓	240	
137	ë	163	ú	189	╜	215	╫	241	±
138	è	164	ñ	190	╛	216	╪	242	≥
139	ï	165	Ñ	191	┐	217	┘	243	≤
140	î	166	ª	192	└	218	┌	244	⌠
141	ì	167	º	193	┴	219	█	245	⌡
142	Ä	168	¿	194	┬	220	▄	246	÷
143	Å	169	⌐	195	├	221	▌	247	≈
144	É	170	¬	196	─	222	▐	248	°
145	æ	171	½	197	┼	223	▀	249	•
146	Æ	172	¼	198	╞	224	α	250	·
147	ô	173	¡	199	╟	225	β	251	√
148	ö	174	«	200	╚	226	Γ	252	n
149	ò	175	»	201	╔	227	π	253	2
150	û	176	░	202	╩	228	Σ	254	■
151	ù	177	▒	203	╦	229	σ	255	
152	ij	178	▓	204	╠	230	µ		
153	Ö	179	│	205	═	231	τ		

ASCII CHART

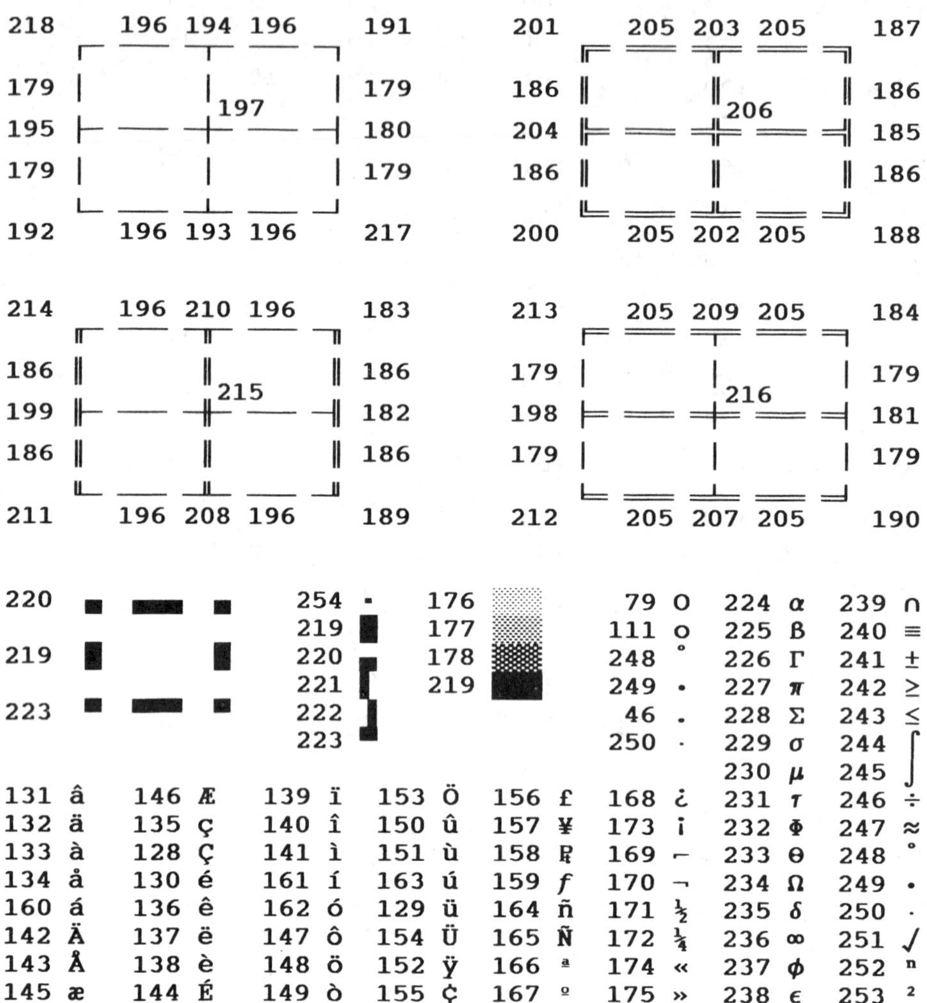
218 196 194 196 191
179 179
197
195 180
179 179
192 196 193 196 217
201 205 203 205 187
186 186
206
204 185
186 186
200 205 202 205 188
214 196 210 196 183
186 186
215
199 182
186 186
211 196 208 196 189
213 205 209 205 184
179 179
216
198 181
179 179
212 205 207 205 190
220
219
223
254 219 220 221 222 223
176 177 178 219
79 O
111 o
248 °
249 •
46 .
250 ·
224 α
225 ß
226 Γ
227 π
228 Σ
229 σ
230 µ
239 ∩
240 ≡
241 ±
242 ≥
243 ≤
244 ⌠
245 ⌡
131 â 146 Æ 139 ï 153 Ö 156 £ 168 ¿ 231 τ 246 ÷
132 ä 135 ç 140 î 150 û 157 ¥ 173 ¡ 232 Φ 247 ≈
133 à 128 Ç 141 ì 151 ù 158 ₧ 169 ⌐ 233 Θ 248 °
134 å 130 é 161 í 163 ú 159 ƒ 170 ¬ 234 Ω 249 •
160 á 136 ê 162 ó 129 ü 164 ñ 171 ½ 235 δ 250 ·
142 Ä 137 ë 147 ô 154 Ü 165 Ñ 172 ¼ 236 ∞ 251 √
143 Å 138 è 148 ö 152 ÿ 166 ª 174 « 237 φ 252 ^{n}
145 æ 144 É 149 ò 155 ¢ 167 º 175 » 238 ε 253 ^{2}

Appendix B

Due to the length of this book, source code listings are not reproduced here. All source code is available on the disk accompanying the book.

Index

D

E

O

M&T BOOKS

A Library of Technical References from M&T Books

Paradox Queries: A Developer's Reference
by Dan Ehrmann

Destined to become the standard Paradox reference, this book teaches database developers the techniques for incorporating queries into their programs. It includes step-by-step instructions plus solid code examples programmers can drop straight into their applications. Covers Paradox for Windows and Paradox for DOS. Disk includes sample tables, source code, and a collection of query tools.   612 pp. approx.

Book/Disk $39.95   #3116

Level: Intermediate-Advanced

Paradox Queries: The Basics
by Dan Ehrmann

The companion volume to *Paradox Queries: A Developers Reference*, this comprehensive guide will teach you query techniques in every version of Paradox, including Paradox for Windows and Paradox SE, 3.5, and 4.0 for DOS. Written for both users and developers, *Paradox Queries: The Basics* provides detailed information on using queries in day-to-day applications. Readers will learn new techniques for extracting information from tables, methods for inserting, deleting, or changing large amounts of data, and tips on pitfalls to avoid. This book includes a 3 1/2" disk that includes sample tables and all of the code described in the book. It also contains an extensive collection of query tools to boost productivity.

Book/Disk $39.95   #2535

Level: All

1-800-628-9658

M&T BOOKS

A Library of Technical References from M&T Books

Developing Paradox Databases: An Object-Based Approach by Gary Entsminger

A comprehensive guide to developing modifiable databases with Paradox for Windows, Borland's object-based and event-driven database system. You'll learn its visual programming style and how to use its easily accessible language, ObjectPAL to develop powerful Paradox for Windows applications. You'll also learn how to organize, code, and test applications, how to use memory efficiently and ways to extend Paradox for Windows using ObjectPAL, DDE, OLE, and other languages. Disk includes source code, numerous illustrations, exercises, and sample applications.

Book/Disk	$39.95	#2969

Level: Intermediate

FoxPro 2: A Developer's Guide Expert Guide for Industrial-Strength Programming by Jeff Winchell

A team of expert FoxPro developers put this one together—definitely industrial strength! Start with the strategies for developing database applications and implementing relational database design. Advanced FoxPro users get valuable insights into keyboard macros, event-driven programming, and tips for optimizing hardware and software performance. Plus FoxPro's application programming interface as it relates to Watcom C, Assembler, and the Macintosh. 503 pp.

Book	$29.95	#0834
Book/Disk	$39.95	#0842

Level: Advanced

1-800-628-9658

A Library of Technical References from M&T Books

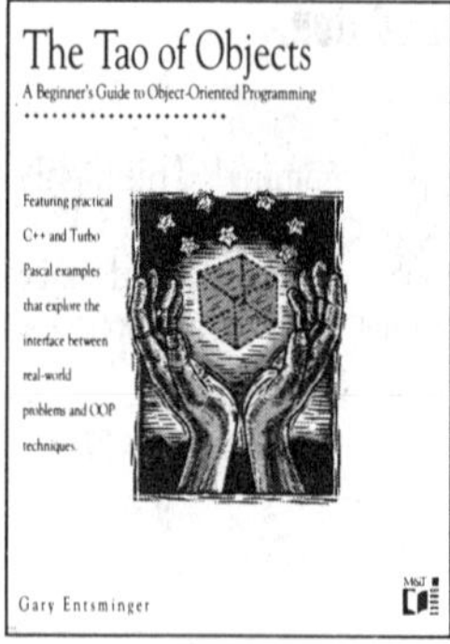

The Tao of Objects: A Beginner's Guide to Object-Oriented Programming by Gary Entsminger

The Tao of Objects is a clearly written, user-friendly guide to object-oriented programming (OOP). Easy-to-understand discussions detail OOP techniques teaching programmers who are new to OOP, where and how to use them. Useful programming examples in C++ and Turbo Pascal illustrate the concepts discussed in real-life applications. 249 pp.

Book $26.95 #1555

Level: Beginning

C++ Components and Algorithms by Scott Robert Ladd

It's true: experienced C programmers always need the kind of comprehensive tools that can help them develop and maintain powerful C++ applications. This excellent volume is where you can find them—all of them! Memory management, indexed files using B-Trees, mathematical programming, adaptive algorithms and more. The in-depth discussions and numerous source code examples are geared toward an understanding of C++'s inner workings. The programs and classes presented are compatible with various C++ compilers, making them valuable to a wide audience of C programmers. All source code included on disk in MC/PC-DOS format. Now you can C more than ever! 512 pp.

Book/Disk $39.95 #2276

Level: Advanced

1-800-628-9658

A Library of Technical References from M&T Books

The Data Compression Book by Mark Nelson

An authoritative guide for advanced C programmers. Details various data compression techniques, explaining the theory behind each and showing how to apply them to significantly increase your system's storage capacity. MS/PC-DOS disk contains sample source code. 527 pp.

Book	$29.95	#2144
Book/Disk	$39.95	#2160

Level: Advanced

Delivering Electronic Mail: Installing and Troubleshooting Electronic Mail Systems by Phillip Robinson

Network administrators: if you're responsible for installing, maintaining, and troubleshooting an electronic mail system, this is the one for you! Addresses concerns of choosing a system and provides a thorough overview of the different types of E-Mail systems available. Helps you select the system most appropriate for your needs. 352 pp.

Book	$29.95	#1709

Level: Beginning - Advanced

1-800-628-9658

A Library of Technical References from M&T Books

Internetworking
A Guide to Network Communications
LAN to LAN; LAN to WAN
by Mark A. Miller, P.E.

This is how to put it all together — from "big picture" to vital details, from LAN to WAN and back again! Discover the essentials of building communications facilities such as leased lines and T-1 circuits and find out which is most viable for your network. Plus a guide to internetworking standards, designs and applications, as well as in-depth discussions of the function of repeaters, bridges, routers, and gateways. Also examined: x.25, TCP/IP and XNS protocols in addition to the specific internetworking capabilities and inter-operability constraints of the most popular networks. An essential guide for network managers working with internetworks. 425 pp.

Book $34.95 #1431

Level: Beginning - Advanced

Troubleshooting Internetworks
Tools, Techniques, and Protocols
by Mark A. Miller, P.E.

This is the one for all network managers, supervisors, and administrators responsible for the managing a complex internetwork. It's a vital reference that covers all the essentials of internetwork troubleshooting, from selecting analysis tools to analyzing the internetwork protocols of popular networks. Detailed investigations of AppleTalk, VINES, DECnet, NetWare and SNA. Offers immediate and effective solutions to common and not-so-common problems. This is the companion volume to *Internetworking: A Guide to Network Commmunications* by the same author. 528 pp.

Book $34.95 #2365

Level: Advanced

1-800-628-9658

ORDER FORM

To Order:

Return this form with your payment to M&T Books, 115 West 18th Street, New York, NY 10011 or **call toll-free 1-800-628-9658.**

ITEM #	DESCRIPTION	DISK	PRICE
		Subtotal	
		NY residents add sales tax ____%	
		Add $4.50 per item for shipping and handling	
		TOTAL	

Charge my:

❑ **Visa**

❑ **MasterCard**

❑ **AmExpress**

❑ **Check enclosed, payable to M&T Books.**

CARD NO. ______________________________

SIGNATURE ______________________ EXP. DATE __________

NAME ______________________________

ADDRESS ______________________________

CITY ______________________________

STATE ______________________ ZIP __________

M&T GUARANTEE: If your are not satisfied with your order for any reason, return it to us within 25 days of receipt for a full refund. Note: Refunds on disks apply only when returned with book within guarantee period. Disks damaged in transit or defective will be promptly replaced, but cannot be exchanged for a disk from a different title.

Tell us what you think and we'll send you a free M&T Books catalog

It is our goal at M&T Books to produce the best technical books available. But you can help us make our books even better by letting us know what you think about this particular title.Please take a moment to fill out this card and mail it to us. Your opinion is appreciated.

Tell us about yourself

Name____________________

Company____________________

Address____________________

City____________________

State/Zip____________________

Title of this book?

Where did you purchase this book?

- ☐ Bookstore
- ☐ Catalog
- ☐ Direct Mail
- ☐ Magazine Ad
- ☐ Postcard Pack
- ☐ Other

Why did you choose this book?

- ☐ Recommended
- ☐ Read book review
- ☐ Read ad/catalog copy
- ☐ Responded to a special offer
- ☐ M&T Books' reputation
- ☐ Price
- ☐ Nice Cover

How would you rate the overall content of this book?

- ☐ Excellent
- ☐ Good
- ☐ Fair
- ☐ Poor

Why?

What chapters did you find valuable?

What did you find least useful?

What topic(s) would you add to future editions of this book?

What other titles would you like to see M&T Books publish?

Which format do you prefer for the optional disk?

☐ 5.25" ☐ 3.5"

Any other comments?

☐ Check here for M&T Books Catalog

M&T BOOKS

3191

NO POSTAGE
NECESSARY
IF MAILED
IN THE
UNITED STATES

BUSINESS REPLY MAIL

FIRST CLASS MAIL PERMIT 1184 NEW YORK, NY

POSTAGE WILL BE PAID BY ADDRESSEE

M&T BOOKS

Att: Special Markets
115 West 18th Street
New York, NY 10011

PLEASE FOLD ALONG LINE AND STAPLE OR TAPE CLOSED